A HISTORY OF CURRENCY IN THE UNITED STATES

A HISTORY OF CURRENCY IN THE UNITED STATES

(REVISED EDITION)

WITH NEW CHAPTERS ON THE MONETARY AND FINANCIAL DEVELOPMENTS IN THE UNITED STATES FROM 1914 TO 1922 AND A PREFACE BY MRS. HEPBURN ON THE AUTHOR'S RELATION TO THE ESTABLISHMENT OF THE FEDERAL RESERVE SYSTEM

BY

A. BARTON HEPBURN, LL.D.

LATE CHAIRMAN OF THE ADVISORY BOARD OF THE CHASE NATIONAL BANK OF NEW YORK; SOMETIME COMPTROLLER OF THE CURRENCY, SUPERINTENDENT OF BANKS OF THE STATE OF NEW YORK, PRESIDENT OF THE NEW YORK CHAMBER OF COMMERCE, PRESIDENT OF THE NEW YORK CLEARING-HOUSE, CHAIRMAN OF THE CURRENCY COMMISSION OF THE AMERICAN BANKERS ASSOCIATION, AND MEMBER OF THE FEDERAL ADVISORY COUNCIL OF THE FEDERAL RESERVE SYSTEM

"It is only by a Sound System of Money and Banking that a Nation can Achieve Real Financial Independence and Power"

REPRINTS OF ECONOMIC CLASSICS

AUGUSTUS M. KELLEY · PUBLISHERS
NEW YORK · 1967

First Edition 1903
(New York: The Macmillan Co, 1903)
Revised Edition 1915
Revised & Enlarged Edition 1924

Reprinted 1967 by
AUGUSTUS M. KELLEY · PUBLISHERS

LIBRARY OF CONGRESS CATALOGUE CARD NUMBER
67-27414

PRINTED IN THE UNITED STATES OF AMERICA
by SENTRY PRESS, NEW YORK, N. Y. 10019

PREFACE TO REVISED EDITION

It was my husband's intention to devote a chapter in the revised edition of this book, on which he was at work at the time of his death, to the story of the relation of the Currency Commission of the American Bankers Association, of which he was Chairman, to the agitation which preceded the passage of the Federal Reserve Act and to the Federal Reserve Act itself. This chapter was never finished. From rough notes in my possession, however, and from my recollections of various episodes, concerning which he talked with me from time to time, I shall try in this preface to work out a somewhat more personal story, which will exhibit the part which my husband took in these events, and which will make clear his attitude toward the various questions of policy which came up. The matter in quotation marks which follows is taken from the notes which Mr. Hepburn left. There will be necessarily an indefiniteness in chronology, as Mr. Hepburn did not have time to work over the matter of dates, and as my own recollections are indefinite regarding them.

"A thirty years' struggle for currency reform finally resulted in the Federal Reserve Law. Experience with various panics and quasi-panics inspired a growing belief on the part of business men and others that our currency system was archaic and needed a general revision in the interest of commerce and the promotion of business.

"Banks could only issue currency against government bonds with a margin to protect the currency and insure redemption. It followed naturally that banks had to invest more in bonds as security than they were allowed to issue in currency. They thereby locked up funds and diminished their power to aid commerce, instead of increasing it.

"Periodic currency stringencies exemplified the defects of our system. In a currency stringency, the banks were powerless to afford relief. President Roosevelt finally took the subject up and indicated to the American Bankers Association, while the bankers were assembled in convention in Kansas City, that if the convention would appoint a Commission of not less than fifteen, fairly representative of all sections of the country, who would agree upon a bill reforming the currency, he would adopt it as his own, would recommend it as his own, place it before Congress in a message and use all his power to put it through.

"This was a great opportunity and promised success. We embraced it with alacrity. The Commission was created and we presently assembled in Washington and held a continuous session for some time, studying the subject. After a brief adjournment, we convened again and agreed upon a bill, a copy of which was submitted to the President.

"In due course a close friend of the President and former member of his Cabinet conveyed the information that the President would like suggestions as to how the matter should be treated in his Annual Message to Congress. Our suggestions were very carefully written out with due reference to the forthcoming bill and submitted. In due course it was returned with certain changes and the query as to whether it was agreeable to the Commission. The changes were mostly those of style and were accepted forthwith.

"I convened the Commission at Washington at the opening of Congress, full of hope and confidence, but doomed to disappointment. Nothing of the matter agreed upon appeared in the President's Message. Our surprise and disappointment were great. When we called upon the President, he greeted us with, 'I had to do it. I know you are disappointed, and it ought to have gone through. But Aldrich and Cannon said it would demoralize things, and they claimed it was included in the agreement which I have with them that I won't interfere in the tariff, in return for which they let me have my way with certain reforms. But I do not think the currency was included. Go ahead with your bill, introduce it and pass it if you can. I won't hinder, if I can't openly help you.'

"This was the origin of the Currency Commission of the American Bankers Association, the personnel of which appears elsewhere." (Page 394.)

Both Senator Aldrich and Honorable Joseph G. Cannon were strongly opposed to any "tinkering" with the currency. Mr. Hepburn told me at one time of a visit which Mr. Cannon paid him at his office at the Bank in which Mr. Cannon said that they had great trouble in controlling Roosevelt, and that just then Mr. Roosevelt was inclined to take up the subject of currency and, for all he knew, the tariff. Mr. Cannon said, "Don't you know him and can't you see him and put him right? I am headed for Oyster Bay and that is my mission." Mr. Hepburn told him that he thought the currency was very much in need of revision, and that if he talked with President Roosevelt he would urge it upon him. As to reducing the tariff, Mr. Hepburn said he was not so clear, but that he was inclined to the view which the President was suspected of entertaining. Mr. Cannon thereupon withdrew his invitation to my husband to go with him to Oyster Bay.

Senator Aldrich likewise objected very much to "meddling with the currency system." He said to my husband, "——— ——— says (naming a prominent New York Banker) that our currency is as good as gold. Why not let it alone?" Mr. Hepburn replied, "The currency is both as good as gold and as bad as gold, namely, quite inelastic." Senator Aldrich introduced a bill creating a National Monetary Commission to make a study of the currency and to determine whether any legislation was required. He frankly told Mr. Hepburn that his purpose in doing this was to sidetrack the matter. He created this Commission knowing that all proposed legislation would be referred to it, and that the Commission would thereby obtain control of the situation.

The Currency Commission of the American Bankers Association, however, immediately had introduced and referred to the National Monetary Commission projects for legislation, and asked for hearings. Senator Aldrich objected to having hearings. The Currency Commission of the American Bankers Association thereupon inspired a lot of telegrams from leading bankers throughout the country, especially members of the clearing house committees in the different cities. The result was that they overwhelmed Senator Aldrich with telegrams which were filed away without reading or perhaps even counting. Senator Aldrich stopped by while passing through New York to tell my husband to "call off" these telegrams, saying that they had the opposite effect from what was desired, and that he was not to be bulldozed into doing anything. Mr. Hepburn invited the Senator to luncheon and told him that next day he would receive a large number of telegrams from bankers whom he could not ignore. There was a good deal of badinage between them, and Senator Aldrich finally told Mr. Hepburn that he was going to Europe to see some "real bankers" who could give him information as to whether currency reform, involving an elastic currency and a central bank, was as necessary as the Currency Commission of the American Bankers Association indicated.

The elaborate investigation of the National Monetary Commission is of course well known.

As the investigation progressed, Senator Aldrich was convinced, and he generously and frankly told Mr. Hepburn so. Senator Aldrich prepared and sponsored the well-known Aldrich plan "which provided for a central bank in this country, with currency predicated upon the normal assets of a bank instead of requiring the banks to go outside their legitimate field to buy government bonds upon which to secure their currency."

The Aldrich plan came too late. The political tide had turned. A Democratic victory gave the lower house to the Democrats in the election of 1910. There was not enough time in the short session of Congress which followed for Senator Aldrich to put his bill through, and with the next election in 1912 the Democrats came into control of all branches of the Government.

The failure of the Aldrich plan was a great disappointment to my husband. The Currency Commission of which he was head did not, however, cease its activity in the effort to help in formulating a scientific law. On pages 397–410 of the present volume will be found a document drawn up by the Commission on June 19, 1913, at a special meeting at Atlantic City, which sets forth its views. It was the belief of my husband and his associates that a central bank, which would pool all the gold reserves of the country, was necessary if our banking system was to be made panic proof. The legislation devised by the Democratic leaders provided for a system of regional Federal Reserve banks, eight to twelve in number, and the bankers took an attitude of opposition to this. They felt that such a system could not stand the strain of a crisis, that there would be danger of some of the weaker Federal Reserve banks going under, with resultant loss of confidence in others, if a period of severe strain should come. The central point in my husband's mind was that no legislation could be adequate which did not provide for the *pooling of gold reserves.*

Shortly before the Federal Reserve Act was introduced, Mr. Hepburn and I were invited to a dinner in New York at which we met a member of President Wilson's cabinet, a leading Senator, and a leading member of the House of Representatives, who were all actively interested in the bill. They told Mr. Hepburn that they understood that he was opposed to the bill, and that they had not asked him to come with a view to making him change his mind. Taking for granted his opposition to the measure as a whole, they still wished the benefit of his advice as a practical banker on points of detail, and they asked him to go with them over the whole measure, and to state to them his opinion as to how this and that feature of the bill would work in practice. Mr. Hepburn did this at length, and various minor changes were made in the measure as a result of this interview.

At various times Mr. Hepburn was consulted by one or another of the men most interested in the measure, among them Dr. H. Parker Willis and Mr. Carter Glass. My husband entertained a high regard for both these gentlemen.

Throughout the whole of the discussion of the Federal Reserve Act, Mr. Hepburn held tenaciously to the view that a pooling of gold reserves was necessary, and he early made the suggestion that if it could be made compulsory for one Federal Reserve bank to rediscount for another the most serious point in his objection to the proposed system would disappear.

Finally Mr. Hepburn and President Wilson had an interview, at the Pan-American Conference (I think) in Washington, at which it developed that the difference in viewpoint between them was not nearly as sharp as had appeared. Almost as soon as they had shaken hands, Mr. Wilson said in substance that he and Mr. Hepburn did not disagree with reference to the banking problem, and added that if the bill passed it would be administered to the entire satisfaction of the banking fraternity. Mr. Hepburn said, "You cannot do that as it now stands, but if you will give the Federal Reserve banks the right to rediscount for one another and make them do it, it will work that way;" *i. e.*, as a central bank. The President agreed to do this.

The clear idea which my husband brought away from the conference was that Mr. Wilson didn't want it announced that the American Bankers Association had agreed to let the bill go through. He had secured the support of interests which were not friendly to the banks for the Federal Reserve Act, and he wished to keep that support. Mr. Wilson was himself condemnatory of the attitude the banks had taken. "He practically requested me not to come out in favor of the bill, but to pass the word around in New York, so that the bill would be sure to go through."

After this conference my husband's attitude towards the measure changed. He undertook to coöperate with the Administration in the way he felt the Administration preferred to have him coöperate. He ceased opposition to the measure, and he quietly informed his friends in Congress and among the bankers that the measure as amended, to provide for rediscounting by one Federal Reserve bank for another, should be allowed to go through. He held that this provision made the Federal Reserve System in effect a central bank. During the crisis of 1920–21, when one of the regional banks had used up all but 2% of its own gold reserve, but still stood strong because it could replenish its gold by rediscounting with other Federal Reserve banks, as well as on other occasions when the inter-regional rediscounting provision was particularly helpful and necessary, Mr. Hepburn used to refer with a good deal of satisfaction to his part in bringing about this provision in the Act.

The preceding edition of this book brought the story of American currency through the crisis of 1914 which followed the outbreak of the great World War. The present edition carries the story on almost to the time of my husband's death early in 1922. The revision of this book was the uppermost literary problem in Mr. Hepburn's mind during the last year of his life. The new material added in the present edition begins with Chapter XXVI, on page 446.

I cannot close this preface without expressing my gratitude to various friends who have made it possible for this book to appear. Dr. Benjamin M. Anderson, Jr., Economist of the Chase National Bank, has brought the loose ends together and has supervised the publishing of the new edition. Professor

John Bates Clark of Columbia University has gone over the manuscript. Mr. James F. Hughes, Dr. John K. Towles, Miss Georgia L. Baxter, and Miss Grace M. Kerr of Dr. Anderson's office have all aided in the critical revision of the manuscript, have prepared new statistical tables and the additional bibliography, and have revised the index.

EMILY EATON HEPBURN.

471 Park Avenue,
New York City.
December 3, 1923.

PREFACE

For three centuries this continent has been inhabited by white men. The financial experience that accompanied the development of the territory now comprised within the United States, from an aboriginal wilderness to its present proud position in the sisterhood of nations, contains much that is crucial and many severe lessons. In the beginning there was a period of barter and trade during which commodity paid for commodity. It frequently happened, however, that a man wishing to purchase goods did not have for exchange anything which the vendor desired; this, and the difficulty of making change, inspired the colonial governments to provide a currency and to give it a fixed value in trade and taxes. At first articles of real value that would go without a government fiat were selected, such as beaver skins, musket balls, corn, etc.; later, printed money with government fiat was resorted to, in many cases with unfortunate results. At the very threshold of our existence our forebears, crudely, but nevertheless conclusively, illustrated the superiority of a currency unit which possessed commercial value and would circulate because people wanted it, over a currency which represented the *ipse dixit* of government.

All of the original thirteen colonies had the same environment and the same experience. Printing money was very easy and seemingly inexpensive, since it avoided taxes at the moment. It was in consequence carried to extremes, depreciated and was largely repudiated when it came to final redemption. This currency suffered the vicissitudes inherent in its nature, precisely as did the French assignats under John Law. The Continental Congress duplicated the experience of the colonies with fiat money, not because they did not realize the danger, but because the Congress had no power to levy taxes and hence no power to borrow money. Apparently no other resources were available, coherent action by the separate colonies, with the imperfect means of communication, being impossible. Again the same issue was raised, following the Civil War; the greenback party, which favored paying the national debt in legal tender paper money, — compelling the holders of interest-bearing obligations of the United States to accept non-interest-bearing obligations in full payment and satisfaction, — obtained a very general support and threatened the honor of the government. The same principles, or want of principles, were presented in the free-silver campaign that followed the greenback craze; the purpose was to take silver and coin it into dollars whose face value was largely in excess of its commercial value, the difference, or seigniorage, so called, representing the fiat of the government. This issue was settled by the gold standard act of 1900. Fortunately, all the schemes of dishonest finance have been signally defeated by the people and now we are reaping our reward. We stand forth preëminently as a nation whose credit firmly based upon the gold standard is unimpaired, whose exchange is at a premium the world over, presaging a period of a world-wide financial growth and development. The story of our financial history, from the early beginnings to the very superior Federal Reserve system upon which we have just entered, has all the quality and charm of romance, alike interesting and instructive. This experience should be of great value as a guiding influence in aiding us to fortify our present commercial standing and banking power.

This country is governed by public sentiment, which, when properly informed, may be trusted to reach a wise conclusion, as clearly shown in the defeat of greenbackism and the free-coinage-of-silver propaganda. My aim is to place before the public all the essential facts as to currency, coinage, and banking, from the wampumpeage currency of the colonies to the notes of our Federal Reserve Banks, together with the indispensable political history connected therewith.

I have indulged in no attempt at fine writing, but have endeavored to recite the facts clearly and succinctly in proper sequence. Few have access to economic libraries covering the period and the subjects treated in this volume, and few could conveniently make use of such libraries even if at hand. This volume is a busy man's library, each subject being fairly treated, while the Bibliography points the way to further and more extended research. In the chapter on Colonial Currency I have made use of the experience of Pennsylvania, because accurate data was easily obtainable, and also because Pennsylvania's experience covered all phases of the subject. I have also made large use of the experience of Massachusetts, and to a lesser extent Virginia, Rhode Island, New Jersey, and the other colonies, thereby fairly covering the subject and bringing out its obvious lessons.

The chapter on Continental Currency, from the confederation until the retirement of this currency in 1793, is very complete.

The basis of this book is "The Contest for Sound Money," published in 1903; but that earlier work has been rewritten and supplemented so that as now issued it covers the period from the adoption of the United States Constitution down to the present time. It deals fully and explicitly with our coinage laws and coinage by our mints; it gives the complete history of the national banking system, and contrasts and compares the banking systems of the various states; it relates the history of the legal tender notes and discusses them as a substitute for taxation, touching upon the political history of the period inasmuch as the question of the legality of these notes was made a political issue; the history of the silver controversy is fully told, especially from the so-called "crime of 1873," when the silver dollar was demonetized, down to the gold standard act of 1900; the various international efforts in favor of the bimetallic standard are likewise set forth.

The panic of 1907 showed the imperative necessity of improving our credit and currency systems. The National Monetary Commission — Aldrich Commission — dealt with the subject exhaustively and procured, reported to Congress and published to the country full data of the laws and practices of other nations as well as our own, and laid the foundation for action. The last Congress, under President Wilson, acted, and the result is the very satisfactory Federal Reserve Law. Our national experience leading up to this law and the influence which focalized in its enactment are fully treated, as well as the abnormal conditions presented by the European cataclysm in 1914, and the problems and opportunities offered to the United States.

CONTENTS

CHAPTER I

COLONIAL CURRENCY

CHAPTER II

CONTINENTAL CURRENCY

CHAPTER III

SOUND MONEY IN NATIONAL POLITICS

CHAPTER IV

THE COINAGE SYSTEM, 1776–1789

CHAPTER IX

PAPER CURRENCY, 1837–1849

CHAPTER X

PAPER CURRENCY, 1850–1860

CHAPTER XI

LEGAL TENDER NOTES, 1861–1865

CHAPTER XII

LEGAL TENDER NOTES, 1866–1875

CHAPTER XVII

NATIONAL BANKING SYSTEM, 1861–1875

CHAPTER XVIII

NATIONAL BANKING SYSTEM, 1876–1882

CHAPTER XIX

NATIONAL BANKING SYSTEM, 1883–1890

CHAPTER XX

SILVER CONTEST OF 1896; 1891–1896

CHAPTER XXI

GOLD STANDARD ACT OF 1900

CHAPTER XXVII

FOREIGN EXCHANGE DURING THE WAR

CHAPTER XXVIII

THE WAR AND THE FEDERAL RESERVE SYSTEM

CHAPTER XXIX

CHANGES IN THE CURRENCY DURING THE WAR—MONETARY HERESIES

CHAPTER XXX

THE POST-WAR BOOM AND THE CRISIS OF 1920

CHAPTER XXXI

THE GOLD AND REDISCOUNT POLICY OF THE FEDERAL RESERVE BANKS

A HISTORY OF CURRENCY IN THE UNITED STATES

A HISTORY OF CURRENCY IN THE UNITED STATES

CHAPTER I

COLONIAL CURRENCY

AFTER the declaration of independence from Great Britain, the confederated colonies, through the Continental Congress, assumed to control national affairs, the conduct of the resulting war, the equipment and maintenance of the army, and the financing of various national needs.

In order to properly understand and appreciate the history of the coinage and currency of the United States, it is necessary to recall the existing conditions in respect to money matters at the birth of our nation, by presenting a brief history and characterization of the experience of the colonies in dealing with currency problems.

The original settlers upon this continent obtained a precarious foothold, some failing and some surviving. They were in the main very poor in purse; the personnel was composed of those who fled from least desirable conditions in the hope of betterment; they brought little money, and from the outset the want of a currency to satisfy their meagre demands in trade was one of their great hardships. Barter was, of course, available, but to buy or sell and receive the equivalent in units of generally recognized value, was impossible, in the absence of a standard currency. Like all primitive peoples, they adopted primitive forms of currency.

Hume defines currency — "The instrument which men have

agreed upon to facilitate the exchange of one commodity for another." It has been aptly said that "coin is to money as species to a genus"; coin is usually the basis, but only a part of the circulating medium; various commodities at various times have been by law made currency.

The Latins measured the value of property in cattle; Pliny tells us the first Latin coins were stamped with a cow. The Latin word *pecus*, meaning flocks or herds, thus came to mean money or property and gave us the derivative pecuniary. Homer tells us that the brazen armor of Diomedes was valued at nine oxen and the golden armor of Glaucus at one hundred oxen. Currency has frequently been made from leather, notably by King John of France, who had each piece marked by a silver nail. Adam Smith in his "Wealth of Nations," tells us that iron nails in a village in Scotland, dried cod in Newfoundland, sugar in several of the West Indian islands, and hides in other countries, were substitutes for coin. In Russia the word for money, kung, also means marten. Whales' teeth are said to be used as money by the Fijians, and red feathers by the South Sea Islanders. Salt is still a favorite currency in Central Africa.

The early settlers had no mints save the earth that stored the precious metals, and no banks save the soil and the waters. Naturally they made currency of products derived from these sources. Fish, corn and especially peltry, which was abundant and eagerly sought by Europeans, were commonly used as currency. Corn was used as a generic term, including all grain, even peas. Court fines were imposed in commodities. The following quotations are taken from the colonial decrees and court records of Massachusetts: "Sir Richard Saltonstall is fined four bushells of malte for his absence from Court." [1] "Chickataubott is fyned a skyn of beaver for shooteinge a swine of Sir Richard Saltonstall." [2] "It is ordered that corne shall passe for

[1] Mass., Sept. 28, 1630; Felt, Massachusetts Currency, p. 14.
[2] Id., June 14, 1631, p. 15.

payment of all debts at the usuall rate it is solde for, except money or beaver be expressly named."[1] This made it legal tender.

In order to protect their coin and beaver skins, which were almost as valuable, "It is ordered that noe planter within the limits of this jurisdiction, returneing for England, shall carry either money or beaver with him, without leave from the Governor, under paine of forfeitinge the money and beaver so intended to be transported."[2] "It is ordered that hereafter farthings shall not passe for currant pay. It is likewise ordered, that muskett bulletts of a full boare shall pass currantly for a farthing a peece, provided that noe man be compelled to take above 12^{d} att a tyme of them."[3] We also find this decree: "Whereas two former lawes, the one concerning the wages of workemen, the other concerning the prizes of comodyties, were for dyvers good consideracons repealed this present Court, nowe for avoydeing such mischiefes as may follow thereupon by such ill disposed persons as may take liberty to oppresse and wronge their neighbours by takeing excessive wages for worke, or unreasonable prizes for such necessary merchandizes or other commodyties, as shall passe from man to man; — It is therefore nowe ordered y^{t} if any man shall offend in any of the said cases against the true intent of this lawe, hee shall be punished by fine or imprisonment according to the quality of the offence, as the Court upon lawful tryall and conviction shall judge."[4]

This was not a dead letter. "Joshua Huyes hath forfect V^{s} for knyves, and iiii^{s} VI^{d} for scythe, which hee solde for above iiii^{d} in the shilling proffitt."[5]

Legislation to prevent extortion on the part of labor lends a sharp contrast to the trend of labor legislation at the present time. Governor Winthrop says, "I may report a passage

[1] Id., Oct. 18, 1631, p. 16.
[2] Id., Mar. 6, 1632, p. 16.
[3] Id., Mar. 4, 1635, p. 20.
[4] Id., Sept. 2, 1635, p. 20.
[5] Mass. Colonial Records, Oct. 5, 1635.

between one of Rowley and his servant. The master being forced to sell a pair of his oxen to pay his servant his wages, told his servant he could keep him no longer, not knowing how to pay him next year. The servant answered him, he could serve him for more cattle. 'But what shall I do,' saith the master, 'when my cattle are all gone?' The servant replied, 'You shall then serve me, and so you may have your cattle again.'"[1] The troubles incident to capital and labor are ever with us.

The Marquis Chastelleux after visiting the colonies, wrote: "The tobacco warehouses, of which there are a number in Virginia, are under the direction of public authority. There are inspectors, nominated to prove the quality of the tobacco brought by the planters, and if found good they give a receipt for the quantity. The tobacco may then be considered as sold, those authenticated receipts circulating as money in the country. For example, suppose I have deposited 20 hogsheads of tobacco in Petersburg, I may go fifty leagues thence to Alexandria or Fredericksburg and buy horses, clothes or any other article with those receipts, which circulate through a number of hands before they reach the merchant who purchases the tobacco for exportation."[2] These receipts were not made to circulate as money by law, but having an intrinsic value, they did perform the office of currency from an early date almost to the nineteenth century.

The Indians along the seacoast used as currency wampumpeage, made from shells in the form of beads, brightly polished and very beautiful; in strings or ropes they were very ornamental. There were two kinds, black, made from quohaug, and white, made from periwinkles. Both the English and the Dutch made use of this currency and the stress was so great that several times the colonies put a fixed value upon wampum

[1] Winthrop, Vol. I, p. 220.
[2] Travels in North America, Dublin, 1789, Vol. II, p. 131.

by law. In 1643 Massachusetts made it a legal tender for any sum not exceeding 40 shillings, fixing the value of the white beads at 8 and the black at 4 to the penny. In 1649 in Rhode Island black peage was fixed at 4 a penny. In 1658 all peage was fixed at 8 a penny, but white peage was receivable for taxes at only 6 a penny. The making of wampumpeage was an industry that appealed to the white man, the quantity was multiplied and the value was so greatly reduced that in May, 1662, Rhode Island forbade its receipt for taxes.

Prior to 1763 France was in possession of Canada, and until its acquisition by the English there was almost continual war between those countries, which of course involved their respective colonies. Massachusetts made the first emission of paper money, in 1690, to pay her soldiers just returned from an expedition to Canada. The issue presently depreciated to 14*s*. to the pound and was called in. From that time forward, Phillips says, Massachusetts "continued to emit such sums as were needed for the Treasury, and once in a while to call in" for cancellation "a parcel by a tax." In 1714, they emitted a bank (as it was called) of £50,000. Massachusetts went beyond all other colonies in the amount of her issues, perhaps because she surpassed all others in the volume of her business.[1] Dr. Douglas estimates that in 1748 the following amounts of paper money emissions were in circulation in the colonies named:

Massachusetts	£2,466,612
Connecticut	281,000
Rhode Island	550,000
New Hampshire	450,000

In December, 1748, Massachusetts received from England a large sum to reimburse her for expenses incurred in the war with France and Canada, and made arrangements to retire the

[1] Historical Summarization of New England, by Dr. Douglas; see Phillips, Paper Currency, Vol. I, p. 108.

greater part of her outstanding circulation with these funds, supplemented by taxation. In a very few years thereafter her paper money circulation ceased. The price at which she retired her circulation is not directly stated, but from current quotations and from fair inference it must have been about 20 per cent.

In 1652, Massachusetts erected a mint in Boston, to coin silver of sterling alloy into 12*d*, 6*d* and 3*d* pieces, the intrinsic value being less than British pieces by 2*d* in the shilling.[1] A law forbade other coins than these and British coins to circulate in the colony. An attempt was made to prevent the exportation of these coins, but in 1748 they had nearly all disappeared, driven out by the depreciated paper currency.

All the original thirteen colonies made use of paper money issues, called by somewhat differing names, but all possessing the same general characteristics, and all being the direct promise to pay of the colony. This currency was usually made legal tender; severe penalties were imposed for refusal to sell goods and receive payment in this paper money at par and the penalty for counterfeiting in many instances was made death.

The experience of Pennsylvania is typical of all the colonies. This state is selected, because as she began the issue of paper money at a comparatively late date (1723) the records are more complete, and her experience presents the best and the worst as well.

The fact that nearly all manufactured articles came from abroad and the colonists had nothing but raw material with which to offset such importations, made a strong demand upon the metallic money of the colonies for export in settlement of trade balance. This demand was in itself hard enough to contend with, and when the emission of paper money became general and depreciated so rapidly, it inevitably drove the better money abroad.

[1] Phillips, Paper Currency, I, p. 109.

In March, 1723, Pennsylvania passed an act for the emission of £15,000 in bills of credit, the argument being that "the government is bound to supply a circulating medium for traffic, for those who are its dependents," and the fact being that the community were suffering for want of a good currency. Previously the Committee on Grievances had referred to the House the question "Whether the raising the cash or striking paper money will be most to the advantage of the Province? But humbly presume if dollars were raised to *five shillings* a piece, it might be of benefit, and they think it would be impracticable to prevent the exportation of specie; they are of opinion, that if a law was made to make the country produce, at market price, pay for servants, goods imported, and to discharge judgments and executions, it would be of public service."[1] A law was passed in accordance with this report, in February, 1723.

The £15,000 in bills were to be loaned at 5 per cent. interest on real estate or upon silver plate, at 5 shillings per ounce, to be deposited at the loan office. The notes were payable, one-eighth of the principal annually, together with interest; they were a full legal tender; refusal to receive them as such voided the debt or forfeited the commodity. This issue was very conservative in amount, the notes were well secured and were of great service to the community. The legislature of Pennsylvania had before it the unfortunate experience of other colonies, and was at the time flooded with their depreciated notes.

In 1726 the amount of currency was £45,000. These notes passed at par and their very excellence attracted counterfeiting; they were counterfeited to an alarming extent, chiefly in Ireland, and sent hither; all this was done notwithstanding the act provided that counterfeiting should be punished by the loss of both ears, by a fine of £100 and the payment of double the value of the loss sustained by those who suffered from the counterfeits.

[1] Phillips, Paper Currency, I, p. 12.

In case of inability to pay these sums, the offender was sold into service for seven years.[1]

The reissue of the amounts paid in in annual instalments had been authorized, and as the expiration of the eighth year approached, May, 1729, another issue of £30,000 was authorized, in order to prevent contraction; these bills were to be loaned upon the same terms as the previous ones, one-sixth of principal and interest payable annually. In 1731, on expiration of the eight-year period, the previous issues were renewed by law and £40,000 of new bills authorized to be exchanged for bills issued prior to August 10, 1728, which bills, if not exchanged by March 1, were to be irredeemable.

In 1739 the total issue had grown to £80,000. The penalty for counterfeiting was changed to death and the former penalties were applied to those who raised notes to a larger amount. These notes were intrinsically good, circulated freely at par, and drove the notes of other colonies out of circulation in Pennsylvania; they were not, however, good in payment of debts abroad and suffered a depreciation when compared with exchange on London.

In 1746 £5000 were issued to help support the expedition against Canada. A long controversy now ensued between the Assembly and the Governor, who, inspired by the Proprietaries,[2] who sought personal immunity from taxation, was opposed to an undue issue of paper money, and also insisted that such acts should be suspended until the King's pleasure should be known.

In 1754 the House adopted the following resolutions:[3]

"*First:* That it is necessary the paper money of this Province should be reëmitted for a further time.

[1] Phillips, I, p. 16.

[2] Proprietaries were the financial backers of the Colony and in a certain sense the owners.

[3] Phillips, I, p. 21.

"*Second:* That there is a necessity of a further addition to the paper money of this Province.

"*Third:* That there is a necessity that a sum should be struck to exchange the ragged and torn bills now current by law in this Province."

The Governor insisted upon his contention, and even vetoed an issue of £30,000 for the King's use in support of Braddock's expedition.

This attitude of the Assembly foreshadowed a departure from the conservatism that had thus far characterized their note issues, which were secured, drew interest and were sought by other colonies and circulated without discount. The volume of business, both domestic and foreign, had grown and prosperity was general. Capital was urgently needed, as it ever is in new countries, for various purposes, and the easiest way to raise it seemed to be to borrow from the future by emitting bills for the future to pay. The constant disagreements between the Assembly and the Proprietaries, as to taxation, made note issues the easier if not the better way. The idea that the government can create wealth by its fiat had grown with the success that attended these earlier issues. Even Benjamin Franklin seemed impressed with this idea.

The Assembly, by persistence, tired out the Governor, who finally consented that the Proprietaries be taxed the same as others. After Braddock's defeat £60,000 was voted for the King's use, £55,000 of which was to be emitted in bills of credit, dated January 1, 1756, and to be redeemed by taxation. In August following, £30,000 were issued, to run for ten years. In 1757–8–9, £300,000 were issued, and in June, 1759, £36,650 further were issued "to reimburse the military agent of the colonies at Philadelphia." This act was vetoed by the King, but the money had already been issued; it was thereupon called in. During the next ten years £175,000 was authorized, and £200,000 called in.[1]

[1] Phillips, I, p. 25.

The course of events in Pennsylvania duplicates the experience of all other countries, as well as of the other colonies, and shows how inflation tends to grow with leaps and bounds, when once it gains a foothold.

In 1763 Parliament passed a law forbidding any bills of credit to be made legal tender, hoping thereby to stem the tide of inflation that had possessed all the colonies.[1] Private individuals and firms throughout the colonies had, to some extent, issued promissory notes payable on demand and attempted, with indifferent success, to circulate them as money. In 1766 an association of merchants in Philadelphia sought to meet the alleged demand for circulation by emitting £20,000 in £5 notes, with interest at 5 per cent. This action was not in contravention of any law but was frowned upon generally and presently abandoned. In 1769 the colony authorized two issues amounting to £30,000. In 1771, because of fear of an attack by the French, £15,000 was issued for the defense of Philadelphia, most of which was used for municipal purposes, the war not having materialized.

In 1772, £25,000 was emitted for the support of the government; in 1773 £12,000 for the erection of a lighthouse at Henlopen, and another issue of £6000 followed in 1775. A second issue in 1773 was for £150,000 and attempted unsuccessfully to restore the loan system. In this year counterfeiting had increased to such an extent that the government offered a reward of £500 for the detection of the guilty ones.[2]

In 1775 an issue was authorized to build a jail, known as Walnut Street Prison. Here Americans captured by the British were imprisoned while Philadelphia was in their hands; here also was the great financier, Robert Morris, imprisoned when reverses had exhausted his fortune and his credit. Roused by the Battle of Lexington, the Assembly created a Committee

[1] Gouge, Paper Money, II, p. 23.
[2] Phillips, I, pp. 28, 29.

of Safety to look after the interests of the colony and authorized an issue of £35,000 as a defence fund.

The Revolutionary War changed the currency question materially. The provinces advanced to the dignity of States and the currency was issued thereafter in conjunction with and under the direction of the Continental Congress. Thereafter there were three kinds of paper currency: that issued by the States, that issued by the Continental Congress, and that issued by the States and Congress jointly. Of course the colonial currency was continued by refunding and otherwise. The notes of the *colony* of Pennsylvania suffered comparatively little depreciation. New Jersey issued her last notes as a colony in 1769,[1] having issued a total of £347,500, of which £190,000 were at the time unredeemed. This amount was not large and depreciation was not very great. Rhode Island had a large amount outstanding, and in February, 1769, 6*s*. lawful money was ordered to be reckoned equal to £8 old tenor, in payment of taxes. Virginia first issued notes in aid of Braddock's expedition against Fort Duquesne, but issues thereafter were frequent and for various purposes. They were made legal tender, severe penalties imposed for refusal to trade or sell goods and take such notes at par; the penalty of death for counterfeiting did not prevent rogues from conducting a thriving industry in that line; depreciation was very great.[2]

Illustrating intercolonial currency troubles, the Governor of Massachusetts, in February, 1744, said, "of Rhode Island bills, now in circulation, and amounting to £440,000, £350,000 are passing in Massachusetts, and also £50,000 in Connecticut. On these two sums the people here have lost, by the fall of them, £25,000 in the last nine months. . . . This and other such losses equal £180,000. Not only this, but their bills reduce the value of those issued by Massachusetts."[3]

In 1749–53, Massachusetts "sunk" its paper money, mainly

[1] Phillips, I, p. 75. [2] *Ibid.*, I, pp. 196, 197. [3] Felt, p. 115.

from reimbursement funds, £180,000, received from Parliament on account of aid rendered by Massachusetts in the Canadian wars. Some funds were raised by taxation. The depreciation is illustrated by the scale of valuation put upon notes for redemption; those bills issued in 1728 varied in proportion from 16–18 shillings to the ounce of silver; the depreciation increased with each subsequent issue; in 1738 the proportion of bills was 28–29 to the ounce and in 1748 37–38–40 to the ounce.[1] Each issue was separately valued and the growing depreciation of each subsequent issue was at the time justified by the Province by the fact that the people who took the notes knew of their then depreciation, and hence would suffer no greater loss comparatively, by having a less value put upon the later issues; at the Town House, Boston, £1,792,236–5–1 was burned, which left about £132,000 outstanding. This action gave Massachusetts a good and sound currency, although the depreciated notes of other colonies were plentiful. Realizing the danger from unrestrained inflation, Parliament enacted, in 1763, a law "to prevent paper bills of credit, hereafter to be issued in any of His Majesty's colonies or plantations in America, from being declared to be a legal tender in payment of money, and to prevent the legal tender of such bills as are now subsisting from being prolonged beyond the periods for calling in and sinking the same."[2]

The effect of this law was to materially reduce the volume of notes. The volume of money in the whole thirteen colonies, at the beginning of the Revolutionary War, was estimated by Peletiah Webster, a very able contemporary writer, "at $12,000,000, or perhaps not more than 10,000,000 hard dollars in value," at least two-fifths of which was specie.[3]

The characteristics of the colonial currency presented in this chapter reflect the experiences of all the other colonies as well as those chosen for the purpose of typical illustration.

[1] Felt, p. 135. [2] Phillips, II, p. 24.
[3] Peletiah Webster's Essays, 1790. Gouge, II, p. 24.

CHAPTER II

CONTINENTAL CURRENCY

ON May 10, 1775, the Continental Congress reassembled in Philadelphia, representing thirteen colonies with a population slightly exceeding 3,000,000 people, and with a circulating medium, both coin and paper, carefully estimated to be $12,000,000. It had been the policy of Britain to keep the colonies dependent, and to keep them defenceless was the best way of accomplishing that result. The colonies had no money in their treasuries, no factories which could manufacture arms or munitions or clothing, not even the implements of industry. The British navy not only endangered their commerce, but practically closed to them the ports of the world. The colonies had no borrowing credit abroad and the nation was a hope as yet without tangible existence. Never was war against a great nation undertaken under more discouraging circumstances. Notwithstanding the distressing experience of the colonies with their government issues of currency and its sad depreciation, there seemed no other resource left to the Continental Congress, and therefore the issue of Continental currency was authorized at the very inception of this national movement, May 10, 1775.[1] These notes were made full legal tender by Congress and eventually by all the States, following the lead of Rhode Island; in August, 1775, Rhode Island made Continental notes full legal

[1] Subsequent issues were made Nov. 29, 1775; Feb. 17, May 9 and July 22, 1776; Feb. 26 and May 20, 1777; Apr. 11, Sept. 26, 1778; Jan. 14, 1779; Mar. 18, 1780. An issue of notes in fractions of a dollar was authorized, but never emitted.

tender and imposed the same penalties for counterfeiting and raising and refusing to take the same at par, that applied to her own notes; she resolved "that any person who refused such money ought to be considered an enemy to the credit, reputation and happiness of the colonies, and wholly destitute of the regard and obligation he was under to his country . . . and should be debarred from all communication with good citizens." [1]

On January 11, 1776, Congress, following a preamble,

> "RESOLVED, Therefore, that any person who shall hereafter be so lost to all virtue and regard for his country, as to refuse to receive said bills in payment, or obstruct or discourage the currency or circulation thereof, and shall be duly convicted by the committee of the city, county or district, or in case of appeal from their decision, by the assembly, convention, council or committee of safety of the colony where he shall reside, such person shall be deemed, published and treated as an enemy of his country and precluded from all trade or intercourse with the inhabitants of these Colonies."

In other words, persons who refused to take these notes as the equivalent of coin, were made outlaws. Nevertheless depreciation began, and even on June 4 the Virginia convention appointed a committee to inquire into the cause of the depreciation of Continental money.[2]

The above facts are significant as showing how utterly powerless the fiat of government is when it seeks to reverse economic law. Determined effort was made to enforce the law and compel people to take this currency at par. Thomas Fisher, being convicted, pleaded "that from conscientious motives their House could not accept this kind of money, as it is issued for the purposes of war." This was the plea generally made and as the whole community was guilty, it sufficed to evade or mitigate punishment. Sometimes apologies were accepted, as in the case of William Gilliland, as follows:

[1] Am. Archives, Series 4, Vol. II, p. 232, etc.
[2] *Ibid.*, Vol. VI.

"I, the subscriber, have been so very wicked and abandoned as to speak at sundry times disrespectfully of the Honorable the Continental Congress, and have also endeavored to depreciate their currency, for which detestable conduct I have deservedly been confined in the jail of this county by the committee of said county, but being now fully convinced of the heinousness and horrible tendency of such conduct, do hereby and in the fullest manner, most sincerely beg pardon of my justly incensed countrymen, and do promise hereafter never to be guilty of the like, but in all instances to conform to such rules and regulations as may be instituted by that very respectable body, for the preservation of our invaluable but invaded rights and liberties; and do further request that this my acknowledgement be made public, that others may be deterred from following my shameful and wicked practices." [1]

In January, 1777, depreciation was so great that Congress appealed to all States to make Continental money legal tender for public and private debts and that a refusal to accept such money should extinguish the debt. They asked the States to call in and "sink" their State currency in order to appreciate the currency of Congress; and as the States were committed to the redemption of Continental currency in proportion to population, the requests of Congress were generally complied with. Counterfeiting was very general among the colonies; the currency was counterfeited by the British and sent here as one means of destroying the American credit; a shipload of counterfeit Continental money, coming from Britain, was captured by an American privateer; and persons accompanying flags of truce made use of the occasion to disseminate counterfeit money.

In November, 1776, Congress authorized a lottery as a means of raising money, but it did not succeed, as people would not pay coin for a chance to draw Continental dollars. Congress, in the year 1778, appealed to the States to raise $5,000,000, by taxes, and pay the same into the Continental Treasury, and again asked them to sink their State issues, saying among other things, "no truth being more evident than that where a quantity

[1] Force's Am. Archives, Series 4, Vol. IV.

of money of any denomination exceeds what is useful as a medium of commerce, its comparative value must be proportionately reduced." [1]

The States complying with the requests of Congress undertook to fix the price of labor, the charges of innkeepers, the price of articles manufactured or imported, indeed of everything except military stores. The winter at Valley Forge was succeeded by a spring of great gloom, until news of the alliance with France arrived; this put great heart and courage into the Americans. The volume of Continental currency at this time was $55,500,000 and had depreciated to six for one in April. Upon news of this alliance in May, it appreciated to four for one. More issues and more depreciation followed, and in 1779 the Continental currency totaled $130,052,080. Congress realized that more paper issues would depreciate the existing issue to an amount greater than the proposed issue would realize, but Congress could not levy taxes; it could only apportion these among the States and ask them to raise the amount by taxation, which the States neglected to do.

The tax that the people suffered, by loss from depreciated paper, was far greater than a direct tax of the amount necessary to carry on the war would have been. Public meetings in Philadelphia, Boston and elsewhere, and meetings of different military organizations, violently denounced the constantly soaring prices of the necessaries of life and constantly depreciating currency, and charged it all to the extortionate greed of the people who would not sell and take the current paper money at its face value.

The total volume of Continental money, "old tenor," was $357,476,541. [2]

There were also so-called "new tenor emissions," in 1780–81 amounting to $2,070,485, put in circulation through the several

[1] Phillips, II, 76.

[2] Gouge, II, p. 25.

State treasuries.[1] These notes were the direct obligation of the State with the guarantee of Congress imprinted on the back.

On the 31st of May, 1781, by Act of Congress, Continental bills ceased to circulate as money, and provision was made for refunding the same, but they were bought for speculation thereafter at from 400 for 1 up to 1000 for 1.[2]

The appeals of Congress to the States for real money to be raised by taxation are pathetic; they also asked for taxation to be paid in Continental notes, such notes to be cancelled, fully realizing that the public must believe that the redemption of currency was certain, in order to give it value; they asked that the States issue a currency called the "new tenor," which should be guaranteed by Congress (.6 going to the State and .4 to Congress), hoping that the specific joint obligation would command confidence. The country thus had three kinds of money, — the notes directly issued by Congress, called old tenor, notes directly issued by the States, and notes jointly issued by the several States and Congress, called "new tenor." Every artifice of legislation was resorted to in an effort to force the circulation of these notes at par; the States by legislation enthusiastically coöperated with Congress in exercising the full power of government for this purpose. The notes were made full legal tender and refusal to accept them forfeited the debt and incurred other money penalties, pillory, imprisonment, loss of ears even, and being outlawed as enemies of their country. Their struggle for national existence intensified their efforts to make their fiat money as good as coin money, and all to no avail. Their experience ought to negative for all time the idea that the government can impart intrinsic value by its mere fiat and thus make the fiat paper money of the government the equal of commercially good money, money which the consensus of opinion declares to be good, either because its substance has commercial value or because its redemption is assured in money possessing com-

[1] Am. Almanac for 1830.

[2] Gouge, II, p. 26.

mercial value. The government can tax, and the power to tax means the power to destroy. It was by imposing an extraordinary tax upon State bank circulation that our national government in 1864 destroyed and drove out of circulation State banknotes. The government can kill by its mandate, but it cannot create value; it cannot breathe into substance of no inherent value, the quality of worth which commercial and economic law gives to another substance. Congress is entitled to leniency of judgment, however, seeking, as they were, to create a democratic government of a kind unprecedented, and at the same time waging war with a great and powerful nation. They learned their lesson and learned from bitter experience that their vigorous attempts to force a depreciated currency upon an unwilling people was bad government, bad economics, bad morals.

Having learned its lesson, Congress boldly repudiated and ignored its former policy to compel the acceptance of these notes by the people as the equivalent of coin, and on July 28, 1780, enacted:[1]

> "RESOLVED, That the principal of all loans that have been made to these United States, shall finally be discharged by paying the full current value of the bills when loaned;" (not face value, but market value at time of issue), "which payment shall be made in Spanish milled dollars, or the current exchange thereof in other money, at the time of payment. That the value of the bills when loaned, shall be ascertained for the purpose above mentioned, by computing thereon a progressive rate of depreciation, commencing at the first day of September, 1777, and continuing to the 18th day of March, 1780, in geometrical progression and proportion to the time, from period to period, as heretofore stated, assuming the depreciation at the several periods to be as follows: On the first day of March, 1778, one dollar and three-quarters of a dollar of the said bills for one Spanish dollar; on the first day of September, 1778, as four of the former for one of the latter; on the first day of March, 1779, as eighteen of the former for one of the latter; and on the eighteenth day of March, 1780, as forty of the former for one of the latter, etc. etc. etc."

[1] Tracts 3744, D., Phila. Library.

This was done, and to illustrate: $100 in bills on March 18, 1780, were redeemed at $2.50; a large percentage of repudiation, and yet the debates characterized the idea of redeeming these notes at any price above their actual value at the time of issue, as "criminal folly."

The currency issued by the various States suffered greater depreciation than that of Congress, and was redeemed at very much less than its face value.

Articles of Confederation were adopted November 15, 1778, and gave Congress coördinate power with the states to emit bills of credit, but no power to levy taxes. Sad experience wrought a rapid revolution in public sentiment, and the new constitution which was adopted and went into effect in 1789, forbade any state to coin money, emit bills of credit or make anything but gold and silver coin a legal tender. This was the beginning of a better condition of finance. State issues soon disappeared, and Continental bills as well. They were called in by fixing a date after which they should be of no value; in the meantime they could be refunded into various state or national obligations provided for such purpose by laws of the states and of Congress.

No sooner had their independence been acknowledged, than other troubles of a serious character confronted Congress. The national spirit had not been aroused except as to coöperation for mutual defence. That danger removed, local jealousies asserted themselves. Each state had large indebtedness, chiefly contracted for the general good, and which they wished the general government to assume. The apportionment of the national debt to the different states gave rise to much controversy and bitterness. It was at this juncture that the genius of Alexander Hamilton came to the rescue. No man in history has shown more creative ability; confronted with unprecedented problems, without historical precedent to point to their solution, he evolved a plan that satisfied all parties and solved all difficulties. He proposed that the general government assume all war debts of the states, and proposed a protective tariff upon imports as a means of raising revenue to meet the same. The "infant industries" of the states sorely needed protection to enable them to establish manufactures in competition with the old world. The commerce of the seas being no longer disturbed, increasing revenue from the tariff imposed realized in full measure their hope and expectation. Congress assumed claims of the States to the amount of $21,500,000.[1]

The table on page 22, prepared by the Treasury Department, gives very full information as to the adjustment of these claims.

From January, 1780, until the close of the war, there was a plentiful supply of coin. England spent large sums in supplies for her troops and ships and it is estimated that France spent $3,000,000 here for the support of her soldiers and ships which she, as our ally, had sent to aid us against the British. Congress had also effected loans abroad which gave us additional specie.

The Bank of North America was chartered by Congress and went into operation January 7, 1782, at Philadelphia. It also received charters from several States. Congress took stock to the extent of about $254,000 as against about $70,000 taken by citizens.[2] The bank was of little aid in the prosecution of the Revolutionary War, having commenced business after Cornwallis' surrender (October 9, 1781), but it was effective as an aid to commerce and trade.

The colonies could hardly have achieved their independence, at least not at that time, without the aid of France. France furnished them arms and munitions, at the inception of the war, to the amount of $200,000. France not only recognized and welcomed the United States into the sisterhood of nations, but entered into a treaty of alliance, in 1778, one article of which pledged the colonies not to make peace until England recognized their complete independence; she gave them confidence and

[1] Laws of the U. S., Aug. 4, 1790. [2] Gouge, II, p. 34.

credit by making them loans; she sent soldiers and sailors to their assistance and spent much good, hard money in the United States, in support of her army and navy, following the treaty of alliance. Washington's army, in 1781, after a hard winter at Morristown, was in no condition for a campaign, and almost in a state of mutiny because they had not been paid in over a year. French money enabled Washington to pay and equip his army and go south in pursuit of Cornwallis. The French fleet, under De Grasse, defeated the British fleet and drove them out of the Chesapeake, thereby depriving Cornwallis of all hope of reënforcements from the British troops stationed in New York, and also cutting off all hope of escape by sea. When Cornwallis was finally rounded up at Yorktown, gazing toward the bay, he looked into the guns of 36 ships of the line of France. He was confronted on land by 7000 French veterans, well armed and equipped and well officered under Rochambeau and Lafayette. Washington had, in addition, 5500 regulars and 3500 militia. A hopeless battle resulted in Cornwallis' surrender. It was the last battle of the war; our independence was won, but, in self-gratulation, let us not forget the magnitude of our obligation to France. Her motives in aiding us may not have been altogether altruistic, may have been inspired by hostility for England as well as love for us; even so, the service rendered is in no degree diminished. The sustaining influence of this help from France, upon our currency and credit, is plain and was far-reaching. Our nation was born amid the martial airs and chivalric deeds of France, and was consecrated by the blood of her soldiers and sailors. If we love our country and cherish our institutions and our freedom, our hearts should ever and always go out to France in gratitude and love.

ABSTRACT OF THE BALANCES DUE TO AND FROM THE SEVERAL STATES, ON THE ADJUSTMENT OF THEIR ACCOUNTS WITH THE UNITED STATES, BY THE GENERAL BOARD OF COMMISSIONERS APPOINTED FOR THAT PURPOSE, UNDER THE SEVERAL ACTS OF CONGRESS, FOR THE FINAL SETTLEMENT OF THE STATE ACCOUNTS, PER THEIR REPORT OF THE 27TH JUNE, 1793.

STATES	Sums allowed to the Credit of the Several States, with Interest to the 1st January, 1790	Advances made by the United States to the Several States, together with the Assumption of the State Debts and Interest to the 1st January, 1790	Balance due to the Several States	Population of the United States answering to the Rule prescribed in the Constitution of the United States	Proportion of the Several States of $77,666,678, the aggregate Amount of the Balances (payable by each State according to Population)	Sums due to Creditor States	Sums due by Debtor States	Proportion of the Several States' Debts authorized to be funded by the 13th Section of the Act 4th August, 1790	Amount of debt funded by each State under the said section
New Hampshire	$4,278,015.02	$1,082,594.02	$3,198.061	141,722	$3,120,006	$75,055	....	$300,000	$282,595.51
Massachusetts	17,964,613.03	6,258,880.03	11,705,733	475,327	10,456,932	1,248,801	....	4,000,000	3,981,733.05
Rhode Island	3,782,974.46	1,977,608.46	1,805,366	68,446	1,505,755	299,611	....	200,000	200,000.00
Connecticut	9,285,737.92	3,456,244.92	5,829,493	236,841	5,210,372	619,121	....	1,600,000	1,600,000.00
New York	7,179,982.78	1,960,031.78	5,219,951	331,590	7,294,797	....	$2,074,846	1,200,000	1,183,716.69
New Jersey	5,342,770.52	1,343,321.52	3,999,449	179,569	3,050,419	49,030	....	800,000	695,202.70
Pennsylvania	14,137,076.22	4,690,686.22	9,446,390	432,879	9,523,099	....	76,709	2,200,000	777,983.48
Delaware	739,319.98	229,898.98	609,421	55,540	1,221,849	....	612,428	200,000	59,262.65
Maryland	7,568,145.38	1,591,631.38	5,975,514	278,514	6,127,154	....	151,640	800,000	517,491.08
Virginia	19,085,981.51	3,803,416.51	15,282,565	699,265	15,383,444	....	100,879	3,500,000	2,934,443.29
North Carolina	10,427,586.13	3,151,358.13	7,276,228	353,523	7,777,310	....	501,082	2,400,000	1,793,803.85
South Carolina	11,523,299	5,780,264.29	5,743,035	206,235	4,537,057	1,205,978	....	4,000,000	3,999,650.73
Georgia	2,993,800	1,415,328.86	1,578,472	70,842	1,558,484	19,988	....	3,000,000	246,030.73
	$114,409,303.10	$36,742,625.10	$77,666,678	3,530,393	$77,666,678	$3,517,584	[1]$3,517,584	$21,500,000	$10,271,814.74

Treasury Department, Register's Office, February 9, 1831. T. L. SMITH, *Treasurer*.

[1] New York, Pennsylvania, Delaware, Maryland, Virginia and North Carolina have never paid their debit balances.

CHAPTER III

SOUND MONEY IN NATIONAL POLITICS

OUR laws with reference to paper currency have been largely influenced by the distribution of governmental authority peculiar to the United States, and entirely separate and distinct interests have thereby been brought into antagonism and have militated against the adoption of the most desirable currency system.

From the Declaration of Independence until the close of the Civil War in 1865, the United States as a nation was in a formative period. The thirteen colonies had organized a confederacy to resist oppression from abroad, but with insufficient and ill-defined powers, and as soon as they had fought to a successful issue and been recognized as an independent nation, they began to be jealous and distrustful of the powers which must necessarily be given to the general government in order to form a permanent nation. Oppressive debt, disorganized business and depreciated currency presented grave economic problems for solution, at a time when the greater and graver problem of creating a government based upon the consent of the governed, evidenced by popular suffrage, must first be solved, in order that it might in turn bring order, credit and prosperity out of existing chaos. The colonies were held together by the cohesive force of self-preservation in the presence of the arms of a powerful and aggressive foe. When this pressure was once removed, the tendency toward separate action and assertion of antagonistic interests on the part of the colonies became pronounced.

Tenacious of their liberties, the people were greatly impressed with possible danger from an arbitrary exercise of power on the part of a central government, and in framing the Constitution the powers of the several states were subordinated to the national government with halting jealousy and only where deemed indispensable. The nation was thus started with a dual sovereignty. The citizens owed allegiance to the states in which they lived, as well as to the nation, and the respects in which each was paramount were as to many questions left in the realm of debate. Seven of the original thirteen states accompanied their ratification of the Constitution with proposed amendments, and many states seemed to regard its obligations lightly. Withdrawal from the Union was freely discussed as an alternative and by no means impossible remedy for unsatisfactory treatment.

In 1798, Kentucky, roused by its opposition to the alien and sedition laws passed by Congress, adopted resolutions reciting, among other things, that the national government was created by a compact among the states and "was not made the exclusive or final judge of the extent of the powers delegated to itself, but that, as in all other cases of compact among powers having no common judge, each party has an equal right to judge for itself as well of infraction as of the mode and measure of redress." Virginia passed nearly identical resolutions in 1799. In other states similar doctrines were at times proclaimed, notably at a later period by the abolitionists of the North, who advocated withdrawal from the Union to escape the partnership in the toleration of slavery.

If the House of Representatives, the Senate and the President concur as to an act of legislation, it becomes a law. If any question as to its constitutionality arises, the theory of the Constitution is that such question is to be determined by the Supreme Court, there being thus four separate parties whose concurrence is necessary before a law becomes final and binding beyond question. The Kentucky resolutions sought to introduce a fifth party and to assert that each state as a party to the compact of federation might determine for itself the limitation of power which the general government possesses.

This doctrine, in all its refinement, culminated in the nullification ordinance adopted by South Carolina in November, 1832, which declared the United States tariff law "null and void, and no law, nor binding on this state, its officers or citizens," and no duties were to be paid in that state and no appeal to the Supreme Court of the United States was to be permitted. The energetic determination of President Jackson to enforce the law, coupled with the "Clay Compromise," a modification of some of the law's most objectionable provisions, deferred but did not settle the constitutional issues involved.

The status of slavery in the Constitution was the occasion of prolonged controversy; and by its terms as finally settled, the importation of slaves could not be prohibited for twenty years, and three-fifths of the slave population was to be counted in determining the basis of representation of the several states in Congress and in the Electoral College. Each state was allotted two senators, and representatives were apportioned according to population. The number of votes to which each state became entitled in the Electoral College, which chooses the President and Vice-president, was and still is equal to its congressional representation, that is, its senators and representatives combined. Allowing three-fifths of the slave population, while not enjoying the suffrage, to be counted in determining the representative population, gave to the white population of the slaveholding states a preponderating influence in national affairs, which was bound to provoke controversy. In laying the foundation of the nation, the framers of the Constitution also laid the foundation of an "irrepressible conflict," and the opposition to slavery which found expression in the constitutional debates was continued with growing intensity, although usually as a moral rather than political question. Its abolition in the northern states, owing very largely to climatic conditions, as well as for ethical reasons, made the question of slavery a sectional one.

The first pronounced conflict arose over the admission of Missouri as a state in 1818–1819. It was admitted in 1821 as a slave state, after the "Missouri Compromise" (Act of March 2, 1820) had provided that slavery should forever be excluded from all national territory west of Missouri and north of 36° 30′ (the southern boundary of the state). In 1846 the "Wilmot Proviso," an amendment to an act appropriating money with which to purchase territory from the government of Mexico, proposed to exclude slavery and involuntary servitude forever from all territory so acquired. It was adopted by the House, but later reconsidered and defeated. This episode marked the formation of a political party, whose avowed and direct purpose was to prevent the extension of slavery in the territories of the United States. Their propaganda was followed by a powerful and continuous onslaught upon the institution of slavery on moral and religious grounds, and created a strong sentiment in favor of its abolition, which ultimately became effective.

Slavery, involving enormous property interests, depended for protection and championship upon the several state governments, and this fact throughout this period gave to the doctrine of state rights and "state sovereignty" its principal element of strength. Largely inspired by this influence, the power given to the general government under the Constitution was rigidly construed, circumscribed within the narrowest limits, and any attempt at liberal construction or enlargement with reference to any subject was tenaciously fought by the champions of state rights. All efforts by the general government to regulate banking and currency encountered the opposition of the strict constructionists in all its virulence as well as that of the state bank interests. The power of Congress to appropriate money for national highways was questioned, and no relaxation or liberalization of constitutional provisions was permitted, lest it should form a precedent that might militate against the slaveholding interests.

The preservation of the Union is traceable to the fact that the National or Federal party controlled the councils of the government during its earlier years. In this connection too much praise cannot be bestowed upon the genius and statesmanship of Hamilton, the judicial wisdom and statesmanship of Marshall. It will appear in the following history that whenever national sentiment and national influence have moulded legislation and controlled the general government, enhanced prosperity has ensued, as during the periods of the first and second United States banks and that of the national banking system. Whenever the disintegrating influence involved in the doctrine of state sovereignty has been paramount, adverse conditions have prevailed, as during the period following the expiration of the charter of the first United States Bank (1811) until the second bank was well under way, and the period between the expiration of the charter of the second bank (1836) and the creation of the national banking system (1863).

The right of secession, and the doctrine of state sovereignty as it had been proclaimed, as well as slavery itself, were buried, and the permanency of the Union and the paramountcy of the general government settled, by the verdict of the Civil War (1861–1865).

The government had been in the habit of borrowing money in the form of notes; for instance, under the administration of President Buchanan, December 23, 1857, it authorized the issue of $20,000,000 of notes, running for a period of one year and bearing interest at a rate to be fixed by the Secretary of the Treasury, not exceeding 6 per cent. These notes were receivable for "all debts of the United States of any character whatever." Another issue, not exceeding $10,000,000, was authorized December 17, 1860, to run for a period of one year and bear interest. They were sold at auction to the responsible party who would bid par and the lowest rate of interest. The acts of July 17 and August 5, 1861, and February 12, 1862, authorized an issue of $60,000,000 of demand notes. The act of February 25, 1862, authorized an issue of $150,000,000 in Treasury notes, which were designed to refund or retire all demand notes theretofore authorized. These notes were made "receivable in payment of all taxes, internal duties, excises, debts and demands of every kind due to the United States, except duties on imports, and of all claims and demands against the United States of every kind whatsoever, except for interest upon bonds and notes, which shall be paid in coin, and shall also be lawful money and a legal tender in payment of all debts, public and private, within the United States, except duties on imports and interest as aforesaid."

The act of July 11, 1862, authorized a similar additional issue of $150,000,000. This act also provided for the funding of any notes outstanding, and the 6 per cent. bonds.

On January 17, 1863, by joint resolution of Congress, providing for the immediate payment of the army and navy of the United States, an issue of $100,000,000 was authorized, not to bear interest and not to be in denominations of less than $1. They were legal tender except in payment of duties on imports and interest on the public debt. These notes were straight fiat money, not drawing interest, not convertible into bonds drawing interest.[1]

It thus appears that Congress, spurred by "military necessity," the necessity of preserving national existence, against its proclaimed conviction as to its constitutional powers, and despite all its previous experience, went to the limit in creating an irredeemable fiat currency with legal tender power. These notes were thus forced into circulation in payment of the current indebtedness of the government and have ever since formed an important part of the circulation of the country, the amount at the present time being $346,000,000.

[1] The government at intervals publishes a document containing United States laws relating to loans, money, banking and coinage from 1790 down to the date of publication. Full particulars of all legislation may be had by reference to this volume.

As soon as the war was over, the constitutionality of the act creating such notes a legal tender was raised in the courts. The matter came before the Supreme Court twice without a decision, but finally, in 1884, nearly a century after our existence as a nation, the Supreme Court decided that Congress had the power to issue full legal tender notes at any and all times, in its discretion, and in effect decided that all sovereign powers pertaining to government were reposed in Congress except where specifically prohibited, or reserved to the states. Salmon P. Chase was Secretary of the Treasury at the time these legal tender issues were authorized by Congress, and approved the same. He was Chief Justice of the United States in 1884, when the question of their constitutionality was finally passed upon, and voted with the minority against the right of Congress to issue paper money and make the same a legal tender in payment of debts.

We have already seen that vigorous measures of taxation would have saved the colonies and Continental Congress from the appalling loss which a badly depreciated currency brought upon all branches of industry and trade. Had Congress possessed the courage to adopt measures of taxation, which would have produced large revenues, they would have saved the country from the evils of inflation, depreciation and subsequent contraction which inevitably ensued.

It seems strange, while all recognized the desirability of having the coinage regulated by the central government, so much so that the power was given exclusively to Congress in the Constitution, thus insuring uniformity throughout the nation, that there should not have been an equal desire to have the paper currency regulated by the same central authority and thus likewise made uniform and good throughout the length and breadth of the land. Such, indeed, was the design of Hamilton and Marshall, but there was a powerful party opposed to the issue of paper currency in any form by the general government. The matter having been left in doubt in the organic law, political exigencies controlled the question and the creation and regulation of paper currency were for years left to the different states.

There is always difficulty in changing existing conditions when by so doing you disturb vested interests and interfere with established business. Precedent and habit are important factors in public as well as private affairs. But the failure earlier to appreciate and adopt a national system of paper currency can only be explained by the jealous desire on the part of the states to minimize the powers of the general government.

Whether it be a great university, a great industrial enterprise or a great nation, successful conduct and maximum development depend upon efficient, intelligent central control. The unity of the nation, the paramount sovereign powers of the central government over all questions except as clearly limited by the Constitution, have been settled by force of arms, by public sentiment, by law and judicial interpretation.

Naught but a national currency will now be tolerated. Such a currency we have, and the problem is to improve the system upon lines requisite to give the greatest measure of utility possible and make the currency in fact what it is in theory, the handmaiden of commerce and the corner-stone of prosperity. The experience of the past yields present wisdom and future guidance. The experience of the colonies and the states presents the money question as affecting individuals and government in every conceivable phase. Sound principle and false theory are wrought out in the fierce fires of controversy and proved or disproved by the severe test of experience, and yield their lessons of value for all charged with the duty and responsibility of citizenship.

Sound money means money made of (or unquestionably redeemable in) a commodity which has a stable value in the markets of the world independent of fiat. Sound money as applied to coin means money wherein the commercial value of the bullion equals its coinage value. Sound money as applied to paper or token money of any kind means that which is redeemable in money wherein the commercial value of its bullion equals its coinage value.

The term "sound money" doubtless originated from the auricular test commonly applied to coins. The counter or other convenient surface offering an opportunity, the coin is dropped thereon, and its quality depends upon whether the resulting ring possesses the true sound or not.

The test of sound money varies with different periods, and is determined by varying conditions. The term has, however, a general significance easily understood, is concise, cogent and seems to have found a permanent place in our economic literature.

Nomenclature

The coins of various countries take their names, largely, from the weight of the precious metal contained, from the power under which they were issued and also from the devices appearing upon the coins.

Shekel was a weight of the Hebrews — *As* a Roman weight — *Denarius*, Roman — *Denier*, French, and *Dime*, United States; all mean tenths of the principal coin. The English *Pound* was formerly a Troy pound of sterling silver. The *ducat* (*duke*), *sovereign*, *crown* or *krone*, the *imperial*, *louis d'or*, *friedericks d'or*, *napoleon* and others take their names from the authority which issued them.

Other coins take their names from devices which they bear — *florin* (flower), *escudo* (shield), *eagle* (United States $10), *condor* (South America). *Dollar* comes from the German *thaler*, also the *rigsdaler* of Scandinavia and *rixdaler* of the Dutch. The United States dollar is based upon the Spanish *milled* dollar, which long circulated in our country and was for periods a legal tender; milled refers to the corrugated edge, now so common in coins, which was devised to prevent debasement by clipping or otherwise; clipping or sweating was bound to be apparent by removing the milled edges. The Mexican *peso* consisted of eight *reals* (rey, king); they circulated extensively in this country; these *reals* (nominal value 12½¢) were called *shillings* in some sections, *bits* and *levies* in others. *Franc* comes from the Francs, who settled or overran France and adjoining countries; under various names, but with identical value, this coin has been copied in many countries.

CHAPTER IV

Coinage System

1776–1789

The American colonies, prior to the Confederation in 1778, had almost as many systems of money as there were distinct colonies. Inasmuch as the majority of the inhabitants were of British birth and traded chiefly with the mother country and with each other, and as pounds, shillings and pence had thus become the money of account, the monetary units were in some measure similar, although, as frequently occurs in colonies, the money of account imposed by the mother country differed from the money in actual use.

The colonies generally reckoned in pounds, shillings and pence, but in actual transactions other coins, chiefly the Spanish dollar and its subdivisions, constituted the medium of exchange. The gold coins in use other than British pieces were the French guinea and pistole, the Portuguese moidore and johannes or "joe," the Spanish doubloon and pistole. Silver coins in circulation other than British were the French crowns and livres and the Spanish pieces, the latter being, as before stated, most prevalent.[1]

The people were naturally compelled to find an equivalence between the money of account and that of exchange, and hence the practice of reckoning the dollar at so many shillings obtained. The valuation varied in different colonies. In what is known as New England and in Virginia the dollar was six shillings; in

[1] MS. Reports, Committee on Finance, Continental Congress, Vol. 26; reprinted in International Monetary Conference, 1878, p. 422.

New York and in North Carolina it was valued at eight shillings; in Georgia at five; in South Carolina at thirty-two and one-half; and in the remaining four colonies at seven and one-half.[1]

The shillings here referred to evidently differed in value and were not in fact the English shillings, for it is declared in a law of Massachusetts of 1750, that the value of the English shilling was equal to one and one-third of the Massachusetts shillings. The "shillings" of most of the other colonies must have been worth much less, therefore, in English coin. The established rate of exchange with London was four shillings and sixpence to the dollar.

Jefferson stated that the tenth part of a Spanish dollar was known as the "bit," yet in states other than Virginia the term was applied to the eighth of a dollar, the same as the "York shilling," and to this day in the western and southwestern sections of the country the quarter-dollar is called "two bits."

The Continental Congress undertook the task of creating a uniform system out of this apparent chaos at a time when the actual currency in circulation was depreciated paper. It may be said to have fixed upon the *unit* finally adopted as early as 1775, when it authorized the issue of notes payable in "Spanish milled *dollars*," [2] but it was not finally and specifically determined upon until several years later.

In April, 1776, the Continental Congress appointed a committee of seven "to examine and ascertain the value of the several species of Gold and Silver coins, current in these colonies, and the proportions they ought to bear to Spanish milled dollars." [3]

[1] Report of Robert Morris, Supt. of Finance, Vol. 1, p. 289.

[2] Mass. 23d George II, Ch. 5 provides that all payments after March 31, 1750, "shall be understood and are hereby declared to be in silver, at six shillings and eight pence per ounce, and all Spanish milled pieces of eight of full weight shall be accounted, taken and paid at the rate of six shillings, etc." The value of a guinea was fixed at 28 shillings; crown at 6 shillings, 8 pence; English shilling at 1 shilling, 4 pence, Massachusetts currency; a Johannes at 48 shillings; Moidore at 36 shillings; pistole at 22 shillings.

[3] Journal Continental Congress; reprinted in International Monetary Conference, 1878, p. 419.

The committee reported, in September following, a resolution fixing such values for the several kinds of coin in circulation, under which the English shilling was rated at two-ninths of a dollar, or about $22\frac{2}{9}$ cents, deduction being made for abraded coins. This resolution also fixed the value of gold bullion at $17 and of silver bullion at $\$1\frac{1}{9}$ per ounce Troy, thus attempting to establish a legal ratio between gold and silver of 15.3 to 1.[1]

The Articles of Confederation were adopted in 1778, became effective in 1781, and continued in force during the remainder of the Revolution and until 1789, when the present Constitution went into operation. Article IX. provided that

> "The United States in Congress assembled shall also have the sole and exclusive right and power of regulating the alloy and value of coin struck by their own authority or by that of the respective states."

Thus the states retained the power to coin money coördinately with the Confederation, but the power to regulate its value was given to Congress.

In August, 1778, after the completion of the Articles of Confederation, Congress appointed a committee with Robert Morris as chairman, to consider the state of the money and finances of the United States. Morris was subsequently appointed Superintendent of Finance, but apparently no definite action was taken until January, 1782, when he was instructed to prepare for Congress a table of rates at which the various foreign coins should be received at the Treasury of the United States. On January 15 Morris submitted a comprehensive report[2] on a coinage system, in which he pointed out the need not only of a uniform system of coins, but of legal tender provisions as well.

After discussing the ratio of silver to gold and the fluctuations in the market value of the precious metals, he concluded that

[1] MS. Reports, Committee on Finance; reprinted in International Monetary Conference, 1878, p. 422.

[2] MS. Reports, Superintendent of Finance, Vol. I; reprinted in International Monetary Conference, 1878, p. 425.

the money standard for the United States ought to be affixed to silver. He favored a coinage charge, urged that the money unit should be very small, and that the decimal system be established.

After suggesting that the Spanish dollar had undergone the least change in intrinsic value, he recommended a money unit which would be the 1440th part of a dollar, or a quarter of a grain of pure silver. Such a unit agreed without a fraction with all the differing valuations of the dollar in the several states. Of these units he proposed that 100 constitute the lowest silver coin, to be called the cent, containing, therefore, 25 grains of silver, to which he proposed adding for alloy two grains of copper; five of these cents to constitute a piece to be called the quint; and ten, or one thousand of the original units, a piece to be called the mark. He favored a ratio between silver and gold of 14½ to 1. He recommended the establishment of a mint and the coinage of the pieces suggested. Congress on February 21, 1782, approved this recommendation and directed Morris to report a plan therefor.[1] This was the first action toward establishing a federal mint.

In December, 1782, Morris recommended to Congress a resolution fixing a valuation of foreign coins, measured in dollars, in order to prevent their exportation, which was denuding the country of specie. In April, 1783, he submitted to Congress specimens of coins prepared by him, and asked further consideration of his mint and coinage proposition. Both these matters were referred to a committee, which did not report for some time.

Meanwhile Jefferson had taken up Morris's plan for a coinage system and submitted a substitute. He recommended the adoption of the Spanish dollar as the unit, as best answering all requirements, and easy of adoption because then practically in

[1] Journal Continental Congress; International Monetary Conference, 1878, p. 432.

general use. His system comprised a gold coin of ten dollars, the unit or dollar of silver, the tenth of a dollar, also of silver, and the one hundredth of a dollar of copper, and supplemental thereto a half dollar, a double tenth (twenty cents), and a twentieth of a dollar. He criticised Morris's plan as less easy of adoption and more laborious in operation than the purely decimal system.

As to the contents of the dollar, he recommended finding the average weight of pure silver in the dollars then in use and adopting the resulting weight, to be coined at a fineness of eleven-twelfths. He proposed fixing a proportion between gold and silver coinage at the average ratio of the nations trading with the United States, which would probably be 15 to 1, and also that the coins provided should be made lawful tender unless diminished in weight. Jefferson's paper was also referred to a committee, which did not, however, reach a conclusion until May, 1785. Morris had meanwhile retired from the Finance Department.

The system recommended was as follows: Ratio of the metals, 15 to 1; a gold piece of five dollars; a silver dollar or unit, containing 362 grains of pure silver; 50, 25, 10, and 5 cent pieces of silver; all gold and silver coins to be eleven-twelfths fine, with a coinage charge of 2 to 2¼ per cent.; two copper coins of one cent and one-half cent respectively.[1]

Action upon the report as a whole was postponed, but in July, 1785, the following resolutions, fixing upon three fundamental propositions, were adopted by Congress: —

"That the money unit of the United States of America be one dollar."

"That the smallest coin be of copper, of which 200 shall pay for one dollar."

"That the several pieces shall increase in decimal ratio." [2]

[1] MS. Reports, Committee on Finance, Vol. 26; International Monetary Conference, 1878, p. 445.

[2] Journal Continental Congress; International Monetary Conference, p. 448.

In April, 1786, the Board of Treasury submitted to Congress three alternative propositions concerning the weight and fineness of the coinage proposed, as exhibited in the table below.

WEIGHT OF PURE METAL

	Silver Dollar	Gold Dollar	Ratio
	grains	grains	
I.	375.64	24.6268	15.253 to 1
II.	350.09	23.79	14.749 to 1
III.	521.73	34.782	15 to 1

Congress on August 8, 1786, passed a resolution fixing the fineness of gold and silver coins at eleven-twelfths, the dollar or unit to contain 375.64 grains of pure silver. It provided for mills, or 1000ths of a dollar, as the lowest money of account, and coins as follows: half cents and cents of copper; dimes or tenths of a dollar, double dimes (20 cents), half dollars and dollars, of silver; five dollars and ten dollars, of gold; the latter being coined at 24.6268 grains pure metal to the dollar, thus giving the ratio 15.253 to 1 as above stated. The copper coinage was to be at the rate of 100 cents for $2\frac{1}{4}$ pounds avoirdupois of copper.

Finally, pursuant to a report of the Board of Treasury of September 20, 1786, Congress on October 16 of that year passed the ordinance establishing the mint.

The mint price of standard gold, eleven-twelfths (or $.916\frac{2}{3}$) fine, was fixed at $209.77 and of standard silver, of the same fineness, at $13.777, for the pound Troy, with a coinage charge of 2 per cent., giving a ratio of 15.22 to 1. Deposits of gold or silver were to be paid for, 95 per cent. in gold or silver and 5 per cent. in copper coin.

The act never became fully operative. Only copper coins were actually struck under this law, and these were made receivable for taxes and public dues to the extent of 5 per cent. in any payment, all other copper coins being excluded. After September 1, 1787, foreign copper coins were to cease to be current, and copper coins struck by the states were rated by weight at the value fixed by the coinage law of August 8, 1786, viz., 100 cents for $2\frac{1}{4}$ pounds.

The financial as well as the general economic condition of the country at this time was so unsettled, that it became obvious to most of the leading men in the colonies that a more stable form of government for the confederation was absolutely necessary. A convention of the states was called to meet in Annapolis, Maryland, in 1786. Nothing came of this, and another convention met in Philadelphia in 1787. Although primarily assembled to consider economic questions, the deliberations of the convention ultimately produced a new form of government, the present Constitution (without the amendments).

Respecting the coinage system that instrument provides

"ART. 1. SEC. 8. The Congress shall have Power . . .
To coin Money, regulate the Value thereof, and of foreign Coin."

"SEC. 10. No State shall . . . coin Money; make any Thing but gold and silver Coin a Tender in Payment of Debts."

Thus the states surrendered the right to coin money, the power over the standard becoming an exclusively federal function.

STATISTICAL RÉSUMÉ

COMMERCIAL RATIO OF SILVER TO GOLD

Soetbeer's Estimate based on Hamburg Prices

Year	Ratio	Year	Ratio	Year	Ratio	Year	Ratio
1775	14.72	1779	14.80	1783	14.48	1787	14.92
1776	14.55	1780	14.72	1784	14.70	1788	14.65
1777	14.54	1781	14.78	1785	14.92	1789	14.75
1778	14.68	1782	14.42	1786	14.96	1790	15.04

Production of Gold and Silver

The most reliable data respecting the world's production of gold and silver toward the close of the eighteenth century give the following *annual averages:* —

Decade	Gold	Silver
1761–1780	$13,761,000	$27,133,000
1781–1800	11,823,000	36,540,000

No reliable data for annual periods are available, the above estimates being conclusions reached by Soetbeer after the most exhaustive study of the subject ever attempted.

The evidence all tends to verify the general conclusion that the production of gold diminished and that of silver increased, thus accounting for the fall in the market price of silver as indicated in the table of ratios.

The production of precious metals in the United States prior to 1800 was insignificant in amount.

CHAPTER V

COINAGE SYSTEM

1790–1829

THE new form of government was nominally put into operation on March 4, 1789. Actually the transition was very deliberate. Washington was not inaugurated as President until April 30, and the Treasury Department was not provided for by law until the following September.

Alexander Hamilton was the first Secretary of the Treasury, and soon after organizing the Department he set himself the task of establishing a comprehensive federal monetary system. He first took up the question of the public debt, then the establishment of a banking system, and on January 21, 1791, presented to Congress his justly celebrated report upon the establishment of a mint and a coinage system for the United States.

He examined this comprehensive subject in all its aspects and ramifications, presenting the facts and arguments bearing upon both sides of each question, and after careful analysis reached the following conclusions: —

1. That the dollar, because it had been in actual use as the measure of values in practically all of the states, was the most suitable unit for the proposed system; that it was of the utmost importance to define as exactly as possible just what the dollar was, in order that neither debtors nor creditors might be injuriously affected. The dollars in existence varied considerably, Spain having degraded or changed the standard at different times. He therefore recommended a dollar containing 371.25 grains

of pure silver, as best expressing the actual average value of the coin in use.

2. That the decimal system was of demonstrated superiority over the duodecimal of Great Britain.

3. That inasmuch as the undervaluation of either metal would cause its exportation, thus shifting the standard to the other, which might result injuriously, and since it was very desirable to have coins of both metals in actual use, the ratio should conform as nearly as possible to the commercial ratio, rather than follow any specific European precedent. He therefore recommended the ratio of 15 to 1.

4. That the silver dollar was the equivalent of 24.75 grains of gold, and therefore a gold dollar containing that quantity of metal be also provided for, in order that there might be a unit coin in each metal.

5. That the fineness of the coins should be eleven-twelfths or .916⅔, corresponding with the British standard of fineness for gold; the alloys being for gold coins, silver and copper; for silver coins, copper only.

6. That no mint charge should be imposed upon the bullion brought for coinage, the cost thereof being properly a general charge rather than one to be imposed upon specific individuals, and to impose a charge might influence prices in international relations, being in effect a reduction of the standard of the coin, as compared with bullion.

7. That foreign coins should be permitted to circulate for one year, that thereafter certain foreign pieces might be tolerated for another year or two; anticipating that the mint would be prepared to provide all the coin needed, he concluded that after three years the use of foreign coins should be prohibited.

Hamilton's report was reviewed by Jefferson, who, in a short letter, expressed concurrence upon the bimetallic proposition and other features of Hamilton's plan.

Congress gave Hamilton's recommendation attention and

passed a resolution for the establishment of a mint on March 3, 1791, but it was not until April 2, 1792, after being spurred by President Washington, that the act establishing a coinage system was finally passed.

The act, after providing for the organization of the mint directed, in Section 9, the coinage of the following pieces: —

Denominations		Weight in Grains	
		Gross	Fine
Gold	Eagles, $10	270	$247\frac{4}{8}$
	Half Eagles, $5	135	$123\frac{6}{8}$
	Quarter Eagles, $2\frac{1}{2}$	$67\frac{4}{8}$	$61\frac{7}{8}$
Silver	Dollars or Units	416	$371\frac{4}{16}$
	Half Dollars	208	$185\frac{10}{16}$
	Quarter Dollars	104	$92\frac{13}{16}$
	Dismes	$41\frac{3}{5}$	$37\frac{2}{16}$
	Half Dismes	$20\frac{4}{5}$	$18\frac{9}{16}$
Copper	Cents	264	264
	Half Cents	132	132

(The act of March 3, 1849, provided for the coinage of gold dollars and double eagles.

The act of February 21, 1853, provided for $3 gold pieces.

The act of September 26, 1890, abolished the coinage of $3 and $1 pieces.)

Section 10 provided for devices on coins.

Section 11 fixed the ratio at 15 to 1, the language being: —

"That the proportional value of gold to silver in all coins which shall by law be current as money within the United States, shall be as fifteen to one, according to quantity in weight, of pure gold or pure silver; that is to say, every fifteen pounds weight of pure silver shall be of equal value in all payments, with one pound weight of pure gold, and so in proportion as to any greater or less quantities of the respective metals."

Section 12 fixed the standard of fineness for the gold coins at eleven-twelfths, the British standard, equal to $.916\frac{2}{3}$, the alloy to be silver and copper, not to exceed one-half of the former metal.

The fineness of the silver coins was by Section 13 fixed at 1485 parts pure metal and 179 parts copper alloy, equal to .89243.[1]

No charge was imposed for coining the bullion brought to the mint, unless the depositor preferred to have payment immediately, instead of awaiting the coinage of the bullion, in which case a deduction of one-half of one per cent. was to be made. A strict provision against giving preference to depositors was included in Section 15.

Section 16 declared that the gold and silver coins provided for "shall be a lawful tender in all payments whatsoever," abraded coins being legal tender for the relative weight thereof.

After prescribing directions for the officers and imposing the penalty of death for fraudulently debasing the coinage or embezzlement on the part of such officers, the act concluded (Sec. 20) with the provision that "the money of account of the United States shall be expressed in dollars, dismes or tenths, cents or hundredths, and milles or thousandths," and that the accounts of public officers were to be kept and proceedings of courts to be had accordingly.

When the act first passed the Senate it provided for an impression on the coins of the head of the President for the time being, in imitation of the coinage of most European countries. This proviso was stricken out in the House of Representatives, and after some discussion the Senate concurred.

Much to Hamilton's chagrin the business of the mint was attached to the Department of State, under Jefferson, and not until after Hamilton, when resigning, called attention to this anomaly, was it transferred to the Treasury Department.[2]

[1] It appears that notwithstanding the statute, the first and second directors of the mint coined dollars at the fineness of .900, thus giving them 374.4 grains of pure metal. This appears to have been tacitly sanctioned by both Jefferson and Hamilton. The ratio was thus altered to 15⅛ to 1. See White's Report, No. 496, 22d Congress, 1st Sess., p. 17; quoted by Watson, Hist. of Amer. Coinage, p. 230.

[2] Life of Hamilton, Vol. VI., p. 186.

This legislation based upon the report of Hamilton was the first attempt in the world to adopt *by law* a bimetallic standard with all the requisite features of free and unlimited coinage of both metals and giving full legal tender power to both.

Hamilton's conception of the proper ratio was not far out of the way, as is shown by the table giving the commercial ratio for the period. Hamilton was *not* aware that the relative production of silver was increasing, so that the commercial ratio would very soon be changed, and naturally when in 1803 France adopted a ratio of $15\frac{1}{2}$ to 1 the disappearance of gold from this country resulted. It was thus early in the history of the United States demonstrated that it was impossible for any one country to maintain *independently* a ratio between the metals differing materially from that fixed by the world's markets.

On May 8, 1792, Congress passed an act providing for the purchase of 150 tons of copper for the coinage of cents and half cents, and that when $50,000 of these pieces had been struck, public notice be given that after six months from that date no other copper pieces were to pass current, or be offered, paid, or received in payment for any debt, etc., under penalty of forfeiture and fine, recoverable by the informer.

The first coins were struck in October, 1792, being a small amount of half dimes, referred to in President Washington's address to Congress at its following session: —

> "There has also been a small beginning in the coinage of half-dismes, the want of small coins in circulation calling for the first attention to them."

The weight of the copper coins was reduced by the act of January 14, 1793, to 208 and 104 grains respectively. By the act of March 3, 1796, further reduction in weight by proclamation of the President was authorized.

Sundry other acts relating to the mint and coinage were passed prior to the general revision of 1834. It is necessary to note only the following: —

March 3, 1796, authorizing a charge upon bullion deposited for coinage if below the standard.

April 24, 1800, March 3, 1823, and May 19, 1825, further providing for charges upon bullion deposits not suitable for immediate coinage, whether above or below the standard.

It was not until February 9, 1793, that Congress modified the existing valuations of foreign coins.[1] From and after the first of July following the date of the act, British and Portuguese gold pieces were to pass current and be *legal tender* at the rate of 100 cents for every 27 grains' weight, French and Spanish gold pieces at 100 cents for $27\frac{2}{5}$ grains, the difference being due to the greater fineness of the gold coin of the first-mentioned countries. Silver coins were rated as follows: the Spanish dollar if weighing 17 pennyweight 7 grains, at 100 cents, and proportionately for lighter coins; French crowns at 110 cents, if weighing 18 pennyweight 17 grains, and proportionately for parts of a crown.

It provided further, that after three years from the date of the beginning of the coinage of gold and silver at the mint (to be proclaimed by the President) no foreign coins *except the Spanish dollar and parts thereof*[2] were to be legal tender. Other foreign coins received by the United States thereafter were to be recoined into coins prescribed by the mint act.

The coinage of the mint was not sufficiently large, however, to provide for the country's needs, and accordingly the above-mentioned act giving legal tender power to foreign gold and silver coins was renewed without change by the acts of February 1, 1798, and April 10, 1806.

The act of April 29, 1816, again continued the provision for three years, including the French five-franc piece; this was again continued by the act of March 3, 1819, until November 1, 1819, for gold coins (after which date they were no longer legal

[1] Fixed by tariff law of July 31, 1789.

[2] Subsequent legislation did not alter this proviso; thus the Spanish dollar and its subdivisions continued legal tender until 1857.

tender) and until April 29, 1821, for the French silver coins. The act of March 3, 1821, continued the same provision as to the French pieces for two years more, and the act of March 3, 1823, for four years from that date. On the same day, foreign gold coins were made receivable in payment for public lands, in order to facilitate their sale to immigrants.

Notwithstanding this action favorable to foreign coin and notwithstanding that a substantial supply of gold came from the Spanish and French traders in the southwest, enabling the mint to coin considerable sums annually, the exports of gold practically drained the country of that metal. During the third decade of the nineteenth century it disappeared from circulation.

This movement was stimulated, not only by the French coinage law of 1803, which fixed a ratio of 15½ to 1, but also by the conditions during the War of 1812 and the adoption of the gold standard by England in 1816, with a subsidiary silver coinage at the ratio of 16 to 1.

During a considerable period after the refusal to renew the charter of the first bank of the United States, depreciated paper was the chief currency, — a condition not remedied until after the second bank was chartered in 1816.

Respecting silver, the country was not much more fortunate, for although the mint was turning out large amounts of the new coinage, the actual specie in use continued to be Spanish piastres (or dollars), and the subdivisions thereof, as a rule much cheapened by abrasion. Although somewhat less in weight than the Spanish pieces, the American dollars were accepted *by tale* throughout the West Indies and were exported for that reason. Spanish and Mexican pieces were imported, and those of full weight, or nearly so, were recoined into dollars at the mint, the depositors reaping the profit.

President Jefferson undertook to check this business in 1806 by directing that the mint suspend the coinage of the dollar pieces. This suspension continued until after the legislation of 1834. A similar fate befell the fractional coins, which were equally valuable for export, and the result was that the Americans were coining for other people while actually using worn foreign coin.

The evils of the disordered metallic currency grew intolerable, and Congress became impressed with the necessity for action. In consequence, numerous reports were prepared and laid before that body, but, as will appear, no action was taken until 1834.

In 1817 the Senate requested John Quincy Adams, then Secretary of State, to prepare a report upon weights and measures, which was not, however, submitted until 1821.

In connection with the general subject Adams discussed the coinage system,[1] prefacing it with a criticism of the law fixing the par of exchange for the pound sterling at $4.44, when in fact the value of the pound was $4.56572 in gold and owing to the demonetization and lower rating of silver in England, $4.3489 when reckoning in the white metal. It is not necessary to follow and verify Adams's calculations; suffice it to say that this very low rating of the pound served to embarrass transactions involving international exchange.

Adams also pointed out that the ratings in the acts governing the valuations of foreign coins were inaccurate. He did not discuss the question of the ratio specifically, but provided those who desired to do so with valuable and accurate material relative to the weights of coins. The inevitable deduction from the facts he presented and his reasoning based thereon is that he regarded the ratio very much at fault.

Although not free from errors, Adams's paper shows great labor and research upon a subject concerning which at that time very little material was available to the student.

In the meantime the House of Representatives had referred to a committee the question "whether it be expedient to make

[1] See International Monetary Conference, 1878, p. 490.

any amendment in the laws which regulate the coin of the United States and foreign coins respectively," which reported, January 26, 1819, a bill recommending that the gold coins be reduced in weight from 24.75 grains to 22.798 grains, that a seigniorage of 14.85 grains pure silver to the dollar be charged for coinage, and that the legal tender of silver coin below the dollar be limited to five dollars. This is the first suggestion that fractional silver be made subsidiary.

After discussing the various ratios prevailing, the report concludes as follows: —

"As the committee entertain no doubt that gold is estimated below its fair relative value, in comparison to silver, by the present regulations of the Mint; and as it can scarcely be considered as having formed a material part of our money circulation for the last twenty-six years, they have no hesitation in recommending that its valuation shall be raised, so as to make it bear a juster proportion to its price in the commercial world. But the smallest change which is likely to secure this object (a just proportion of gold coins in our circulation) is that which the committee prefer, and they believe it sufficient to restore gold to its original valuation in this country, of 1 to $15\frac{6}{10}$."[1]

The coinage charge imposed by this bill would have made the ratio of the bullion actually 15 to 1. Congress, however, took no action.

On March 1, 1819, the House directed Crawford, Secretary of the Treasury, to report, among other matters, "such measures as, in his opinion, may be expedient to procure and retain a sufficient quantity of gold and silver coin in the United States." A very able state paper was prepared by Crawford in response to this resolution and presented to the House in February, 1820.[2]

He argued that the difference of 1 per cent. between the Spanish and American dollar would have retained the latter in

[1] Abridgment of Debates, Vol. 6, p. 273.

[2] See International Monetary Conference, 1878, p. 502.

circulation if the former had not been made legal tender. In discussing the ratio he correctly alleged that the derangement was due to the appreciation of gold, and urged that no injustice would result from a change in the ratio which would make it correspond to the market value. He recommended the ratio of 15.75 to 1 as best calculated to correct the disparity, as it would cause the importation and retention of gold, and would not cause silver to go out unless the state of the foreign trade warranted. Upon the other hand he pointed out that the retention of a metallic currency was dependent upon the volume of paper currency in use (a subject also discussed in his report), that in fact the value of gold and silver had been materially affected by the general use of paper in leading countries, followed by the suspension of specie payments, and subsequently by efforts to resume.

Crawford's report was referred to a select committee which in February, 1821, reported conclusions agreeing with his. It was pointed out that a gold coinage amounting to $6,000,000 had practically disappeared from use, that this was unquestionably due to the ratio of 15 to 1 under which the gold coins were more valuable for export than for home use, the difference being about sixty cents upon every $15 or three half eagles.

Secretary Crawford, in a letter to a committee of the House of Representatives in February, 1823, apparently modified his view as to the ratio somewhat. He said: —

"In terminating this letter I feel it my duty to observe that the relative current value of gold and silver differs materially from that established by the laws of the United States. The consequence has been that the gold coin of the United States has always been exported whenever the rate of exchange between the United States and the commercial nations of Europe has been in favor of the latter. If the gold coins of the United States should be made equal in value to sixteen times the value of silver coins of the same quantity of pure silver, they would be exported only when the rate of exchange should be greatly against the United States." [1]

[1] Abridgment of Debates, Vol. 7, p. 429.

In a report submitted to the House by a committee having under consideration the valuation of foreign coins, in 1823,[1] it is stated that the coinage of gold and silver at the mint had been in excess of $20,000,000, whereas the amount of specie in the country, inclusive of foreign coin, was estimated at $16,000,000 (less by $1,500,000 than in 1804), and by far the greater part of the coin in the country consisted of French silver pieces, which, it will be recalled, had full legal tender power. It was upon the recommendation of this committee that this power was continued until 1827.

In the Senate at about the same time (January, 1819) the Finance Committee had reported upon a resolution as to the "expediency of prohibiting by law the exportation of gold, silver, and copper coins," concluding that it was *not* expedient. Three quotations from this report are of interest: —

> "Of the inefficiency, if not entire impotence, of legislative provisions to prevent the escape of the precious metals beyond the territorial limits of the Government, the history of all countries in which the power of legislation has been thus exercised, bears testimony. . . . Indeed, no error seems more entirely renounced and exploded, if not by the practice of all nations, at least in the disquisitions of political economists, than that which supposed that an accumulation of the precious metals could be produced in the dominions of one sovereign by regulations prohibiting their exportation to those of any other. . . . In short, it is the opinion of your committee, that commerce is always destined to flourish most where it is permitted to pursue its own paths, marked out by itself, embarrassed as little as possible by legislative regulations or restrictions."[2]

For more than a decade this question had thus been before Congress without definite progress toward the adoption of a remedy. Meanwhile the opposition to the bank of the United States (described in a later chapter), had begun, and materially interfered with calm, deliberate action.

[1] *Ibid.*, p. 427.

[2] *Ibid.*, Vol. 6, p. 190.

STATISTICAL RÉSUMÉ

Commercial Ratio of Silver to Gold

Soetbeer's Estimate based on Hamburg Prices

Year	Ratio	Year	Ratio	Year	Ratio	Year	Ratio
1793	15.00	1802	15.26	1812	16.11	1822	15.80
1794	15.37	1803	15.41	1813	16.25	1823	15.84
1795	15.55	1804	15.41	1814	15.04	1824	15.82
1796	15.65	1805	15.79	1815	15.26	1825	15.70
1797	15.41	1806	15.52	1816	15.28	1826	15.76
1798	15.59	1807	15.43	1817	15.11	1827	15.74
1799	15.74	1808	16.08	1818	15.35	1828	15.78
1800	15.68	1809	15.96	1819	15.33	1829	15.78
1801	15.46	1810	15.77	1820	15.62	1830	15.82
		1811	15.53	1821	15.95		

Production of Gold and Silver

Decade	World		United States	
	Gold	Silver	Gold	Silver
1801–1810	$118,152,000	$371,677,000	——	Insignificant
1811–1820	76,063,000	224,786,000	——	
1821–1830	94,479,000	191,444,000	$715,000	

Coinage of the United States

Years	Total Gold	Silver Dollars	Fractional Silver
1792–1795 . . .	$71,485.00	$204,791.00	$165,892.80
1796–1800 . . .	942,805.00	1,052,667.00	17,103.95
1801–1805 . . .	1,533,267.50	182,059.00	287,889.00
1806–1810 . . .	1,717,475.00		3,099,217.25
1811–1815 . . .	1,345,925.00		2,622,316.50
1816–1820 . . .	1,820,585.00		3,348,494.45
1821–1825 . . .	600,315.00		5,844,178.95
1826–1830 . . .	1,302,777.50		10,936,868.00

Imports and Exports of Gold and Silver, United States

Prior to 1821 the commercial movement of precious metals was not separately reported; nor were the exports and imports of silver correctly given separate from gold, until 1864.

Years	Imports	Exports
1821–1825	$31,062,367	$43,472,833
1826–1830	38,081,413	28,065,712

CHAPTER VI

COINAGE SYSTEM

1830–1860

THE ratio existing during the period from 1820 to 1830, by consensus of opinion, undervalued gold. The only differences of opinion related to the proper ratio to be adopted and the correlated question whether gold or silver should be the standard.

On May 4, 1830, Secretary Ingham, of the Treasury, in response to a resolution of the Senate of December 20, 1828, requiring him to "ascertain, with as much accuracy as possible, the proportional value of gold and silver in relation to each other; and to state such alterations in the gold coins of the United States as may be necessary to conform those coins to the silver coins, in their true relative value," presented a report upon the subject containing the most thorough and exhaustive treatment it had received up to that date.

He insisted that the loss of gold by the country was by no means entirely due to the undervaluation in ratio. He adduced the fact that prior to 1821 the market value in the United States had not varied materially from the mint value, and contended that the introduction of bank paper had been the chief cause of the exportation of gold. He argued that the exportation of gold alone did not cause serious trouble, but that actual distress ensued when silver also went abroad, leaving the country inadequately supplied. He set forth with great force the futility of endeavoring to maintain a bimetallic standard, and urged the adoption of a single standard, and that silver. He favored silver because contracts in the country had been for many years based upon the silver dollar, and also because no exact adjustment of the relation of the two metals could be maintained with any degree of permanence, and silver *could* be retained at home by reducing the mint value of gold. The country could not possibly get along without silver, whereas it could without gold by the use of sound bank currency. As to the ratio, he suggested that, since the market ratio appeared to be about 15.8 to 1, and it was desirable under his plan to have gold at a slight premium, the coinage ratio should be 15.625 to 1.

Secretary Ingham addressed many persons familiar with the subject, for information, and he thus obtained much valuable material which was published with his report.[1]

Gallatin, who had been Secretary of the Treasury under Jefferson, contributed a lengthy letter and statistical information. He favored the adoption of the French bimetallic system, ratio 15½ to 1, with coins .900 fine. He criticised the English single gold standard, with its "adulterated silver currency," but not with his usual perspicacity. His general conclusion was that the bimetallic standard should be adopted for the reason that the fluctuations of gold and silver would be less than that of one metal only. If a single standard were selected, silver was preferable to gold because it was then the existing standard metal, was more abundant, requiring a greater premium before it could be exported, and was the only means of suppressing small notes, the worst form of paper currency.

Very valuable statistical and other data relative to exchange, premium on gold, coins, etc., covering many years, were furnished by Samuel Moore, Director of the Mint, and by John White, Cashier of the Bank of the United States.

The views of Alexander Baring, the famous banker of London, upon the single gold standard system of England, in which

[1] Printed in full in International Monetary Conference, 1878, p. 558.

he expressed decided preference for the double standard at $15\frac{1}{2}$ to 1 and voiced existing dissatisfaction with the new British system, were also reprinted in the report.

Ingham's report unquestionably influenced many of the leading men in Congress. To counteract the tendency toward the single standard Senator Sanford of New York, in December, 1830, reported a bill for the continuation of the double standard at the ratio of 15.9 to 1, altering the weight of the gold coins only. The bill was ably supported in the committee's report [1] which formed the basis of two reports to the House of Representatives in 1831,[2] one on silver and the other on gold, by Representative C. P. White, also of New York. The latter made two further reports in March and June, 1832.[3] Together, these five reports constitute an encyclopædia of the then existing information on the subject. The House Committee opposed the double standard because of "the impossibility of maintaining both metals in concurrent, simultaneous, or promiscuous circulation," urged that the single standard was the nearest approach to stability precluding the need of further legislation with each change in relative commercial value, and asserted that if a metallic circulation were desired, notes of ten dollars and under must be prohibited.

White would not admit, as Sanford claimed, that injurious consequences would ensue if one of the metals were rejected. He recommended the adoption of the ratio of 15.625 to 1 and .900 as the standard of fineness. As to this ratio, he regarded it the utmost limit to which the value of gold could be raised if silver was to be retained, and finally he stated that "the standard ought to be legally and exclusively, as it is practically, regulated by silver."

The influence which the large volume of small notes exer-

[1] Senate Reports, 21st Congress, 2d Sess., No. 3.

[2] House Reports, 21st Congress, 2d Sess.

[3] *Ibid.*, 22d Congress, 1st Sess., Nos. 278, 496.

cised in driving out coins was fully appreciated in the House Committee reports.

The discussion proceeded without action for two years longer. In February, 1834, White again reported upon the subject, repeating his former bill and recommendations.[1]

In May the banks of New York, under the lead of Gallatin, then president of one of them, sent a memorial to Congress asking for the enactment of a law to coin gold at the rate of 23.76 grains of pure and 25.92 grains standard metal to the dollar.[2] This would have continued the fineness of the coin at .916$\frac{2}{3}$ (or eleven-twelfths) and, since the silver dollar remained unchanged, would have resulted in a ratio of 15.625 to 1. They also asked that the silver dollars of the Latin-American states and the five-franc pieces of France be made legal tender as well as the Spanish dollars, at their proper mint values. These coins had in fact become the chief elements in the country's specie circulation, and some action was necessary to provide a sufficient volume of legal tender money.

Later in the session, when the desire for action became pressing (and only one week before the act of 1834 was actually passed), White completely changed his position and reported a bill which practically favored the gold instead of the silver standard, fixing a ratio of about 16 to 1. What the influences were which caused such a radical change does not clearly appear. Many of his followers, for he had become the recognized leader on the subject in the House, severely criticised his course.

From the speeches of Benton, the champion of gold in the Senate, it would appear that the policy of adopting a ratio that undervalued silver, according to the judgment of all expert economists, and thus cutting loose practically from both Great Britain and France, was influenced by the desire to place the country in position to draw, in competition with Spain, the

[1] *Ibid.*, 23d Congress.

[2] International Monetary Conference, 1878, p. 679.

precious metal product of Mexico, Central and South America. The Spanish ratio had for years been 16 to 1, and it was presumed that this caused the flow of gold from the Spanish-American countries to the former mother country, even after the separation of those colonies between 1820 and 1830.[1]

There is evidence that the action was in part influenced by the fact that gold had been found in North Carolina and Georgia. The production there had been increasing until the annual output was nearly one million dollars, and indeed the people of that section of the country believed that the new Eldorado had been discovered. (In 1835 mints were established at Dahlonega, Ga., and at Charlotte, N.C.) The argument that prosperity, so long absent from the states, would be restored if this gold product could be kept at home, proved very captivating, and in order to make assurance doubly sure the ratio was made sufficiently advantageous to retain that gold beyond peradventure.

Benton said: —

> "Gold goes where it finds its value, and that value is what the laws of great nations give it. In Mexico and South America, the countries which produce gold, and from which the United States must derive their chief supply, the value of gold is 16 to 1 over silver; in the island of Cuba it is 17 to 1; in Spain and Portugal it is 16 to 1; in the West Indies, generally, it is the same. It is not to be supposed that gold will come from these countries to the United States, if the importer is to lose one dollar in every sixteen that he brings; or that our gold will remain with us, when an exporter can gain a dollar upon every fifteen that he carries out. Such results would be contrary to the laws of trade, and therefore we must place the same value upon gold that other nations do, if we wish to gain any part of theirs, or to regain any part of our own."

He made his acknowledgments "to the great apostle of American liberty" (Jefferson) for the wise, practical idea that the value of gold was a commercial question, to be settled by its value in

[1] Benton, Thirty Years' View, p. 436.

other countries. He had seen that remark in the works of that great man, and treasured it up as teaching the plain and ready way to accomplish an apparently difficult object; and he fully concurred with the Senator from South Carolina (Mr. Calhoun) that gold in the United States ought to be the preferred metal; not that silver should be expelled, but both retained; the mistake, if any, to be in favor of gold, instead of being against it.[1] Looking to the actual and equal circulation of the two metals in different countries, he noted that this equality and actuality of circulation had existed for above three hundred years in the Spanish dominions of Mexico and South America, where the proportion was 16 to 1. White gave up the bill which he had first introduced and adopted the "Spanish ratio." John Quincy Adams said he would vote for it, though he thought gold was overvalued, but if found to be so, the difference could be corrected thereafter.[2]

Speaking of the domestic supply of native gold, Benton said that no mines had ever developed more rapidly or promised more abundantly than those in the Southern states. In the year 1824 they were a spot in the state of North Carolina, they are now a region spreading into six states. In the year 1824 the product was $5000, in 1832 he claimed the product in coined gold was $868,000, in uncoined as much more, and the product of 1834 was computed at $2,000,000, with every prospect of continued and permanent increase. The probability was that these mines alone, in the lapse of a few years, would furnish an abundant supply of gold to establish a plentiful circulation of that metal if not expelled from the country by unwise laws.

It was on June 21, 1834, that the White substitute bill was introduced. In one week it became law, only thirty-six representatives and seven senators voting against it upon final passage. It is apparent that the action was taken from a desire to accomplish something quickly. Political exigency rather

[1] *Ibid.*, p. 443.

[2] *Ibid.*, p. 469.

than careful deliberation caused the House to ignore the ratio of 15.625, which was held by White two years before to be the "utmost limit to which the value [of gold] could be raised," and to favor 16 to 1, without regard to the commercial ratio.

The only change made by the act of June 28, 1834, respecting the coinage, was to alter the weight of the gold coins, giving them 23.2 grains of pure gold and 25.8 standard to the dollar. This changed the fineness to nearly .900, instead of .916⅔. The resulting ratio was 16.002 to 1. Another act, passed the same day, provided that foreign gold coins were to be received and pass current at the new ratings which the preceding law established.

As the Spanish-American colonies were now separate states, their silver coinage was, by another act of June 28, 1834, made receivable the same as the "Spanish dollars" if of full weight. In fact, they superseded the Spanish coins which had been issued from the same mints. Few, if any, of the "Spanish milled dollars" that came to the United States were coined in Spain.

The legislation of 1834 left the silver dollar exactly as the act of 1792 had fixed it. When in 1836 it was found desirable to revise the laws regulating the mint, a bill containing thirty-eight sections was introduced, and several important changes in coins were included. This bill passed January 18, 1837. Section 8 prescribes that the standard of fineness for both gold and silver coins shall be .900, thus avoiding the awkward fraction fixed by the law of 1792. The weight of pure silver in the dollar remained the same, 371.25 grains; the gross weight was altered from 416 to 412.5 grains, and fractional pieces were changed in proportion. The legal tender power of all silver pieces remained unchanged. The fineness of the gold coins was slightly increased to make it exactly .900. The eagle thus weighed 258 grains, of which 232.2 grains were pure gold. The ratio became 15.988 to 1, the same as it is to-day. The difference is so slight that the custom has become universal to characterize the present coinage ratio as "16 to 1," thereby ignoring the fractional difference of .012. The coinage of both metals was made free and unlimited, and in fact the coinage of silver dollars was resumed.

The above-mentioned ratio placed a valuation upon gold of 52 cents per ounce higher than that generally prevailing in Europe. It made the silver dollar worth $1.03 measured by the gold dollar. Ere long silver began to depart for Europe, where the ratio of 15½ to 1 prevailed, and also to India, which had adopted the single silver standard in 1835 at the ratio of 15 to 1. The commercial ratio of gold to silver did not equal our coinage ratio until 1874, silver all this time commanding a small premium. Although trade balances were for a number of years adverse, the placing of investments abroad proved more than an offset and the stock of gold in the country increased. Notwithstanding the continual export of United States silver coin, the influx of silver coins from Central and South America, which had been made legal tender, prevented any serious shortage of small coins for some time.

The legal rate of the pound sterling was $4.44 4/9 as fixed by the revenue act of July 31, 1789 (prior to the first coinage law) under which imported wares from British sources were appraised. Adams tells us that this rating was in accord with the valuation of the silver dollar that had been adopted by the Continental Congress by the ordinance of 1786.

The customs rating was $4.44 4/9, the actual rating $4.566, and thus the quotations of exchange at par prior to 1834 were in figures 102.7. No legal change was made after the alteration of the weight of the gold coin in 1834–1837, yet by that alteration the 113.001 grains of pure gold in the pound sterling, estimated in dollars of 23.22 grains pure gold, gave $4.86⅔. The difference between this last-mentioned equivalent and the one of 1789 amounts to 9½ per cent.,[1] and hence from 1837 onward the

[1] Hunt, Merchant's Magazine, Vol. I., p. 536.

par of exchange was expressed with a nominal premium figure, thus 109½, notwithstanding an act of 1842 which rated sterling at $4.84 in payments by and to the Treasury. This anomaly continued until 1873.[1]

The gold fields of the South proved disappointing, but California, recently acquired from Mexico, proved an Eldorado indeed, yielding $10,000,000 in 1848 and $40,000,000 in 1849. In the following decade the annual output continued large, the maximum being $65,000,000 in 1853. This enormous production dazzled the world at that time, attracted foreigners and foreign capital, and proved of the greatest value to our currency and credit. But the country was denuded of silver, only the abraded foreign coins remaining in circulation. The inconvenience suffered by the public for want of small change became a crying evil, and Congress was impressed with the necessity for action.

Thomas Corwin, Secretary of the Treasury, in an elaborate report early in 1852,[2] recommended the reduction of the amount of silver in coins as the only remedy, and suggested that the weight of all silver pieces, including the dollar, be reduced so as to give the ratio of 14.88 to 1.

Senator Hunter, in the same year, made a comprehensive report[3] in which he referred to the fears existing that the great gold production would unsettle values. This he believed would not result, in view of the great increase of wealth and capital, if natural laws were permitted to operate. But paper currency was interfering with natural laws. He favored a system of subsidiary silver coinage in place of bank-notes of smaller denominations than one dollar which had become prevalent. He added, "The great measure of readjusting the legal ratio between gold and silver cannot be safely attempted until some permanent

[1] See Chapter XII.
[2] Special Report, Finance Report, 1852.
[3] Senate Reports, 32d Congress, 1st Sess., No. 104.

relations between the market values of the two metals shall be established."

The act of July 3, 1852, established the mint in San Francisco, to provide for the official handling of the large gold product of the Pacific slope.

Corwin, in January, 1853, again called attention to the general conditions, saying that no indication of relief was near, but rather a prospect of reduced supplies of silver. He added: —

"This state of things has banished almost entirely from circulation all silver coins of full weight, and what little remains in the hands of the community consists principally of the worn pieces of Spanish coinage of the fractional parts of a dollar, all of which are of light weight, and many of them ten or twenty per cent. below their nominal value." [1]

He discussed the objection which had been seriously raised that the proposed silver currency could not, without a violation of contracts, be made a legal tender for the payment of debts, and that the gold thereafter would be the only legal tender. He said: —

"It is true that heretofore the laws of the United States have recognized the coin of either metal as a legal tender, and if it was at the option of the creditor to select what he would receive there would be a very serious objection to changing either the weight or standard fineness of any portion of the coin. But this is not the fact, as it rests with the debtor to say with which description of coin he will pay his debts, and the natural and inevitable consequences of the premium which silver now bears have been to establish, practically, gold as the only legal tender."

These efforts finally resulted in the act of February 21, 1853, which provided that after June 1, 1853, the weight of the half dollar or piece of fifty cents should be 192 grains, the quarter dollar, dime, and half dime respectively one-half, one-fifth, and one-tenth of the weight of the half dollar; that the fineness should continue at .900; and that the silver coins thus ordered should

[1] Finance Report, 1853.

be legal tender in payment of debts for all sums not over five dollars. The mint was authorized to purchase silver bullion for coinage, and further deposit for coinage into fractional silver pieces for private account was prohibited, but the deposit of gold and silver for casting into bars or ingots of either pure or standard metal at a charge of one-half of one per cent. was permitted. The law also authorized the coinage of $3 gold pieces. The coinage of $20 gold pieces had been previously authorized in 1849.

The weight thus prescribed for the small silver coins, 384 grains of standard silver or 345.6 grains fine to the dollar, gave, as compared with gold, the ratio of 14.882 to 1, but as it proved, the question of the ratio of these coins was of no importance so long as it reduced their value below the export point. In a short time the country possessed a fairly adequate supply of small silver.

The act of 1853 did not disturb the coinage of silver dollars. It related solely to the establishment of a subsidiary currency of silver to take the place of fractional bank-notes and to establish a circulation of domestic coin in place of the light-weight foreign coins. Yet speaking on the question in the House, Chairman Dunham of the Ways and Means Committee said:[1] —

> "We propose, so far as these coins are concerned, to make silver subservient to the gold coin of the country. We intend to do what the best writers on political economy have approved, what experience, where the experiment has been tried, has demonstrated to be the best, and what the Committee believe to be necessary and proper, to make but one standard of currency and to make all others subservient to it. We mean to make gold the standard coin, and to make these new silver coins applicable and convenient, not for large but for small transactions."

Farther on in his speech he said: —

> "Another objection urged against this proposed change is that it gives us a standard of currency of gold only. . . . The constant though some-

[1] Congressional Globe, XXVI., p. 190.

times slow change in the relative value of the two metals has always resulted in great inconvenience and frequently in great loss to the people. Wherever the experiment of a standard of a single metal has been tried it has proved eminently successful. Indeed, it is utterly impossible that you should long at a time maintain a double standard. The one or the other will appreciate in value when compared to the other. It will then command a premium when exchanged for that other, when it ceases to be a currency and becomes merchandise. It ceases to circulate as money at its nominal value, but it sells as a commodity at its market price. This was the case with gold before the act of 1834, but it is now the case with silver. Gentlemen talk about a double standard of gold and silver as a thing that exists, and that we propose to change. We have had but a single standard for the last three or four years. That has been and now is, gold. We propose to let it remain so and to adapt silver to it, to regulate it by it."

Despite this manifest purpose the silver dollar remained in the law, with full legal tender power equally with gold.

The principal opponent of the bill was Andrew Johnson of Tennessee, later Vice-President and President. The following extract from his remarks is of interest: —

"I look upon this bill as the merest quackery — the veriest charlatanism — so far as the currency of the country is concerned. The idea of Congress fixing the value of currency is an absurdity, notwithstanding the *language* of the Constitution — not the meaning of it. . . . If we can, by law, make $107 out of $100,[1] we can, by the same process, make it worth $150. Why, Sir, of all the problems that have come up for solution, from the time of the alchemists down to the present time, none can compare with that solved by this modern Congress. They alone have discovered that they can make money — that they can make $107 out of $100. If they can increase it to that extent they can go on and increase it to the infinity, and thus, by the operation of the mint, can the Government supply its own revenues. The great difficulty of mankind is solved, the idea that so much money is wanted all over the world is at length at an end." [2]

[1] The act of 1853 altered the value of the silver in the subsidiary coin about 7 per cent.

[2] Congressional Globe, XXVI., p. 475.

By an act of March 3, 1853, the date fixed for the beginning of the subsidiary coinage was changed from June 1 to April 1, 1853, and the weight of the three-cent silver piece was changed to correspond with the new standard for subsidiary coin. Over $1,000,000 in these pieces had been coined at the lower fineness under the law of March, 1851, showing the great need for small coin, especially for postage, which was then three cents.

Another act of the same date provided for the establishment of an assay office at New York and permitted the deposits therein of gold and silver bullion, dust or foreign coin, for manufacture into bars or coin at the will of the depositor and the issue of certificates of deposit for the kind of metal deposited, which certificates were made receivable in payment of customs dues at the port of New York, for sixty days from date thereof.

The estimates of specie in the country show an increase of $170,000,000 from 1841 to 1861. Of this increase $130,000,000 occurred subsequent to the year 1849. The principal cause was, of course, the domestic production of gold, which was in large measure retained despite the exports due to adverse trade balances and the inflated condition of the paper currency from 1850 to 1860.[1]

Australia as well as California had become a large producer of gold, and the commercial ratio of silver to gold continued to rise under the influence of this largely increased production. In 1853 the ratio rose above 15½ and did not again recede to that point until 1861. For the year 1859, 15.19 was recorded. The premium on the silver dollar was four to five per cent. No dollars could have circulated under these conditions, and hence but few were coined. The government actually coined less than 2,800,000 of these pieces from 1834 to 1861.

The final act in the series to establish a currency of domestic coin, in place of the depreciated foreign pieces, became law February 21, 1857. It repealed all statutes permitting the cir-

[1] Treasury Circular of Information, No. 113, 1900, pp. 61, 62.

culation of and giving legal tender power to foreign coins, excepting only the Spanish-American fractional silver pieces, which were to be received only at government offices at a greatly reduced rate and at once recoined. Changes were made in the minor coins, nickel being then first used in combination with copper. The coinage of the half cent was discontinued and the weight of the cent was reduced from 168 to 72 grains.

The act also transferred from the Secretary of the Treasury to the Director of the Mint the duty of annually reporting the values of foreign coins, and required the latter officer to make his reports to the Secretary of the Treasury instead of to the President.

A review of the history of the coinage laws prior to 1861 shows that all the leaders in the government of the country were convinced of the imperative necessity of uniformity in the standard of value as represented by coin. Hence there was no contest over the provision in the Constitution which deprived the several states of the power to coin money and fix the value of coins. Nor was there a difference of opinion between the chief party leaders at the outset (Hamilton and Jefferson) upon the question of the advisability of a concurrent use of both gold and silver at the ratio of 15 to 1. Being unable to foresee the eventual change in the commercial ratio, no provision was made for an alteration in the legal ratio.

Hesitating to depart from the bimetallic policy adopted under the inspiration of these men, the followers of both in Congress did not venture upon a radical change such as Great Britain had made, but endeavored first by the legislation of 1834 and 1837 to adjust the legal to the commercial ratio, the disparity in which had deprived the country of gold currency; and later, in 1853, by reducing the amount of silver in the fractional coins they sought to retain the same in circulation as the small change of everyday transactions by making the coins worth more as money than they were as bullion for export. For nearly half a century prior to 1853 the people had suffered from a dearth of coin and especially fractional parts of a dollar, with all the economic disturbances resulting therefrom.

Notwithstanding the declared purpose in 1853 to establish the single gold standard, the bimetallic law remained, and silver dollars, equally with gold, possessed full legal tender power. The failure of Congress to provide a sound coinage system with a single standard of value materially affected the paper currency system, which is now to be discussed, and left the seed from which was to grow the greatest monetary heresy of modern times, destined to threaten the welfare of the people for a quarter of a century.

STATISTICAL RÉSUMÉ

Commercial Ratio of Silver to Gold

1831........15.72	1838........15.85	1845........15.92	1852........15.59
1832........15.73	1839........15.62	1846........15.90	1853........15.33
1833........15.93	1840........15.62	1847........15.80	1854........15.32
1834........15.73	1841........15.70	1848........15.85	1855........15.38
1835........15.80	1842........15.87	1849........15.78	1856........15.38
1836........15.72	1843........15.93	1850........15.70	1857........15.27
1837........15.83	1844........15.85	1851........15.46	1858........15.38
	1859........15.19	1860........15.29	

World's Production of Gold and Silver

(Amounts in millions of dollars)

Period	Annual Average		Per Cent by Value	
	Gold	Silver	Gold	Silver
1831–1840	13.5	24.7	35.2	64.8
1841–1850	36.4	32.4	52.9	47.1
1851–1855	132.5	36.8	78.3	21.7
1856–1860	134.1	37.6	78.1	21.9

The great increase in production of gold, shown in the above table, accounts for the marked rise in the price of silver, as indicated by the fall in the commercial ratio.

EXPORTS AND IMPORTS, UNITED STATES

Years	Exports		Imports	
	Gold	Silver	Gold	Silver
1831–1835	$7,963,900	$17,873,605	$8,351,935	$42,974,961
1836–1840	13,578,435	17,423,953	25,588,296	30,554,104
1841–1845	10,724,258	19,705,113	21,525,334	19,771,321
1846–1850	20,695,177	13,886,373	31,739,452	13,799,885
1851–1855	184,017,429	13,145,180	13,960,026	11,799,057
1856–1860	279,790,526	18,158,678	23,845,192	28,083,659

GENERAL STATISTICS, PRECIOUS METALS, UNITED STATES

(Amounts in millions of dollars)

Year	Gold Exports	Gold Imports	Silver Exports	Silver Imports	Domestic Coin Exports	Production of Gold	Gold Coinage	Silver Coinage
1831	0.9	0.9	6.0	6.4	2.1	0.5	0.7	3.2
1832	0.6	0.7	3.6	5.2	1.4	0.7	0.8	2.6
1833	0.5	0.6	1.7	6.5	0.4	0.9	1.0	2.8
1834	0.3	3.8	1.4	14.1	0.4	0.9	4.0	3.4
1835	0.6	2.3	5.1	10.8	0.7	0.7	2.2	3.4
1836	0.3	7.2	3.7	6.2	0.3	0.7	4.1	3.6
1837	1.9	2.4	2.8	8.1	1.3	0.7	1.1	2.1
1838	0.7	11.7	2.3	6.1	0.5	0.6	1.8	2.3
1839	2.9	1.2	4.0	4.4	1.9	0.6	1.4	2.2
1840	1.5	3.1	4.7	5.8	2.2	0.5	1.7	1.7
1841	0.8	1.3	6.4	3.7	2.7	0.6	1.1	1.1
1842	1.1	0.8	2.5	3.3	1.2	0.7	1.8	2.3
1843	0.3	17.1	1.1	5.3	0.1	0.8	8.1	3.8
1844	1.2	1.6	4.1	4.2	0.2	0.9	5.4	2.2
1845	2.2	0.8	5.6	3.3	0.8	1.0	3.8	1.9
1846	1.6	0.9	1.9	2.9	0.4	1.1	4.0	2.6
1847	1.0	21.6	0.9	2.5	0.1	0.9	20.2	2.4
1848	8.4	3.4	4.8	3.0	2.7	10.0	3.8	2.0
1849	1.0	4.1	3.4	2.6	1.0	40.0	9.0	2.1

Production of silver in the United States for the period, $500,000.

The silver coinage included only 1,017,500 silver dollars.

Domestic coin exports included both gold and silver, but the Mint reports include them with the gold. The figures are presented as the best available, without claiming accuracy.

COINAGE, UNITED STATES

YEARS	TOTAL GOLD	SILVER DOLLARS	FRACT. SILVER
1831–1835	$8,631,700	——	$15,371,605
1836–1840	10,146,100	$62,305	11,909,529.60
1841–1845	20,214,180	567,218	10,841,782
1846–1850	69,001,515	435,450	10,518,680
1851–1855	214,142,519.50	107,650	22,864,243
1856–1860	130,264,446	1,527,930	23,132,280

GENERAL STATISTICS, PRECIOUS METALS, UNITED STATES

YEAR	GOLD EX-PORTS	GOLD IMPORTS	SILVER EX-PORTS	SILVER IM-PORTS	DOMES-TIC COIN EX-PORTS	PRO-DUCTION OF GOLD	GOLD COIN-AGE	SILVER COIN-AGE
1850	2.5	1.8	3.0	2.9	2.0	50.0	32.0	1.9
1851	4.8	3.6	6.6	1.9	18.1	55.0	62.6	0.8
1852	2.6	3.7	2.6	1.8	37.4	60.0	56.8	1.0
1853	1.9	2.4	2.0	1.8	23.5	65.0	39.4	9.1
1854	2.5	3.0	0.7	3.7	38.1	60.0	25.9	8.6
1855	1.2	1.1	1.1	2.6	54.0	55.0	29.4	3.5
1856	0.9	1.0	0.7	3.2	44.1	55.0	36.9	5.1
1857	5.2	6.7	3.9	5.8	60.1	55.0	32.2	5.5
1858	7.6	11.6	2.6	7.7	42.4	50.0	22.9	8.5
1859	3.6	2.1	2.8	5.3	57.5	50.0	14.8	3.3
1860	1.5	2.5	8.1	6.0	56.9	46.0	23.5	2.3

The production of silver in the United States was only $1,150,000.

The silver coinage included only 1,682,080 silver dollars.

Domestic coin exports included both gold and silver, but the Mint reports include them with the gold. The figures are presented as the best available, without claiming accuracy.

CHAPTER VII

Paper Currency

1775–1811

The history of our country shows that the people have experimented with every known description of paper currency. The history of the colonial paper issues would form a bulky volume.

Prior to 1775 every one of the colonies had at one time or another made use of note issues, and in some cases issues were made by private banking concerns. The issues were made to obviate raising revenue by taxation and also to supply circulating medium; owing to the scarcity of coin, notes of denominations as low as threepence were issued during that period and are still in existence. Massachusetts appears to have taken the lead in this as well as in many other matters, and as early as 1690 issued "bills of credit" to pay soldiers.[1] No adequate provision was made for the redemption of the notes issued by the colonies and depreciation followed; this proved equally true where the currency was given legal tender power.

When an issue had depreciated to such an extent as to be thoroughly discredited it would be redeemed at a percentage, and sometimes a very small percentage, of its par value, in a new issue put forth with solemn pledges for its redemption, which new issue underwent in turn a like depreciation. The losses suffered by New England on account of depreciated paper currency prior to the Revolution were much greater proportionately

[1] Knox, United States Notes, 1.

than the losses sustained by the other colonies, and this section also was more prolific in schemes with reference to currency. All the bitter experiences which the colonies separately suffered were again to be experienced by the Federation.

The Continental Congress was powerless to impose taxes, and hence unable to make loans; consequently, burdened with the duty of prosecuting a war, no other recourse than note issuing seemed possible. Accordingly, on June 22, 1775, but not without considerable opposition, a first issue of what was afterwards known as Continental currency was authorized, in denominations from $1 to $20, to the amount of $2,000,000.

Issue succeeded issue, as we have seen in Chapter II, until depreciation was so great and the country so flooded with currency that further issues ceased to be an available resource. Legal tender laws did not avail; we find these words in a protest at that time: —

> "If public confidence was wanting tender laws could not replace it. . . . If the paper were of full value it would pass current without such aid; if it were not, then to compel persons to receive it at its nominal value would be an act of dishonesty."[1]

Fine, imprisonment, forfeiture of claim, outlawry (any one convicted "shall be deemed, published and treated as an enemy of his country and precluded from all trade or intercourse with the inhabitants," etc.), death, as penalties for refusal to take such notes at their face value, failed to make them pass except at such a price as the public deemed them to be worth in coin. The impotence of governmental fiat in the creation of value was painfully and most expensively illustrated. The aggregate issues of Continental currency totaled $357,000,000, which likely included some reissues. After the adoption of the Constitution, Congress in 1790 provided for its redemption, at 100 to 1, if notes were presented prior to September 30, 1791;[2] the time limit was

[1] Phillips, Paper Money, II. [2] U. S. Statutes, Vol. I.

subsequently extended until December 31, 1797.[1] The loaning of real money to the United States by France was the vitalizing force that gave life to our finances, as French arms gave victory to our cause. It was natural that Congress, after its costly experience with government currency, should revert to bank currency as the safer and better expedient.

Congress authorized in 1781 the establishment of the Bank of North America, the first incorporated bank in the country, still in existence in Philadelphia as a national bank.[2] The capital was $400,000, of which the government took $250,000, but sold its holdings in 1783, being induced to do so by extreme financial needs. The bank's charter was perpetual, and a number of the states granted it local charters. It rendered the government valuable assistance and commanded general confidence, its note issues soon finding their way into general use, and circulating at par.

In 1784 the Bank of New York, New York City, and the Massachusetts Bank, Boston, were organized and are both now doing a successful business, the former under its original name; the latter, June 27, 1903, acquired control of the First National Bank and absorbed the same, at the same time adopting its name and is now doing business as the First National Bank of Boston. Alexander Hamilton was a controlling influence in the organization of the Bank of New York, and drew its charter, which, however, was not granted by the legislature until 1791. These three institutions were the only ones which preceded the establishment of the Bank of the United States. Their notes gave the people an excellent paper currency which served as an educating influence against "fiat money" schemes, the disastrous effects of which led to the adoption of sounder principles in framing the Constitution in 1787. That instrument, which went into effect in 1789, provided as follows: —

[1] *Ibid.*

[2] It was in a sense the successor of an informal banking association organized in Pennsylvania a few years earlier, to assist the Continental Congress.

ART. I. SEC. 8. "The Congress shall have power . . . to borrow money on the credit of the United States, . . . to coin money, regulate the value thereof, and of foreign coin."

ART. I. SEC. 10. "No state shall . . . coin money, emit bills of credit, make anything but gold and silver coin a tender in payment of debts, pass any . . . law impairing the obligation of contracts."

Fresh from their experiences with continental paper currency, so disastrous to all, it would appear reasonable to assume that the intention of the framers of the Constitution was to prohibit all issues of legal tender paper by Congress. George Bancroft contends, in antagonism to the Supreme Court, that the record of the proceedings of the convention leaves no doubt of such intention.

Upon the question whether the power to "emit bills of credit," as stated in the draft of the Constitution then under consideration, should be given the United States, Gouverneur Morris, in opposition, remarked that "if the United States have credit, such bills will be unnecessary; if they have not, will be unjust and useless." He was vigorously supported by other delegates. Ellsworth said it was a favorable moment to "shut and bar the door against paper money." Wilson said that the striking out of the provision would "remove the possibility of paper money." Langdon preferred rejecting the whole plan rather than retain the three words "and emit bills." Madison, who hesitated to strike out the words, finally assented after having, as he said, satisfied himself that it would not disable the government from using its credit, but would cut off the pretext for a paper currency and particularly for making bills a tender either for public or private debts.[1]

The words were stricken out by a vote of four to one, and unquestionably the convention intended to withhold from the federal government the power to create paper money with legal tender attributes.

[1] Bancroft, A Plea for the Constitution, quoting Elliot's Debates.

The foregoing comments are here briefly introduced in chronological order, but will again be referred to in discussing government paper currency issues in later years.

The course pursued by the "fathers" respecting bank paper currency under the Constitution will now be considered.

In reply to an order from Congress, to inform that body what further provisions he deemed necessary to establish the public credit, Alexander Hamilton, in December, 1790, submitted his plan for the establishment of a Bank of the United States, similar in its constitution to the Bank of England. He regarded it necessary, owing to the lack of knowledge of the functions of banks, to devote a large portion of the report to that subject. He showed very lucidly how the system of discounts and credits and the use of checks operated to supplement the stock of coin and foster trade and commerce. He demonstrated that the organization of such a bank of issue would enable the country to obtain a manifold use of the volume of coin available, would aid the government in obtaining loans in sudden emergencies by having the capital concentrated, would facilitate the payment of taxes by extending credit and also furnish a convenient medium for remittance from place to place, which latter function would be further facilitated by the system of branches proposed. The bank would serve as the receiver and disburser of public funds, and the money derived from taxes would not be locked up awaiting the government's expenditures, but remain all the while in circulation. He thus anticipated the arguments against the present subtreasury system.

He controverted the current charges that banks "serve to increase usury," that they "tend to prevent other kinds of lending," "furnish temptations to overtrading," "afford aid to ignorant adventurers," "give to bankrupt and fraudulent creditors fictitious credit," and "have a tendency to banish gold and silver from the country."

Upon the last point he remarked: —

"A nation that has no mines of its own must derive the precious metals from others; generally speaking, in exchange for the products of its labor and industry. The quantity it will possess will, therefore, in the ordinary course of things, be regulated by the favorable or unfavorable balance of its trade; that is, by the proportion between its abilities to supply foreigners, and its wants of them, between the amount of its exportations and that of its importations. Hence, the state of its agriculture and manufactures, the quantity and quality of its labor and industry, must, in the main, influence and determine the increase or decrease of its gold and silver. If this be true, the inference seems to be that well constituted banks favor the increase of the precious metals. It has been shown that they augment, in different ways, the active capital of a country. This it is which generates employment, which animates and expands labor and industry. Every addition which is made to it, by contributing to put in motion a greater quantity of both, tends to create a greater quantity of the products of both, and, by furnishing more materials for exportation, conduces to a favorable balance of trade, and consequently to the introduction and increase of gold and silver."

These statements of rudimentary banking principles and defence of the character and purpose of banks sound very droll, read in the light of the wonderful development of modern banking, and yet the primitive conditions demanded such an exposition and such defence.

Comparing a government currency with a bank currency, he said: —

"Among other material differences between a paper currency issued by the mere authority of government and one issued by a bank, payable in coin, is this; that in the first case there is no standard to which an appeal can be made as to the quantity which will only satisfy or which will surcharge the circulation; in the last that standard results from the demand. If more should be issued than is necessary it will return upon the bank. Its emissions, as elsewhere intimated, must always be in a compound ratio to the fund and the demand, whence it is evident that there is a limitation in the nature of the thing; while the discretion of the government is the only measure of the extent of the emissions by its own authority."

State banks, he showed, could not serve the government as well as a federal corporation, being unable to furnish adequate security for public moneys, and not being amenable to Congress or federal authority. He would have favored the utilization of the Bank of North America under its perpetual charter from the Continental Congress had the bank not been handicapped by the acceptance of charters from several states. Even its original charter from Congress, in Hamilton's opinion, required material amendment to serve the purpose he had in view.

The bank charter bill passed Congress substantially in the form presented by Hamilton, despite the objections of most of the adherents of Jefferson and Madison, who opposed it upon constitutional as well as other grounds.[1] The Cabinet of Washington was evenly divided upon the question, but the bill received Washington's approval on February 25, 1791. Before it was approved, Hamilton prepared a masterful argument upon the subject of its constitutionality, in reply to Jefferson and Edmund Randolph, who advised against approval on the ground that it was not authorized by the Constitution.[2]

This was practically the first important crossing of swords between the strict constructionists of the organic law and those who believed in broader lines of interpretation. In the final analysis the argument turned upon the question of the expressed and the implied powers of the federal government. While practically admitting that there was no express grant of power to Congress to create corporations, Hamilton urged that implied powers were equally authoritative — that the sole question was whether the end to be served came within the scope of the federal authority and needs — "within the sphere of the specified powers." If this were answered affirmatively, the means necessarily employed to accomplish such end must be constitutional. For example, under the expressed power of regulating commerce,

[1] Clarke and Hall, Documentary History of Bank of United States.
[2] *Ibid.*

lighthouses, etc., were provided for, and the power thus implied to establish lighthouse service was also a sovereign and unlimited power.

He then proceeded to show how the incorporation of the bank was a means to the end of facilitating the government's fiscal operations, as well as establishing a broader and stronger credit and currency system for the entire country, promoting uniformity in those important particulars, and hence the general welfare, functions which the state banks could not possibly exercise to advantage.

Replying to Jefferson's contention that while convenient this was not necessary, and that necessity constituted the only valid reason for exercising implied powers, he maintained that to define that word so narrowly would lead to a restriction of the powers of the federal government which would largely defeat the purpose of the Constitution. The following quotation contains the gist of his argument: —

> "This general principle is inherent in the very definition of government, and essential to every step of the progress to be made by that of the United States; namely, that every power vested in the government is, in its nature, SOVEREIGN, and includes, by force of the term, a right to employ all the means requisite and fairly applicable to the attainment of the ends of such power and which are not precluded by restrictions and exceptions specified in the Constitution, or not immoral, or not contrary to the essential ends of political society."

The argument of Hamilton was adopted by Chief Justice Marshall in sustaining the United States Bank charter, and later by the Supreme Court in upholding the legal tender power of United States notes. Hamilton's position was endorsed by Washington, and in several instances when amendatory acts were passed by Congress, Jefferson, when he became President, interposed no objection nor did the charter ever come for review before the Supreme Court. The charter of the second bank did, and since many of the points at issue in 1791 were then reviewed and determined, and since it was the first comprehensive exposition of the scope and principles of the Constitution, I insert here the syllabus and also excerpts from the opinion of Chief Justice Marshall.

The terms of the charter were not in question — the constitutional power of Congress to grant any bank charter of any kind was determined; that was the issue before the courts, raised as to the Second United States Bank.

SYLLABUS

McCulloch *vs.* Maryland, 4 Wheaton 413

"Congress has power to incorporate a bank.

"The government of the Union is the government of the people; it emanates from them; its powers are granted by them; and are to be exercised directly on them, and for their benefit.

"The government of the Union, though limited in its powers, is supreme within its sphere of action; and its laws, when made in pursuance of the Constitution, form the supreme law of the land.

"There is nothing in the Constitution of the United States, similar to the articles of confederation, which exclude incidental or implied powers.

"If the *end* be legitimate and within the scope of the Constitution, all the *means* which are appropriate, which are plainly adapted to that end, and which are not prohibited, may constitutionally be employed to carry it into effect.

"The power of establishing a corporation is not a distinct sovereign power or end of government, but only the means of carrying into effect other powers which are sovereign. Whenever it becomes an appropriate means of exercising any of the powers given by the Constitution to the government of the Union, it may be exercised by that government.

"If a certain means to carry into effect any of the powers, expressly given by the Constitution to the government of the Union, be an appropriate measure, not prohibited by the Constitution, the degree of its necessity is a question of legislative discretion, not of judicial cognizance.

"The act of 10th April, 1816, c. 44, to 'incorporate the subscribers to the Bank of the United States,' is a law made in pursuance of the Constitution. The Bank of the United States has, constitutionally, a right to establish its branches or offices of discount and deposit within any state.

"The state within which such branch may be established, cannot, without violating the Constitution, tax that branch.

"The state governments have no right to tax any of the constitutional means employed by the government of the Union to execute its constitutional powers.

"The states have no power, by taxation, or otherwise, to retard, impede, burden, or in any manner control the operations of the constitutional laws enacted by Congress, to carry into effect the powers vested in the national government.

"This principle does not extend to a tax paid by the real property of the Bank of the United States, in common with the other real property in a particular state, nor to a tax imposed on the proprietary interest which the citizens of that state may hold in this institution, in common with other property of the same description throughout the state."

* * * * * * * * * *

The Chief Justice said: —

"Although, among the enumerated powers of government, we do not find the word 'bank' or 'incorporation,' we find the great powers to lay and collect taxes; to borrow money, to regulate commerce; to declare and conduct a war; and to raise and support armies and navies. . . . A government, entrusted with such ample powers, on the due execution of which the happiness and prosperity of the nation so vitally depends, must also be entrusted with ample means for their execution. . . .

"The government which has a right to do an act, and has imposed on it the duty of performing that act, must, according to the dictates of reason, be allowed to select the means; and those who contend that it may not select any appropriate means, that one particular mode of effecting the object is excepted, take upon themselves the burden of establishing that exception. . . .

"But the Constitution of the United States has not left the right of Congress to employ the necessary means, for the execution of the powers conferred on the government, to general reasoning. To its enumeration of powers is added that of making 'all laws which shall be necessary and proper, for carrying into execution the foregoing powers, and all other powers vested by this Constitution, in the government of the United States, or in any department thereof.' . . .

"The word 'necessary' is considered (by counsel for the state) as controlling the whole sentence, and as limiting the right to pass laws for the execution of the granted powers, to such as are indispensable, and without which the power would be nugatory. That it excludes the choice of means, and leaves to Congress, in each case, that only which is most direct and simple. Is it true, that this is the sense in which the word 'necessary' is always used?

* * * * * * * * * *

"To employ the means necessary to an end, is generally understood as employing any means calculated to produce the end, and not as being confined to those single means without which the end would be entirely unattainable.

* * * * * * * * * *

"To have declared that the best means shall not be used, but those alone without which the power given would be nugatory, would have been to deprive the legislature of the capacity to avail itself of experience, to exercise its reason, and to accommodate its legislation to circumstances.

* * * * * * * * * *

"Take, for example, the power 'to establish post offices and post roads.' This power is executed by the single act of making the establishment. But, from this has been inferred the power and duty of carrying the mails along the post road, from one post office to another. And, from this implied power, has again been inferred the right to punish those who steal letters from the post office or rob the mail. It may be said, with some plausibility, that the right to carry the mail, and to punish those who rob it, is not indispensably necessary to the establishment of a post office and post road. This right is indeed essential to the beneficial exercise of the power, but not indispensably necessary to its existence.

* * * * * * * * * *

"Yet all admit the constitutionality of a territorial government, which is a corporate body.

"If a corporation may be employed indiscriminately with other means to carry into execution the powers of the government, no particular reason can be assigned for excluding the use of a bank, if required for its fiscal operations. To use one, must be within the discretion of Congress, if it be an appropriate mode of executing the powers of government. That it is a convenient, a useful and essential instrument in the prosecution of its fiscal operations, is not now a subject of controversy. All those who have been concerned in the administration of our finances, have concurred in representing its importance and necessity; and so strongly have they been felt, that statesmen of the first class, whose previous opinions against it had been confirmed by every circumstance which can fix the human judgment, have yielded those opinions to the exigencies of the nation.

* * * * * * * * * *

"It can scarcely be necessary to say, that the existence of state banks can have no possible influence on the question. No trace is to be found in the Constitution of an intention to create a dependence of the government of the Union on those of the states, for the execution of the powers assigned to it. Its means are adequate to its ends, and on those means alone was it expected to rely for the accomplishment of its ends. To impose on it the necessity of resorting to means which it cannot control, which another government may furnish or withhold, would render its course precarious, the result of its measures uncertain, and create a dependence on other governments, which might disappoint its most important designs, and is incompatible with the language of the Constitution. But were it otherwise, the choice of means implies a right to choose a national bank in preference to state banks, and Congress alone can make the selection."

The charter was an exclusive one for twenty years. The capital was fixed at $10,000,000 divided into shares of $400 each, the government taking one-fifth. Small investors in the shares were protected by being given a relatively greater voting power, and no one was allowed to cast more than thirty votes; foreign shareholders had no votes. Twenty-five directors were to govern the institution. The government's shares were to be paid for with money borrowed from the bank, repayable in instalments. No specific authority to issue notes was conferred, this being apparently understood to exist without a special proviso, but other parts of the act referred to the notes to be issued, and the notes were to be included in the liabilities. The notes and other debts (exclusive of deposits) were not to exceed the capital of the bank, directors being liable for such excess. Furthermore, the notes while payable on demand in coin were to be "receivable in all payments to the United States." Branches were authorized to be opened at any place in the United States, and the Secretary of the Treasury was empowered to require reports and to inspect the *general* accounts upon which such reports were based. The bank was not allowed to hold real estate beyond that necessary for offices, etc., unless acquired in satisfaction of preëxisting debt. It was prohibited from loaning more than $100,000 to the United States or more than $50,000 to any state, or making any loans to a foreign prince or state, unless sanctioned by Congress. It was not permitted to deal in stocks and bonds (except to sell those it acquired at the outset), or, generally, in anything but bills of exchange and bullion, nor was it to charge more than 6 per cent. upon loans or discounts. A very important provision was that three-fourths of the stock had to be paid for in 6 per cent. bonds of the United States then being issued. Thus the government was to be materially assisted at the outset in floating its loans.

The stock of the bank was considerably oversubscribed in two hours after the books were opened. Thomas Willing, President of the Bank of North America and a former partner of Robert Morris, was the first President.

The bank began business in Philadelphia, branches being eventually opened in New York, Boston, Baltimore, Washington, Norfolk, Charleston, Savannah and New Orleans. The government almost immediately became a borrower from the bank, its loans totaling $6,200,000 at the close of 1795, and ultimately it was compelled to realize upon its shares in the bank to repay in part the debt. In 1802 it ceased to be a shareholder, having, however, realized a net profit of nearly 57 per cent. upon its investment.

No reports of the bank's condition seem to have been required by the Treasury, and only two reports are known to exist, having been communicated to Congress by Secretary Gallatin in 1809 and 1811.[1] The rate of dividend paid (in excess of 8 per cent.) indicates that it was a very successful enterprise, besides being of incalculable benefit to the government in its most trying

[1] Gallatin's Reports, Finance Reports, Vol. I.

days during the period under review. From the reports in question it is gleaned that its circulation was $4,500,000 to $5,000,000, individual deposits $8,500,000 in 1809 and $5,900,000 in 1811, loans about $15,000,000, specie about $5,000,000. The latter of the two reports was for a date within a few months of the expiration of its charter.

Aside from the service to the government which the bank performed admirably, as testified to by Gallatin, Jefferson's Secretary of the Treasury, it exercised a most salutary influence upon the currency. Its own issues were never very large compared with its specie reserve, it issued no notes under ten dollars and it checked undue expansion on the part of the state banks, which now were increasing in number annually, by forcing redemption in specie when occasion warranted.[1]

The bank issued post notes, that is, post-dated notes, which, as a rule, were payable thirty days after the post date; they ran for various periods and differed from the usual promissory note only in having the bank back of them.

Although the charter was not to expire until 1811, a petition from the bank for its renewal was presented to Congress early in 1808. It was referred to committees, and Gallatin was directed to submit his views on the subject. He favored a new charter rather than a renewal, but was unquestionably favorable to the use of such a bank, particularly for the collection, safe keeping, and transmission of public moneys, and as an aid to the government in respect to loans.[2] The strongest objection to the renewal was the fact that $7,200,000 of the $10,000,000 capital was owned abroad. He therefore recommended a national bank, capital $30,000,000, two-sixths to go to the shareholders of the existing bank, three-sixths to the United States and the states, and one-sixth to the public, both the federal and the state governments to have a voice in the direction; the United States to receive interest on its deposits in excess of

[1] Gallatin's Reports, Finance Reports, Vol. I.

[2] *Ibid.*

$3,000,000, and in emergencies to be accommodated with loans to the extent of $18,000,000 at 6 per cent.

In 1810 a committee reported a bill upon the lines indicated by Gallatin, simply grafting the new features on Hamilton's act of 1791.[1] Subsequently another bill was reported to renew the charter for twenty years with some such modifications as recommended by Gallatin, excluding the participation of the states. In January, 1811, Gallatin submitted the second of the reports of the condition of the bank, already referred to. Another bill for renewal was introduced and pressed. An extended debate ensued, in the course of which the entire question was thoroughly discussed. Much of the opposition was based on constitutional objections. In the House the bill was defeated by the close vote of 65 to 64. In the Senate, Crawford, (afterwards Secretary of the Treasury) favored the renewal, in a strong report, believing, like Gallatin, in the great practical utility of the bank. He obtained from Gallatin a forcible plea for his bill, in which the inability of state banks to serve the desired purpose was conclusively shown. Crawford pointed out that despite the admitted usefulness of the bank and its influence upon the country's prosperity, the legislators were being carried away by the supposed public sentiment against the bank. Henry Clay opposed the bill upon constitutional grounds; he also appears to have been afraid of foreign control. The vote in the Senate was 17 to 17, and Vice President George Clinton gave the casting vote against the bill. So renewal was defeated. A petition from the bank for a brief extension in order to wind up its affairs was likewise negatived. Clay in the Senate made the committee report against the petition, saying that inasmuch as the original act was unconstitutional, any extension would be equally so. In the House the same reason was given for refusal.[2]

The Bank was required to report its condition to the Secre-

[1] Clarke and Hall, History of the Bank of the United States. [2] *Ibid.*

tary of the Treasury as often as required, not exceeding once a week. Such reports were not made public, being considered confidential, but that they were made is sufficiently shown by the writings of Jefferson, Gallatin and others who could not otherwise have obtained the data which they present. The fact that no such records now exist justifies the conclusion that they were burned; it will be remembered that the Treasury Department was burned in August, 1814, when Washington was occupied by the British, and was burned again in March, 1833. Had such reports been preserved, they would have been of great value to economists and publicists.

The assets of the institution were acquired by Stephen Girard, who continued the business in Philadelphia as Girard's Bank, which still flourishes there under a national charter.

In the final liquidation it paid $434 for each of its $400 shares, after having paid dividends averaging 8½ per cent.[1]

In 1784 there were but three state banks, with a capital of $2,100,000. From the meagre reports available it is gathered that the number increased to 28 in 1800 with $21,300,000 capital; in 1805 there were 75 with over $40,000,000 of capital; and in 1811 there were 88 with nearly $43,000,000 of capital. Of these last mentioned 47 with $12,200,000 capital were in New England, where the laws imposed wholesome regulation, particularly in Massachusetts, which required public reports from 1803. Although the systems in other states were with rare exceptions very carelessly supervised, or not at all, and charters were granted as spoils of party in some, the circulation issued relative to the specie holdings was not excessive in volume until after 1811.[2]

In 1806 Vermont had organized a bank, with branches, owned and operated exclusively by the state. Kentucky in the same

[1] Knox, History of Banking.

[2] See Crawford's Report of 1820, also Gallatin, Currency and Banking System, 1831.

year, Delaware in 1807, and North Carolina in 1810, each chartered a bank in which the state took a substantial stock interest.

Taken all together the period covered by the two decades during which the first United States Bank existed was one of prosperity, perhaps without parallel in any new country after an impoverishing war, and although natural advantages and the energies of the people had much to do with this prosperity, it is but just to give credit to the fathers of the Republic for their foresight in laying its foundations, and especially to the genius of Hamilton, who at the age of 32 took charge of the Treasury Department, and for about six years had the almost exclusive direction of the economic affairs of the new nation. His four reports on the Public Credit, the Establishment of a Coinage System, on the Bank, and on Manufactures and Tariff, constitute a monument to the incomparable ability of this greatest of all our financial ministers.

STATISTICAL RÉSUMÉ

Estimates of Bank Capital and Circulation, and the Money in the Country for Various Dates to 1811

Compiled from Crawford's Reports and Elliot's Funding System

(In millions except in last column)

	Banks (including Bank of United States after 1790)			Money Volume			
	Number	Capital	Circulation	Specie	Total	Population	Per Capita
1784	3	2.1	2.0	10.0	12.0	3.0	$4.00
1790	4	2.5	2.5	9.0	11.5	3.8	3.00
1795	24	21.0	16.0	19.0	35.0	4.5	7.77
1800	29	31.3	15.5	17.5	33.0	5.3	6.22
1805	76	50.5	26.0	17.5	43.5	6.2	7.00
1811	89	52.7	28.1	30.0	58.1	7.3	8.00

It is reported that in 1811 the banks held about $15,000,000 of specie. Statements purporting to give specie holdings prior to that date are misleading.

CHAPTER VIII

Paper Currency

1812–1836

The currency history of the country for the quarter-century following the expiration of the charter of the First Bank of the United States is divisible into three almost equal periods, — the disorganized condition of the currency during and following the War of 1812, and the struggle for its reformation, which extended to 1820; a period of sound currency under regulation by the Second Bank of the United States followed and continued until 1829; then began the war upon the Bank resulting in the failure to renew its charter and the downfall and breaking up of the system of which the Bank had been the controlling influence.

Statistics relating to banking and currency from 1812 to 1834 are exceedingly meagre. Subsequent to 1834, pursuant to a resolution of Congress directing the collection and reporting of information, the Treasury reports contain fairly satisfactory data. Secretary Crawford,[1] and afterward ex-Secretary Gallatin,[2] undertook to give some comparative figures for certain years. For the period from 1821 to 1828, inclusive, the only available statistics are found in the reports of the Massachusetts banks (required by state law from 1803) and those of the Second Bank of the United States, also required by law.

The second war with Great Britain began in 1812. The government found it necessary to borrow money and, as pre-

[1] Report of 1820, in full in International Monetary Conference, 1878, p. 502.

[2] Currency and Banking System, 1831.

dicted by Hamilton, Gallatin, and Crawford, the state banks proved unequal to the emergency. Instead of the anticipated contraction of banking facilities after the liquidation of the First Bank, a rapid expansion had taken place, but much of the alleged bank capital was fictitious, a large number of banks having been organized upon capital represented by notes of hand of the subscribers.

Crawford estimated that in the four years, 1811–1815, the number of banks increased from 88 to 208, the capital from less than $43,000,000 to over $88,000,000, and the circulation from $23,000,000 to $110,000,000. In 1816 there were 246 banks with $89,400,000 capital. For 1817 the number of banks is not given, but the capital is estimated at $125,700,000. In 1820 there were 307 banks, but the capital was only $102,100,000. Adequate legal restrictions were wanting in most of the states, and notes were issued with ease and without regard to capital or specie holdings. In order to increase the volume as much as possible, since note-issues were their principal means of making loans and discounts, a mass of small denominations, some as low as six cents, were issued. Adding to this the stress of war and the consequent hoarding of specie, suspension of coin payments naturally followed. Most of the banks outside of New England suspended in August, 1814. The depreciation of Southern and Western bank-notes was most severe. At Baltimore, where notes from Southern banks were found in greatest abundance, the discount on some issues reached 23 per cent. In New York and Philadelphia 16 per cent. was the maximum discount. Boston and New England notes alone were quoted on a par with specie. The range of the discounts by years was: 1814, 10 @ 20 per cent.; 1815, 2 @ 21½ per cent.; 1816, 1¾ @ 23 per cent.; and 1817, the year of resumption, 2½ @ 4½ per cent. Lack of specific information prevented the public from exercising a wise discrimination, as between banks, and hence they discriminated against localities. As late as 1823 discounts reaching a maximum of 75 per cent. upon notes of certain Kentucky banks are recorded.[1]

The funds of the government were deposited in many of these banks throughout the country, and when suspension took place amounted to $9,000,000. Congress, in 1812, had been compelled to resort to an issue of "Treasury Notes" (the first since 1781) to cover short term loans. Five separate issues were authorized during the war. At first all were interest-bearing, payable in one year and in denominations of $100 only. Later notes of $50, $20, and $5 were authorized; the $5 notes, however, did not bear interest. They were not made legal tenders, the proposition to do so having been promptly defeated; but being receivable for all public dues, and payable to public creditors, they circulated freely. In all $60,500,000 were authorized, but less than $37,000,000 were actually issued.[2] These notes were all funded into bonds or paid, except a very few which were probably destroyed or lost.

The government did not succeed in disposing of its obligations at par. An official report shows that of the $80,000,000 of bonds and notes placed during the War of 1812, owing to the discounts thereon and the depreciated currency received in payment therefor, the Treasury actually obtained only $34,000,000.[3] In other words, had the Treasury been able to dispose of its notes and bonds at par in coin, and had its balances in the various state banks been available, a loan of $34,000,000 properly financed would probably have covered the expenses of the war, for which, ultimately, the people paid $80,000,000 and interest. Gallatin, in reviewing the period, expressed the opinion unequivocally that, had the Bank of the United States been rechartered, suspension of specie payments would have been avoided and so this loss, enormous for that period, would not have been incurred.[4]

[1] Gouge, History of Paper Money. [2] Bailey, National Loans.

[3] McDuffie's Report on Bank of United States, 21st Congress, 1st Sess.

[4] Gallatin, Currency and Banking System.

Many of those in Congress who had aided in defeating the renewal of the federal bank charter began to see the error of that policy. It will be recalled that a change of one vote in each House of Congress would have carried one of the measures proposed. Even Madison, now President, who in 1791 was the leader of the opposition to the First Bank charter, modified his opinions. The "object lesson" had been an instructive one.

Jefferson advised Madison to propose the issue of government currency, $20,000,000 annually so long as needed, and appeal to the states to relinquish the right to establish banks of issue.[1] This appears to be the first important suggestion for a government note-issue.

Early in 1814 New York members in Congress presented a petition for the establishment of a national bank with a capital of $30,000,000.[2] The House Committee reported adversely, upon constitutional grounds. Calhoun, then a representative from South Carolina, endeavored to have such a bank established in the District of Columbia, which, being under exclusive federal jurisdiction, made the measure constitutional. A bill for this purpose was reported in February, but was soon dropped. In October the Secretary of the Treasury, A. J. Dallas, upon request from the House Committee on Ways and Means to furnish suggestions for the maintenance of the public credit, submitted a report[3] strongly favoring a national bank. Jeffersonian though he was, and in the cabinet of Madison, Dallas said that if after twenty years of tacit sanction of the old bank charter the Constitution had not been amended upon this question, he considered himself justified in regarding it settled in favor of the constitutionality of the charter. He regarded such an institution "the only efficient remedy for the disordered condition of our circulating medium." He recommended a $50,000,000 bank, two-fifths

[1] Bolles, Financial History of United States.

[2] Clarke and Hall, Documentary History of Bank of United States.

[3] Finance Reports, Vol. II.; also Clarke and Hall's History.

of the capital to be taken by the United States, $6,000,000 to be paid in specie by outside subscribers, $24,000,000 in the recent issues of public debt, and the $20,000,000 taken by the United States to be also paid for in such obligations; the bank to loan the government $30,000,000, and the government to have five of the fifteen directors and the right of inspection.

Calhoun proposed a substitute bill providing that all the shares were to be open to public subscription, and omitting the required loan to the government. Another bill, containing a clause permitting the bank to suspend coin payments during the war, was introduced. The suspension clause was rejected by the casting vote of Speaker Langdon Cheves (afterwards president of the Second Bank). Daniel Webster, with his accustomed vigor and eloquence, also opposed the suspension clause. Amended in various particulars the bill finally passed, but since the capital was reduced to $30,000,000 and no loan to the government was provided for, Dallas pronounced the measure inadequate and President Madison vetoed it on January 30, 1815.[1]

Among the objections urged by Madison was that the bank would be compelled to maintain coin payments, thus restricting note circulation and diminishing the bank's usefulness during the war period.[2]

The war came to an end soon thereafter, but the disordered condition of the currency required attention, and Madison, at the opening of the next Congress, December, 1815, gave special attention to the subject in his message.[3] He referred to the absence of specie and the need of a substitute; if state banks could not supply a uniform national currency, a national bank might; if neither could, it might "become necessary to ascertain the terms upon which the *notes of the Government* (no longer required as an instrument of credit) shall be issued, upon motives of general policy, as a common medium of circulation." The

[1] Clarke and Hall, History of Bank of United States. Messages of Presidents, Vol. I. [2] Messages of Presidents, Vol. I. [3] *Ibid.*

exigency must have been great indeed to produce such a change of views since the days when he sat in the Constitutional Convention.

Dallas in his annual report for 1815 again discussed the subject, concluding that "the establishment of a national bank is regarded as the best, and perhaps the only adequate resource"; believing that such a bank would aid and lead the state banks in the work of restoring credit, public and private.[1] He recommended a capital of $35,000,000, three-fourths government bonds, one-fourth specie (the capital to be afterwards augmented to $50,000,000 by Congress, the additional $15,000,000 to be taken by the states); the United States to take $7,000,000 of the capital and to have one-fifth of the directors; the bank to pay $1,500,000 for the charter out of its earnings. Suspension of coin payments was not permitted, branches were allowed, and the ordinary government business was to be transacted without charge.

Calhoun reported a bill to the House upon the lines suggested by Dallas. Webster desired to reduce the capital. Clay, now in the House, favored the bill, explaining that his former opposition in the Senate to a national bank was due to supposed instructions from the Kentucky legislature, to the supposed desire of his constituents, and to his conviction that the *necessity* for using an implied constitutional power did not exist; now the case was different; such a bank was indispensable to remedy existing evils. The bill passed the House March 14, 1816, by a vote of 80 to 71. It received the support of Calhoun, Clay, and Ingham (afterwards Secretary of the Treasury); Webster and most of the Whigs voted against it, objecting finally to the participation of the government in the bank. (The Jeffersonians were to have control.) The vote was by no means sectional. The Senate passed the bill in April, and it was approved by Madison on the 10th of that month.[2]

[1] Clarke and Hall, History of Bank of United States; also Finance Reports, Vol. II.

[2] Clarke and Hall, History of Bank of United States.

The Second Bank's charter was drawn largely upon the lines devised by Hamilton for that of the First Bank. Numerous provisions repeat his language word for word. The capital was fixed at $35,000,000, three and one-half times that of the First Bank, with shares of $100 (instead of $400) each. The government took one-fifth of the stock, paying for it with its obligations in instalments, the last one being paid in 1831. Of the remaining $28,000,000, one-fourth was to be paid for in specie, the balance in specie or government bonds, in three equal half yearly instalments. No single subscription for more than three thousand shares was to be accepted unless the full amount subscribed for by others had not been taken prior to the date fixed. The restrictions upon voting the shares which the first charter contained, were repeated. There were twenty-five directors, as in the First Bank, but now the government had one-fifth of the board, to be appointed by the President.

In lieu of making a loan to the government, the Bank paid a bonus of $1,500,000, and it was to act as the fiscal agent of the government, including the transfers of funds, without compensation. The deposit of public moneys was to be made in the Bank and branches where they existed, unless otherwise directed by the Secretary of the Treasury, and when that officer gave such directions he was to report his reasons therefor to Congress. The Bank was empowered to establish branches anywhere, with a local organization, and it had to have a branch in the District of Columbia and in every state where two thousand shares of its stock were held. Reports were to be made to the Secretary of the Treasury as often as required, and the Bank was subject to his inspection and to that of a committee of Congress.

The note-issuing function was more specifically provided for than in the first charter. Denominations under $5 were prohibited and all under $100 were to be payable to bearer on demand. The suspension of coin payments of notes and deposits was prohibited, subject to a penalty of 12 per cent. per annum. As in the old charter the liabilities, other than for deposits (therefore including note issues), were not to exceed the amount of the capital, unless authorized by Congress, and directors were personally liable for any excess. The notes of the Bank were to be receivable in all payments to the United States.

The provisions relative to the holding of real estate, dealing in anything but exchange and bullion, and demanding more than 6 per cent. upon loans, were the same as in the old charter. The sale of the government bonds held by the Bank was limited to $2,000,000 a year, and if sold in this country they were first to be offered to the government at current rates. Congress agreed further to incorporate no other banks, except in the District of Columbia, during the life of the charter.

The shares were not fully subscribed at once, and Stephen Girard ultimately took the unsubscribed 30,383 shares.

The Bank opened for business on January 17, 1817. The second instalment of subscriptions to shares was then due, but neither this nor the third was paid in promptly and according to the charter. In order to encourage payment the Bank management was unwisely indulgent; the Bank made loans to stockholders upon their subscription stock, accepted the notes of specie-paying banks as coin, and made payment in this manner so easy that the Bank received less than $2,000,000 (instead of $7,000,000) in specie, and $15,430,000 in government bonds, instead of $21,000,000 as expected. The Bank was thus weakened in its capitalization and had to contend with adverse trade balances, which resulted from large importations from abroad during 1816–1818; foreign exchange was at a premium, which means that gold was really at a premium. Consequently the bank was compelled in 1818 to import specie. The officers permitted the transfer of the shares upon the books of the Bank before they were fully paid for. A number of the officers and directors speculated in the stock of the Bank, discounting their loans for the purpose at the Bank or its branches. The first two years' operations showed losses, due largely to this speculation, of more than $3,500,000; nevertheless it paid dividends.

On November 30, 1818, the House of Representatives appointed a committee to investigate the Bank's affairs. In its report made by John C. Spencer, afterwards Secretary of the Treasury, in February following, the speculations and other derelictions above referred to were published.[1] The Bank was nearly insolvent and had violated its charter; nevertheless the House refused to declare it forfeited, preferring that the shareholders correct the mismanagement. In March, 1819, Langdon Cheves became president and under his able and conservative administration, covering four years, the evils were corrected and the Bank became very prosperous. From 1823 to the expiration of the charter Nicholas Biddle was president of the institution.

Coin payments were not at once restored. Secretary Dallas had endeavored, but without success, to prepare the way in 1816, by urging the state banks to resume,[2] but the existing conditions were very profitable to them, and they were not inclined to do so. The greater their note-issues and the longer specie resumption was delayed, the larger would be their dividends. In October, 1816, Dallas was succeeded by Crawford, who continued the efforts for resumption and finally succeeded in having July 1, 1817, fixed as the date for its beginning. Crawford felt, however, that the Bank's assistance was requisite and accordingly influenced it to negotiate an agreement with the state banks in the principal cities, to resume on February 20 instead of July 1.

This proved more easily said than done. The country was unquestionably short of specie. The Bank could not, as has been stated, obtain its required quota without importation and there appears to have been a premium on foreign exchange the greater part of the years 1817 and 1818, so that the imported specie

[1] House Reports, 15th Congress, 2d Sess. [2] Finance Reports, Vol. II.

promptly returned abroad. This served to aid the state banks to continue redundant paper issues. The Spencer committee laid a large portion of the blame for this upon the Bank, declaring that its measures were not sufficiently vigorous. The problem which confronted the Bank was, however, a formidable one. The Treasury had turned over to it nearly $11,000,000 of "public deposits" from the state banks, consisting largely of depreciated paper. Specie resumption meant contraction of state bank circulation and serious curtailment of credits which they had extended. The United States Bank could not, owing to its lack of strength in specie, safely supply the credit thus curtailed and at the same time maintain coin payments. A too rapid contraction necessarily tended to precipitate disaster. While the management of the Bank in the first and second years of its existence was open to serious criticism (the speculative tendency of the time having unquestionably influenced many of those who had the business in charge), some of the subsequent currency difficulties might have been avoided if the Bank's policy of compelling the *gradual* retirement of state bank-notes had been continued.

Nevertheless, in obedience to the desire of Congress, the Bank acted more vigorously. The volume of notes in the country, which in 1815 stood at $110,000,000, and probably higher in 1816 and 1817, was reduced by the end of 1819 to $45,000,000.[1] The volume of specie was practically unchanged. Loans were violently contracted, prices necessarily fell seriously, "hard times" came upon the land and propositions to issue government paper, as is usual under such conditions, were numerous. Secretary Crawford, asked by the House of Representatives for his views upon this as well as the general subject of the currency, vigorously and successfully opposed the propositions. Without discussing the question of the constitutionality of such a measure, which he assumed was not intended to be put before

[1] See Crawford's Report, in International Monetary Conference, 1878, p. 502.

him, he asserted that "as a measure of alleviation, it will be more likely to do harm than good," pointing out, as if he had lived through the later period when a similar policy prevailed (1862–1879), the effects of such a paper currency upon practically all lines of human activity.

Much of the disturbance during this period was no doubt due to the great fluctuation in exchange between the states of the East, and those of the West and South. The latter, owing largely to their limited and widely distributed population, were continually at a disadvantage, and this condition was largely responsible for the unstable character of the banks in those sections and the resulting discount on their notes. The government drew large sums from the people in those states in payment for public lands, whereas the bulk of the disbursements were made in the East. The Bank endeavored to alleviate this condition by redeeming its notes, no matter where issued, at any of its branches at par, thus affording a medium of exchange available throughout the country. It was compelled to modify this policy in 1818, when it found that the operation caused embarrassment, serious enough to threaten suspension.[1] Its notes thereupon depreciated somewhat excepting as to the three New England branches; but the amount of depreciation was inconsiderable, ranging from 1 per cent. in the early years to $\frac{1}{2}$ and $\frac{1}{8}$ per cent. later. All notes were redeemed at Philadelphia as well as at the places of issue; notes of five dollars were redeemed at all offices, and at times all notes were received at all the offices from individuals, but not from banks.

Another practice of the Bank which led to criticism was the issue of "branch drafts" drawn for five dollars, ten dollars, and twenty dollars, by the branches upon the parent bank in Philadelphia, which practically circulated as notes of the Bank and were treated as such in its reports. This was done at first (1826) to obviate the great labor of signing notes that the law

[1] Cheves's Report in Goddard's History of Banks.

imposed upon the president and cashier of the parent bank, a task which on account of the large volume of circulation they were physically unable to perform, and which Congress, notwithstanding repeated petitions, refused to alter.[1] The practice eventually became so general, and partook so much of the nature of "kiting," that it was regarded as unwise. At one time these drafts constituted one-third of the circulation.

The presentation of local bank-notes for redemption by the United States Bank, instead of paying them out in the regular course of business, aroused antagonism which many of the state banks fostered for their own advantage. In Kentucky, Ohio, Georgia, and Maryland particularly, the friction became serious. It was upon the question of taxing the Bank in the last-mentioned state that the Supreme Court upon appeal finally settled the controversy, prohibiting state interference with the Bank.[2]

Nevertheless in Ohio the Bank was declared an outlaw for resisting exorbitant taxation, and the entire machinery of the state government was used against it for a time. In Georgia a law was passed virtually justifying creditors of the Bank in refusing payment of their debts to it. Kentucky passed "stay" laws practically relieving debtors of their obligations. For presenting notes of local banks for payment in specie, the Bank was regarded as a criminal; the people there seemed to think it the duty of the Bank to lend its capital to the state banks without interest (by holding or paying out their notes) although many of these local banks were by no means substantial institutions.

Notes of country banks were received by the government for taxes and in payment for land sold; these notes were deposited with the United States Bank and credited to the government as cash; the notes of many banks were not good and many that were good were at a discount; these notes were received by and passed

[1] Clarke and Hall, Documentary History of Bank.

[2] McCulloch *vs.* Maryland; see Chapter VII., *ante*.

upon as to goodness by the Revenue Collectors and Land Agents, neither possessing training to insure their competency; nevertheless the Bank was expected to receive these notes and credit them at par. In self-protection the Bank received such notes in special deposit, subject to collection, and not as cash, but the Secretary of the Treasury would not permit this practice. The effort to control the redundant state bank circulation by enforcing specie redemption, and the responsibility of discriminating as between the different state banks was largely transferred from the Treasury to the Bank; inevitably the state banks became intensely hostile, the more so as they regarded the United States Bank as a business rival; any course tending to contract the volume of currency found many assailants and was generally unpopular. The hostility incurred by the Bank, in doing its duty under these trying circumstances, laid the foundation for the opposition that prevented the renewal of its charter.

As has been stated, the Second Bank began under conditions and with incompetent administration calculated to defeat the object of its creation. Its circulation in 1818 had expanded to nearly $10,000,000, an amount not warranted by the specie it held. Cheves corrected this, and under his management the amount of the circulation exceeded $6,000,000 only in three monthly statements, the amount having been as frequently under as over $5,000,000, and at times it held more specie than the notes outstanding. The discounts showed a conservative policy, absolutely necessary in this critical period. In 1817 the deposits were usually in excess of $12,000,000, continuing so until near the end of 1818; during Cheves's term the minimum was $4,700,000, the maximum $8,600,000.

In September, 1819, the Bank had eighteen branches, of which only five were north of the parent office at Philadelphia, showing the disposition to establish them where credit was most needed. The Baltimore branch was the most important, and five others did a larger business than the branch at New York.

Conditions changed somewhat; the distribution of the Bank's activities throughout the country, the different localities served and the extent of the service is fairly well shown by the following statement showing the location of branches in 1825, and the volume of loans and exchange carried at each:—

	Loans and Bills of Exchange
Baltimore	$4,281,000
Boston	2,011,000
Charleston, S.C.	3,795,000
Chillicothe, Ohio	461,000
Cincinnati	1,478,000
Fayetteville, N.C.	549,000
Lexington, Ky.	1,062,000
Louisville, Ky.	1,197,000
Middletown and Hartford, Conn.	618,000
New Orleans	3,472,000
New York	5,118,000
Norfolk	696,000
Philadelphia	4,507,000
Pittsburg	815,000
Providence, R.I.	599,000
Portsmouth, N.H.	442,000
Richmond	1,316,000
Savannah	776,000
Washington	1,335,000

There was not sufficient central control exercised over the branches to prevent loss in extending credit and make the bank administration a homogeneous whole.

The statistics of state banks prior to 1817, such as they are, show conclusively that the general practice was to organize banks mainly for the purpose of issuing notes, and then exert political influence to obtain government deposits. The policy of having the states interested as shareholders and participate in the profits operated to prevent the exercise of restraining power by the states except in a very limited degree.

Not since the continental days had the country had such a wretchedly bad circulating medium as from 1812 to 1819. It was composed of a relatively small amount of notes of sound banks, an almost equally large amount of counterfeits, and a mass of paper the value of which could rarely be known from one day to another. The location of many "banks" was practically unknown, and many of them had failed. Their notes were nevertheless in use; others deliberately repudiated their notes, still others pretended falsely to redeem upon demand. Other corporations and tradesmen issued "currency." Even barbers and bartenders competed with the banks in this respect. Altogether it appears marvellous that, when nearly every citizen regarded it his constitutional right to issue money, successful trade was possible at all.

The influence upon public men and Congress by individuals and corporations who were profiting by the demoralized conditions of the currency is wonderful, almost incredible. Politics of the present time seem pure compared with those of that period.

Congress passed a resolution on April 26, 1816, declaring

> "That the revenues of the United States ought to be collected and received in the legal currency of the United States, or in Treasury notes, or in the notes of the Bank of the United States, as by law provided and declared,"

and requiring the Secretary of the Treasury to adopt such measures as he deemed necessary, to cause, *as soon as may be*, all taxes to be so collected and paid, and that after the first day of February, 1817, no taxes, etc., "ought to be collected or received otherwise than in the legal currency of the United States, or Treasury notes, or notes of the Bank of the United States, as aforesaid."

Dallas's successor (Crawford) under the authority of this resolution gently but firmly brought about a reform, first by persuasion, ultimately by publishing the names of the banks whose notes were not to be received for public dues. The great care exercised by him in this enormous task of endeavoring to obtain for the Treasury the revenue to which it was entitled, without precipitating a crisis, is shown in a large volume of correspondence preserved in the annals of the government.[1] Every possible subterfuge to foist upon the Treasury depreciated and worthless paper was used. Notes passing current in one locality at par could be paid out by the government in another only at a considerable discount, and in places where local notes were really at par in specie depreciated paper imported from other points for the specific purpose was paid to the Treasury. These devices in a multitude of varying forms had to be met by Crawford and afterwards by the Bank. Ultimately, however, they brought order out of chaos, but the losses were enormous.

Gallatin, writing in 1831, gives a list of 165 banks that failed between 1811 and 1830, most of them undoubtedly "going to the wall" between 1817 and 1821.

Crawford states in his special report early in 1820 that the *worst* of the troubles resulting from the war and the inflation of the currency had then practically passed, and soon thereafter the monetary conditions, the industries of the people, and the finances of the government gradually improved. The reduction of the federal debt began, the antagonism to the Bank was somewhat abated, and it prospered so that its shares were at a premium of 20 to 25 per cent.

Sounder principles in state bank currency regulation were introduced. In a number of the states the business of banking was placed under supervision, the issue of "currency" by persons or associations not authorized to do banking business prohibited, and penalties for non-redemption of notes were provided. The evil of small note-issues was not materially checked, however.[2]

The practice of having the states more or less interested in the banks by the ownership of stock increased, in most cases with disastrous results. The state bank of South Carolina, owned entirely by the state, was one of the few that made a satisfactory showing during this period.[3]

[1] American State Papers, Vol. III.

[2] Knox, History of Banking; Sumner, History of Banking.

[3] *Ibid.*

That restraining force which legislation failed to provide was, in New England, supplied by the banks themselves. Profiting by the lesson taught by both Banks of the United States, Boston banks undertook to regulate the currency by compulsory redemption. The Suffolk Bank led in this movement, and the system which developed was known by its name.[1] Practically this bank, with the coöperation of six other Boston banks, organized a clearing-house for notes of outside institutions, by establishing a redemption fund in the Suffolk Bank. The banks which entered the system would have their notes received at par in Boston, the financial centre, and would be called upon for redemption only at specified periods by the Suffolk, which would receive in redemption, also at par, any notes of banks in good standing in lieu of specie. Banks which refused to enter the "system" were called upon to redeem their notes in specie on demand. The result of this system was that banks which had a redundant circulation were compelled to contract to reasonable limits. On the other hand, the Boston redemption gave their notes a more extended circulation, and the people were not subjected to the onerous discounts which country bank-notes otherwise suffered in the money centres. This loss had been from 3 to 5 per cent. The New England Bank of Boston had reduced it to less than 1 per cent., the actual cost of sending notes for redemption, but the Suffolk reduced it even more, so that ultimately the cost was only 10 cents per $1000, and this was borne by the banks.[2]

These results were not accomplished without much opposition. The practice of making a bank keep its promise to pay specie when it did not provide for redemption at Boston was deemed arbitrary, but the communities securing a sound currency heartily approved, and almost all of the banks in New England found it to their interest to enter the system.

The "Safety Fund System" was adopted by statute in New

[1] D. R. Whitney, The Suffolk Bank.

[2] Sound Currency, Vol. II.

York State in 1829,[1] when the legislature was considering the renewal of a large number of expiring charters. It required the banks so rechartered, and any others desiring to come under the system, to contribute to a joint fund for the redemption of notes and payment of deposits of any of their number which should be overtaken by disaster. The system was adopted by only a few of the existing banks, and, as will be seen later, was not a success.

What the Suffolk system was doing for New England, the Bank of the United States was endeavoring to accomplish for the rest of the country, particularly for the South and West, although necessarily upon different lines. It had no redemption fund, but it was the government fiscal agent, and exercised the power of regulation by means thereof. Banks not in good standing found their notes rejected by government officers and specie redemption was required of them. Although firm in these requirements to maintain notes at or near par, the bank cultivated friendly relations with state banks wherever it could. It received their notes, when good, for government dues and paid the Treasury drafts with its own. Some of them acted as its agents at points where it had no branches. It continuously had large balances with them and carried their notes. In 1819 the amount due it from various state banks was over $2,600,000 on current accounts and nearly $1,900,000 on account of their notes which it held. Its own circulation at the time amounted to $6,600,000. In later years the total of items due it by state banks at the periods of its annual reports was lowest in 1826 at $1,860,000 and highest in 1832 at $6,100,000, the average being about $3,500,000.[2]

The policy of Cheves to limit discounts and note-issues was generally adhered to by Biddle, but as the business of the country improved, that of the bank correspondingly increased. The statement at the end of the chapter, giving the condition of the bank annually, is one of the most interesting exhibits in the monetary history of the United States.

[1] Knox, History of Banking. [2] See statement at end of chapter.

The average of deposits rose to $14,500,000 for the period 1823–1832, the annual average never falling below $10,000,000 and rising to nearly $23,000,000 in 1832. In that year the "Bank War" became active and the business of the institution diminished. The loans and discounts kept pace fairly with the deposits, the minimum being about $28,000,000, the maximum about $66,000,000 (in 1832). The holdings of bonds and stocks reached a maximum in 1825 of $18,400,000, and diminished to nothing as the government debt was paid off.[1]

The circulation of the Bank, even when "branch drafts" were included, was never excessive. The maximum prior to 1836 was $21,300,000 (1832), but up to 1824 it never exceeded $6,000,000, and the specie holdings were frequently in excess of the notes until after that year. Even in the later years (prior to 1832) the specie never fell below 40 per cent. of the notes outstanding, and was usually in excess of 50 per cent.

The evidence is conclusive that the Bank was, after reorganization by Cheves, and particularly under Biddle's régime, a strong institution, a valuable auxiliary to the government, a bulwark against rotten bank-note issues, a most serviceable instrument to the trade of the country, and in its international relations a protection to American industry and commerce. In his annual report for 1828[2] Secretary of the Treasury Rush, reviewing his administration, sets forth all these facts. He said: —

"This capacity in the Treasury to apply the public funds at the proper moment in every part of a country of such wide extent, has been essentially augmented by the Bank of the United States. The department feels an obligation of duty to bear its testimony, founded on constant experience during the term in question, to the useful instrumentality of this institution in all the most important fiscal operations of the nation. . . . It receives the paper of the state banks paid on public account in the interior, as well as elsewhere, and by placing it to the credit of the United States as cash, renders it available wherever the public service may require. . . . Such, also, is the confidence reposed in the stock of the Bank of the United States,

[1] See statement at end of chapter. [2] Finance Reports, Vol. II.

that it serves as a medium of remittance abroad in satisfaction of debts due from our citizens to those of other countries, which otherwise would make a call upon the specie of the country for their discharge. Nor are these all the uses of this institution in which the government participates. It is the preservation of a good currency that can alone impart stability to prosperity, and prevent those fluctuations in its value, hurtful alike to individual and to national wealth. This advantage the bank has secured to the community by confining within prudent limits its issues of paper, whereby a restraint has been imposed upon excessive importations, which are thus kept more within the true wants and capacity of the country. Sometimes judiciously varying its course, it enlarges its issues, to relieve scarcity, as under the disastrous speculations of 1825. The state banks following, or controlled by its general example, have shaped their policy towards the same salutary ends, adding fresh demonstrations to the truth that, under the mixed jurisdiction and powers of the state and national systems of government, a national bank is the instrument alone by which Congress can effectively regulate the currency of the nation. . . . A paper currency too redundant, because without any basis of coin, or other effective check, and of no value as a medium of remittance or exchange beyond the jurisdiction of the state whence it had been issued, a currency that not unfrequently imposed upon the Treasury the necessity of meeting, by extravagant premiums, the mere act of transferring the revenue collected at one point to defray unavoidable expenditures at another; — this is the state of things which the Bank of the United States has superseded. In the financial operations of the Nation, as in the pecuniary transactions between man and man, confidence has succeeded to distrust, steadiness to fluctuation, and reasonable certainty to general confusion and risk. The very millions of dollars not effective, of which the Treasury for many years has been obliged to speak, is but a remnant of the losses arising from the shattered currency, which the bank, by a wise management of its affairs, has cured."

In December, 1827, a resolution to sell the shares in order to profit by the premium (then 23½ per cent.) was defeated in the House of Representatives, only 9 votes favoring, 174 opposing.[1] The hostility seemed to have nearly disappeared under these conditions.[2] Gallatin wrote that in 1829 the currency of the country was as sound as could be expected under any system of paper money.[3]

[1] Abridgment of Debates. [2] Parton, Life of Jackson, Vol. III., p. 256.
[3] Gallatin's Writings, Vol. VIII., p. 390.

It was therefore a surprise to the country that President Jackson as early as 1829, more than six years before the expiration of the Bank's charter, announced his opposition to its renewal. The language he used in his message to Congress was as follows: —

"The charter of the Bank of the United States expires in 1836, and its stockholders will most probably apply for a renewal of their privileges. In order to avoid the evils resulting from precipitancy in a measure involving such important principles and such deep pecuniary interests, I feel that I cannot, in justice to the parties interested, too soon present it to the deliberate consideration of the legislature and the people. Both the constitutionality and the expediency of the law creating this bank are well questioned by a large portion of our fellow-citizens and it must be admitted by all, that it has failed in the great end of establishing a uniform and sound currency.

"Under these circumstances, if such an institution is deemed essential to the fiscal operations of the government, I submit to the wisdom of the legislature whether a national one, founded upon the credit of the government and its revenues, might not be devised which would avoid all constitutional difficulties, and at the same time secure all the advantages to the government and country that were expected to result from the present bank."[1]

South Carolina's legislature immediately took up the suggestion of a *national* bank,[2] looking upon it as in line with its own state bank policy, and estimating the demand of the country for currency (and banking capital) at $1,000,000,000, it recommended that the United States issue that amount of currency pledging its faith to its redemption, apportion it as banking capital to the several states to be used by them or farmed out to corporations, the states to guarantee the federal government against any loss that might result and to pay 1 per cent. for its use. No official action appears to have been taken by other states.

Both houses of Congress referred the subject to committees. The report of the committee to the House (1830) was very volu-

[1] Messages of Presidents, Vol. II. [2] Niles Register, 1830.

minous,[1] and its chairman (McDuffie, S. C.), after a complete presentation of the facts, defended the federal bank policy. He reviewed the question of its constitutionality and utility, as well as the expediency of Jackson's recommendation of a "national bank" founded on the credit of the government. Upon the first point he recalled that most of the leading opponents, both in the legislative and in the executive departments of the government, taught by the "very brief but fatal experience" (1811–1816), yielded their views, and the judicial department had unanimously decided the question of the constitutionality of the charter. He argued that the power to regulate the value of money given by the Constitution to Congress unquestionably carried the power to establish efficient means to that end. He forcibly and conclusively controverted Jackson's assertion that the Bank had failed to serve the purpose for which it was established, and demonstrated that the paper currency had been made uniform and sound.

Jackson's national bank plan was fairly "riddled." It was the general opinion that it would ultimately result in merely a government note-issue, and the impossibility of providing a satisfactory currency of this character, subject as it would be to partisan influences, was conclusively demonstrated.

In the Senate the recommendation of Jackson met a similar reception. The report (made by Smith of Maryland) maintained that a sound and uniform currency system existed, provided by the Bank of the United States, and that there were "insuperable and fatal" objections to the scheme proposed by Jackson, which the committee pronounced impracticable. Both houses were favorable to the Bank.

Notwithstanding this advice of his friends in Congress (for the committees were both controlled by Jacksonians), and notwithstanding the opinions of all but one member of his Cabinet,

[1] House Reports, 21st Congress, 1st Sess. Also in Clarke and Hall, History of Bank of United States.

which included Ingham as Secretary of the Treasury, Jackson repeated his attack upon the Bank in his message in 1830 and in a milder form in 1831. It was well known to the leaders, as Adams showed in his report in 1832, although not fully understood by the public until later, that he was secretly influenced by a cabal of lesser politicians, generally known as the "Kitchen Cabinet" (with Amos Kendall, afterward Postmaster-general, at its head),[1] whose motives were anything but patriotic. They used Secretary Ingham to open an attack upon the management of the Bank's branch in New Hampshire upon allegations which proved entirely unfounded. The cabal ultimately forced Ingham, who believed in the Bank, out of the Cabinet.[2]

The question of rechartering soon became one on which the political parties divided. Clay, then the Whig candidate for presidency, espoused the cause of the Bank, and upon the advice of the leaders of that party, Biddle early in 1832 petitioned Congress for a renewal of the charter. Jackson and his partisans regarded this as a challenge to battle, and Benton assumed the leadership of the opposition.[3] In the House, Polk, afterwards President, was the anti-Bank leader. Benton was in fact opposed to all bank currency, entertaining the opinion, which he aired upon every possible occasion, that the country would be more prosperous with a circulation composed of coin only.

In March, under the influence of Benton, a committee of the House of Representatives was appointed to examine the Bank. The report[4] was in three parts, one adverse to the Bank by the majority (including Clayton of Georgia, the chairman), the second favorable to the Bank, by McDuffie, and the third by John Quincy Adams, also favorable, and giving special prominence to certain features. In many particulars the Clayton attack

[1] Sumner, History of Banking in United States; Horace White, Money and Banking, pp. 288–291; Niles Register; Duane's Narrative.

[2] Niles Register.

[3] Benton, Thirty Years' View, Vol. I., p. 236.

[4] House Reports, 22d Congress, 1st Sess.

(openly fathered by Benton) was frivolous. Usury, the issue of "branch drafts" already referred to, selling foreign coin, domestic exchange and stocks, non-user of charter by refusing to issue notes at certain branches, making donations for roads and canals, building and renting houses, were the principal criticisms, and were manifestly made in order to create political capital. Upon none of these charges would serious-minded individuals have justified a discontinuance of the Bank. The criticisms applied to its administration rather than the Bank itself. One charge that the Bank purchased newspaper support by granting a loan was fully disproved, one of the members of the majority acquitting the Bank of any such motives.[1] On the other hand, it developed that some members of the cabal had failed in their purpose to drag politics into the management of one of the branches, for their pecuniary benefit, which indicated the motive for their secret machinations. This evidence, as well as Biddle's masterly defence of the Bank, was suppressed by Clayton but brought out by Adams.[2] The chief witness against the Bank (Whitney) was subsequently proven guilty of perjury; nevertheless he was received into the "Kitchen Cabinet"[3] in good fellowship.

A bill for the extension of the charter was reported, in the Senate from a committee headed by G. M. Dallas (son of the former Secretary) and Webster, and in the House from McDuffie's committee (Ways and Means). Dallas thought the time inopportune, a presidential campaign being at hand, but he supported the measure heartily. The Senate bill passed. It provided for an extension of the charter for fifteen years, upon the payment of an annual bonus of $200,000. It also contained a provision (to which Dallas had objected) compelling the Bank to accept its own notes from state banks no matter where issued

[1] R. M. Johnston, who, however, admitted that he had not looked at a document.
[2] House Reports, 22d Congress, 1st Sess.
[3] White, Sound Currency, Vol. IV., No. 18.

or where tendered. "Branch drafts" were prohibited, but subordinate officers were permitted to sign notes, and Congress reserved the right to prohibit notes under $20. The vote on the bill in the upper house was 28 to 20, in the lower one 107 to 85. Jackson vetoed the measure (July 10, 1832), and it failed to command the necessary two-thirds to pass it over the veto.

Jackson's objections[1] were (1) that the recharter continued a practical monopoly, (2) benefited the shareholders by giving them a valuable gratuity, (3) foreigners held a large part of the shares, and in case of war the Bank could be used by the enemy, (4) finally that it was unconstitutional. He waived aside the argument that the liquidation of so large a concern would cause disturbances, and held that neither he nor Congress was bound by the decision of the Supreme Court that the charter was constitutional. Upon this last point Madison had just previously published a letter in which he radically disagreed with Jackson.[2]

The Supreme Court had passed upon the charter of the Bank, and held it constitutional ten years prior to Jackson's attack in 1829. It seems strange therefore that he should make the principal ground for vetoing the renewal bill the unconstitutionality of the original charter. His position that his oath to support the Constitution bound him to support it as he construed it and not as interpreted by the Courts, was untenable. The President, of all persons, is bound by the Constitution and laws as interpreted by the Supreme Court. Jackson believed the Bank was being used in opposition to him politically, and the subsequent virtual alliance between the Whig party and the Bank would indicate that his belief may have been well founded. Be this true, he had wantonly begun the attack when he, as a statesman, should have sought to correct the management rather than destroy the Bank. It seems strange that political fortune could induce men to attack with such vehemence an institution when the inevitable effect

[1] Messages of Presidents, Vol. II.

[2] Letter to C. J. Ingersoll, Clarke and Hall's History, p. 778.

must be to jeopardize the national interests of the whole people. Our fathers had many virtues which it is well to emulate, but in respect to political rancor and partisan vindictiveness the present is certainly a great improvement upon the period under discussion.

It should be borne in mind that the constitutional objection which confronted every attempt to exercise any power not specially delegated to Congress was brought forward by representatives of the slave states. The agitation against slavery kept its champions constantly on the alert lest some precedent be established that might tend to provoke national interference with that institution. The less the power conceded to Congress, and the greater the power reposed in the states, the less likelihood there would be of outside interference either by law or by failure to suppress efforts constantly being made to aid slaves in escaping. Vermont and Kentucky were admitted as states at the same time, and when Maine applied for admission she was kept waiting pending the controversy over the question of slavery in Missouri. Nothing was permitted to be done which tended to impair the relative power of the slaveholding interests. This policy of minimizing the powers of the general government is largely responsible for the failure to provide a national currency free from the evils which seemed inseparable from a currency issued under the heterogeneous laws of the states. In criticising Jackson for overthrowing the Second Bank it should be borne in mind that the Whig party under the leadership of Clay sought to gain power by forcing the renewal of the charter forward as a political issue.

Jackson's veto caused great excitement, and was used to aid him in his campaign for reëlection (1832). The friends of the Bank were equally active, and public meetings were held at which Jackson was denounced in unmeasured terms.

Naturally the great majority of the business men of the day ranged themselves with the Bank party, which gave Jackson's partisans an additional weapon, reënforcing the cry of "monopoly" and "wealth" with which they were inciting the masses to believe that their liberties were in danger. Unfortunately for the Bank Biddle took an active part in the contest, which soon became personal, although he insisted that he was merely defending the Bank against the unwarranted attacks of the cabal. It thus gave some color to the charge that this powerful institution was using its untold millions, including the government's money on deposit with it, to defeat the popular idol, the hero of the War of 1812. In fact the total sum used by the Bank for "literature" during the campaign did not amount to $250,000,[1] and no evidence that it used its power in business lines (by refusing discounts, etc., as was charged) was produced. Jackson was reëlected by a larger electoral vote than in 1828, although the popular vote was smaller.

In his message in December, 1832,[2] Jackson suggested to Congress that the government deposits be transferred, in whole or in part, from the Bank to the state banks. He said: —

> "Such measures as are within the reach of the Secretary of the Treasury have been taken, to enable him to judge whether the public deposits in that institution may be regarded as entirely safe; but as his limited power may prove inadequate to this object, I recommend the subject to the attention of Congress, under the firm belief that it is worthy of their serious investigation. An inquiry into the transactions of the institution, embracing the branches as well as the principal bank, seems called for by the credit which is given throughout the country to many serious charges impeaching the character, and which if true, may justly excite the apprehension that it is no longer a safe depository of the money of the people."

He also recommended the sale of the government's shares in the Bank.

Secretary McLane had stated in his report in 1831[3] that —

> "It must be admitted, however, that the good management of the present bank, the accommodation it has given to the government, and the

[1] Report of Government Directors, Finance Reports, Vol. III., and Congressional Report of 1832.

[2] Messages of Presidents, Vol. II. [3] Finance Reports, Vol. III., p. 222.

practical benefits it has rendered the community, whether it may or may not have accomplished all that was expected from it, and the advantages of its present condition, are circumstances in its favor entitled to great weight, and give it strong claims upon the consideration of Congress in any future legislation on the subject."

These considerations induced him to recommend a recharter with modifications, at the proper time. In 1832 he directed a special examination of the Bank and its branches, which the "Kitchen Cabinet" expected would prove it to be insolvent. To their disappointment the examiner reported that the Bank had upward of $42,000,000 in excess of its liabilities, hence more than $7,000,000 in excess of its stock obligation.[1] The House of Representatives after an examination of the Bank by the Committee on Ways and Means, by a vote of 109 to 46, declared by resolution that the public funds were absolutely safe in the Bank, and by a vote of 102 to 91 opposed the sale of the shares. In the report by Verplanck of the committee it was shown that in sixteen years the transactions of the government had aggregated $440,000,000, and not one dollar had been lost. Polk in the minority report expressed serious doubts as to the safety of the public funds.[2]

Immediately after the adjournment of Congress, in March, 1833, Kendall and his associates began the work of utterly destroying the Bank. Soon after the reinauguration of Jackson, plans were devised to use the provision of law authorizing the Secretary of the Treasury to place the government moneys elsewhere (provided he explained his reason to Congress), as the first measure in the renewed warfare. McLane refused to be a party to this transaction and was made Secretary of State, W. J. Duane being appointed to the Treasury. State banks had been negotiated with by Kendall in order to be prepared. Jackson read to his cabinet in September a paper in which the plan was set forth. He felt that in reëlecting him the people had decided against a recharter.

[1] Niles Register. [2] House Reports, 22d Congress, 2d Sess., No. 121.

All the old charges were rehearsed. The Bank had opposed his reëlection and should be punished. A majority of the cabinet, including McLane, Duane, and Cass, did not favor the step proposed. Duane, who was not favorable to the Bank's recharter, particularly opposed the plan as unwise, arbitrary, uncalled for, a breach of faith, and dangerous because no other *safe* depository could be found. Duane stated that not only had he refused, when urged by the "irresponsible cabal," to change the system, but had been promised by the President that he would be allowed to manage his department without interference, particularly upon this point. Upon being *ordered* to "remove the deposits" by Jackson, Duane flatly refused, declaring such action unconscionable and opposed to the express will of Congress, and denying the power of the President under the law to *order* the Secretary of the Treasury to do so.[1] Jackson promptly removed Duane and appointed in his stead Taney, then Attorney-general and afterwards Chief Justice of the Supreme Court, who at once signed the order for the removal of the deposits. Many of Jackson's friends condemned his policy in this respect.

At first the process adopted was not to *remove* the deposits from the bank, but to place the revenues as received in state banks, drawing on the Bank for all disbursements. Later deposits were actually transferred.

Deprived speedily of one-half of the public money, and its total deposits shrinking to nearly $10,000,000, the Bank was necessarily obliged to curtail its loans, which caused a stringency, for which it was again attacked. Actually, the curtailment was less than three-quarters of the loss of deposits. Biddle, knowing the unscrupulousness of the cabal, conducted the business most cautiously. Kendall showed his real object in a published letter, in which he said that the bank only continued to exist because of Taney's forbearance, and apparently gave it only a forty days' lease of life.[2] No measure was too contemptible for Kendall to

[1] Duane's Narrative. [2] White, Money and Banking.

employ. The invariable custom of advising the Bank of Treasury drafts was at his instigation abrogated and secret drafts for over two and a quarter millions were issued, transferring deposits to pet state banks, with the hardly disguised purpose of causing a "run." [1]

When Congress met in December the President and Secretary Taney reported upon the subject.[2] The Senate, then anti-Jackson, refused to confirm Taney's nomination made during recess. In the House the Jacksonians controlled and voted 132 to 82 that the Bank ought not to be rechartered, and 118 to 103 that the deposits should not be returned to the Bank.[3] Levi Woodbury became Taney's successor in the Treasury.

In the Senate Clay had a resolution passed (23 to 18) calling upon the President to say if the published paper purporting to be the one read to the cabinet in September was genuine, and asking that the Senate be furnished with a copy.[4] Jackson declined, standing upon his constitutional rights. Thereupon the Senate passed a resolution declaring that in his action relating to the public revenues the President had exceeded his powers, and another, supported by Webster, which pronounced the reasons given by Secretary Taney for removing the deposits "unsatisfactory and insufficient." [5] Jackson sent in a message protesting against the first resolution. After long discussion the Senate by a vote of 27 to 16 refused to receive the message, regarding it as a breach of its privileges on the part of the President and denying his right to protest to the Senate against any of its proceedings.[6]

The House of Representatives again ordered an examination of the Bank, to which it did not, in the opinion of the majority of the committee (Jacksonian), submit gracefully. The minority, headed by Edward Everett, contended that the Bank had shown

[1] Niles Register. [2] Finance Reports, Vol. III. Special Report on Removal.
[3] Williams, Statesman's Manual, Vol. II. [4] Benton, Thirty Years' View.
[5] Statesman's Manual. [6] *Ibid.*

every disposition to aid the examination of the affairs relating to the question of violation of the charter, which was the limit of the power of the committee and which the majority had endeavored to transcend.[1] The Senate also ordered an examination which was reported by Tyler (afterward President) and was favorable to the Bank.[2] No specific action was taken, but the President felt called upon to send a special message to Congress criticising the Bank's action at that time.[3] In the Senate Jackson's nominees for government directors of the Bank were not confirmed; the vote stood 30 to 11. In December, 1834, in his annual message to Congress,[4] the Bank is characterized as "the scourge of the people." All his former charges were repeated, and he recommended the sale of the government holdings of stock and the repeal of that part of the charter making the Bank's notes receivable for public dues. He averred that events had proved that the Bank was unnecessary, that the state banks had been found fully adequate to serve the government, and would soon be in position to supply all the wants of the people, and that if the states reformed their systems, prohibiting small notes, the country would in a few years have as sound a currency as any.

In the interval the Bank had obtained a charter from the state of Pennsylvania and continued business under it after March, 1836, when its federal charter expired. The government continued to hold the shares until liquidation.

In December, 1836,[5] Jackson's last message complained that the Bank had not yet settled its affairs and was doing a number of things which he disapproved. He again referred to the state banks, representing that their services to the government were far greater than those rendered formerly by the Bank. But he also showed that little progress had been made in retiring small

[1] Statesman's Manual.
[2] Senate, Doc. 17, 23d Congress, 2d Sess.
[3] Messages of Presidents, Vol. III.
[4] *Ibid.*
[5] *Ibid.*

notes, and that the state banks had entered into speculation in public lands and resorted to inflation in order to do so.

In his "farewell address" (March, 1837),[1] he launched his final bolt against the Bank, including the entire paper currency system, banks generally, the "moneyed interests" and their encroachment, as dangerous to the liberties of the people.

Woodbury's report for 1836 was a confession that the state banks were using the public deposits both speculatively and to increase their note-issues, which had been expanded fully 50 per cent. since 1833; nevertheless the public moneys were regarded safe.

With the destruction of the Bank perished by far the best instrumentality for furnishing the people of the United States a sound paper currency that could be devised under the circumstances and conditions then prevailing. It merited and received the commendation of a host of the ablest men of the country, who in other particulars differed radically from the political views of the Federal Party. That its *destruction* was planned, and not regulation or reformation of the defects which experience brought to light, is clearly shown by the evidence. The men behind the scenes endeavored to use the Bank for their own ends, and failing, resolved to destroy it, and circumstances so shaped events that Clay, the inveterate opponent of Jackson, became its champion, thus further involving it in the maelstrom of politics.

The Bank and its management were not perfect, but every defect which had manifested itself could have been easily remedied, and indeed most of them were provided for in the proposed new charter.

Webster, in discussing another subject, after stating that the question of recharter was settled not to be reopened until the people called for it, expressed his judgment on the Bank in the following words:[2] —

"The bank has been assailed by party, mainly, as I believe, because it would not yield itself to party objects. No cry was raised against its con-

[1] *Ibid.* [2] Webster's Works.

stitutionality, no doubt expressed on that point, till its directors had resisted suggestions, the effect of which would have been to render the bank a servile instrument in the hands of political men. In my judgment, those directors were entirely right, and the country, I think, should rejoice that they staked and risked the continuance of the charter on that point. They could easily have secured the renewal of their charter. A little compliance would have done the whole business. They were courted before they were denounced. If, in 1829 and 1830, they would have consented to make a partnership with the Treasury, and to yield themselves to power, they would have been commended, extolled in many a message and report, and enabled to take their own time for a renewal. The bank has fallen in its independence, and by reason of its independence. It should be proud so to have fallen; and it is much better for the country that it should thus fall, than that it should purchase a prolonged existence by rendering itself a tool of party power.

"It is well known to be my opinion that direct injustice was done to the bank in the withdrawal of the deposits; and injustice has been done to it also, as I think, by the gross and unfounded imputations made upon its general management. The bank now, for many years, has accomplished every object intended by its establishment. It has reformed the currency, sustained it when reformed, and upheld a system of internal exchange, safe, cheap and of unprecedented and unparalleled facility. No country has seen the like; nor shall we see it soon again when the operations of the bank shall cease. The directors, of late years especially, have had a most difficult and undesirable duty to perform; but they have performed it, as I think, with entire uprightness and great ability. Every fair investigation has proved this, and the state of the bank itself, the best of all proofs, abundantly shows it. The time will come, I am sure, when justice will be done them, universally, as it is done them now by those who have sought for information, and have formed their judgments with candor and good sense."

Ingham in 1832 (after his retirement from the Treasury) said: [1] —

"The bank has purified one of the worst currencies that ever infested any country or people. It consisted of mere paper, of no definite value, accompanied by worthless tickets issued from broken banks, petty incorporations and partnerships, in almost every village. Instead of this, the

[1] Niles Register.

United States Bank has given us the best currency known among nations. It supplies a medium equal in value to gold and silver, in every part of the Union. It preserves with a steady and unerring power a uniform and equal value in the paper of the local banks; gives stability and certainty to the value of all property, and to the incalculable benefits of internal commerce; it maintains domestic exchanges, at a less premium than it would cost to transport specie; and enables the government to transmit its funds from one extremity of the Union to another, without cost, without risk, without pressure upon the section from which they are withdrawn, and with a despatch which is more like magic than reality."

The political rancor and sordid motives which entered into this controversy over the renewal of the charter are in sad contrast to the exalted patriotism and statesmanlike qualities usually ascribed to the "fathers." The best evidence of its strength and the highest compliment to its condition is found in the fact that it could withstand as it did the onslaught of President Jackson, backed by the whole power of his administration.

When it is borne in mind that the means of communication with the remote parts of the country were exceedingly primitive (no railways existing), the undisputed fact that the Bank raised the credit of the bank circulation throughout the Union, made transfers at little or no cost, and reduced the cost of exchange to a minimum, prove its great value to the country. McDuffie states that in 1830 only the banks in North Carolina were not specie-paying.

Altogether it was a reactionary victory over the intelligence of the day, and the people paid roundly for it. Practically all those who by reason of their study and experience had actual knowledge of the subject opposed the destruction of the Bank as a positive evil which would result in an unsound currency, just as they opposed the violent alteration of the ratio of coinage.

Students of the history of the period of the Second Bank give the same credit for a good degree of success in accomplishing the purpose for which it was created. They acquit the Bank management of the serious charges made against them, and trace the charges to selfish interests, mainly political. This is a fair statement of the conclusions of Dr. Dewey, who wrote the history of the Second Bank of the United States for the National Monetary Commission, and also of Prof. Catterall, who perhaps has made a more thorough and exhaustive study of the Second Bank than any other writer.

As was generally foreseen, the removal of deposits caused the organization of a large number of state banks. The revenues were about to accumulate in the Treasury, the public debt having been entirely paid, and holding public moneys by political favor became an important feature in banking. The number of banks increased from 1830 to the end of 1836, from 330 to 788,[1] and the note-issues from under $49,000,000 to $149,000,000. Thus the circulation of the country which in 1829 was about $7 per capita and then regarded by Gallatin as "sound," was increased to $15 per capita, an amount equalled only in the days of continental currency.[2] The government had in 59 state banks nearly $50,000,000, before any law regulating the deposits became effective. Speculation in public lands, in payment for which the government accepted almost any form of paper, assumed tremendous proportions. Congress was asked to stop the speculation by restricting the funds receivable to specie, but the counter-influence was too great and the defective measure passed for that purpose did not receive Jackson's approval. Congress had adjourned and Jackson undertook by means of a Treasury circular to require specie for land purchases. This caused a violent collapse of the speculation and serious troubles generally, notably in the West.

The act of June 23, 1836, regulating deposits, directed the Secretary of the Treasury to select, in each state, banks which in his judgment were in a satisfactory condition, in which to deposit the revenues subject to the Treasury drafts. The limit of deposits was 75 per cent. of paid-up capital, the banks were required to report their condition periodically to the Secretary, to

[1] Report on Banks, 1863. [2] See table at the end of chapter.

credit all deposits as specie and pay specie on demand for Treasury drafts, to make transfers and perform such other functions as the Bank of the United States was required to by its charter. The Secretary might also require further security from the banks if in his judgment it was requisite. He was required to report his selections or changes in depositories to Congress, to discontinue depositories that suspended specie payments, or issued notes under five dollars, and to receive for public dues no notes of banks issuing denominations under five dollars. He was given power to require depository banks to have a reasonable amount of specie on hand. For deposits in excess of one-fourth of the capital banks were to pay interest at 2 per cent. per annum, and the banks were subject to examination. Transfers of deposits, excepting on account of public business, were especially prohibited. This was due to the alleged practice of making transfers to accommodate certain banks.

This law Jackson deemed onerous upon the banks.

The same act provided that the surplus in the Treasury in excess of $5,000,000 for a working balance be deposited with the states, in proportion to their representation in Congress, in four equal instalments, beginning January 1, 1837, provided the states authorized their treasurers to receive the money and pledge its return on demand of the Secretary of the Treasury. Although the act specifically provided that the funds were to be held as "deposits," the general opinion was that they were given to the states. This measure was finally passed after years of discussion on the subject and after a bill to donate the money to the states had been vetoed as unconstitutional. The amount finally transferred was $28,101,644.

The prospect of the transfer of such a large sum from the depository banks to the states served to add to the general tendency to expansion, and the usual results followed.

The act of 1836 providing for the deposit of public funds in state banks, was designed to accomplish several improvements in the currency which under other conditions would probably have been realized. It brought a considerable number of banks throughout the country under the supervision of the Treasury Department, and the importance given these institutions in their localities by being depositories, so regulated, could not have failed to exercise an influence upon others. It also contemplated in an indirect manner the ultimate elimination of small notes, instead of going directly at this evil by taxing them out of existence as Gallatin had proposed. It further undertook to compel maintenance of specie payments by making it profitable. But the act came too late: Jackson and Woodbury had repeatedly asked for it in vain, and when it came, the provision for distribution of the surplus and Jackson's specie circular deprived the country of whatever good results might have been expected from it.

The following data of the depository banks at about this period are of special interest.[1]

	In Millions		
	36 Banks April 1, 1836	36 Banks June 1, 1836	59 Banks Nov. 1, 1836
Capital	43.7	46.4	77.6
Circulation	28.8	28.0	41.5
Public deposits	36.8	41.0	49.4
Other deposits	15.5	16.0	26.6
Due banks	15.4	17.1	24.1
Other liabilities	12.6	13.8	24.6
Total	152.8	162.3	243.8
Loans and discounts	101.6	108.5	164.0
Specie	10.9	10.5	15.5
Notes of other banks	11.1	11.0	16.4
Due from other banks	15.9	17.9	26.6
Other resources	13.3	14.4	21.3

Considering the circulation alone the specie fund was fairly satisfactory, but when public deposits are included the reserve was rather slender.

[1] Finance Reports, Vol. III.

For the purpose of winding up the business of the government with the Bank of the United States, several acts were passed: April 11, 1836, to discontinue the functions of the Bank in connection with government loans; June 15, 1836, repealing the section of the charter which made the notes of the Bank receivable for public dues; June 23, 1836, appointing the Secretary of the Treasury agent to settle for the government's shares in the Bank.

The United States derived a profit of over $6,000,000 on its investment.[1] It will be recalled that its subscription was paid for with 5 per cent. obligations. They amounted to: —

Principal	$7,000,000.00	
Interest	4,950,000.00	$11,950,000.00
The Bank paid in settlement for the same	9,424,750.78	
The dividends paid amounted to	7,118,416.29	16,543,167.07
Profit		4,593,167.07
Bonus paid by the Bank for the charter		1,500,000.00
Making a total of		$6,093,167.07

Although both Jackson and Benton charged that the Bank was not getting ready to wind up its affairs, the fact is that prior to the determination to continue under a state charter, the Bank took definite steps toward liquidation, disposing of its branches and converting its resources into short paper and increasing its cash, as the following table shows:[2] —

ITEMS REPORTED AS OF APRIL 1, EACH YEAR, IN MILLIONS

	1831	1832	1833	1834	1835
Total loans	58.5	69.9	64.8	54.8	60.1
Bills of exchange	14.7	21.5	22.7	18.7	22.9
Circulation	18.2	21.4	18.0	17.5	20.5
Specie	12.5	7.0	9.0	10.2	16.4

The public deposits at the last-mentioned date were about 1.5 millions.

[1] Finance Report, 1876, p. 127. [2] Niles Register.

The statistics of the banks of Massachusetts, the only state that furnished continuous returns from an early date (1803), afford an indication of the results which would have been possible in the whole country had anything like sound principles prevailed. The number of banks, their capital and circulation, grew almost normally and steadily during the entire period from 1803 to 1836. There was no great expansion when the first Bank of the United States expired, no suspension in 1814, hence no contraction necessary in 1819. During the existence of the Second Bank, the banks increased gradually and steadily. This was not accomplished without many sad experiences, but the people profited by these and remedied the evils in order to avert the greater ones which afflicted others. From 1784 to 1836 only ten banks in Massachusetts suspended or discontinued business; the total losses to the shareholders and to the public were estimated at $300,000.[1] Gallatin's list of banks that failed between 1811 and 1830 includes only 6 of Massachusetts, as against 16 of Pennsylvania and 18 of Kentucky.[2]

[1] Knox, Finance Report, 1876, p. 132.
[2] Gallatin, Currency and Banking System.

STATISTICAL RÉSUMÉ

(Amounts in millions of dollars)

BANK STATISTICS, 1812 TO 1837

State Banks

Estimates prior to 1834

YEAR	NUMBER	CAPITAL	DEPOSITS	CIRCULATION	SPECIE	LOANS
1813	—	65.0	—	62–70	28.0	117
1814	—	80.4	—	—	—	—
1815	208	88.1	—	90–110	16.5	150
1816	246	89.4	—	110	19.0	—
1817	—	125.7	—	—	—	—
1819	—	125.0	—	45–53	21.5	157
1820	307	102.1	31.2	40.6	16.7	—
1829	329	110.1	40.8	48.3	14.9	—
1830	330	110.0	39.0	48.4	13.5	160

No data available for 1812, 1818, and from 1821 to 1829. Figures given for 1820 and 1829 are Gallatin's; those prior to 1820, Crawford's; for 1830 the statement is composite, and probably erroneous. All are to a great extent based upon actual figures, supplemented by estimates.

Official Reports after 1834

JANUARY 1	NUMBER	CAPITAL	DEPOSITS	CIRCULATION	SPECIE	LOANS
1834	506	200	76	95	26	324
1835	704	231	83	104	44	365
1836	713	252	115	140	40	457

No returns in 1834 from Del., N.J., S.C., Ga., Fla., La., Ark., Ky., Ohio, Ind., Ill., Mich., Mo.

No returns in 1835 from Del., Md., N.C., Ark.

No returns in 1836 from N.J., R.I., Ark.

No returns in 1837 from Ark.

Incomplete returns in 1835 from S.C. and Ohio.

Massachusetts Banks

1803 to 1837

Year	Number	Capital	Deposits	Loans	Circulation	Specie	Notes of Other Banks
1803	7	2.2	1.5	3.9	1.6	1.1	0.4
1808	16	6.0	2.5	7.4	1.0	1.0	0.5
1811	15	6.7	3.4	10.1	2.4	1.5	0.3
1815	25	11.5	4.1	13.7	2.7	3.5	0.4
1817	26	9.3	3.5	12.6	2.5	1.6	0.7
1820	28	10.6	3.2	13.5	2.6	1.3	0.9
1825	41	14.5	2.7	22.0	4.1	1.0	0.7
1830	63	19.3	3.6	28.0	5.1	1.3	1.4
1835	105	30.4	12.9	48.3	9.4	1.1	2.1

Bank of the United States [1]

Beginning of	Deposits	Loans	Bonds, Etc.	Circulation	Specie	State Bank Notes	Due from Banks	Due to Banks
1817	11.2	3.5	4.8	1.9	1.7	0.6	8.8	—
1818	12.3	41.2	9.5	8.3	2.5	1.8	2.2	1.4
1819	5.8	35.8	7.4	6.6	2.7	1.9	3.2	1.4
1820	6.6	31.4	7.2	3.6	3.4	1.4	3.0	2.1
1821	7.9	30.9	9.2	4.6	7.6	0.7	1.3	2.1
1822	8.1	28.1	13.3	5.6	4.8	0.9	2.8	2.0
1823	7.6	30.7	11.0	4.4	4.4	0.8	1.4	1.3
1824	13.7	33.4	10.9	4.6	5.8	0.7	2.7	1.0
1825	12.0	31.8	18.4	6.1	6.7	1.1	2.2	2.4
1826	11.2	33.4	18.3	9.5	4.0	1.1	1.2	0.3
1827	14.3	30.9	17.8	8.5	6.5	1.1	2.1	0.3
1828	14.5	33.7	17.6	9.9	6.2	1.4	0.4	3.2
1829	17.1	39.2	16.1	11.9	6.1	1.3	2.2	1.4
1830	16.0	40.7	11.6	12.9	7.6	1.5	2.7	—
1831	17.3	44.0	8.7	16.3	10.8	1.5	2.4	0.7
1832	22.8	66.3	—	21.4	7.0	2.2	4.0	2.0
1833	20.3	61.7	—	17.5	9.0	2.3	6.8	2.1
1834	10.8	54.9	—	19.2	10.0	2.0	4.9	1.5
1835	11.8	51.8	—	17.3	15.7	1.5	6.5	3.1
1836	5.1	59.2	—	23.1	8.4	1.7	4.1	2.7

[1] Finance Report, 1876, p. 193.

NOTE. — The government deposits have never reached $10,000,000, and were, in the earlier period, never more than $6,000,000. After 1827 the discounts included important amounts of domestic bills of exchange; in the last four years this item constituted from 25 to 40 per cent. of the total. The item "due to banks" prior to 1828 was composed entirely of European credits, and that "due from banks" included large sums abroad in many of the years. Circulation is *net*, and includes "branch drafts."

CIRCULATION OF THE COUNTRY

YEAR	SPECIE	BANK NOTES		TREASURY NOTES	TOTAL	POPULATION	PER CAPITA
		State	U. S.				
1813	30	62	——	9	101	7.9	$12.78
1814	28	70	——	11	109	8.2	13.30
1815	25	75	——	24	124	8.5	14.58
1816	23	68	——	18	109	8.7	12.53
1817	22	75	1.9	5	104	8.9	11.68
1818	20	60	8.3	1	89	9.1	9.78
1819	20	45	6.6	——	72	9.3	7.74
1820	24	41	3.6	——	69	9.6	7.19
1821	23	40	4.6	——	68	9.9	6.87
1822	18	40	5.6	——	64	10.2	6.27
1823	17	41	4.4	——	62	10.5	5.90
1824	19	42	4.6	——	66	10.9	6.06
1825	18	43	6.1	——	67	11.2	6.00
1826	20	44	9.5	——	74	11.5	6.43
1827	21	46	8.5	——	76	11.8	6.44
1828	23	47	9.9	——	80	12.2	6.55
1829	26	48	11.9	——	86	12.5	6.88
1830	32	48	12.9	——	93	12.8	7.26
1831	32	61	16.3	——	109	13.2	8.26
1832	30	70	21.3	——	121	13.6	8.90
1833	31	73	17.5	——	121	14.0	8.64
1834	41	95	19.2	——	155	14.4	10.76
1835	51	104	17.3	——	172	14.8	11.62
1836	65	140	23.7	——	229	15.2	15.06

NOTE. — In this table the specie is given for 1820 and 1830–1836 as usually accepted, although the movement abroad, as shown in the next table, does not warrant the conclusions. It should be borne in mind that from 1814 to 1817 specie was hoarded, hence not actually in use.

The notes of state banks are based on Gallatin's and Crawford's estimates, the latter appearing to have been excessive, the former, too conservative.

SPECIE AND TRADE MOVEMENT AND EXCHANGE

Net Import, +. Export, –.

YEAR	SPECIE	MERCHANDISE	EXCHANGE ON LONDON
1821	– 2.4	– 0.1	3¾ @ 12½ premium
1822	– 7.4	+ 18.5	8½ @ 13 "
1823	– 1.3	+ 4.2	5 @ 12½ "
1824	+ 1.4	+ 3.2	7½ @ 11¼ "
1825	– 2.6	– 0.5	5 @ 10½ "
1826	+ 2.2	+ 5.2	7¾ @ 12¼ "
1827	+ 0.1	– 3.0	10 @ 11½ "
1828	– 0.8	+ 17.0	9½ @ 11 "
1829	+ 2.5	– 0.3	8½ @ 10 "
1830	+ 6.0	– 8.9	6 @ 9¾ "
1831	– 1.7	+ 23.6	6 @ 10¾ "
1832	+ 0.3	+ 13.6	7 @ 11 "
1833	+ 4.5	+ 13.5	5 @ 9 "
1834	+ 15.8	+ 6.3	– 2 @ 8 "
1835	+ 6.7	+ 21.5	7½ @ 10 "
1836	+ 9.1	+ 52.2	7 @ 10½ "

It is quite evident from the above table that a considerable amount of foreign capital came to the country after 1830. It was estimated that the debt abroad probably exceeded two hundred millions in 1835. At that time (no United States bonds being outstanding), the bonds of the states of New York, Pennsylvania, Ohio, Louisiana, Mississippi, Alabama, Florida, and Indiana were quoted in London; also certain bank shares and canal company bonds.

CHAPTER IX

Paper Currency

1837–1849

Briefly recapitulated the conditions affecting the currency early in 1837 were as follows: the Bank of the United States had acted as regulator of the circulation of state banks by refusing the notes of doubtful concerns and requiring the redemption of others; now, since its federal charter had expired and it was operating under a charter from the state of Pennsylvania, it necessarily ceased to perform that function and was merely a very largely capitalized state institution. This check upon the state bank issues having been removed and the enticing prospect of obtaining public deposits being held out by the Jackson administration resulted, as it did in 1811–1817, in a large increase in the number of state banks and an inordinate inflation of both notes and discounts. Many banks were conducting business without a dollar of actual capital paid in, and a majority were subject to no legal restriction. The distribution to the states of the surplus in the Treasury caused a number of the states to create "fiscal banks," and the others selected state banks as public depositories; thus this large sum was transferred from "pet" federal to "pet" state depositories. These transfers naturally necessitated the calling of loans, for the federal depositories had loaned the funds, and a general curtailment of credits ensued, thereby involving domestic exchange in more or less confusion.

The states had undertaken various enterprises to employ the surplus, the first instalment of which was paid in January, 1837, and an era of unbounded speculation set in.

The federal government under the existing regulation (the "specie circular") required payments to it for public lands (a large source of revenue) to be made in specie, and other taxes were to be collected in the notes of specie-paying banks. Congress received at this time, and ignored, a petition from the Board of Trade in New York, which, foreseeing trouble, asked for a reëstablishment of a national bank for the regulation of the disordered currency and exchanges.

Van Buren, who became President in March, 1837, continued Woodbury as Secretary of the Treasury and adhered to Jackson's policy.

After the second instalment of surplus had been paid to the states in April, the serious nature of the financial and commercial situation became very apparent. A public meeting in New York in that month appointed a committee of fifty, with Gallatin at its head, to appeal to the administration to abandon a policy which threatened destruction of the material interests of the nation. Over two hundred and fifty failures had already occurred.[1]

In May specie payments were suspended and the people were compelled to take irredeemable bank-notes, as well as "shinplasters" of all sorts, in order to carry on the necessary transactions of each day. On May 15 Van Buren called Congress to meet in special session the following September. Notwithstanding many depository banks had suspended and the Treasury funds were running low or becoming unavailable by reason of the inability of the state bank depositories to make payment when required, Woodbury in July paid the third instalment of the surplus to the states (over $9,300,000), and in so doing barely escaped defaulting in his own payments.[2]

[1] Sumner, History of Banking.

[2] Finance Reports, Vol. III.

When Congress met, Van Buren in his message, a most discursive document, recounted the events and cast upon the banks, depositories included, the blame for the deranged business conditions. These institutions, which but nine months before had been declared by Jackson to be satisfactorily performing their functions, and thereby demonstrating that a national bank was unnecessary, were now denounced by his official successor as unfaithful to their trusts. He believed the government should sever all connection with banks, collect its revenues in specie only and keep the same in its own possession until needed for disbursements.

Secretary Woodbury reported that funds in only six out of the eighty-six depository banks were available; five others had in a measure been able to meet the demands of the Treasury; his nominal balance was $34,000,000, but of this $28,101,644 had recently been transferred to the states, and over $5,000,000 was in suspended banks, leaving him actually but $700,000; he had arranged to have the revenues retained by the collectors and receivers subject to Treasury drafts, instead of depositing the same in banks as formerly.

To meet the pressing obligations Congress did not call upon the states to repay the deposits recently made with them, but an act of October 2 postponed the payment of the fourth instalment until January 1, 1839, at which time there proved to be no surplus to transfer. On October 12, an act was passed providing for an issue of $10,000,000 of one year Treasury notes, receivable for public dues and bearing not to exceed 6 per cent. interest, and also an act postponing the payment of customs bonds. On October 16, Congress took away from the Secretary of the Treasury the power to recall the deposits with the states, reserving the right to itself.

The amount which had been paid in the three instalments, as given above, it may be remarked, remains "on deposit" to this day, and is carried on the books of the Treasury as "unavailable."[1] Its recall has on several occasions been suggested. On the other hand, a number of the states have, even in recent years, asked for the fourth instalment, which, however, has never been distributed.

Van Buren's recommendations for an independent treasury were formulated into a bill, reported by Silas Wright (N.Y.) in the Senate, where it passed over Clay's vigorous opposition by a vote of 26 to 20; in the House, however, a contingent of Jacksonians who favored banks refused to act with their party, and the measure was defeated 120 to 107.

The Whigs, under the lead of Clay and Webster, insisted that a national bank was the only adequate remedy for the existing evils. The chief need was a uniform currency system with a proper regulation of the issues of the local banks, which only a central bank could enforce. Van Buren's supporters, under the lead of Wright and Benton, declared that the Bank of the United States had been unable to prevent over-issues; that it was no part of the government's duty to regulate exchange; that the people wanted a separate subtreasury system; that the public money would be more secure in subtreasuries than in banks; that by this system the use of specie would be encouraged and the depreciated bank-notes rejected, thus leading to a uniform currency.

Webster declared the subtreasury plan unworthy of a civilized nation; would keep from general use the sums which the government would receive; was practically hoarding money; would result in contracting the volume of currency; was illogical and unsound.

Other Whigs and some conservative Democrats regarded the scheme as an attack on the whole credit system, sure to lead to contraction of the currency, besides increasing the presidential patronage and power.

Calhoun, now again with the administration, admitted that

[1] Finance Report, 1902, p. 183.

a central bank was the true remedy, but as he believed it unconstitutional, he supported the subtreasury plan in part, although finally voting against it.

Congress, inspired by President Van Buren, again considered the subject. The opposition received encouragement from resolutions of the legislatures of Tennessee, Pennsylvania and New Jersey, instructing their senators to vote against it. One New Jersey senator refused to obey his instructions, and the bill passed the Senate in March, 1838, by a vote of 27 to 25; the House again rejected it by a majority of 14.

The opposition developed the argument that the scheme was but a continuation of the suggestion of Jackson's message of 1829 for the ultimate establishment of a treasury bank; the great bank had been destroyed, and it was now the turn of the lesser ones to go, and the subtreasury plan would develop into a powerful political machine, giving the President control of the nation's purse and patronage.

These arguments were combated with ability by the Democrats, who maintained that they were for a constitutional treasury system and were not attacking the banks; that the remedy against hoarding, as alleged, was to have no surplus to hoard; that it was much better for the people to have the government look after its own finances and not be meddling with the banks; that the Whigs themselves admitted that most of the local banks were unsafe depositories.

The Treasury funds ran very low in May, 1838, due to the fact that Congress had not provided for the reissue of the Treasury notes that were received for taxes. The balance was down to $216,000 at one time, and Van Buren sent a special message to Congress in May asking for relief. Accordingly Congress at once passed an act permitting the reissue of the $10,000,000 authorized in 1837. In July it passed an act prohibiting the United States Bank (of Pennsylvania) from reissuing the old Bank's notes, issued while it was doing business under its federal charter; and another act prohibiting notes under $5 in the District of Columbia. Congress also abrogated the "specie circular," issued by order of President Jackson.

Van Buren repeated his recommendations in December, 1838, arguing that giving the banks public deposits merely induced expansion of an undesirable kind. As to the national bank plan, he was gratified that Congress did not, as in 1816, permit the suspension of coin payments to lead to a reëstablishment of so dangerous an institution. The policy of depositing public money in banks he regarded as a scheme for the benefit of the few against the rights of the community at large.[1]

In the canvass of 1838 for the election of representatives in Congress the subtreasury plan received much attention. The result was almost a defeat for the adherents of Van Buren, the control of the House turning upon the contested election of five Whigs from New Jersey. The Democrats were seated.

In his message in December, 1839, Van Buren made his final effort to have his pet scheme become law. He said that the existing embryonic subtreasury system had worked well and economically; the second suspension of coin payments in 1839 emphasized the need of becoming absolutely independent of the banks; speculation was too large a part of the business of banks; the dependence of banks upon each other, subjecting the country institutions to those of the cities, and the latter to those of London, practically placed the business of every hamlet in the country under the influence of the money power of Great Britain; every new debt contracted in England affected the currency throughout this land, thus subjecting the interests of our people to whatever measures of policy, necessity, or caprice were resorted to by those who control credits in England; the impropriety of using institutions thus affected as public depositories was obvious — the independence of the government would be impaired by thus placing its fiscal affairs in the control of foreign

[1] Messages of Presidents, Vol. III.

moneyed interests; holding public deposits induced banks to favor heavy taxes, large appropriations, and a surplus; the same objection applied to the use of bank-notes for revenue payments; he insisted upon payment in specie, instead of letting the banks hold the specie and the government take their promises to pay; the supposed danger of confining the payments to specie did not really exist; only four to five millions would be necessary, the government's drafts being used in large measure in lieu of the actual coin; moreover, the use of coin would tend to bring more into the country to meet the demand; the argument against banks applied equally against one central bank; the difference was only in degree; he believed that the states would remedy the evils of the depreciated currency by legislation; legislation and inflexible execution of the laws were necessary, and the federal government should coöperate on the lines he suggested to bring about the reform.[1]

Congress had again authorized the reissue of the Treasury notes of 1837 and practically extended the limit to $15,000,000. The issues and reissues amounted to over $31,000,000, but the limit was never exceeded. These notes were not authorized without much opposition on constitutional grounds. Benton particularly opposed the small denominations; Clay and Webster also opposed small notes.

The interest ran from 1 per mille to 6 per cent., the former rate on the smaller notes, which prevented their remaining out. The notes were for a time below par, but at other times commanded a premium of 5 per cent.

Congress also took up the subtreasury bill. It was debated even more fully than before, but practically few new arguments were adduced on either side and the discussion was largely political. The bill passed the Senate by a vote of 24 to 18 and the House by 124 to 107, was signed by the President July 4, 1840, and at once put in operation.

[1] Messages of Presidents, Vol. III.

The act provided for the collection, safe-keeping, transfer, and disbursement of public moneys by the Treasury through treasurers and receivers-general, of whom a definite number were to be appointed for the purpose; public money was not to be loaned or deposited in bank, under severe penalties, except that when a large surplus was on hand it might be specially deposited in banks designated by the Secretary, but could not be loaned by the banks; the banks so used were to receive $\frac{1}{8}$ per cent. commission; officers handling the funds were to be bonded; vaults were to be built, etc. The specie clause, an important feature which nearly killed the bill, was modified so as to have all public dues paid one-fourth in specie for the first year and an additional fourth each succeeding year until the whole was so payable.

Under the lead of the safety fund banks of New York, whose period of suspension had been limited by law to a year, resumption of coin payments began in May, 1838, but general resumption was not brought about until February, 1839, after several sessions of a convention of bankers in Philadelphia. It proved to be short-lived. The total note-issues had, it is true, been contracted, apparently by $33,000,000, but in many sections coin payment was merely nominal, and thus the conservative banks, which actually paid out coin, at the same time receiving notes of other banks, were the sufferers, being loaded up with notes that were practically irredeemable. The contraction and general liquidation had not been sufficient. Biddle's bank particularly failed to serve as a regulator; on the contrary, from its preponderating size it was the greatest source of embarrassment. Suspension of specie payments again took place in November, 1839, and continued until 1842.

The question of the constitutionality of note-issues of banks owned or controlled by states, came before the Supreme Court of the United States from Georgia and Kentucky in 1824 and 1829; the question was finally decided early in 1837. It was argued that as a state could not emit "bills of credit," it could not authorize such emissions through a bank which it owned in whole or part. The decision (Briscoe *vs.* Bank of the Commonwealth of Kentucky, 11 Peters 257) held that in order to give notes the character of "bills of credit" they must be issued by the state on the faith of the state, and be binding on the state. The notes of the bank named were not such, but ordinary banknotes, and hence constitutional issues. Justice Story dissented. In the case of Craig *vs.* Missouri, in 1830 (4 Peters 410) it was decided that certificates issued by a state, made receivable for taxes and salaries, were bills of credit and prohibited by the Constitution.

The notes of state banks were quoted at varying rates of discount. Thirty-five per cent. discount on Mississippi notes is the lowest quoted during 1838 for notes that actually passed at all. During suspension of coin payments domestic exchange fluctuated violently; bills on Southern points were quoted from 5 to 25 per cent. discount. The brief resumption in 1839 restored rates to quasi-normal conditions, the maximum discount being 4½ per cent. The second suspension again brought about heavy discounts, continuing until 1842, the greatest being 17 per cent. on Mobile; Cincinnati and Nashville falling at times to 16. The lowest rate of discount at New Orleans was 10.[1]

All interests suffered greatly from the unsettled policy of the government. The continuing controversy between the supporters of a United States bank as against utilizing the state banks, and the controversy between the advocates of an independent treasury and those who insisted that banks in some form must be used in order to keep current funds in current use, rendered the policy of the government dependent upon whichever interest happened to be in power. That these political agitations served to delay resumption is unquestionable.

The United States Bank, as we have seen, was continued with its $35,000,000 capital under a Pennsylvania charter and continued to exercise a very extensive influence both at home and

[1] Finance Report, 1876, pp. 197, 198.

abroad. Biddle had purchased the shares of the old Bank from the government at about 115½ and disposed of the new ones abroad at 120 to 126. Through his influence millions of dollars were brought from Europe and invested in the South and West. No one better than he understood the *whole* situation. When suspension of coin payments came in May, 1837, his bank also suspended. In his opinion liquidation was unavoidable, but at the same time he employed his credit abroad to bring about indulgence to debtors here, and in view of the fact that the debt held abroad was then about $200,000,000, this service was of great value.

However, he became involved in a gigantic cotton speculation (that staple having become the principal export commodity), which resulted in heavy losses; his personal prestige suffered from continued and virulent political attacks, and altogether his position was rendered untenable. He resigned from the bank in 1839, leaving it, as he claimed, prosperous; but after three assignments and two attempts at resumption, all in 1841, the institution succumbed, due no doubt to its having undertaken too great a load under the unfavorable business conditions. Its notes and deposits were paid in full, but the stockholders lost all, and Biddle was impoverished by the catastrophe.[1]

The statements of the bank during its existence as a state institution show (in millions of dollars): —

UNITED STATES BANK OF PENNSYLVANIA [2]

YEAR	LOANS	STOCKS AND BONDS	SPECIE	DEPOSITS	NET FROM STATE BANKS	CIRCULATION	DUE ABROAD	OTHER LIABILITIES
1837	57.4	—	2.6	2.3	1.2	11.4	6.9	—
1838	45.3	14.9	3.8	2.6	—	6.8	12.5	8.0
1839	41.6	18.0	4.2	6.8	4.6	6.0	12.8	9.3
1840	36.8	16.3	1.5	3.3	4.7	6.7	5.0	8.1

[1] Sumner, History of Banking in United States.
[2] Finance Report, 1876, p. 193.

These figures indicate the great efforts which were made to maintain the bank in a dominating position and yet conserve its strength; there was no undue expansion of its circulation and a fair reserve of specie; but doubtless the items of loans and securities included a large amount of paper made worthless by the disasters of 1837; the losses must have been enormous to entirely dissipate the capital.

Had Biddle avoided speculation, pursued a conservative course, and maintained specie payments instead of suspending (which he professed he was able to do), the Treasury would, as Gouge pointed out, have been morally compelled, under the law of 1836, to use his bank as one of the very few specie-paying banks, and the effect of this would have so influenced Congress as to cause the defeat of the subtreasury plan.

A comparison of the condition of the state banks generally is rendered impracticable by reason of the imperfect returns prior to 1834, the first year for which a compilation appears in the Treasury reports. That the expansion was quite general appears certain, and that it was greatest in the South and West is also demonstrable. From the most complete unofficial statement published the following is abstracted (amounts in millions): —

All Banks	1834	1837	Increase
Capital	200	291	91
Circulation	95	149	54
Deposits	76	127	51
Loans	324	525	201

Comparing 1837 with 1835, the following data are presented from the official sources, the same states being used in each case: —

	Capital	Circulation	Deposits	Specie	Loans
5 New England States: —					
1835	53	17	18	2	79
1837	65	19	20	3	97
4 Middle States: —					
1835	51	24	30	11	94
1837	67	41	47	10	135
9 Southern States: —					
1835	57	26	17	8	87
1837	98	54	39	14	180
5 Western States: —					
1835	8	6	4	3	12
1837	14	13	16	6	29

Circulation increased in the eastern group $19,000,000, and loans $59,000,000, whereas in the much more sparsely populated states of the South and West the note-issues increased $35,000,000 and loans $110,000,000.

Deprived of the steadying force and conservative influence of a national bank, and taught by the disastrous experiences of the several years following the expiration of the charter of the Second United States Bank, some of the states seemed to realize an added sense of responsibility and enacted banking laws based upon sound and conservative principles and provided for intelligent and adequate supervision. In Massachusetts, where thirty-two banks had discontinued, the new law provided for examinations by state commissioners annually, and specially if found desirable. The Suffolk Bank system continued, with some improvements, and doubtless served to avert greater disaster to New England banks. Rhode Island restricted loans and circulation of banks. Its banks, as well as those of Connecticut, weathered the storm of 1837–1840 without a failure.

In New York the safety fund, apparently through inadvertence in legislation, was made applicable to all the indebtedness of the banks, and proved altogether inadequate. The principle established was correct, and had the law providing for the same been drawn with sufficient detail and with sufficient solicitude for its enforcement, its practical working would have vindicated the principle. A careful analysis shows that slight changes would have achieved well-recognized success instead of failure. The principle made the banks mutually insure the redemption of the notes of all by contributing to a safety fund an amount annually which any bank could well afford to pay for the privilege of note-issue. Each bank contributed annually an amount equal to ½ per cent. of its capital until the same equalled 3 per cent. of the total bank capital. The tax should have been predicated upon the volume of note-issues. Had care been taken to prevent over-issues, and had the fund been limited in its application to the circulation of the banks, it would have been sufficient to protect all note holders from loss, as shown by Millard Fillmore in his report as Comptroller of the state of New York (1848). The legislature felt impelled to waive the penalty of forfeiture of charters, on account of suspension of coin payments, which the law provided, because of adverse business conditions, but more especially because suspension had been very general throughout the country. Prior to this period all bank charters had been granted by special act of the legislature, and were regarded as patronage to be extended to political favorites.[1] To avoid the scandals growing out of this practice and to avoid the just charge of monopoly, a "free banking" law was passed in 1838.

As finally adjusted, the law provided that one or several persons might qualify and enjoy the right of issuing notes to circulate as money. By depositing with the state comptroller stocks of the United States, of the state of New York, or of any other state approved by the comptroller and by valuation made equal to a 5 per cent. stock of the state of New York; or by depositing bonds bearing not less than 6 per cent. secured by mortgage on productive, unencumbered real estate worth double the amount

[1] Fillmore, Report of Comptroller, New York, 1848.

of the mortgage; the right to receive circulating notes for an equal amount was established. In case of default these securities were to be sold and the notes redeemed with the proceeds. Interest on the securities deposited was paid to the party depositing the same, so long as there was no failure to redeem notes and the security was deemed adequate. Provision was made for the surrender of notes and the return of securities. The state in no wise guaranteed the notes. A reserve of at least 12½ per cent. in specie was required, and refusal to redeem notes brought a penalty of 14 per cent.

Under this system the number of banks at once increased rapidly. Individuals in need supplied mortgages to be deposited as a basis for circulation upon condition of obtaining accommodations. Very many if not most of the banks organized under this law were started for the sole purpose of issuing notes, and were not banks of discount and deposit. They simply converted the securities which they deposited with the state authorities into bank bills. Had the note-issues been merely an incident or adjunct to a regular banking business the system would have had a fairer test. It was not, however, comparable to the safety fund system, since no bond-secured circulation can possess elasticity. The first case of failure occurred in 1840, and the bank's securities realized sixty-eight cents on the dollar of its note-issues. Mortgages were not convertible, and the legislature in 1843 limited securities which might be deposited to stocks of the state of New York. Later the act was amended so as to include United States bonds. In order to prevent individuals residing in one place from issuing notes payable in another, a law was passed requiring all interior banks to redeem their notes either in New York or Albany at not exceeding 1 per cent. discount (subsequently made ¼ per cent.), and later that no one should transact the business of a banker except at his place of residence, and still later all banks were required to be banks of discount and deposit as well as of circulation. In 1846 the new constitution prohibited organization of banks except under the general law, prohibited the legislature from authorizing the suspension of specie payments, imposed the double liability of shareholders, and made note holders preferred creditors.

The legislature seemed disposed to correct the faults of the system, and had not the Civil War intervened it is fair to assume the New York bank system would have been perfected. From the passage of the free banking act up to 1850, thirty-two banks failed, entailing a loss upon note holders of $325,487, some paying as low a percentage as thirty cents on the dollar. From 1850 to 1861, twenty-five failures entailed a loss upon note holders of only $72,849.[1] Notwithstanding the crisis in 1857 these statistics show an improving condition.

The free banking system with bond-secured circulation was adopted in many other states, notably Illinois, Indiana, and Wisconsin. In many it met with unfortunate results, in some with indifferent success. The first effect was inflation of note-issues. Note-issues were the one certain resource for obtaining credit, and public sentiment would not apply wholesome restraint and enforce conservative management. The system in our principal states was rapidly improving, however, when the crisis of the Civil War overtook the country, and that resulted in substituting what every interest and every industry required — a national system of currency.

The condition of Michigan banks during this period gave the name "red dog" and "wild cat" currency to the notes of the mushroom banks generally. A dog in red color and the wild cat were common imprints upon their current bills. Michigan had (1839) endeavored to imitate Indiana with a state bank and branches, but while the plan was the same, the management was radically different, to the cost of the note holders. Two of these Michigan banks held $1,800,000 public moneys when their capital as reported was less than $600,000 and specie $122,000.[2]

[1] White, Money and Banking.

[2] Finance Report, 1876, p. 200.

In many of the states the suspension of coin payments for a limited time was legalized, and stay laws[1] again appeared upon the statute books.

The banks of states (*i.e.* banks in which states were interested as owners of stock) proved in most instances costly experiments. Political influences entered into the management and control in many commonwealths to the great detriment of their business interests, and where states had issued bonds to capitalize such banks, the people had them to pay by means of taxation. There were, however, notable exceptions. As before stated, Delaware and South Carolina had very successful state banks.

The Indiana state bank was phenomenally successful. It consisted of ten branches, each with a capital of $160,000, the parent bank located at Indianapolis being practically a board of control, and exercising its banking functions through its branches. The bank was chartered for a period of twenty-five years immediately after Jackson's veto of the renewal charter of the Second United States Bank, and was exclusive in character. The state owned one-half the stock, and individuals one-half, all of which was paid in in specie. The state issued bonds with which to raise funds for its part of the capital, and also advanced to individuals 62½ per cent. of their subscriptions, taking a lien upon their shares, and also real estate security as collateral to such advances. The president and four directors of the parent bank were chosen by the legislature, and one director by the private stockholders of each branch. The assets of each branch belonged to its shareholders exclusively, and the branch was managed by the local shareholders subject to the parent board at Indianapolis, which alone could declare dividends. In this manner each branch reaped the benefit of superior management and greater earnings, and had every incentive to energy and conservatism.

Each branch was liable for the debts of every other branch,

[1] Sumner, History of Banking in United States.

and in case of insolvency its indebtedness must be liquidated within one year. This induced an interested if not a jealous watchfulness of each other, and a most intelligent and vigorous system of examination and supervision on the part of the central board. Loans exceeding $500 could only be made by a five-sevenths majority of the board, the vote and the names to be entered on the minutes, and officers and directors could not vote upon a proposition in which they were financially interested. Directors were individually liable for any loss resulting from loans made in violation of the law unless they could prove they voted in opposition. Favoritism in loans to officers and directors was forbidden. The insolvency of any branch was presumptively fraudulent, and unless the fraud was disproved, the directors were liable without limit for the debts. After their estates were exhausted the other stockholders were liable for an amount equal to the par of their stock. Any director in order to protect his estate must be prepared to prove good faith, and this insured a high degree of efficiency and conservatism. Loans upon their own stock were forbidden. (See statement, pp. 159, 160.)

The debts to or from any branch except on account of deposits could not exceed twice the capital stock. The intended and actual effect of this provision was to limit the circulating notes to twice the capital. Rediscounts or loans to banks at that time were very uncommon. No bank would borrow from another and pay interest thereon when it could issue its circulating notes without interest. Each branch redeemed its notes in specie on demand and was compelled to receive the notes of all other branches. The notes were signed by the president and issued to the branches by the parent bank. Discounts could not exceed two and one-half times the capital. Restriction upon voting the shares prevented monopolization.

The bank was liquidated at the expiration of its charter, netting stockholders $153.70 in addition to good dividends, which it paid regularly. The state realized, after the payment of principal and interest of the bonds issued in capitalizing the same, $3,500,000 net profit.[1]

This was a model bank in every respect. With independent ownership of assets and joint liability for debts, the greatest degree of efficiency and watchfulness was secured in the separate branches, and though widely separated, they were for all essential purposes closely woven together as one harmonious whole. It is an exemplary illustration of the efficacy of branch banking as a system. It is an equally potent illustration of the safety and efficiency of credit or asset currency when administered by a good system with competent management. It also presents supervision and examination in its ideal form. Examination by a government examiner, compensated by a lump sum without regard to the time expended or labor involved, is very valuable; but examination by an expert banker, an accountant, a judge of credits who inventories both assets and liabilities, knows the symmetry and proportion of banking in that particular locality, and can judge intuitively whether in any department or in any respect the rules of prudence have been infringed; who, in short, sees all and judges all through the eye of a stockholder and from the standpoint of dividends — such examinations are effective, are ideal.

To-day deposits are the main instrumentality which enables banks to extend loans and discounts to their patrons. Capital and surplus are the margin of safety that commands public confidence. Circulating notes are a trivial factor at best with individual banks, and really do not count at all, since more money is invested in bonds as security than is received in return in notes. At that time deposits were a meagre factor and circulating notes counted twice as much as capital stock, even in this strong and conservative bank. Circulating notes counted in much greater ratio in less conservative banks, and were practically the only resource in many. This explains why the people clung to and

[1] White, Money and Banking.

supported the note-issuing function of banks when security was so meagre and inevitable losses so great. There was practically no other resource for extending loans to them. Bank-notes were the most convenient means of utilizing loans in the circumscribed limits of trade at that time. Credits on the books of the banks to be utilized by checks and drafts were little used.

The severe strictures upon the banks owned and conducted by states are as a general proposition wholly justified. The state bank of Indiana was an honorable exception. It maintained the highest credit at all times and supplied the needs of the commercial public. Its notes were at all times redeemed in specie, even in the panic of 1857, when all the banks in the Eastern states and in New York (except the Chemical) were forced to suspend.

The state of Louisiana in 1842 enacted a general banking law which embodied the sound principles of banking which experience with state and United States banks had demonstrated. It also contained some restrictions, which, however practical then, would interfere with legitimate business now. No bank could have less than fifty shareholders owning not less than thirty shares of stock each, hence minimum capital of $150,000. Specie reserve of 33⅓ per cent. against all liabilities was required; all banks were to be examined by a board of state officers quarterly or oftener; directors were personally liable for all loans approved by them and which were made in violation of law; no bank could pay out any notes but its own; all banks were required to pay their balances to each other every Saturday under penalty of being put in liquidation. The above requirements were wholesome and in the interest of good banking, and afford the first instance of a legal requirement of a definite reserve. Some other requirements that seem to reflect somewhat upon the standard of commercial honor at that time were as follows: no commercial paper having more than ninety days to run could be discounted or purchased, and none could be renewed; if any paper was not paid at maturity or a request for its renewal made, the account of the party was to be closed and his name posted as a delinquent and other banks advised; any director being absent from the state for more than thirty days or failing to attend five successive meetings was deemed to have resigned and the vacancy filled at once. This law was in successful operation until interrupted by the events of the Civil War in 1862.

The state bank of Ohio (organized in 1845) was similar to the state bank of Indiana. Any number of banks not less than seven might compose its branches; these might be existing banks or those organized for the purpose; it started with a capital of $3,300,000; the branches could issue notes in a ratio graduated to their capital; for the first $100,000 of capital, $200,000 of notes; for $200,000 capital, $350,000 notes, the relative amount of notes diminishing as the capital increased; the branches were required to maintain a reserve fund with the central board of control equal to 10 per cent. of their circulating notes; the central board of control could invest this in bonds of Ohio or the United States or in real estate mortgages, the interest inuring to the respective branches; all branches were jointly liable for the notes of each, but not for its general debts; in case of failure of any branch to redeem its notes, the board of control immediately assessed the branches pro rata and raised sufficient funds to redeem such notes, and then reimbursed the branches as soon as the assets in the safety fund could be reduced to cash for that purpose, and in turn reimbursed the safety fund from the assets of the failed branch, the claim for such reimbursement having a prior lien. The bank ceased to exist with the expiration of its charter in 1866, the national bank system having rendered state banks less desirable. It had thirty-six branches, and was well managed and successful.[1]

Van Buren's victory in establishing the subtreasury system was short-lived. In the presidential contest of 1840, the sub-

[1] White, Money and Banking.

treasury question being at issue, the Whigs elected Harrison and a Congress (both houses) by large majorities. Van Buren, in his last message (December, 1840), insisted that the subtreasury system was working satisfactorily; nevertheless, its abolition had apparently been decreed by the popular vote. Harrison called Congress to meet in extra session on May 31, but he died in April, and the Whig leaders who had nominated and elected Tyler as Vice-President because of his views against the subtreasury act, found, when he succeeded to the presidency, that he did not agree with Clay, the actual leader of the party. The act repealing the subtreasury law passed by a vote of 29 to 18 in the Senate and 134 to 87 in the House, and became a law August 9. The repeal of the deposit act of 1836 was also speedily accomplished. Meanwhile Tyler's Secretary of the Treasury, Thomas Ewing, had, by request of Congress, prepared the President's plan for a "fiscal bank," to be located in the District of Columbia: capital $30,000,000, of which the United States was to take two-tenths, the states three-tenths, to be paid for by the United States in place of the "fourth instalment of surplus," not yet distributed, and to which the states seemed to think they had a claim; with branches to be located in the states *only after their assent.* The latter proviso was the chief point of controversy. Under the influence of Clay this feature of the bill was remodelled so as to provide that unless the legislatures actually dissented at once it was to be presumed that they had no objection. The Senate passed it 26 to 23, the House 128 to 97. Tyler vetoed this bill in August, 1841.

The special features of the bill were: that the parent bank was to make no loans except to the government in accordance with law; dividends were limited to 7 per cent., any surplus earnings to go to the government; the debts were limited to 1¾ times the capital and $25,000,000 in excess of deposits; loans were not to be renewable and were to cease when circulation reached more than thrice the specie on hand; dealing in stocks and commodities was prohibited. The objection of Tyler (a Virginian and strict constructionist) was chiefly that it was unconstitutional to authorize branches in the states without their consent, but he also objected to giving the bank the discounting privilege.[1]

The actual difference between the bill drafted by Ewing for the President, and that reported by Clay and passed was very slight.

The will of the people as expressed at the polls was ignored, the establishment of a central bank and thereby a uniform system of paper currency, national in character, was also defeated by this hair-splitting construction of the Constitution, extreme assertion of state sovereignty, and jealous determination to minimize the powers of the federal government.

The Whigs were angered by the veto upon such a slender pretext. Webster, who was Secretary of State, counselled yielding, since the end was to obtain a means of regulating the currency, equalizing exchanges, and taking care of public moneys. It was reported that Tyler had agreed to sign the Ewing bill. He outlined in his veto message the kind of a bill he would sign; accordingly such a bill was drawn and approved by Webster, who took it to Tyler, who also approved it, whereupon Congress passed it September 3. In the meantime John Minor Botts, representative from Virginia, had written a violent letter in which Tyler was charged with currying favor with the Democrats. The letter was published, and naturally Tyler was offended. He then desired, as Ewing says, to have the bill postponed, which did not, however, suit the Whigs, and the legislation was hurried through as stated. Tyler vetoed the bill on September 9, and the Whigs could not pass it over the veto. The entire cabinet thereupon resigned, excepting Webster, who remained for some time in order to complete with dignity certain important negotiations with foreign countries.[2]

[1] Messages of Presidents, Vol. IV.
[2] Statesman's Manual, Vol. II.

Ewing in his letter of resignation pointed out the inexplicable inconsistencies of Tyler's second veto, declaring unequivocally that the very features objected to were approved by Tyler before the bill was introduced, and some of them included upon his own suggestion. He properly resented Tyler's action in having him (Ewing) prepare a bill upon lines to satisfy the earlier objections, and then vetoing it without consulting him. These statements of Ewing's were publicly confirmed by at least two other members of the cabinet, showing such a breach of faith toward the Secretary of the Treasury as made his remaining in office impossible.[1]

From the evidence it was clear (1) that Tyler was desirous of establishing some form of fiscal corporation to perform the functions set forth above, (2) that he was hypercritical and hair-splitting on the constitutional point, (3) that in view of the Botts letter the Whigs should have postponed action as Webster said, (4) that notwithstanding the Botts letter, which did not alter the facts, Tyler was not justified in vetoing the bill which he had previously approved; by so doing he placed his personal feelings above his public duty respecting a great public measure.

Webster's view that Tyler was sincerely trying to adjust his constitutional views to the occasion, appears to be borne out by the second veto message in which Tyler literally implored Congress not to press the differences on this measure to a rupture of harmony. Postponement for more deliberation was asked, in terms which showed anxiety.

The Democrats could not resist exulting, and the Whig leaders denounced Tyler, declaring political coöperation with him at an end. But many, like Webster, believed in waiting. The new cabinet included a number of distinguished Whigs, Walter Forward becoming Secretary of the Treasury.

With both the subtreasury act and the deposit law of 1836 repealed, the Treasury fell back upon the system in use prior to the establishment of the First Bank of the United States, a sort

[1] Statesman's Manual, Vol. II.

of half independent treasury, half bank-deposit system. The Treasury was at this time still borrowing money.

The congressional election of 1842 was won by the Democrats, the Senate remaining Whig, and legislation was therefore blocked.

Interest-bearing Treasury notes were issued quite extensively during these years, in the usual form.

In 1844 the Whigs with Clay as candidate for the presidency suffered severe defeat. Polk, formerly Speaker, was chosen.

Tyler had continued in his messages to urge his plan upon Congress, but without avail. He referred to the use by the people of the Treasury notes as evidence that his plan of using such notes secured by a specie reserve would have proved satisfactory.

Polk had continually been opposed to the national bank. In his message, December, 1845, he also opposed the use of state banks upon constitutional grounds, pointing out that as there were only four banks in the country when the Constitution was adopted, it could not have been contemplated holding public money anywhere but in a national treasury. He therefore urged the establishment of a "constitutional treasury," a more elaborate measure than that of Van Buren, to absolutely divorce the government from the banks, and prevent the latter from using the public moneys for private gain.[1] He was ably supported by his Secretary of the Treasury, Robert J. Walker (Miss.), who took the extreme view that it was necessary to exclude bank-notes from the revenues entirely, because it would be useless to have an independent treasury receiving and disbursing bank paper.

The advocates of a national bank, as the proper solution of the currency difficulties and the best instrumentality through which the government could transact its fiscal affairs, failed to establish such an institution, owing to the successive vetoes of Tyler. If with both branches of Congress in political accord and favorable they failed to establish a national bank, one was

[1] Messages of Presidents, Vol. IV.

not likely to be established under any circumstances, and public sentiment turned in other directions. The evidence was cumulative and clear that the state banks could not be relied upon, and under the circumstances no doubt public opinion favored the subtreasury measure. The act was clearly a device to protect the government's money and at the same time avoid any regulation of the currency by the federal government, under the plea that Congress had no constitutional power over the same. If Congress were conceded the undelegated power to regulate paper currency, other similar powers might be assumed, for instance the power to interfere with slavery.

Congress took up the subject at once, and after long debate passed Polk's measure, in the House by 123 to 67, in the Senate by 28 to 24. It was approved by the President August 6, 1846.

Thus in a government for the people and controlled by them, it was claimed by the leaders in public life of that day that no matter how imperfect, unsafe, or disgraceful, even, the existing paper currency systems might be, there was no remedy which could provide a safe, sound, and uniform paper medium. So the make-shift to provide only for the safety of the government revenues was enacted, supported solidly by those who, under Benton's lead, insisted that the country's business could be done by the use of specie only, arguing that the example of the government would be followed by all.

The chief features of the act were the prohibition against depositing public moneys in banks, or disposing of them in any manner other than in payments of Treasury drafts or transfer orders. The officers of the government were required to hold the funds "safely" in the meantime; revenues were after January 1, 1847, all to be paid in specie or Treasury notes, and severe penalties for disregard of the act were imposed.

Years elapsed before the officers of the government were provided with proper facilities for safely handling funds. Gouge, the official examiner of subtreasuries, reported in 1854 that

Western depositories were inadequately protected. He found, for example, the subtreasury at Jeffersonville, Indiana, in a tavern adjoining the bar-room, with which it was connected by a door with glass lights, so that the subtreasurer might, when in the bar-room, see into his office. The entrance for the public was through a back passage under a stairway. The office was divided into two rooms by a temporary partition, lighted by a single window defended by iron grates. The silver was kept in wooden boxes, the gold in an iron safe. The subtreasurer slept in one of the rooms with his weapons.[1]

The requirement that all payments be made in specie was not rigidly carried out. It was, indeed, practically impossible at post-offices, etc., but in the main Walker was gratified with the result.

The war with Mexico occurred at this period (1846), and the government being constrained to borrow made use of its notes to the extent of $20,000,000, which paid current expenditures and went into general circulation as money. Bond issues were also resorted to, and were in part used to fund the notes above mentioned.

Both Polk and Walker pointed with pride to the "constitutional treasury" which had by preventing inflation and suspension during the war period enabled the government to issue its notes freely and sell its bonds at a premium. Such were the facts. True, the war was a short one, and not nearly so expensive as that of 1812; furthermore, the existing banks had but recently passed through a period of liquidation and contraction, bringing about sounder conditions, all of which served to aid the Treasury. Polk maintained that the country was saved from the effect of the crisis of 1847 in Great Britain by the check both upon bank-note inflation and the resulting speculation.[2]

The execution of the law showed many defects which both Polk and Walker asked Congress in vain to remedy. The war

[1] Finance Report, 1854. [2] Messages of Presidents, Vol. IV.

and the tariff occupied the legislators' attention. The issues growing out of the tariff caused the defeat of Polk and the success of the Whigs with Taylor in the presidential contest of 1848.

Whenever specie payments were suspended there occurred a marked increase in the number of banks, because the profit upon circulation was large, and under meagre laws and lax supervision the liability almost insignificant. From 1837 to 1840 the number of banks increased 113, the nominal capital $68,000,000; by 1843 the resumption of coin payments had become quite general and the number had diminished 210, the capital $130,000,000. Note-issues, which it will be recalled aggregated $149,000,000 in 1837, now amounted to less than $59,000,000. The liquidation had reduced the money supply per capita from $13.87 to $6.87; needless to add that the number of failures was without precedent in the country's history. The estimate of losses during the period was nearly $800,000,000.

The banks which were founded upon a flimsy basis were of course the first to go to the wall, but many which had been properly organized also suffered extinction. The catastrophe was so general and widespread that the subject of banking reform was taken up seriously, as we have seen. In sixteen of the states the New York plan of free banking with bond deposit to cover circulation and the double liability of shareholders was copied. Quite a number of states experimented with banking laws that had been tried elsewhere and found wanting and with schemes which had never been tried.

Regarding only the safety of the federal revenues, in view of the condition of the banks and their currency, the subtreasury act was a proper measure. It served its purpose so well during this period only because conditions were exceptionally favorable. Secretary Walker claimed for it the credit of having caused the $22,000,000 net import of specie in 1847 to be put into circulation instead of being used by the banks, as formerly, to inflate their note-issues.[1] In fact, however, when the bank reports were published later, it appeared that the banks had absorbed fully one-half of this coin and increased their circulation by $23,000,000. Indeed, the financial transactions of the government for a number of years after 1846 were relatively so insignificant in volume that the question whether upon the whole the "constitutional treasury" was detrimental or not was subjected to no real test. President Taylor in his first message (1849) gave the subject only three lines, leaving it to the wisdom of Congress to retain or repeal the law, and Congress took no action.

It is worthy of note that Congress had devised no method of ridding the people of depreciated paper; not even the small bills (under $5), against which so much had been said, were done away with.

Reference has been made in previous chapters to the dissatisfaction of the Southern and Western states due to the disadvantage under which they labored owing to inadequate banking facilities. The following table gives for the several sections the banking power, composed of capital, circulation, and deposits of reporting institutions, and the relative amount per capita (excluding slaves in the Southern states).

	Banking Power (In Millions)			Per Capita		
	1830	1840	1850	1830	1840	1850
New England	54	89	114	$27.66	$39.98	$41.89
Middle	107	131	185	25.87	25.64	27.95
Southern	80	196	117	15.54	48.75	22.28
Western	7	38	35	4.47	11.29	6.35
Total	248	454	451	19.33	26.64	19.47

NOTE. — For 1830 the figures include the Bank of the United States distributed according to branches, but omitting $14,000,000 of capital invested in United States bonds.

[1] Finance Report, 1847.

The table illustrates not only the disparity referred to, particularly in the Western states, but also the location of the enormous expansion in 1840.

STATISTICAL RÉSUMÉ

(Amounts in millions of dollars)

CONDITION OF BANKS, 1837 TO 1849

YEAR	NO.	CAPITAL	CIRCULATION	DEPOSITS	SPECIE	LOANS
1837	788	291	149	127	38	525
1838	829	318	116	85	35	486
1839	840	327	135	90	45	492
1840	901	358	107	76	33	463
1841	784	314	107	65	35	386
1842	692	260	84	62	28	324
1843	691	229	59	56	34	255
1844	696	211	75	85	50	265
1845	707	206	90	88	44	289
1846	707	197	106	97	42	312
1847	715	203	106	92	35	310
1848	751	205	129	103	46	344
1849	782	207	115	91	44	332

THE STATE BANK OF INDIANA

YEAR	LOANS	SPECIE	OTHER ASSETS	NOTES	DEPOSITS	CAPITAL	SURPLUS
1835	1.8	0.8	1.9	1.5	0.4	1.2	—
1838	4.2	1.3	1.1	3.0	0.4	2.2	0.3
1841	4.7	1.1	1.0	3.1	0.3	2.7	0.3
1844	3.5	1.1	1.4	3.1	0.3	2.1	0.3
1847	3.8	1.1	2.1	3.6	0.6	2.1	0.5
1850	4.4	1.2	1.5	3.4	0.6	2.1	0.8
1853	5.1	1.3	1.5	3.8	0.7	2.1	1.0
1856	5.0	1.1	1.9	3.4	0.6	2.1	1.3

Loans include advances to the state and bonds.

CIRCULATION, 1837 TO 1849

YEAR	BANK NOTES OUT-STANDING	SPECIE IN U.S.	TOTAL MONEY IN U.S.	SPECIE IN TREASURY	MONEY IN CIRCU-LATION	POPULA-TION	PER CAPITA
1837	149	73	222	5	217	15.7	$13.87
1838	116	88	204	5	199	16.1	12.33
1839	135	87	222	2	220	16.6	13.26
1840	107	83	190	4	186	17.1	10.91
1841	107	80	187	1	186	17.6	10.59
1842	84	80	164	—	164	18.1	9.02
1843	59	90	149	1	147	18.7	7.87
1844	75	100	175	8	167	19.3	8.68
1845	90	96	186	8	178	19.9	8.95
1846	106	97	203	9	193	20.5	9.43
1847	106	120	226	2	224	21.1	10.59
1848	129	112	241	8	232	21.8	10.66
1849	115	120	235	2	233	22.5	10.34

CHAPTER X

Paper Currency

1850–1860

The element of federal politics incident to the competition for public deposits having now been definitely eliminated from the banking business, commercial banking developed in a greater degree than ever before. Issuing currency, instead of being the primary object of banking, began to be regarded as of less importance in most of the older sections of the country.

The distressing experiences already described produced a revulsion of sentiment in some of the states which led to the severest restrictions upon all banks by legislation and in a few by constitutional amendment. Nine states had no banks in 1852.[1] After a few years this rigidity relaxed and local bank-note issues were again reported from nearly all of the states. The scarcity of silver coin, discussed in another chapter, had caused a large increase in small note-issues.

Many states adopted the New York free banking and bond deposit plan, but not without modifications that operated more or less to neutralize its beneficial features. Bonds of states that afterwards depreciated, railway bonds some of which proved of little value, and miscellaneous securities, were permitted to be used as a basis for circulation, entailing losses upon the note holders. Many banks reported no deposits and no specie, the bonds deposited to secure circulation being all the protection note holders could expect.

[1] Sumner, History of Banking in United States.

The publication of reports of condition, now required by law in many states, no doubt assisted in correcting many evils and removed much of the mystery which had surrounded the business.

In New England compulsory specie reserve laws were enacted, and other wise legislation, supplemented by the Suffolk system, served to maintain prompt redemption and a safe bank currency, acceptable almost everywhere in the Union. In 1858 the Suffolk Bank made over that special business to the Bank of Mutual Redemption, organized for the purpose by country banks. In 1856 the Boston Clearing-house was established, following the lead of New York City, where a similar institution was organized three years earlier.

The New York State Banking Department was established in 1851. The Metropolitan Bank of New York City was established to act as a central redemption bank (like the Suffolk) in the same year. These circumstances and the establishment of the clearing-house in New York City in 1853 brought about a much more stable and secure system of paper currency.

In New York weekly reports were required to be made to the clearing-house by the associated banks, and in 1858 a fixed ratio of cash reserve to be held against deposit liabilities was agreed upon. The clearing of checks obviated the use of currency to a considerable extent, and in other particulars the association of the banks of the city, voluntarily imposing restrictions upon their business, contributed greatly to make them strong and influential.

There is one fundamental principle underlying the clearing-house system. Each bank settles its daily business with all the other banks of the city precisely as it would if there were but one other bank in the city. For instance, the First National Bank delivers to the clearing-house at ten o'clock A.M. every day all the debit items it holds against all the other banks and receives credit for the amount by the clearing-house. The clearing-house in turn, having received the same from the other banks, delivers to the First National all the items which all the other banks of the city hold against it and debits the First National with the amount. The First National is either debit or credit according to whether the amount of checks, etc., it brought to the clearing-house exceeds or is exceeded by the amount of checks, etc., which the other banks brought against it, and pays or receives the difference or balance in cash, as the case may be. The average daily exchanges of the New York banks for the year ended September 30th, 1914, were $296,238,762.28 and the average balances paid in cash were $16,926,228.72. The average daily use of money was lessened by the clearing-house system of exchanges by $279,312,533.56, being the difference between the cash actually used and the amount of the checks exchanged. The system not only minimized the use of actual cash, but removed the risk involved in sending so much cash about the streets and greatly reduced the expense involved in messengers, runners, and book-keeping.

The making of the settlement at the clearing-house involves only about forty-five minutes on the average. The payment of debit balances is made at a bank's convenience any time prior to 1.30 P.M., at which time all credit balances are paid.

The clearing-house fixed a cash reserve and bound each member to maintain the same; and took the public into its confidence by publishing weekly reports of condition showing the standing of each bank. This action, more than any legislation, more than anything else, aided in building up a sense of moral responsibility to the public, on the part of banks throughout the country, in restraining the undue expansion of note-issues and the many other reprehensible practices which characterized the banking of that period.

Philadelphia banks organized a clearing-house in 1858. Pennsylvania enacted a redemption law similar to that of New York and also prohibited notes under $5. The latter provision was likewise embodied in the laws of Maryland, Virginia, Alabama,

Arkansas, Louisiana, Kansas, and Missouri,[1] one of the objects being to enforce the use of silver and gold in the smaller transactions of daily barter. It failed for want of coöperation among the states. A similar effort failed many years later, when the Treasury tried to enforce the general circulation of the silver dollars coined under the act of 1878. The people demanded small notes.

Notwithstanding the strength of the state bank of Indiana, the state itself was for a time the favorite place for incubating note-issuing "banks" without capital, banking offices, or furniture. A circular letter which was issued, offering aid to any one desiring to start such a bank, stated that the sole cost necessarily incurred in starting a $100,000 "bank" would be $5000 for plates to print the notes and expenses, including compensation to the promoter, and $5000 as margin to carry the necessary bonds to be deposited.[2] The owner of the "bank" could as well reside in New York as Indiana.

A notable instance of the opposite extreme was "George Smith's money." These notes were issued by the Wisconsin Marine and Fire Insurance Company, which was controlled by George Smith. The company clearly had no right to issue circulating notes, but the notes were convertible into specie at all times with such absolute certainty that they passed at par everywhere, and for years constituted the best currency in the Northwest.[3]

It was necessary to exercise great discrimination as to the notes of certain sections and certain banks, which were at a discount of from one to fifty per cent. In order to feel assured that a note when tendered was good, one of the numerous "bank-note detectors" had to be consulted, and it was exceedingly difficult for those weekly publications to keep pace with the brisk

[1] Sumner, History of Banking in United States.

[2] Hunt's Merchant's Magazine, Vol. XXXVIII., p. 261.

[3] White, Money and Banking.

"bank starter" and "note issuer." Says Sumner in his History of Banking: —

"The bank-note detector did not become divested of its useful but contemptible function until the national bank system was founded. It is difficult for the modern student to realize that there were hundreds of banks whose notes circulated in any given community. The bank-notes were bits of paper recognizable as a species by shape, color, size and engraved work. Any piece of paper which had these came with the prestige of money; the only thing in the shape of money to which the people were accustomed. The person to whom one of them was offered, if unskilled in trade and banking, had little choice but to take it. A merchant turned to his 'detector.' He scrutinized the worn and dirty scrap for two or three minutes, regarding it as more probably 'good' if it was worn and dirty than if it was clean, because those features were proof of long and successful circulation. He turned it up to the light and looked through it, because it was the custom of the banks to file the notes on slender pins which made holes through them. If there were many such holes the note had been often in bank and its genuineness was ratified. All the delay and trouble of these operations were so much deduction from the character of the notes as current cash. A community forced to do its business in that way had no money. It was deprived of the advantages of money. We would expect that a free, self-governing, and, at times, obstreperous, people would have refused and rejected these notes with scorn, and would have made their circulation impossible, but the American people did not. They treated the system with toleration and respect. A parallel to the state of things which existed, even in New England, will be sought in vain in the history of currency."

The following statement illustrates the condition of the currency from the detector's point of view: —

	1856	1862
Number of banks reported	1409	1500
Number whose notes were not counterfeited . .	463	253
Number of kinds of imitations	1462	1861
Number of kinds of alterations	1119	3039
Number of kinds of spurious	224	1685

This does not include notes in circulation of suspended banks, whose value was so doubtful pending liquidation that the discounts thereon were always heavy.

An examination of the reports of the banks indicates that upon the whole the general business was regulated in greater measure by the demands of trade and less by speculative ventures than in any previous period. The circulation bore a fair relation to the specie, and deposits constituted an increasing portion of the amounts loaned.

The great weakness of the banks of the Western states was their investments in "stocks" (securities generally); fully one-half of their capital was so invested, whereas New England and Middle state banks showed but 2 per cent.

Owing to the non-enforcement of laws requiring redemption of notes, it had become the habit of bank officers and others to regard the presentation of notes for *redemption* in specie as an act to be reprobated, manifesting a desire to injure the bank and through it the community where it was located.

As has been stated, the operation of the subtreasury act exerted little influence upon the currency so long as the federal revenues were not largely in excess of expenditures. Repeatedly the secretaries of the Treasury reported that no disturbance had been experienced — indicating that the fear that such an event might occur was lurking in their minds.

In 1853–1854 the surplus revenue assumed considerable proportions, and Secretary Guthrie found it advisable to use it to relieve stringencies in the money market by the purchase of bonds at extraordinary premiums.[1] On one occasion he paid as high as 21 per cent. premium. He did not hesitate to say that he regarded it necessary to avert a panic, and he repeated the operation on several other occasions for the same reason.

Guthrie gave the subject of the currency much attention during his administration of the Treasury (1853–1857).

[1] Finance Reports, 1853 and 1854.

In 1855[1] he reviewed the history of banks from 1790. He expressed himself in no uncertain language upon the laxity of the state governments in failing to properly regulate the note-issues, and especially to abrogate the use of small denominations. Like his predecessors of the Jackson school, however, he saw no way to coerce the states or the banks: several judicial decisions (the Briscoe case already referred to and the case of Darrington *vs.* Bank of Alabama, 13 How. 12) had settled the question of the constitutionality of state bank issues, and he regarded it too late then (1855) to have the courts retrace their steps, nor could he hope for the coöperation of the states, influenced as they were by local interests. He said, however, that if the states continued this policy Congress would be justified in levying a tax on the notes that would in effect abrogate the power.

In his last report (1856), however, Guthrie confessed that a purely specie currency was out of the question; he estimated the volume of small notes ($5 and under) at $50,000,000, but regarded it premature to tax them out of existence, recommending a constitutional amendment giving Congress the power to regulate these issues. He added: —

"At present, an attempt to prohibit and restrain the issue and circulation of small notes, by a resort to taxation, or by applying bankrupt laws to these corporations, would be premature. In my former reports the subject has been brought to the attention of Congress, with a view to the full consideration of the evil and danger to our currency, from their continued use, under the hope that Congress or the states authorizing their issues, would take action, to extend the restriction and make it general.

"If the small notes are withdrawn and prohibited, it is believed the operations of the Treasury, in the collection and disbursement of the national revenue, would be as salutary a restraint upon the banks and upon commercial transactions as could be interposed, *and all-sufficient to secure as sound, healthy, and uniform a currency as it is practicable to have.*"

The Treasury at this time held, in coin, $30,000,000 surplus. In order to save the expense of transferring specie from de-

[1] Finance Report, 1855.

positories where it accumulated beyond the local needs, the Treasury entered upon the business of selling drafts, thus assuming the function of dealing in domestic exchange, which had been regarded so pernicious when done by the Bank of the United States.

Disbursing officers of the government, to whom large sums were from time to time advanced, continued to deposit these funds in the banks until an act of 1857 (repeatedly asked for by every Secretary of the Treasury since 1846) compelled the deposit in the subtreasuries, the payment to be made by checks instead of by cash, — another departure from the original plan.

The banks had during the period prior to 1857 become heavily interested in railway construction which at this time assumed very extensive proportions. So large a part of their funds were tied up in this relatively permanent form of investment, that they found it impossible in the summer and fall of 1857 to satisfy the demand for commercial discounts. Rates of interest became exorbitant. The troubles began in August and became quite general by October, when the New York City banks, except the Chemical, suspended specie payments, followed generally by all the banks in the country excepting South Carolina, Louisiana, the state banks of Ohio and Indiana, and a few others.

New York City was and had been for years the actual monetary centre of the country; its banking capital had steadily grown from $20,000,000 in 1840 to $25,400,000 in 1849, $35,500,000 in 1852, $55,000,000 in 1856, and $65,000,000 in 1857. The associated banks of the metropolis were looked to for leadership.

It is therefore of special interest to note their condition during the year of the crisis. The specie in the New York subtreasury is also given in the following table [1] (in millions of dollars): —

[1] Compiled from Hunt's Merchant's Magazine.

Date	Capital	Loans	Specie	Circulation	Deposits	Sub-treasury
Jan. 3	55.2	109.1	11.2	8.6	95.8	11.4
April 11 . . .	59.5	115.4	10.9	8.8	96.5	15.2
Aug. 1 . . .	64.6	120.6	12.9	8.7	94.6	12.2
Oct. 3 . . .	65.0	105.9	11.4	7.9	68.0	7.7
Dec. 5	63.5	96.3	26.1	6.6	78.5	4.0

The loans had reached a minimum of $95,000,000 on November 28, the deposits $53,000,000 and specie $7,800,000 on October 17.

The tremendous increase in railway construction, especially in the Central and Western states, was the most important factor in bringing about the stringency of 1854 and finally the crisis of 1857. In 1850 there were 9021 miles of railway in operation; in 1854, 16,726; in 1857 the number was 24,503; this represented an increase of railway securities of nearly $600,000,000, more than half of which was issued in 1854–1857.

For the preceding seven years the country's imports exceeded exports more than $300,000,000, and all but $50,000,000 of this sum was covered by net exports of specie. The foreign holdings of our securities, estimated at $261,000,000 in 1852, were in 1857 placed at $400,000,000.

With but a limited foreign market for the large mass of securities and a home market incapable of absorbing them, the banks of the country unwisely undertook to carry them, to the detriment of the mercantile community. In order to meet the strain, the total circulation of the banks of the country expanded until the money per capita was over $16 in 1854; in the two following years contraction took place, but in 1857 the general expansion was in even greater proportion. (See table at end of chapter.)

The New York City banks were subjected to a steady drain of specie by the subtreasury, owing to the large importations, and at the same time were pressed for loans. They had expanded their credits to the limit of prudence in August, and began to contract existing loans at a rapid rate and refused applications for new ones, endeavoring in this way to avoid suspension which was prohibited by the state constitution.[1]

A desperate struggle ensued. Notes of country banks were rushed for redemption, and failure to redeem promptly caused reports of failures of such banks. The telegraph, then lately come into general use, spread the news and was named as one of the "causes of the crisis." Bank shares which had been at par sold under 40, stocks fell from 10 per cent. to 40 per cent., and foreign exchange broke more than 10 per cent. without bringing specie.[2] The Treasury had begun early in the year to buy government bonds in small amounts, and the banks were disposed to look to it for further help. Secretary Howell Cobb increased his purchases, but the withdrawal of deposits exceeded $40,000,000 in ten weeks, thereby greatly diminishing the specie fund, finally causing suspension of the banks October 14.

It should be noted that the courts decided that the constitutional provision against suspension was not applicable so long as a bank was not actually insolvent.[3] The suspension of note redemption was only for a short time; the suspension of the payment of deposits was longer, and under the circumstances loans and discounts were out of the question.

Speaking of the great withdrawal of deposits the Superintendent of the Bank Department of New York said: —

> "The great concentrated call loan was demanded, and in such amounts that a single day's struggle ended the battle; and the banks went down before a storm they could not postpone or resist. . . . The most sagacious banker, in his most apprehensive mood, never for a moment deemed it possible to have a general suspension in this state from a home demand for coin, while coin itself was at little or no premium with the brokers." [4]

[1] Sumner, History of Banking.

[2] Hunt's Merchant's Magazine, Vol. XXXVII.

[3] *Ibid.*

[4] Report, 1857.

The banks in the Central and Western states being the largest holders of railway securities suffered more than those of the South. Indeed, in some parts of the South the crisis was hardly felt.

After the suspension in New York the Treasury continued to buy bonds, gold arrived from California and from abroad, and on December 12 the banks were able to resume. Other Eastern banks resumed early in 1858; Western and Southern banks delayed much longer.

Over 5100 failures with liabilities of nearly $300,000,000 were recorded. Prices of stocks, breadstuffs, and other commodities fell ruinously, imports diminished immediately, many cargoes being returned without landing. The exchanges at the New York Clearing House diminished 43 per cent.

Says Sumner: —

"The suspension was preceded by a desperate struggle between all the banks themselves, and distrust and fear of currency was more apparent among them than with the public generally. The banks began a savage contraction, being in no position whatever to meet the crisis by bold loans to solvent borrowers. It was afterwards said, with great good reason, that the panic was entirely unnecessary and need not have occurred, but the banks put all the pressure on their loans to merchants because they could not recall those to the railroads."[1]

President Buchanan and Secretary Cobb were most severe in their denunciation of the banks. The former in his message[2] said that such revulsions must occur when 1400 irresponsible institutions are permitted to usurp the power of providing currency, thus affecting the value of the property of every citizen: this power should never have been dissevered from the money-coining power exclusively conferred upon the federal government; unfortunately, as it was, nothing could be done; a national bank, even if constitutional, would not serve the purpose, as was

[1] History of Banking in United States.

[2] Messages of Presidents, Vol. V.

shown by the history of the Second Bank. Referring to the existing systems he pointed out that only in one state, Louisiana, were banks required to keep adequate specie reserves; according to the standard adopted by Louisiana, the banks should have had one dollar in three against notes and deposits, whereas they had only $58,000,000 of specie against $445,000,000 of those obligations, considerably less than one in seven; slight pressure for cash thus inevitably brought failure. He favored a compulsory bankrupt law for banks failing to meet their obligations, and even suggested depriving banks of the note-issuing power altogether.

Cobb insisted that the disbursements of specie by the sub-treasuries had aided in restoring coin payments, and contrasted the conditions with those of 1837. He thought so well of the independent treasury that he urged the several states to adopt the same system for their own affairs.[1] Ohio actually did so in 1858.

The Treasury suffered in its revenue by the diminished imports, and the act of December 23, 1857, authorized covering the deficit by the issue of $20,000,000 in 6 per cent. one-year Treasury notes. In June, 1858, the Treasury was authorized to issue a fifteen-year 5 per cent. loan for $20,000,000. In 1859 authority was given to reissue the Treasury notes of 1857, and the amount used, including reissues, was $52,778,900. Most of them actually remained out until 1860. Thus the people suffered from taxation in addition to their losses on account of the ill-regulated currency system.

The aggregate bank returns for 1858 showed a contraction of deposits and circulation from $445,000,000 to $340,000,000 and an increase of specie to $74,000,000. Loans were diminished fully $100,000,000, of which $43,000,000 occurred in the banks of New York State alone. The banks of the latter state were also credited with almost the entire specie increase for that year.

[1] Finance Report, 1857.

At the end of this period (1861) the number of banks had increased to 1601, their capital to $697,000,000; circulation had again gone beyond the $200,000,000 point, and deposits to $257,000,000. Against the total of these obligations of $460,000,000 they had nearly $88,000,000 specie, or nearly one dollar in five.

The following table shows the distribution by sections and for certain states, of the deposits, circulation, and specie in millions, and the relation of specie holdings to circulation and deposits, in 1861: —

States	Deposits	Circulation	Specie	Specie to Notes. Per Cent.	Specie to Both. Per Cent.
New England	41.9	33.1	10.4	31.4	13.8
Massachusetts	34.0	19.5	8.8	45.1	16.4
Middle	152.0	53.4	39.0	73.0	18.9
New York	114.8	28.2	26.4	93.6	27.2
Southern	42.5	61.9	30.2	48.8	29.0
Louisiana	17.1	6.9	13.7	198.5	57.0
Western	15.8	38.2	9.6	25.0	17.7
United States	257.2	202.0	87.7	43.8	19.2

The Louisiana system thus appeared in the front rank as far as security was concerned. New York and the Middle states, as well as the Southern states, reported conditions superior to those of New England. Indeed it was only after the crisis that the banks in the latter section were led to increase their specie. In prior years the specie of New England banks was usually less than 13 per cent. on their circulation.

In 1860 and early in 1861 the deficits in the revenue again compelled the Treasury to resort to loans and Treasury notes which were negotiated at a discount. This latter circumstance was due to the impending civil war and not to currency conditions. The amount authorized was $20,000,000; including reissues the amount used was $45,364,450.

The sectional disparity in banking and currency facilities largely disappeared during this period, the Southern states having been fairly well supplied, as the following table shows. (As before, the slave population is excluded in reaching a per capita.)

States	Banking Power (in Millions)		Per Capita	
	1850	1860	1850	1860
Eastern . . .	114	209	$41.39	$66.89
Middle	185	371	27.95	44.35
Southern . . .	117	223	22.28	33.69
Western . . .	35	83	6.35	8.52
United States .	452	886	19.47	27.98

The conditions existing from 1850 to 1861 were truly anomalous. The currency systems of the several states were as a rule based upon laws which on their face were fairly complete and conservative. In the aggregate, so far as the reports enable one to determine, the conditions were not radically unsound, and yet, owing to want of supervision and non-enforcement of the laws, they furnished the country a paper currency in large part so disreputable as to cause amazement that the people tolerated the same and endured the robbery which was thereby imposed upon them. Refusal to redeem notes was in most states an infraction of the law, to be followed by the forfeiture of the charter of the offending bank, and yet the law was habitually disregarded.

Banking conditions for the whole period of national existence prior to the Civil War may be classified as follows: —

1. First United States Bank (1791–1811). Sound bank currency.

2. Interval (1812–1816). State bank currency inflation, suspension, disasters involving enormous losses.

3. Second United States Bank (1817–1836). At first unsettled

conditions as to currency and business, then sound paper currency by reason of United States Bank enforcing redemption of state bank notes and formulating a standard of credit to which the state banks in competition were obliged to conform; then during the last years of its existence unsettled conditions owing to political power exerted to prevent renewal of bank's charter.

4. 1837–1846. Inordinate inflation, suspension, and losses measured by the hundred millions, withdrawal of government funds from the banks, with the declared hope of preventing undue expansion of bank-note issues by so doing.

5. 1847–1860. Banking becoming more conservative; deposits counting more and note-issues less as a means of extending credit; note-issues, however, unrestrained and entailing enormous losses upon the people; failure of subtreasury to restrain or control banking methods, but disastrously interfering with business by withdrawing from the channels of trade, and locking up, funds which should have been current.

It is notable that only during the existence of a central bank did the country enjoy for extended periods a currency that could be regarded as sound, with domestic exchange reasonably well regulated, and discount rates fairly equitable in different sections. So long as the bank was limited in its charge for discounts by its charter, local banks were necessarily influenced in adjusting their rates; so long as the bank through its branches furnished exchange at rates which were not an exorbitant tax upon trade, other banks had to do the same; and so long as the bank enforced redemption of notes and accepted only those convertible into specie for payments to the Treasury, the local banks could not inflate their issues and found it profitable to maintain convertibility.

The Jacksonian Democrats, in contradistinction from other Democrats, like Gallatin, Dallas, Crawford, having taken position against the central bank system, and having by fortuitous circumstances maintained control of legislation for a long period, conceived the idea that currency and business evils could be regulated by the subtreasury system. Although they suffered defeat at the polls in 1840, their plans were materially aided by Tyler's weakness and virtual desertion of his party and the consequent failure to establish a central bank. In the meantime the judicial department of the government had declared that the state bank issues were constitutional. Thus the subtreasury act came into popular favor and became law; at its best it was only a partial remedy.

The states which endeavored by the enactment of the bond deposit plan to remedy the currency evil imagined that they had done all that was requisite, but in the absence of compulsory provision for reserves and redemption, and the lax enforcement of the laws which existed, undue expansion was not prevented and illegitimate evasions went unpunished. Van Buren, Tyler, and Buchanan, as well as secretaries of the Treasury during the period after 1837, saw clearly wherein the states were derelict and appreciated fully the extent of the legalized misappropriation of the people's property resulting therefrom. Their narrow political tenets, however, rendered them blind to the fact that Congress had the power by taxation to extirpate the evil and afford the people protection. Their shuffling policies are well illustrated by the historic enunciation of Buchanan in another instance when he declared that the states had no right to secede, but that there was no power in the Constitution to coerce a sovereign state. To paraphrase, the state bank systems of currency were almost criminally wrong and unjust, but there was no power in the Constitution, ordained though it was "to establish justice," to prevent the wholesale fraud upon the people which the lax currency systems of the states engendered. The Civil War resulted in enfranchising the slaves. It also liberated the whole people from evils of state-bank currency.

Respecting the several issues of Treasury notes prior to the Civil War, it is interesting to note that the first emission of this form of "bills of credit" (1812) was made during the administration of Madison, and although a question as to the constitutionality arose, it was determined in favor of the issue both by Congress and the President. It was, however, held beyond the power of Congress to give the notes the legal tender function, but they were made receivable for all public dues. Later issues were authorized in the administrations of Van Buren, Tyler, Polk, and Buchanan, all of them "strict constructionists." Both Jefferson and Tyler favored the use of these notes as currency, and when they were issued in small denominations, they actually became for short periods a part of the circulation of the country.

Hamilton's views on the subject were expressed in his report on the bank plan, as follows: "The emitting of paper money by authority of government is wisely prohibited to the individual states by the Constitution, and the spirit of that prohibition ought not to be disregarded by the government of the United States."

STATISTICAL RÉSUMÉ

(Amounts in millions unless otherwise indicated)

CIRCULATION, ETC.

Year	Estimated Bank Notes Outstanding	Estimated Specie in United States	Total Money in United States	Specie in Treasury	Money in Circulation	Population	Per Capita	New York Clearing-House Transactions
1850	131	154	285	7	278	23	$12.02	——
1851	155	186	341	11	330	24	13.76	——
1852	172	204	376	15	361	25	14.63	——
1853	188	236	424	22	402	26	15.80	——
1854	205	241	446	20	426	26	16.10	5750
1855	187	250	437	19	418	27	15.34	5363
1856	196	250	446	20	426	28	15.16	6906
1857	215	260	475	18	457	29	15.81	8333
1858	155	260	415	6	409	30	13.78	4757
1859	193	250	443	4	439	31	14.35	6448
1860	207	253	442	7	435	31	13.85	7231

Bank Statistics

Year	State Banks							Savings Banks		
	Number	Capital	Circulation	Deposits	Specie	Loans	Stocks	Deposits	Number Depositors (000's)	Average Deposit
1850	824	217	131	110	45	364	21	43	251	$173
1851	879	228	155	129	49	414	22	50	277	182
1852	—	—	—	—	—	—	—	59	309	193
1853	750	208	146	146	47	409	22	72	366	198
1854	1208	301	205	188	59	557	44	78	396	196
1855	1307	332	187	190	54	576	53	84	432	195
1856	1398	344	196	213	59	634	49	96	488	196
1857	1416	371	215	230	58	684	59	99	490	201
1858	1422	395	155	186	74	583	60	108	539	201
1859	1476	402	193	260	105	657	64	129	623	207
1860	1562	422	207	254	84	692	70	149	694	215

No returns for 1852. 1533 very imperfect.

CHAPTER XI

Legal Tender Notes

1861–1865

There was never any reasonable doubt as to the power of Congress under the Constitution to charter a bank, and the Supreme Court settled the question early in the period of the Second United States Bank. The contention that Congress had no such power was fostered as a political issue, as in the case of Jackson, affording, as it did, an opportunity to decry monopoly and assail the money power; but the chief strength of this contention came from the champions of state sovereignty and a strict construction of the Constitution, who feared that liberalizing that instrument might give encouragement to the opponents of slavery and endanger its extension into the territories, and indeed might disturb its maintenance where it already existed.

It seems equally clear that the framers of the Constitution intended to prohibit Congress from issuing paper currency and making the same legal tender. At the time the Constitution was adopted, the country was at the climax of its suffering from legal tender notes issued by the colonies and Congress, as set forth in Chapter I. Although the purpose to prohibit seems clear, the language failed to carry out the intent, as appears from the decision of the courts that Congress has that power in a practically unlimited degree. No history of our currency struggles would be complete that did not fully cover this phase of our experience.

The financial and monetary conditions which confronted the administration of Lincoln in 1861 were such as would have severely taxed a finance minister with the genius of Hamilton and the wide experience of Gallatin. The nation was at the brink of civil war, the outcome of which could not be foreseen. Its debt of about $76,000,000 was greater than at any time since the period following the War of 1812, and most of this debt had been created during years of peace. The nation's credit was poor, its securities having been sold at more than 10 per cent. below par by the outgoing Secretary of the Treasury.

The currency consisted of about $250,000,000 of specie and $200,000,000 of state bank notes, and whilst the 1600 banks, as a whole, possessed a fair quantity of specie (probably 45 per cent. of their note-issues), most of it was held by the banks in the money centres. The condition of the paper circulation was very far from satisfactory. Great dissimilarity in the laws governing banks in the several states precluded uniformity, security, or safety. There was no central place of redemption, hence most notes were at a discount, varying with the distance from the bank of issue. It was estimated that there were 7000 kinds and denominations of notes, and fully 4000 spurious or altered varieties were reported.

The government's funds were held in the subtreasuries and mints, in specie, but the amount was small, the revenues having been for some time insufficient to meet the expenses. The tariff law passed on March 2, 1861, had not yet become effective. The Treasury possessed power, granted by the Congress which had just expired, to issue bonds and Treasury notes. As the bonds would not bring par (some selling at 94, others as low as 86), Treasury notes were issued, since, being receivable for duties, they were approximately worth par.

Government needs became more pressing as the impending war developed, and Congress was called in extra session July 4, 1861. Secretary Chase, in his report to Congress,[1] estimated the sum required at $318,000,000 and recommended both taxation

[1] Finance Report, July, 1861.

and loans. His plan embraced taxation sufficient to cover the ordinary expenses of the government, interest on the debt, and provision for the sinking fund, the extraordinary expenses to be covered by loans. His scheme for borrowing included non-interest-bearing notes payable on demand, interest-bearing notes for short terms, and bonds for long terms; the first to be convertible into the second, and the second into the third, form of obligation. Thus he expected to avert the evil which many of his predecessors experienced, of being compelled to receive for payments to the Treasury the notes of state banks, most of which were fluctuating in value, and might even become valueless on his hands. He hoped that $100,000,000 of the loan might be placed abroad, but this hope was not realized. While thus suggesting notes to circulate as money, he urged great care "to prevent the degradation of such issues into an irredeemable paper currency, than which no more certainly fatal expedient for impoverishing the masses and discrediting the government of any country can well be devised."

Congress adopted Chase's plan in the act of July 17, 1861, which authorized the borrowing of $250,000,000, either in 6 per cent. twenty-year bonds, or 7.30 per cent. three-year Treasury notes in denominations not less than $50, or in one-year 3.65 per cent. notes, or non-interest-bearing notes of less than $50, redeemable on demand. Notes under $10 were prohibited, and the demand notes were not to exceed $50,000,000. These might also be issued to pay public creditors and be redeemed in 7.30's, and when redeemed they might be reissued at any time prior to December 31, 1862, provided the total limit of the loan was not exceeded. The amending act of August 5, 1861, provided for the exchange of the 7.30 notes into bonds, the limit of the loan ($250,000,000) not to be exceeded; for the issue of "demand" notes of $5; directed that the latter class be receivable for all public dues; furthermore, suspended the subtreasury act of 1846, so far as to permit the moneys received from loans to be deposited in "solvent, specie-paying banks" and drawn upon for payments. It will be observed that the demand notes were not made specifically payable in coin, but were universally regarded as coin notes, since no other legal tender money existed at the time.

In his report in December, 1861, Chase, still hopeful of an early cessation of the war, discussed two plans for the currency. He pointed out that the banks in the states in rebellion had about one-fourth of the estimated circulation for the whole country, and that of the remaining $150,000,000 a very considerable part was of doubtful value in an emergency. He ventured the opinion that the issue of state bank notes was not constitutional, and proposed that the large amount thus practically borrowed, without interest, from the people by state banks, should, by legislation, be made to inure to the advantage of the general government. An issue of government notes would, in his opinion, serve the purpose of furnishing a uniform circulating medium, and at the same time aid the government in its emergency; but the dangers of overissue, inadequate provision for redemption, and consequent depreciation were, he thought, so great as to outweigh the advantages. He therefore recommended a national bank currency secured by bonds, which would yield all that a government issue could, and not be open to the same criticism.

The Treasury had met its immediate needs up to this time with demand and 7.30 notes, a sale of two lots of $50,000,000 each of the latter having been "underwritten" and "placed" by the banks of New York, Philadelphia, and Boston. Chase had arranged with the banks for a further placing of $50,000,000 in 6 per cent. bonds on a 7 per cent. basis, and there was an understanding that still another $50,000,000 would be taken in January, 1862. He also issued the Treasury notes authorized by the laws of the previous Congress.

At the special session of Congress in July, Chase had estimated the government's expenditures for the fiscal year at $318,000,000.

In his December report[1] the estimate was increased over $200,000,000, and at the same time he showed that the revenue would fall far below the amount he had expected. Figures of such unusual magnitude at that time were appalling, and had a most depressing effect. An international complication arose at this time which had a far-reaching influence upon the finances of our country. The confederate government sought to send representatives abroad, presumably to negotiate for the recognition of the Confederacy by European nations, and also to negotiate for loans. Captain Wilkes, commanding the *San Jacinto*, forcibly took from the British steamer *Trent*, plying between Havana and Southampton, two commissioners of the Confederacy, Messrs. Mason and Slidell. There was great rejoicing over this capture throughout the country, and Captain Wilkes was thanked by Congress. When the news of the capture reached England, the greatest indignation was aroused over what was deemed a wanton insult to the British flag. The surrender of the prisoners and an apology were demanded, coupled with instructions to the British Minister in Washington to ask for his passports in case the demands were not complied with. The patriotic fervor with which the capture had been received and applauded made it exceedingly difficult and certainly distasteful for the administration to comply with the British demands, and yet the alternative seemed war with a great and powerful nation, in addition to the struggle with the Confederacy. Calm consideration showed the British position to be well taken, and the demands were therefore complied with. The news of the British demand was received in New York December 16, and precipitated a *quasi* panic.

Chase, as authorized in placing his loans with the banks and through them, had utilized the banks as temporary depositories of the proceeds of the loans. They rightfully expected these funds to remain on deposit and be checked out to meet the govern-

[1] Finance Report, December, 1861.

ment's needs as they arose. Chase, however, construed the subtreasury act rigidly and required the transfer of the funds in specie to the Treasury. This at once deprived the banks of a large part of their reserve, created a money stringency, and coupled with the appalling expenditures of the government and the *Trent* affair resulted in suspension of specie payments near the close of December, 1861. The banks had at the time, according to their reports, $102,000,000 of specie against $184,000,000 of notes. The Treasury was compelled to suspend specie payments also, and the Secretary was forced to readjust his plans.

He still urged his bank-note measure, and a comprehensive bill for the purpose was introduced in Congress. A bill to issue more government notes was also prepared, which being shorter and less complex in its nature, appealed to Congress and was given precedence. Chase, harassed by inability to place bonds or 7.30 notes, with demands upon him amounting to a million and a quarter dollars daily, not only assented to the latter measure, but urged its speedy adoption. As demand notes at the time were not redeemed in coin "on demand," the Treasury found it difficult to pay them out. Banks and others were refusing them. It was therefore proposed to make the new issue legal tender, which Chase also urged upon Congress very reluctantly and under the plea of necessity.

Unlike Hamilton, he failed to grasp the principles of finance as applied to government. Instead of seeking the best way he seems to have sought the easiest. The most easily available resource which the government had was the issuance of United States notes with legal tender power. These were immediately available for the payment of the government's obligations. Whenever bonds were issued the element of time necessarily entered in order to negotiate their sale. Secretary Chase made a great mistake in not asking for largely increased taxation immediately at the outbreak of the war. The patriotic spirit of the country would undoubtedly have insured compliance with his request, thereby avoiding the occasion for issuing so great a volume of legal tender notes. Adams, in Public Debts, lays down the governing principle in such emergencies as follows: —

> "It is a recognized fact that self-governing peoples are stronger for tax purposes than the subjects of a monarchical state, for their will lies more closely to the heart of the state. But the administration of a self-governing people should never undertake a war in favor of which there is no strong sentiment. As things go, then, in democratic countries, it does not appear that loans to the full extent of extraordinary demands are necessary, and there is no question as to the superiority of taxes over loans when their use will not curtail industrial energy. The measure of this first money-tax should be the popular enthusiasm for the war."

Taught by experience, Chase recognized this principle later. He said to Congress in 1863 that it was not too much, and perhaps hardly enough, to say that every dollar raised by taxation for extraordinary purposes or reduction of debt is worth two in the increased value of national securities. He excused his failure to ask for additional taxation immediately because of the impossibility of realizing in advance the long continuance and enormous expenditure involved in the war.[1]

Pending the discussion of the measure, Congress on February 11 authorized the issue of $10,000,000 more "demand notes." The legal tender act of February 25, 1862, provided for the issue of $150,000,000 United States notes (of which $60,000,000 were to redeem the demand notes) to be "lawful money" and legal tender for all debts, public and private, except customs duties and interest on the public debt, both of which were to be payable in coin. No denominations less than $5 were to be issued. They were made convertible into 6 per cent. five-twenty year bonds, and receivable at par the same as coin for all loans to the government, and when received by the Treasury might be reissued. The act further provided for the issue of $500,000,000

[1] Finance Report, 1863.

of the bonds mentioned above, to fund the notes, or to be sold at the market value for coin, or for any Treasury notes authorized to be issued. The coin from customs revenues was pledged for the interest on the debt and the creation of a sinking fund. The Treasury was further empowered to issue, in exchange for notes, temporary loan certificates in sums not less than $100, running not less than thirty days, with interest not more than 5 per cent., the amount not to exceed $25,000,000. The act also exempted securities of the United States from state and municipal taxation.

This measure caused much discussion, both in and out of Congress. There was no precedent for, and apparently every reason against, constituting the notes money and making them legal tender. Lincoln and Chase very reluctantly accepted it as a necessary evil. The Committee on Ways and Means was evenly divided on the question of favorably reporting the bill. Thaddeus Stevens (the Republican leader in the House), Spaulding, and others of the dominant party, declared the measure warranted only by the necessities of the war, *the saving of the Union*. Nevertheless such Republicans as Morrill, of Vermont, and Conkling, and nearly all the Democratic representatives, led by Pendleton and Vallandigham, opposed it as unnecessary, inexpedient, and unconstitutional. In the Senate Fessenden, Sherman and Sumner gave reluctant assent, the first named opposing and voting in favor of omitting the legal tender clause. Among those afterwards prominent in currency legislation who favored the bill were Windom, Kelley, Hooper, Morrill (Me.); and among the opponents, Morrill (Vt.), Cox, and Holman. The bill passed the House by a vote of 93 to 59; in the Senate the legal tender clause was retained by a vote of 22 to 17, and the bill passed by 30 to 7, only 3 Republicans voting nay.

Opinion in banking and business circles was divided, but leading Chambers of Commerce passed resolutions urging the adoption of the measure, and popular opinion was generally favorable.

Chase in his letter to the House Committee said that he felt —

"a great aversion to making anything but coin a legal tender in payment of debts. It has been my anxious wish to avoid the necessity of such legislation. It is, however, at present impossible, in consequence of the large expenditures entailed by the war, and the suspension of the banks, to procure sufficient coin for disbursements, and it has, therefore, become indispensably necessary that we should resort to the issue of United States notes."[1]

He urged such legislation as would "divest the legal tender clause of the bill of injurious tendencies, and secure the earliest possible return to a sound currency of coin and promptly convertible notes."

Spaulding said: —

"The bill before us is a war measure, a measure of *necessity*, and not of choice. . . . These are extraordinary times, and extraordinary measures must be resorted to in order to save our government, and preserve our nationality."

The tax and banking measure proposed would operate too slowly to provide means to continue the war.

Stevens said: —

"No one would willingly issue paper currency not redeemable on demand and make it a legal tender. . . . I look upon the immediate passage of the bill as essential to the very existence of the government. Reject it, and financial credit, not only of the government, but of all the great interests of the country, will be prostrated."

Pendleton, opposing, said, as to the constitutionality: —

"I find no grant of this power in direct terms, or, as I think, by fair implication. It is not an accidental omission; it is not an omission through inadvertency; it was intentionally left out of the Constitution, because it was designed that the power should not reside in the federal government."

Conkling on the same subject said: —

"Had such a power lurked in the Constitution, as construed by those who ordained and administered it, we should find it so recorded." The

[1] Shuckers, Life of Chase.

"universal judgment of statesmen, jurists, and lawyers has denied the constitutional right of Congress to make paper a legal tender for debts to any extent whatever."

Morrill of Vermont spoke of it as "a measure not blessed by one sound precedent, and damned by all!" He characterized it as of doubtful constitutionality, immoral, a breach of the public faith. He predicted that it would increase the cost of the war, banish all specie from circulation, degrade us in the estimation of other nations, cripple American labor, and throw larger wealth into the hands of the rich; that there was no necessity for so desperate a remedy.

In the Senate Fessenden said: —

"The . . . clause making these notes a legal tender is put upon the ground of absolute, overwhelming necessity; . . . the question then is, does the necessity exist? . . ."

He would

"take the money of any citizen against his will to sustain the government, if nothing else was left, and bid him wait until the government could pay him. It is a contribution which every man is bound to make under the circumstances. We can take all the property of any citizen. That is what is called a forced contribution. . . . The question after all returns: Is this measure absolutely indispensable to procure means? If so, as I said before, necessity knows no law. . . . Say what you will, nobody can deny that it is bad faith. If it be necessary for the salvation of the government, all considerations of this kind must yield; but to make the best of it, it is bad faith, and encourages bad morality, both in public and private. Going to the extent that it does, to say that notes thus issued shall be receivable in payment of all private obligations, however contracted, is in its very essence a wrong, for it compels one man to take from his neighbor, in payment of a debt, that which he would not otherwise receive, or be obliged to receive, and what is probably not full payment."

Collamer said that the men of the period of the adoption of the Constitution always

"entertained the opinion that the United States could have nothing else a tender but coin. While they lived there never was such a thing thought of as attempting to make the evidences of the debt of the government a legal tender, let their form be what they might."

There were two modes of replenishing the Treasury; one was by taxation, and the other was by borrowing. To borrow money there must be a lender and a borrower, and both should act voluntarily, and not compel the lender to part with his money without an inducement. "The operation of this bill is not anything like as honorable or honest as a forced loan."

Sherman said that the legal tender clause was necessary to make the notes acceptable; it was after all a mere temporary expedient necessary to save the government.

"I am constrained to assume the power, and refer our authority to exercise it to the courts. I have shown . . . that we must no longer hesitate as to the necessity of this measure. That necessity does exist, and now presses upon us."

He thought himself required to vote for all laws necessary and proper for executing the powers given to uphold the government.

"This is not the time when I would limit these powers. Rather than yield to revolutionary force, I would use revolutionary force."

Howe said: —

"Those who deny the constitutional authority to pass this bill must deny its necessity or its propriety, . . . ought to show us some plan for avoiding it, some measure adequate to the emergency, and more proper than the one proposed by this bill. . . . It is evident that no substitute can be provided except it be taxation or direct loans."

Taxation alone could not provide the vast sums required, and direct loans were equally impracticable.

J. A. Bayard said: —

"No one can deny the fact that in contracts between man and man, and in government contracts to pay money, the obligation is to pay intrinsic value. If you violate that by this bill, which you certainly do, how can you expect that the faith of the community will be given to the law which you now pass, in which you say that you will pay hereafter the interest on your debt in coin? Why should they give credit to that declaration? If you can violate the Constitution of the United States in the face of your oaths, in the face of its palpable provision, what security do you offer to the lender of the money?"

Sumner said: —

"Surely we must all be against paper money, we must all insist upon maintaining the integrity of the government; and we must all set our faces against any proposition like the present, except as a temporary expedient, rendered imperative by the exigency of the hour."

Lincoln, engrossed with a multitude of onerous duties, approved the act without comment.

Much opposition was caused by the clause inserted by the Senate, which provided for payment of interest on bonds in coin, which practically meant a discrimination in favor of one class of creditors, and, as Stevens said, depreciated at once the money which the bill created.

It is obvious that few of the men charged with affairs believed the legal tender act constitutional. It was considered warranted only by extreme necessity, as a temporary measure, to save the Union and hence the Constitution itself. Had the banks been able to maintain specie payments and aid the Treasury in greater measure, and had the banks and the people accepted the demand notes, the legal tender provision would have been unnecessary.

It will be observed that the act did not specify how or when the notes were payable, nor was any other provision, except the convertibility into bonds, made for their eventual retirement. The power to reissue them when received into the Treasury contemplated their continuous circulation until Congress directed otherwise. The faces of the notes bore the simple statement that "The United States will pay the bearer — dollars."

Congress passed additional tax laws, but these did not produce funds at once. An act of March 1, 1862, adopted Chase's recommendation that certificates of indebtedness, to run one year, at 6 per cent., be issued to public creditors who would receive them, and one of March 17, authorizing him to purchase coin with any securities authorized to be issued upon terms which appeared to him advantageous; increased the limit of temporary loan certificates to $50,000,000; and made the demand notes legal tender. It also permitted the issue of new for worn notes.

The effect of the act of February 25 upon the general status of the currency was at first not specially marked. The premium on coin, which had earlier in the month reached 4¾, was at the end of it only 2¼ per cent., and in March and April ranged from two and a fraction down to one. Demand notes, being receivable for customs, were approximately equal to coin. The new notes literally took the place of the coin in circulation and were rapidly absorbed, few being presented for conversion into the 6 per cent. bonds waiting for them at the Treasury. In May the premium on specie advanced beyond 4, and in June rose to 9¼. One hundred and forty-seven million dollars of both kinds of notes were in use, but did not return to the Treasury in sufficient volume to enable it to maintain payments. Chase accordingly asked in June for authority to issue an additional $150,000,000 of legal tender notes. Congress gave the required authority by the act of July 11, 1862, reserving, however, $50,000,000 of the notes for the redemption of temporary loan certificates, which the act permitted the Secretary to expand to a total of $100,000,000. Congress also adopted Chase's recommendation that $35,000,000 of the notes to be issued be in denominations less than five dollars.

The total disappearance of specie caused trouble in providing small change. The people had resorted to a variety of substitutes, including postage stamps, which suggested the authorization by the act of July 17, 1862, of an issue of stamps, and later of currency, for fractional parts of a dollar, at first in the form of postal stamps engraved on the notes, subsequently in other forms. This currency was made "receivable," at first for all dues, later for all except customs, in sums not over five dollars, and was exchangeable for legal tender notes in like sums. The amount was not limited by this act. The issue of tokens or currency under one dollar by others was strictly prohibited.

In his report for December, 1862, Chase estimated that he would have to borrow nearly $300,000,000 for the remainder of the fiscal year (to June 30, 1863) and $600,000,000 for the following year, unless the war happily came to an end. In the discussion of the manner of borrowing he treated the currency question at great length, pointing out that the state banks had increased their note-issues by $37,000,000, deposits by $80,000,000, and discounts by $70,000,000. He argued that this expansion, and not the issue of legal tender notes, had caused the exports of, and the premium on, coin (now 34 per cent.), since the government notes outstanding amounted to $210,000,000, only a trifle more than the coin in circulation in 1861, at the time of suspension. While admitting that the issue of more notes was an easy way for the government to pay the expenses, to do so to any material extent would prove calamitous, a "disastrous defeat of the very purposes sought to be obtained by it." A small addition to the volume might, however, not be unsafe. But he much preferred the adoption of the pending measure for a national bank currency, which would enable him to dispose of bonds, then not readily salable. He recommended taxing the state bank notes so as to limit and reduce the volume and permit United States notes to fill the need for increased currency until the national bank system should supply the demand. In this way he suggested that $50,000,000 more of legal tender notes might be useful within the year, and a like amount the following year.

President Lincoln in his message at this time (December, 1862) referred to the currency as follows:[1] —

[1] Messages of Presidents, Vol. VI.

"The suspension of specie payments by the banks, soon after the commencement of your last session, made large issues of United States notes unavoidable. In no other way could the payment of the troops, and the satisfaction of other just demands, be so economically or so well provided for. The judicious legislation of Congress, securing the receivability of these notes for loans and internal duties, and making them a legal tender for other debts, has made them a universal currency; and has satisfied, partially, at least, and for the time, the long-felt want of an uniform circulating medium, saving thereby to the people immense sums in discounts and exchanges.

"A return to specie payments, however, at the earliest period compatible with due regard to all interests concerned, should ever be kept in view. Fluctuations in the value of currency are always injurious, and to reduce these fluctuations to the lowest possible point will always be a leading purpose in wise legislation. Convertibility, prompt and certain convertibility into coin, is generally acknowledged to be the best and surest safeguard against them; and it is extremely doubtful whether a circulation of United States notes, payable in coin, and sufficiently large for the wants of the people, can be permanently, usefully, and safely maintained.

"Is there, then, any other mode in which the necessary provision for the public wants can be made, and the great advantages of a safe and uniform currency secured?

"I know of none which promises so certain results, and is, at the same time, so unobjectionable, as the organization of banking associations, under a general act of Congress, well guarded in its provisions. To such associations the government might furnish circulating notes, on the security of United States bonds deposited in the Treasury. These notes, prepared under the supervision of proper officers, being uniform in appearance and security, and convertible always into coin, would at once protect labor against the evils of a vicious currency, and facilitate commerce by cheap and safe exchanges.

"A moderate reservation from the interest on the bonds would compensate the United States for the preparation and distribution of the notes, and a general supervision of the system, and would lighten the burden of that part of the public debt employed as securities. The public credit, moreover, would be greatly improved, and the negotiation of new loans greatly facilitated by the steady market demand for government bonds which the adoption of the proposed system would create.

"It is an additional recommendation of the measure, of considerable weight, in my judgment, that it would reconcile, as far as possible, all existing interests, by the opportunity offered to existing institutions to reorganize under the act, substituting only the secured uniform national circulation for the local and various circulation, secured and unsecured, now issued by them."

The report on state banks for January 1, 1863 (the last published by the Treasury), showed that their circulation was nearly $239,000,000 and specie $101,000,000.

The army being unpaid and Chase being, as he stated, unable to sell bonds "at the market price," a joint resolution, authorizing the immediate issue of $100,000,000 of legal tender notes, was passed on the 17th of January, 1863. "Inability to sell bonds at the market price" meant that offering any large quantity would break the market price and force a lower quotation.

In approving this resolution Lincoln sent a message to Congress cautioning against further note-issues.

The act of March 3, 1863, authorized borrowing $300,000,000 for the current fiscal year (to June 30), and $600,000,000 for the next. As to the *forms* of the obligations, the Secretary was given wide discretion, as the circumstances required; first, bonds, payable in not less then ten nor more than forty years, the interest payable in coin, not to exceed 6 per cent., issuable in exchange for notes or other evidences of debt; second, notes payable in not exceeding three years, at interest not to exceed 6 per cent., in amount not to exceed $400,000,000; these notes might be made legal tender for their face, and be exchanged into the ordinary legal tender notes, for which purpose, *exclusively*, *another* $150,000,000 of the latter was provided (this last-mentioned authority was not, however, used by Chase); third, legal tender notes in amount $150,000,000 for ordinary purposes of the government; fourth, fractional currency to the limit of $50,000,000; fifth, the issue of gold certificates for coin and bullion, and to an amount equal to 20 per cent., in excess of the actual deposit of gold. The act also provided for a tax of 2 per cent. upon state bank notes and for a prohibitive tax of 10 per cent. upon fractional note-issues, and permitted sales of bonds *below* the market value, for which Chase asked.

But the most important feature, after the first section, was the proviso that after July 1, 1863, the legal tenders could no longer be exchanged for bonds, practically repudiating the pledge made in 1862, thus diminishing the value of the notes and conducing to their remaining in circulation when not needed for that purpose. This proviso, which had also been asked for by Chase to aid in disposing of bonds, was regarded by the majority in Congress as in the nature of a limitation, and not a breach of the contract. Shortly before adjourning Congress passed the national currency act, for which Chase had striven so assiduously in his attempt to give the country a safe and uniform paper medium. (This is fully discussed in another chapter.)

The premium on coin had advanced to 60 in January and to 72½ in February; in March it receded, falling as low as 39. The Treasury was, however, still unable to float bonds in sufficient volume, and was compelled to use its note-issuing powers. By end of June $90,000,000 more of the new legal tenders had been put out, making a total of over $367,000,000 in circulation on that date.

Before presenting his annual report to Congress in December, 1863, Chase had begun the issue of one and two year interest-bearing notes, and under his discretionary power he made them legal tenders. In his report he showed that the tax laws produced much less than had been expected, and estimated an increase of the debt to June 30, 1864 (over the same date in 1863), of nearly $685,000,000, and for the following year $545,000,000. He entertained the hope, however, that internal revenue receipts would thenceforward increase and the war expenses diminish. Discussing the currency, he recommended that no further legal tender note-issues be made, as the increase beyond the $400,000,000 authorized (besides $50,000,000 for reserves) would certainly cause great depreciation. The country could not absorb more. He expected good results from the national banking law, under which bonds would be taken and a sound note-issue take the place of the state bank currency.

Congress authorized further issues of bonds, the prepayment of interest on the debt for a period of one year if the Secretary deemed it wise, and by the act of June 30, 1864, authorized the further issue of interest-bearing notes to run not more than three years, at interest not to exceed 7.30 per cent. These notes might be made legal tender for their face value, but were not to be in denominations under $10. The act also gave the Secretary authority to exchange notes of all kinds provided the limits fixed by law were not exceeded, and definitely provided that the issue of non-interest-bearing legal tender notes, which had become distinguished from other Treasury notes by the title "United States Notes" (and colloquially by the term "greenbacks"), should never exceed $400,000,000, besides $50,000,000 to be used as a reserve for the temporary loan certificates. The limit of issue of these last-named obligations was extended to $150,000,000, the limit of interest raised to 6 per cent., and the newly created national bank notes were made receivable for such loans. The same act provided that the interest-bearing notes authorized were not to be legal tender for redemption of notes of banks. The national bank act was on June 3, 1864, amended in very important particulars.

The sales of bonds were for a time quite active, but Chase's attempt to float 5 per cents proved abortive, and such were the demands upon the Treasury for war expenses that he found it necessary to increase the issue of the one and two year 5 per cent. notes already referred to, to $211,000,000, and begin the issue of three year notes just authorized, making them 6 per cent. compound interest, instead of 7.30 per cent. They were also made legal tenders for their face value. Such extreme use of the legal tender power shows to what extent the credit of the government under such enormous borrowing had become impaired. By

June 30, 1864, there were in round numbers about $650,000,000 of legal tender notes of all kinds in existence. The interest-bearing varieties were not all in active circulation, but were used in reserves of banks, thus performing some of the money functions.

From December, 1863, the premium on gold rose steadily until it reached 86 in May. In order to check speculation Congress authorized the Secretary to sell coin accumulated in the Treasury beyond its needs; and on June 17, 1864, passed an act forbidding all sales of gold and foreign exchange on "time" contracts, and prohibited brokers from selling gold anywhere except at their offices, thereby hoping to break up the "gold exchange." This resulted in a rise in the premium to 185. The act was repealed on July 6, 1864. This short period sufficed to convince Congress of the futility of attempting to regulate the premium upon gold by legislation. On the first of July it became known that Chase had resigned, and the gold premium fluctuated between 122 and 150. Fessenden, who as Chairman of the Senate Finance Committee was fully conversant with all fiscal measures, became his successor.

Fessenden, adhering to Chase's policy in general, continued the issue of compound interest notes, with which he retired the short term 5 per cent. notes and issued in addition some $55,000,000 more than was necessary for such retirement (the total issue having been $266,000,000). Experiencing difficulty in placing bonds, he also made use of 7.30 notes, but without the legal tender power, to which, as has been shown, he seriously objected.

The expansion of the currency occasioned by the continued use of United States notes was at this time increased by national bank issues, which began to appear in considerable volume. On the other hand, the expansion was modified considerably by the very rapid disappearance of state bank circulation. Fessenden estimated that in November, 1864, the amount of the latter was $126,000,000. National bank notes at the time amounted to

$65,000,000, the legal tender issues of all classes to $675,000,000, thus giving an aggregate of $866,000,000.[1] The gold premium fluctuated quite violently, ranging in March, 1865, between $48\frac{1}{3}$ and 101, but diminishing after July.

In the act of March 3, 1865, complying with Fessenden's recommendations, $600,000,000 were provided for in bonds or Treasury notes convertible into bonds, interest on the former not to exceed 6 per cent., on the latter 7.30 per cent., and none were to be made legal tenders. Practically all the remaining needs of the government growing out of the war were supplied by means of this new issue of 7.30's (of 1864–65) of which approximately $830,000,000 were used. The interest as well as the principal was made payable in currency, and they were known as currency bonds. In the revenue act of March 3, 1865, Congress laid such a tax upon state bank notes (10 per cent.) as to practically prohibit their use, and they gradually disappeared.

The provisions of the national bank act of June 3, 1864, constrained the banks to become large owners of legal tender notes as well as of United States bonds. The banks were required to provide for the redemption of their notes in "lawful money," and to maintain reserves of such money for this purpose as well as against deposits. Many of these legal tender notes bore interest and hence were a profitable form of reserve. The non-interest-bearing ones were needed for current use. These wants necessarily employed a substantial amount of the several forms of legal tender notes. The act also provided that national banks might be designated as depositories of public money, upon giving security to the satisfaction of the Secretary in "government bonds and otherwise."

Before the close of the fiscal year 1865 (in April), the war ceased and the restoration of the finances to a peace basis could be considered. Fessenden returned to the Senate and was succeeded (March 4) by Hugh McCulloch, whose long experience

[1] Finance Report, 1864.

with the state bank of Indiana and as the first Comptroller of the Currency under the national banking law peculiarly fitted him for the great work.

A brief review and correlation of the portentous events crowded into this short space of four years is requisite. Chase was the guiding spirit of the fiscal affairs of the Nation. Never before or since had a finance minister wielded such power as was placed in his hands. In reviewing the manner in which the power was used due consideration must be given to the unprecedented conditions with which he had to contend. Without experience as a financier, he was required to provide for the expense of a gigantic war rendered extravagantly costly by inexperience, want of preparation, and failure to even approximately foresee its magnitude and duration. The cost averaged over $2,000,000 a day for the entire period, and at its maximum called for a daily expenditure of nearly $3,000,000. He was confronted with a Treasury without funds, a shattered public credit, an insufficient revenue, and a heterogeneous state bank currency of fluctuating and uncertain value. He adopted at the outset a policy of providing a homogeneous circulating medium which would be safe alike for government and individual, and of issuing notes fundable into interest-bearing bonds. Believing that the volume of specie in the country, under the influence of adverse foreign trade balances and other demands, was totally inadequate to maintain coin payments for the enormous volume of transactions which would become necessary, unless an auxiliary were provided, he preferred risking the danger involved in the issue of the demand notes of the government rather than that certain to follow from the acceptance of state bank notes.

While Chase's distrust of state banks was extreme, and he was too rigid in his requirements in connection with the execution of the law authorizing him to deposit public moneys with them (a course which contributed materially to force suspension of coin payments), it is nevertheless true that the banks as a whole were unable to finance the extraordinary needs of the government, and it would have been unwise to rely upon them. The people were not prepared to absorb the enormous loans which the government had to make, and the banks could not invest all their funds in such loans. No loans could be placed abroad. The issue of United States notes, to circulate as money, under the circumstances seems to have been unavoidable and hence justifiable. It has been fully shown that both Lincoln and Chase, as well as Congress, believed it imperatively necessary a little later to give these notes legal tender power. Viewed in retrospection it seems to have been quite unnecessary. It is by no means fair, however, to judge the acts of men, who could only conjecture the future, by the standard of events as they afterwards transpired. The country was rudely awakened from a long period of profound peace. It was quite accustomed to the issue of "state sovereignty" and "popular sovereignty." Nullification by South Carolina in Jackson's time was recalled. The "Missouri Compromise," the Kansas-Nebraska controversy, and other important incidents had familiarized the North with the contention of the slave states. The North did not realize that the South was determined to put the issue to the exhaustive test of final arbitrament by the sword. The best evidence of this is Lincoln's first proclamation calling for troops. Seventy-five thousand was the number asked for, and ninety days the period of enlistment.

Nations, like individuals, should live within their income, and current taxes should always equal current expenses, including, of course, interest on any indebtedness. According to principles laid down by publicists and economists, extraordinary expenses, as in case of war, should be met by a judicious apportionment of increased taxation and loans. It is deemed just that a portion of extraordinary expenditure, whether incurred in war or for public utility or permanent improvement, be devolved upon the succeeding generation, which is profited thereby, by means of loans payable at a future date. Had Chase applied this principle in his demands from Congress in July, 1861, it would have stood him in good stead. Congress, beyond question, would have complied, and much embarrassment on account of loans and full tender notes would have been avoided. In saying this I do not forget that Lincoln's administration felt the necessity of winning victories at the polls as well as in the field, and cherished a wholesome and proper dread of the effect upon the public of largely increased taxation.

The one fixed purpose of Secretary Chase was to supplant the onerous, costly, and insecure state bank circulation by a safe, efficient national bank circulation secured by government bonds and further protected by a lawful money reserve against both circulation and deposits. In this way he expected to find a large demand and permanent use for both bonds and legal tender notes. Had Congress promptly created the national banking system instead of waiting until 1863, the Secretary's hopes would undoubtedly have been largely realized, and the volume of legal notes issued would have been very much less. The power of the state banks was enormous, and they looked upon the idea of conversion into national banks under the proposed law with conservative fear. The treatment of the two United States banks at the hands of Congress was not at all reassuring. It is not surprising, however regrettable, that their influence should have so long defeated the national system and left the Secretary to meet his responsibilities by means of Treasury note-issues.

It would seem that a suspension of coin payments was inevitable, even had it not been precipitated by the events heretofore recounted. The great expansion of trade, caused primarily by the enormous government purchases, required a larger volume of money. Without credit for its securities abroad and with an adverse foreign trade balance, the country could not retain its specie, much less draw from abroad. Expansion of paper currency under either state or national authority was sure to follow. Had Chase adhered to state banks the reserves would have proved inadequate to maintain coin payments, and the country would have been flooded, as before, with an irredeemable currency varying in value from good to worthless. United States notes and national bank notes would at least be uniform and ultimately redeemed, and the advantages of such circulation, instead of swelling private profits, would inure to the benefit of the government and be applied to the saving of the Union. Chase could not but choose the latter. Fully appreciating the danger of a redundant issue of government notes, he endeavored to limit the volume, but conditions forced him to issue more and more, in the face of depreciation. He did so, doubting their legality, and hoping and believing that the national bank circulation when created would take their place and admit of their retirement. In a formal communication to Congress he later condemned his own policy in issuing so many notes in lieu of imposing greater taxation. As Chief Justice he pronounced the legal tender notes he had issued unconstitutional — a most unique commentary upon his own administration, and one that is surely without parallel.

The chain of causes and effects may be recapitulated as follows: Utter failure to foresee the probable length and magnitude of the war, hence failure to provide largely increased taxation, always unpalatable to short-sighted legislators; first, resort to note-issues rendered necessary by the absence of a reputable currency system and of credit abroad through which specie could be drawn; the vain desire not to sell bonds at a discount, and consequent inability to sell them as rapidly as needs arose; wretched military administration and waste in innumerable ways; suspension of coin payments precipitated by unwise management and foreign complications; forced legal tender currency loans and expansion of prices, checking commodity exports and increasing expenses; heavy exports of specie naturally following; more legal tender currency, with further rise in prices and increase in expenses; repudiation of right to fund legal tender notes into bonds; wild speculation in specie which extended into all lines of business, enriching the shrewd few at the expense of the many. Net result, — ultimate cost to the people very much more than it would have been had they been taxed more heavily at the outset.

As Franklin had pointed out in the days of continental currency, the people actually paid exorbitant sums *indirectly* because they did not pay the lesser amounts *directly*. It has been said that the "greenbacks" saved the Union. Be this as it may, it is certain that had a great national bank or a system of national banks existed, and had a proper scheme of taxation been adopted, the same result would have been accomplished at far less cost; and while suspension of coin payments would probably have been inevitable, the premium upon gold would have been controllable and prices kept within limits.[1]

STATISTICAL RÉSUMÉ

National Finances (in millions of dollars)

(The government fiscal year ends June 30.)

Fiscal Year	Revenue			Expenses			Deficit	Debt	
	Customs	Other	Total	Ordinary	Interest	Total		Outstanding	Increase
1861	40	2	42	63	4	67	25	91	26
1862	49	3	52	456	13	469	417	524	433
1863	69	43	112	694	25	719	607	1120	596
1864	102	141	243	811	54	865	622	1816	696
1865	85	237	322	1218	77	1295	973	2681	865

[1] See Mitchell, Sound Currency, Vol. IV., No. 8.

CIRCULATION (in millions, except last column)

FISCAL YEAR	SPECIE	U. S. NOTES	BANK NOTES		FRACTIONAL CURRENCY	TOTAL	IN TREASURY	IN CIRCULATION	POPULATION	PER CAPITA
			State	National						
1861	250	——	202	——	—	452	4	448	32	$14.00
1862	25	150	184	——	—	359	24	335	25	13.40
1863	25	391	239	——	20	675	79	596	26	22.66
1864	25	447	179	31	23	705	36	670	27	24.81
1865	25	431	143	146	25	770	55	715	30	23.83

Specie includes after 1861 only the amount estimated in use on the Pacific Slope. Population reduced by that of states in rebellion.

EXPORTS AND IMPORTS (in millions of dollars)

FISCAL YEAR	MERCHANDISE		EXCESS	SPECIE		EXCESS
	Exports	Imports	+ Imports − Exports	Exports	Imports	+ Imports − Exports
1861 . . .	220	289	+ 69	30	46	+ 16
1862 . . .	191	189	− 2	37	16	− 21
1863 . . .	204	243	+ 39	64	10	− 54
1864 . . .	159	316	+ 157	105	13	− 92
1865 . . .	166	239	+ 73	68	10	− 58

THE GOLD PREMIUM AND PRICES

(See Sound Currency, Vol. III., No. 17.)

CALENDAR YEAR	PREMIUM ON GOLD			GOLD VALUE OF PAPER			GOLD PRICES U.S.	WAGES IN GOLD	PURCHASING POWER OF WAGES	COST OF GOLD IN LABOR
	High	Low	Average	High	Low	Average				
1860	——	——	——	——	——	100	100.0	100.0	1.000	1.000
1861	——	——	——	——	——	100	94.1	100.7	1.050	.993
1862	34.0	1.1	13.3	98.5	75.6	88.3	101.6	101.2	1.009	.988
1863	72.5	22.1	45.2	79.5	62.3	68.9	91.1	81.9	9.73	1.221
1864	185.0	51.5	103.3	64.3	38.7	49.2	110.7	66.6	9.00	1.500
1865	134.4	28.5	57.3	73.7	46.3	63.6	107.4	94.5	7.80	1.057

CHAPTER XII

Legal Tender Notes

1866–1875

The expenses of the government did not become normal until some years after the close of the war. A great army had to be disbanded and many obligations remained to be paid. McCulloch reported (December, 1865) that the debt had increased during the fiscal year nearly $942,000,000; he estimated a deficit in the revenue for 1866 of $112,000,000, but a surplus in 1867 of almost the same amount. The total debt at its maximum, in August, 1865, stood at $2,845,900,000. It was expected that it would reach $3,000,000,000, but by this time the revenues increased and expenditures diminished. The fiscal year 1866 showed $290,000,000 surplus instead of the $112,000,000 deficit as estimated. Provision had been made for funding the floating debt, and this process, as well as the reduction, began in the fall of 1866. The debt in August, 1865, was composed of

Bonds	$1,109,600,000
Interest-bearing legal tenders	250,900,000
Non-interest-bearing legal tenders	433,200,000
7.30's	830,000,000
Temporary debt and other forms	222,200,000
The annual interest charge was in excess of	150,000,000

McCulloch directed special attention to the currency portion of the debt, urging preparation for resumption of specie payments and ultimate repeal of legal tender acts. The United States notes, popularly called "greenbacks,"[1] were a convenient form of money and a non-interest-bearing loan, hence their retention was urged on the double ground of convenience and economy. To these the Secretary opposed, first, the extra-constitutional exercise of power warranted only by war; second, the breach of faith involved in failure to redeem; third, the evil effects which would follow the continuance of the inflated currency. He recommended that the legal tender power of the interest-bearing notes be discontinued after maturity, and that he be authorized to sell bonds to retire these as well as the non-interest-bearing notes (greenbacks). He warned Congress against a continuance of the policy of an inconvertible currency, predicting that, unless remedied, the question would become a political one, and few less disturbing to the welfare of the country could be imagined.

McCulloch estimated the amount of currency on October 31, 1865, at $704,000,000, not including $205,000,000 of interest-bearing legal tenders (nor the 7.30's); of the interest-bearing notes about $30,000,000 and some of the smaller 7.30's were circulating as money. The bank-notes included in the above total he placed at $250,000,000, of which $65,000,000 were state bank-notes, the remainder national bank issues; of the latter class $115,000,000 might still be issued within the legal limit, some of which would, however, replace the state bank issues. The premium on coin which in the early months of the year stood at over 100 (reaching 133¾), fell as low as 28⅝, closing in December at 45½.

President Johnson supported the recommendations of McCulloch in his message. He said: —

[1] The word "greenback," applied to the first legal tender notes issued by the government in 1862 because of the prevailing color of the back of the notes, is generally used as a comprehensive term including all legal tender notes issued prior to the law of 1890. It is used interchangeably with the term "United States notes" but colloquially is much more popular.

"It is our first duty to prepare in earnest for our recovery from the ever-increasing evils of an irredeemable currency, without a sudden revulsion and yet without untimely procrastination." [1]

A considerable number of public men were inclined to regard the war debt as only partially obligatory upon the Nation, owing to the fact that depreciated currency had been received for the greater part of it, and urged that payment in coin commanding a high premium ought not to be insisted upon. They doubtless had in mind the fact that Congress redeemed the "continental currency" at a discount of 100 to 1.

This led to the adoption, on motion of Representative Randall (Dem., Pa.), afterwards Speaker, of the following declaratory resolution in the House on December 5, 1865, with but one dissenting vote: —

"RESOLVED, That, as the sense of this House, the public debt created during the late rebellion was contracted upon the faith and honor of the Nation; that it is sacred and inviolate and must and ought to be paid, principal and interest; that any attempt to repudiate or in any manner to impair or scale the said debt shall be universally discountenanced, and promptly rejected by Congress if proposed."

McCulloch had actually begun the retirement of greenbacks out of the surplus revenues. The House of Representatives on December 18, 1865, indorsed his policy by almost unanimous vote, and the act of April 12, 1866, authorized him to fund all notes into bonds or sell bonds to retire notes, provided the total debt was not increased. The act contained the limitation that not more than $10,000,000 of the "greenbacks" be retired in the ensuing six months, and $4,000,000 monthly thereafter. Other acts provided for nickel coins of three and five cents to retire those denominations of the fractional paper currency.

This salutary legislation was not secured without opposition from those who might have been expected to favor it. Stevens,

[1] Messages of Presidents, Vol. VI.

who had proclaimed in 1862 that the "greenbacks" were only a temporary expedient, was content to continue them as a debt not bearing interest. Boutwell (afterwards Secretary) appeared to believe that Congress should not interfere with events which would bring about resumption of coin payments automatically. Senator Sherman (also later Secretary) believed that if the Treasury simply met current obligations, no power could delay resumption beyond a year and a half.

The authority conferred by the act of March 3, 1863, to issue gold certificates was first made use of by McCulloch on November 13, 1865. The act of July 13, 1866, amended the act imposing a tax of 10 per cent. on state bank circulation, making it apply to individuals as well as to banks. This effectually prohibited their further use. The premium on coin fluctuated during the calendar year 1866 between 67¾ and 25½ per cent., averaging 40$\frac{9}{10}$, making the average value of the notes about 71 per cent.

In his report for 1866 McCulloch showed that he had reduced the debt from August, 1865, $164,000,000, and had a larger cash balance by $42,000,000. The funding had progressed satisfactorily. Nearly $100,000,000 of the interest-bearing legal tenders were out of the way, and "greenbacks" had been reduced by nearly $43,000,000, standing at $390,195,785. The financial operations were no doubt greatly facilitated by the increased investment of foreigners in our securities, thus enabling the country to retain a substantial part of its gold product. McCulloch estimated in 1866 that $600,000,000 of such securities ($350,000,000 in United States bonds) were held abroad. The amount of specie in the country, estimated at $66,000,000 in 1865, was in 1867 given as $139,000,000.

Criticised for holding so large a balance in the Treasury which might have been used in great measure to save interest, he pointed out the necessity for keeping the Treasury strong in order to maintain the stability of the irredeemable currency, regarding this end much more important to the people than saving some interest. His purpose was to hold a reserve against these issues precisely as a bank would, selling gold when in his judgment advisable to reduce the premium, to limit depreciation of the notes. To correct the evils which would unquestionably enrich the few at the expense of the many, he recommended contraction, tariff revision, and refunding the debt; and also an amendment of the national banking law to compel banks to redeem their notes at the Atlantic cities as well as at their counters.

The act of March 2, 1867, authorized 3 per cent. temporary loan certificates to take up a part of the 6 per cent. compound interest legal tender notes, thus substituting a form of obligation not legal tender. The certificates were, however, made available for bank reserves, and thus served as a substitute for "lawful money." The issue was limited to $50,000,000.

A very substantial sentiment had by 1867 manifested itself against the retirement of legal tender notes, against the national banks, and favorable to paying the public debt in greenbacks. The word "contraction" was made to appear to the masses as signifying a monstrous power which would not unlikely rob them of their daily bread. The greenbacks outstanding had been reduced to $356,000,000, and the average gold premium in 1867 was 38.2 per cent.

President Johnson's message for 1867 showed that he had not escaped the political influence of the day. He favored measures looking to resumption of coin payments, but, he added, a "reduction of our paper circulating medium need not necessarily follow." He declared it was unjust to pay bondholders in coin and other creditors in depreciated paper. He was endeavoring to obtain the support of the "greenback" element for a renomination. A wave of economic heresy had struck the people, especially in the West. Crop failures, high prices, speculation, and resulting business troubles gave strength and numbers to the movement. The greenbacks were regarded as the means of curing the evils which in fact they caused. The Democratic party, which had opposed the legal tender acts as unconstitutional, now became their especial advocate. Pendleton, who in 1862 vigorously denounced the first act, now aiming for the presidency in 1868, led the movement in favor of perpetuating the greenbacks.

Many of the Republican leaders, anticipating defeat unless their sentiments were modified, yielded to the storm. Senator Sherman, who had predicted resumption before 1868, and who had expressed the opinion that the paper currency was not redundant at a time when the premium on coin was nearly 50 per cent., now believed it proper to pay the bonds in greenbacks, and in deference to public opinion proposed to stop contraction. Senator Morton, of Indiana, favored more note-issues. Thus a Republican Congress, which had in December, 1865, "pledged coöperative action" toward resumption by retirement of the notes, and early in 1866 had passed a law authorizing contraction, in February, 1868, passed an act suspending the authority and prohibiting further reduction of the currency by retiring notes. President Johnson, then at odds with Congress, and uncertain as to the best policy, did not approve the act, nor did he veto it, but allowed it to become law without his approval.

The act of June 25, 1868, authorized the increase of 3 per cent. certificates to the amount of $75,000,000 to retire the remaining compound interest notes. A bill passed both houses of Congress on July 27, 1868, providing for refunding the debt at lower interest rates, but Johnson failed to approve the measure, and it lapsed by the adjournment of Congress.

The national conventions of 1868 adopted the following platform resolutions respecting the debt and the currency question: —

Republican Platform, at Chicago, May.

"We denounce all forms of repudiation as a national crime, and the national honor requires the payment of the public indebtedness in the utmost good faith to all creditors at home and abroad, not only according to the letter, but the spirit of the laws under which it was contracted. The national debt, contracted as it has been for the preservation of the Union for all time to come, should be extended over a fair period for redemption. It is the duty of Congress to reduce the rate of interest thereon whenever it can honestly be done.

"That the best policy to diminish our burden of debt is to so improve our credit that capitalists will seek to loan us money at lower rates of interest than we now pay, and must continue to pay so long as repudiation, partial or total, open or covert, is threatened or suspected."

Democratic, at New York, July.

"Payment of the public debt of the United States as rapidly as practicable; all moneys drawn from the people by taxation, except so much as is requisite for the necessities of the Government, economically administered, being honestly applied to such payment, and where the obligations of the Government do not expressly state upon their face, or the law under which they were issued does not provide that they shall be paid in coin, they ought in right and in justice, to be paid in the lawful money of the United States.

"Equal taxation of every species of property according to its real value, including Government bonds and other public securities.

"One currency for the Government and the people, the laborer and the office-holder, the pensioner and the soldier, the producer and the bondholder."

The sound element in the Republican party having thus been able to stem within its ranks the tide of repudiation, and having nominated Grant, whose popularity as a hero of the war unquestionably assisted them materially, the greenback movement received a check at the polls.

Although discouraged by the reactionary legislation of Congress, McCulloch nevertheless continued, in his report in December, 1868, to urge upon that body the need of bringing the currency to a coin basis.

He estimated the amount of American bonds held abroad at $850,000,000, of which $600,000,000 were in "governments."

In his message of December, 1868, Johnson repeated his views on the currency of the previous year, and came out more broadly in favor of "scaling" the public debt, which brought forth the following resolution in the Senate: —

"RESOLVED, That the Senate, properly cherishing and upholding the good faith and honor of the nation, do hereby utterly disapprove of and condemn the sentiments and propositions contained in so much of the late annual message of the President of the United States as reads as follows:

"'It may be assumed that the holders of our securities have already received upon their bonds a larger amount than their original investment, measured by a gold standard. Upon this statement of facts, it would seem but just and equitable that the six per cent. interest now paid by the Government should be applied to the reduction of the principal in semi-annual instalments, which in sixteen years and eight months would liquidate the entire national debt. Six per cent. in gold would at present rates be equal to nine per cent. in currency, and equivalent to the payment of the debt one and a half times in a fraction less than seventeen years. This, in connection with all the other advantages derived from their investment, would afford to the public creditors a fair and liberal compensation for the use of their capital, and with this they should be satisfied. The lessons of the past admonish the lender that it is not well to be over anxious in exacting from the borrower rigid compliance with the letter of the bond.'"

The hard fight that the friends of sound money had to make can well be imagined when the President, the official representative of the nation, in his message to Congress, urged such repudiation.

The Senate resolution was passed by a strict party vote of 43 to 6; and in the House a similar resolution was passed by 155 to 6; not voting 60.

Subsequently a section in the fourteenth amendment to the Constitution settled the question in the following terms: —

"The validity of the public debt of the United States, authorized by law, including debts incurred for payment of pensions and bounties for services in suppressing insurrection or rebellion, shall not be questioned. But neither the United States nor any State shall assume or pay any debt or obligation incurred in aid of insurrection or rebellion against the United States, or any claim for the loss or emancipation of any slave; but all such debts, obligations, and claims shall be illegal and void."

On February 19, 1869, Congress passed an act prohibiting national banks making loans on collaterals of United States notes or national bank-notes, a practice which might obviously be used to cause a considerable contraction of the currency.

A bill was also passed on March 3, 1869, to strengthen the public credit by a declaration of the purpose of the government to pay bonds in coin, and legalizing coin contracts, as recommended by McCulloch; but Johnson refused to approve it, and Congress having adjourned the same day, it failed to become law.

In his inaugural address, on March 4, 1869, President Grant said: —

> "A great debt has been contracted in securing to us and our posterity the Union. The payment of this, principal and interest, as well as the return to a specie basis, as soon as it can be accomplished without material detriment to the debtor class or to the country at large, must be provided for. To protect the national honor every dollar of government indebtedness should be paid in gold, unless otherwise expressly stipulated in the contract. Let it be understood that no repudiator of one farthing of our public debt will be trusted in public place, and it will go far toward strengthening a credit which ought to be the best in the world, and will ultimately enable us to replace the debt with bonds bearing less interest than we now pay."

George S. Boutwell succeeded McCulloch as Secretary of the Treasury in March.

Congress was called in extra session by Grant at once, and on the 18th of March the act to strengthen the public credit, already referred to, became law, but without the coin contract clause. It declared the purpose of the United States to pay its notes and bonds in coin or the equivalent, solemnly pledging the faith of the nation to such payment, and "to make provision at the earliest practical period for redemption of United States notes in coin"; another declaration was that no bonds would be paid before maturity unless greenbacks were convertible into coin at the option of the holder or unless at such time bonds bearing a lower rate of interest could be sold for par in coin.

The coin contract clause was stricken out by a vote of 82 to 56 in the House and 28 to 15 in the Senate; the bill passed by 97 to 47, and 42 to 13 respectively.

It should be borne in mind with reference to the word "coin" as used in the several statutes that the silver dollar was at this time worth in the market about 4 per cent. more than the gold dollar.

This declaration no doubt served its purpose but, as will be seen, it was not acted upon, so far as notes were concerned, for nearly six years, and not actually made effective until nearly ten years thereafter. Bonds were in fact almost immediately "paid before maturity," although the sale of lower rate bonds at par for coin did not begin until 1871. The volume of greenbacks remained practically undisturbed at $356,000,000 for nearly five years, and then the amount was not reduced but *increased.* This was the interpretation given the declaration "earliest practical period" to which the faith of the nation was pledged.

The Democratic state platforms still opposed the policy above outlined; that of the Ohio convention of July 7, 1869, contained the following: —

"RESOLVED, That exemption from tax of over $2,500,000,000 Government bonds and securities is unjust to the people, and ought not to be tolerated, and that we are opposed to any appropriation for the payment of the interest on the public bonds until they are made subject to taxation.

"That the claim of the bondholders that the bonds which were bought with greenbacks, and the principal of which is by law payable in currency, should, nevertheless, be paid in gold, is unjust and extortionate, and if persisted in will force upon the people the question of repudiation.

"That we denounce the national banking system as one of the worst outgrowths of the bonded debt, which unnecessarily increases the burden of the people $30,000,000 annually, and that we demand its immediate repeal."

That of Iowa, a week later, contained the following: —

> "That we favor a reform in the national banking system looking to an ultimate abolishment of that pernicious plan for the aggrandizement of a few at the expense of the many."

It soon became obvious that the plan of the new administration differed from that of McCulloch although officially announcing the same end in view, resumption. For while both Grant and Boutwell urged consideration of the subject and early legislation (but with due regard for the "debtor class"), the policy carried out in the absence of legislation was to reduce the debt, under the sinking fund law of 1862, thus raising the national credit, and cause a change in the trade conditions which would bring specie into the country, or at least enable the country to hold part of its own product. In this manner it was expected that coin and paper would come to a parity. The result was apparently favorable, as the net exports of specie fell off more than 50 per cent. The country's stock of coin was increased, and although the maximum premium for coin was higher than in the previous year, reaching 62½ per cent., the minimum was much lower, 19½, and the average for the year was only 33 against 39$\frac{7}{10}$ the year before. The average value of greenbacks in coin thus rose to 75.2 per cent. Boutwell redeemed over $75,000,000 of bonds in nine months, paying for them in coin, retiring them at a little over 88 per cent.

President Grant in his message, December, 1869, said:—

> "Among the evils growing out of the rebellion and not yet referred to, is that of an irredeemable currency. It is an evil which I hope will receive your most earnest attention. It is a duty, and one of the highest duties, of government to secure to the citizen a medium of exchange of fixed, unvarying value. This implies a return to a specie basis, and no substitute for it can be devised. It should be commenced now, and reached at the earliest practical moment consistent with a fair regard to the interests of the debtor class. Immediate resumption, if practicable, would not be desirable. It would compel the debtor class to pay, beyond their contracts, the premium on gold at the date of their purchase, and would bring bank-

ruptcy and ruin to thousands. Fluctuation, however, in the paper value of the measure of all values (gold) is detrimental to the interests of trade. It makes the man of business an involuntary gambler, for, in all sales where future payment is to be made, both parties speculate as to what will be the value of the currency to be paid and received. I earnestly recommend to you, then, such legislation as will assure a gradual return to specie payments, and put an immediate stop to fluctuations in the value of currency.

"The methods to secure the former of these results are as numerous as are the speculators on political economy. To secure the latter I see but one way, and that is, to authorize the Treasury to redeem its own paper, at a fixed price, whenever presented, and to withhold from circulation all currency so redeemed until sold again for gold."

The legal tender notes were treated as if they had "come to stay," their ultimate retirement *in toto* was no longer considered, and the newly given pledge of Congress to make the notes convertible into coin before paying off bonds not due and payable was not referred to.

One circumstance remains to be noted. Although the act of 1866 provided that greenbacks were to be retired and cancelled and there had been destroyed some $77,000,000, reducing the volume to $356,000,000, it was urged that since the maximum issue authorized by the act of June 30, 1864, had been fixed at $400,000,000, and the act not repealed, the difference between that sum and the existing amount, viz. $44,000,000, was a "reserve" available to the Treasury. Under this supposed authority Boutwell had issued in 1869 $1,500,000 of notes from the "reserve," but had retired them again soon thereafter. This remarkable construction of the status of cancelled and retired notes subsequently led to actions which for a time threatened serious results.

Speculation in gold was very active during the year, at one time in midsummer reaching unprecedented proportions. Unscrupulous speculators, believing that the Treasury policy of not selling its specie would render such an operation easy, undertook to "corner" gold, causing serious disaster to those compelled to use it; but the Treasury did sell gold in time to avert a general panic. Congress ordered an investigation, which disclosed a thoroughgoing conspiracy in which several persons supposed to be close to the administration were implicated.

Congress on July 14, 1870, authorized the refunding of the 6 per cent. bonds into 5, 4½, and 4 per cents. Amendments for funding the greenbacks into bonds and for retiring them before unmatured bonds were paid, were defeated, and also one to scale the debt. On February 14, 1870, the House of Representatives voted that the business interests of the country required "an increase in the volume of circulating currency," and favored a bill "increasing the currency" to the amount of at least $50,000,000; and on March 21 that the interest-bearing debt "should not be increased by causing a surrender of any part of our present circulating medium not bearing interest, and the substitution therefor of interest-bearing bonds."

In the Senate on February 24, 1870, the following was agreed to:—

> "Resolved, That to add to the present irredeemable paper currency of the country would be to render more difficult and remote the resumption of specie payments, to encourage and foster the spirit of speculation, to aggravate the evils produced by frequent and sudden fluctuations of values, to depreciate the credit of the nation, and to check the healthful tendency of legitimate business to settle down upon a safe and permanent basis, and therefore, in the opinion of the Senate, the existing volume of such currency ought not to be increased."

But no further action was taken.

On July 12, 1870, an act was passed to retire the 3 per cent. certificates and issue $54,000,000 additional national bank-notes, an amendment to retire greenbacks as bank-notes were increased being voted down.

While this measure was under discussion the anticipated decision of the Supreme Court that the legal tender acts as applied to preëxisting contracts were unconstitutional, was published.

No effort was made by Congress or the administration to conform to this decision; on the contrary, steps were taken to secure its reversal.

In order to enable banks to have a form of money in large denominations, available as reserves and convenient in paying large sums, Congress, June 8, 1872, authorized the issue of certificates, bearing no interest, for deposits of greenbacks, in denominations of $5,000 and $10,000. These were issued only to national banks, were payable to order, were counted as reserve, and intended to be used in settling balances at clearing-houses.

The currency question played a subordinate part in the presidential contest of 1872 (Grant-Greeley). The platforms of the two parties were practically identical. That of the Republicans contained the following: —

> "We denounce repudiation of the public debt, in any form or disguise, as a national crime. We witness with pride the reduction of the principal of the debt, and of the rates of interest upon the balance, and confidently expect that our excellent national currency will be perfected by a speedy resumption of specie payment."

The Democratic-Liberal-Republican platform contained the following: —

> "The public credit must be sacredly maintained, and we denounce repudiation in every form and guise. A speedy return to specie payment is demanded alike by the highest considerations of commercial morality and honest government."

By 1872 there had been a large increase in national bank-notes, and a slight increase in the average gold premium, due to the inflation, had appeared. Boutwell held that Congress and the country were opposed to contraction, so that the only alternative to bring about resumption was to await the increased need for circulation by the natural growth of population and business. Both Grant and his Secretary occupied an "opportunist" attitude toward the currency during his first term, in strong contrast to the vigorous sound money attitude of McCulloch.

The second decision of the Supreme Court (reversing the former decision), published early in the year, had declared the legal tender notes constitutional. The Court, however, seemed to base its approval of the act upon the necessities growing out of the war. It left a doubt as to whether they could be issued in time of peace and in the absence of some crucial necessity.

Boutwell had again in 1872 issued a small amount of his so-called "reserve" of greenbacks. This led to an examination of the question by the Finance Committee of the Senate early in 1873. Boutwell justified the issue, but Sherman, speaking for the committee, disagreed with him, stating that greenbacks once "retired and cancelled," as provided by the act of 1866, could no more be reissued than the bonds and interest-bearing notes retired and cancelled under the same law. No legislation in relation to the matter resulted.

On February 12, 1873, the act revising the coinage laws, which eliminated the silver dollar and made the gold dollar the unit of value, was passed. This is fully discussed in another chapter.

Sherman in vain endeavored during the winter of 1872–1873 to obtain consideration of a bill providing for resumption by January 1, 1874, and for "free banking."

In his inaugural address in March Grant, in pledging himself to a program for his second administration, included as one feature "the restoration of our currency to a fixed value as compared with the world's standard—gold, and if possible to a par with it." Economic conditions had now reached a climax. The long-continued period of speculation and inflation had reached a limit. Early in 1873 the coin value of the greenbacks, which had in January, 1872, risen to nearly 92, fell below 85. When the crop-moving period came, a sharp stringency in money manifested itself, a severe panic involving a large number of important concerns and spreading over the entire country followed, and since the government was the creator and regulator of the country's currency, the Treasury was naturally appealed to for relief.

William A. Richardson, then Secretary, with the full approval of the President, purchased bonds with a large part of the so-called greenback reserve. By the end of December he had added $22,000,000 to the outstanding greenbacks by issuing part of those which had been "retired and cancelled" by McCulloch under the act of 1866, and he continued the policy until the amount so added was nearly $29,000,000. In his report, rendered early in December, no mention is made of this issue, but the purpose to make use of the "reserve" in the absence of congressional action was declared. Richardson pointed out the total absence of flexibility in the currency as an evil which should be remedied, and suggested a restricted reserve of greenbacks to be used in emergencies and legislation which would prohibit, or at least restrict, the payment of interest on deposits by the banks.

The President gave the currency considerable space in his message. He regarded the accumulation of gold, by increasing our commodity exports, as essential, and for this purpose the industries must be encouraged by sufficient currency; not inflation, but "just enough," combined with elasticity. "The exact medium is specie; . . . that obtained, we shall have a currency of an exact degree of elasticity." He thought the panic proved the greenbacks to be the best currency "that has ever been devised," because during the panic they were hoarded like gold. In his opinion the currency was not redundant.

Whatever else may be said of the discussions of the President and Secretary, it must be admitted that these and the panic stirred Congress to action. The House began in January, 1874, consideration of measures to amend the currency acts, and to provide for free banking. The latter feature will be considered in another chapter; those relating to greenbacks were numerous: —

1. To issue notes, payable in gold in two years from date, at the rate of $4,000,000 monthly, in lieu of the greenbacks.

2. To apply the sinking fund solely to the extinction of the greenback debt.

3. As national bank-note issues increase cancel a like amount of greenbacks, down to $300,000,000.

4. To issue notes and 3.65 bonds interconvertibly, limit of notes otherwise to be $400,000,000.

5. Substitute greenbacks for national bank-notes, redeeming the 5.20 bonds on deposit to secure the same, in such notes.

6. Repeal the legal tender act, to go into effect July 1, 1876, notes to be funded into bonds.

The Senate was engaged with measures of similar scope and import. A bill finally passed in April fixing the maximum amount of greenbacks at $400,000,000, and national bank-notes at the same amount. The vote was 29 to 24 (19 not voting) in the Senate, 140 to 102 (48 not voting) in the House. Congress practically divided geographically, the Eastern members being arrayed against the bill, with Ohio as the dividing line. The measure was known as the "inflation bill," and public meetings were at once held to denounce it, and to influence Grant to use the veto power, it having been reported upon good authority that he might approve the bill. The movement was successful, and the veto came April 22. In his veto message, Grant questioned whether the bill would actually increase the currency, but if it did, it must be regarded a departure from true principles of finance and the pledges made by Congress and the Executive. Until the government notes were convertible into coin, free banking would not be safe, and in order to provide for such convertibility, the revenues would have to be increased.

A second bill was passed June 20, 1874, limiting the maximum of greenbacks to $382,000,000, and providing for the redistribution of bank issues and the substitution for the reserve required on circulation of a 5 per cent. redemption fund to be maintained in the Treasury. It also authorized the retirement of circulation by deposits of legal tenders with the Treasury. The Treasurer was thereafter required to redeem all national bank-notes upon presentation.

The congressional elections in 1874 changed a Republican majority of 110 into a minority of 71. No doubt this was due largely to "hard times," following the panic. It certainly roused the Republicans and inspired them to redeem their long-neglected pledges.

Benjamin H. Bristow followed Richardson as Secretary of the Treasury in June, and proved a worthy successor of McCulloch as a vigorous champion of sound finance. He regarded the failure to provide for resumption a breach of the Nation's pledges. The United States notes were merely a temporary expedient, warranted only by the exigency of the war. Resumption was essential to the honor of the government and the general welfare. To accomplish this, contraction was necessary, and he recommended legislation which would fix a day in the near future when the notes would cease to be legal tender as to contracts thereafter made, also the conversion of the notes into bonds or their redemption in coin.

Grant also adopted stronger language. The failure to make the notes equal to gold was not honorable, and it should be no longer delayed; the duty to act rested with Congress; no real prosperity could be expected unless this first duty was attended to. He recommended a measure removing the limitation upon the volume of national bank-notes, popularly termed "free banking." The premium on gold fluctuated during the year between $14\frac{3}{8}$ and 9 per cent., averaging $11\frac{2}{10}$, and giving an average value to the greenbacks of 89.9.

The Republicans still having control of Congress for the short session ending March 3, 1875, Sherman immediately prepared a bill which, while by no means as satisfactory as might have been expected, was all that in his opinion Congress would assent to. It provided for the retirement of the fractional currency with subsidiary silver coin; the repeal of the gold coinage charge; free banking and the retirement of greenbacks to the extent of 80 per cent. of new bank-note issues, until the amount of the former was reduced to $300,000,000; the redemption of greenbacks in coin on and after January 1, 1879; authorized the use of the surplus coin in the Treasury for this purpose and the sale of bonds without limit to provide such further coin as might be needed. The bill was reported from the Finance Committee December 21; passed the Senate December 22 by a vote of 32 to 14 (27 not voting); passed the House January 7, 1875, 136 to 98 (54 not voting). Not one Democratic vote was cast in favor of the measure, and a number of the extreme sound money Republicans in the House voted against it, as not sufficiently strong. Grant approved the bill January 14.

Thus the authors of the legal tender acts, nearly a decade after the disappearance of the only justification for these acts, and after repeated violation of pledges, finally provided for convertibility of notes into coin at a fixed date. The resumption act did not permit the retirement of the greenbacks below $300,000,000, and was cleverly silent upon the question of reissue within the limit, but, obviously, the intention was to retain the currency in use. It gave the Secretary of the Treasury as great, if not greater, powers than the act of 1866, against which Sherman and other majority leaders had protested. Conditions made this necessary, but no more in 1875 than in 1866. On the day the act was signed gold closed at 12½ per cent. premium.

The history of this decade is but a repetition of the experience of every nation with fiat money. The first step taken, the rest follows easily — inflation, delusion of the people, breach of faith, disaster. Had the Nation been actually impoverished so that recuperation was long and tedious, some excuse might be found in such conditions. But the Nation was rich enough to reduce its debt during the period by $650,000,000. The use of one-third of that amount in retiring the legal tender debt would probably have brought about specie payments by 1870, and the application of two-thirds would have extinguished it altogether. This would have given the country a stable currency, would have raised the credit of the Nation much more rapidly, and would have saved the people great losses due to depreciation arising from the subsequent troubles.

The political leaders were "opportunists," bent upon retention of power, and willing in order to accomplish this purpose to delude the people with the false notions of wealth engendered by such a currency. Wittingly or unwittingly, these leaders helped to engraft upon the public mind, as a sound economic proposition, the absurdity that a currency which fluctuated daily and on some single days lost a tenth of its purchasing power, was the "best that could be devised." It is interesting to note that the surplus gold received from customs which was sold by the government at a premium from 1866 to 1876 exceeded $500,000,000.

The strength of the opposition to resumption and retirement of the greenbacks was located south of the Potomac and west of the Alleghanies, and the reason for this was the same which, as far back as the Jackson days, operated as an obstacle to sound currency legislation, viz. a lack of adequate banking facilities, adverse exchange conditions, and much higher interest rates. This great and growing agricultural section was suffering from conditions which were absent in the eastern sections, and blindly casting about for a remedy, advocated "more paper money." They thought they wanted more currency; what they needed was more capital. The leaders seemed incapable of meeting and solving the problem thus presented, and it was much easier to placate the people with more or less inflation than to devise legislation which would actually bring relief.

Having in mind continually the facts that the legal tender notes were of doubtful constitutionality, were to be but a temporary expedient, were at a fluctuating discount and hence a delusive measure of values, the lack of wisdom in the legislative halls is illustrated in this brief chronological record: —

1862, February .	$150,000,000 legal tender notes. Temporary issue, fundable into bonds.
July . . .	$150,000,000 more.
1863, March . .	$150,000,000 more. Funding right repealed.
1864, June . .	Limit of notes $400,000,000, and $50,000,000 more for reserve.
1865, December .	Almost unanimous declaration of representatives for contraction looking toward retirement.
1866, April . .	Law providing for contraction, to promote specie payments.
1868, January. .	Contraction suspended. Volume of notes, $356,000,000.
1869, March . .	Public Credit Act. Notes payable in coin and to be made so before bonds are redeemed.
1869–1873 . . .	Hundreds of millions of bonds redeemed. Notes still at a discount.
1873, December .	Reissue of so-called reserve. Increasing notes to $382,000,000. No objection from Congress. Resumption bill defeated.
1874	Inflation bill passed and vetoed. Act fixing maximum of notes at $382,000,000.
1875	Resumption act passed. Specie payments by 1879. Volume of notes to be reduced to $300,000,000.

STATISTICAL RÉSUMÉ

National Finances (in millions of dollars)

Fiscal Year	Revenues			Expenses			– Deficit + Surplus	Debt	
	Customs	Other	Total	Ordinary	Interest	Total		Outstanding	+ Inc. – Dec.
1866 . .	179	341	520	386	133	519	+ 1	2762	+ 81
1867 . .	176	287	463	203	144	347	+ 116	2659	– 103
1868 . .	164	212	376	230	140	370	+ 6	2594	– 65
1869 . .	180	177	357	190	131	321	+ 36	2541	– 53
1870 . .	195	201	396	164	129	293	+ 103	2432	– 109
1871 . .	206	168	374	158	126	284	+ 90	2319	– 113
1872 . .	216	149	365	153	117	270	+ 95	2207	– 112
1873 . .	188	134	322	180	105	285	+ 37	2149	– 58
1874 . .	163	137	300	194	107	301	– 1	2156	+ 7
1875 . .	157	127	284	172	103	275	+ 9	2138	– 18

CIRCULATION

(In millions of dollars, except last column)

Fiscal Year	Specie	U. S. Notes	Bank-notes		Fractional Currency	Total	In Treasury (Paper only)	In Circulation	Population	Per Capita
			Nat'l	State						
1866	25	401	281	20	27	754	81	673	35.5	$18.99
1867	25	372	299	4	28	728	66	662	36.2	18.28
1868	25	356	300	3	33	717	36	681	37.0	18.39
1869	25	356	300	3	32	716	51	665	37.8	17.60
1870	25	356	300	2	40	723	48	675	38.6	17.50
1871	25	356	318	2	41	742	26	716	39.6	18.10
1872	25	356	338	2	41	762	24	738	40.6	18.19
1873	25	356	347	1	45	774	23	751	41.7	18.04
1874	25	382	352	1	46	806	30	776	42.8	18.13
1875	25	376	354	1	42	798	44	754	44.0	17.16

The Treasury held substantial amounts of gold and the banks some, but this was not used except for special purposes. The amount of interest-bearing notes, not included, which probably circulated during the earlier years (1866–1868) did not exceed $25,000,000 to $35,000,000.

EXPORTS AND IMPORTS

(In millions of dollars)

Fiscal Year	Merchandise			Specie		
	Exports	Imports	Excess + Imports − Exports	Exports	Imports	Excess of Exports
1866	349	435	+ 86	86	11	75
1867	295	396	+ 101	61	22	39
1868	282	357	+ 75	94	14	80
1869	286	417	+ 131	57	20	37
1870	393	436	+ 43	58	26	32
1871	443	520	+ 77	98	21	77
1872	444	626	+ 182	80	14	66
1873	522	642	+ 120	84	21	63
1874	586	567	− 19	66	28	38
1875	513	533	+ 20	92	21	71

THE GOLD PREMIUM AND PRICES

Year	Premium on Gold			Gold Value of Paper			Gold[1] Prices U. S.	Wages[2] in Gold	Purchasing Power of Wages	Cost of Gold in Labor
	High	Low	Average	High	Low	Average				
1866 . .	67.8	25.5	40.9	78.6	66.0	71.0	134.0	111.1	.971	.900
1867 . .	46.4	32.0	38.2	74.3	69.7	72.4	123.2	121.8	1.129	.821
1868 . .	50.0	32.1	39.7	74.4	68.7	71.6	125.6	119.1	1.094	.839
1869 . .	62.5	19.5	33.0	82.3	71.8	75.2	112.3	123.5	1.232	.809
1870 . .	23.3	10.0	14.9	90.3	82.4	87.0	119.0	136.9	1.281	.730
1871 . .	15.4	8.4	11.7	91.5	87.3	89.5	122.9	150.3	1.333	.664
1872 . .	15.4	8.5	12.4	91.7	87.4	89.0	121.4	153.2	1.367	.652
1873 . .	19.1	6.1	13.8	92.1	84.9	87.9	114.5	147.4	1.385	.678
1874 . .	14.4	9.0	11.2	91.2	89.1	89.9	116.6	145.9	1.348	.685
1875 . .	17.6	11.8	14.9	88.9	85.4	87.0	114.6	140.4	1.318	.712

SALES OF GOLD BY THE TREASURY

(Amounts in millions)

Year	Amount	Premium	Average Rate	Year	Amount	Premium	Average Rate
1867 . . .	38.4	14.2	37%	1872 . . .	77.6	9.4	12%
1868 . . .	54.2	21.9	41	1873 . . .	77.0	11.6	15
1869 . . .	32.0	12.4	39	1874 . . .	38.0	5.0	13
1870 . . .	65.1	15.3	24	1875 . . .	33.4	4.0	12
1871 . . .	72.4	8.9	11	1876 . . .	26.2	3.8	14
				Total . .	514.3	106.5	21%

[1] Basis of 100 for 1860. [2] *Ibid.*

CHAPTER XIII

Legal Tender Notes

1876–1890

Resumption of specie payments had been decreed by the act of 1875, but Western Democrats soon began to talk of repealing the act. The House of Representatives would presently be organized by their party for the first time since the outbreak of the war. It proved, however, that almost all of the Eastern members of that party opposed repeal, while a substantial number of Western Republicans favored it. The premium on gold rose considerably on account of these manifestations. It reached a maximum of $17\frac{5}{8}$, and the average for the year was $14\frac{9}{10}$ per cent., lowering the average value of the greenback to 87 compared with 89.9 the previous year.

Bristow, in December, 1875, reported the redemption of nearly $9,000,000 of legal tender notes under the resumption law, but insufficient internal revenues compelled him to sell gold derived from customs, thus preventing its accumulation preparatory to resumption. The national banks had made use of the privilege under the recent law of depositing "lawful money" with the United States Treasurer to retire their circulation, to the extent of over $37,500,000, so that there was an actual contraction going on. The policy of paying and retiring the government's interest-bearing debt was continued during the year, over $30,000,000 of the revenue being so applied.

A number of bills to nullify or repeal the resumption law were presented in the House and considered by the Banking and Currency Committee, but the presidential contest (of 1876) was at hand, and the Democratic leaders were cautious. Repeated attempts to have the measures brought before the House were defeated until August, when Cox (New York) reported a bill to repeal the clause in the act providing for redemption of United States notes in coin on January 1, 1879, which passed, 106 to 86 (93 not voting). Only 11 Republicans voted aye, while 28 Democrats voted nay. Upon the question of repealing the entire act the vote was 111 to 158 (not voting 20), only 9 Republicans voting aye and 61 Democrats nay. Upon the proposition that the Constitution did not confer on Congress the power to make notes legal tender in time of peace, the vote was 97 to 146 (46 not voting); only 9 Democrats favored and 11 Republicans opposed.

A Democratic caucus measure proposed, in lieu of the resumption law of 1875, an accumulation in the course of ten years of a coin reserve by the government and banks equal to 30 per cent. of the notes of each. It failed to pass in the House, the vote being 81 for and 157 against.

The Republican national platform of 1876 indorsed the policy of resumption. The Democrats, Tilden being their candidate, denounced the Republicans for the delay, of which they had been guilty, in bringing about resumption, and declared the redemption clause of the act of 1875 a hindrance to resumption.

This year is marked by the separation of the extreme paper money advocates from the two main parties and the organization of the "Greenback" party as a political force. It nominated Peter Cooper for the presidency, demanded the repeal of the resumption act, favored the issue of legal tender notes interconvertible to and for 3.65 per cent. bonds, the abolition of bank currency, and the continuation of the fractional currency.

The results of the election showed that the people had lost confidence in the Republican party. Their policy lacked the vigor of sincerity in dealing with monetary affairs. They had for fifteen years controlled the government in all its branches, and yet had failed to redeem their pledges. Their reconstruction policy in the South evinced a desire seemingly to build up and develop a political force rather than build up and develop the country so lately devastated by war. The result of the election was close, and the final ascertainment and counting of the deciding votes subjected our institutions and our electoral machinery to a severe strain. Congress and the whole country as well were absorbed in the controversy, and no legislation of a general nature was attempted.

Under the process of redemption under the act of 1875, the volume of legal tenders had been reduced to $367,500,000. New bank circulation amounting to $18,000,000 had been issued, but the banks had at the same time retired circulation to the net amount of $29,100,000. The premium on gold averaged 11½ per cent. for the year. The relative commercial value of gold and silver was gradually changing. In 1873 the market value of the silver dollar was about 3 per cent. greater than the gold dollar, and this fact explains the ease with which the demonetization law passed Congress.[1] Gold was the cheaper metal, and legislators seem prone to favor the standard which tends toward the greater volume of money. The greater relative production of silver had changed the relative price, and the privilege of free coinage of silver would furnish silver producers a steady market for their product at a price much in advance of its commercial value. Their keen sagacity lost no time in seeking through Congress to remonetize the silver dollar. The proposition was well received by the general public, who had since 1834 known silver as an appreciated and not a depreciated metal. The lower House voted to remonetize silver 167 to 53, and from this Congress dates the birth of the silver party, destined to play such an important part in fiscal and monetary affairs during the ensuing quarter of a century.

President Hayes in his inaugural, March 4, 1877, briefly but

[1] See Chapter XV.

firmly supported resumption. He appointed John Sherman Secretary of the Treasury, and plans were at once matured to insure the successful execution of the resumption law. In Congress the House was again Democratic, although by a smaller majority, — 20. In the Senate the Republicans had only 38 votes to 37 Democrats and one independent, David Davis (Ill.), heretofore a member of the Supreme Court.

Ewing (Dem., O.) at once introduced in the House a bill to repeal the resumption clause of the act of 1875, and reported it favorably from the Banking and Currency Committee, October 31. Fort (Rep., Ill.) presented a measure for the same purpose differently worded, which latter measure passed November 23, by a vote of 133 to 120, 27 Republicans (practically all Western men) voting for it and as many Democrats, from the East, against it. Among the Democrats favoring the measure was Carlisle, afterwards Secretary of the Treasury; voting against it was Foster, Republican, also later Secretary. The bill went to the Senate, but remained in the Finance Committee until April 17, 1878.

In December Secretary Sherman reported favorable progress in refunding the debt and the sale of bonds to procure gold for resumption purposes. The premium on gold had fallen so that notes were worth $97\frac{3}{8}$ per cent. The outstanding legal tenders had been reduced to $351,300,000. The trade balance continued favorable, helping him to secure gold. He urged a firm maintenance of the resumption policy — to reverse it would impair the public credit. It will be remembered that under the act of 1875, as new national bank circulation was taken out United States notes were to be retired to the extent of 80 per cent. of such amount. He anticipated that bank-notes would not be taken out in sufficient volume to reduce the United States notes under the 80 per cent. proviso to the minimum of $300,000,000, hence he recommended funding the excess into bonds, or if the silver dollars were remonetized, these might be used for that purpose.

He said that the act of 1875 did not clearly state whether the notes redeemed after 1879 might be reissued, but he thought they might be. "A note redeemed in coin is in the Treasury, and subject to the same law as if received for taxes or as a bank-note when redeemed by the corporation issuing it." He thought it well to settle the question by legislation, as his views were controverted. This would involve the question of making the notes permanent currency, and he used all the old arguments in favor of doing so with or without the legal tender quality.

He remarked: —

"The Secretary ventures to express the opinion that the best currency for the people of the United States would be a carefully limited amount of United States notes, promptly redeemable on presentation in coin, and supported by ample reserves of coin, and supplemented by a system of national banks, organized under general laws, free and open to all, with power to issue circulating notes secured by United States bonds deposited with the government, and redeemable on demand in United States notes or coin. Such a system will secure to the people a safe currency of equal value in all parts of the country, receivable for all dues, and easily convertible into coin. Interest can thus be saved on so much of the public debt as can be conveniently maintained in permanent circulation, leaving to national banks the proper business of such corporations, of providing currency for the varying changes, the ebb and flow of trade."

National bank-note issues had diminished in volume, and the fractional currency had been practically replaced by silver coin. The economic conditions of the country were still unsettled, and as usual this was charged to the policy of currency contraction, the resumption law being especially attacked.

We have seen that by the aid of a few Republican votes the bill to repeal the resumption act passed the House. In the Senate, on April 17, 1878, it was reported by Ferry (Rep., Mich.) with a substitute making United States notes receivable in payment or redemption of bonds, and after October 1, 1878, for customs, and providing that the volume in existence at that date was to be the permanent volume and reissuable. By a vote of 30 to 29 this was substituted for the House bill, and then passed by the Senate by 45 to 15. Ten Democrats voted against the House bill and 9 Republicans voted for it.

The House had tired of waiting for the Senate, and on April 29 passed a bill introduced by Fort (Rep., Ill.) to suspend the cancellation of redeemed United States notes, and directing their reissue. The vote stood 177 to 35, the negative vote including only 7 Democrats. Only the strongest representatives could resist the tide; Foster and McKinley voted for it and Garfield against it. The Senate passed this bill May 28 by a vote of 41 to 18, having first rejected Bayard's amendment that such reissued notes were not to be legal tenders. The affirmative vote included Blaine, Davis, and Windom; the negative Bayard, Conkling, Hoar, and Morrill. Generally speaking, the negative vote was from the Eastern states. Sherman favored the measure, and hence Hayes approved it on May 31 without a protest. The volume of notes then, as to-day, was $346,681,016.

Thus Republican votes assisted the Democrats in emasculating the measure to which the former had "pointed with pride," in the previous campaign platform. A veto by Hayes, in the face of the overwhelming votes in both houses of Congress, would very likely have been overridden. It is obvious that the approval of this act was contrary to his convictions, and that but for Sherman's leanings to the policy of continuing the United States notes as a permanent part of our currency, our financial history might have been altered by a vigorous veto of this reactionary measure.

Congress on February 28, 1878, passed the act remonetizing the silver dollar over the veto of the President. (Discussed in another chapter.) Silver certificates were also provided for in this act. The silver movement developed rapidly in both parties during 1877–1878. The "Greenback" party had conventions in many of the states and controlled a substantial vote. It had become a force in certain sections, and each of the old parties shaped platforms to gain its support, as well as that of the silver advocates. The election of 1878 gave the Democrats the House by a majority of 19, and the coöperation of 16 Greenbackers. The Senate became Democratic by 12 majority.

Despite all these political machinations against the gold standard and resumption, gold, which in January stood at 102, fell below 101 in April, and never thereafter reached that figure. In December it was but $\frac{1}{10}$ of 1 per cent. premium, and resumption, so far as equality of notes and gold was concerned, was practically accomplished. Many there were, even astute bankers, who believed even in December, 1878, that resumption would fail; but Sherman had made adequate preparation, and the economic conditions had grown month by month more favorable to his plans. As stated officially in his report in December, 1878, Sherman had acquired a gold fund of over $133,000,000, of which $96,000,000 had been derived from bond sales, the balance from surplus revenues, the income of the government having improved as "hard times" passed. He had suspended the issue of gold certificates; had arranged that the Treasury use the New York clearing-house to facilitate and cheapen the collection and payment of checks and drafts, with only partial use of cash, at the point where three-fourths of his payments were made; had concentrated his coin in New York, where alone under the act of 1875, notes could be presented for redemption, and had resolved to receive the legal tender notes for customs without legislation — a privilege he could in the absence of law revoke at any time. He feared that a law making United States notes receivable for customs would deprive the government of the power to exact coin, and might prove embarrassing if an emergency arose. He expressed the view that the act of 1878 prohibiting further cancellation of notes was wise, and stated his purpose to pay either gold or silver in redemption of notes, as preferred by the holder, but reserving to the government the right, which it had under the law, to pay in either.

In his message Hayes recommended that no financial legislation be undertaken to disturb the "healing influences" then at work. The House, notwithstanding, took up the amended repeal bill of the previous session, but on Garfield's motion it was "laid on the table," 141 to 110. Only 5 Republicans voted favorably to the measure, 27 Democrats against it. Thus the reactionary policy was definitely checked. At this time the fractional silver coin had become redundant, and by the act of January 9, 1879, its redemption in "lawful money" was provided for.

Sherman had to use the same means for resumption proposed by McCulloch, but did so only after much shifting, and in a manner which after all left much of the evil unremedied. While his remarkable changes of policy served to delay resumption, it should be borne in mind that he had much opposition within as well as without his party. He probably went as far in support of sound finance as he could without suffering political defeat. An uncompromising position by the Republican party in favor of retiring the greenbacks, or redeeming them in coin at an earlier day, would doubtless have resulted in placing the opposition in control. In view of that party's attitude, it leaves room for doubt whether after all the halting and vacillating course of the Republican party, typified by Sherman, did not eventuate in the greater good to the country.

No disturbance of currency conditions appeared for some time after resumption. Abundant crops, a large, favorable trade balance, larger investments by foreigners in our securities, caused an enormous inflow of gold. The refunding of the debt proceeded rapidly. Sherman contracted in one day for the placing of nearly $150,000,000 of bonds. Even the issue of the silver dollars and the fall in their commercial value could not affect the progress to solid prosperity, and the Republicans naturally took credit for the "good times" which resulted.

A bill for the free coinage of silver passed the House in May, 1879, but was defeated in the Senate. The reason for referring to it here is to recall one section (introduced by Ewing, Dem., O.), proposing that the government buy bullion at market price, issue certificates against the same, and retain only 40 per cent. of the dollar coined from the bullion as a reserve for their redemption. This passed 106 to 105, Speaker Randall voting aye; only 2 Republicans voted for, and 12 Democrats against, it. A subsequent vote eliminated the section from the bill.

Political conventions of the opposition still declared resumption a failure, in the local campaigns of 1879. Ewing, the author of the repeal bill, candidate for governor of Ohio, was badly beaten by Foster, and the Democratic-Greenback fusion in other states met a similar fate.

Sherman reported in December, 1879, that only about $11,000,000 of notes had been presented for redemption in coin, and the Treasury gold stock had increased nearly $20,000,000. He recommended that the legal tender proviso as to greenbacks be repealed as to future contracts, letting the notes sustain themselves by their convertibility into coin and their receivability for public dues. Thus the question of the constitutionality of making the reissued notes legal tender in time of peace, now before the courts, would be finally determined.

The free banking law had not added materially to the volume of bank-notes, which, as Sherman reported, stood at $337,000,000. Thus with $305,800,000 estimated gold, $121,400,000 silver, and $346,600,000 greenbacks, the supply of money was $1,110,800,000. Of this amount, averaging nearly $23 per capita, $260,000,000 was in the Treasury, leaving for general use about $17 per capita.

In his message Hayes congratulated Congress on the successful execution of the resumption act. He urged action, however, to retire the greenbacks, it being his conviction that the issue of the notes was, except in extreme emergency, "without warrant of the Constitution and a violation of sound principles."

In the House, in April, 1880, Weaver, the Greenback leader, introduced a resolution declaring against bank-notes and favoring the substitution of legal tenders, which was voted down 85 to 117 (not voting 90). Only one member classed as Republican voted for, and 29 Democrats against, it. The resolution also favored the coinage of more silver dollars, and their use in redeeming bonds.

In the presidential contest of 1880 Sherman's chance for the Republican nomination was clearly destroyed by his unstable record on the money question prior to 1877, but the dominating influence of Ohio was so great that Garfield obtained the nomination. The Republicans in their national platform made no promises for the future as to the currency, and seemed content to rest upon their laurels. The Democrats declared for "honest money, — gold, silver, and paper convertible into coin on demand," and the strict maintenance of public faith. Tilden, the logical nominee, was apparently undecided as to acceptance, owing to delicate health, and General Hancock became the nominee. The Greenback party nominated Weaver as its candidate, upon the platform which embodied his resolutions above referred to. Garfield won by a small plurality of the popular vote, but a large majority in the electoral college. Weaver received over 300,000 votes, against 81,000 for Cooper in 1884. The House of Representatives elected comprised, Republicans 150, Democrats 137, Greenbackers 10. The Senate was again evenly divided, counting Davis of Illinois against the Republicans.

Sherman in December, 1880, reported that only $706,658 notes had been presented for redemption in coin during the year, and his available coin was over $141,000,000, a portion being silver. He regarded the notes in form, security, and convenience the best circulating medium known — a burdenless debt. He concluded that the legal tender quality was not necessary to make them useful, and even if deprived of that, they would be the "favorite money of the people." Indeed he regarded the currency system of the United States the best ever devised. This happy but short-sighted optimism reads strangely in the light of the calamity which the Nation suffered during Cleveland's second administration on account of this "favorite money of the people."

On the other hand, Hayes, in his last message, reiterated that the notes should be retired. As a war measure they served their purpose, but their indefinite employment was not warranted. They were a debt and, like any other debt, should be paid and cancelled; their retirement was a step to be taken toward a safe and stable currency. How statesmanlike this reads in contrast with the sentiments of his shifty Secretary!

The greenback agitation had given way to that for silver, in which the advocates of inflation found an easier field for the work. The silver law had increased the "stock of money" by nearly $73,000,000, but only $45,500,000 in dollars and certificates were in circulation, the remainder being in the Treasury, a useless asset. Sherman had indeed, under the law providing for free transportation of coin, effected a larger distribution by offering silver payable in Western and Southern points at par in exchange for gold in New York. The continual issue of silver already threatened the Treasury's reserves.

Congress, during the short session after the election, passed a bill to refund the 5 per cent. and 6 per cent. bonds maturing in 1881 into 3 per cents. The Republicans solidly opposed this measure because the new bonds were limited in amount to $400,000,000, and one section of the bill required national banks to use them exclusively as security for circulation. The bill also authorized the temporary use of the coin reserve in redemption of bonds. Hayes vetoed it upon the first-mentioned ground on the last day of the session.

This was the condition when William Windom succeeded Sherman in March, 1881, in the cabinet of Garfield, whose untimely death prevented him from impressing his views upon the legislation of that period. Windom remained in the Arthur cabinet for a time, and during the summer, when the 6 per cent.

and 5 per cent. bonds matured, was able, by reason of the general prosperity, to extend most of them at 3½ per cent., the principal payable at the pleasure of the government, which proved to be one of the most brilliant operations in our financial history. The amount of bonds maturing at that time was $671,500,000, of which $597,800,000 were "continued," the remainder redeemed. The saving of interest was on the basis of nearly $10,500,000 annually, and the cost of the operation was not quite $10,500.

Windom returned to the Senate in November, and his place was taken by Charles J. Folger, of New York, who had in former years been Assistant Treasurer in New York City.

In Congress two measures, separately introduced, finally became law in one act, — the extension of charters of national banks, many of which would soon expire, and the 3 per cent. refunding bill. The opposition to the former measure was pronounced, but unavailing. This is known as the act of July 12, 1882, and beside the chief features named above, provided for the issue of gold certificates, making them receivable for all public dues; both these and the silver certificates were made available for bank reserves, and national banks were forbidden to be members of any clearing-house where silver certificates were refused in payment of balances (which latter proviso was particularly directed against the New York Clearing House). It further provided that the issue of gold certificates be suspended whenever the gold reserved for the redemption of notes fell below $100,000,000, the first legal recognition of the necessity of the "reserve."

At this time it was estimated that the stock of money in the country amounted to over $1,409,000,000, of which the Treasury had $235,000,000. The stock was composed of $506,700,000 gold, $197,000,000 silver, the fixed amount of greenbacks ($346,681,000), and nearly $359,000,000 of national bank-notes. The Treasury had over $35,000,000 in silver dollars in excess of certificates (hence absolutely unavailable) and was coining more.

The era of great prosperity was on the wane, but so long as the tide was favorable, the silver inflation at the rate of nearly $28,000,000 annually was not generally marked. A combination of circumstances again gave the Democrats the control of the House of Representatives, this time by a plurality of seventy-seven. Many states that had been strongly Republican reversed their votes, Massachusetts electing General Butler, now a Greenback-Democrat, governor, by a handsome plurality.

In the year 1883 little occurred directly affecting the legal tender notes, but the continued increase of silver and silver certificates began to show serious results. The national bank currency diminished, and greenbacks being preferred to silver were held back from the Treasury in payments. The government had to use its gold or force out silver only to have it return after a very brief circulation. The growing fear that the continued purchase and coining of silver would eventually disturb the basis of values was accentuated by reactionary business conditions, which, growing in intensity, resulted in a sharp stringency in the money market in May, 1884, — a virtual panic. It was not of long duration, in its intensity, but had a pronounced effect upon business and a very potential influence in the ensuing presidential campaign. During the panicky period the New York City banks, owing to the contraction of their cash reserves, due to hoarding money, as well as the general drain upon their resources, used a device which had been resorted to before on several occasions, to provide an "inter-bank" currency for the purpose of settling debit balances at the clearing-house. Loan certificates were issued by the clearing-house upon deposits of securities by banks amounting in the aggregate to $24,915,000. The first certificates issued bore date May 15.

It was at this time that the Supreme Court decided, with but one dissenting voice, that the power to issue legal tender notes in time of peace as well as in time of war was accorded by the Constitution. In consequence, amendments to the Constitution prohibiting making aught but gold and silver legal tender were proposed, but not acted upon.

The presidential campaign (Blaine-Cleveland) was conducted upon lines other than the money question. Both parties wished to appear favorable to silver, and both protested that they favored sound money, the Republicans calling for "the best money," the Democrats for "honest money." The Greenback party, nominating General Butler for the presidency, claimed that the Supreme Court had upheld their chief tenet, demanded the substitution of greenbacks for bank-notes, and took special credit for forcing remonetization of silver and suspension of greenback retirement, the two unsound measures of 1878.

The people not only chose Cleveland President, but a House of Representatives strongly Democratic. The Senate continued Republican. The Greenbackers polled 133,000 votes, less than one-half as many as in 1880, and thereafter the party as such disappeared.

Folger died early in 1884, was succeeded by Gresham, previously Postmaster-general, who, however, remained but a few months at the head of the Treasury, resigning to become Circuit Judge. Arthur then turned to Hugh McCulloch and prevailed upon him again to take charge of the Treasury Department for the short period remaining of his administration. With a gold reserve rapidly diminishing, silver payments appeared at several times almost inevitable. The supply of money in circulation was estimated at $1,244,000,000, giving a per capita of $22.65, nearly $6 more than in 1879.

In his report for 1884 McCulloch asserted that, so long as the government issued notes, a reserve must be maintained, and correctly forecast the future in these words: "Many persons regard legal tender notes as being money, and hold that no means should be provided for their redemption. That this is a delusion will be proven whenever there is a large demand for gold for export. They are not money, but merely promises to pay it, and the government must be prepared to redeem all that may be presented, or forfeit its character for solvency."

Silver dollars alone were really available in substantial amounts, but for these there was no demand. From January 1 to August 12 the gold had diminished $39,000,000, and the silver had increased by more than $21,000,000. McCulloch recommended the retirement of all notes under $10 to increase the use for silver and the suspension of coinage of the "white metal."

Early in 1885 McCulloch, with a shrinking gold reserve and only a small balance of greenbacks, actually paid the clearing-house at New York silver certificates. That body had revoked its resolution not to use silver in its transactions; but, by tacit understanding, no member had ever tendered silver up to this time. Prompted by a request not to embarrass the incoming administration, McCulloch did not persist in this policy.

Daniel Manning became Secretary of the Treasury in the Cleveland administration in March, 1885. The uselessness of calling Congress in extra session was understood, and measures to tide over the dangers from inflation were undertaken by the executive alone. In order to conserve the gold balance, soon reduced to $115,000,000, bond purchases were for a time suspended, and extraordinary efforts were made to put silver into circulation. Under his discretionary power the Secretary discontinued the issue of $1 and $2 greenbacks (silver certificates were then limited to $10 and upwards), and the silver dollar surplus of $71,000,000 was somewhat reduced. The New York City banks exchanged with the Treasury nearly $6,000,000 in gold for subsidiary silver coin.

By the time Congress assembled in December, 1885, the Treasury was in much better condition, but still unsafe so long as the laws remained unchanged. Manning, in his report, emphatically attributed the danger to two laws, — the silver purchase act of February, 1878, and the act of May, 1878, suspending the retirement of greenbacks, which, he said, indefinitely postponed fulfilment of the solemn pledge of the public credit act of 1869. He earnestly recommended the repeal of both of these acts, but his argument was directed particularly against the silver law.

Cleveland, in his message, devoted special attention to the evil of the silver purchase and coinage law, by which the Treasury was compelled to pay out $27,000,000 of gold annually for silver, a policy which would soon bring about the single silver standard. Congress was deaf to admonition. A provision was, however, inserted in one of the appropriation acts (August 4, 1886), authorizing the issue of silver certificates in denominations of $1, $2, and $5, which put a substantial amount of silver into use, thereby relieving the Treasury. The country was also recovering rapidly from the effects of the depression following the panic of May, 1884. Revenues increased, and so did the surplus, and the gold reserve was replenished.

In the House Morrison (Dem., Ill.) introduced on July 14 a resolution directing the use of the money in the Treasury in excess of $100,000,000 (including the gold reserve) in buying bonds at the rate of $10,000,000 per month. McKinley (Rep., O.) proposed an amendment providing that the $100,000,000 gold, having been accumulated under the resumption act as a reserve fund for the redemption of greenbacks, be maintained for that purpose, and not otherwise used. This was defeated by a vote of 119 to 154. Only five Republicans voted against the amendment, and 13 Democrats, chiefly New York members, voted for it. Morrison's measure passed 207 to 67. The 13 Democrats again voted against it, but over 50 Republicans voted for the resolution. Manning, to whom the resolution had been referred for his opinion, expressed himself vigorously against it.

The Senate amended the resolution so as to give the Treasury a working balance of $20,000,000, and authorized the President to suspend the operation of the measure in case of exigency. The vote was 42 to 20. The negative vote included Beck, Ingalls, Plumb, Voorhees, Wilson of Iowa, and others favorable to the "more money" policy. The House agreed to the amendments August 4; but as Congress adjourned that day, and the President declined to sign it, the measure failed.

In his report for 1886 Manning recommended the application of the large and growing Treasury surplus to the redemption of the legal tender notes, gradually substituting the silver certificates for the notes, thus accomplishing the extinction of a debt actually due without contracting the currency, and at the same time aiding the Treasury in putting its silver funds in circulation. Discussing the decision of the Supreme Court, he urged that the power of making the notes legal tender was not exercised "in relation to any power to borrow money," for money is the standard and measure of the wealth borrowed. Changing the standard in the act of borrowing was "cheating or enriching the lender. Such proceedings found no defender among the lawyers, statesmen, or people . . . not until after 1861, when a great danger had beclouded most men's perceptions of financial as well as constitutional law, was a legal tender money made out of the debts of the United States; not until the infection spread was it ever deliberately argued that any representative of the unit of value could justly be suffered to be made, or to abide, in permanent depreciation and disparity therewith."

He further urged that whether lawful or not to issue such notes after redemption and twenty-one years after the exigency which called them into existence had passed, every argument now forbade the continuance of the "legalized injustice." If the power had been conferred upon Congress by the Constitution, it should now be abrogated. "No executive and no legislature is fit to be trusted with the control it involves over the earnings and the savings of the people."

How unfortunate that Manning's recommendations were not

adopted. The first and perhaps the greatest error committed in our financial legislation, after the issue of the legal tender notes, was the repeal of the law permitting them to be funded into government bonds. This closed the door to their retirement and, in the absence of affirmative legislation, left them as a permanent feature of our currency system.

In July, 1886, the silver funds in the Treasury amounted to over $96,000,000, the gold fund had reached $160,000,000, and the outstanding volume of national bank circulation was $311,000,000. The per capita circulation was about $22. Taxation was by no means burdensome, and yet the surplus over expenditure was constantly accumulating in the Treasury. The people were content with the tax budget, and certainly no more fitting or desirable conditions for retiring the legal tender notes could be hoped for. The sin of omission on the part of Congress at this time was most grievous.

Manning was succeeded by Charles S. Fairchild in 1887. The growing surplus in the Treasury had absorbed money from the channels of circulation to such an extent as to embarrass business and occasion uneasiness. Fairchild met the situation and established the policy of depositing receipts from internal revenue with designated national bank depositories, properly secured by United States bonds. About $40,000,000 of the internal revenue was thus placed instead of locking up the money in the subtreasuries.

The year's changes in the Treasury's cash are interesting. Nearly $17,000,000 silver funds had gone into circulation, in addition to the amount coined from monthly purchases of silver bullion, the minimum of which purchase was fixed at $2,000,000. The gold fund was over $200,000,000. The outstanding national bank circulation was reduced to $279,000,000. The reduction of bank circulation was effected chiefly by the deposit of "lawful money" with the Treasury under the act of June 20, 1874. This fund in the Treasury had gradually grown so that now it amounted to over $100,000,000, awaiting the presentation of bank-notes for redemption.

Cleveland made the surplus the paramount subject of discussion in his message to Congress. Instead, however, of urging retirement of greenbacks with the unused and unnecessary funds in the Treasury, he proposed revision and reduction of the tariff and thereby gave to the Republicans an issue which encompassed Cleveland's defeat in the ensuing presidential campaign.

A resolution to use the surplus in excess of $100,000,000 again passed the House, without a division. The form was modified from that of the previous years by the insertion of the words "not otherwise specially reserved." In the Senate it came up early in 1888 and Plumb (Rep., Kan.) proposed an amendment to issue in lieu of national bank-notes retired, Treasury notes redeemable in coin, to be legal tender for all debts public and private. The redemption fund was to be increased pro rata and not to be less than 25 nor more than 30 per cent. of the outstanding notes of both kinds. Morrill (Vt.) moved to table the amendment, which was agreed to by a vote of 23 to 22. A little later Plumb offered the same proposition, omitting the words "public and private." Morrill again moved that it lie on the table, which was defeated, 24 to 24, and the Plumb amendment as modified then passed, 28 to 21. Beck (Dem., Ky.) proposed an amendment directing the purchase of silver bullion to the amount of national bank-notes retired, in addition to the purchases under the Bland act, the bullion to be coined and certificates issued, as provided by the act of 1878, which was carried by a vote of 38 to 13, March 26, 1888. Allison, Cameron, Cullom, and thirteen other Republicans voted for it. The bill failed in the House. These proposed amendments to the law and the votes thereon are interesting as showing at a very recent date the attitude of the two great parties and prominent men in relation to greenbacks, silver, and national bank circulation.

Cleveland's pronounced and somewhat extreme anti-protection attitude upon the tariff precipitated many speeches in Congress made for general distribution and general effect, and roused the Republicans to press forward the policy of protection as the cardinal issue before the people.

For the time being the money question again took subordinate position in the campaign. The platform of the Republicans indeed declared for "sound money," both gold and silver, and *denounced the attempt of the Democrats to demonetize silver.* The efforts of both parties in turn to convince the silver advocates that "Codlin, not Short" was their friend, is rather amusing. The Democrats, seriously divided between the sound views of the eastern wing, which was in position to dictate the nominee (Cleveland), and those of the western wing, which was for "more money" of any kind, — paper or silver, — were obviously in no condition to make a decisive declaration. Thus the tariff became the general issue.

The Greenbackers had returned to their respective affiliations, but there were evidences that a third party, formed by separation of dissatisfied elements from both parties, chiefly in the agricultural sections, would at an early day bring the money question to the front. Cleveland received a plurality of the popular vote in November, but the electoral vote went to Harrison, the House also becoming Republican. The Senate continued Republican by two majority.

Fairchild's second report was an able presentation of the financial situation. He urged reduction in taxation and relief from the danger involved in the continual purchase and coinage of silver. Congress had granted authority which was asked for to purchase unmatured bonds at a premium with the surplus, and this resulted in a material reduction of the debt, although by expensive means.

The net silver in the Treasury had been reduced to $54,000,000, the net gold remained about $200,000,000, and public deposits in national banks amounted to $50,000,000. The "lawful money" fund deposited with the United States Treasury by national banks for the purpose of retiring their notes stood at $86,000,000.

Again in power March 4, 1889, in both houses of Congress and the Executive Department, the Republicans were bent upon aggressive legislation. Windom was appointed Secretary of the Treasury. He continued the policy of reducing the debt by bond purchases, diminishing the gold fund somewhat, but the silver funds even more, bringing the latter down to $32,000,000. Under the pressure of these issues national bank-notes were retired from circulation so rapidly that the volume fell below $200,000,000. The silver question received Windom's special attention. The party leaders were convinced that something had to be done, but since Cleveland had favored the suspension of purchases and coinage of silver, this was not the policy to be adopted. With the desire to satisfy both the agricultural sections, again clamorous for "more money," and the mercantile communities, who urged the suspension, Windom, after an elaborate discussion, recommended a silver measure, which, because its result was a large addition to the volume of legal tender paper, will be outlined here.

He proposed to "issue Treasury notes against deposits of silver bullion at the market price of silver when deposited, payable on demand in such quantities of silver bullion as will equal in value, at the date of presentation, the number of dollars expressed on the face of the notes at the market price of silver, or in gold, at the option of the government, or in silver dollars at the option of the holder"; and to repeal the compulsory feature of the coinage act of 1878; these notes to be receivable for all public dues the same as the silver certificates. He urged that this would give the country a "paper currency not subject to undue or arbitrary inflation or contraction, nor to fluctuating values," "as good as gold," "an absolutely sound and perfectly convenient currency . . . to take the place of retired national bank-notes . . . meet the wants of those who desire a larger volume of circulation . . . and not encounter the opposition of those who deprecate inflation." He was convinced that the public sentiment demanded the continued use of silver in some form, and he regarded the proposed plan as the least dangerous form of so doing.

Windom's course in the Senate showed that he was a follower of Sherman, classifiable as a moderate paper money man, as distinguished from the inflationists like Morton, Logan, and Ferry. He would no doubt have favored the soundest system of money had it been politic to do so, but it was not, in his judgment, wise to fly in the face of the people. Few men could have so skilfully devised a plan calculated to satisfy the silver advocates, the Greenbackers, the gold men, and the inflationists, as well as those who favored contraction.

The plan was hailed by a majority in Congress as a solution of a troublesome problem which the legislators feared to undertake. Nevertheless they were not satisfied to adopt Windom's plan without tinkering, as the law, which is known as the act of July 14, 1890, shows. Congress insisted upon making the notes legal tender, fixed the amount of silver to be purchased monthly, and in other particulars changed the plan. In addition, the national bank-note redemption fund, now amounting to $54,000,000, was "covered into the Treasury," to be used as an asset, the obligation to redeem the bank-notes being assumed as a part of the public debt. The ultra silver element in the two parties was sufficiently strong, if united, to pass a free coinage bill had this measure been defeated. Indeed the Senate had passed such a bill by a vote of 42 to 25, and the Democrats in the House favored it, but they failed to obtain the support of the silver Republican representatives.

This law, popularly called the Sherman Act, and fully set forth in the discussion of silver legislation in another chapter, caused inflation of the currency by about $50,000,000 in legal tender notes annually, without increasing the gold reserve fund. At the same session acts were passed under which the revenues were reduced by over $50,000,000, largely by removing the duty on sugar, and the pension disbursements increased by about the same amount, a remarkable trio of laws, after a long period of inactivity on the part of Congress.

The popular demand for "more money," which during this period influenced political leaders, was based upon false premises. It came from the large agricultural sections and less developed portions of the country. Noting these vast undeveloped resources, and foreseeing the fortunes which could be speedily made by their rapid development, they exerted their political energies to increase the volume of currency, seemingly expecting that in some undefined way the increase would inure to their benefit. They seemed oblivious to the fact that however great the volume of currency, no one could receive any portion of it except by giving something of value in exchange, either labor or property. As before stated, these sections needed more capital, not more currency.

That the alleged need for "more money" was fictitious or greatly exaggerated, is demonstrated by the fact that the national bank circulation diminished during the decade (1880–1890) from $359,000,000 to $186,000,000. This was the only form of paper money which was to an appreciable degree affected as to volume by the demands of trade, and the evidence is conclusive that it diminished chiefly because there was no legitimate demand for the continued large volume. The reported gold stock showed an increase of $343,000,000, and the silver supply was augmented $310,000,000; the growth of available money was much greater than the increment in population and trade, for the amount per capita of money outside the Treasury was in 1880 $19.41, in 1890 $22.82.

STATISTICAL RÉSUMÉ

(Amounts in millions unless otherwise indicated)

NATIONAL FINANCES

Fiscal Year	Revenue			Expenses			Surplus	Debt	
	Customs	Other	Total	Ordinary	Interest	Total		Outstanding	+ Inc. – Dec.
1876	148	142	290	165	100	265	25	2105	– 33
1877	131	150	281	144	97	241	40	2095	– 10
1878	130	127	257	134	103	237	20	2150	+ 55
1879	137	135	272	162	105	267	5	2183	+ 33
1880	187	147	334	169	96	265	69	2072	– 111
1881	198	163	361	177	83	260	101	1986	– 86
1882	220	184	404	187	71	258	146	1820	– 166
1883	215	183	398	206	59	265	133	1686	– 134
1884	195	154	349	190	55	245	104	1586	– 100
1885	181	143	324	209	51	260	64	1540	– 46
1886	193	143	336	192	51	243	93	1495	– 45
1887	217	154	371	220	48	268	103	1367	– 128
1888	219	160	379	215	45	260	119	1293	– 74
1889	224	163	387	241	41	282	105	1171	– 122
1890	230	173	403	262	36	298	105	1067	– 104

CIRCULATION

Fiscal Year	Specie	Subsidiary Silver	N. B. Notes	U. S. Notes	Fractional Currency	Total	In Treasury	In Circulation	Population	Per Capita
1876	25	27	333	370	34	790	63	727	45	$16.12
1877	25	41	317	360	20	763	41	722	46	15.58
1878	41	61	324	347	17	790	61	729	48	15.32

CIRCULATION — (*Continued*)

Fiscal Year	Gold and Gold Certificates	Silver Dollars and Certificates	Subsidiary Silver	U.S. Notes	N.B. Notes	Total	In Treasury	In Circulation	Population	Per Capita
1879	246	41	70	347	330	1034	215	819	49	$16.75
1880	352	70	73	347	344	1186	212	974	50	19.41
1881	478	95	74	347	355	1349	235	1114	51	21.71
1882	506	123	74	347	359	1409	235	1174	52	22.37
1883	542	152	75	347	356	1472	242	1230	54	22.91
1884	546	180	75	347	339	1487	243	1244	55	22.65
1885	588	208	75	347	319	1537	245	1292	56	23.02
1886	591	237	75	347	311	1561	309	1252	57	21.82
1887	654	277	76	347	279	1633	316	1317	59	22.45
1888	706	310	76	347	252	1691	319	1372	60	22.88
1889	680	344	77	347	211	1659	278	1381	61	22.52
1890	695	380	77	347	186	1685	256	1429	63	22.82

EXPORTS AND IMPORTS

Fiscal Year	Merchandise			Specie		
	Exports	Imports	Excess + Imp. − Exp.	Exports	Imports	Excess + Imp. − Exp.
1876	540	461	− 79	57	16	− 41
1877	602	451	− 151	56	41	− 15
1878	695	437	− 258	34	30	− 4
1879	710	446	− 264	25	20	− 5
1880	836	668	− 168	17	93	+ 76
1881	902	643	− 259	19	110	+ 91
1882	751	725	− 26	49	42	− 7
1883	824	723	− 101	32	28	− 4
1884	741	668	− 73	67	37	− 30
1885	742	578	− 164	42	43	+ 1
1886	679	635	− 44	72	39	− 33
1887	716	692	− 24	36	60	+ 24
1888	696	724	+ 28	46	59	+ 13
1889	742	745	+ 3	97	29	− 68
1890	858	789	− 69	52	34	− 18

THE GOLD PREMIUM AND PRICES [1]

Year	Premium on Gold			Gold Value of Paper		
	High	Low	Average	High	Low	Average
1876	15.0	07.0	11.5	92.5	87.4	89.6
1877	07.9	02.5	04.8	97.3	93.9	95.5
1878	02.9	00.0	00.8	99.9	97.5	98.6

[1] After 1878 there was no premium on gold.

CHAPTER XIV

Legal Tender Cases in the Supreme Court

The question of taxing certificates of indebtedness and legal tender notes came before the Supreme Court for review on writs of error and was decided in 1868. The first-named form of security was declared not subject to municipal taxation in the case of The Banks *vs.* The Mayor (7 Wall. 16) and the tax was declared unconstitutional. In another case, Bank of New York *vs.* Supervisors (7 Wall. 26), it was held that although the greenbacks circulated as money, they were also obligations of the United States, and hence not taxable.

Respecting legal tender, it was held in Lane County *vs.* Oregon (7 Wall. 71) that taxes laid by a state were not "debts" within the meaning of the legal tender act. In Bronson *vs.* Rodes (7 Wall. 229) it was held that an express contract to pay coin was not dischargeable with legal tender notes, one Justice (Miller) dissenting from the decision.

As to the validity of the act of Congress taxing state banknotes 10 per cent., it was held in Veazie Bank *vs.* Fenno (8 Wall. 533) that the act was constitutional, the federal government having the power to tax out of existence such form of currency in order to make room for another form if national in character. Two Justices, Nelson and Davis, dissented.

It was also held that the shares of stock in a national bank were subject to state tax even though the entire capital of the bank were invested in United States bonds. The tax was held to be in the nature of a franchise tax or license to do business, and hence within the power of the state to impose.

The main question, whether the legal tender acts themselves were constitutional, did not come before the Supreme Court until 1867, and the decision was not published until February 7, 1870. (Hepburn *vs.* Griswold, 8 Wall. 603.) Circumstances attending this decision and its subsequent reversal (Legal Tender Cases, 1871, 12 Wall. 457) caused so much comment at the time that they will be given place here.

The Court in 1867 consisted of eight members, as follows: Chief Justice Chase, formerly Secretary of the Treasury, whom Lincoln appointed in 1864 upon the death of Chief Justice Taney, and who had for some time been regarded as more of a Democrat than a Republican; Justices Grier, Nelson, Clifford, and Field, looked upon as Democrats; and Justices Miller, Davis, and Swayne, regarded as Republicans. An act of Congress of July 23, 1866, provided that the Court be reduced to seven members, the reduction to be effected by not filling the next vacancy caused either by death or retirement. While the first legal tender case was pending, a decision against the validity of the act was anticipated, and an act was passed in April, 1869, to take effect December 1, 1869, restoring to the Supreme Court the previous membership of nine. It was expected that Justice Grier would soon retire, thus enabling the appointment of two justices with Republican antecedents and favorable to the view of that party — that the greenbacks were, and should remain, lawful money.[1]

The case, as stated, came before the Court in 1867, but owing to its importance was held for reargument until 1868, and was actually decided November, 1869, by the expected vote, 5 to 3. The form of the opinion was, as is the custom, submitted to conference and adopted January 29, 1870, and would have been published two days later, but a week was given to the dissenting Justices (Miller, Davis, and Swayne) to prepare their views.[2] On February 1, 1870, Justice Grier retired, and on the 14th of that month William Strong of Pennsylvania was appointed in

[1] Schuckers, Life of Chase.

[2] Chase in the dissent, 12 Wall.

his stead by President Grant. In March following Joseph P. Bradley of New Jersey was appointed to fill the place which the act of April, 1869, had "revived." Both of these appointees were known to favor the legal tender act, Justice Strong, when on the bench in his own state, having written an elaborate opinion declaring it constitutional.

The decision in Hepburn *vs*. Griswold was written by Chief Justice Chase, who thus passed upon the validity of his own acts as Secretary of the Treasury. The debt in this case had been contracted in 1860 and fell due February 20, 1862 (five days prior to the approval of the legal tender act). It was not paid, nor was payment tendered, until March, 1864.

The opinion held that the act by its terms was manifestly intended to apply to all debts, those contracted before as well as those incurred after the act (from this there was no dissent); that therefore the act impaired the obligation of contracts, compelling a creditor to receive $1000 in paper, in lieu of coin, when in fact $1000 in coin was at the time equal to $2000 or more in paper, and thus an arbitrary injustice would be done. The power to do this was not granted by the Constitution, either expressly or impliedly, and all power of Congress is limited by the fundamental law. Not only may specifically expressed powers be exercised, but it is within the power of Congress by implication to employ such means, not prohibited by nor repugnant to the Constitution, as were necessary and appropriate to execute any of the express powers. The power to determine what shall be legal tender is a governmental one, and in the United States vested in Congress so far as relates to *coins;* but this grant of power does not carry with it that of clothing paper with the same quality. The emission of Treasury notes was, as a form of borrowing, held to be valid, but this did not carry with it the power to make them legal tender. Manifestly, if Congress were clothed with power to adopt any and all means it saw fit in executing the express powers granted by the Constitution, it had absolute power, which was not consistent with American ideas of government.

It was denied that giving the notes legal tender power was "appropriate" or "plainly adapted" to the purpose in view. It did not save them from depreciation but added to the long train of evils which irredeemable currency always brings, and since the result necessarily was an impairment of existing contracts and also the taking of private property (so large a portion of which consisted of contracts) without due process of law, the act was inconsistent with and prohibited by the Constitution.

In dissenting, Justice Miller urged that under the express power to declare war, support an army and navy, borrow money and pay national debts, provide for the common defence and general welfare, Congress had, in the emergency, no other recourse to save the government and the Constitution; the legal tender act furnished the means, the ordinary use of the government's credit having failed; it was passed reluctantly only after it had become imperative; that if, as the Court had just previously ruled (Veazie Bank case), in order to provide a national currency either by means of government notes or national bank-notes, Congress could place a prohibitive tax on state bank-notes, how much more appropriate and effectual for the purpose it was to give the government notes legal tender power; undoubtedly contracts were impaired, but the states, not Congress, were prohibited by the Constitution from enacting laws impairing the validity of contracts; national bankruptcy laws are constitutional although they clearly impair contracts; as to taking property without due process of law, the legal tender act does so indirectly, but so do other acts for great national purposes — the tariff laws, a declaration of war, additional bond issues depreciating those already out; moreover, by declaring the act void all business would be disturbed, millions of dollars sacrificed, and thus great injustice done. In conclusion, the choice of means, the degree of necessity, lay with Congress, and were not questions for the Court to determine.

So the legal tender act was declared unconstitutional. It was currently reported at the time that Chase, Nelson, and Clifford held that the act was void for all purposes; Grier and Field only as to preëxisting contracts. The decision occasioned no surprise and made no disturbance, as it was confidently believed that the Court, enlarged by the new appointees, would reverse the decision when occasion arose. The occasion was not long delayed. In the December term of 1870 several cases came up and were decided in May, 1871, the decisions being published in January, 1872. The public expectation was realized, and the former decision reversed by a vote of 5 to 4.

The opinion of the Court was written by Justice Strong, a concurring opinion by Justice Bradley, and dissenting opinions were filed by Chief Justice Chase, Justice Clifford, and Justice Field. The manner in which this important decision was brought about was severely criticised as a radical departure from the settled practice of the Court, and it was reported that, for the first time in its history, heated arguments and recriminations were heard at its sessions.[1]

Justice Strong gave as a reason for reopening the question, the plea that the Court had not been full when Hepburn *vs.* Griswold was decided. To this Chase replied by pointing to the dates (heretofore stated), from which it is apparent that until the act of April, 1869, took effect (December, 1869), the Court was full, with a membership of eight, and would have been full if there had been but seven, so a full Court *heard* and decided the case. The form of the opinion was not agreed upon until after December, 1869, but the Court might then have been full had the President made an appointment, which he delayed until 1870, obviously because the vote would still have been against the validity of the act, and Justice Grier would not accommodate the President by retiring prior to the filing of the opinion.

[1] Schuckers, Life of Chase.

The revised opinion of the Court stated that if the United States could not *in any emergency* make Treasury notes legal tender, as other sovereignties did, the government was without the means of self-preservation; if the legal tender acts were held invalid, great business derangement, distress, and rankest injustice would be caused, since almost all contracts made since 1862 were made with the intent to discharge them in legal tender notes which had become the universal *measure of values;* debtors would have a large percentage added to their obligations; no distinction could be made as to debts preëxisting; the act affected all obligations; the incompatibility of laws with the Constitution must be plain before they can be declared invalid, for the presumption was in favor of laws of Congress being constitutional; the general purpose of the Constitution must be considered and the intent of the framers discovered; it could not name specifically every power to be exercised, and the manifest object being to establish a sovereign government, every means not prohibited could be employed, *especially for its preservation;* the "general welfare" clause (Article I, Section 8) provides for that; the reasons for the first ten amendments to the Constitution were clearly to prohibit certain powers supposed to be deducible from the original document; if then the object were one for which the government was framed, the means conducive to the end were to be determined by Congress, if necessary, appropriate and not prohibited, nor could the degree of necessity be reviewed by the Court; it must therefore be clearly shown that the means were *not* appropriate, and due weight must be given to the exigencies of the case; at the time of the passage of the acts the Treasury was empty, the credit exhausted, the army unpaid, and the existence of the government at stake; the legal tender notes saved the country from disaster; if nothing else *could* have saved it, no one would question the power of Congress to take the course it did; even if other means might have been employed, the Court could not therefore interfere, as the choice lay with Congress; but there were no other means; the then head of the Treasury Department (Chase) had seen no way to avoid the necessity; the legal tender notes having proved effective, the act must have been appropriate to the purpose; and if, as had been admitted in the Veazie Bank case, Congress could tax state bank currency to enable a national currency to circulate, it could certainly choose the more direct means of making the latter legal tender; to the objection that the clause authorizing the coinage of money and fixing the value thereof by implication excluded the power to make paper legal tender, it was maintained that such a rule of construction was out of harmony with the entire history of the court; indeed it might more logically be held that as the states were prohibited from making aught but coin legal tender, it was intended that the federal government should have that power as other governments had; whatever power over the currency existed was vested in Congress; if the power to declare what is and shall be money is not vested in Congress, it is annihilated; if this was intended, would it not, as in other cases where governmental powers were *prohibited*, have been definitely stated? in the absence of such a prohibition, is it not reasonable to say that it was intended to be used under the grant of the power to regulate the value of money? as to the impairment of contract obligations by the acts, it has been held repeatedly that contracts to pay money generally are obligations to pay that which is money when payment is to be made; the coinage law of 1834 changed the weight of gold coins, and certainly could not be held unconstitutional; it was denied therefore that the acts did impair the obligation of contracts, since every contract to pay money is subject to the constitutional right of Congress over money; Congress is not prohibited from passing such a law; both expressly and by implication is the power given, as in bankrupt laws, declaration of war, embargo laws, tariff laws, and laws changing the coinage; all take from the worth of contracts and indirectly take private property, but they are part of the legitimate governmental functions which private contracts cannot defeat; however harsh or unjust, these considerations alone do not make them unconstitutional; as to the alteration of the standard of value, the acts do not make paper a standard of value; it is not claimed that this power to issue rests on the power to coin money or regulate its value; it is not asserted that Congress can make anything which has *no value* money; but Congress has the power to enact that the government's promise to pay money shall be money *for the time being*, equivalent in value to the representative of value determined by the coinage acts; the legal tender acts fix no standard of value, nor do they make money of that which has no intrinsic value.

In dissenting, Chief Justice Chase asserted that it was the plain duty of the Court to declare unconstitutional any act of Congress not made in the exercise of express power, or coming within Marshall's rule that it is "necessary and proper," if under an implied power; Congress may not adopt any means it may deem fit, even to carry out an express power; the means must be "necessary and proper," and the Court is to determine the question; the necessity, however, need not be absolute; the power to tax state bank-notes was exercised under the express grant to regulate the value of money; the occurrences of the war did not make the acts necessary; the notes would have circulated without the legal tender power, to which he had reluctantly assented as Secretary of the Treasury, only because he could not otherwise get authority to issue notes that were necessary; the legislation he favored contemplated notes receivable for public dues, which function would have fully served the purpose; giving them compulsory circulation by the acts in question was an element of depreciation, a declaration that the government was insolvent; every honest purpose would have been served without making them legal tender; the acts were really harmful, and largely increased the debt by the inflation consequent upon the great depreciation which these notes suffered; not only were they not necessary, but they directly violated the express provisions of the Constitution; to be warranted, laws must be not only not prohibited by, but also consistent with, the Constitution in letter and spirit, as Marshall stated; the powers cited under which Congress may impair contracts or take private property are undisputed express powers; bankrupt laws are the only ones which Congress may pass directly affecting contracts; implied powers require different construction; Congress no doubt had the power to issue notes, and it was also its duty to establish a standard of value, in order to measure values, but *every presumption* is against the interpretation that aught but gold and silver could be adopted for the purpose; all legislation contemporaneous with and subsequent to the adoption of the Constitution and all judicial decisions until 1862, as well as all the facts in our history, sustain this view; the published discussions of the framers of the Constitution, from which their intent must be deduced, show that they intended to cut off every pretext for making paper legal tender; Webster's opinion was unequivocal that Congress had no power to make paper legal tender, and the Court had frequently held that coin alone constituted a legal tender under the Constitution; it cannot be disguised that an exigency, not entirely free from a political coloring, influenced the rehearing and the decision of 1872; tried by the cold facts of history, the conclusion that the framers of the Constitution intended to absolutely prohibit the issue of paper as money with legal tender power seems unavoidable; that the majority opinion was somewhat influenced by its probable effect is shown by the two opening paragraphs, in which the great distress likely to follow an affirmation of the decision in Hepburn *vs.* Griswold was set forth; the "debtor class," a phrase then very much in vogue among politicians, was referred to in sympathetic terms. It is difficult to see how the *legal* status of the measure could be affected by the question whether debtors or creditors were upon the whole more numerous, or whether debtors were suffering more at the moment than creditors suffered when they were compelled to accept depreciated paper on anterior contracts; moreover, the Court seemed to lose sight of the fact that its decision continued a depreciated currency, from which the masses always suffer most and the shrewd minority profit most.

The evidence, however, is all but conclusive that the war could not have been carried on and the Union saved without a United States note-issue, and that the note-issue would not have been successful without the forced currency feature was evidently the opinion, at the time, of Lincoln, Chase and the leaders in Congress.

Justice Strong, despite the sweeping character of his opinion, qualified the power of Congress over the legal tender feature by the phrase "for the time being." Granted that the exercise of power was necessary, it was the almost unanimous opinion of those in Congress who voted for the act that it was but a temporary expedient; as such it was a necessary and proper public policy; although an evil, the remedy was to be speedily applied when the emergency passed. Virtuously indignant at the suggestion that they were about to create paper money, the leaders pledged a retracing of steps when the object was accomplished. They broke their pledges, for practically the same men were at the helm in 1865 and in 1868.

The Court incidentally pointed out the underlying purpose of the first and second legal tender acts, which was that the notes should be funded at the option of the holder. The provision in the act of March 3, 1863, which repealed the funding pledge, is responsible for the trouble incident to the legal tender notes. Had that privilege been continued, these notes would have largely disappeared and national bank-notes have taken their place. The maintenance of a necessary volume of currency would doubtless have brought about free banking at an earlier date, and the trials and tribulations which this "temporary" currency in the forty years of its existence has brought the nation would have been in large measure avoided.

The Court had settled the right of Congress to issue legal tender notes in an emergency, but could these notes be reissued in time of peace? Had Congress the power to issue, at any time in its discretion, legal tender notes? This question was brought before the Court in the case of Juilliard *vs.* Greenman (110 U. S. 421, 1884) and argued by General Benjamin F. Butler and Senator George F. Edmunds respectively for and against the unlimited power of Congress to issue such notes.

The majority of the Court (Justice Field alone dissenting) held that the Constitution created a national sovereignty, quoting the grants of express powers to lay taxes, to borrow money, to regulate commerce, to coin money and regulate its value, and the power to make all laws necessary and proper to carry into effect these and all other powers vested in it by the Constitution. It was repeated from previous decisions that the necessity need not be absolute and indispensable, and the power might include all means appropriate in the judgment of Congress. Expressly prohibited from making anything but gold and silver a tender, or passing laws impairing the obligation of contracts, the states could not exercise these powers. The question whether the framers intended to likewise prohibit the federal government from issuing paper money and making it a legal tender for private debts, in view of the silence of the Constitution, was answered in the negative; the power to borrow and emit evidences of debt (*i.e.* bills of credit) was not contested; the power to create banks for the issue of notes was likewise conceded; as a logical consequence Congress has the power to issue its own bills of credit in such form and with such qualities as currency as accord with the usage of sovereign governments. The authority to confer the legal tender quality is incident to the powers referred to and universally understood to belong to other sovereignties, and not being prohibited, it was within the power of Congress.

The power is as broad as that of coining money and regulating commerce, nor is it restricted by the fact that the value of contracts may be affected. And the question whether the issue is to be made in times of special exigency, such as war, or generally in times of peace, is one solely for Congress to determine.

Justice Field, dissenting, maintained that the history of the events preceding the adoption of the Constitution left no room for doubt as to the intent of those who framed the instrument, respecting legal tender paper and impairment of contracts. The analogy of power exercised by other sovereignties was not pertinent, since the organic law clearly limited the powers of Congress. Neither the needs of the government nor the fact that the Constitution was silent on the subject could give the power. The power to borrow money did not include the power to make the notes issued legal tender as to private contracts, thus giving the debtor special privileges to pay his creditor less value than he agreed. Such a power would enable the government to interfere with all property rights; nor was the power incident to that of coining money, which did not mean coining anything but metals. To claim such power was logically claiming the power to debase the coinage, acknowledged by all to be monstrous iniquity.

Manifestly, if the power is not granted it is withheld, and to construe it as impliedly granted it must not only be appropriate, not prohibited, but, as Marshall also said, consistent with the letter and spirit of the Constitution. Since the United States notes had been greatly depreciated and might again be so, oppression and injustice resulted, and a law promoting either of these conditions was not consistent with the Constitution. He reminded the majority that upon the subject of laws impairing the obligation of contracts Marshall had also said, "It is against all reason and justice, for a people to intrust a legislature with such powers; and, therefore, it cannot be presumed that they have done it" (3 Dall. 388).

If Congress has the power claimed by the majority, it may issue such notes indefinitely and pay its bonds with them, no matter how depreciated. Why then should the government continue paying interest on the bonds when the principal might be paid in a day?

The historian George Bancroft maintained, in reviewing the decision,[1] that the evidence was complete that it was the unalterable purpose of the framers of the Constitution to prohibit legal tender paper. He declared the dictum that the federal government had sovereign powers to be revolutionary. Its powers were clearly *limited*. It had no inherent sovereignty, but only that delegated to it by the Constitution. European sovereignties had *not* the power of making notes legal tender. The attitude of Bancroft illustrates the frame of mind in which the decision was received by many of our strongest and best men.

When the federal Constitution was created and adopted the people were in a revulsion of feeling over the suffering caused by the great depreciation of the Continental currency. It depreciated on every one's hands. The Continental Congress redeemed some of its issues at an enormous discount in new issues that in turn suffered a great depreciation. There is no doubt that the framers of the Constitution intended, and thought they had succeeded in, prohibiting Congress from issuing an irredeemable currency and making the same a tender for debt. The federal government was a compromise in which the states sought by united strength to command respect and achieve consequence in the sisterhood of nations, at the same time jealously retaining their local sovereignties in order to avoid the dangers which experience had taught them to apprehend from a strong central government. In respect to intercommunication they were remote from one another with the means of travel existing at the time, and naturally wished their local governments interfered with as little as possible. The adoption of the

[1] Bancroft, A Plea for the Constitution.

federal Constitution gave to the people two sovereigns — a double allegiance. The question, which was to be paramount, state or nation, was an active issue until settled by the sword and sealed in favor of the nation, by the surrender at Appomattox. A strengthening of the central government inevitably ensued. State sovereignty ceased to be an influence, and the courts were left free to discriminate between what the framers of the Constitution had done and what they thought they had done.

Above all things the framers of the Constitution intended to create a perpetual government, and when the life of the government was at issue the technical reading of the Constitution yielded perforce to broader lines gauged by the civic and economic changes which a century had wrought. The law of self-preservation construed the Constitution broadly as to the power of Congress over currency, in the interest of preserving the government.

CHAPTER XV

Silver Question

1861–1878

The demand for more money seems to be ever popular with the general public; at least such is the view of politicians. The vacillating course of the leaders of both of the great political parties, evidenced by their votes, diverse in character, at different stages of the silver controversy, indicates plainly that they were seeking to follow public sentiment and insure their own continuance in office, rather than seeking to furnish the best currency system for the promotion of commerce and trade, and a system which would best serve the interest of labor and the small trader as well. So many and such flagrant misstatements were made as to the demonetization of silver in 1873, that I have deemed it well to give the history of silver legislation in great detail.

"Capital is that portion of all the previous product of a nation which at any given time is available for new production. This will be a certain amount of tilled land, houses, buildings, stock, tools, food, clothing, roads, bridges, etc., which have been made and are ready for use in producing, transporting, and exchanging new products. These things are all the product of labor, and require time for their production. Nothing but labor spent upon them can produce others, and time is required for this labor to issue in new and increased possessions. Currency only serves to distribute this capital into the proper hands for its most efficient application to new production. Banks, it must be repeated, only facilitate the transfer of capital from hands where it is idle into hands by which it will be usefully employed. Currency, therefore, is not capital, any more than ships are freight; it is only a labor-saving machine for making easy transfers. Banks do not create wealth, they only facilitate its creation by distributing capital in the most advantageous manner. If, therefore, currency is multiplied, it is a delusion to suppose that capital is multiplied, or, if 'money is plenty,' by artificial increase of its representatives, it is only like increasing the number of tickets which give a claim on a specific stock of goods — the ticket-holders would be deceived and could, in the end, only get a proportional dividend out of the stock."[1]

For a quarter of a century the standard of value was imperilled, business disturbed, and the value of all property subjected to uncertainty by a propaganda on the part of a large portion of our people laboring under the conviction that *currency was capital* and that the free coinage of the silver product of our mines, at the behest of any one choosing to present the same at the mints, would add that vast sum to the capital of the country in form adapted to current use. The fiat of the government can impart legal tender quality to currency, either coin or paper, but its value as expressed in articles of commerce — what it will buy — is determined by its commercial value or by its convertibility into money whose commerical value is equal to its nominal currency value.

During the Civil War the coins of the United States disappeared from circulation owing to the premium thereon following the suspension of coin payments in December, 1861. The only exception was in the country west of the Rocky Mountains, where the gold product of California assisted the people there, so far away from the seat of war and possessing but indifferent means of communication with the rest of the country, to maintain the coin standard. The specie in the rest of the country was in the Treasury, in banks or in private hoards, there being no substantial amount of coin in circulation outside the Treasury after 1863–1864.

The country exported the greater part of its estimated stock of coin, $250,000,000 (1861), and its annual product besides.

[1] Sumner, A History of American Currency.

The mints coined from 1861 to 1867 the following amounts: —

Gold coin	$230,358,000
Silver dollars	306,000
Subsidiary coin	8,731,000
Minor coin	5,638,000

The commercial ratio of silver to gold fluctuated between 15.35 and 15.57 to 1, indicating a value for the silver dollar of from $1.04 to $1.02½.

In 1867 an international monetary conference met in Paris at which this country was represented. This body among other things recommended the adoption of the single gold standard and an international coin. The latter proposition was favorably received. The Senate Finance Committee (June 9, 1868) made a report recommending the coinage of a dollar 3½ cents less in value than the existing one, thus making it equal to 5 francs. It was expected also that the British sovereign would be so modified as to make it exactly 25 francs or five of the proposed dollars. Nothing further was done in the matter.

The production of silver in the United States, which in 1861 was estimated at $2,000,000, steadily increased, chiefly due to the rich discoveries in Nevada; by 1868 the product was $12,000,000, in 1872 $28,750,000. The coinage of silver dollars increased at once, and from 1868 to 1872 over 3,200,000 of them were struck, and practically all were exported.

The Franco-German War at this time (1870–1871) had a most important and far-reaching effect upon the monetary standards of the world. The brilliancy of the German campaign and the triumph of her arms placed the new empire in the front rank of military powers. She received an enormous war indemnity from France, 5,000,000,000 francs ($965,000,000), all of which was paid in a comparatively short time after the conclusion of peace. The prestige of her arms and the condition of her treasury greatly facilitated the work of welding together the separate states, commercially as well as politically, into one harmonious whole. The dream of the Hohenzollern was realized and a unified Germany was the result. The commercial aspirations of the German Empire proved equal to its military ambition, and turning to Great Britain, the chief commercial nation, as an exemplar, its banking system was copied largely and the gold standard adopted. The coinage of the country, which differed in the separate states, was unified, and the sale of the greater part of the old silver pieces was determined upon. France, in order not to be swamped with the white metal at its open mints, suspended silver coinage for the public, and the other nations belonging to the Latin Union followed her example.[1] The action of these nations in suspending the free coinage of silver has been held by many to be the principal cause of the fall in its commercial value.

Contemporaneously with these events Congress was at work upon the revision of the mint laws, and its labors resulted in what is known as the coinage law of 1873. This revision was the result of several years of work and discussion, begun in 1869 by John Jay Knox under the direction of Secretary Boutwell. The report and draft of the bill were transmitted to the Senate early in 1870, referred to its Finance Committee, and ordered printed. The House received the documents in June, 1870.

The original bill made the gold dollar the unit of value, discontinued the coinage of the silver dollar, the half dime and three-cent piece, and the report not only called attention to the proposed discontinuance, but discussed the reasons for doing so. It had been proposed to have a dollar, subsidiary in character, of 384 instead of 412½ grains, with legal tender power the same as subsidiary pieces, but this was finally eliminated from the bill. Obviously the reason for recommending the discontinuance of the old dollar of 412½ grains was that its value (some 7½ per cent. greater than that of the subsidiary silver) was then $1.02 in the world's markets. It was not provided for in any draft of the

[1] The Latin Union consists of France, Italy, Switzerland, Belgium, and Greece.

bill from the first to the passage thereof in 1873. The section omitting it (15th, afterward 16th) never mentioned it at any stage.

The bill was reported, with amendments, to the Senate, December, 1870, debated and passed by a vote of 36 to 14 on January 10, 1871. Senator Sherman voted against, and Senator Stewart of Nevada for, the bill, but there was no division on the question of omitting the silver dollar and no amendment was offered to restore the same.

The bill reached the House January 13 and went to the Coinage Committee. It was not acted upon in that Congress, however, and in the next Representative Kelley (Rep., Pa.) reported the same bill from the committee after it had, as he said, "received as careful attention as I have ever known a committee to bestow on any measure." Subsequently it was amended to include a 384-grain dollar; on April 9, 1872, it was debated and every section discussed. The fact that the bill made gold the sole standard was also debated, Kelley stating that it was "impossible to retain the double standard." He called attention to the fact that the old silver dollar was worth more than the gold dollar, remarking also that "every coin that is not gold is subsidiary." On May 27, 1872, it passed by a vote of 110 to 13; the negative vote was not due to the omission of the silver dollar.

The Senate amended the bill January 17, 1873, with a provision for the unlimited coinage of a "trade dollar" of 420 grains, commercially worth more than the Mexican dollar, to compete with the latter in the Oriental trade. Thus amended it became a law on February 12, 1873.[1] It was therefore before Congress nearly three years, printed at least ten times, debated on several occasions, and attention was directed to the omission of the old silver dollar. Nevertheless Kelley, a few years later, said that

[1] History of the Coinage Act of 1873, being a complete record of all documents issued and all legislative proceedings concerning the act. Public document printed in 1900.

he "did not know that the bill omitted the silver dollar," and Stewart with others declaring that the bill was passed surreptitiously, denounced the legislation as the "crime of 1873." Yet in 1874 (February 11) Senator Stewart in a speech in the Senate on another measure had said, "I want the standard GOLD." Later he asserted that he was not aware until 1875 that the dollar had been omitted from the bill of 1873. Kelley, who stated, when reporting the bill, that it had been studied by the Coinage Committee line for line and word for word, and had announced that the bill contemplated establishing the single gold standard, declared in 1877 that the demonetization was an unexplained mystery to him. It is unnecessary to say that it was the *duty* of Kelley, Stewart, and all the others then in Congress to *know* what they were legislating upon. If, therefore, the act was wrong they are themselves guilty of wrong, and their professed ignorance (in Kelley's case disproved by the facts) is merely an aggravation of the offence. The truth is that the growing political strength of the silver advocates alarmed many men who voted for the law of 1873, and they thought it better politics to explain their vote as an unwitting act rather than to attempt to justify it.

I have given the history of the demonetization of the silver dollar fully, to show the utter falsity of the oft-repeated charge that it was accomplished surreptitiously.

The act of 1873 altered the coinage laws in several other particulars. The charge on gold coinage was reduced to one-fifth of 1 per cent.; a three-dollar piece of gold was provided for; the subsidiary coinage was modelled after that of France as to weight, giving 25 grammes (185.8 grains) to the dollar in such coins instead of 184 grains; and these coins were continued legal tender to the amount of $5. Trade dollars were to be coined for the public, but subsidiary pieces only on government account.

An act of March 2, 1873, reformed the absurd method of

quoting the par of exchange with Great Britain, which continued as a relic from the old act of 1789, at the ancient rate of $4.449 to the pound sterling, notwithstanding the act of 1842, wherein $4.84 had been adopted as the par for payments by or to the Treasury. Thereafter the pound was to be rated at $4.8665, its actual value.

The law of January 14, 1875 (resumption act), repealed the coinage charge for the purpose of attracting gold to the mints, and provided for the issue of subsidiary silver to redeem the fractional currency, and the act of March 3, 1875, provided for the coinage of a twenty-cent piece in exact proportion to the other subsidiary coins.

The fractional currency was presented for redemption slowly, wherefore the act of April 17, 1876, provided for the issue of subsidiary coin in other payments, and the joint resolution of July 22, 1876, extended the limit of issue of such coin to $50,000,000.

The same enactment revoked the legal tender power of the trade dollar, inadvertently given to it as to subsidiary pieces by the act of 1873. It further provided that the Secretary of the Treasury might suspend its coinage when satisfied that there was no export demand, and inasmuch as these dollars had made their appearance in the country's circulation, it seemed that the coinage of $36,000,000 was in excess of the demand.

Returning now to the silver dollar. Although the act of 1873 omitted it from the coins provided for, and prohibited its coinage, it did not revoke the legal tender function of the dollars then in existence; but on June 22, 1874, Congress adopted a revision of the statutes then in force, and Section 3586, purporting to represent the law as it then stood, provided that "the silver coins of the United States shall be a legal tender at their nominal value for any amount not exceeding five dollars in any one payment." It was contended that this abrogated the full legal tender power of the existing dollars; on the other hand, it was held that a mere revision could not repeal the statute. No occasion then arose for determining this question.

How and when the agitation to restore silver to free coinage actually began, seems in doubt, but the increased production in the far Western states, now averaging $40,000,000 annually, and the fall in price under the influence of diminished demand, unquestionably were the causes. The greater demand for gold coincident with the diminution of product, brought the commercial ratio of the metals to 17.5 to 1.

On July 19, Bland (Dem., Mo.) reported a bill in the House which provided for coin notes to pay for unlimited deposits of gold or silver, repayable on demand *in kind* (bars or coin), and for the coinage of a 412.8-grain silver dollar; the notes to be receivable for all public dues and the coins to be full legal tender. As a substitute for this, on July 24, Kelley endeavored to pass a free coinage bill (previously introduced by him) under suspension of the rules (requiring a two-thirds vote). The motion was defeated 119 to 66 (99 not voting), 32 Republicans voting favorably, 27 Democrats against. Bland later made a similar attempt, which was also defeated. The votes, however, demonstrated the ability of the silver men to pass such a bill. A compromise measure was therefore introduced, and passed August 15, 1876, to appoint a commission to inquire into the whole subject and report to Congress.

The commission was to consist of three senators, three representatives, and not to exceed three experts, who were to inquire: —

First. Into the change which had taken place in the relative value of gold and silver; the causes thereof, whether permanent or otherwise; the effects thereof upon trade, commerce, finance, and the productive interests of the country, and upon the standard of value in this and foreign countries.

Second. Into the policy of restoration of the double standard in this country; and if restored, what the legal relation between silver and gold should be.

Third. Into the policy of continuing legal tender notes concurrently with the metallic standards, and the effects thereof upon the labor, industries, and wealth of the country; and

Fourth. Into the best means for providing for facilitating the resumption of specie payments.

The commission consisted of Senators Jones (Rep., Nev.), Bogy (Dem., Mo.), and ex-Secretary Boutwell; Representatives Gibson (Dem., La.), Willard (Rep., Mich.), and Bland (Dem., Mo.), W. S. Groesbeck, of Ohio, Francis Bowen, of Massachusetts, professor in Harvard; and George M. Weston of Maine as secretary. It gave the matter undivided attention and presented a voluminous report, March 2, 1877,[1] discussed below.

The political platforms in 1876 were silent on the subject; it had not developed sufficiently to permit declaration.

Bland could not await the report of the commission, of which he was a member. In December, 1876, he again pushed his bill, but ultimately preferred the Kelley substitute, which on the 13th of the month passed the House by a vote of 167 to 53. In the Senate the Finance Committee reported it back without recommendation, desiring to await the report of the commission.

The report of the majority of the Silver Commission (an exhaustive document), favoring remonetization, was written by Senator Jones. Bogy, Willard, Bland, and Groesbeck concurred. Separate reports were presented by Boutwell and Bowen, Gibson concurring in the latter. Of the majority, Jones, Bogy, and Willard favored the coinage at the ratio of 15½ to 1, like that of France and the Latin Union; Groesbeck and Bland preferred the existing 16 to 1.

The majority contended that the fall in price of silver had not been due to increased production but to practical demonetization in so many countries at the same time; that there was an exaggerated idea of the volume of the silver product, whereas the gold product was actually diminishing, and by the stimula-

[1] Senate Report, No. 703, 44th Congress, 2d Sess.

tion of its use by the adoption of the single gold standard the price of silver was further depressed; the double standard was advocated as having a compensatory influence tending to preserve and not depress prices, so that prices would not be violently depressed, as was sure to follow if the demonetization were persisted in; there were no new circumstances warranting the change from bimetallism; open mints in France and the United States would overcome the effects of fluctuation; the entire volume of coin money governed prices, and to reduce the volume would be an unjust interference with the course of prices; decreasing volume and the resulting fall in prices were more disastrous than war, pestilence, or famine, as history showed.

Respecting the duty of the United States, they urged that with an enormous debt which was payable by the terms of the law, and equitably as well, in silver dollars, the proposition to make it payable in gold alone was to impose onerous and oppressive obligations upon the people; the existing economic troubles in the entire commercial world were due to a diminishing money supply; they insinuated that an international conspiracy was afoot to establish the gold standard and thus lay burdens upon the masses, pointing, as evidence, to the international conference of 1867, Sherman's bill to make gold the sole standard thereafter, and also to the act of 1873.

The questions propounded were substantially answered as follows: —

That the change in the relative value of the metals would not be permanent unless general demonetization took place, in which case the most serious consequences, social, industrial, political, and economical would follow.

That the double standard should be restored in order to avert the danger threatening the entire world.

That paper could not be maintained concurrently with coin unless its market value was made equal to coin by convertibility.

That convertibility by means of resumption, extremely difficult with coinage of both metals, would be impracticable with gold alone.

As stated, three of the majority members favored the ratio $15\frac{1}{2}$ to 1, in order to bring about concurrent action with France and the Latin States.

Boutwell opposed the remonetization unless by international agreement; otherwise in his opinion silver would flow to this country in such quantities that it would force the country upon a depreciated silver standard; he admitted that demonetizing one metal increased the purchasing power of the other, reduced prices and increased the burden of debts; the use of both metals furnished a more stable standard; the United States should delay action until coöperation could be secured.

Professor Bowen's view, concurred in by Gibson, was that the change in relative values was due to the fluctuation of silver, which was caused by increased product and diminished use, proof of its unfitness as a money metal; whether permanent or not, was impossible to determine; he regarded the double standard an illusion; silver was further unfitted except for subsidiary purposes by reason of bulk; the concurrent use of government paper would be unjust, since its redemption had been pledged; resumption was indeed practically at hand.

In 1877 Western Republican platforms called loudly for remonetization, Iowa and Ohio taking the lead. Even Pennsylvania joined in the demand. The Democrats denounced the demonetization as a "Republican outrage," although Democrats had voted for the bill of 1873 quite as solidly as Republicans.

The Hayes administration with Sherman as Secretary of the Treasury began March 4, 1877. In negotiating a new contract for the sale of bonds the question arose whether the new obligations would be payable in gold. The refunding act of 1870 provided that the obligations were to be payable in "coin of the *present* standard value." Inasmuch as the legal tender power of the silver dollar was apparently not affected by the act of

1873, and certainly was an existing power in 1870, the question was pertinent. Sherman answered that the bonds would be payable "in coin" as required by the law, but that they would bear date as issued (1877) "when only one kind of coin is a legal tender for all debts." After some discussion the matter was referred to Attorney-General Devens, who ruled that the bonds could not be made payable "in gold coin"; that under the statute of 1870 they were unquestionably redeemable in "coin of the standard value as it existed at the date of the act"; and that all the bonds would stand alike, no matter when issued, unless the law should be altered.[1]

Obviously the bonds authorized to be sold for resumption purposes (act of 1875) fell within the same category; and the legal tender notes were to be redeemed in *coin;* gold was not specified. Upon the other hand, in 1875 gold was, by the act of 1873, the unit of value; and according to the Revised Statutes (1874, already quoted), the silver coins were not legal tender above $5. The point could have been determined by reference to Congress, but that body was for silver by a large majority, and the administration was afraid to appeal to it.

Bland again introduced his free coinage bill, and it passed under a suspension of the rules November 5, 1877. The vote, 163 to 34 (not voting 92), indicates that many representatives dodged the question; the negative vote included only 10 Democrats, Hewitt among these, and on the Republican side, Frye and Reed; the affirmative included such Democrats as Carlisle, Cox, Ewing, Morrison, and such Republicans as Foster, McKinley, Cannon, Kelley, and Keifer.

The bill was as follows: —

"That there shall be coined, at the several mints of the United States, silver dollars of the weight of 412½ grains troy of standard silver, as provided in the act of January 18, 1837, on which shall be the devices and superscriptions provided by said act; which coins together with all silver

[1] Specie Resumption, etc., Ex. Doc., No. 9, 46th Congress, 2d Sess.

dollars heretofore coined by the United States, of like weight and fineness, shall be a legal tender at their nominal value, for all debts and dues public and private, except when otherwise provided by contract; and any owner of silver bullion may deposit the same at any United States mint or assay office, to be coined into such dollars for his benefit upon the same terms and conditions as gold bullion is deposited for coinage under existing laws.

"All acts and parts of acts inconsistent with the provisions of this act are repealed."

In the Senate Allison reported the bill November 21, with an amendment proposing, in lieu of free coinage, the government purchase of a limited amount (not less than $2,000,000 nor more than $4,000,000 monthly) of bullion and coinage on its own account, leaving the dollars full legal tender, which was adopted by 49 to 22.

Meanwhile President Hayes in his first message in December took up the subject, earnestly urging Congress to consider the implied breach of faith respecting the public debt involved in the proposed silver measure, and the interference with the pending reduction of the interest rate; this involved a loss greater than the supposed gain of paying in a cheaper dollar; while opposed to the disparagement of silver, he recognized that equality with the commercial ratio was not attainable, hence the cheaper coin would drive the better abroad; and recommended a dollar that would approach nearer the commercial value of silver with only limited legal tender power; without this, only mischief and misfortune would flow from free silver coinage.

Secretary Sherman in his report [1] practically stated the same points in another form. He asked that the bonds issued from 1873 to date, amounting to nearly $593,000,000, be exempted from the operation of the proposed silver law, having been paid for in gold; but he also favored the pledge of gold payments for all bonds.

[1] Finance Report, 1877.

He insisted that to coin a dollar worth 9 per cent. less than gold would drive out gold, just as it was driven out under the act of 1792, and the same as silver was driven out under the rating in 1834; that a dollar subsidiary in character, with limited legal tender power, would be a great public advantage, unlimited coinage a great public injury.

When the Senate resumed consideration of the Bland Bill, amendments to coin a heavier dollar, to accord more nearly with the commercial ratio, were defeated (49 to 18) by the combination of the extreme and the moderate silver advocates. An amendment to make the dollars redeemable in gold, and one which made the dollars *not* a tender for customs or interest on the public debt, were defeated. An amendment providing for the issue of silver certificates on deposits of dollars in the Treasury, and making such certificates receivable for all public dues and reissuable, was adopted; also an amendment calling for an international conference on silver, one providing that silver dollars were to be tenders only when not otherwise expressly stipulated and not at all for redemption of gold certificates. The final vote on the bill, February 15, 1878, was 48 to 21.

The House passed it, February 21, as amended by the Senate, 203 to 72; Hayes vetoed the bill on the 28th, and it was promptly passed over the veto on the same day; House 196 to 73, Senate 46 to 19. Among the Republicans voting to override the veto were Representatives Butler, Charles Foster, William McKinley, and Kelley, Senators Allison, Matthews, and Windom. Supporting Hayes were Representatives Hale, Reed, Garfield, and Frye; Senators Blaine, Conkling, Dawes, Hoar, and Morrill (Vt.).

The vote in both houses was sectional rather than partisan, only a few members of Congress, except from the East, opposing the measure.

Hayes's reasons for his veto were chiefly that making the dollars and certificates receivable for customs would soon deprive the country of its gold revenues; that the public credit was affected by making the debt payable in silver, thus practically scaling it 8 to 10 per cent.; over $580,000,000 of the bonds had been issued since the act of 1873; gold was received for them, and the subscribers were practically assured that they would be paid in gold; the government received the benefit of a lower interest rate by such assurance; while some measures should be adopted to retain the use of silver as money of the country, this measure violated the obligation of the Nation, the keeping of which "transcends all questions of profit or public advantage."

> "It is my firm conviction that if the country is to be benefited by a silver coinage, it can be done only by the issue of silver dollars of full value, which shall defraud no man. A currency worth less than it purports to be worth will in the end defraud not only creditors, but all who are engaged in legitimate business, and none more surely than those who are dependent on their daily labor for their daily bread."

Senator Matthews (Rep., O.) on January 16, 1878, introduced a *concurrent* resolution (not requiring the President's approval and hence only declaratory) with long preambles, declaring that the bonds of the United States were payable in silver dollars, and that making such dollars legal tender in payment of public debt was not a violation of the public faith nor in derogation of rights of public creditors. The preamble argued that the act of 1869 made the obligations payable in *coin;* all bonds issued under the funding acts of 1870 and 1871 were payable in coin of the then standard, which (being prior to 1873) included the silver dollar. The resolution was adopted 43 to 22. All amendments were voted down, and one to the preamble reciting that only some 8,000,000 silver dollars had been coined from 1792 to date, that the coin was obsolete and had no existence when the bonds were authorized, that the coinage act of 1873 had made gold the standard, that creditors had a right to expect gold, that the government ought not to take advantage of obsolete laws, and that the dollar was worth only 92 cents, received only 17 affirmative votes, 13 being Republican. Only the strong sound money men supported the amendments.

In the House the resolution passed, January 29, by 189 to 79, the vote being practically the same as the subsequent vote on the silver law. A new form of currency inflation was thus found in the use of silver.

The intensity of the silver propaganda is shown by the fact that the legislature of Illinois had, in May, 1877, passed an act to make all silver coins, the standard of which had been declared by Congress, a legal tender. Governor Cullom vetoed the act. Whether free coinage would have materially raised the price of silver, is doubtful. The compromise measure fathered by Senator Allison was not likely to "restore the value" of silver, hence Bland's persistence in pushing the free coinage measure after the compromise had passed.

In accordance with the second section of the act of 1878, the chief commercial nations were invited by the President to send delegates to a conference to meet in Paris in August, to consider the adoption of

"a common ratio between gold and silver, for the purpose oi establishing, internationally, the use of bimetallic money, and securing fixity of relative value between those metals; such conference to be held at such place, in Europe or in the United States, at such time within six months, as may be mutually agreed upon by the executives of the governments joining in the same whenever the governments, so invited, or any three of them, shall have signified their willingness to unite in the same."

Eleven countries replied favorably and were represented; the United States by ex-Senator Fenton (N.Y.), Groesbeck (O.), Francis A. Walker (Mass.), with S. Dana Horton as secretary.

At the conference the American delegates found the representatives of European countries well informed, and many well disposed toward international bimetallism. Others, however, were content to let the United States solve its problem alone.

The several propositions from the Americans, looking to the general reopening of the mints to coinage upon an agreed ratio which could be maintained, were thoroughly discussed and a mass of valuable material was laid before the body; but the conference finally dissolved on August 29 without results. The propositions were as follows: —

"I. It is the opinion of this assembly that it is not to be desired that silver should be excluded from free coinage in Europe and in the United States of America. On the contrary, the assembly believe that it is desirable that the unrestricted coinage of silver, and its use as money of unlimited legal tender, should be retained where they exist, and, as far as practicable, restored where they have ceased to exist.

"II. The use of both gold and silver as unlimited legal-tender money may be safely adopted; first, by equalizing them at a relation to be fixed by international agreement; and, secondly, by granting to each metal at the relation fixed equal terms of coinage, making no discrimination between them."

The European delegates replied that they recognized: —

"I. That it is necessary to maintain in the world the monetary functions of silver as well as those of gold, but that the selection for use of one or the other of the two metals, or of both simultaneously, should be governed by the special position of each State or group of states.

"II. That the question of the restriction of the coinage of silver should equally be left to the discretion of each state or group of states, according to the particular circumstances in which they may find themselves placed; and the more so, in that the disturbance produced during the recent years in the silver market has variously affected the monetary situation of the several countries.

"III. That the differences of opinion which have appeared, and the fact that even some of the states, which have the double standard find it impossible to enter into a mutual engagement with regard to the free coinage of silver, exclude the discussion of the adoption of a common ratio between the two metals." [1]

France, which had been expected to lead in support of the bimetallic proposition, while favoring it in theory, felt it impracti-

[1] International Monetary Conference, 1878, Senate Ex. Doc., No. 58. 45th Congress, 3d Sess.

cable to agree at the time, and certainly could not at any ratio other than her own, 15½ to 1; Great Britain had sent delegates without power to commit the government, and these delegates (having had the benefit of the report of a British silver commission in 1876–1877), while desiring the continued use of silver as money on account of India, could not favor the double standard; Germany had refused to send delegates, being satisfied with her newly adopted gold standard; Russia and Austria, silver standard countries with actually depreciated paper currencies, might be favorable at some time; Belgium and the Scandinavian states, as also Switzerland, favored gold; Italy alone, also suffering from depreciated paper, favored immediate adoption of the American proposal.

Consequent upon the publication of the deliberations of the conference there arose in the United States a distinct body of conservative silver advocates, logically favoring bimetallism, but insisting that the policy was proper only in the event of international action embracing practically all of the commercial nations. They cultivated relations with similar bodies abroad, and were sufficient in number when acting with the gold standard advocates in the two leading parties to thwart the efforts of those who agitated for free coinage by the United States alone. These bimetallists naturally labored for and fully expected another conference, basing the expectation upon the constantly diminishing gold product, which they concluded would not suffice for the world's needs.

STATISTICAL RÉSUMÉ

(Amounts in millions)

Production of Gold and Silver, Ratio, etc.

Year	World			United States				Bullion Value of Silver Dollar	Price of Ounce of Silver
	Gold	Silver		Gold	Silver		Ratio		
		Commercial Value	Coining Value		Commercial Value	Coining Value			
1861	123	46	46	43	2	2	15.50	$1.031	$1.333
1862	123	48	46	39	5	5	15.35	1.041	1.346
1863	123	48	46	40	9	9	15.37	1.040	1.345
1864	123	48	46	46	11	11	15.37	1.040	1.345
1865	123	47	46	53	12	11	15.44	1.035	1.338
1866	150	58	56	54	10	10	15.43	1.036	1.339
1867	130	57	56	52	14	14	15.57	1.027	1.328
1868	130	57	56	48	12	12	15.59	1.025	1.326
1869	130	57	56	50	12	12	15.60	1.024	1.325
1870	130	57	56	50	17	16	15.57	1.027	1.328
1871	116	84	82	44	24	23	15.57	1.025	1.326
1872	116	84	82	36	29	29	15.63	1.022	1.332
1873	96	82	82	36	36	36	15.93	1.004	1.298
1874	91	71	72	34	37	37	16.16	.989	1.279
1875	98	78	81	33	31	32	16.64	.961	1.242
1876	104	78	88	40	35	39	17.75	.900	1.164
1877	114	75	81	47	37	40	17.20	.930	1.202
1878	119	85	95	51	40	45	17.12	.932	1.154

Exports and Imports of Specie, and Coinage

Fiscal Year	Gold			Silver			Coinage of	
	Exports	Imports	Excess + Imp. − Exp.	Exports	Imports	Excess + Imp. − Exp.	Gold	Silver[1]
1861	27	42	+ 15	2	4	+ 2	83	4
1862	35	14	− 21	1	3	+ 2	21	1
1863	62	6	− 56	2	4	+ 2	22	1
1864	101	11	− 90	5	2	− 3	20	1
1865	58	6	− 52	9	3	− 6	28	1
1866	71	8	− 63	15	3	− 12	31	1
1867	39	17	− 22	22	5	− 17	24	1
1868	73	9	− 64	21	5	− 16	19	1
1869	36	14	− 22	21	6	− 15	18	1
1870	34	12	− 22	25	14	− 11	23	1
1871	67	7	− 60	32	14	− 18	21	3
1872	50	9	− 41	30	5	− 25	22	3
1873	45	9	− 36	40	13	− 27	57	4
1874	34	20	− 14	33	9	− 24	35	7
1875	67	14	− 53	25	7	− 18	33	15
1876	31	8	− 23	25	8	− 17	47	25
1877	26	26	− 0	30	15	− 15	44	28
1878	9	13	+ 4	25	16	− 9	50	29

[1] Coinage of dollars prior to 1878 amounted to 3,900,000, of which 2,500,000 were coined from 1871 to 1873.

CHAPTER XVI

Silver Question

1879–1890

The silver advocates in Congress were by no means satisfied with the Bland-Allison law, and during the summer of 1878 the subject was again agitated in the political field. The Republican state platforms favored "both gold and silver," but Western Democrats declared persistently for free coinage, as did the "Greenbackers." The congressional elections resulted rather favorably to the silver advocates, but they were unable to rely fully on their forces.

When Hayes sent in his second message (December, 1878), resumption was practically at hand. He said that, with views unchanged, he had had the silver law of 1878 carried out faithfully, to afford it a fair trial. He recommended therefore that Congress abstain from disturbing business by legislation or attempts thereat, and allow the people to have an opportunity to bring about an enduring prosperity. Secretary Sherman announced that while maintaining that the resumption act contemplated redemption of notes in *gold*, he would use either metal, as holders of notes might demand, reserving the legal option, however, to pay in either.

At this time the ratio of silver to gold was (average) 17.92, and the bullion value of the silver dollar 93.2 cents.

In February, 1879, a bill to make gold and silver coin interchangeable was defeated in the House, 101 to 136; one to pay out legal tender notes for any coin brought to the subtreasury in New York, by 105 to 129; and bills to redeem trade dollars and recoin them into standard dollars were also defeated.

In the following Congress, the first session of which assembled in March, a free coinage measure, reported by A. J. Warner (Dem., O.), passed the House by 114 to 97, 6 Republicans favoring and 8 Democrats opposing it. An attempt to limit the coinage to domestic product was defeated by 105 to 130, and one to provide for a 460-grain dollar by 52 to 176. A proposition to make gold and silver certificates legal tender was negatived by 73 to 135.

In the Senate the free coinage bill was sent to the Finance Committee, from which it was reported adversely by Senator Bayard at the following session, and a resolution by Senator Vest (Dem., Mo.), declaring free coinage necessary to supply the needed volume of money, was sent to the same committee, for burial, by a vote of 23 to 22, 4 Eastern Democrats voting with the majority.

The House passed a resolution, by a vote of 143 to 79, with considerable support from the Republican side, directing the Secretary of the Treasury to pay out the silver dollars in the Treasury the same as gold.

A bill was passed at this session (June 9, 1879), for the redemption of subsidiary coin in lawful money and for its issue in exchange for lawful money in sums or multiples of $20. This action was due to the existence of a troublesome surplus of such coin caused, not by excessive coinage, but by the return from abroad of pieces of the old coinage banished during the war period.

At this time a bill proposing a solution of the silver question by the minting of a "goloid" dollar containing both metals, was favored by Stephens (Dem., Ga.), formerly Vice-President of the Southern Confederacy. It proposed, also, to adopt the system for international use by coining a four-dollar piece. The measure, however, never got beyond the committee stage.

In his report for 1879 Secretary Sherman reported that no effort had been spared to put silver into circulation, but only 13,000,000 of the dollars were then in use out of a coinage of 45,000,000; the coin could be maintained at par only by holding a great part of it in the vaults of the Treasury; he accordingly urged limitation of the coinage to preserve the parity with gold.

President Hayes recommended that the Treasury be authorized to suspend coinage of silver when parity was endangered. He expressed the belief that international agreement upon a ratio was possible, and hoped no legislation other than that recommended be undertaken, in order to avoid disturbances.

Congress, in appropriation acts now, and annually thereafter, provided for the distribution, free of expense, of silver dollars from mints and Treasury offices, the cost to be charged against the "silver profit fund"; *i.e.*, the amount representing the difference between the cost of the bullion and the nominal value of the dollars coined therefrom, sometimes also called "seigniorage."

The Senate, also Democratic, nevertheless contained a sufficient number of anti-silver Democrats from the East to defeat any free silver measure, and hence no further attempts were made to press such bills. But Representative Weaver of Iowa, later Greenback candidate for the presidency, offered in the House a proposition to redeem bonds in silver, opening the mints to the free coinage of silver to provide means. This was defeated 85 to 117. The substance thereof became one of the cardinal principles announced in the platform of that party in the summer of 1880.

The principal parties omitted silver from their platforms in the presidential contest of 1880. It was an important and exciting issue, however, in very many congressional districts. Garfield, conspicuous for sound money views, was elected President, and with him a Republican Congress.

In his report for 1880, Secretary Sherman stated that the amount of silver was already in excess of the demand; popular objection to the dollars arose from their bulk and their known deficiency in value; less than $26,000,000 were in use out of nearly $73,000,000 coined, and less than $20,000,000 were floated by representative certificates, thus leaving $27,000,000 idle in the Treasury — almost the year's coinage. The average bullion value of the dollars was about 88½ cents. Sherman had adopted a policy of furnishing silver certificates, free of exchange charge, at Southern and Western points, for deposits of gold at New York.

President Hayes forcibly urged the suspension of coinage in his message for 1880. It was demonstrated that the coinage law of 1878 would not raise the commercial value of silver, and indeed its price had fallen. He also recommended increasing the amount of silver in the dollar.

With the silver situation thus remaining undetermined, and the conditions in France, Italy, India, and other countries becoming more serious owing to the steadily diminishing supply of gold and the steadily falling price of silver, opinion in both England and Germany underwent a change. Leading advocates of the single gold standard altered their views. France now consented to join this country in an invitation to another conference to devise a "system for the establishment by means of an international agreement of the use of gold and silver as bimetallic money, according to a settled relative value between these two metals." (The ratio was now about 18 to 1.)

The conference met at Paris in April, 1881.[1] England, on account of India, was seriously interested, and Germany was also represented. In all, eighteen countries sent delegates, our own being ex-Secretary of State William M. Evarts (N.Y.), ex-Senators Allen G. Thurman (O.) and Timothy O. Howe (Wis.),

[1] International Monetary Conference, 1881, House Misc. Doc., No. 396, 49th Congress, 1st Sess.

with S. Dana Horton as expert. The membership of the conference in general was more favorable to bimetallism than that of the previous one.

The questions considered were concisely these: —

Has the fall of silver been hurtful to prosperity; is it desirable that the relation be made more stable?

Has the fall been due to increased product or to legislation?

Can stability be restored if a large group of states remonetize silver under unlimited coinage of full legal tender pieces?

If so, what measures should be taken to reduce fluctuation of the ratio to a minimum?

It was apparent that most of the Europeans imagined that the United States was interested because she was a great producer of silver. Germany at this time still had a very large stock of its old coins unsold. Great Britain, on account of India, showed a desire to have all others extend the use of silver in order to raise the price.

Long intervening recesses prolonged the conference until July. France and the United States finally joined in a declaration answering the questions practically thus: —

That the fall of silver was injurious, and establishing a fixed ratio would be beneficial; international agreement for free and unlimited coinage of both metals at a fixed ratio would cause and maintain stability; the ratio of 15½ to 1 was most suitable; England, France, Germany, and the United States, with the concurrence of others, could by convention secure and maintain the stability of the ratio adopted.

Germany and England declined to enter into such a compact. The conference adjourned for politeness' sake to April 12, 1882 — to enable France and this country to work out a plan. Actually, as it proved, the adjournment was *sine die.*

Opinion here now took in large measure the view, as Secretary Folger expressed it in his report for 1881, that Europe was in fact more deeply interested in the solution of the silver question than the United States, that therefore the suspension of all coinage by us would tend toward the adoption of the bimetallic policy. Folger urgently recommended such action, since the supply of dollars was now in excess of the home demand, and further coinage would bring us to the single standard. He had been able to increase the dollars in use to $34,000,000, the certificates to $59,000,000, leaving in the Treasury some $11,000,000 net of silver funds.

In January, 1882, Congress called for a report upon silver purchases, which when furnished showed that 92,550,000 fine ounces had been acquired at a cost of $95,119,000, being coined into 105,380,000 silver dollars. The Treasury had in the forty-six months bought only the minimum amount fixed by the law.

In the House an attempt was made under the lead of Dingley (Rep., Me.) to suspend coinage of silver and the issue of silver certificates, but it failed.

The act of July 12, 1882, authorized the issue of gold certificates, and made these as well as silver certificates available for bank reserves. It also prohibited any national bank from being a member of any clearing-house where silver certificates were refused in settlement of balances.

In 1882 Folger had been able to put into circulation only about 1,000,000 silver dollars, and the silver certificates in use were less than the year before, so that practically the entire purchase of silver for the year, some $27,000,000, was idle in the Treasury, having displaced gold or legal tenders to that extent.

The well-known opposition of President Arthur made further efforts to pass a free coinage measure useless, and no attempt was for a time made in that direction; but the silver advocates tried unsuccessfully to enact a law for the redemption of trade dollars and their recoinage into standard dollars. The bill failed in the Senate.

McCulloch became Secretary near the end of 1884, which gave him an opportunity to point out vigorously the danger threatening the country from silver. A believer in bimetallism *under international agreement*, he nevertheless saw the futility of the policy now obtaining in the United States. A continuation of this policy would either impair the gold reserve or compel the use of silver for payment of *gold obligations*, thus bringing about the silver standard. The silver funds in the Treasury had increased to $53,000,000. The reduction of tariff and other taxes by the act of March 3, 1883, caused a temporary shrinkage of revenues which presently made it much more difficult to carry a large volume of idle silver.

The annual gold product of the world had now fallen below $100,000,000 and that of silver was over $115,000,000, the United States furnishing $30,000,000 of the former and $46,000,000 of the latter.

Grover Cleveland had been elected President, and a portion of his party was definitely opposed to silver. Anticipating that he would in his inaugural express himself hostile to silver, 95 Western Democrats early in 1885 addressed a letter requesting him not to do so. He replied (February 24), forcibly declaring his belief that a financial crisis would follow a continuance of the coinage of silver; that the gold reserve was practically already impaired. The silver advocates retorted by pointing out that France with $850,000,000 gold maintained $600,000,000 silver; arguing that we had $600,000,000 gold and only $200,000,000 silver, and that if the Secretary of the Treasury would only pay out more silver and less gold, the gold reserve would not be endangered.

The silver advocates persisted in the belief that the Treasury was not only indifferent in getting silver into circulation, but were inclined to the opinion that obstacles were actually placed in the way. In February, 1885, the House passed a resolution asking the Secretary of the Treasury a number of questions on the subject, designed to inform the House as to the action of his department. Secretary McCulloch replied frankly, demonstrating not only that both dollars and certificates were paid out as largely as was possible, but showing that both forms returned to the Treasury in the revenues as fast as, and sometimes in greater volume than, he disbursed them; 40 per cent. of the customs revenue was now paid in silver certificates; the gold currency was preferred, and was very largely withheld in payment of taxes and duties; the silver issue had reached the saturation point. Yet upon this showing the House refused, in the same month, to suspend the further coinage of dollars, 118 to 152. So the Treasury was compelled to pay out current money and increase its supply of those forms which were not current. The country barely escaped going upon a silver basis.

President Cleveland and his Secretary of the Treasury, Daniel Manning, immediately adopted vigorous measures to prevent a catastrophe. By at once curtailing the issue of small legal tender notes (which was in the discretion of the Secretary), room was made for a larger volume of silver dollars; by using legal tender notes in disbursements, and avoiding when possible the payment of silver certificates, a smaller proportion of the revenues was received in that form; and the gold reserve, which in May had fallen to $115,000,000, was increased. Secretary Manning also acquired from the New York banks nearly $6,000,000 in gold in exchange for subsidiary silver coin, of which there was a surplus on hand. By suspending bond purchases the Treasury by December had $148,000,000 gold in its reserve, and also over $76,000,000 of idle silver. These makeshifts served to tide over the interval until the regular session of Congress, to which Secretary Manning, in his report (December, 1885), presented an exhaustive, learned review of the silver question.

He urged a suspension of the coinage of dollars in order that the status of silver might become more definitely determined. The country had now 215,000,000 of the dollars which could be maintained at parity only by stopping further output; to continue the coinage under existing conditions was merely inviting disaster.

President Cleveland devoted serious attention to the subject in his first message. He asserted that the vital part of the act of 1878 was that looking to an international bimetallic agreement; that endeavors in this line had failed, thus leaving the United States alone to battle for silver — a losing contest. An examination of conditions abroad convinced him that no help was to be expected so long as the present policy was persisted in. Indeed, the further accumulation of dollars at the peculiar ratio of 16 to 1, not anywhere else in use, made the chance for an agreement more remote; the supply of dollars now far exceeded the demand; by suspending further coinage, however, these might be ultimately absorbed in the circulation; the plea that the continuation was for the benefit of the "debtor class" implied that this class was dishonest, which he denied; nor would a depreciated dollar help them in the end.

In Europe a marked depression in trade became manifest at this time. In England a commission was appointed to examine the subject, and out of this came eventually a gold and silver commission. In other nations also the question of silver was being considered.

Congress had again called upon the Treasury for a full report as to its action respecting silver, to which Secretary Manning replied (March 3, 1886). The questions embraced the authority for the loan of gold from the New York banks, the amount of free silver in the Treasury, and bonds subject to redemption not paid, implying that the silver could have been used for the payment of debt, and finally asking as to the future policy.

Secretary Manning replied that the loan of gold from the New York banks was made by exchanging subsidiary silver for gold with an agreement to change back when the condition of the treasury warranted. He referred to no authority therefor, as the transaction was regarded as an exchange presumably permitted by the act of 1879.

He further stated that there had been no disparagement of any form of money by the Treasury; each citizen was paid in his own choice of currencies on hand. He had by much labor increased the circulation of silver dollars by $11,500,000. He pointed out that silver certificates, if issued beyond the actual needs, would necessarily flow back into the Treasury, and silver dollars would not circulate if one and two dollar notes were furnished. Interest-bearing debt subject to call amounted to $174,000,000, but to force silver out for this would precipitate the silver basis. On the other hand, there was $346,000,000 of debt in the shape of legal tender notes, the payment of which had been pledged in 1869, but which under the act of May 31, 1878, he was compelled to reissue when paid; these could be replaced by silver certificates; the country desired to remain bimetallic; free coinage, or the continuation of the limited coinage, would bring silver monometallism, under which all the surplus silver of Europe would ultimately come here for gold; until the coinage was discontinued it was useless to talk of bimetallism.

The sole action taken by Congress was to authorize the issue of silver certificates of the denominations of $1, $2, and $5, by an amendment tacked to an appropriation act. These certificates gradually began taking the place of greenbacks.

Congress endeavored to force Manning to use the accumulating surplus in the purchase of bonds, but he felt that unless he was able to hold a large surplus, he would be hampered by the large silver balance.

In his report for 1886 Manning reviewed the silver question at home and abroad, and again concluded that the only hope lay in the cessation of silver purchases under the act of 1878, thereby causing a change of sentiment in Europe, which was content to look on while we carried the load.

Opinion in Europe was undergoing a change: 243 members of the British Parliament had petitioned that the Gold and Silver Commission inquire into the subject and suggest remedies to be obtained either by sole or concurrent action by the British government. The fall of prices was having its influence.[1]

On March 3, 1887, an act was passed (becoming law without the President's signature) to redeem trade dollars, not mutilated, for a period of six months; $7,689,000 were so redeemed and recoined into dollars and smaller pieces.

Europe had again been sounded as to international action, but entirely without result. Edward Atkinson, the delegate, returned without the slightest hope of the success of the movement in Europe. President Cleveland had, however, taken strong ground favoring the reduction of tariff taxes to check the growing surplus. This surplus could be used only in redemption of bonds, which meant retiring national bank currency, leaving in turn a "vacuum" for gold or silver. Even if the tariff were lowered, the increased imports of goods would tend to cause exports of gold and the vacuum would have to be filled by silver. Europe did not fail to see this and awaited the issue. No legislation followed, but the discussion served to keep silver in the background, although in the presidential campaign of 1888 the subject took a more prominent position than ever before. The Republicans denounced Cleveland's policy as an attempt at silver demonetization. The majority of the Democrats, favorable to silver, were yet unable to dictate the platform, and appreciating the necessity of renominating Cleveland, their declaration was drawn by the eastern wing of the party. It favored both "gold and silver."

Harrison defeated Cleveland, and his administration was tacitly pledged to "do something for silver."

In 1888 the report of the British Commission appeared.[2]

[1] Russell, International Monetary Conferences.

[2] See Senate, Misc. Doc., No. 34, 50th Congress, 2d Sess.

The opinion of the twelve commissioners was unanimous as to the causes of the disturbance of the bimetallic par and the disastrous fall in prices resulting. They said: —

"The action of the Latin Union in 1873 broke the link between silver and gold, which had kept the price of the former, as measured by the latter, constant at about the legal ratio; and when this link was broken the silver market was open to the influence of all the factors which go to affect the price of a commodity. These factors happen since 1873 to have operated in the direction of a fall in the gold price of that metal, and the frequent fluctuations in its value are accounted for by the fact that the market has become fully sensitive to the other influences to which we have called attention above,"

viz., the great increase in production of silver and diminution of the gold product, increased use of gold and diminished use of silver, resulting from changes in currency systems, the sale of silver by Germany, the removal of the steadying force of the Latin Union.

As to remedies, the commission was evenly divided. One-half headed by Lord Herschell rejected bimetallism and recommended no change in the British system. They said: —

"In our opinion it might be worth while to meet the great commercial nations on any proposal which would lead to a more extended use of silver, and so tend to prevent the apprehended further fall in the value of that metal, and to keep its relation to gold more stable.

* * * * * * * * * *

"Though unable to recommend the adoption of what is commonly known as bimetallism, we desire it to be understood that we are quite alive to the imperfections of standards of value, which not only fluctuate, but fluctuate independently of each other; and we do not shut our eyes to the possibility of future arrangements between nations which may reduce these fluctuations.

"One uniform standard for all commercial countries would no doubt, like uniformity of coinage or of standards of weight and measure, be a great advantage. But we think that any premature and doubtful step might, in addition to its other dangers and inconveniences, prejudice and retard progress to this end.

* * * * * * * * * *

"Under these circumstances we have felt that the wiser course is to abstain from recommending any fundamental change in a system of currency under which the commerce of Great Britain has attained its present development."

The other half of the commission contended that if the Latin Union's system of bimetallism had steadied the bullion market, as admitted, such a system of free coinage by *all* nations upon an agreed ratio certainly would. They said: —

"Neither metal alone exists in sufficient quantity to serve as a sole standard without causing such a change in the level of prices as to amount to a financial and commercial revolution; but we cannot doubt that if a sufficiently wide area of agreement between the leading commercial countries can be secured, this most important result may be effectually attained and a great international reform successfully accomplished.

* * * * * * * * * *

"Failing any attempt to reëstablish the connecting link between the two metals, it seems probable that the general tendency of the commercial nations of the world will be towards a single gold standard.

"Any step in that direction would, of course, aggravate all the evils of the existing situation, and could not fail to have a most injurious effect upon the progress of the world.

"A further fall in the value of silver might at any moment give rise to further evils of great and indefinite magnitude in India, while a further rise in the value of gold might produce the most serious consequences at home.

"No settlement of the difficulty is, however, in our opinion, possible without international action.

"The remedy which we suggest is essentially international in its character, and its details must be settled in concert with the other powers concerned.

"It will be sufficient for us to indicate the essential features of the agreement to be arrived at, namely, (1) free coinage of both metals into legal tender money; and (2) the fixing of a ratio at which the coins of either metal shall be available for the payment of all debts at the option of the debtor.

* * * * * * * * * *

"We therefore submit that the chief commercial nations of the world, such as the United States, Germany, and the States forming the Latin

Union, should in the first place be consulted as to their readiness to join with the United Kingdom in a conference, at which India and any of the British colonies which may desire to attend should be represented, with a view to arrive, if possible, at a common agreement on the basis above indicated."

One of the six reporting against bimetallism later came out strongly in favor of it.[1]

The document was a lengthy and scholarly production; its burden was naturally India and her relations to the mother country. Congress ordered it printed for distribution here, and it gave both the international bimetallists and the free coinage advocates much material for study and discussion.

By 1888 the national bank circulation had largely made way for silver certificates. Nearly $230,000,000 of the latter were now in existence; about 60,000,000 of the dollars were actually in circulation. The Treasury had only $30,000,000 free. Gratifying as this was from one point of view, Secretary Fairchild nevertheless urged action to remove the danger of going to a depreciated silver basis. He still hoped that before a crisis was reached international action would relieve the situation. The feature of the Treasury condition which attracted most attention was the rapid increase of the gold reserve which had during Fairchild's term gone beyond $200,000,000, standing at the end of March, 1888, at almost $219,000,000.

This was the political situation respecting silver: A large majority of the Democrats in both houses of Congress favored free coinage; a sufficient number of Republican senators were also pledged to that policy to make it easy to pass a bill through the Senate; in the House the Republican majority was small, and while a large majority of representatives of that party were opposed to free coinage and a lesser number, but still a majority, were opposed to enlarging the use of silver, it was clear that if *nothing were done* a sufficient number of Republicans would

[1] Leonard Courtney.

join the silver Democrats in passing a free coinage law. The party was at the same time pledged to tariff legislation, and Harrison, as well as McKinley, who was the House leader, deemed the tariff of paramount importance and believed some silver legislation was necessary for the purpose of averting free coinage and preventing the defeat of tariff legislation. The silver Republicans used their power to attain their ends without disguise.

The task of meeting the political exigency fell to Windom, who had been chosen Secretary of the Treasury by Harrison. Windom's Treasury report for 1889 included a most elaborate review of the silver question. Silver had now fallen so that the ratio was 22 to 1, giving the silver dollar a bullion value of about 72 cents. The world's product of gold was $123,000,000, that of silver $155,000,000. The United States had coined 343,500-000 silver dollars, of which only 60,000,000 were in use, but 277,300,000 were in the Treasury represented by certificates, leaving free in the Treasury only 6,200,000.

While the prediction of danger from our financial policy had not been fulfilled, it was due to favorable conditions of trade, large crops, and general prosperity, which served to postpone the crisis. Silver had continued to fall despite the large purchases by the government.

Windom proposed the following: —

> "Issue Treasury notes against deposits of silver bullion at the market price of silver when deposited, payable on demand in such quantities of silver bullion as will equal in value, at the date of presentation, the number of dollars expressed on the face of the notes at the market price of silver, or in gold, at the option of the government; or in silver dollars at the option of the holder. Repeal the compulsory feature of the present coinage act."

The price was not to exceed $1 for 412½ grains of standard metal.

In support of the measure he argued that while satisfying the demand for the continued use of silver, it provided a note-issue which could not depreciate, hence was *sound;* would enhance the value of silver to a point where free coinage would be safe; prevented contraction by supplying the place of bank-notes rapidly being retired, yet would not cause inordinate or unhealthy expansion; would if successful point a way for other nations to take. Loss to the government by reason of depreciation of the bullion was exceedingly remote, but even if it came to pass, the government having assumed the duty of providing currency must stand it; nor could an opportunity be given for speculation in silver, the option to redeem in gold being a sufficient check; no flood of silver need be feared to cause undue inflation, because being taken at the *market price* it would not pay Europe to surrender her coins; he estimated the surplus product of silver at 40,000,000 ounces, and the proposed law, if limited, would at the maximum take 50,000,000 ounces; there was no substantial stock on hand anywhere; he preferred that there be no limit on the amount; if any limit were deemed advisable it should be by excluding foreign silver altogether.

Assuming, as Windom did (for he was impressed by the Western view), that some action to take care of silver was requisite, this measure was perhaps the least objectionable. Harrison in his message declared in favor of some legislation to increase the use of silver without the danger of a silver basis. He had not had an opportunity to study the Windom plan, but approved its general lines.

The measure was introduced in January, 1890, but the tariff bill had precedence. Congress debated long, and only by a vote of 120 to 117 was ready to consider it in June, and then the Committee on Coinage reported a much altered bill. It directed the purchase monthly of $4,500,000 worth of silver with an issue of Treasury notes, which were to be legal tender, with free coinage when silver reached parity (16 to 1). Bland moved to recommit the bill and order the committee to report a free coinage bill, which was defeated 116 to 140.

The committee's bill passed the House by a majority of 16, no Democrats voting in its favor. In the Senate numerous amendments were proposed. One striking out the legal tender feature of the notes, by Morrill, was defeated 14 to 50 (Carlisle voting for it, Sherman against). One to strike out the free coinage proviso was lost by 16 to 46. Finding themselves strong enough, the silver advocates in the Senate finally substituted a free coinage bill by a vote of 42 to 25, 14 Republicans voting aye and 3 Democrats nay. After a severe contest in the House in which McKinley led the almost solid Republican vote, the Senate free coinage bill was disagreed to, 135 to 152, and the bills went to conference, where, largely under Sherman's lead, the House bill was remodelled into the shape in which it finally passed on July 14, 1890, in the House by 123 to 90 (116 not voting) and in the Senate by 39 to 26; both were strict party votes, for it was a purely administration measure.

This act, sometimes known as the "Sherman law," provided for a compulsory purchase by means of an issue of legal tender Treasury notes of 4,500,000 ounces of pure silver monthly, at the market price, not to exceed $1 for 371.25 grains of pure silver (equal to $1.2929 per ounce). Dollars were to be coined for one year, and thereafter only as they were required for redemption of notes, which were made redeemable in gold or silver dollars at the government's option. No greater or less amount of notes was to be outstanding than the cost of the bullion and the dollars coined therefrom in the Treasury, and silver certificates might be issued on the surplus dollars coined (in other words on the "seigniorage"). The act also declared it the purpose of the government to maintain gold and silver at a parity; the fund of lawful money held for redemption of notes of liquidating or reducing banks was "covered into the Treasury" instead of being held as a trust fund, the notes to be redeemed to be treated as debt of the United States.

The measure as passed was obviously not as safe or conservative as that planned by Windom; but the friends of silver demanded a larger measure of "protection" for the white metal than Windom had accorded it.

Thus "something was done for silver." The tariff bill was also passed, reducing revenues $50,000,000; and a pension bill ultimately calling for an additional annual expenditure of $50,000,000 also became law.

The prospect therefore was that the surplus would be annually cut down $100,000,000, and that the inflation of the circulating medium would be at the rate of over $50,000,000 annually, less the reduction in bank-notes. A definite increasing liability against the gold reserve was created without enlarging the reserve. Careful students of the situation calculated that in eighteen months a crash would come, but they had not given full credit to the nation's resources.

STATISTICAL RÉSUMÉ

(Amounts in millions)

PRODUCTION OF GOLD AND SILVER

Year	World			United States				Average Price of Ounce of Silver
	Gold	Silver		Gold	Silver		Ratio	
		Commercial Value	Coining Value		Commercial Value	Coining Value		
1879	109	84	96	39	35	41	18.39	$1.124
1880	106	86	97	36	35	39	18.05	1.145
1881	103	90	102	35	38	43	18.25	1.132
1882	102	98	112	33	41	47	18.20	1.136
1883	95	99	115	30	40	46	18.64	1.109
1884	102	91	105	31	42	49	18.61	1.111
1885	108	98	118	32	43	52	19.41	1.065
1886	106	93	121	35	39	51	20.78	.995
1887	106	94	124	33	40	53	21.10	.979
1888	110	102	141	33	43	59	22.00	.940
1889	123	112	155	33	47	65	22.10	.935
1890	119	132	163	33	57	70	19.75	1.046

THE PURCHASE AND COINAGE OF SILVER

Fiscal Year	Ounces Fine	Cost	Average Price per Ounce	Bullion Value of Silver Dollar	Coinage of Silver Dollars	Silver Certificates Out	Silver Dollars Out	Net Silver Dollars and Bullion in Treasury
1878 . .	11	13	$1.2048	$.9318	22	—	1	15
1879 . .	19	22	1.1218	.8676	28	—	8	33
1880 . .	22	25	1.1440	.8848	27	6	19	44
1881 . .	20	22	1.1328	.8761	28	39	29	27
1882 . .	21	24	1.1351	.8779	28	55	32	36
1883 . .	23	26	1.1174	.8642	28	73	35	44
1884 . .	22	24	1.1120	.8600	28	96	40	43
1885 . .	22	24	1.0897	.8428	29	102	39	68
1886 . .	23	23	1.0334	.7992	31	88	53	96
1887 . .	26	26	.9810	.7587	34	142	56	80
1888 . .	25	24	.9547	.7384	32	200	56	54
1889 . .	26	25	.9338	.7222	35	257	54	33
1890 . .	28	27	.9668	.7477	37	297	56	27

EXPORTS AND IMPORTS OF SPECIE

Fiscal Year	Gold			Silver		
	Exports	Imports	Excess −Export +Import	Exports	Imports	Excess −Export +Import
1879	5	6	+ 1	20	15	− 5
1880	4	81	+ 77	13	12	− 1
1881	3	100	+ 97	17	11	− 6
1882	33	34	+ 1	17	8	− 9
1883	12	18	+ 6	20	11	− 9
1884	41	23	− 18	26	15	− 11
1885	8	27	+ 19	34	17	− 17
1886	43	21	− 22	30	18	− 12
1887	10	43	+ 33	26	17	− 9
1888	18	44	+ 26	28	15	− 13
1889	60	10	− 50	37	19	− 18
1890	17	13	− 4	35	21	− 14

CHAPTER XVII

National Banking System

1861–1875

Bank currency in the United States in 1861, as has been shown, was issued wholly under state authority and was far from creditable to a nation boasting advanced civilization. In the Eastern states and a few others salutary laws had led to systems which were sound, but in the greater part of the country, owing to lax legislation and want of supervision, bank-notes passed at varying rates of discount and were counterfeited to an extent that was appalling.

The conditions precipitated by the Civil War were therefore favorable to the creation of a national currency, uniform in character and based upon lines of conservatism and safety. The basic principles underlying the National Bank Act and bank legislation in many of the states were evolved by Alexander Hamilton in preparing the charter for the first United States Bank. The laws of several states, especially those of New York, were copied in preparing the provisions of the National Bank Act.

The federal government was in pressing need of money. Bonds could not be readily sold for coin, and Secretary Chase would not accept state bank-notes, even had the subtreasury law of 1846 permitted his doing so. Chase recommended a national currency system based upon government bonds. The bill for this purpose, drawn upon the lines suggested by the Secretary, was introduced in Congress by Representative Spaulding (N.Y.) in the winter of 1861–1862. It was necessarily a lengthy measure, and the exigencies of the war devolved great labors upon Congress. It was not acted upon until the succeeding session, and the result was, as we have seen, the legal tender government note-issue. Chase was persistent in urging upon Congress the double advantage of his plan, at once making a market for government bonds and furnishing the people with a safe and uniform currency.

The legal tender issue, owing to its doubtful constitutionality and its dangerous facility of expansion, was regarded as temporary, and no one contemplated its retention as a permanent part of our currency system. Lincoln, in his message, strongly urged the speedy enactment of the proposed law.[1] The act passed both houses of Congress and was approved February 25, 1863, just one year after the approval of the legal tender act. A considerable number of Republicans and practically all the Democrats opposed the measure. The debate showed that the intention was to supplant state bank circulation, and this intensified the opposition. The authors of the measure contemplated that the currency created would ultimately supplant the United States notes. Sherman, in debate, alluding to the latter form of notes, said that they could "be used only during the war. The very moment that peace comes, all this circulation . . . will at once be banished. . . . The issue of government notes can only be a temporary measure." Spaulding regarded it as "the commencement of a permanent system for providing a national currency."

The act provided for a bureau in the Treasury Department to be in charge of a Comptroller of the Currency under the general direction of the Secretary, to report directly to Congress. This bureau was given supervision of the banks to be established under the act and the currency issued by them. Hugh McCulloch was appointed the first Comptroller.

[1] See page 193.

In order to constrain state banks to nationalize, their notes were by the act of March 30, 1863, taxed two per cent., just double the tax imposed upon national currency. Four hundred banks were immediately organized, but defects in the law were at once discovered, and upon the recommendation of Treasury officials it was revised by the act of June 3, 1864. The act passed the House by a vote of 80 to 60, no Democrats favoring it and only two Republicans opposing it, in the Senate by 30 to 9, no Democrats favoring and three Republicans opposing. Under its provisions any number of persons not less than five might form a banking association. The minimum capital was fixed at $50,000 for places under 6000 population, $100,000 for places not exceeding 50,000, and $200,000 for larger cities. One-half of the capital was required to be paid in cash before beginning business, the balance in 10 per cent. monthly instalments. Shareholders were liable for debts of the bank to an amount equal to the par of their stock. Each bank was required to deposit with the Treasury United States bonds bearing not less than 5 per cent. interest to the amount of one-third of its capital (but in no case less than $30,000), to be held to secure circulation, which might be issued to the extent of 90 per cent. of the market value of the bonds (not to exceed 90 per cent. of par), but not in excess of the bank's capital. Notes might be in denominations from $1 to $1000 and were to bear a certificate on their face that bonds of the United States were held by the Treasury to secure them, the name of the bank, and signatures of its officers. They were made redeemable on demand in "lawful money" (*i.e.* legal tender), receivable for all public dues except customs and for all payments by the United States except interest on the public debt and redemption of national currency. The volume of notes was limited to $300,000,000, of which one-sixth might be under $5 until after the resumption of specie payments, when none under $5 were to be issued. Banks might reduce their bond deposits to the minimum required by surrendering their notes for cancellation. They were required to receive each other's notes at par and not to pay out notes of banks failing to redeem on demand.

Seventeen reserve cities were designated by the act. The banks in these were required to hold a 25 per cent. reserve on circulation and deposits, one-half of which might be to their credit with an approved reserve agent in the city of New York, banks in the latter city being required to keep a 25 per cent. cash-in-bank reserve. All other banks were required to keep 15 per cent. reserve on circulation and deposits, three-fifths of which might be to their credit with a bank approved by the Comptroller of the Currency in any of the reserve cities. When reserves were impaired no new loans were to be made until the same were restored, and if not restored within thirty days after notice from the Comptroller, a receiver might, with the approval of the Secretary of the Treasury, be appointed. A receiver might also be appointed for failure to redeem notes or provide for their redemption at the reserve agencies. In case of receivership the bonds were to be sold by the Comptroller and the bank's circulation retired with the proceeds. If there were a deficit the amount thereof was a paramount lien upon all the bank's assets.

The banks might transact a general banking business. Loans in excess of 10 per cent. of the capital to any one person or concern were forbidden, bona fide discount or purchase of bills receivable excepted. Interest rates were regulated. Banks were forbidden to acquire real estate other than for their necessary use, unless the same was taken for preëxisting debts. Before dividends were declared, 10 per cent. of the profits were required to be passed to a surplus fund until it should equal 20 per cent. of the capital. A tax of ½ per cent. semiannually was imposed upon circulation and ¼ per cent. each upon capital and deposits, in lieu of all other federal taxes. Charters extended for a period of twenty years from date of incorporation, but dissolution might be effected by a two-thirds vote of shareholders, in which case notes were to be advertised for and redeemed. After one year, however, the bank might deposit with the Treasury lawful money to redeem the notes and receive back the bonds held. Periodical examinations, full and verified quarterly reports, and monthly reports of the principal items, were required. The total debts of a bank, aside from its notes and deposits, were not to exceed its capital. Provision was made for the conversion of state banks into the national system. National banks might be designated by the Secretary of the Treasury as government depositories for all revenues except customs, such deposits to be secured to the satisfaction of the Secretary "by government bonds and otherwise." Congress reserved the right at any time to amend or repeal the act.

By the end of 1864 there were 638 banks, with a capital of over $135,000,000 and circulation of nearly $67,000,000. They owned at that time $176,500,000 government bonds, and had helped to place with the public a much larger amount. The government's deposits with them amounted to nearly $38,000,000.

The state banks experienced little difficulty in redeeming their notes in greenbacks and constantly maintained a very large volume in circulation. Under the laws of many states bank-notes were issued against the credit or general assets of the banks and where a deposit of security was required it was easier or more profitable to comply with the state laws than to deposit United States bonds as required by the National Bank Act. The amount of notes which might be issued was less restricted under the state laws and altogether banking under the state systems was more profitable. The currency was not nationalized, and the national system as a market for bonds was disappointing.

Therefore, on March 3, 1865, a revenue law imposed a tax of 10 per cent. upon state bank-notes paid out by any bank, national or state, and also provided that state banks with branches might come into the national system and retain their branches. In 1866 the 10 per cent. tax was extended to state bank-notes used in payment by any one. This legislation very soon caused the disappearance of all such notes and was a powerful factor in inducing state banks to organize under the national system. At the end of 1865 there were 1582 national banks with over $400,000,000 capital, owning $440,000,000 of bonds, with circulation amounting to $213,000,000. They also had outstanding over $45,000,000 of notes issued by those which had been state institutions.

The act of March 3, 1865, regulated the proportion of note-issues of largely capitalized banks, diminishing the ratio as the capital increased, and provided that one-half of the maximum circulation ($300,000,000) was to be apportioned among the states according to population, the other half "with due regard to banking capital, resources, and business." This law was the result of a tendency, anticipated in the original currency act, towards a monopolization of the new bank issues by Eastern banks. The Southern states, recently restored to the Union, had now to be provided for. The limit of circulation was soon reached.

Let us now turn to the state banks and record the conditions at the period of the disappearance of a system which had existed for thirty years, despite its glaring defects and the want of security, uniformity, and stability of the notes issued thereunder. In the states which formed the Southern Confederacy there were in 1861 about 250 banks, capitalized at $110,000,000, with $68,000,000 of note circulation and $31,000,000 in specie. With some notable exceptions these were the worst of the note-issuing banks of that period. The system of banks in the remainder of the country at this time was not materially different as to currency and supervision from that existing in the period of 1857–1860 already described. The war gave a wonderful impetus to business. The repeated issue of United States notes, suspension of specie payments, and general inflation of values gave to state banks, with their facility for note expansion, a great opportunity to make money. It was only natural that they should resist the establishment of a national currency system.

The Treasury reports upon the condition of state banks were not continued after 1863. From Secretary Chase's reports it appears that in 1861 there were 1601 state banks, with a capital of $429,600,000; in 1863, 1466 banks, with a capital of $405,000,000. The circulation, which in 1861 was $202,000,000 and in 1862 only $184,000,000, had risen to nearly $239,000,000 in 1863, an increase of $55,000,000 coincident with the issue by the government of $400,000,000 legal tender notes. This was the largest amount of state bank-notes ever reported. In the year when the new system was born the old one showed the maximum note-issue, as if to challenge its competitor. With the power of the federal government behind it, however, the national system was rapidly growing. In January, 1864, state bank circulation was estimated at $170,000,000, and on July 1, at $126,000,000. The power of Congress to tax the notes of state banks out of existence was contested and carried to the Supreme Court, which sustained the law (Veazie Bank *vs.* Fenno, 8 Wall. 533).

The interest-bearing legal tender notes which were held by the banks in their reserves matured in 1867. It was feared that their retirement and the consequent substitution of non-interest-bearing United States notes would occasion a contraction of the currency and interfere with business prosperity. Hence the act of March 2, 1867, authorized the issue of $50,000,000 of 3 per cent. temporary loan certificates payable on demand, and the act of July 25, 1868, permitted the use of $25,000,000 more, to take the place of the maturing interest-bearing notes in bank reserves; the maximum issue was about $60,000,000.

The national currency was absolutely secured by government bonds and passed at par throughout the length and breadth of the land. It presented a strong contrast to the old system of state bank circulation, consisting of more or less doubtful promises to pay and costing the public through discount and losses at its best about 5 per cent. per annum. But the national bank circulation was limited to $300,000,000, and notwithstanding the apportionment act of 1865 the larger portion had been obtained by the Eastern states. This gave rise to the cry of monopoly. The advocates of more money and cheap money obtained a ready audience, producing a practical recurrence of the events of 1832. There arose a substantial party in 1867 which favored the substitution of legal tender notes for bank-notes, and in fact the national system suffered a precarious existence for the next ten years, with strong probabilities of its abandonment. Secretary McCulloch felt constrained to defend the system from the attacks of the anti-bank element, which had the aid of the friends of the old state banks. The following summary of his arguments is interesting. The national system had been adopted not to do away with state banks but to supersede a very defective bank currency with a national one; the legal tender notes were only temporary currency, the national bank-notes were proposed as a permanent currency; the legal tenders were subject to inflation, depreciation, and other evils; the national bank-notes could easily be regulated and kept from depreciating; moreover, to supersede them now would inevitably cause a crisis; on the other hand the Nation was bound in honor to retire the greenbacks and the policy of contraction of these notes was the only proper one in view of the redundancy of paper money and the imperative duty of resuming coin payments at an early date; an increase of greenbacks, such as was contemplated by the anti-bank men, would render resumption much more difficult and cause irretrievable losses; in order to provide the sections inadequately supplied with circulation, he recommended a redistribution by law; he regarded it unwise to increase the volume of notes until after the resumption of coin payments. The circulation per capita at this time was $18.28, against $13.35 for 1860 and $23.80 for 1865.

It is interesting to note the earnestness with which Comptroller Hulburd in 1867, 1868, and 1869 denounced the payments of interest on deposits by New York banks as an element of danger. He argued that interest attracted large deposits of money from the interior when not needed for local purposes, which money to be available must necessarily be loaned to brokers on call; the latter were able to lock up money and raise rates of interest by means of over-certification, resulting in a money stringency and general disturbance when these loans were necessarily called in order to admit of sending the money back to the interior to again serve the local demand. Why brokers as a class should be subjected to the charge of a desire to raise money rates does not appear.

Secretary Boutwell in 1869 strongly indorsed Comptroller Hulburd's recommendations and favored a law absolutely prohibiting the payment of interest on deposits and limiting collateral loans to 10 per cent. of a bank's capital. He was also satisfied that the practice of certifying checks, even when funds were in bank to the credit of the drawer, was fraught with evil and should be entirely prohibited. It is indeed strange that so absurd a proposition could emanate from the chief financial officer of the government.

On February 19, 1869, an act was passed prohibiting making loans either upon legal tender notes or national bank-notes as collateral; this was designated to prevent contraction. On March 3, 1869, a law authorized the Comptroller to fix the dates of reports at his discretion, not less than five each year, and required reports of earnings and dividends semiannually; another prohibited certification of checks in excess of the drawer's balance.

The absolute inelasticity of the bank circulation became an important question. The authorized $300,000,000 had been absorbed, and no new banks could be organized except as old ones went out of business. Only fifteen banks had failed, and only fifty-six had gone into voluntary liquidation up to the close of 1869. Moreover, the government was about to retire the 3 per cent. reserve certificates which would cause a greater demand for United States notes for reserve purposes, thereby contracting the currency. In February, 1870, the House of Representatives, by a vote (110 to 73) which was practically sectional rather than partisan, passed a resolution declaring that the country required more money and directed the Banking and Currency Committee to prepare a bill for an increase of $50,-000,000. After great labor Congress, on July 12, 1870, passed an act to increase the circulation of national banks $54,000,000. This was to take the place of the 3 per cent. reserve certificates about to be retired. The act also provided for a reapportionment of the circulation by taking from banks in states having more than their share, according to wealth and population, and assigning it to banks in states having less. The proportion in the Eastern and Middle states was then some $80,000,000 in excess, the South being entitled to $57,200,000 more than it had. The act also limited the amount of circulation of banks thereafter organized to $500,000 and authorized national gold banks. This latter provision was practically confined to the Pacific slope where specie payments had not been suspended. The issues of these banks were limited to 80 per cent. of the par value of bonds deposited, were redeemable in gold on demand, and gold reserves of 25 per cent. were to be maintained; the banks were not required to take the notes of other banks nor to provide for redemption in the East.

During the discussion of this measure propositions were introduced, but defeated, to repeal the 10 per cent. tax on state bank-notes, to fix maximum discount rates at 7 per cent., to prohibit the payment of interest on deposits, to pay no interest on bonds while on deposit to secure circulation, and to substitute United States notes for bank-notes.

On June 8, 1872, the Treasury was authorized to receive

on deposit legal tender notes (greenbacks) and issue therefor non-interest-bearing currency certificates in denominations of not less than $5000. These certificates were a convenient form of bank reserve and were especially useful in the settlement of large clearing-house balances.

Statesmen and economists were much in need of some central reservoir of information in regard to all banks and banking institutions, state as well as national. To provide accurate statistical information of such character the act of February 19, 1873, provided that the Comptroller should report the condition of state banks and other financial institutions annually. In order to comply with this requirement the Comptroller corresponds with the supervisory departments of the different states, as well as with the various institutions directly and submits the most accurate data obtainable.

In September, 1873, there occurred a monetary panic in New York, causing a suspension of cash payments for forty days and carrying down many business houses. The unfortunate experience of this trying period greatly emphasized the defects in the currency system. The Treasury aided in relieving the stringency by bond purchases and by the very questionable course of issuing greenbacks "in reserve," that is, greenbacks that had once been redeemed and retired.

The New York banks presently lost $35,000,000 of cash and for relief were compelled to resort to clearing-house loan certificates, issued upon securities hypothecated, and used in settlement of debit balances at the clearing-house. The maximum amount of this auxiliary currency used was $26,565,000.

President Grant, in his message in December, suggested that the crisis may have been a blessing in disguise and cautioned Congress to heed the lesson and provide against its recurrence. Elasticity of the currency and the prevention of speculative use of reserves, the prohibition of interest on deposits, the requirement of reserves to be kept at home, the redemption of notes by banks, and "free banking" (*i.e.* removing the limit on circulation and facilitating its retirement) were among the remedies he suggested. The interconvertible bond plan, under which banks could obtain government notes at any time by depositing bonds, returnable when the notes were returned and bearing no interest while on deposit, was also recommended.

Congress, regarding the proper remedy an increase of paper money, immediately took up the question and after consideration of numerous propositions finally passed an act increasing national bank-notes and legal tender notes to $400,000,000 each, prohibiting interest payments on balances held as reserve on circulation, requiring accumulations of coin by banks for redemption of notes and requiring three-fourths of the reserves to be kept in cash in bank. Grant, after much urging, vetoed the measure, calling attention to the fact that $25,000,000 of bank currency was still subject to reapportionment to states having a deficiency. When that was taken up and specie payments restored it would be time to consider the demand for "more money."

Congress thereupon passed the act of June 20, 1874, providing that in lieu of the required reserve (25 and 15 per cent. respectively) for redemption of circulation, lawful money to the extent of 5 per cent. of the circulation should be deposited and maintained in the Treasury and the current redemption of notes was thereafter to be made at the Treasury and by the Treasurer instead of by reserve agents. The 5 per cent. fund was to be counted as part of the reserve on deposits. This obviously released from reserve requirements a considerable amount of lawful money, estimated by Comptroller Knox in 1874 at over $20,000,000. The act also provided that banks might deposit lawful money in the Treasury for the reduction or retirement of their circulation and receive back their bonds pro rata. The notes were then to be redeemed out of this fund by the Treasury. The bonds on deposit were not to be reduced below the minimum requirement. Under this provision currency reapportionment was facilitated as banks were by the act compelled to surrender excess circulation; the amount available for redistribution was $80,000,000. The maximum circulation issuable remained at $354,000,000. A "free banking" provision was presented as an amendment to the bill but defeated, as were also amendments to replace bank-notes with greenbacks, regulate discount rates, and require *all* reserves to be kept in cash-in-bank. The latter proviso at one stage had passed both houses of Congress but was finally lost; the measure passed by very large majorities.

It appears that all the Comptrollers of the Currency down to and including Knox recommended the prohibition of interest upon deposits by reserve banks, and stringent measures against over-certification of checks, believing that the payment of interest abnormally increased the deposits of interior banks in New York City while the certification of checks facilitated the use of the same by stock exchange brokers. This money being in use by the brokers when required for crop-moving purposes was what occasioned the annual stringency in money in the fall of the year. Secretary Bristow disapproved the prohibition of interest upon deposits, as a discrimination against national and in favor of state banks, but suggested a tax upon all interest-bearing deposits as a means of discouraging the practice.

The strong position against the payment of interest on deposits by banks, taken by the various Comptrollers of the Currency and Secretaries of the Treasury down to 1874, possesses peculiar interest in view of the fact that since 1901 the government itself has required interest upon its deposits in banks.

The political revolution in 1874, by which the Republicans for the first time since 1859 lost control of the House of Representatives, was also largely caused by the halting, hesitating, shuffling, and changing positions which they occupied with reference to the retirement of the greenbacks, the resumption of specie payments and the question of sound money generally; the public generally felt that a change might prove beneficial, and this feeling was certainly justified by events. Stung by defeat and brought face to face with the political consequences of their insincere and opportunist method of meeting these questions, they strove to regain lost ground and win back the confidence and support of the business interests of the country. In the short session of the old Congress (1874–1875) the Republicans vigorously pushed a specie resumption measure, coupled with free banking, which finally became law January 14, 1875. It repealed all limits on the volume of national bank-notes, thus doing away with the necessity for redistribution; it was passed by a strict party vote, with a small body of extreme sound money Republicans opposing the measure.

The passage of the resumption act marks a period in the life of national banks. At this time there were 2027 of these associations with capital of $496,000,000, circulation $331,000,000, individual deposits $683,000,000, loans $956,000,000, government bonds $413,000,000, specie $22,000,000, legal tenders $116,000,000, and 5 per cent. fund with the Treasury $21,000,000. One hundred and seventy-eight banks had gone out of business in the eleven years; thirty-seven of these failed, twelve of them ultimately paid their debts in full, and the balance paid a very large percentage of their indebtedness; all their notes were paid in full.

The earnings of the national banks calculated upon capital and surplus had diminished from an average of 11.8 per cent. in 1870, the first year this information was reported, to 10.3 per cent. in 1874; dividends averaged in 1870 10.05 per cent., and in 1874 9.9 per cent.; a generally higher ratio of earnings prevailed in the West and South.

The incomplete reports of state banks covered only 551, with capital of $69,000,000, deposits $166,000,000, loans $176,000,000, cash $28,000,000. Many of the states still neglected to require reports from banks.

STATISTICAL RÉSUMÉ

(Amounts in millions of dollars)

Condition of National Banks, 1864 to 1875

(at dates nearest January 1)

Year	Number	Capital	Deposits	Circulation	Cash	Loans
1864	139	15	19	—	5	11
1865	638	136	221	67	77	166
1866	1582	403	552	213	207	501
1867	1648	420	588	291	207	609
1868	1682	420	562	294	175	617
1869	1628	419	585	294	118	645
1870	1615	426	555	293	136	689
1871	1648	435	517	296	107	726
1872	1790	460	617	318	124	819
1873	1940	483	611	336	134	886
1874	1976	490	553	341	160	857
1875	2027	496	694	331	139	956

Condition of State Banks, 1861 to 1875, so far as obtainable

Year	State Banks						Savings Banks			Clearings, New York
	Number	Capital	Deposits	Circulation	Cash	Loans	Depositors (000's)	Deposits (Millions)	Average Deposit	
1861	1601	430	257	202	88	697	694	147	$211	5,916
1862	1496	420	297	184	102	648	788	169	215	6,871
1863	1466	405	394	239	101	649	887	206	232	14,868
1864	1089	312	—	163	51	—	976	236	242	24,097
1865	349	71	—	—	—	—	981	243	247	26,032
1866	297	66	—	—	—	—	1067	282	265	28,717
1867	272	65	—	—	—	—	1188	337	284	28,675
1868	247	66	—	—	—	—	1310	393	300	28,484
1869	259	67	—	—	—	—	1467	458	312	37,407
1870	325	87	—	—	—	—	1631	550	337	27,804
1871	452	111	—	—	—	—	1902	651	342	29,301
1872	566	122	—	—	—	—	1993	735	369	33,844
1873	—	43	111	—	11	119	2186	802	367	35,461
1874	—	59	138	—	27	154	2293	865	377	22,856
1875	551	69	166	—	28	176	2360	924	392	25,061

CHAPTER XVIII

National Banking System

1876–1882

The changes in the National Bank Act in 1875 broadened the scope and increased the power of national banks with respect to currency by removing all limitation upon the volume, thereby making banking free. This made it possible to organize banks *ad libitum* in the South and West and tended to relieve in a measure the disadvantages which caused so much just complaint from those sections owing to the inadequacy of currency and credit facilities. Rich in natural, undeveloped resources these sections needed capital for their development. What they thought they needed was currency and believing United States notes most likely to meet their wants, the agitation against national banks and in favor of the substitution of greenbacks for bank-notes continued. Although bank organization and the issue of bank currency was now absolutely free the cry of monopoly was still maintained.

Comptroller Knox in elaborate reports in 1875 and 1876, in which the history of banking and bank currency in the United States from the beginning of the government was reviewed, demonstrated that the national system with uniform national currency, was vastly superior to any that had preceded it. The cost of domestic exchange which in 1859 averaged 1 per cent. had, largely by the national system, been reduced to a small fraction of that rate.

Against the charge that the national banks made enormous profits, he showed that, taxation considered, the earnings were actually less than those of banks outside the system not subjected to the onerous restrictions of the federal law. The voluntary surrender of over $50,000,000 of notes by the banks, he contended, was proof absolute that the profit on circulation could not be as large as alleged.

Under the law the Comptroller appoints receivers for failed national banks, fixes their compensation, adjusts differences, and approves compromises in reducing the assets of failed banks to cash. By means of bank examiners he is fully advised as to conditions. By means of hard and painstaking work he is able to exercise an intelligent judgment and reach a satisfactory conclusion as to the value and adjustment of claims, thereby effecting compromises, speedy settlement and payment, avoiding expensive litigation and delay, realizing a much larger net amount for the payment of creditors, and securing to them their dividends in a much shorter space of time. The Comptroller sustains the same relation to a failed national bank and the receiver, that the court in any of our states does to a failed corporation and the receiver of the same. His powers are parallel and coincident. The cheapness and celerity and high percentage of dividends realized in the settlement of failed national banks compared with the administration of corporate receiverships in our different states is most gratifying and highly complimentary to the national system as administered by the Comptroller of the Currency.

A very important feature of the national banking system is the supervision exercised by official examiners. The statute provides that the Comptroller, with the approval of the Secretary of the Treasury, shall "appoint a suitable person or persons to make an examination of the affairs of every banking association, who shall have power to make a thorough study of all the affairs of the association, and, in doing so, to examine any of the officers and agents thereof on oath; and shall make a full and detailed report of the condition of the association to the Comptroller." The above provision is wisely made very general in its terms; there is practically no limit to the power of the examiner so long as he is right; the good the examiners do is largely of a negative character, in preventing wrongs and mismanagement which otherwise might exist; such work necessarily does not come to the public notice, and the system therefore does not receive the credit it is entitled to; they do not always detect bad management and prevent bank failures, but their restraining and corrective influence is of the greatest value.

Requiring banks to publish not less than three reports of condition annually upon blanks furnished and in a form prescribed by the Comptroller of the Currency necessarily compels the banks' bookkeeping to conform to such requirements. It compels system and method in the conduct of each bank's affairs and insures uniformity throughout the nation; this provision is most wholesome and far-reaching in its effect upon the conduct of a bank's business; the data thus obtained and collected afford most valuable information as to business and economic conditions.

Notwithstanding free banking, the banks did not avail of the opportunity to increase their circulation as had been expected, proving that the demand for "more money" on the part of the South and West simply expressed the need of more capital. Eighteen million dollars of new circulation had been issued under the law of 1875, and hence nearly $14,500,000 of greenbacks had been retired. The privilege of reducing circulation by deposit of "lawful money" was made use of to such an extent that there was a net contraction of national bank circulation of nearly $40,000,000 since the act became operative; thus the contraction of paper currency was fully $54,000,000. On the other hand, the operation of the changed law with respect to reserve against circulation released $14,000,000 of legal tenders, resulting in a net contraction of $40,000,000. The ability to retire circulation by depositing lawful money and the right to increase at any time gave to the currency a measurable degree of flexibility.

During the two years following the enactment of the law of 1874 fully two-thirds of the national bank-notes outstanding were redeemed through the 5 per cent. fund and new ones issued, thus furnishing the public a cleanly and wholesome currency.

In 1878 a determined effort was made to supplant national bank currency with legal tender notes. The Greenback party favored this movement. Representative Ewing (Dem., O.), one of the chief leaders of the movement, introduced an elaborate bill for the purpose in the House. The measure was defeated by the very close vote of 110 to 114, a dozen Democrats voting against the measure and as many Republicans for it. This vote greatly encouraged the "Greenbackers" to continue their efforts.

In February, 1878, Congress passed the silver purchase and coinage law, under which a new form of paper currency (silver certificates) was provided, and in May, 1878, another act, under which the further retirement of greenbacks was prohibited. Both these measures were intended to operate against the extension of bank-note issues; bank circulation had increased during the year but slightly, and mainly owing to the organization of new banks.

The national bank system received but indifferent support from Secretary Sherman, who expressed himself in favor of the continuance of the bank currency at least until 1883, when the first of the charters were to expire; the subject could then be discussed with the public mind better prepared to consider it; he also opposed the retirement of the greenbacks.

Notwithstanding the continuing warfare made upon them, the banks worked zealously to aid the government in meeting the requirements of the resumption law and very materially strengthened their gold reserves to bring their notes to par in specie.

In 1879, specie payments having been resumed, business materially revived; the circulation of banks showed a substantial increase, although the capital had diminished; the issue of the 4 per cent. bonds at or near par helped to make circulation profitable; on the other hand, the increased demand for circulating media was now in considerable measure supplied by gold and by silver dollars and certificates representing the same.

Comptroller Knox reported (1880) that the banks held $100,000,000 in specie, and as evidence of an improved condition generally, presented a table showing a material lessening of prevailing rates of interest in different localities. New York and Philadelphia rates were from 3 to 5 per cent., Boston and Baltimore, 5 per cent., Chicago, 4 to 7 per cent., St. Louis, 5 to 7 per cent., Cleveland and Milwaukee, 6 to 8 per cent., St. Paul, 7 to 10 per cent., Omaha, 10 per cent., Denver, 10 to 15 per cent., and California, 8 to 12 per cent., in the South, 7 to 10 per cent., except in New Orleans, where 4 to 6 per cent. prevailed. The increase of circulating media since resumption had been $248,000,000, of which $176,000,000 was gold, $51,000,000 silver, and $20,000,000 bank-notes. Attention was also directed to the average size of loans and discounts by banks — $1082 for all. The Southern and Western states averaged $750, whereas the average of the Bank of France was $188.80, the Imperial Bank of Germany, $402.55. The Bank of France showed over 2,000,000 transactions of less than $100 each, whereas our national banks showed but 251,000 of such transactions.

Congress passed a refunding measure providing for 3 per cent. bonds, which were to be the only bonds available to secure bank circulation. The measure also repealed the provision for reducing circulation by deposit of lawful money, and contained other restrictions and objectionable features. The bill reached President Hayes on the last day of his term, March 3, 1881, and was at once vetoed. In his messages and by his veto power President Hayes proved a strong and firm defender of the national credit and the principles of sound money throughout his administration.

In the absence of a refunding law, Secretary Windom, during the summer of 1881, extended $538,000,000 of 5 and 6 per cent. bonds at 3½ per cent. interest, redeemable at the pleasure of the government. The banks held about $250,000,000 of these bonds.

Comptroller Knox obtained and reported data showing the actual amount of cash that entered into the transactions of all national banks on two business days, viz. June 30 and September 17, 1881. The average transactions represented by checks were 95.1 per cent. and 94.1 per cent. respectively, the balance being in actual money. Of the cash, paper currency represented 4 per cent. and 4.36 per cent. respectively, coin supplying the balance. Banks outside of reserve cities showed 81.7 per cent. of checks on both days.

A curious and interesting controversy arose at this time over the proper construction of the term "lawful money," permitted to be deposited as a part of the 5 per cent. redemption fund with which to retire circulating notes, — curious because it shows the tenacity with which the advocates of legal tender notes insisted that they should be used on all occasions. It was later paralleled by the fatuous devotion of the advocates of silver. The statute provided that the Treasury was to redeem bank-notes in "United States notes" and "legal tender notes." The term "lawful money" had become interchangeable, in the minds of legislators, with "legal tender notes," and they insisted that it did not include coin. The Treasury, strange to say, clung to this narrow construction. The banks maintained that gold coin and silver dollars were "lawful money." The Attorney-general, to whom the subject was referred, decided that when a payment was required to be made in promises to pay dollars, the dollars themselves could be used for that purpose.

A bill permitting the extension of the charters of existing banks for a period of twenty years, after a long and determined opposition, became a law on July 12, 1882. The advocates of more money, however, succeeded in incorporating into the act a provision limiting the amount of bank-notes which might be retired to $3,000,000 per month (except when bonds securing the circulation were called for redemption), and banks reducing their circulation were prohibited from again increasing their note-issue for the period of six months. Gold certificates were provided for, and these, as well as silver certificates, were to be available for bank reserves.

To prevent alleged discrimination against silver certificates, national banks were prohibited from being members of a clearing-house where such certificates were not taken in payment of balances. This was aimed at the New York clearing-house, which immediately thereafter repealed its rule forbidding the use of silver certificates in the settlement of balances. Provision was made for a 3 per cent. bond payable at the pleasure of the government, to be used in funding the extended 3½ per cents. The minimum bond deposit with the United States Treasury for banks capitalized at $150,000 or less was fixed at one-quarter of their capital. This allowed a minimum bond deposit of $12,500. Provision was made for retiring the notes of banks whose charters were extended, and all gain by the loss or destruction of bank-notes inured to the benefit of the government. The over-certification of checks was also forbidden under severe penalty.

This legislation was obviously a compromise, although in many respects favorable to the banks. For everything that was obtained by the friends of the banks something had to be yielded. The expansionists succeeded in interfering with the sole provision for flexibility by limiting the power of retiring notes at the pleasure of the banks. An amendment to substitute greenbacks for national bank-notes received only 71 votes and the votes on other amendments showed that the greenback influence in Congress was on the wane.

This act extending the charters of national banks seemed to mark another period and settle the status of the system. Since then little serious effort has been made to legislate them out of existence or to rescind their power to issue circulating notes, although it had been impossible to obtain any legislation which would give to bank currency greater flexibility and make it responsive to the needs of commerce.

Shortly after the enactment of the law of 1875 bank capital reached a maximum of $505,000,000. It fell to $454,000,000 in October, 1879, recovering to $477,000,000 July 1, 1882. Circulation (not including that against which lawful money had been deposited) showed a minimum of $298,000,000 and a maximum of $325,000,000, both in 1881. Individual deposits at the beginning of the period were $683,000,000, at the end $1,067,-000,000, and loans increased from $956,000,000 to $1,209,000,000. Gauged by their capital the banks could have issued $121,000,000 more notes than they had outstanding on July 1, 1882, but the demand for bank-notes was lessened by the existence at this time of $54,500,000 silver certificates which had come into use. The increase in the number of banks was only 212, of which 124 were added in the last year. The losses sustained after the panic of 1873 and the disturbances in 1876–1877 were so large that the aggregate surplus fund was reduced to $114,000,-000 (from $130,000,000). This was recovered during 1880–1882. Earnings receded from 9.7 per cent. to 5.1 per cent., recovering to 8.9 per cent. Forty-nine banks failed, 25 of which suspended in 1877–1878. Of the failed banks 21 paid creditors in full, and the balance nearly in full. The tax paid by the banks on circulation in 1864–1882 amounted to $50,700,000, and the tax on capital and deposits to $62,600,000, a total of $113,300,000. In addition, state taxes now averaged more than $8,000,000 annually, so that the rate of taxes paid yearly was equal to 3.7 per cent. on the capital.

Despite the utmost freedom given by the act of 1875 to bank

circulation, the Western and Southern states still had only $105,000,000, against $250,000,000 in the Middle and Eastern states.

State banks, of which only incomplete reports were available, showed an increase of 121 in number and $23,000,000 in capital. They had since 1875 increased their surplus from less than $7,000,000 to more than $23,000,000, their deposits by $116,000,000, and their loans by $96,000,000.

The relative supply of banking facilities of the several sections of the country is concisely stated in the following table compiled from the reports of the Comptroller of the Currency. Savings banks are here included, which give the Eastern and Middle states a great preponderance. The savings banks of California in the same manner increase the per capita of the Western section. An almost total absence of such institutions in the Southern states is a remarkable fact in the economic history of that section.

States	Banking Power (In millions)		Per Capita	
	1870	1880	1870	1880
Eastern	637	707	$182.51	$176.37
Middle	1046	1335	107.64	113.50
Southern	147	158	11.23	10.36
Central	311	462	27.65	26.86
Western	61	140	60.61	73.07
All	2202	2802	57.09	55.88

The increase in banking power in the Southern and Central states did not keep pace with the growth of population, which accounted for the strength there of the "greenback movement."

STATISTICAL RÉSUMÉ

(Amounts in millions of dollars)

Condition of National Banks

(at dates nearest January 1)

Year	Number	Capital	Deposits	Circulation	Specie	Legal Tenders	Loans
1876	2086	505	629	315	17	102	963
1877	2082	497	631	292	33	92	929
1878	2074	477	615	299	33	97	882
1879	2051	462	707	304	41	99	824
1880	2052	454	766	322	79	66	934
1881	2095	459	1018	317	107	65	1071
1882	2064	466	1115	325	114	68	1169

State Banks and Trust Companies

Year	State Banks[1]					Trust Companies
	Number	Capital	Deposits	Cash	Loans	Aggregate Resources
1876	633	80	158	30	179	128
1877	592	111	227	37	267	124
1878	475	95	143	32	169	111
1879	616	104	167	39	191	112
1880	620	91	209	55	207	127
1881	652	93	261	41	251	157
1882	672	92	282	42	272	195

[1] This table has little value for comparative purposes; reports from six to twelve states are missing after 1876, but again included in later years.

NEW YORK CLEARING-HOUSE AND SAVINGS BANKS

YEAR	NEW YORK CLEARING-HOUSE EXCHANGES	SAVINGS BANKS, U. S.			FAILURES	
	(Millions)	DEPOSITORS (000's)	DEPOSITS (Millions)	AVERAGE DEPOSIT	NUMBER (000's)	LIABILITIES (Millions)
1876	21.597	2369	941	$397	9	191
1877	23.289	2395	866	361	9	191
1878	22.508	2401	880	366	10	234
1879	25.178	2269	802	354	7	98
1880	37.182	2336	819	351	5	66
1881	48.565	2529	892	353	6	81
1882	46.552	2710	967	357	7	102

UNITED STATES BONDS, AND BANK CIRCULATION

YEAR (JUNE 30)	TOTAL BONDED DEBT	HELD AS SECURITY FOR CIRCULATION	NATIONAL BANK CIRCULATION	+ INCREASE − DECREASE	SILVER CERTIFICATES IN CIRCULATION	PRICE OF BONDS[1]	
						High	Low
1865	1110	236	131	+ 105	——	112⅜	103½
1866	1213	327	268	+ 137	——	114¾	103¾
1867	1634	341	292	+ 24	——	113¼	106½
1868	2092	341	295	+ 3	——	118⅛	108⅜
1869	2167	343	293	− 2	——	125	111
1870	2051	342	292	− 1	——	118½	112⅜
1871	1953	360	316	+ 24	——	119⅜	110¼
1872	1845	380	327	+ 11	——	113¾	107¾
1873	1760	390	339	+ 12	——	116¼	106¼
1874	1789	391	339	——	——	117	111
1875	1773	376	318	− 21	——	119	113⅝
1876	1761	341	294	− 24	——	119	110⅜
1877	1762	339	290	− 4	——	112⅝	105¼
1878	1845	350	300	+ 10	——	107⅜	103
1879	1952	354	307	+ 7	——	104¼	99
1880	1775	362	318	+ 11	6	113⅝	103
1881	1690	360	312	− 6	39	118⅝	112⅜
1882	1514	358	309	− 3	55	121¾	117¼

[1] 6's of 1881, to 1872; 5's of 1881, to 1878; 4's of 1907 later.

CHAPTER XIX

NATIONAL BANKING SYSTEM

1883–1890

DURING the period now under discussion the banks were a neglected factor in the currency affairs of the country; the government seemingly having assumed the province of furnishing circulating media, no legislation relating to banks was enacted or seriously considered.

In May of 1884 a serious financial crisis, produced by conditions in the country generally, but practically limited in its manifestation to New York City, caused numerous suspensions, including two large national banks. The crisis was caused largely by undue expansion of loans induced by speculation in securities. The New York banks again issued clearing-house loan certificates to be used in settling debit balances, the first bearing date May 15, and the maximum amount being $24,915,000. They were practically retired by July 1. The fact that the certificates were promptly issued served to restore confidence in a short time, and prevented more serious consequences.

The withholding of money from deposit in banks and savings banks, the strengthening of their cash resources by interior banks, which caused a corresponding reduction of their balances in New York, necessarily produced a stringency. Any degree of fear or anxiety which induces the wage-earners employed by our large stores, factories, railroads, and employers of labor generally, to keep the money received from the pay roll instead of depositing or spending the same, materially and immediately affects the volume of money in circulation. The banks under the rigid currency laws were powerless to afford relief. They could not buy bonds required to be deposited as security for circulation without investing more money in such bonds than they would receive as circulation in return. Had they borrowed the bonds it would have required about forty-five days after depositing them before the circulation could be prepared for delivery. The banks protected and retained their cash reserves by suspending cash payments as between themselves, and using loan certificates in payment of clearing-house debits. The crisis thus proclaimed undoubtedly drove money into hiding and prevented the banks from strengthening their reserves by the usual receipts of currency.

The important and valuable function which clearing-house certificates perform, and the only one which justifies their use, is the temporary inflation of currency which they in a manner produce. A bank may deposit with the clearing-house $1,250,000 of its assets and receive $1,000,000 of loan certificates. It then can loan to its customers $1,000,000 and meet and pay the checks drawn against such loans, in the clearing-house exchanges, with the $1,000,000 loan certificates it has received. It may then deposit the assets taken for said $1,000,000 of loans with the clearing-house and receive $800,000 in loan certificates. It could then in turn loan its customers $800,000 and settle for the same through the clearing-house exchanges with the $800,000 of loan certificates received, and so on. This illustration is given to show the extent to which banks might extend accommodations to their customers without the use of actual currency. Of course the issuing or withholding of loan certificates rests wholly with the clearing-house authorities, and each particular application is determined by them upon its merits. The beneficial results which these loan certificates have produced rest wholly upon the fact that the banks while maintaining their reserves by retaining their currency have been enabled to extend to the public whatever assistance it may have required. A statement of the several issues of such certificates at New York appears on page 353.

Their charters had been extended under the law of 1882, and the banks were recognized as a permanent part of our monetary system, but many things militated against the increase of their note-issues. As we have seen, the 3 per cent. bonds, constituting a large portion of the public debt, were redeemable at the pleasure of the government, and were being rapidly retired with the large Treasury surplus and were liable to be called at any time. Hence they were undesirable as a basis for note-issue since, in case the bonds were redeemed, a bank would have to purchase and substitute others. All other issues of government bonds commanded high premiums, the 4 per cents standing at 129, which rendered the issue of circulation based upon them unprofitable.

Another powerful factor in reducing bank circulation was the fact that the government was purchasing silver, coining silver dollars, and issuing certificates, at the minimum rate of $2,000,000 per month, and using all the power of the Treasury to force them into circulation in order to prevent going upon a silver basis. The crusade in favor of free coinage of silver monopolized the attention and sympathy of Congress to such an extent that it continuously refused to permit banks to issue circulation to the par of bonds, retaining the limit at 90 per cent. notwithstanding the fact that the bonds commanded a premium of nearly 30 per cent. The entire absence of elasticity, which every bond-secured currency must possess, as well as the growing premium on and lessening volume of United States bonds, induced economists to consider a bank currency without such bonds as security, which would be quite as safe and more responsive to business necessities. Comptroller Henry W. Cannon, who succeeded John Jay Knox in 1884, was the first official to discuss and recommend such a currency issue. He suggested as security a guarantee fund to be accumulated from the tax on circulation, the gain on lost notes, and the interest on the redemption fund in the Treasury.

Examining and analyzing the statistics of the 104 national banks that had failed up to that time, with a view to demonstrating the securities to note holders under the proposed plan, he said: —

"The experience with these 104 banks shows almost conclusively that if their issues to the amount of 65 per cent. of their capital had been secured by a deposit of bonds to an equal amount, the remaining 25 per cent. might have been issued without other security than a first lien on the general assets; and if a safety fund had been in existence it would in the case cited have been drawn upon to the extent of $62,000 only upon a circulation amounting to $5,464,700. For a beginning, therefore, it might be safe to authorize banks to issue circulation amounting to 90 per cent. of their capital, 70 per cent. to be secured by an equal amount of United States bonds at par value, the remaining 20 per cent. being issued without other security than a first lien on such assets. But if the law should provide for the accumulation of a safety fund in the manner suggested, then as such safety fund increased the percentage of circulation unsecured by bonds might be increased as the diminution of the public debt might require and the safety fund warrant."

William L. Trenholm became Comptroller of the Currency in 1886. In that year Congress authorized banks, by a two-thirds vote, to increase their capital or change their location, and in 1887 prescribed conditions under which cities might become reserve and central reserve cities. Chicago and St. Louis became central reserve cities like New York, and three reserve cities were added. At this time a question arose as to the legality of using bonds on which interest had ceased (after being called for redemption), as security for circulation. The Attorney-General decided that under the law such bonds were not available and must be replaced.

Although by 1887 banks had increased largely in number and their capital had also grown, their circulation was reduced to $167,000,000. A presidential election was at hand, and the trend of public sentiment and political conditions is suggested by the fact that the oft-repeated proposition to substitute greenbacks for national bank-notes was defeated, at this time, by the close vote of 23 to 22 in the Senate.

Secretary Fairchild had endeavored to counteract the absorption of money by the Treasury by depositing surplus revenues with banks. There were 290 bank depositories at this time, and they held $60,000,000 of the Treasury surplus amply secured by government bonds. The Republicans severely criticised this policy in the ensuing campaign as opening the door to political favoritism. They have since paid Mr. Fairchild the compliment of adopting and extending his policy. The number of such depositories, May 1, 1903 (under Secretary Shaw and President Roosevelt), was 257, and the amount of surplus Treasury money on deposit with them was $142,959,727.12.

Benjamin Harrison became President in 1889, and early in his administration Edward S. Lacey was appointed Comptroller of the Currency. The new administration secured no more attention for its recommendations relative to bank currency than did its predecessor. The all-absorbing, crucial question was how to placate the silver advocates and still remain upon a gold basis.

William Windom had succeeded Fairchild as Secretary of the Treasury, and following the logic of the campaign began reducing the Treasury funds in banks. As the surplus locked up in the Treasury was thus increased, the year 1889 closed with an uneasy feeling in the money market, rates for a period ruling from 30 to 40 per cent. Windom's plan for the placation of the silver interests and the utilization of silver eventuated in the law of 1890, fully discussed in another chapter.

The enormous Treasury surplus had been made prominent in the presidential campaign, and the relief determined upon was reduction of taxation. The protection influence dominated, and the McKinley act of 1890 retained the duty upon articles produced in this country and removed or reduced the duties upon sugar and other large revenue-yielding commodities not produced to any considerable extent in the United States.

During the summer and early fall of that year the money

stringency, which had been foreshadowed by the growing surplus, occurred, and the application of the Treasury funds to bond redemptions amounted to over $100,000,000. Aside from the much criticised policy of depositing money in banks, the only means of counteracting the demoralization of business whenever the government's income exceeds its expenditures under our subtreasury system of withdrawing money from channels of trade, is the "steady by jerks" method of buying bonds, first practised by Secretary Guthrie in 1854, and continued by every Secretary since that day, when the surplus was large. It was the only recourse available to Windom under the circumstances. In the month of September alone over $62,000,000 was disbursed by the Treasury for bonds and anticipated interest payments. The suspension of Barings in November of this year caused a severe crisis in London and produced scarcely less effect in New York. The Bank of England came to the rescue and eventually restored the Barings to solvency.

The underlying fear that the monetary policy of the government would eventually force the country upon a silver basis rendered the business interests peculiarly sensitive. Credit was easily disturbed and withheld. Under the circumstances the gravity of the situation in London easily precipitated a *quasi* panic in New York, and the banks again resorted to clearing-house loan certificates on November 12. The date of the last issue was December 7, and final retirement occurred February 7, 1891. The total issue was $16,645,000 and the maximum amount outstanding at one time was $15,205,000. Boston and Philadelphia banks adopted the same course to relieve the stringency, the former issuing $5,065,000 and the latter $8,820,000 of such auxiliary currency. No attempt was made by Congress to provide means whereby the banks could afford relief under such circumstances to all sections of the country, instead of leaving relief to clearing-house loan certificates available only in the large cities, amounting to a partial suspension of currency payments and producing evil results which approximate the amount of good they do.

In 1890 Comptroller Lacey obtained data showing the amount of domestic exchange drawn by the national banks during the year. For the purpose of verification he obtained similar facts in 1891. These data showed the amount in the aggregate to be $13,000,000,000, and he estimated that the state banks drew half as much more, making an aggregate of $19,500,000,000. Sixty per cent. of the total was drawn upon New York. The cost, or charge for exchange, as reported by national banks, varied from 1 cent to 21 cents per $100 and averaged 8½ cents. At the rate of 1½ per cent., prevailing in 1859, the cost to the people of the exchange thus furnished by national banks would approximate $195,000,000, whereas the cost in 1890 was slightly over $11,000,000. This reduction in cost of exchange was not due entirely to the national banking system, but that system contributed largely to bringing about such saving.

The national banking system, designed, as we have seen, to give the people a permanent paper currency, lacked the necessary support even in the ranks of those who had created it. Only by the most strenuous efforts was the system able to survive the political attacks upon the one hand and the untoward conditions of a decreasing volume and enhancing prices of bonds, producing diminution of profits, on the other. Moreover, the introduction of the two forms of silver paper (certificates and Treasury notes of 1890) materially lessened the demand for bank-notes. Nevertheless, as a system of banks of deposit and discount, under the regulation of federal law, it kept pace with the commercial development of the country. Its growth was especially marked in the states from which the principal opposition came. Of the 1545 active banks added to the list since 1882, Texas had contributed 195, Missouri 61, the Dakotas 67, Kansas 134, Nebraska 127, and Iowa 75.

The act of July 14, 1890, directed that the funds held in trust in the Treasury for redemption of these notes be turned into the general cash of the Treasury, and the notes assumed as part of the public debt.

The earnings of the banks calculated upon capital and surplus ranged between 6.9 per cent. and 8.9 per cent., and dividends, on capital alone, from 8.6 to 7.8 per cent., with a declining tendency.

Greater efforts than ever before were made during the period to obtain fuller data relating to state banks, private banks, and trust companies. The report for 1891 showed the following comparison as to state banks (in millions): —

Year	Number	Capital	Deposits	Loans	Total Resources
1881	652	92.9	261.4	250.8	438.8
1891	2572	208.6	556.6	623.2	906.0

While the increase thus shown was no doubt in part due to the more complete returns in the latter year, it is obvious that these banks more than doubled in number and importance during the decade. Examination shows that this was due in great measure to the fact that the national system proved less inviting to capital in the sections showing the greatest growth. The provisions of state laws for small banks, capitalized at $10,000 or even less, accounted for much of this preference.

Trust and loan companies showed increased resources for the same period from $156,500,000 to $536,600,000 and savings banks deposits grew from $891,900,000 to $1,623,500,000.

Appended is a table showing the aggregate banking power of the country, indicating the per capita, and illustrating further the great lack of banking facilities in the sections which continually clamored for measures calculated to result in unsound currency. The two phenomena are unquestionably correlated. The higher interest rates exacted in localities not well supplied with capital and credit facilities — a disparity which is a serious burden upon all productive industry — tends to induce those who suffer therefrom to support any means suggested to remedy the evil, and too often the proposed remedies have been such as would actually render conditions worse.

States	Banking Power (In millions)		Per Capita	
	1880	1890	1880	1890
Eastern	707	1229	$176.37	$261.86
Middle	1335	2410	113.50	170.92
Central	462	1184	26.86	54.29
Southern	158	387	10.36	21.15
Western	140	403	73.07	107.15
All	2802	5613	55.88	89.85

STATISTICAL RÉSUMÉ

(Amounts in millions of dollars)

Condition of National Banks

(at dates nearest January 1)

Year	Number	Capital	Deposits	Circulation	Specie	Legal Tenders	Loans
1883	2308	485	1080	315	106	77	1230
1884	2529	512	1120	305	114	91	1307
1885	2664	524	1002	280	140	95	1234
1886	2732	529	1126	267	165	79	1344
1887	2875	551	1188	202	167	74	1470
1888	3070	581	1279	165	159	82	1584
1889	3150	594	1382	144	173	92	1677
1890	3326	618	1480	126	171	94	1812

UNITED STATES BONDS AND BANK CIRCULATION

YEAR (JUNE 30)	TOTAL BONDED DEBT	HELD AS SECURITY FOR CIRCULATION	NAT'L BANK CIRCULATION	+ INCREASE – DECREASE	SILVER CERTIFICATE CIRCULATION	+ INCREASE – DECREASE	PRICE OF BONDS[1]	
							High	Low
1883	1389	353	312	+ 3	73	+ 18	125⅛	118½
1884	1277	331	295	– 17	96	+ 23	124⅞	118½
1885	1247	312	269	– 26	102	+ 6	124⅜	121⅜
1886	1196	276	245	– 24	88	– 14	129⅜	123
1887	1072	192	167	– 78	142	+ 54	129⅝	124½
1888	1001	178	155	– 12	201	+ 59	130	123¾
1889	880	148	129	– 26	257	+ 56	129⅞	126¼
1890	776	145	126	– 3	298	+ 41	126½	121½

STATE BANKS, TRUST COMPANIES, PRIVATE BANKS

YEAR	STATE BANKS					TRUST COMPANY RESOURCES	PRIVATE BANK RESOURCES
	NUMBER	CAPITAL	DEPOSITS	CASH AND CASH ITEMS	LOANS		
1883	754	103	335	78	322	212	394
1884	817	110	325	82	331	240	—
1885	975	125	344	87	348	248	—
1886	849	110	343	91	331	278	—
1887	1413	141	447	111	436	319	174
1888	1403	155	410	105	432	384	164
1889	1671	167	507	133	505	441	143
1890	2101	189	553	121	582	504	164

MISCELLANEOUS FINANCIAL

YEAR	CLEARING-HOUSE EXCHANGES (In millions)		SAVINGS BANKS			FAILURES	
	NEW YORK	UNITED STATES	DEPOSITORS (000's)	DEPOSITS (Millions)	AVERAGE DEPOSITS	NUMBER (000's)	LIABILITIES (Millions)
1883	40,293	51,731	2876	1025	$356	9	173
1884	34,092	44,200	3015	1073	356	11	226
1885	25,251	41,474	3071	1095	357	11	124
1886	33,375	49,294	3158	1141	361	10	115
1887	34,873	51,147	3418	1235	361	10	168
1888	30,864	49,541	3838	1364	355	11	124
1889	34,796	56,175	4021	1425	354	11	149
1890	37,661	60,624	4258	1525	358	11	190

[1] 4's of 1907.

CHAPTER XX

Silver Contest of 1896

1891–1896

The retention of the national bank system was virtually settled by the law of 1882 enabling banks to extend their charters for a period of twenty years. Although opposition did not thereafter cease, it very materially subsided. The Supreme Court having decided that Congress had unlimited power to issue legal tender notes at any time, these notes became a settled factor in our currency system, with little hope of their retirement. The status of silver was undetermined and in sharp controversy, — free coinage at the ratio of 16 to 1 being the contention of one party and the repeal of the existing silver purchase law being the contention of the friends of the gold standard. Gold was the standard of value, but silver was being purchased at the rate of 4,500,000 ounces per month and legal tender coin notes issued in payment therefor. It was only a question of time when the continued purchase of this vast amount of silver, practically redeemable in gold, would exhaust the credit of the government and force it upon a silver basis. The question whether the standard should be gold or silver was paramount, and all forms of our currency were so closely related to the standard that they will be considered together in this and the following chapter.

The financial and monetary conditions of the whole commercial world were affected by the position which this country had assumed respecting silver. By careful management the gold surplus of the Treasury had been increased to nearly $219,000,000 in 1888. The estimated stock of gold in the country at the same time was over $700,000,000. We had retained all of our gold product, then averaging more than one-quarter of the world's output, and had imported more than we exported.

The embarrassment of Baring Brothers of London, which culminated in November, 1890, precipitated a severe stringency in the money market in London which had its counterpart in New York. The Barings were financing vast undertakings in South America and elsewhere, which they were unable to carry through. The Bank of England took charge of their affairs, managed the same most successfully, and eventually restored the Barings to solvency and strength. In order to do this the Bank of England at that time found it convenient to borrow from the Bank of France $15,000,000 in gold. The incident was regarded as a warning and in order to strengthen their reserves European banks generally began to make extraordinary efforts to obtain gold from all points, but mainly from the United States. The Bank of England, by raising its discount rate and by raising the price which it will pay for gold bars or foreign coin, can measurably protect its gold supply. In addition to these safeguards the Bank of France goes farther and refuses to pay notes and drafts entirely in gold, offering a portion in gold and the balance in silver, or exacts a premium on gold desired for export. The United States Treasury has no safeguards whatever against withdrawals of gold, and hence ours is the easiest market from which other nations' necessities may be supplied.

By the end of the fiscal year 1890 over $54,000,000 gold had been exported notwithstanding a favorable trade balance, showing conclusively a return of American securities from abroad. The inflation resulting from the silver purchase act made money easier and accelerated the drain of gold. Following the return flow of money to New York after the crops of 1890 were harvested, heavy exports of gold were resumed in January, 1891, the net exports for the fiscal year having been $68,000,000. General business activity and a continuous demand for money, in the fiscal year ending June 30, 1892, together with a favorable trade balance resulting largely from bountiful crops in 1891 and a general shortage in Europe, caused heavy importations of gold, so that the net loss in that year was only $500,000. In July large exports again began. The banks finding it impracticable to furnish the gold from their vaults, exporters of gold were paid in notes and thus the demand was transferred to the Treasury, and as a consequence its gold reserve steadily diminished. In the seven months following June, 1892, more gold was drawn out of the Treasury in redemption of legal tender notes than in the thirteen years preceding.

The hope that the purchase of silver under the law of 1890 would restore that metal to a parity with gold was not realized. The rise in price to $1.21 per ounce fine ($1.2929 being par) was largely speculative and was followed by a rapid decline. The monometallists experienced the sad satisfaction of having their predictions verified; the bimetallists saw their arguments against independent action proven by the test of experience. The keen foresight of the business world clearly perceived the impending struggle and realized the baleful effect upon all forms of industry whatever the eventual result might be. New enterprises were abandoned, present business was curtailed, and the more timid proceeded to hide their talent in a napkin.

The party in power was held responsible for unsatisfactory conditions, and the congressional election in 1890 gave the Democrats a majority of 149 in the House. This spurred the Republicans in the remaining short session (1890–1891) to endeavor to pass some decisive legislation. A bill was reported in the Senate providing for an increased purchase of silver under the law of 1890 for a period of one year, in order to absorb the surplus in the market, which seemed to keep down the price. The silver Republicans held the balance of power and uniting with the silver Democrats passed a measure for free coinage pure and simple by a vote of 39 to 27. Fifteen Republicans voted for and

18 Democrats against it; the House voted down all attempts to consider the bill. Windom died, and was succeeded by Charles Foster, of Ohio. The Treasury note-issues continued, and silver fell to 96 cents per ounce.

Harrison, in pursuance of authority granted him by Congress, invited the principal nations to join in another conference to consider the question of international bimetallism which was held in 1892. Harrison believed that the scarcity of gold in Europe would incline European nations to favor international bimetallism and hence urged the accumulation of gold in the Treasury. He felt satisfied that we could maintain parity, expressed sympathy with the silver producers and was gratified that the surplus was not large and no longer deposited in banks.

Notwithstanding the pendency of this international conference, those favoring independent free coinage persisted in their efforts to force action in both branches of Congress in the session of 1891–1892. The silver advocates in the Senate were strongly re-enforced by members from the recently admitted Rocky Mountain states and proceeded to pass a bill for free coinage at the ratio of 16 to 1 by a vote of 29 to 25. Seven Democrats, including Carlisle, opposed it. The House rejected the bill by a vote of 136 to 154, the negative including 94 Cleveland Democrats.

In the political campaign of 1892 the Republican platform declared for both gold and silver and for international bimetallism. The Democratic platform, dictated by the Cleveland wing of the party, denounced the silver purchase law as a "cowardly makeshift," demanded that both gold and silver should be used without discrimination and declared in favor of the repeal of the 10 per cent. tax on state bank-notes. An important element, particularly representatives from the South, regarded the restoration of state bank circulation as the best solution of the currency question and a popular substitute for the silver issue in the campaign.

A new party appeared in the field, composed largely of the old

Greenback element, called the "People's Party," afterward "Populist," and nominated Weaver, of Iowa, for the presidency. The declarations of its state conventions favored various "isms," including subtreasuries in every important locality for the reception of wheat and other farm products, and the issue of paper money against the same, in a manner similar to the issuing of notes against silver bullion purchased. In the national Populist platform gold monometallism was declared a "vast conspiracy against mankind"; a circulation of $50 per capita was demanded. Silver demonetization, it was asserted, added to the purchasing power of gold, and the national power to create money had been used to favor the bondholders. The fact that a candidate appealing for public support as the representative of such policies polled 1,041,000 votes and actually carried four states and received one electoral vote in each of two other states is a strong commentary upon the vagaries of human nature.

Cleveland was elected over Harrison with a Democratic House of Representatives; the Senate was also Democratic, with a majority in favor of the free coinage of silver.

The international conference on silver, called by Harrison, met in Brussels in November following the election. The United States were represented by Senator Allison (Ia.), Senator Jones (Nev.), Representative McCreary (Ky.), ex-Comptroller of the Currency H. W. Cannon, Prof. E. B. Andrews of Brown University, and E. H. Terrell, United States Minister to Belgium. Twenty countries were represented, one of Great Britain's delegates being a member of the banking-house of Rothschild.

The delegates from the United States were instructed to endeavor to secure international bimetallism or, failing in that, action tending to a largely increased monetary use of silver to arrest depreciation. They soon found the former proposition to be out of the question. A sentiment favorable to an increased use of silver was manifest but no practical method could be agreed upon. France would not support any measure which would increase its stock of silver. Great Britain, manifestly concerned chiefly on account of India, seemed anxious that the price of silver be kept steady, but evidently did not intend to change her monetary system. The conference adjourned in January until May, 1893, and again to November, 1893, but never reassembled.

The United States were ably represented at this conference by men schooled in economics and possessed of practical experience as well. The subject was exhaustively discussed and thoroughly considered. Of course their efforts in favor of international bimetallism were largely compromised and nullified by the determined and persistent effort in Congress to force independent action in favor of free coinage at a ratio differing from that obtaining in Europe. The European delegates naturally regarded the formal action of Congress as more representative of public sentiment, and a better indication of probable action on the part of the United States, than any presentation which our delegates were able to make. As negotiators in the interest of silver their power was impaired by the fatuous zeal of silver advocates at home. It should be stated in explanation that the most ardent advocates of free silver regarded the conference as a means devised to postpone the accomplishment of their purpose and enable the party in power to hold the support of the silver Republicans in the pending presidential campaign.

Although barren of affirmative results the conference was productive of one great good: it served to concentrate the thought and the study of all nations upon this question and its failure to reach any agreement convinced all that the relative value of silver and gold, in the future as in the past, would be determined by the laws of trade and not by international agreement. It demonstrated the impossibility of international bimetallism. The leading European nations were quite satisfied with the gold standard and in no mood for monetary experiments apparently in the interest of commercial rivals. The settled judgment in favor of the single gold standard and the firm determination on the part of the leading European nations to adhere to the same was clearly apparent. That the question of a single gold standard or a single silver standard was the leading issue to be fought out in the United States was equally apparent. With all thinking men bimetallism was impossible. The question was, silver or gold.

In the presidential contest of 1892 the Democratic platform favored the repeal of the prohibitive tax on state bank circulation. The Democrats elected their President, and controlled Congress. Their candidates, and presumably their platform, had been indorsed at the polls. A serious attempt to restore state bank circulation was anticipated. It was known that the incoming administration would exert its influence to secure the repeal of the Silver Purchase Law, and it was feared that the restoration of state bank circulation might be necessary in order to command the support of the representatives from the South. Comptroller Hepburn, in his report, presented the objections to such a policy, and reviewed the history of state banks and state bank circulation in contrast with the existing national system, showing from statistics the saving in exchange, the greater economy, greater safety, and general superiority of the national system; he also urged that greater elasticity be given the national bank currency by removing the limitations upon the retirement and reissue of circulation; he also elaborated and recommended a plan for the refunding of the presently maturing government bonds into a long-time, low-rate bond; this would result in the saving of interest to the government and at the same time furnish a more desirable basis for note-issues. Such a measure was eventually embodied in the refunding act of March 14, 1900.

The condition of the Treasury upon the eve of the change in administration (March 4, 1893) was far from satisfactory. The cash balance available for current payments was about $24,000,000. The gold reserve was maintained above $100,000,000, which had come to be regarded the danger line, only by extraordinary efforts, the Treasury obtaining gold from the banks in exchange for other forms of currency. The condition of the Treasury which confronted President Cleveland upon resuming office was in sharp contrast with the $196,245,980 gold reserve and $70,158,461 other available cash balance which he left upon retiring from office in March, 1889. His administration was embarrassed for want of funds to meet current expenses without trenching on the gold reserve necessarily maintained to insure the redemption of legal tender notes upon presentation. There was another circumstance which tended still further to reduce the lessening revenues. The Democrats favored a revision of the tariff, a policy to which Cleveland was pledged. Business interests affected by customs laws naturally halted, pending action by Congress. Manufacturing diminished materially, labor was unemployed, consumption was reduced and the government's income necessarily fell off.

Carlisle, who had been an ardent advocate of the free coinage of silver, became Secretary of the Treasury. But for the well-known attitude of President Cleveland on the money question Carlisle's selection might have occasioned uneasiness. The gold exports continued and the reserve, in April, fell below the $100,000,000 mark. The administration had not up to this time had occasion to clearly define its policy respecting the Treasury notes of 1890, which were by their terms redeemable *in coin*, and hence, if the government chose, in silver dollars. Considerable alarm had been caused by the reported decision of Carlisle to redeem these notes in silver, hence Cleveland declared his purpose to redeem them in gold and to exercise all the powers of his great office for the maintenance of gold payments. Fear of a silver basis prevailed, especially abroad, owing to the weakness of the Treasury, and every express steamer brought in American securities and took away gold. The net loss during the fiscal year 1893 amounted to $87,500,000.

The crisis which resulted was severe and its effects enduring. Fear of going upon a silver basis roused the banking and business interests to united action. Within the period of six weeks in midsummer the banks, at great expense and notwithstanding adverse exchange conditions, imported $50,000,000 of gold. The usual form of transaction was to purchase the gold to arrive, with clearing-house funds, the premium ranging from 1 to 3 per cent.

President Cleveland convened Congress in extra session in August. In his message the disturbed condition of business was attributed to the silver law of 1890, and its repeal was strongly recommended. He pointed out that in three years the Treasury had lost $132,000,000 of gold and gained $147,000,000 of silver; if this continued all its funds would soon be in silver, and the maintenance of parity between silver and gold impossible; the government had no right to impose upon the people a depreciated currency nor to experiment with currency plans rejected by the leading civilized nations.

He experienced great difficulty in inducing his own party to sustain him. After a long struggle, terminating November 1, with the aid of Republican votes in the Senate the silver purchasing section of the law of 1890 was repealed; amendments proposing free coinage at various ratios and the restoration of the act of 1878 were defeated; in the Senate the vote was 43 to 32, only 20 Democrats favoring the repeal and 9 Republicans opposing; in the House the vote stood 239 to 109, only 22 Republicans voting in the affirmative. This repealing act declared it to be the policy of the United States to maintain parity of its gold and silver coins by international agreement or otherwise.

The discontinuance of silver purchases after such a protracted struggle did not restore confidence at once because those in Congress who favored "more money" and were in the majority, kept urging the free coinage of silver, increased greenback issues, repeal of the tax on state bank-notes and other measures calculated to unsettle public confidence. A general feeling of uneasiness pervaded the country. Interior banks had over $200,000,000 of reserve deposits in New York. As the Treasury reserve gradually diminished, they became impressed with a desire to strengthen their position at home and the withdrawal of a large portion of their New York deposits followed. This in turn necessitated curtailing and calling loans and general liquidation ensued. Reserves of the New York banks fell below the legal requirement. Money on call rose at one time to 74 per cent. Time loans to other than regular customers of the banks were exceedingly difficult to obtain. During the crisis, money was hoarded, and despite the great supply (nearly $24 per capita) a currency "famine" ensued and premiums as high as 4 per cent. were paid for currency of any kind, even silver dollars. The banks in the principal Eastern cities were compelled to curtail cash payments. The use of clearing-house loan certificates in large amounts was resorted to throughout the country as well as various other forms of obligation designed to perform the functions of currency.

Shortly after the panic or currency famine of 1893, by means of extensive correspondence with every considerable place in the country, the writer obtained statistics which justify the estimate that there were issued fully $100,000,000 of clearing-house certificates used in settlement between banks, of certified checks, certificates of deposit, cashier's checks in round amounts (as $1, $5, $10, $20, and $50), due bills from manufacturers and other employers of labor, and clearing-house certificates, in round amounts (in the case of Birmingham, Ala., as small in amount as 25 cents), all designed to take the place of currency in the hands of the public. Clearing-house certificates, issued and used in settling debit balances between banks, were not, but all of the other above-described evidences of debt which were issued to circulate among the public as money, were clearly subject to the 10 per cent. tax enacted for the purpose of getting rid of state bank circulation.

This temporary currency, however, performed so valuable a service in such a crucial period, in moving the crops and keeping business machinery in motion, that the government, after due deliberation, wisely forebore to prosecute. In other words, the want of elasticity in our currency system was thus partially supplied. It is worthy of note that no loss resulted from the use of this makeshift currency.

The Clearing-House Association of New York, in 1893, issued their first certificates June 21, their last September 6. All certificates were finally retired November 1. The total amount issued was $41,490,000. The maximum outstanding at any one time was $38,280,000. The rate of interest paid thereon by the banks to the Clearing-House Association was 6 per cent. The Philadelphia Clearing-House Association issued $11,465,000, and that of Baltimore $1,475,000 in certificates, practically coincident with the New York issue as to time, and similar as to conditions. The Boston banks issued $11,695,000, bearing interest at 7 3/10 per cent.; the first issue bore date of June 27, and the final retirement was October 20. The aggregate maximum amount issued in these four cities was $66,125,000.

As heretofore stated, this currency famine caused a forced importation of about $50,000,000 of gold in the face of adverse exchange rates and hence at a premium. By means of borrowed bonds national bank circulation was increased. The process was slow, and the worst of the stringency was over before the time required in which to procure notes from the Treasury had elapsed. The scarcity of currency forbade discrimination and the gold imported found its way largely into the Treasury and served materially to strengthen the reserve.

Commercial agencies reported the suspension of 15,000 individuals and concerns with liabilities aggregating $347,000,000. One hundred and fifty-eight national banks and 425 other banks and trust companies, largely located in the South and West, suspended. Eighty-six of the national banks and many of the

LOAN CERTIFICATES OF THE NEW YORK CLEARING HOUSE

Loan Comm. of	Date of First Issue	Date of Last Issue	Date of First Cancellation	Date of Final Cancellation	Aggregate Issue	Max. Amount Outstanding	Date	Rate of Interest	Nature of Collateral
1860	Nov. 23, 1860	Feb. 27, 1861	Dec. 12, 1860	March 9, 1861	7,375,000	6,860,000	Dec. 22, 1860	7 p. c.	U. S. Stocks; Tr'y notes; Stocks of State of N. Y.
1861	Sept. 19, 1861	Feb. 17, 1862	Oct. 7, 1861	April 28, 1862	22,585,000	21,960,000	Feb. 7, 1862	6 p. c.	Temporary receipts of U. S. for purpose of Gov't Bonds.
1863	Nov. 6, 1863	Jan. 9, 1864	——	Feb. 1, 1864	11,471,000	9,608,000	Nov. 27 to Dec. 1, 1863	6 p. c.	U. S. or N. Y. State Stocks, Bonds, etc., or temporary receipts as in 1861.
1864	March 7, 1864	April 25, 1864	April 20, 1864	June 13, 1864	17,728,000	16,418,000	April 20, 1864	6 p. c.	Same as in 1863; comm. of that year continued.
1873	Sept. 22, 1873	Nov. 20, 1873	Oct. 3, 1873	Jan. 14, 1874	26,565,000	22,410,000	Oct. 3, 1873	7 p. c.	Bills receivable; Stocks, Bonds & other securities.
[1] 1884	May 15, 1884	June 6, 1884	May 19, 1884	Sept. 23, 1886	24,915,000	21,885,000	May 24, 1884	6 p. c.	do
1890	Nov. 12, 1890	Dec. 22, 1890	Nov. 28, 1890	Feb. 7, 1891	16,645,000	15,205,000	Dec. 12, 1890	6 p. c.	do
1893	June 21, 1893	Sept. 6, 1893	July 6, 1893	Nov. 1, 1893	41,490,000	38,280,000	Aug. 20 to Sept. 6, 1893	6 p. c.	do
1907	Oct. 26, 1907	Jan. 30, 1908	Nov. 14, 1907	Mch. 28, 1908	101,060,000	88,420,000	Dec. 16, 1907	6 p. c.	do
1914	Aug. 3, 1914	Oct. 15, 1914	Aug. 26, 1914	Nov. 28, 1914	124,695,000	109,185,000	Sept. 25, 1914	6 p. c.	do

[1] All Certificates were cancelled by August 25, 1884, except part of those issued to the Metropolitan National Bank, which were gradually retired as the bills receivable became due and were paid.

others subsequently resumed. Clearing-house exchanges for the year showed a falling off of $13,800,000,000, of which 74 per cent. was in the city of New York. Savings bank deposits were reduced $36,000,000, the resources of national banks diminished $350,000,000, and those of state banks $53,000,000.

It had become apparent that the international conference on silver would not reassemble. The British government had closed the mints of India to the free coinage of silver and endeavored to maintain a fixed par of exchange between the mother country and the dependency. Silver fell to 78 cents per ounce, giving a ratio to gold of 26½ to 1. This further depression of the price of silver added materially to the difficulties and embarrassments of the United States Treasury in its struggle for the maintenance of the gold standard. As marking the trend of thought and events in the world it undoubtedly confirmed and strengthened the advocates of the gold standard.

The usual result followed this money stringency. Currency in hiding came into circulation, business stagnation lessened the demand and a plethora ensued. The expenditures of the Treasury exceeded its receipts at the rate of $7,000,000 monthly. The Treasury was obliged to use the gold, which it had accumulated as a reserve, to meet its current expenses.

Carlisle, in his report to Congress, asked for authority to make temporary loans to cover revenue deficits and also for specific authority to issue bonds for gold for the purpose of increasing the gold reserve. He urged that so long as the Treasury was charged with the functions of a bank of issue ample provision for the redemption of its notes should be made. Congress disregarded his recommendation. In January, 1894, the gold reserve fell below $66,000,000, and there was but $18,000,000 other available cash. He was therefore compelled to exercise the authority granted by the Resumption Act of 1875, and determined to issue ten-year five per cent. bonds, as authorized by the Refunding Act of 1870, to the amount of $50,000,000.

He proceeded without consultation with the leading bankers of the country and especially avoided New York. He endeavored to float the loan by popular subscriptions and appealed to the country at large for that purpose. The attempt was unsuccessful. He then came to New York, convened the leading bankers at the subtreasury and announced that less than $5,000,000 subscriptions had been received. He said to the bankers present in substance: Unless you take this loan it will be a failure; just what effect its failure will have upon the business interests which you represent, you, gentlemen, are better able to judge than I am; what the political effect will be I can perhaps better judge than you; all business interests and all classes of people are suffering, and have been for many months; the silver purchasing provision of the law of 1890 was denounced as the cause, and its repeal advocated as a remedy; you, gentlemen, joined if you did not lead in this sentiment; the President convened Congress, the law was repealed — not promptly, as it should have been, but it was repealed, nevertheless; the troubles seemed to continue without abatement; then it was proclaimed that the gold reserve was impaired, hence the credit of the government endangered, and must be restored in order to restore confidence and credit generally, and bonds should be issued for that purpose; well, we offer you the bonds; if you take them and give the government gold, I think the situation will be relieved; if you refuse, the bond issue is a failure; in that case, I think an act to coin the seigniorage in the Treasury or issue silver certificates against the same will pass both houses of Congress almost immediately; the friends of silver will then say to the President: "You have tried Wall Street's remedy twice, and each time it has failed; now try ours;" under the circumstances I very much fear that the President in his poverty will be compelled to sign such a bill; if this bond issue is taken, the situation will be relieved, and should a bill to coin the seigniorage reach the President, he will certainly veto it.

John A. Stewart replied: "Of course we will take the loan; we have known all along that in the end you would have to come to us; we have anticipated this interview, and are prepared to take the loan." The loan was promptly taken. A substantial amount of gold came into the Treasury from the vaults of the banks. A portion, however, was furnished by withdrawal from the Treasury for that purpose by means of greenbacks. This in no wise interfered with the success of the loan, as the government's stock of cash was so low that it was obliged to pay out gold for current purposes.

The Secretary's power to issue bonds was questioned in Congress, and a resolution was introduced to prohibit the payment of interest on the bonds sold. A labor organization attacked the Secretary's authority in a legal proceeding in the federal courts, which, however, ruled in his favor.

Carlisle was severely criticised in some quarters for not resorting to bond issues at an earlier period in order to protect his reserves and prevent a general feeling of distrust from taking possession of the country. Sentiment or fear is an important element in every financial crisis, but the success of the Secretary's policy depended upon public support, and perhaps the delay in issuing bonds was necessary, in order that the people as a whole might realize the danger so apparent to statesmen and financiers and thus justify the remedy. The continuance of distrust is amply evidenced by the fact that by the first of September $75,000,000 of gold had been exported and the gold reserve was down to $55,000,000.

The silver bullion purchased under the act of 1890 had cost $156,000,000. The average cost per ounce was 92.5 cents. This bullion would produce when coined 218,000,000 silver dollars, yielding a seigniorage or profit between cost and coinage value of about $62,000,000. A part of this bullion had already been coined, so that the remainder would produce a seigniorage of about $55,000,000. Congress proposed to anticipate the coinage of this bullion, regard the last-mentioned sum as already coined, and direct the issue of silver certificates to that amount. This ingenious inflation measure is the one alluded to by Carlisle in his interview with the New York bankers. It passed in April, but Cleveland, after some deliberation, during which earnest protests were poured in upon him, vetoed it.

This Congress repealed the law of 1862 and later ones exempting the United States notes and certificates circulating as money from taxation. A law was passed reducing tariff rates generally, but designed to provide for a larger revenue from sugar and other articles. It failed to produce any material increase of revenue immediately, owing, very likely, to the depressed condition of trade and industry. The business troubles were in large part due to the fact that the government's income did not equal its expenditure and Congress was properly held reponsible for failure to give the country a measure that would produce sufficient revenue to meet the ordinary expenditure of government.

In November a further issue of $50,000,000 5 per cent. bonds under the authority of the Resumption Act became necessary. Carlisle, in his report, urged the retirement of the greenbacks and, among other things, formulated an elaborate currency scheme, whose principal features were the impounding in the Treasury of legal tender notes as part security for national banknotes and permitting state banks to issue notes under certain restrictions. The monthly inflation of the currency by the purchase of silver bullion having ceased, the time seemed propitious for improving and popularizing the national bank circulation. The American Bankers' Association, meeting in Baltimore in 1894, developed a bank-note issue system, afterward known as the Baltimore plan. It proposed to permit note-issues under federal supervision to the extent of 50 per cent. of the paid-up, unimpaired capital of banks, subject to ½ per cent. taxation, and an additional note-issue equal to 25 per cent. of the capital, subject to a much heavier tax in order to insure its retirement when the necessity for its issue had disappeared. The notes were to be a first lien upon the assets of the bank (including the double liability of shareholders), and a 5 per cent. guarantee fund (in addition to the 5 per cent. redemption fund) was to be provided and maintained for the redemption of notes of failed banks, this fund to be replenished if need be, by enforcing the prior lien. The silver sentiment of the country was so strong that no currency scheme, however well devised, could obtain a hearing.

The House of Representatives elected in 1894 was strongly Republican and that party also regained control of the Senate. President Cleveland, who had vigorously supported the recommendations of Secretary Carlisle on the subject of the gold reserve and legal tender notes, sent a special message to Congress on January 9, 1895, asking for authority to issue a 3 per cent. fifty-year gold bond, the proceeds to be used to retire and cancel the legal tender notes. He believed that the time had come when the Treasury should be relieved from the "humiliating process of issuing bonds to procure gold to be immediately drawn for purposes not related to the benefit of the government or our people." Over $300,000,000 notes had been redeemed in gold, yet they were all in existence and mainly in circulation. More than $172,000,000 gold had been paid out by the Treasury in redemption of notes during the year.

One month later, Congress having failed to act, and the continuing exports having reduced the gold reserve to less than $42,000,000, Cleveland informed Congress that, in order to maintain gold payments, he had been compelled to authorize a special contract (with a syndicate) to procure gold under the old law of 1862 (referred to, *ante*, p. 185) continued as section 3700 of the Revised Statutes. The contract called for the purchase of gold to the value of $65,116,244, by the sale of $62,315,400 4 per cent. thirty-year *coin* bonds at 104.496; if, however, Congress would authorize a 3 per cent. *gold* bond, the same would be taken at par by the syndicate and result in an ultimate saving of over

$16,000,000; inasmuch as the coin bonds would doubtless be paid in gold at maturity, such legislation should be promptly passed in order that the above-mentioned sum might be saved. Congress refused by a vote of 120 to 167 to grant the authority asked for and the more expensive course had to be adopted. Four per cent. bonds issued in 1877 had but recently been quoted at 129.

Under this contract the syndicate not only undertook to furnish the gold, but to take none from the Treasury with United States notes, to actually import one-half of the sum contracted for, and to do all in its power to prevent exports of gold during the period of the contract. The importation of so much gold necessarily implied the lapse of a very considerable period of time. Obviously these conditions were of the greatest importance to the Treasury under the circumstances. The syndicate, which included the Rothschilds, was managed by J. P. Morgan. By the establishment of a large credit abroad and by a combination of all foreign exchange houses on this side, it was able to carry out the undertaking. The syndicate furnished over $16,000,000 more gold than their contract called for by exchanging the same with the Treasury for other forms of money.

The action of the administration received the severest criticism in Congress, especially from its own party. A committee was appointed by the Senate to investigate the subject, upon the allegation of irregularities, but the result was unimportant except as it furnished a basis for political speeches. The business interests of the country, on the other hand, applauded the measure as sound and imperatively necessary. The drain of gold ceased at once and by the end of February the reserve stood at $84,000,000 and in June had increased to $107,500,000. The tide turned, however, and by January 1, 1896, the gold reserve had reached the very low point of $50,000,000.

Carlisle met the situation promptly, and sold in the ordinary way $100,000,000 thirty-year 4 per cent. coin bonds. The aggregate bids for the same amounted to over $568,000,000, and the loan was placed at 111⅛. The success of this bond sale in relieving the situation shows plainly that insufficient revenue was one of the principal troubles. The net loss of gold by export in the fiscal year 1894 was over $4,500,000, in 1895 $31,000,000, and in 1896 $80,500,000. The gold production of the world, especially in the United States, showed a marked increase in 1891, and continued to increase steadily from year to year. Coincident therewith the trend of sentiment throughout the world was strongly toward the gold standard. Austria and Russia had adopted this policy and were actively accumulating gold.

In his report for 1895, Carlisle showed a continuing deficit in revenue but a growing cash balance from the sale of bonds. He ably defended his policy to restore the nation's credit, which had been seriously undermined by long adherence to a false monetary system; he urged Congress (Republican in both branches) to provide for the cancellation of the legal tender notes; he also recommended the authorization of branch banks to supply the smaller towns with facilities not obtainable under the national bank act. Cleveland forcibly urged that the government notes should be funded into bonds, not only to avoid the expense of further bond issues made in order to procure gold but, much more, to save the cost to the people of periodic crises incident to the circumstances compelling such issues of bonds.

The report of Comptroller Eckels reflected the generally unsatisfactory condition of business throughout the country; the number of national banks had increased only sixty-nine in the two years 1894 and 1895; their circulation in October, 1895, as in 1893, amounted to $182,000,000. His report of 1894 contained a most valuable abstract of the banking systems under state laws and of foreign countries. In 1895 he presented a report on the use of credit instruments in retail transactions and one giving the number of depositors in national banks classified by their average deposits.

The per capita circulation in July, 1895, was $22.93, and one year later $21.10; the supply, however, was more than equal to the demand. Every bond issue had involved a money stringency of greater or less degree followed by the usual plethora. The change in the tariff law had had an unsettling effect, and the business of the country generally was unsatisfactory because of the absence of stable conditions which would enable business men to forecast future results with a reasonable degree of certainty. The lessening per capita circulation, lower prices, and hard times produced a condition of mind throughout the country peculiarly favorable for the campaign of the silver propaganda. The movement in favor of free coinage, managed by skilful leaders with ample means at their command, spread rapidly. Pamphlets, books, speeches, and newspapers favoring that policy were distributed plentifully. Every phase of the question was discussed with consummate ability and with arguments well calculated to impress the public.

European bimetallists were also exceedingly active. In both Germany and England, where the opposition had been strongest, opinion had apparently altered to such an extent that the outlook for an international agreement was considered favorable. Before adjourning in March, 1895, Congress had appointed three members of each house a delegation to confer with European representatives. The agitation for independent action by the United States became so strong that the "internationalists" soon became convinced that the question would have to be determined at the polls. Local conventions of the Populists, more numerously attended than ever before, declared unequivocally for independent action and liberation of the people from the alleged slavery to the "money power." The conduct of the Treasury, the redemption of notes in gold alone when the silver dollar was also full tender, the bond sales to buy gold, and the ranging of the entire banking community against free coinage, were especially denounced. Never before was the country roused to such a degree of excitement by an economic question.

Republican conventions in the Western states also leaned toward silver, but the national convention opposed free coinage, except under international agreement, and gold was, after much discussion, indorsed as the standard of value. Their candidate, McKinley, was equally cautious and hesitating in the early portion of the campaign.

The Democratic national convention was controlled by the anti-Cleveland wing of the party, which was prepared to coalesce with the Populists. Its platform favored free coinage of silver. The logical nominee, Bland, was passed by because it was feared he could not rally the full support of the radical Populists. Bryan was nominated. The Populists also nominated Bryan but named a separate candidate for second place.

The campaign which followed was, despite the attempt to make the tariff the principal issue, determined mainly on the question of the gold or silver standard. McKinley finally came out unreservedly for gold, and the question was comprehensively discussed.

The Republicans desired to hold as large a portion of the silver vote within their organization as possible and their campaign, especially in certain localities, was more in the nature of an appeal to the advocates of silver than an earnest attempt to show the error of their position and danger to the material interests of the country in case their policy should prevail. The public were therefore dependent upon the independent press and *quasi*-independent element in both political parties for sound money literature and sound money arguments. In this connection most valuable and most effective service was rendered by the National Sound Money League under the leadership of such men as Henry Villard, J. Sterling Morton, John K. Cowen, M. E. Ingalls, George Foster Peabody, Horace White, J. Kennedy

Tod, H. P. Robinson, John B. Jackson, James L. Blair, Louis R. Ehrich, E. V. Smalley, A. B. Hepburn, and many others.

They published in Chicago a paper known as *Sound Money*, which was gratuitously distributed to the press of the country, to public speakers, and to leaders and moulders of thought. In this manner they furnished data and arguments in the interest of right thinking and right voting. They as well as other economists contributed largely to its columns. They raised large sums of money, which were thus expended in a purely academic campaign. The dishonesty of free coinage of silver at the ratio of 16 to 1, when the commercial ratio was more than twice as great, was boldly proclaimed, and logic reënforced by history adduced in demonstration. From the non-partisan character of their organization they were able to reach and command the attention of people who would have rejected similar matter emanating from a political organization.

The contentions of the silver men may be summarized as follows: —

1. Demonetization of silver had deprived the people of one-half the primary money made available by nature.

2. This great contraction of money, increased by the falling off in the production of gold, had caused the steady downward trend in prices since 1873.

3. The consequent enhancement of the purchasing power of gold enormously increased the obligations of the debtors having deferred payments to make.

4. These unsatisfactory conditions would be aggravated by concentrating upon one metal only the measuring of values and debt-paying power; while the alternative existed of paying in either metal, the danger of inordinate enhancement of one was neutralized.

5. The farmer was under the gold standard compelled to compete with producers in other lands (India, etc.), where labor was cheap and the silver basis prevailed.

6. The United States should take the lead by opening the mints to free and unlimited coinage of silver, which would surely bring silver to parity and compel other nations to do likewise.

7. The United States required a larger volume of money, and free coinage was the proper way of increasing it, especially as the country produced so much silver.

The international bimetallists generally agreed with the contentions 1 to 4, but insisted that independent action by the United States would defeat the object in view and place the country on a silver basis to the lasting detriment of all interests.

The gold advocates maintained: —

1. That the volume of money had actually increased in greater ratio than population, and that the growing use of credit instruments had added to the media of exchange.

2. That the fall in prices was due chiefly and probably wholly, to improved methods of production, and had no relation to the demonetization.

3. That producers were also consumers and hence had to pay less for commodities, so that relatively they were not injured by the fall in prices.

4. That the theory of having two standards was a delusion. Only one thing could actually be a standard. That in fact gold was the only standard, silver being measured by it.

5. That free coinage meant depreciated money than which no device was more potent in cheating both the producer and consumer. It would precipitate the country upon a silver basis with gold at a fluctuating premium as in Mexico, not only contracting the volume of money but causing untold injury to all interests.

6. That Europe would only be too glad to have the United States take up the silver burden alone, enhancing the value of Europe's stock of silver, but would not follow the example.

7. That the volume of money was then greater than the needs of the country and when greater needs manifested themselves the supply would come from abroad in the shape of gold and from the product of our own mines at home, the output of which was now rapidly increasing.

The silver men appealed to the farmers as producers. The opposition appealed to the workmen, especially in manufacturing lines, and the tariff question was dexterously used to supplement their arguments in favor of an honest dollar. The division of parties was almost sectional. Eastern Democrats refused to follow the leaders of the West and South and the Central Western states were looked upon as the battle-ground. They generally joined with the East and Bryan's defeat was regarded as a declaration by the Nation in favor of the gold standard. The popular vote was, McKinley 7,164,000, Bryan 6,562,000. Fortified and encouraged by such a vote, the silver advocates had no idea of abandoning the contest.

The exports of gold, as before stated, continued in large volume during the latter half of the fiscal year, — January to July, 1896. Thereafter imports exceeded exports. During this movement, the withdrawals of gold from the Treasury were in excess of the exports and continued when exports ceased, showing that the fear of Bryan's election and a silver standard caused hoarding. Fully $50,000,000 was withdrawn from the Treasury because of this fear. The gold reserve, which had risen to $129,000,000 in March, fell to less than $101,000,000 in August. After the election the gold reserve steadily increased.

The average price of silver, which had fallen below 63½ cents per ounce in 1894, recovered to 67½ cents in 1896; but after the election a downward movement set in from which there was no reaction for several years.

Both Carlisle and Cleveland, in their last communications to Congress, elaborated and vigorously argued for the retirement of the legal tender notes. In order to meet their redemption the people had incurred obligations in the form of bonds in excess of $262,000,000, which would require, if held to maturity, a further payment for interest of $379,000,000, making a total cost of $641,000,000 on account of these notes, and the notes were still outstanding and unpaid. This form of currency, designed as a temporary expedient, and retained because of its supposed economy (being a non-interest-bearing loan), had proven most burdensome and costly both in direct taxation and indirect injury to business affairs. Untoward events would again produce similar results unless these notes were finally retired.

When Cleveland assumed office March 4, 1893, he found a gold reserve of $103,284,219, and other available cash in the Treasury $20,843,869. When he retired from office in March, 1897, he left $148,661,209 gold reserve, and $64,176,047 other available cash, showing an increase of Treasury cash of $88,709,168. The four bond issues placed during his administration netted the Treasury $293,388,061, hence $204,678,893 of the money received from bond sales were used for current expenses. The ordinary expenses of government, by the accepted principles of good administration, should be met by current taxation. The tariff and revenue law passed during the Cleveland administration failed to produce needed revenue which would unquestionably have averted a very large part of the troubles experienced by the administration and by the public generally. Carlisle was forced to issue bonds under existing authority to replenish the gold reserve. The gold thus received was paid out in redemption of legal tender notes, which had immediately to be used, together with some of the gold, to meet current expenses. Had he possessed other money for current use, and thus been able to impound the redeemed notes, the gold reserve would have been more easily maintained. He was forced to proclaim the weakness of the Treasury and assail the credit of the government with each bond issue, made ostensibly for the purpose of maintaining the gold reserve, but in part as well for the purpose of meeting the ordinary expense of government. Had Congress granted the authority asked to borrow for temporary purposes upon exchequer notes, smaller bond issues would have been required and less trouble and distrust would have been experienced.

The national banks were constantly growing in importance and usefulness as banks of deposit and discount. Their safe and conservative management had won for them a place in public confidence and favor unsurpassed by the best institutions in any country. The silver controversy had for several years commanded the attention of Congress to the exclusion of legislation affecting bank circulation. The condition and changes sufficiently appear in the statistics following.

STATISTICAL RÉSUMÉ

(Amounts in millions)

National Finances

Fiscal Year	Revenue			Expenditures			− Deficit + Surplus	Outstanding Debt	+ Increase − Decrease	Price of 4's of 1907	
	Customs	Other	Total	Ordinary	Interest	Total				High	Low
1891	220	173	393	318	38	356	+ 37	1006	− 61	122	116
1892	177	178	355	322	23	345	+ 10	968	− 38	118⅛	114
1893	203	183	386	356	27	383	+ 3	961	− 7	115	108
1894	132	166	298	340	28	368	− 70	1017	+ 56	116	112½
1895	152	161	313	325	31	356	− 43	1097	+ 80	113⅝	110
1896	160	167	327	317	35	352	− 25	1223	+ 126	112½	106

Circulation

July 1st	Gold [1]	Silver [1] Dollars	Subsidiary Coin	U. S. Notes	Treasury Notes	National Bank-notes	Total	In Treasury	In Circulation	Population	Per Capita
1891	647	388	78	347	50	168	1678	180	1498	64	$23.41
1892	664	389	77	347	102	173	1752	151	1601	66	24.44
1893	598	391	77	347	147	179	1739	142	1597	67	23.85
1894	627	395	76	347	153	207	1805	144	1661	68	24.28
1895	636	401	77	347	146	212	1819	217	1602	70	22.93
1896	599	422	76	347	130	226	1800	294	1506	71	21.10

[1] Includes certificates.

Exports and Imports and Gold Movement

Fiscal Year	Merchandise			Silver			Gold			Notes Redeemed in Gold	Gold Reserve
	Exports	Imports	Excess −Exp. +Imp.	Exports	Imports	Excess −Exp. +Imp.	Exports	Imports	Excess −Exp. +Imp.		
1891	884	845	− 39	24	26	+ 2	86	19	− 67	6	118
1892	1030	827	− 203	34	29	− 5	50	50	—	9	114
1893	848	866	+ 18	42	34	− 8	109	21	− 88	102	95
1894	892	655	− 237	51	20	− 31	77	72	− 5	85	65
1895	808	732	− 76	48	20	− 28	67	36	− 31	117	108
1896	883	780	− 103	61	27	− 34	112	34	− 78	159	102

Production of Gold and Silver

Calendar Year	World			United States			Price of Silver	Commercial Ratio	Bullion Value of Dollar
	Gold	Silver		Gold	Silver				
		Coining Value	Commercial Value		Coining Value	Commercial Value			
1891 . . .	131	177	136	33	75	58	$.98800	20.92	.764
1892 . . .	147	198	133	33	82	56	.87145	23.72	.674
1893 . . .	157	214	129	36	78	47	.78030	26.49	.604
1894 . . .	181	213	104	40	64	31	.63479	32.56	.491
1895 . . .	199	217	110	47	72	36	.65406	31.60	.505
1896 . . .	202	203	106	53	76	40	.67565	30.59	.522

THE SILVER ACQUISITION

Fiscal Year	Bullion Purchased			Coinage of Dollars	Stock of Dollars	Dollars Out	Certificates Out	Net Silver in Treasury	
	Fine Ounces	Cost	Average					Dollars	Bullion
1891 [1]	3	3	$1.0901						
1891	48	51	1.0451	24	391	59	307	22	32
1892	54	51	.9402	6	397	57	327	5	77
1893	54	45	.8430	1	398	57	327	7	118
1894	12	9	.7313	3	401	53	327	16	127
1895	—	—	——	1	402	52	320	30	124
1896	—	—	——	20	422	52	331	36	119

NATIONAL BANKS

(AT DATES NEAREST JANUARY 1)

Year	Number	Capital	Surplus	Deposits	Circulation	Specie	Legals	Loans
1891	3573	658	215	1515	123	190	88	1932
1892	3692	677	228	1620	135	208	103	2001
1893	3784	690	240	1778	146	210	109	2167
1894	3787	682	247	1553	180	251	163	1872
1895	3737	666	245	1719	169	218	157	1992
1896	3706	657	246	1734	185	207	131	2041

STATE BANKS, ETC.

Year	State Banks						Total Resources		
	Number	Capital	Surplus	Deposits	Cash	Loans	Trust Companies	Private Banks	Savings Banks
1891	2572	209	60	557	108	623	537	152	1855
1892	3191	234	67	649	130	700	600	147	1964
1893	3579	251	74	707	137	758	727	108	2014
1894	3586	244	74	658	145	666	705	105	1981
1895	3774	250	74	712	143	693	807	130	2054
1896	3708	240	71	696	128	697	855	94	2143

[1] Under law of 1878 to August 14, 1890.

MISCELLANEOUS FINANCIAL

Year	Clearing-house Transactions		Savings Banks			Failures	
	New York (Millions)	U. S. (Millions)	Depositors (000's)	Deposits (Millions)	Average	Number (000's)	Liabilities (Millions)
1891 . . .	34,054	57,299	4533	1623	358	12	190
1892 . . .	36,280	60,884	4782	1713	358	10	114
1893 . . .	34,421	58,881	4831	1785	370	15	347
1894 . . .	24,230	45,028	4778	1748	366	14	173
1895 . . .	28,264	50,975	4876	1811	371	13	173
1896 . . .	29,351	51,936	5065	1907	377	15	226

CHAPTER XXI

Gold Standard Act of 1900

1897–1902

The gold standard advocates, who hoped that McKinley's election would be accepted as a final declaration in favor of the gold standard and that legislation would be speedily enacted, under the influence of his administration, insuring such result, were doomed to disappointment. McKinley was a safe exponent but not a moulder of public sentiment. His characteristics in this respect earned him the criticism of always "keeping his ear to the ground." The leaders of the Republican party were still influenced by the habit of deference to silver advocates and silver interests and the very large vote cast for Bryan, under stress of a presidential campaign, was a tangible evidence of strength and distinct source of inspiration far outweighing any sense of discouragement involved in his defeat. McKinley's congressional record upon the question of the standard justified the silver advocates in expecting no drastic measures at his hands, and the record of other Republican leaders fortified the hope of sufficient Republican assistance to defeat such measures should they appear. The gold standard had distinctly triumphed, but the lines of battle were still drawn, astute generals were deploying for position on either side, and the struggle was to be finally determined in the presidential contest of 1900.

McKinley was easily persuaded that one more effort to secure international agreement in favor of the enlarged use of silver as money should be made. The troubles of Great Britain in preserving even approximate stability in ratio between the rupee and the pound, among other causes, had precipitated a general discussion of the subject in Europe and perhaps justified this attempt on the part of our government. Senator Wolcott (Colo.), ex-Vice-President Adlai Stevenson, and General Charles J. Paine were sent abroad as commissioners. They visited the different capitals of Europe, were pleasantly received, but elicited no responsive interest. The complete failure of the mission was so generally anticipated in advance that it produced no appreciable effect upon public sentiment at home.

A deficit in revenue of $18,000,000 estimated for 1897 was not disturbing, because the cash balance, including the gold reserve, was nearly $213,000,000, resulting from the proceeds of the bond sales in 1894–1896. The fact that Cleveland's struggle to maintain the gold standard was largely caused and greatly intensified by insufficient revenues was fully understood and appreciated. In fact the most serious criticism upon Cleveland's administration is his failure to influence legislation which would presently produce revenue sufficient for his needs.

McKinley convened Congress in extra session and an act increasing the tariff generally, including a reimposition of part of the duty on sugar, which had been abolished by the McKinley act of 1890, soon produced sufficient revenue.

Lyman J. Gage, for more than a generation a successful banker in Chicago, had been appointed Secretary of the Treasury. He brought his long experience and study to the work of solving the currency problem and before the regular session of Congress opened had elaborated a complete plan well worthy of adoption which was submitted to that body in December, 1897. His purpose was, as he expressed it, to put the country squarely upon a gold basis.

The business interests of the country were keenly alive to the necessity for action and under the leadership of H. H. Hanna delegates from all sections assembled in convention at Indianapolis. The meeting was thoroughly representative in character, including some of the ablest men in the country. A very able commission was created, including Senator George F. Edmunds as chairman, and ex-Secretary Charles S. Fairchild and J. Laurence Laughlin, among its members, to prepare a comprehensive measure or proposed law for currency and coinage reform, together with an academic discussion of the whole subject, for submission to Congress, and to the public generally. Their report, an octavo volume of 600 pages, showed great research, was forceful, lucid, convincing, and had great influence upon the public mind; this octavo volume was distributed gratuitously, all important libraries receiving a copy. During the early period of our history, stenography was unknown and printing but little developed, hence records were meagre, libraries almost negligible and important documents were preserved in a very few places. Many important historical documents were published in full in this volume and thus made accessible to the general public; for this reason reference is frequently made to this volume because the original data are out of reach of the general public. This convention was, perhaps, the most influential single influence in favor of the gold standard and currency based upon commercial assets.

The friends of the gold standard became aggressive, and presented to Congress a proposition to redeem silver dollars in gold. This roused the silver leaders who repelled it as an attack upon the legal tender quality of the "dollar of our daddies," and the Senate passed a resolution against the proposition; the House, however, refused to concur. The whole trend of the administration toward the establishment of the single gold standard, slow though it was, gave to Bryan and his lieutenants great hope of political success in the ensuing campaign.

The declared issue had theretofore been between the single silver standard, toward which the country had been so rapidly tending prior to the repeal of the silver purchase law, and the bimetallic standard with a strong tendency to the single gold standard. Aggressive action in favor of the latter was likely to concentrate all other elements in opposition, and the silver advocates scented future victory in the situation. They were doomed to disappointment. The Spanish War, which occurred at this time (1898), united the patriotic sentiment of the country in support of the administration. Republicans no longer entertained any doubt of McKinley's reëlection and assumed a bolder attitude in favor of the gold standard.

An almost continuous rebellion against Spanish rule had existed in Cuba for more than a quarter of a century. The military occupation of the island necessarily interfered with commercial relations with the United States. Exorbitant and unusual tariff exactions were imposed, coupled with unexplained and prolonged delay in passing goods, both for export and import, through the custom-houses, producing conditions inimical to successful business; and these conditions were modified only by the improper use of money with customs officials. Self-respecting merchants found it difficult to engage in trade with Cuba. Utter neglect of sanitation in the Cuban ports bred yellow fever without interruption.

Cuban ports were in close proximity to the Gulf ports of the United States, easily reached by the smaller sailing craft, and hence a periodic scourge of the yellow pest was more or less prevalent in our own country. The only means of protecting our own people from this disease seemed to be to compel proper sanitation in Cuba. These conditions were aggravating and long continuance had exasperated people almost to the explosive point. According to the laws of nations no provocation of war existed and yet the happening of any untoward event was bound to precipitate a conflict. The blowing up of the battleship *Maine* in Havana harbor, February 15, 1898, and the death of a large number of American sailors, produced a crisis and the conflict became inevitable.

The recounting of the above events seems justifiable here for the reason that the Spanish War, resulting as it did, greatly strengthened McKinley's administration in the popular mind and nerved the Republican leaders to firm action in behalf of the gold standard, relieved as they were from fear of popular defeat. The war brought other topics to the front and silver lost its commanding interest.

To meet the expenses of the war taxes were increased and a loan of $200,000,000 in 3 per cent. bonds was placed at par. The act authorizing the latter contained a provision which directed a more rapid coinage of silver dollars. It was, in fact, with difficulty that the silver majority in the Senate was restrained from forcing a free silver amendment to this measure, so imperatively demanded by the exigencies of the war. In the House, Bland had proposed the further issue of legal tender notes to cover the cost of the war instead of issuing bonds.

After the tariff revision of 1897 was completed, thus rendering any further change in the near future improbable, the industrial interests rapidly recovered from the depression, and an era of prosperity set in which was materially stimulated by the great demands of the government for war supplies. The world's production of gold steadily increased and the United States, with favorable trade balances and a heavy home output, augmented its gold stock at a rate greater than that shown by any other country. Ability to maintain the gold standard was beyond question.

The number of national banks continued to diminish until July, 1898, when there were but 3582 (compared with 3830 in 1893 and 3634 in May, 1897). Their circulation in July, 1898, stood at $190,000,000. The issue of the 3 per cent. war loan at par enabled the banks to increase circulation at a profit and by December, 1899, it had increased to $205,000,000. The number of banks had in the same period increased 20, but their aggregate capital had diminished over $16,000,000. The circulation of the country was now $25.50 per capita. Silver declined to about 60 cents per ounce, making the market ratio to gold 34 to 1 and the bullion value of the silver dollar about 47 cents.

The Republican leaders in Congress determined in December, 1899, that the time for action on the currency question had arrived. In the House a Republican caucus adopted a bill upon the general lines proposed by the Indianapolis conference but varying in certain particulars. This bill passed in January by a majority of fifty. The Senate passed a separate measure differing in many respects. The two bills went to conference, an agreement was reached early in March, and on the 14th of that month the conference bill passed and was signed by the President.

The act declared the gold dollar to be the standard unit of value and all forms of money issued or coined by the United States were to be maintained at a parity therewith by the Secretary of the Treasury. Both classes of legal tender notes were to be redeemed in such gold coin, the reserve for the purpose to be increased at once to $150,000,000, and maintained, if necessary, by sales of 3 per cent. gold bonds. Notes when redeemed were to be reissued only for gold, but if the gold were obtained out of the general Treasury fund, they might be used for any purpose except to meet deficiencies in revenues. The legal tender quality of the silver dollar remained undisturbed by the law. The monetary functions of the Treasury were separated from those of a merely fiscal character by the establishment of a separate division. Treasury notes of 1890 were to be cancelled as received, and silver certificates substituted therefor; the issue of gold certificates to be resumed and continued unless the gold reserve should fall below $100,000,000, or the greenbacks and silver certificates in the general fund exceed $60,000,000, and the issue of currency certificates to be discontinued. Denominations of paper were regulated as follows: no gold certificates under $20, but one-fourth at least of the issue to be $50 and under; silver certificates, 90 per cent. to be $10 and under, 10 per cent. $20, $50, and $100; greenbacks under $10 to be retired as smaller silver certificates are issued, larger greenbacks to be substituted; $5 national bank notes to be issued only to one-third of the amount taken by each bank; the limit of subsidiary coinage was increased to $100,000,000, the silver on hand to be used for this purpose. The new 3 per cent. government bonds, the 4 per cents of 1907, and 5 per cents of 1904 outstanding were to be refunded in the discretion of the Secretary into 2 per cent. thirty-year gold bonds, upon a 2¼ per cent. income basis, the premium to be paid in cash; national banks were authorized in smaller towns with $25,000 capital; circulation allowed to the par of bonds, and to the full amount of unimpaired capital, and banks depositing the new 2 per cent. United States bonds to be taxed only ½ per cent. annually on circulation, whereas the tax on circulation secured by any other issue remained at one per cent.

By selling to the banks a 2 per cent. bond (at least 1 per cent. under the interest rate which the government would have to pay had the bonds sold on their investment value) and allowing them circulation to the par of the bonds, with a 50 per cent. reduction in the rate of annual taxation, the government became morally obligated to maintain these bonds at par and to protect the currency monopoly which the law gave to the banks; the consideration to the government was a market for its bonds at a very low rate of interest.

The provision of the act of 1882 prohibiting banks retiring circulation from again increasing the same for a period of six months was repealed, but the limit of the amount which might be retired in any one month remained at $3,000,000. The final section disclaims any intention of precluding bimetallism if conditions should prove favorable.

Thus after a struggle covering many years a number of reforms in the monetary system were carried through in a single legislative measure. The opposition at once made itself manifest. The platform of the Democratic-Populist party in Nebraska, which met in convention under the leadership of Bryan five days after the passage of the "gold standard law," declared for free and unlimited coinage of silver and the substitution of greenbacks for national bank-notes. In many of the other states similar declarations were adopted, and although the new issue of "Imperialism," growing out of the war, was for a time prominent in the presidential campaign the actual contest was upon the question of the standard of values and opposition to bank-note currency. All the former arguments for an increased money supply to come from the remonetization of silver, the oppressive effects of the single gold standard, and the inadequacy of the gold supply were rehearsed with little effect as the country was prospering as never before in its history. Prices of agricultural products had risen. The excess of exports over imports had averaged $560,000,000 a year for the preceding three years. The revenues produced a substantial surplus. The world's production of gold was now over $300,000,000 a year, the United States contributing nearly one-fourth, all of which was retained. The money in circulation in the United States had risen to nearly $27 per capita.

Bryan's renomination was a foregone conclusion, and he fatuously insisted upon making the silver question the main issue. The Republicans renominated McKinley, declared for the gold standard and against free coinage of silver and in favor of legislation looking to an equalization of interest rates by enabling the varying currency needs of the seasons and all sections to be promptly met.

McKinley was reëlected by a largely increased majority, and the country accepted the result as indorsing and confirming the action of Congress in adopting the gold standard by the act of March 14, 1900. Good results flowing from this act were speedily manifest. The refunding of the bonds provided for aggregated $352,000,000 and a large amount of the surplus revenue was paid out for premiums in making the exchange. National banks increased 340 in number, the capital was increased $26,500,000 and circulation nearly $86,000,000 compared with September a year before. Of the new banks 123 were converted state banks and 208 were capitalized at the minimum of $25,000. The bond security for circulation included $270,000,000 of the new 2 per cents.

The issue of gold certificates increased materially, and the changes in the denominations of paper money provided for by the law progressed rapidly, the silver certificates taking the place of the smaller denominations of other issues. With large crops to be moved, the country did not suffer from the usual money stringency, owing to the large increase in the gold stock, in bank circulation, and the distribution of the surplus revenue in the process of refunding.

The law of 1900 provided "that the dollar consisting of twenty-five and eight-tenths grains of gold nine-tenths fine, as established by section thirty-five hundred and eleven of the Revised Statutes of the United States, shall be the standard unit of value, and all forms of money issued or coined by the United States shall be maintained at a parity of value with this standard and it shall be the duty of the Secretary of the Treasury to maintain such parity." It did not, however, provide any method by which this parity should be maintained. Secretary Gage in his report for December, 1900, called attention to this omission, and urged that specific power be given. He also renewed his arguments in favor of providing an elastic bank currency. While favoring branch banking, he recognized that public sentiment was averse to such a system, and suggested a federated system or federated bank somewhat analogous to the general government and the states, one of whose principal functions should be the issue of currency. He also recommended that bank-notes be secured, 30 per cent. by a deposit of government bonds, 20 per cent. by a deposit of legal tenders, the remaining 50 per cent. of the issues to be based upon assets and secured by a guaranty fund.

Thus he hoped to accomplish a double reform, the elimination of the greenbacks and an ample paper currency which would not only, as he demonstrated, prove safe to the holder, but would expand and contract as business needs warranted.

The terrible tragedy at Buffalo, which resulted in the death of McKinley and the accession of Roosevelt to the presidency, engrossed not only Congress but the public mind generally. Moreover there was a general feeling that the act of 1900, ratified and confirmed by the popular vote in the election following, had rendered our currency and our standard of values safe and that further legislation had better be deferred until experience had demonstrated its necessity. The prosperity of the country was unprecedented. Enterprises requiring enormous and hitherto unheard-of amounts of capital were undertaken. The growth of banks and trust companies, the underwriting and flotation of securities, the industrial development, the increase of exports without a corresponding increase of imports, — all tended to greatly enlarge the volume of business, and the circulating medium increased in proportion. By 1901 it reached $28 per capita, and continued to grow. A large part of this was in gold, the supply of which increased $429,000,000 from 1897 to 1901. Bank-notes had also increased more than $120,000,000 in that period, while silver issues of all classes showed only the slight increase arising from the seigniorage on the coinage. The character of the increased supply of money in use was therefore sound, and the entire mass was practically continuously employed. Notwithstanding this large volume of money the usual stringency appeared when the crop season arrived. At its minimum of employment in the usual channels of trade, the surplus accumulation in the banks was rapidly absorbed by the speculative demand, stimulated no doubt by the large return of American securities from abroad to pay the enormous trade balances in our favor. Hence, when the maximum demand again recurred in the crop-moving season, stringency manifested itself, aggravated by the accumulation in the subtreasuries of surplus revenues which, despite the laws reducing taxes after the war had closed, the great consuming power of the Nation continued to pour into the government's coffers. There were but two means of returning this money to the channels of trade, — the purchase of bonds at high premiums, inaugurated as we have seen by Guthrie in 1854, and the placing of the surplus in depository banks. Both courses necessarily increased the demand for and the price of government bonds (to be deposited as security for public moneys), which in turn tended to check an increase in bank circulation.

The imperfections of the existing laws relating to currency, and the receipt, safe keeping, and payment of the public moneys by means of our subtreasury system, were illustrated in a practical manner with each recurring fall.

Leslie M. Shaw succeeded Gage as Secretary of the Treasury and when, in the early fall of the year 1902, the same evils manifested themselves he endeavored to alleviate the condition by a broader construction of the law governing public deposits, which provides that such deposits shall be secured to the satisfaction of the Secretary by "deposit of government bonds and otherwise." This he rightly construed as authorizing him to accept approved bonds of states and municipalities as part of such security. By this course an equal amount of government bonds would be released for use to increase the bank circulation. By this process and by the purchase of bonds and anticipation of interest, Shaw rendered some $40,000,000 of surplus available for use in trade channels and induced an increase of bank-notes to about one-half that sum.

The change of sentiment following the evolution of business is well illustrated by the fact that Secretary Shaw recommended depositing government money with the banks at interest, when so many of his predecessors prior to 1878, as well as comptrollers of the currency, had urged that banks be prohibited by law from paying interest on deposits.

The need of giving our currency elasticity in average conditions was generally recognized. Also, the necessity of relieving its rigidity so that the banks might afford relief and preserve values in time of panic was a paramount need in the public mind. For this reason I have set forth in much detail the principal schemes of currency reform.

As has been stated, the British government adopted a monetary policy for India which prohibited the coinage of silver except on government account, and silver coin was made exchangeable at a fixed ratio, approximately 32 to 1, which corresponded with the commercial ratio, silver having fallen to 64½ cents per ounce. Japan adopted a similar policy, and minor countries followed these examples, so that the Oriental silver standard countries of China, Straits Settlements, and the Philippines were the only open markets for silver. Since the latter islands have come under the control of the United States, the gold standard with silver coinage on government account has been decreed by the act of Congress March 2, 1903.

Mexico was a large producer of silver, which constituted her principal export, and was therefore greatly interested in arresting its further depreciation. Her silver piasters had for over a century been the favorite coins of the Orient and their exportation and further use was threatened by the political and other changes in the Philippines and China. Mexico, for this reason, instituted negotiations for an international agreement, between the countries having colonial possessions where silver was in use, to establish a stable ratio if possible between the two metals. China joined Mexico, and the United States, having regard for the interests of the Philippines and having important silver-producing interests, also joined in the movement; and for this purpose a commission composed of Messrs. H. H. Hanna, C. A. Conant, and J. W. Jenks was sent abroad to confer on the subject with the nations concerned, in the hope that some means of preventing the violent fluctuations in the price of silver might be devised and the stability of international exchange insured. This was the last attempt to "do something for silver" by international agreement.

DATA RELATING TO BANKS 1903 AND 1915

	JUNE 1903	JANUARY 1915
Number of national banks	4,939	7,581
Capital	$ 744,000,000	$ 1,066,000,000
Note circulation	413,000,000	849,000,000
Deposits	3,348,000,000	6,668,000,000
Loans	3,415,000,000	6,358,000,000
Cash	552,000,000	663,000,000
Two per cent. bonds held to secure notes	367,000,000	607,000,000
Total bonds to secure notes	375,000,000	897,000,000
Total resources of national banks	6,287,000,000	11,357,000,000
Money in circulation	2,376,000,000	3,545,000,000
Per capita circulation	29.39	35.50

[1] Net amount on which reserve is computed.

NATIONAL FINANCES

(Millions of Dollars)

FISCAL YEAR	REVENUE			EXPENDITURES			+ SURPLUS − DEFICIT	DEBT		PRICE OF 4%'S OF 1907	
	CUSTOMS	OTHER	TOTAL	ORDINARY	INTEREST	TOTAL		NET[1]	+ INCREASE − DECREASE	HIGH	LOW
1897	177	171	348	328	38	366	− 18	987	+ 31	115	111 5/8
1898	150	255	405	406	37	443	− 38	1027	+ 40	114 3/4	108
1899	206	310	516	565	40	605	− 89	1155	+ 128	115 1/8	112
1900	233	334	567	448	40	488	+ 79	1108	− 47	118 1/8	114
1901	239	349	588	478	32	510	+ 78	1045	− 63	115 1/2	112
1902	254	308	562	442	29	471	+ 91	969	− 76	113	108 3/4
1903	284	275	559	477	29	506	+ 53	925	− 44	——	——

[1] Total of debt less cash in the Treasury.

NOTE. — In 1913 the revenues from customs were $318,891,396 and from all sources except postal $747,512,080. The disbursements exclusive of postal were

$748,703,574. The interest-bearing debt amounted to $965,706,610 with an annual interest charge of $22,835,330; the debt bearing no interest, including certificates issued against gold, silver and currency deposited in Treasury, was $1,948,838,753, making the total outstanding principal $2,916,204,913, while the total net debt less cash in the Treasury was $1,028,564,055. The per capita debt in 1903 was $11.44, in 1906, $11.25, in 1908, $10.55, and in 1913, $10.60.

CIRCULATION

Fiscal Year	Gold[1]	Silver[1]	Subsidiary Silver	U. S. Notes	Treasury Notes	National Bank-notes	Total	In Treasury	In Circulation	Population	Per Capita
1897	696	442	76	347	115	230	1906	266	1640	72	$22.87
1898	862	460	76	347	101	228	2074	236	1838	73	25.15
1899	963	470	75	347	94	241	2190	286	1904	74	25.58
1900	1036	491	83	347	75	310	2342	279	2063	76	26.94
1901	1125	520	90	347	48	354	2484	306	2178	78	27.98
1902	1189	540	97	347	30	356	2559	312	2247	79	28.43
1903	1253	554	101	347	19	413	2688	312	2376	80	29.39

[1] Including certificates.

EXPORTS AND IMPORTS AND GOLD MOVEMENT

Fiscal Year	Merchandise			Silver			Gold			Notes redeemed in Gold	Net Gold
	Exports	Imports	Excess Exports	Exports	Imports	Excess Exports	Exports	Imports	Excess −Exports +Imports		
1897	1051	765	286	63	31	32	40	85	+ 45	78	141
1898	1231	616	615	56	31	25	16	120	+ 104	25	167
1899	1227	697	530	57	31	26	38	89	+ 51	26	241
1900	1394	850	544	57	35	22	48	45	− 3	36	221
1901	1488	823	665	64	36	28	53	66	+ 13	24	249
1902	1382	903	479	50	28	22	49	52	+ 3	19	254
1903	1420	1026	394	44	24	20	47	45	− 2	36	252

PRODUCTION OF GOLD AND SILVER

Year	World			United States			Price of Silver	Ratio	Bullion Value of Silver Dollar
	Gold	Silver		Gold	Silver				
		Commercial Value	Coining Value		Commercial Value	Coining Value			
1897	236	96	207	57	32	70	$.60483	34.20	$.467
1898	287	100	219	64	32	70	.59010	35.03	.456
1899	307	101	217	71	33	71	.60154	34.36	.465
1900	255	107	223	79	36	75	.62007	33.33	.479
1901	263	105	226	79	33	71	.59595	34.68	.461
1902	297	86	210	81	30	76	.52795	39.15	.408

SILVER STATISTICS

Fiscal Year	Coinage of Silver Dollars	Stock of Dollars	Dollars Out	Silver Certificates Out	Net Silver in the Treasury	
					Dollars	Bullion
1897	13	442	52	358	32	105
1898	14	456	58	390	12	98
1899	15	471	61	402	7	85
1900	25	496	66	408	16	70
1901	23	520	67	430	24	48
1902	18	543	69	447	25	33

NOTE. — The total stock of silver dollars in the United States on December 31, 1913 was $568,272,478 of which $74,326,345 was outside the Treasury. The total stock of silver coin and bullion on June 30, 1914, was $753,563,709.

NATIONAL BANKS
(In millions)
(AT DATES NEAREST JANUARY 1)

YEAR	NUMBER	CAPITAL	SURPLUS	DEPOSITS	CIRCULATION	SPECIE	LEGALS	LOANS
1897	3661	647	247	1655	211	226	156	1901
1898	3607	630	246	1961	194	252	159	2100
1899	3590	621	247	2319	207	329	136	2214
1900	3602	607	250	2461	205	315	115	2480
1901	3942	632	262	2718	299	360	142	2707
1902	4291	665	287	3074	319	370	151	3038
1903	4766	731	351	3308	335	418	153	3351

OTHER BANKS
(In millions)

YEAR	STATE BANKS						TOTAL RESOURCES		
	NUMBER	CAPITAL	SURPLUS	DEPOSITS	CASH	LOANS	TRUST COMPANIES	PRIVATE BANKS	SAVINGS BANKS
1897	3857	229	77	724	145	670	844	78	2199
1898	3965	234	81	912	144	814	943	91	2241
1899	4191	233	77	1164	217	909	1072	88	2401
1900	4369	237	91	1267	202	1030	1380	127	2625
1901	4983	255	104	1611	310	1184	1615	149	2757
1902	5397	277	111	1698	228	1346	1983	160	2893

MISCELLANEOUS FINANCIAL

YEAR	CLEARING-HOUSES		SAVINGS BANKS			FAILURES	
	NEW YORK	UNITED STATES	DEPOSITORS (000's)	DEPOSITS (Millions)	AVERAGE	NUMBER (000's)	LIABILITIES (Millions)
1897	31,338	54,180	5201	1939	373	13	154
1898	39,853	65,925	5386	2066	384	12	131
1899	57,368	88,829	5688	2230	392	9	91
1900	51,965	84,582	6107	2450	401	11	138
1901	77,021	114,190	6359	2597	408	11	113
1902	74,753	116,022	6667	2750	412	12	117

CHAPTER XXII

DEFECTS OF THE OLD SYSTEM AND PROPOSED REFORMS

THE gold standard was accepted by the country as an accomplished fact, although Bryan and his followers were as determined as ever in their contentions. Judge Alton B. Parker, of New York, a very strong and able man, was made the Democratic nominee for the Presidency in 1904. He required as a condition in accepting the nomination, that all demand for the free coinage of silver be omitted from the Democratic platform. The convention reluctantly complied with Judge Parker's requirements and with undisguised hostility on the part of the ultra-champions of the free coinage of silver at the ratio of 16 to 1.

His opponent was elected by a majority so large that people concluded he had been knifed at the polls by the extreme cheap money element of his party. For a long period no serious attempt was made to reform the unscientific and unsafe currency and credit systems, the evils of which had been so long experienced. Business activity and prosperity were world-wide; existing business was being expanded and new enterprises were being developed; the tall-building craze possessed our larger towns; real estate was being converted into personal property by the fiction of stock and bond capitalization, largely in excess of present values, thus seeking to capitalize the future; latent resources were being wastefully exploited with no thought of conservation; this boom was in evidence in all the great commercial nations, in varying forms germane to local conditions; the world did not possess sufficient mobile capital to supply the demands resulting from this overtrading and overexpansion. To far-seeing men the danger was imminent. A severe break in the price of listed securities in the Spring of 1907 made only too apparent the impending crash which came in the Fall. In Austria, Germany, England and other European countries conditions were just as acute, but those nations were better able to meet the situation; their credit and currency systems were greatly superior to our own.

Panic is business paralysis; it is born of fear; the first result is curtailment or stoppage of the usual business activity accompanied by the hoarding of money, the refusal of credit; the only way to cure a panic is to set business in motion, keep it in motion, that produce may find its way to market, raw material find its way to the factory and be made into goods that people want and for which they are ready to pay; the cure for a panic is to insure a continuance of business activity. The first difficulty to surmount is a money stringency, a currency famine; our national banks could only issue currency secured by government bonds; to buy these bonds, which commanded a premium, as a basis for bank-notes, cost more money than the currency they were permitted to issue amounted to; they lessened their money supply and impaired rather than strengthened their power to serve the public. In case of bond secured currency, the bonds must be worth more than the currency issued, or else the security fails; our banks were unable to relieve the situation by creating currency; there were, in round numbers, 25,000 banks in the country, each maintaining a separate reserve. At the first sign of trouble they naturally sought to increase their cash holdings to make themselves strong, and hence they competed with each other for currency and thus aggravated a stringency which the law should have enabled them to relieve. Not being able to create credit instrumentalities under the law, which would perform money function, they created, through their clearing houses, instruments which did perform a money function, a new credit instrument giving additional banking power. The banks were possessed of ample credits, none better in the world, just such credits as they were chartered to deal in, and yet they were wholly unavailable as a basis for currency; by law they must go outside their regular business and buy bonds for the sole purpose, so far as the bank is concerned, of using them as a basis for circulation; so far as the government is concerned it compelled banks to become purchasers of its bonds.

The many defects of our financial system were overshadowed by the three cardinal weaknesses above mentioned. *First,* — the unavailability of normal bank assets as a basis for bank-notes. The law discriminated against and discredited normal assets by compelling the purchase of bonds to secure circulation. The exigencies of the Civil War justified such action in 1863 but its continuance long after the war had ceased and long after the restoration of normal business conditions was a serious wrong and imposed hardship and loss upon the entire people. *Second,* — the failure to provide a central bank, which, among other things, should provide a central reservoir for reserves, mobilize the reserve money of the country, instead of compelling its decentralization, by forbidding branch banking and forbidding each national bank to do business anywhere except over its own counter, at the place named in its charter. *Third,* — the absolute want of a market for credits in America. Any bank in France can go to the Bank of France with acceptable receivables and receive currency; any bank in Germany can go to the Reichsbank with acceptable commercial paper and receive currency. In America interior banks borrow from banks in metropolitan centres, all tending toward New York. New York's resource was call loans upon the Stock Exchange and the importation of gold from abroad. Small wonder is it that our commercial history has been marked by frequent currency stringencies and panics of more or less severity. In the Fall of 1907, the clearing-house banks of New York held $1,250,000,000 subject to check, the savings banks $1,050,000,000, and the trust companies

$980,000,000, all deposits subject to check; the total of these three items ($3,280,000,000) exceeded the total amount of currency in the country, including that in the United States Treasury. There was a large shrinkage of all New York deposits, especially those from interior banks. It is a custom of interior banks to borrow when necessary to keep intact their due-from-banks reserve. Those who were overextended could not borrow more nor could they reduce their existing debts; this was true of individuals, industrial enterprises and railroads; they had to be carried, and in many cases of acute condition, in order to prevent widespread disaster, additional loans had to be made. The City of New York always has to be financed in a crisis and the bankers had to loan the City $50,000,000 in November and December, 1907, on temporary revenue bonds; $50,000,000 4½ per cent. 50-year bonds were placed in February, 1908. The trouble was nation-wide and the resulting experience brought the defects of our financial system into the keen, bright sunlight of publicity; clearing-house certificates and substitutes for money were issued generally, and the total amount of such substitutes for money may have reached $500,000,000. A. Piatt Andrew, Secretary of the National Monetary Commission, in his "Substitutes for cash in the panic of 1907," furnishes elaborate data upon the crisis of 1907, from which the data and extracts in the following pages are taken: There were issued clearing-house loan certificates for settlement of bank debits; clearing-house certificates in small denominations for general circulation; clearing-house checks, cashiers' checks and pay checks payable only through the clearing-house, in convenient denominations for use as currency, also New York exchange and certificates of deposit in small amounts, usable in passing from hand to hand as bank bills pass. It is not profitable to differentiate between the various kinds and I therefore give the total amount issued by the following cities, each having a population exceeding 25,000:—

Atlanta, Ga.		$1,500,000
Augusta, Ga.		320,000
Baltimore, Md.		3,094,000
Birmingham, Ala.		1,850,000
Boston, Mass.		12,595,000
Buffalo, N. Y.		915,000
Canton, Ohio		810,000
Cedar Rapids, Iowa		154,000
Charleston, S. C.		100,000
Chicago, Ill.		39,240,000
Cincinnati, Ohio		2,200,000
Cleveland, Ohio		3,220,000
Columbus, Ohio		1,220,500
Council Bluffs, Iowa		90,000
Dallas, Texas		90,000
Davenport, Iowa		279,447
Denver, Colo.		750,000
Des Moines, Iowa		1,050,000
Detroit, Mich.		2,145,000
Duluth, Minn.		117,000
Easton, Pa.		136,375
Fort Wayne, Ind.		345,000
Harrisburg, Pa.		357,000
Indianapolis, Ind.		1,650,000
Joliet, Ill.		225,000
Joplin, Mo.		76,400
Kansas City, Mo.		8,001,601
Knoxville, Tenn.		282,500
Lexington, Ky.		20,000
Lincoln, Nebr.		198,000
Little Rock, Ark.		183,000
Los Angeles, Cal.		5,585,500
Louisville, Ky.		2,490,000
Memphis, Tenn.	Circ.	300,000
Milwaukee, Wis.		3,548,000
Minneapolis, Minn.		1,730,000
Nashville, Tenn.		417,000
New Orleans, La.		5,226,000
New York, N. Y.		101,060,000
Oakland, Cal.		1,250,000
Omaha, Nebr.		2,007,000
Peoria, Ill.		227,000
Philadelphia, Pa.		13,695,000
Pittsburg, Pa.		54,445,000
Portland, Ore.		2,422,750
Racine, Wis.		10,000
Sacramento, Cal.		250,000
St. Joseph, Mo.		695,000
St. Louis, Mo.	Circ.	20,965,000

St. Paul, Minn.	1,900,000
Salt Lake City, Utah	1,255,650
San Antonio, Texas	595,500
San Francisco, Cal.	19,729,000
Savannah, Ga.	265,000
Seattle, Wash.	2,850,000
Sioux City, Iowa	245,000
South Bend, Ind.	120,000
Spokane, Wash.	2,076,000
Tacoma, Wash.	500,000
Topeka, Kans.	40,000
Wheeling, W. Va.	195,000
Wichita, Kans.	216,000
Youngstown, Ohio	541,000
	330,066,233

"Financial excitement in 1907 was by no means confined to the larger cities. Limitation of payments and the creation of emergency currency occurred in towns of every degree of smallness all over the country. Our record of such issues is of necessity fragmentary. Names of a number of towns are included where emergency currency was known to have been issued, but from which repeated letters of inquiry failed to elicit any reply as to the amount. Unquestionably, the names of scores of towns in which such currency was employed have not chanced to reach the writer's attention. The table here given presents an explicitly avowed issue of nearly $4,500,000 in the case of 33 towns and cities; but it doubtless includes only a small fraction of what actually existed in the smaller localities of the country during the panic."

Clearing-house certificates originally were confined in their use to the settlement of debit balances at the clearing-house, and they had never been used for any other purpose in New York City. In 1907 they were issued avowedly for general use and in towns where there was no clearing-house.

"In such cases they were issued under the auspices of temporary committees of the local banks, which accepted and held the collateral offered to guarantee their redemption. In Douglas, Ga., for instance, a town with an estimated population of 2500, $50,000 in these so-called 'clearing-house certificates' were issued; in Tifton, Ga., with less than 3000 inhabitants, $50,000 in certificates were also issued; in South Boston, Va., with less than 4000 inhabitants, an issue of as much as $1,000,000 in certificates was made; even in Bishop, Ga., with only 400 inhabitants, a limited amount was issued."

Pay checks mean checks drawn upon a bank by its customers, in amounts corresponding to bank bills, and payable to bearer.

"The pay-check system reached its largest development in Pittsburg, where during the panic some $47,000,000 were issued, much of which was in denominations of $1 and $2.

It is perhaps worthy of record in this connection that in New York the time elapsing between the first issue and the date of final cancellation of the certificates was twenty-two weeks, or three weeks longer than in the crisis of 1893. In Pittsburg, Los Angeles and New Orleans the emergency currency was outstanding also for about five months, but such duration was clearly exceptional. In most places the notes and certificates were rapidly retired soon after the beginning of the new year; *i.e.*, within eight or ten weeks after the date of their first issue.

Surveying the record as a whole, we have here definite figures for $334,000,000 of emergency currency issued during the panic of 1907, classified as follows: —

Clearing-house certificates (large)	$238,000,000
Clearing-house certificates (small)	23,000,000
Clearing-house checks	12,000,000
Cashiers' checks	14,000,000
Manufacturers' pay checks	47,000,000
Total	$334,000,000

Making a very moderate allowance for the cashiers' checks and pay checks issued in cities from which their amounts have not been reported, including many of the largest cities like New York and Philadelphia, we may safely place an estimate of the total issue of substitutes for cash above $500,000,000."

Other unusual means were resorted to in order to relieve people who were unable to meet their obligations because of the paralysis of credit and the dearth of currency.

"Of official encouragement to suspension, singular and striking examples occurred in several states. The most extreme instances were the legal holidays declared by some of the western governors, which were intended to authorize banks, as well as other firms and individuals, to decline payment when unduly pressed or wherever they saw fit. The governor of Nevada was the first to resort to this measure. Beginning on October 24, he declared legal holidays continuously up to and including November 4. On October 28 the governor of Oregon also began declaring such holidays, and he continued to declare them by subsequent proclamations until December 14. In California such holidays were proclaimed without interruption for a still longer period, from October 31 to December 21, thus suspending all debts for more than seven weeks. This method of relieving business involved great inconvenience in unexpected ways. The whole judicial system was thereby brought to a standstill, the courts being even restrained from trying criminal cases. The governor of California very soon felt obliged to call a special session of the state legislature, and so secured authority to declare 'special holidays' during which only civil actions based upon expressed or implied contracts for the payment of money would be precluded."

The above governmental action amounted to decreeing a moratorium. With such an appalling exhibition of the defects in our monetary system we had a right to expect our government to so amend our laws as to prevent a possible recurrence. The American Bankers' Association gave matters serious attention, and in order that its work might be effective, appointed the following commission of representative bankers: A. Barton Hepburn, Chairman, James B. Forgan, Vice-Chairman, Festus J. Wade, Joseph T. Talbert, Charles H. Huttig, John Perrin, Luther Drake, Myron T. Herrick. Sol Wexler, Robert Wardrop, Arthur Reynolds, E. F. Swinney, Jos. A. McCord, W. V. Cox and John L. Hamilton. This commission gave earnest and continued attention to the subject until fairly satisfactory legislation was accomplished in 1914.

Congress (Chap. 229, Laws 1908) passed a law providing for emergency currency, which expired by limitation June 30, 1914; it authorized the formation of currency associations throughout the country, which could utilize their assets as a basis for banknotes, subject, however, to a very high tax. This act, though somewhat crude, proved of the greatest value in the stress of

1914. The same act created the National Monetary Commission and was designed to safeguard the situation until a comprehensive law could be passed as the result of the commission's labors. The commission consisted of nine Senators and nine Representatives, of which Senator Nelson W. Aldrich was Chairman and Representative Edward B. Vreeland was Vice-Chairman. This commission took much time and made an exhaustive survey of the subject of banking, currency and credit; they visited Europe, studied the systems of the principal commercial nations and reported upon the same; the central, or national banks of the different countries were separately reported upon; they procured men of high standing and practical familiarity to write these reports; the Canadian system, our own national bank system, the first and second United States banks, history of the financial crises under the national bank system, the use of credit instruments in making payments in the United States, the independent treasury system, state banks and trust companies, clearing houses, laws of the United States concerning money — making in all 38 pretentious volumes, a good economic library in itself. These books were printed as congressional documents and hence were obtainable without cost by all sections of the country. The educational influence of these volumes and the proposed law reported by the commission, made the legislation of 1914 possible.

Assured that a central bank was impossible, by the leaders of both parties, the American Bankers' Association sought relief by amending the existing National Bank Act — their proposals were remedial and not generic. Their measures were championed by many members in the House, notably Fowler, Hill, Weeks, etc.; their literature, and the speeches of these gentlemen, were widely distributed under the auspices of the Association; the subject was kept constantly before the public, presented in the proper light, and had the effect of wearing away preconceived prejudice and of aiding in final legislation.

Senator Aldrich and his associates went to the bottom of matters and earnestly sought to build upon fundamentals and give the country a monetary system adapted to its needs. The measure submitted provided a central institution with $300,000,000 capital, to be voluntarily subscribed by banks; all earnings in excess of 5 per cent. went to the government; the country was divided into 15 districts, with a branch of the Reserve Association in each district. The Secretary of the Treasury, Secretary of Commerce and Labor, and Comptroller of the Currency were *ex-officio* members of the Reserve Board — 15 were elected by the Boards of the Branches, 12 by the stockholding interests, 12 representing agricultural, commercial and industrial interests, a Governor and two Deputy Governors — 45 in all.

In order that the measure submitted by the National Monetary Commission may be compared with the Federal Reserve law, both are printed in full in the Appendix; they have many points in common. This measure never reached a vote. Senator Aldrich had retired from the Senate, as also many other strong and experienced Republican members; the Progressive or insurgent element in the Republican ranks was quite strong; the Democrats were opposed almost solidly. The rift in the Republican party resulted in the election of Woodrow Wilson to the Presidency by a plurality vote, Taft, the regular Republican candidate, polling fewer votes than Roosevelt, the Progressive candidate; both branches of Congress were also strongly Democratic. Under the leadership of President Wilson, the Democrats adopted an aggressive policy and accomplished very important legislation in respect to tariff reduction, the regulation of big business by the so-called Clayton anti-trust law, the prohibition of interlocking directors and the creation of a permanent commission to regulate industrial and manufacturing enterprises, much as the Interstate Commerce Commission regulates the railroads. Under the insistent leadership of the President, Congress also passed the Federal Reserve Bank law, a measure which, while open to criticism, is a vast improvement upon the old system and as good as could have been fairly expected under all the circumstances. The law, as finally enacted, was a matter of evolution; when the first draft appeared and the serious purpose of the President to force action became apparent, the whole country joined in the discussion. The Senate prepared and sent out a questionnaire, designed to elicit the principles that should govern legislation. The Currency Commission of the American Bankers' Association convened and sought to be helpful by making a seriatim reply, which was sent to the President and the cabinet and to Congress, published and widely distributed. The questions and answers follow: —

ANSWERS PREPARED BY THE CURRENCY COMMISSION OF THE AMERICAN BANKERS' ASSOCIATION

TO QUESTIONS FORMULATED BY A SUB-COMMITTEE OF THE BANKING AND CURRENCY COMMITTEE OF THE UNITED STATES SENATE.

1. What are the essential defects of our banking and currency system?

Answer. (*a*) A principal defect of our system is the absolute rigidity of our currency. A bank in order to take out circulation must invest more money in government bonds than it is permitted to issue in currency, thereby impairing, rather than increasing, its power to aid commerce and trade.

Outside of the three central reserve cities there is no redemption of national bank-notes, except when and as they wear out and become unfit to circulate. This condition is inherent in the system and is certainly unsound.

(*b*) The system lacks cohesiveness, there being no provision for coöperation among the banks in it. Under ordinary conditions this is not so much felt by the banks individually, but under strained financial conditions, when each bank is thrown on its own resources and must in self-protection act independently of all the rest, the lack of a system under which all could coöperate through a common policy of action becomes keenly felt and it becomes evident that what is really lacking is a system.

(*c*) The requirement that the banks must individually control their own portion of the legal reserve money of the country, without being provided with proper means for the protection or replenishment of their legal reserves, is unscientific and economically wasteful.

(*d*) An unsound system of reserves under which in periods of anxiety it becomes necessary in the protection and maintenance of individual reserves for each bank in the national system to contend against every other bank; the dissipation and scattering of the great bulk of the reserve money of the country into a large number of small hoardings, completely destroying in times of stringency the strength and power which might be gained by unification and massing of reserves for the mutual support of the banks and the common good of the public.

(*e*) The use of so much of the legal reserve money of the country in actual circulation for ordinary business purposes is another economical waste. No provision is made for the use of any substitute for legal reserve money as a circulating medium other than the national bank-notes secured by government bonds, which are as inflexible in their volume and therefore as irresponsive to the fluctuating commercial needs for them as the legal reserve money itself. The gold certificates now in circulation, amounting to $1,085,489,000, being merely warehouse receipts for an equal amount of gold in the government treasury, form the most conspicuous example of this economic waste.

(*f*) The lack of elasticity in the circulation, all forms of our present circulating medium being rigidly fixed in amount. The necessities of commerce for a circulating medium are arbitrarily met with a fixed amount of it, which does not respond in its volume to the fluctuating demands. Assuming that the aggregate amount may be just sufficient for an average volume of general business, then there must be a surplus when the volume of business falls below the average and a deficiency when the volume of business rises above the average. The actual condition, however, is that in each year there are seasons in which the needs for circulation are much heavier than they are in other seasons, so that its inadaptability in volume to the legitimate existing demand is constantly felt. We have as a rule either a surplus or a deficiency.

(*g*) The restriction of the use by the banks of their legal reserves and the prohibition of their lending power in the presence of unusual demands upon them, without means of protecting their reserves by the use of any satisfactory substitute therefor, or of replenishing them through adequate rediscounting facilities, which would enable them to convert their available assets into cash or legal reserve.

(*h*) The lack of provision for the organization of American banking institutions in foreign countries, which are necessary for the development of our foreign trade.

(*i*) The independent treasury system, under which the government acts as partial custodian of its own funds, resulting in irregular withdrawals of money from the bank reserves and from circulation and materially interfering with the even tenor of general business.

(*j*) No open market for commercial paper; banks of sufficient capital should be allowed to accept drafts, for a commission, with a view to the sale of the acceptances in the open market, thereby establishing a current market for commercial paper and thus enabling banks to buy, whenever they have an overplus of funds, or sell in this market, whenever they wish to strengthen their position or meet demands against them, or accumulate funds for the use of their regular clientele.

2. *Enumerate concisely its advantages and disadvantages.*

Answer. (*a*) One advantage of our banking system is that it enables each community to organize and control its own banking facilities.

(*b*) It has for half a century provided the government with a market for its bonds. This was a great advantage to the government at the time the banking system was inaugurated and it has since been taken advantage of by the government to reduce by two-thirds the rate of interest on its bonds. On some issues of its two per cent. bonds it has obtained a premium, notwithstanding the fact that without this artificial market their investment value would be about thirty per cent. below par.

(*c*) Another advantage of no small importance in view of the conditions of the bank-note circulation of the state banks at the time the bank act was enacted is that it has provided a bank-note circulation of uniform value, which in spite of its defects is of undoubted strength and stability.

Its disadvantages are covered in the list of its defects. It might, however, be stated as an offset to the advantages referred to, "B" and "C," that the artificial market maintained for government bonds has been so maintained at the expense of the banking development and commercial growth of the country, both of which have been seriously retarded by the costly periodical panics for which the defects of the banking and currency system are principally responsible.

3. *What are the chief purposes to be attained in an improved system?*

Answer. The chief purposes to be attained in an improved system are the correction of the defects of our present system so that it will be placed on a sound and scientific basis and made to respond adequately to the varying requirements of the public in conducting the trade and commerce of the country.

4. *Should national banks continue to have a bond-secured currency?*

Answer. No. In the use of government bonds as security for circulation, the volume of currency, instead of fluctuating with the varying requirements of trade, is limited by the volume of bonds and fluctuates according to their market prices. These prices are determined, not by the general investment value of the bonds, but by the profit possible to banks in using them as security for circulating notes, resulting in artificial stimulation of government bond prices. One unfortunate consequence of this artificial condition is that the nation's bonds, which should be widely held by its citizens as their choicest investment, are held almost exclusively by banks to secure circulation or government deposits.

5. *Should the present requirements of reserves for national banks be reduced, increased or otherwise modified?*

Answer. Whether the present requirements of reserves for national banks should be reduced, increased or otherwise modified depends upon how they are to be controlled and protected. If under a centralized system of control they are to be economically protected by a satisfactory note issue based on an adequate gold reserve and liquid bank assets for use by the banks as circulation in place of reserve money, so that the currency use in commerce of legal tender money would be largely reduced and, if under such control, legal reserve money could be made available to the banks when and as required through proper rediscounting facilities, we believe some modification of the present requirements might safely be made.

6. *Should an elastic currency be authorized by law? If so, should it be limited, and to what amount?*

Answer. Regarding an elastic currency as a vital necessity in connection with the banking and currency system of this country, we believe that such a currency should be authorized by law. The amount of it should be controlled by the gold reserve requirements against it. Such gold reserve should be ample, not less than 50 per cent. as a recognized minimum. A special tax might be levied upon any deficiency of the reserve below the stipulated amount of it, this tax to be increased as the deficiency increases. Such provision would in our opinion prevent over-expansion of the currency.

7. *Should such currency be the notes of the individual banks, or of a central reserve association, or of a number of regional reserve associations, or of the United States Treasury?*

Answer. Preferably by a central reserve association. Good results may be accomplished by a number of regional reserve associations, if the control of their resources were properly placed under central joint control of the government and the banks. Doubtless a safe currency could be issued by the United States Treasury, if the law providing the same were properly drawn, but it would seem difficult if not impossible to provide for its proper expansion and contraction in accordance with the demands of trade. The experience of the world is that it is better for a government to provide for such currency indirectly, through some privately owned corporation under strict governmental supervision, rather than put the credit of the government at issue with every note placed in circulation. Troublesome times come to every community and every nation, and it is better then to have the credit of the bank called in question, than the credit of the government itself.

8. Should these notes be procured from the Treasury on pledge of security and if so, of what should this security consist? Should these notes be a first lien of the government upon the assets of the association or bank to which they are issued?

Answer. If the notes are to be issued by a central reserve association, or by regional reserve associations, against an adequate gold reserve and liquid bank assets belonging to and in possession of these associations, there seems no reason why they should be procured from the Treasury on a pledge of security. They should be made a first lien, not of the government, but of the holders of notes, upon the assets of the association which issues them, but not of the bank to which they are issued, which will in all cases give value received for them.

9. Should all currency be based upon gold? If so, how ought it to be issued and what per cent. of gold reserves should be required?

Answer. Reserve money should preferably be gold, but the proportion of greenbacks and silver now included in our so-called lawful money, if the amounts thereof are not increased, is of diminishing importance and if continued as eligible for reserve will not cause embarrassment. The percentage of reserve money against deposits, whether in the form of deposits subject to check or in the form of circulating notes, should be left to the discretion of the management of the central or regional reserve associations, but if a restriction is imposed it should be in the form of a tax upon the deficiency in reserves when below 50 per cent.

10. If notes are issued to or by an association, what should be the limit in amount of this currency for each association, and should this limit be based on its capital stock and surplus?

Answer. As already stated, notes should be issued preferably by one association, or possibly several regional associations, and their limit should be regulated by the amount of gold reserve such association or associations can command and hold in readiness for their redemption. The business needs for circulation will thus be supplied within the limits of the reserve held by the association or associations responsible for their redemption, and they will automatically respond in volume to the existing demand for them. The association or associations issuing them will be able to check any undue increase in the issue of them by raising the discount rate. As its reserve goes down its discount rate will go up.

11. What device should be provided to force the retirement of this currency in whole or in part when the legitimate demands of trade subside?

Answer. No device will be necessary to enforce the retirement of such a currency when the legitimate demands of trade subside. The volume will automatically adjust itself to the demands of trade.

12. If a tax on this currency payable to the government is provided, should it be graduated so as to increase with the volume of currency issued by the reserve association, or graduated so as to increase with the length of time it is outstanding?

Answer. A tax upon the deficiency in reserve graduated on a scale increasing as the deficiency increases removes all necessity or reason to tax notes either in proportion to volume or to length of time outstanding. The tax might be regulated so as to become prohibitive before the reserve could fall to what might be regarded as the danger point.

13. Should there be a central reserve association with branches, or a number of reserve associations with or without a central control? If a number of reserve associations under central control, should that control be wholly with representatives of the various associations, or wholly by the government, or by giving both representation?

Answer. In our opinion one central reserve association with branches would best serve our present necessities. Failing that, a small number of regional reserve associations, also with branches, might be organized to serve the purpose. The smaller the number of regional reserve associations, however, the more effective the reserve control. If there are to be a number of regional reserve associations, they should be under some kind of central control in which both the government and the various associations should have representation.

Three objections to the regional reserve associations occur to us: First. They will divide the cash reserves of the country into as many different ownerships as there are regional associations. No individual bank can now strengthen its cash reserves without at the same time and to the same extent depleting the reserve of some other bank; so with the regional reserve associations, no one of them will be able to strengthen its cash reserves without drawing them from and reducing to the same extent the reserve of one of the other associations.

Second. In connection with the shipping of reserve money from one section of the country to another. Under one central reserve association with branches this could be accomplished without change of ownership of the money shipped, as it would belong to the one association irrespective of what branch had custody of it. In the case of independent regional reserve associations no such transfer of reserve money could be made from one region to another without a change in ownership. It would increase the reserve of the association that received it and deplete by a similar amount the reserve of the association that ships it. In times of financial stress when each regional reserve association would be husbanding its resources for the benefit of its own constituents this might produce an undesirable and awkward situation, the interests of the various sections of the country being at variance. Such effect will be intensified in direct ratio to the number of regional reserve associations.

And Third. Under one ownership and control of the reserves transfers of funds could under normal conditions be accomplished by book entries rather than by the shipment of money.

14. Should such reserve associations have a geographical territory and exercise the functions of a reserve bank in such territory exclusively; or should member banks of any reserve association be permitted to exercise a choice as to which of the near-by or contiguous reserve associations they should join without regard to fixed territory?

Answer. If in counting their legal reserve balances the banks are to be restricted to their balances with the regional reserve associations it must be remembered that no legal enactment can change the necessity which most of them find for keeping deposit accounts for exchange and collection purposes with banks in the principal business centres of the country. If they are to be compelled to maintain all their reserve balances with the regional reserve associations and are to lose the privilege they now have of including their balances with correspondents at the principal financial centres as part of their legal reserves, they must continue to carry such balances for exchange purposes, even if they cannot include them in their legal reserves, which will materially encroach upon their lending power. This question is further discussed in our answer to Question 24.

15. Should such reserve associations have state bank and trust companies as stockholders; and if so, what requirements should be made of such state banks and trust companies?

Answer. State banks and trust companies should be included as well as national banks. They should be under the same requirements as to capital, surplus and examination.

16. Approximately, how many regional reserve associations should there be if that system is adopted? What, if any, should be the minimum capital stock, and what amount of stock should each member bank hold?

Answer. As already indicated, it is our opinion that the smaller the number of regional reserve associations the better will they be able to command and hold gold and thus to protect the lawful reserves of the banks of the country. We would prefer to have only one association with branches, but if such centralized control of the gold reserves of the country is not acceptable, then we are of the opinion that the number be limited as much as possible. Each regional reserve association could have as many branches as may be necessary in its region. If limited in number the capital supplied by the constituent banks connected with each regional reserve association by contributing ten per cent. of their present capital would be adequate for the use of the regional reserve associations. If on the other hand, there should be a larger number of regional reserve associations, then the capital stock required by each would have to be considered and determined from the standpoint of the aggregate amount of capital of the banks in each district. The participating banks would have to contribute their pro rata share of such amount of capital as might be deemed necessary, which would differ in different localities.

17. How should the directors of a reserve association be elected? What should be their number, powers, and term of office?

Answer. The number of directors of regional reserve associations might properly be fixed at nine, six of whom should be elected by the member banks, of whom three should be bankers and three should fairly represent the agricultural, commercial, industrial and other interests of the region in which the regional reserve association is located and should not be officers, nor, while serving, directors of banks, trust companies or other financial institutions. The remaining three should be appointed by the President of the United States.

The powers of the directors should be practically those of national bank directors. They should have authority to make the by-laws of the association, elect its officers and supervise and direct them in the conduct of its business. Directors should be elected for three years, but the terms of those first chosen should be so arranged that the term of one member of each of the three classes will expire each year.

18. What should be the general nature of the business of such an association?

Answer. Regional reserve associations should act as the principal fiscal agent of the United States for the region in which they are located; buy and sell United States and other government and state bonds; receive deposits from the government and member banks; discount for its members; buy and sell exchange here and abroad; buy and sell gold coin and gold and silver bullion; have similar dealings with other regional reserve associations and any other transactions with them which would insure fullest coöperation for efficiently serving the business interests of the country.

19. Should it accept any deposits other than those of banks and should it be allowed to pay interest on deposits?

Answer. They should not accept any deposits other than those of the government and of the participating banks and they should not pay interest on deposits.

20. Should it discount double-name commercial paper for its member banks on equal terms to all, and should its discount rate be public, subject to change weekly?

Answer. They should rediscount for and with the indorsement of any bank having a deposit with them, commercial paper of short maturity and bills of exchange arising out of commercial transactions. The discount rate, which each regional reserve association should have power to fix for itself, should be equal to all participating banks in the region, should be made public and should be subject to change when in the opinion of the directors a change is desirable.

21. Should it loan directly to member banks with or without collateral security, and should the rate of interest be equal to all, public, and subject to change weekly?

Answer. Regional reserve associations should be permitted to loan directly to member banks against satisfactory collateral security whenever on the representation of the directors of the regional reserve association the central board of control, referred to in our answer to Question *13*, is satisfied that the public interests so require and gives its consent thereto.

22. Should reserve associations be permitted to deal with each other in the purchase and sale of commercial paper, exchange, securities, and gold?

Answer. Yes.

23. Should government deposits be withdrawn from banks and placed with the reserve associations, and if so, how should they be apportioned and what rate of interest, if any, should be paid? Within what time could this be safely done?

Answer. Government deposits should be withdrawn from the banks gradually, over a period of not less than two years, and placed with the regional reserve associations, except in such localities where it is necessary for the government to have bank accounts for its own convenience. The apportionment among the regional reserve associations should be largely a matter of convenience to the government, but as much as possible they should be divided in proportion to the capital of the different associations.

Deposits secured by 2 per cent. bonds should not be withdrawn except as the bonds are taken over from the banks or refunded into bonds bearing such a rate of interest as will make the same worth par without the circulation privilege.

24. Should every national bank be required to keep its reserve with the association to which it belongs except such as it keeps in its own vaults; or should it be permitted to keep any certain per cent. of its reserve with other reserve associations? If so, how much?

Answer. In connection with this question as to whether national banks should be required to keep all their reserves with the regional reserve associations to which they belong, or should be permitted to keep any certain percentage of them with other regional reserve associations, the question arises whether the banks are to keep their active checking accounts for exchange and collection purposes with the regional associations, or not? If each regional reserve association is to handle the exchange and collection accounts of its member banks, then the further question arises, could the regional reserve associations also handle such accounts of the banks outside of their own region? Could, for instance, the regional reserve association located in the city of New York undertake to handle the exchange accounts of the banks all over the country that need New York accounts, and if so, should such banks be permitted to count their balances in the New York regional reserve association as a part of their reserves? In our opinion, the regional reserve associations could not be satisfactorily organized so as to handle economically the enormous amount of work entailed by the keeping of such accounts. We are therefore of opinion that the reserves of the banks kept with the regional reserve associations should be confined to their balances, kept with the regional reserve association in which they are shareholders. The banks in the reserve and central reserve cities now acting as reserve agents should be permitted to continue to so act. The reserves of the banks outside of the reserve cities should be divided equally into three allotments, one-third to be kept in their vaults, one-third to be kept on deposit with the regional reserve association in their own district and one-third on deposit with their duly appointed legal reserve agents in reserve or central reserve cities; the same division of reserves might be applicable to the banks in the reserve cities; and the banks in the central reserve cities might be required to keep one-half of their reserves in their vaults and the other half on deposit with the regional reserve association, which of course would be located in their own cities.

The reserve balances maintained with correspondent banks are the basis of credit as well as other valuable banking privileges extended to the banks maintaining such balances. Being legal reserves the balances are upon the average fairly steady, the amount of daily turnover increasing or diminishing the same as the case may be; in order to have their daily business handled and their exchanges paid and establish a basis of credit, the interior banks must maintain active accounts in important business centres. It follows that if such balances may not count as reserve and funds must in addition be deposited with regional reserve associations, it will materially curtail the loaning power of the country banks, and their power to serve the public. The requirement imposes the heaviest burden upon the banks of the interior which will be under the necessity of carrying with their active correspondents and regional reserve associations combined, much larger balances than now.

25. Should a reserve association be required to maintain a reserve against its deposits, and if so, in what amount and should it consist of gold or lawful money?

Answer. Regional reserve associations should be required to maintain a reserve against their deposits to the same extent required against their note issues with the same penal tax on any deficiency in the required amount. The reserve should consist principally of gold, but if the government greenbacks, Treasury notes, and silver certificates are to continue in use and are not to be increased there seems no good reason why they should not continue to be counted as legal reserve for the regional reserve associations as well as for the banks. The silver certificates and Treasury notes should continue to furnish the small bills for circulation, and the government being responsible for their redemption should maintain a reasonable gold reserve against them.

26. Should the liability of each member bank in a reserve association be limited to its stock subscription? If not, what should be the liability?

Answer. The principle of double liability of stockholders should apply to the regional reserve associations as it now applies to the banks.

27. Should a reserve association have transactions with banks other than its own members, and if so, what character of transactions should be permissible?

Answer. The regional reserve associations should have no transactions with banks other than their own members, except that they should be authorized to maintain accounts and have transactions with selected banks in the financial centres of the principal foreign countries, and to buy and sell exchange and prime acceptances in the open market.

28. Should national banks be permitted, upon payment of a commission, to loan their credit by accepting bills arising out of the ordinary course of commerce, and should reserve associations be permitted to deal in these acceptances in transactions with banks or other reserve associations?

Answer. The accepting of bills arising out of the ordinary course of commerce by the banks should not be confined to national banks as such, but to all banks having a capital of $1,000,000 or over, and which are members of reserve associations; and regional reserve associations should be permitted to deal in such acceptances in their transactions with banks or with other regional reserve associations, or in the open market.

29. Should there be a limit within which banks should be permitted to give acceptances? If so, what limit?

Answer. Banks having less than $1,000,000 capital should not be permitted to accept and accepting banks should be limited in their acceptances outstanding at any one time to an amount equal to their paid-up capital, subject to the statutory limitations as to the amount of loans which may be made to any one individual, firm or corporation.

30. What dividends should reserve associations be permitted to pay their member banks?

Answer. Regional reserve associations should be permitted to pay their member banks out of earnings, dividends of six per cent. per annum.

31. Should any share of the profits of a reserve association be distributed to the member banks in proportion to the average deposit maintained by them during the year?

Answer. We do not deem it advisable that any share of the profits of the regional reserve associations should be distributed to the member banks in proportion to the average deposit maintained by them during the year. This would be equivalent to the payment of interest on balances by the regional reserve associations, which we think should not be permitted.

32. Are you familiar with the recommendations of the National Monetary Commission to Congress in January, 1912? If so, what is your opinion of the plan, and what modifications would you suggest, if any?

Answer. We are familiar with the recommendations of the National Monetary Commission made to Congress in January, 1912, and are on record as having indorsed and recommended that measure.

33. As one of several plans suggested to mobilize the banking reserves and provide elastic currency, it has been suggested that the Treasury Department establish a division to be called a "Federal Reserve Division," which should con-

duct reserve agencies in each reserve city to exercise the functions of the proposed reserve banks; receive capital from member banks to the extent of 10 per cent. of their capital and surplus; pay 5 per cent. interest to the banks upon such capital, but without permitting the banks to manage the reserve agencies directly or indirectly; that such reserve agencies should discount short-term prime commercial paper and furnish Treasury note currency, where needed, to member banks under reasonable safeguards to prevent inflation, thereby mobilizing the reserves and furnishing elastic currency directly to the qualified banks. This suggestion carries with it a more thorough examination of the national banks and makes the indebtedness to the government by such banks a first lien on the assets of the banks. What do you think of such a suggestion?

Answer. It is possible for the Treasury Department to furnish the country with a safe currency. It would be very difficult, if not impossible, to make that currency elastic, in the sense of contracting and expanding according to the needs of the public. The experience of commercial nations is that results can be better accomplished by the creation of a privately owned central organization dominated and controlled by the government, as for instance, the Imperial Bank of Germany, or the Bank of France. It serves to take the matter out of politics.

The great danger is that if borrowers go direct to the Treasury, politics would become an all-important and dominating influence. Our government experienced great difficulty in retiring the greenbacks in gold as presented, at a recent period, although their total amounted to less than $350,000,000. Four bond issues during one administration became necessary to obtain gold for that purpose. If the amount of Treasury notes outstanding were to be multiplied by seven or eight the responsibility resting upon the government would be still greater. With an overflowing Treasury and ample gold no anxiety would be felt, and little difficulty would be experienced in meeting such obligations, but we know from the past that we are bound to have times in the future, when the Treasury will not be overflowing and the gold reserve will be encroached upon, and the credit of the government would then be unnecessarily brought in issue. We cannot have any credit in the country better than that of the government under which we live, and it is for the interest of all to protect that credit against all possible danger. Our own experience for the last fifty years, in fact ever since the creation of our government, as well as the experience of other nations, militate against this general proposition. The policy of the government has been to protect itself against maturing liabilities, by making even its future obligations payable on or after a fixed date at its pleasure. The proposal that it should assume not only large demand liabilities on note issues but also enormous demand liabilities in the form of bank reserve deposits would be a radical and dangerous reversal of its policy.

A. BARTON HEPBURN, New York, Chairman.
JAMES B. FORGAN, Chicago, Vice-Chairman.
FESTUS J. WADE, St. Louis.
JOSEPH T. TALBERT, New York.
GEORGE M. REYNOLDS, Chicago.
JOHN PERRIN, Los Angeles.
LUTHER DRAKE, Omaha.
SOL. WEXLER, New Orleans.
ROBERT WARDROP, Pittsburg.
JOSEPH A. McCORD, Atlanta.
J. F. SARTORI, Los Angeles.
LEVI L. RUE, Philadelphia.
E. L. HOWE, Princeton.
Members of the Currency Commission of the American Bankers' Association, and
ARTHUR REYNOLDS, Des Moines.
First Vice-President of the Association.
FREDERICK E. FARNSWORTH, Secretary.
In attendance at Special Meeting at Atlantic City, N. J., June 18, 19, 1913.

CHAPTER XXIII

Federal Reserve Act of 1913 [1]

The Democrats, since the days of Andrew Jackson, have opposed a central bank; their national platform denounced a central bank and denounced the Aldrich bill as a central bank in disguise. The leaders set about devising a scheme that would accomplish the good results of a central bank and yet avoid the criticism that such a creation would inevitably produce. They divided the country into 12 Federal Reserve Districts, with 12 "Federal Reserve cities" as their banking centers — not one central bank, but 12 banking centres, each national bank being required within thirty days after notice, to subscribe to the stock of the Federal Reserve Bank an amount equal to 6 per-cent. of its capital and surplus; failure to join the Federal Reserve system depriving a bank, upon 30 days' notice, of the power to act as reserve agent, and failure for one year involving its dissolution. It was clearly a force bill, and in case of failure to obtain a sufficient capital from the banks, the public were to be invited to subscribe, and in case public subscriptions were insufficient, in the judgment of the organization committee, they had the power to "allot to the United States such an amount of said stock as said committee shall determine." Only stock of member banks can vote; no bank can commence business with less than $4,000,000; each Federal Reserve Bank has power to establish branches in its own district; each Board consists of nine members. The banks are divided with respect to size, into three groups, as nearly equal in number as may be, so that the large banks, the intermediate and the small banks vote by themselves respectively; a bank with $25,000 capital has the same

[1] The Act is discussed in this chapter in its unamended form.

voting power as a bank with $25,000,000 capital. The law provided for the three directors representing the bank stockholders, and three representing "commerce, agriculture or some other industrial pursuit"; the Federal Reserve Board, consisting of the Secretary of the Treasury, the Comptroller of the Currency, *ex officio*, and five members appointed by the President and confirmed by the Senate, designates the other three directors, one of whom is designated as Chairman of the Board. The stock is not transferable; stockholders receive 6 per cent., if earned, one-half of all other net earnings going to surplus until it equals 40 per cent., all the rest going to the government. State banks and trust companies can become members; Federal Reserve Banks have the general powers of banking; the Federal Reserve Board has power to examine Federal Reserve Banks and require statements and reports, and shall publish a weekly statement of such and a consolidated statement of the condition of all Federal Reserve Banks; has power to require Federal Reserve Banks to rediscount the paper of other Federal Reserve Banks, which centralizes the loaning power of these banks and closely approximates a central bank in this respect; has power to suspend the reserve requirements; has very complete supervisory powers, including suspending the operations of a bank and suspending or removing officers and directors of a Federal Reserve Bank, giving the cause therefor in writing. In short, the dominating power of the Federal Reserve Board is so pronounced that it, in effect, makes of the system created practically a central bank and, needless to add, this is the strongest feature of the system. Under the Act as passed in 1913, the Federal Reserve Banks could receive deposits only from the United States and its member banks, and solely for exchange purposes could receive deposits from other Reserve Banks; could rediscount notes, bills and drafts with not more than 90 days to run; could discount acceptances in connection with international commercial transactions, with not more than three months to run;

could accept drafts or bills growing out of the importation or exportation of goods, having not more than three months to run; could purchase or sell in the open market cable transfers, bankers' acceptances and bills of exchange, within the limitations fixed by the act; they could serve as United States depositories.

The hostility to all banks was so great and the element in the Democratic party favorable to government notes so strong, that the currency provided was made "obligations of the United States," the government being directly pledged to their payment. So long as the Treasury is rich in funds the government can suffer no harm from having its demand "obligations," in the form of currency, outstanding to the total of two or three billions, but in conditions such as existed under President Cleveland's second administration the embarrassment may be serious; and that similar conditions are likely to return is the obvious lesson of history.[1] We have already seen what President Cleveland had to say on this subject.

The law provided that when a Reserve Bank applied for notes "such application shall be accompanied with a tender to the local Federal Reserve Agent of collateral in amount equal to the sum of Federal Reserve notes applied for"; when received, the bank must maintain "reserves in gold of not less than 40 per cent. against its Federal Reserve notes in actual circulation"; the bank gives up its assets and gets in return notes against which it must maintain a 40 per cent. gold reserve and which it must itself redeem. "The Federal Reserve Board requires each Federal Reserve Bank to maintain on deposit in the Treasury of the United States, a sum in gold sufficient in the judgment of the Secretary of the Treasury for the redemption of the Federal Reserve notes issued to such bank," etc.; the bank gives up its assets, and in return, when it receives the Federal Reserve notes, gets a liability.

[1] Federal Reserve notes in circulation, December 23, 1920, amounted to $3,404,931,000.

The above incongruities were the price of the support of the Bryan element of the Democratic party. They sought to curb the money power by decentralizing the banking power of the country, by compelling the withdrawal from large business centres of the large volume of bank balances which had naturally followed business and accumulated there. They compelled each member bank to keep a portion of its required reserve in the Federal Reserve Bank of the district wherein it was located; there are twelve Federal Reserve Districts, each with a Federal Reserve City, the latter being Boston, New York, Philadelphia, Richmond, Atlanta, Cleveland, Chicago, St. Louis, Kansas City, Minneapolis, Dallas and San Francisco; all due-from-banks reserve should be maintained in the Federal Reserve Banks. The Federal Reserve Bank of New York City could have the reserve of its district only, and the other banks in the district could hold no reserve provided for in the act. Banks outside of Reserve or Central Reserve cities should keep 4 per cent. reserve in cash on hand, 5 per cent. with the Federal Reserve Bank and 3 per cent. optional, either on hand or with the Federal Reserve Bank — total, 12 per cent.; member banks in Reserve cities should keep 5 per cent. cash on hand, 6 per cent. with the Federal Reserve Bank and 4 per cent. optional, either on hand or with the Federal Reserve Bank — total 15 per cent.; member banks in Central Reserve cities should keep 6 per cent. cash on hand, 7 per cent. in the Federal Reserve Bank and 5 per cent. optional, either on hand or with the Federal Reserve Bank. This was a material reduction in the reserve requirements of the national bank law, which compelled banks in Central Reserve cities to keep 25 per cent. reserve in cash on hand, Reserve cities 12½ per cent. cash on hand and 12½ per cent. due from reserve agent banks; all other banks were required to keep 6 per cent. cash on hand and 9 per cent. due from approved reserve agents.[1]

There is no justification, either in logic or practical business,

[1] Reserve requirements were still further reduced by amendments of June, 1917.

for requiring any reserve except cash on hand; if banks must be required by law to keep strong, that strength should be in their home office; banks must inevitably keep sufficient balances with correspondents to protect the exchange they draw, else their drafts would go to protest, and there is no need of a law to compel that; they should be allowed to keep their due-from-banks balances wherever required, to meet the exchange requirements of their customers; the doing away with reserve banks would have been wise had the law stopped there, but the Federal Reserve Banks had to be provided with resources, and hence the enforced subscription to their capital stock and enforced maintenance of balances with them. Congress had no thought of inducing the banks to join the system, because it would be for their interest and for the general interest for them to do so; the measure was clearly a force bill and largely justified by the desirability of launching the new system throughout the country in a comprehensive way and with uniformity with respect to time. Congress sought, wisely sought, to create a resource from which currency could be obtained at any time to meet the demands of the country; this they did by leaving the limit that might be issued wholly in the discretion of the Federal Reserve Board. After the law went into effect the chief sponsors of the bill in the House and also in the Senate stated in public addresses that there never could be another panic in this country, because currency without limit could be obtained from the Federal Reserve Banks. These statements failed to discriminate between mobile capital and currency; had they said there could not be another currency famine, they would have been quite justified. The crisis of 1920–1921 proved that the powers of currency issues for preventing industrial depression had been much overestimated.

The preliminary or tentative drafts of the law ignored United States bonds, but it soon became apparent that if the currency system was to be changed the bonds must be taken care of. The government had created a currency monopoly in favor of the banks, thereby constraining the banks to buy government bonds at large premiums, the United States 2 per cents selling many points above par. Now the government proposed to take away the current monopoly and issue the currency direct from the Treasury, secured by the commercial assets of the banks, which would reduce the price of bonds to an investment basis; the bonds, as the plan unfolded, depreciated rapidly, the 2 per cents selling as low as 94; the banks owned $698,064,560 2 per cent. bonds out of a total issue of $730,882,130, or 95 per cent. The law provided for retiring not exceeding $25,000,000 of the 2 per cent. bonds per year at par and interest, and for refunding bonds with the circulation privilege, into 3 per cent. notes and 3 per cent. thirty-year bonds without circulation privilege.

It will be remembered that the United States 2 per cent. bonds, other than the Panama issue, with no due date, are payable at the pleasure of the government. Being a perpetual debenture and yielding only 2 per cent. interest they would, on an investment basis, have sold down to about 70; hence taking away the currency privilege or issuing other currency in competition with the bond secured currency, would have been a breach of implied contract, certainly a breach of faith, on the part of the government. This possible wrong was prevented by the refunding and retirement plan adopted.

The act provides:

"Every Federal Reserve Bank shall receive on deposit at par from member banks or from Federal Reserve Banks checks and drafts drawn upon any of its depositors, and when remitted by a Federal Reserve Bank, checks and drafts drawn by any depositor in any other Federal Reserve Bank or member bank upon funds to the credit of said depositor in said Reserve Bank or member bank. Nothing herein contained shall be construed as prohibiting a member bank from charging its actual expense incurred in collecting and remitting funds, or for exchange sold to its patrons. The Federal Reserve Board shall, by rule, fix the charges to be collected by the member banks from its patrons whose checks are cleared through the

Federal Reserve Bank and the charge which may be imposed for the service of clearing or collection rendered by the Federal Reserve Bank.

The Federal Reserve Board shall make and promulgate from time to time regulations governing the transfer of funds and charges therefor among Federal Reserve Banks and their branches, and may at its discretion exercise the functions of a clearing house for such Federal Reserve Banks, or may designate a Federal Reserve Bank to exercise such functions, and may also require each such bank to exercise the functions of a clearing house for its member banks."

On the face of it, the above provision seeks to make a check on any bank in the system worth par in any part of the country, and inferentially it seeks to induce or constrain all banks to join the system.

Among the good services rendered by the First and Second United States banks was the facilitation and cheapening of exchange and rendering the cost of the same uniform. The Federal Reserve system can and should render a public service along the same lines. Now that their branch system is established, the Reserve Banks very greatly facilitate and cheapen the handling of domestic exchange; they largely avoid cost by offset, but offset is subject to items being good, and that can only be determined when each item reaches the place of payment; exchange between different sections may equalize itself in a round period, a year for instance, but settlements must be made much sooner than that. Comparing the United States with Europe, our European receivables centralize in New York, so do our European payables, and generally offset each other, supplemented as they are by credit received and extended for that purpose, but there comes a condition when the balance, one way or the other, must be paid, in whole or in part, and then gold is exported or imported, as the case may be. Similar conditions confront the Federal Reserve Bank, with respect to different sections of the country, in handling exchange. A check on a Texas bank is not worth par in Maine; a check on a Florida bank is not worth par in Oregon, and whatever cost or expense is involved in making such checks acceptable in paying debts, so far from the place where they are issued, whether it take the form of loss in interest while in transit, or a collection charge, or otherwise, should be borne by the party who receives advantage by the payment, usually the drawer of the check, sometimes the drawee. It would not be right to devolve this expense upon the stockholders in the Federal Reserve Bank. One thing that all banks have to struggle against is "check-kiting"; making country checks worth par in business centres might open up a rich field for that form of misadventure. It was the declared purpose of some Congressmen to make all checks worth par everywhere, at the expense of the banks, and thereby make them practically a part of our currency.

The act creates an Advisory Council equal to the number of Federal Reserve Banks, and elected by the boards of directors of such banks; national banks were empowered to establish foreign branches; the emergency currency act was extended for one year and the restriction of the use of such currency to the banks who had bond-secured currency equal to 40 per cent. of their capital, was removed.

CHAPTER XXIV

General Review

A general review of the monetary history of the entire period of our national existence shows that each generation had to learn for itself and at its own expense the evils of unsound money. The costly experiences of the preceding generation were generally forgotten, and legislators, following rather than leading the people, failed to correct the evils except after long and disastrous delays. So intolerable were the conditions at times that only the unlimited recuperative powers of our rapidly developing and expanding country prevented the overthrow of that standard of value and honor which is recognized by the world as highest and best.

The problem of furnishing a sound and stable medium for a country of such large area, of such diverse interests composed of 48 sovereign states, developing at an unprecedented rate, presents unusual difficulties, and no precedent is furnished by any other country with kindred conditions and analogous experience. Principles remain the same, however, and the obstacles could have been overcome and all questions properly solved had not political ambitions and party advantage exercised such a controlling influence. With the creation of the Federal Reserve Bank let us hope that we have a credit and currency system which will assure stability as to metallic money, security and flexibility as to paper currency, to the end that prices may not be subject to ruthless disturbances and interest rates be reasonably uniform and equitable throughout the land.

The bimetallic theory, however logical in the days of Hamilton, when the production of precious metals was but small and the greater part of the civilized world preferred silver to gold, has been demonstrated to be impossible of realization without substantially universal adoption, which has been shown to be quite impossible. As a practical question bimetallism has been abandoned by all great commercial nations. Whether the enormous production of gold shall ultimately impair its desirability as a standard of value, or, what is more likely, cause the development of entirely novel theories of money, with all the vagaries and unsoundness that inevitably accompany original theories, is a question too remote to have any present utility.

Hamilton's writings, his careful study of the subject, with the end always in view of giving his country a just measure of values, show clearly that to-day he would favor a standard resting upon gold alone; nor is it to be doubted that Jefferson would maintain equally sound and conservative views. The statistics presented show that immediately after the adoption of Hamilton's coinage law the production of silver increased largely, disturbing the commercial ratio between gold and silver. According to Hamilton's theory, this should have been followed by a change in the coinage ratio as early as 1810. In 1834, when such action was taken, the intelligent opinion of the day was ignored and an extreme ratio adopted which reversed rather than corrected the disparity by undervaluing silver. Within a decade the great increase in gold production had enhanced the relative value of silver, and all coins, fractional silver as well, were exported. To correct this and retain small coins for current use the law of 1853 was passed, reducing the amount of fine silver in fractional coins.

The relatively scant product of the white metal for the following twenty years served to demonstrate the wisdom of the law of 1853. Unfortunately the legislators of that day left the silver dollar unit undisturbed, and when silver was again produced in larger quantities (after 1874) the existence of the law of 1837 gave the advocates of free coinage of silver a precedent and prestige which would not otherwise have existed. The act of 1900 leaves the legal tender power of the dollar of 371.25 grains of pure silver exactly as provided in the acts of 1792 and 1837, except where otherwise expressly provided in the contract.

It is only necessary to recapitulate the silver legislation since the beginning of the agitation for remonetization in 1876, in order to appreciate the bearing of the enormous acquisition of silver by the United States and the possible menace which its possession involves. The silver purchased under the laws of 1878 and 1890 amounted to 459,946,701 fine ounces, costing us $464,210,262, an average per ounce of nearly $1.01, parity being $1.2929; the silver dollars coined amount to $565,194,138.

The entire volume of silver and representative certificates may be utilized for the great and growing retail trade of the country so long as business conditions are prosperous, the labor of the country is employed, and the consuming power continues unabated, and issued in small denominations only they may be so chained to the wheels of industry as to prevent them from being a menace to the Treasury. A safe means of avoiding danger to the gold standard from the large volume of silver in our currency is the maintenance of a good Treasury surplus, into which the redundant silver, for which there may be no use as currency, can be absorbed.

While at first gold certificates were permitted to be issued in excess of the gold deposited (law of 1863), the more recent laws governing their issue, as also in the case of silver certificates, require that the full amount of coin shall be held against them. Both forms of certificates are, therefore, merely warehouse receipts. The silver certificates are receivable for public dues and available for bank reserves, but are not legal tenders. These certificates as compared with coin save in transportation as well as in abrasion, cater to a public preference for paper money and seem to be fully established as a permanent part of our currency system.

We have seen that the "fathers" without specifically embodying a prohibition to that effect in the Constitution intended to prevent the issue of governmental legal tender paper, and a tacit understanding that no such power existed guided legislators for seventy-three years. In the evolution of government the conception of federal power under the Constitution was broadened, and found enlarged expression in legislative, executive, and judicial action. The perils and necessities of the government during the Civil War broke the barriers of the strict constructionists, and the powers which a sovereign government needed to exercise were held to be warranted by the Constitution except where specifically prohibited. Relying upon the opinions expressed in debate, it is safe to assert that Congress believed the legal tender act of 1862 unconstitutional when they voted that it become law. They were willing to adopt revolutionary means to overcome revolution. The Rubicon once passed, this law furnished a precedent for others to follow. The Supreme Court in its first decision held the law in large part unconstitutional. The second decision reopened the case, and held that Congress had power to issue legal tender notes "for the time being," having reference to the perils of the government in the exigency of war. Upon the third hearing, in 1884, the Court held that giving the legal tender quality to paper was a sovereign power, exercisable in time of peace as well as in time of war, in the discretion of Congress.

The right to issue bank-notes was made use of by the few banks existing prior to the adoption of the Constitution as a common law right. The banks in the several states continued to exercise this right after the adoption of the Constitution, under their state charters, whether specifically authorized or not. It was generally admitted that such rights existed, that the states, although prohibited from issuing bills of credit to be used as money, could charter corporations with such powers. This granting to their own creatures powers which the states did not themselves possess was assented to and finally confirmed as constitutional by the Supreme Court. Antecedent thereto Hamilton devised the charter of the First Bank of the United States, and assumed for the federal government a similar power, that of creating a corporation to emit paper to circulate as money, which it was generally held at that time the government itself could not do under the Constitution. Marshall in his masterly decision on the charter of the Second Bank of the United States confirmed the federal power to create such a bank, and enunciated principles in construing the Constitution which became the foundation for the broader assumption of power in the legal tender acts of the Civil War.

The volume of legal tender notes of the war period continued as they stood in 1878, after the law forbidding their further retirement, at $346,681,016, less such as have been lost or destroyed. Those issued under the act of 1890, in payment for silver bullion purchased, were retired by the dollars coined from such bullion, such dollars now being largely represented by silver certificates. Aside from the enormous cost to the people through the depreciation of this currency, the maintenance of coin redemption, since resumption was determined upon, has resulted in bond issues, in order to obtain gold amounting to, 1875–1879, $95,000,000 and, 1894–1896, to $262,300,000, together with the interest thereon.

In order to be able to redeem these notes upon presentation, $357,300,000 of interest-bearing bonds of the government have been issued, which the people have paid or must pay. Compare the amount of these bond issues with the amount of legal tender notes outstanding (greenbacks), $346,681,016, and instead of being a "burdenless debt" and the "best currency ever devised," it would seem pregnant with burden as well as danger. These notes when presented for redemption and paid are not cancelled but reissued, and continue to possess all potentiality of further drain upon the Treasury. Experience in 1893–1896 teaches that continuous deficits in revenue will inevitably render the existence of these notes an element of danger. Congress seems to have realized this and sought to guard against it by establishing a gold reserve of $150,000,000. Should the usual banking methods for maintaining the reserve prove unavailing, the act provides: if "said fund shall at any time fall below $100,000,000, then it shall be his [Secretary of the Treasury] duty to restore the same to the maximum sum of $150,000,000 by borrowing money on the credit of the United States," etc. With this power lodged in the hands of the Secretary and this duty imposed upon him, there can be no doubt of the redemption of these notes in gold so long as gold can be borrowed on the credit of the United States. The danger is that still further bonded indebtedness may have to be incurred on account of them. In this connection, it should be borne in mind that all currency to be issued to or by the Federal Reserve Banks is a direct obligation of the United States government, unwisely and unnecessarily made so in deference to the National Democratic Platform and those who favored the money policy therein proclaimed.

Ninety per cent. of silver certificates are now limited to $10, $5, $2, and $1 issues. Gold certificates are limited to $10 minimum. No national bank shall receive or have in circulation at one time more than $25,000 of its own notes of the denominations of $1 and $2. Silver is by law made the only available currency for the small everyday transactions of the people which are so largely effected by actual money rather than by auxiliary credits. Silver is thus laid under contribution to perform the daily exchanges of the workaday world, and cannot leave its task either directly or indirectly to aid in withdrawing gold from the Treasury. It is chained to the wheels of industry. The volume of currency which may be thus safely impounded by an active commercial people, already approximating 100,000,000 and rapidly increasing, is certainly very large, and since the volume of silver is no longer increasing, it is probable that except under extraordinary conditions the gold standard has little to fear from the present amount of silver currency. The prejudice or preference of the American people in favor of paper money precludes the use of coin except to a very limited extent. Bank-notes together with the silver certificates perform all the essential functions of money, except that they do not possess the debt-paying power — are not legal tenders. Our widely extended country, with many commercial and business centres, requires a considerable volume of legal tender money. The custom which avoids the use of coin makes a continual use for legal tender notes. A very large amount is continually in use for bank reserves. These notes are more useful than silver certificates, for while they are both readily redeemable at the Treasury, the notes may be tendered to and forced upon a creditor in satisfaction of his debt. The issue of currency certificates, in denominations of $5000 and $10,000 for legal tender notes deposited, was designed to furnish a currency, convenient in form and size, to enable the banks in large cities to settle their clearing-house balances, which frequently amount to several millions. They proved an equally convenient instrumentality for withdrawing gold from the Treasury. It was easy to present them and demand notes, and then present the notes and demand gold. Such certificates are no longer issued, Treasury gold certificates and clearing-house gold certificates serving the clearing-house needs of the banks. It will in future be much more difficult to accumulate legal tenders in large volume as a means of withdrawing gold from the Treasury as they, to a very large extent, are kept in constant use.

The United States was the last stronghold of silver. The gold standard law of 1900, directly in issue in the Presidential contest of that year, and hence squarely indorsed and ratified by the people, settled the question in the United States in favor of gold.

Nevertheless, our government nursed bimetallism and sent commissioners abroad to try to interest Europe in the subject, until their courteous reception depended upon the character of the government which sent them rather than the subject which they represented. All the great commercial nations adhered to the gold standard. The consensus of opinion of the civilized world, which in commerce makes law and regulates exchange, adopted the gold standard. This fact, borne in upon the public mind in the United States, found its record in the second defeat of Bryanism, and this fact, more potent than statute law, will preserve the gold standard.

When the Federal revenues increased under the independent Treasury system, the government necessarily absorbed and locked up a substantial part of the available supply of money, which tended to produce a stringency. As early as 1853 the Treasury was constrained to "come to the relief of the money market" and return the surplus money to the channels of trade by purchasing government bonds. The government's obligations have been purchased at premiums ranging up to 28 per cent., in order to counteract the workings of the subtreasury system. Could a more severe arraignment or criticism be made upon the system? The only other means of preventing the undue absorption of money by the Treasury was to deposit receipts from internal revenue in banks. From 1837 until the establishment of the national banking system (1863), depositing funds with banks was regarded as dangerous. Indeed, the existing system, under which the public deposits are amply secured by Federal, State and other approved bonds, has been much criticised, especially by the political party (Republican) which subsequently made the largest use of it. Deposits formerly were limited to current internal revenue receipts. However acute the stringency, customs receipts could not be so deposited, nor money transferred from the Treasury. Under the former law customs receipts must be paid directly into the Treasury, and money once in the Treasury can only be gotten out by means of an appropriation of Congress.

In no other civilized country was there ever such an absurd governmental interference with the currency supply, affecting values, promoting speculation, retarding business, and disturbing the welfare of the people. One of the best features of the Federal Reserve Act is that it does away with the bad effects of the subtreasury system.

The Second Bank of the United States had been drawn into the maelstrom of party politics and wrecked. Its continuation after its federal charter had expired, and its ignominious failure as a state institution shed reflex disgrace upon the original bank, and prevented Congress from turning again to a national bank for relief, as it had done in 1816, during the currency demoralization and financial troubles following the War of 1812. The action of Congress, in creating the subtreasury system in 1846 and seeking safety for its own funds regardless of the public, can be explained but not justified; the continuation until 1914 of this system of governmental interference with every man's business, a disturbing factor that must be reckoned with in every business forecast, cannot even be intelligently explained.

There is much to be said in favor of maintaining the reserve and current checking funds in the government's own coffers, and this the Secretary of the Treasury may do under the Federal Reserve Act while placing other funds with the Federal Reserve Banks.

At the inception of our national existence the genius of Hamilton conceived a central bank as the instrumentality through which the fiscal affairs of the government should be conducted. With branches established throughout the country, the standard of banking, the character of currency which this bank established, would become the criterion by which all would be judged. Other banks in order to succeed in competition had to be equally sound, their notes equally sure of redemption. His prescience and wisdom were vindicated by the achievements during the period of the First United States Bank (1791–1811). Public and private credit was raised from almost unprecedented chaos to a very high standard.

The deplorable condition of both currency and credit following the refusal to renew the bank's charter, coupled with the exigencies of the War of 1812, which resulted in chartering the Second United States Bank in 1816 (with the approval of Madison as President and many others who had opposed renewing the charter of the First), may also be noted to the credit of the central bank plan. The Second Bank was discredited by corruption in its early years, and weakly and most unwisely becoming embroiled in politics in its latter years, suffered party defeat and ceased to exist as a national institution with the expiration of its charter. Its early mistakes were corrected, and for many years its career was most honorable and useful. During this period, the central bank system so regulated the currency that its purchasing and debt-paying power was practically stable and uniform, with prompt redemption as well as flexibility of volume. It provided safe depositories for public moneys and transferred the same at little or no cost, developed the use of bank credits, greatly diminished the cost of domestic exchange, and by means of its branches and general powers tended to equalize interest and discount rates. When the system was destroyed, all the evils, which had thus been corrected, reappeared and continued until the era of nationalization which the Civil War brought about.

It must not, however, be inferred that all the state bank systems were bad. In theory many were good, although in practice the conservative restraints were not generally observed. In the earlier periods of our history the issuing of currency was regarded as the principal function of banks. They generally had limited cash capital and small deposits. Auxiliary currency, checks and drafts, that at the present time perform over 90 per cent. of the transactions consummated by the people through banks, were little used. A bank's ability to accommodate the public with loans and discounts depended very largely upon its note-issue. This explains why the people so long tolerated such enormous issues of bank-notes of such uncertain value. In the newer sections the curbing of the power to issue notes was stoutly resented. It was regarded as depriving the locality of the life-blood of its trade notwithstanding the defective character and fluctuating value of such notes. One of the strongest criticisms, and most effective as to public sentiment, against the United States Bank was that it refused to receive the notes of many banks, and promptly presented for redemption such notes as it did receive, instead of paying them out. As the country grew in population and wealth, deposits became a more important factor, and checks and drafts largely superseded currency.

The national banking system was planned to make a market for government bonds and to furnish a currency secured by such bonds which should supplant United States notes, and also to create a demand and use for United States notes in the reserves which the banks were required to hold. Such currency was perfectly safe but not at all responsive to the varying needs of trade. No currency based upon bond security can be elastic. A bank is required to invest as much or more money in the purchase of bonds to secure circulation than the amount of circulation it is permitted to issue. Its ability to extend accommodations to its patrons is thereby limited rather than increased.

Bond security is not essential to a perfectly secured circulation. One life insurance company in New York had outstanding at the end of 1923, 30,221,727 life insurance policies amounting to $9,238,254,068. The company is remarkably strong and well managed. All life insurance the world over is based upon mortuary tables, showing the expectation of human life calculated from statistical experience. The business is safe in all particulars. All fire insurance is based upon statistical history of loss by fire and the percentage of probable loss calculated therefrom. The business is safe if prudently and wisely conducted. How much easier to calculate with certainty the mortality among banks and the percentage of probable loss, in view of supervision, examination, and great publicity, and the elaborate data which they are required to furnish! In 1902 the Treasury Department prepared statistics, showing that for the thirty-nine years that the national banking system had then existed, a tax of $\frac{3}{8}$ of 1 per cent. levied annually upon outstanding circulation would have produced an amount of money sufficient to have redeemed the outstanding notes of every national bank that had failed, without recourse to the bonds held as security or other funds. Undoubtedly the same statement would be true up to the present time. With business certainty, a safety fund and a guarantee fund involving only a moderate tax can be provided which will make note-issues perfectly safe and sound, and with equal certainty currency based upon the normal assets of a bank can be safe and sound.

The experience of other nations furnishes competent evidence upon the question of currency.

The Reichsbank of Germany, prior to 1914, afforded an example of the power and efficiency of a central bank in what it accomplished for the German people and German industry, after the formation of the German Empire. Under wholesome restraint it issued notes sufficient for the needs of business and the volume of notes issued varied with the necessity for their use. — The World War, of course, changed all this.

Dunbar, in his "Theory and History of Banking," states that on more than one occasion the provision for elasticity in the German currency law saved the nation from what would otherwise have been a severe spasm of contraction. It is the consensus of opinion of German financiers that this provision enabled them to pass through the commercial and financial depression during the years 1900 and 1901 with comparative ease, avoiding what otherwise might have entailed serious disaster.

The Dominion of Canada has no central bank; it has 18 banks, with 4,451 branches. Our 12 regional Federal Reserve Banks with the power to create branches, are closely analogous to the Canadian system and make a study of the experience of Canada most inviting.

The working of the Canadian system furnishes a valuable object lesson; expansion and contraction of the currency issued by the banks registers the varying needs of commerce in different seasons; since the maximum currency issue was within the total amount authorized, the needs of commerce and trade must have been fully supplied. There have been very few bank failures in Canada since the creation of its present currency system; note holders were paid in full, and the redemption fund fully restored from the assets of the failed banks.

The Canadian banking system, unlike ours, requires no reserve against deposits and no governmental inspection, although elaborate data are required to be furnished by means of verified monthly reports. It has borne the test of experience, and furnishes good evidence that a currency may be both safe and elastic without pledged security for its redemption, while our experience proves that circulation secured by bonds may be perfectly good, but cannot be elastic. It also proves that currency can be perfectly good without being issued by the government.

As the government's credit improved after the war and the premium upon bonds increased, it became more profitable to sell bonds and retire circulation, and the banks increased their loanable funds by so doing. For this reason bank circulation decreased at a period when the friends of sound money hoped it would increase and thereby aid in retiring the greenbacks. An opposition to the national banking system existed not unlike that which developed against the two United States banks in intensity and virulence. This opposition championed first the greenbacks and later silver. The system had to struggle for existence, and received little consideration and no indulgence in respect to note-issues. As banks of discount and deposit, the growth of the system is simply marvellous. It is preëminently the best and safest system of local banks which the country has ever possessed, made secure and homogeneous by means of federal supervision and comprehensive publicity. It has elevated the general credit, very materially reduced the cost of domestic exchange, furnished circulation at par throughout the country, proved a competent and efficient auxiliary to trade, and paid large tribute to the Treasury for the privilege of so doing.

EXHIBIT OF GROWTH OF NATIONAL BANKS (EXPRESSED IN MILLIONS)

OCTOBER	NUMBER	CAPITAL	SURPLUS AND PROFITS	LOANS	DEPOSITS	CIRCULATION	TOTAL RESOURCES
1903	5,118	758	565	3,425	3,176	376	6,302
1904	5,412	771	583	3,726	3,458	411	6,310
1905	5,833	808	633	4,017	3,989	486	7,563
1906	6,137	835	671	4,299	4,199	518	8,016
1907	6,625	902	750	4,585	4,177	602	8,408
1908	6,853	921	768	4,751	4,548	614	9,027
1909	6,877	945	801	5,129	5,010	658	9,574
1910	7,173	1,003	874	5,467	5,146	675	9,826
1911	7,301	1,025	904	5,663	5,490	697	10,379
1912	7,397	1,046	944	6,041	5,892	714	10,963
1913	7,509	1,059	1,008	6,261	6,052	727	11,302
1914	7,571	1,063	1,018	6,316	6,079	1,018	11,492

This exhibit is the most remarkable that the world has to show of financial institutions operating under identical charters and single supervision.

The taxes paid to the United States during the period 1863–1914 amounted to $208,329,011.86. In addition they paid large amounts to the states where located.

The statistics of insolvency show as follows: —

FAILURES OF NATIONAL BANKS

(Amounts in millions)

Period	Number	Capital	Claims Proved	Paid to Date	Per Cent. Paid
1864 to 1873	34	8.2	14.8	10.6	71.6
1874 to 1883	55	11.7	18.9	13.5	71.4
1884 to 1893	161	24.6	54.5	37.6	69.0
1894 to 1902	156	23.2	51.2	35.3	69.0
1903 to 1915	150	24.9	57.6	41.8	72.6
Total	556	92.6	197.0	138.8	70.05

The circulating notes were of course paid in full upon presentation, and the assets have not been entirely distributed.

In short, as a system of *banking* institutions its value was very great, and its imperfections might have been corrected by intelligent legislation.

STATISTICAL RÉSUMÉ

CIRCULATION OF MONEY IN THE UNITED STATES

(Millions of dollars)

Year	Gold[1]	Silver[1]	Subsidiary Silver	U. S. Notes	Treasury Notes	National Bank-notes	Total	In Treasury	In Circulation	Population	Per Capita Circulation
1904	1328	560	107	347	13	449	2803	284	2519	82	30.77
1906	1476	561	118	347	7	561	3070	333	2737	84	32.32
1908	1618	563	147	347	5	698	3379	341	3038	87	34.72
1910	1636	565	155	347	4	713	3419	317	3102	90	34.33
1912	1818	565	171	347	3	745	3648	364	3284	96	34.34
1913	1871	566	175	347	3	759	3720	356	3364	97	34.56
1915	1816	566	185	347	2	1040	3972[2]	427	3545	100	35.50

[1] Including certificates.
[2] Including $17,199,225 Federal Reserve Notes.

PRODUCTION OF GOLD AND SILVER

(Millions of dollars)

Year	World			United States			Ratio	Bullion Value in Silver
	Gold	Silver		Gold	Silver			
		Commercial Value	Coining Value		Commercial Value	Price of Silver[1]		
1904	347	95	218	80	33	.57876	35.70	.447
1906	403	112	213	94	38	.67689	30.54	.523
1908	442	109	263	95	38	.53490	38.64	.413
1910	455	120	287	96	31	.54077	38.22	.418
1912	466	138	261	93	39	.61470	33.62	.475
1913	458	118	—	89	40	.60458	34.19	.487

[1] Value of a fine ounce at average quotation.

NOTE. — In 1914, the estimated production of gold in the world was $449,224,-983.

EXPORTS AND IMPORTS OF MERCHANDISE, GOLD AND SILVER

(Millions of dollars)

Fiscal Year	Merchandise			Silver			Gold		
	Exports	Imports	Excess Exports	Exports	Imports	Excess Exports	Exports	Imports	Excess – Exports + Imports
1904	1461	991	470	49	28	21	81	99	+ 18
1905	1519	1118	401	49	28	21	93	54	– 39
1906	1744	1227	517	66	45	21	39	96	+ 57
1907	1881	1434	447	57	43	14	51	114	+ 63
1908	1861	1194	667	58	45	13	72	148	+ 76
1909	1663	1312	351	56	44	12	92	44	– 48
1910	1745	1557	188	55	45	10	118	43	– 75
1911	2049	1527	522	65	46	19	23	74	+ 51
1912	2204	1653	551	65	47	18	57	49	– 8
1913	2466	1813	653	71	41	30	78	69	– 9
1914	2365	1894	471	55	30	25	112	67	– 45

BANKING POWER BY SECTIONS

National, State, Savings and Private Banks and Trust Companies

States	Capital, Surplus and Profits, and Deposits (Millions of Dollars)			Per Capita		
	1890	1900	1914[1]	1890	1900	1914
New England .	1,229	1,728	3,065	$261.86	$312.30	$437.85
Eastern . . .	2,410	4,281	9,403	170.92	251.10	408.82
Middle . . .	1,055	1,808	5,632	54.59	75.00	208.60
Southern . .	387	552	2,155	21.15	24.94	79.81
Western . . .	218	306	1,114	54.83	60.16	131.06
Pacific . . .	315	467	1,610	139.15	147.01	255.55
United States	5,614	9,142	22,979	89.83	118.73	232.11

[1] The total banking power of the United States in 1914 (30,011 banking institutions) is computed by the Comptroller of the Currency to be $24,340,090,000, this including estimates for 3246 non-reporting banks.

Other Banks

(In millions of dollars)

Year	State Banks						Total Resources		
	Number	Capital	Surplus	Deposits	Cash	Loans	Trust Companies	Private Banks	Savings Banks
1906	8,862	422	171	2,741	232	2,271	2,959	144	3,583
1908	11,220	503	217	2,937	309	2,436	2,866	162	3,810
1910	12,166	436	188	2,728	241	2,406	4,217	160	4,482
1912	13,381	459	177	2,920	242	2,549	5,107	197	4,923
1914	14,512	501	214	3,227	262	2,880	5,490	197	5,449

MISCELLANEOUS FINANCIAL STATISTICS

Year	Clearings, Bank (Millions)		Savings Banks		Failures	
	New York	United States	Depositors [Thousands]	Deposits [Millions]	Number [Thousands]	Liabilities [Millions]
1904	68,649	112,612	7,035	2,919	12	144
1906	104,675	159,935	8,027	3,300	11	119
1908	79,275	132,095	8,706	3,479	16	222
1910	97,274	163,392	9,143	4,070	13	202
1912	100,743	173,427	10,010	4,452	15	203
1914	83,018	153,830	——	4,935	18	357

The Federal Reserve Bank Act will eventually do away with notes secured by United States bonds, one distinctive feature of the national bank system; it also does away with the power to act as reserve agent for other national banks, and it takes away from the latter United States deposits and places the same with the Federal Reserve Banks; it also admits to full membership banks chartered by state authority—state banks and trust companies; it may make a better and broader system, but it certainly marks the passing of the national bank system as it has existed for over 50 years. The system had its defects and has come in for severe criticism from us all and yet its good qualities were far in the ascendant; it financed the country through 52 years of growth unparalleled in respect to population, the creation of industries, the production and distribution of commodities, the prosperity and happiness of a great people.

CHAPTER XXV

General Review (*Continued*)
and
Federal Reserve Law

The Federal Reserve Act became law December 23, 1913. The President took a long time to select the members of the Federal Reserve Board and the Senate thereafter took a long time to confirm them. Not only was the crop-moving season upon us before the Board was ready for action, but there also occurred the wholly unexpected disruption of commercial and financial relations of the whole world, which followed the war involving Germany, Austria, Servia, Russia, Turkey, England, France, Belgium, Italy and Japan. Orient and Occident, the whole eastern hemisphere was mostly involved. Each nation forbade its citizens to pay indebtedness to citizens of the nations with which such nation was at war; [1] moratoriums and postponement of the payment of debts due, at home and abroad, were decreed; credit was absolutely denied to people of the United States; they were required to pay promptly all due and maturing debts; exchange on Europe had been sold in large amounts in anticipation of cotton and grain bills which would presently come into the market; borrowing through exchange transactions is usual every year in anticipation of our cotton and cereal exports and is good, conservative business, but this year our people were compelled to take up such bills and furnish gold with which to do so; the war

[1] Brussels, March 18, 1915. — The firm of Henri Leten has been fined 20,000 marks ($5000) for violating the order of Gov.-Gen. Von Bissing, prohibiting payments to creditors in England.

assured, every nation began to struggle for gold; presently all European exchanges were closed or constrained by supervision, and the New York Stock Exchange was the only open market left; American securities were sold from abroad as fast as the market would take them without precipitating a panic, in order to make bank credits which could be used to obtain gold for exportation; $28,000,000 securities came over on one vessel.

From January 1, 1914, to August 1, 1914, gold was exported to the amount of $107,516,000. For the week of July 31, 1914, gold was exported to the amount of $24,677,000. The Stock Exchange did not open for business on Friday, July 31. The closing of the Stock Exchange became absolutely necessary. As long as a customer of a bank deposited drafts which were paid through the clearing-house in gold or its equivalent, the bank could not consistently refuse to pay such customer gold when called for; closing the Stock Exchange prevented further sale of securities and prevented gold-exporting houses from receiving checks upon which they could call for gold. The closing of the Stock Exchange was a most serious matter for the New York banks. Interior banks may rediscount or borrow from New York, but the only resources of the New York banks are gold from abroad and call loans upon the Stock Exchange. Gold from abroad was impossible and when the Stock Exchange was closed all their call loans became, *ipso facto*, investments, so far as non-availability was concerned; they were left with no resource but their maturities, and comparatively few were prepared to pay their maturing obligations. On August 3 the clearing-house banks had $471,713,600 in cash and owed out-of-town banks subject to check $853,621,400. Interior banks in the larger cities loan in a very large way, well over $100,000,000, money on call in New York, in order to have a "cold-blooded" resource, available, without compunction, at any time. Of course whenever such loans are called, New York banks must loan funds with which to pay the same. The danger was, that with the Stock Exchange closed and their call loan resource cut off, the interior banks would largely draw down their New York balances. It was necessary that the whole country should be made to realize that these troubles were thrust upon us from abroad; that no one at home was responsible and that all must unite in bearing the burdens. Private wires and long distance telephoning brought St. Louis, Minneapolis, Chicago, Pittsburg, Baltimore, Philadelphia and Boston into one conference; all was harmony, all united to and did meet the situation shoulder to shoulder; credit instruments were provided by the various clearing-houses, which made it easy for the banks to meet the situation. As soon as the clearing-house certificates were resorted to it was easy to prevent gold shipments. A bank receiving large deposits from a depositor could well say, "we receive for these checks only clearing-house funds, not gold, therefore we can only pay your checks through the clearing-house and not in gold." Gold exports were effectively stopped for the time. The trouble and embarrassment were not confined to banks and business men. The greater part of the revenues of the government are derived from customs duties received at the Atlantic seaboard. The absolute stoppage of American credit abroad and the payment of existing commitments with exchange on London ranging as high as $5.08, easily portended a violent reduction of imports from Europe, a corresponding reduction in governmental revenues and the conversion, in the not-distant future, of the Treasury surplus into a deficit. The issuance of clearing-house certificates protected the gold of the United States Treasury and was absolutely needful for such purpose. The Treasury has none of the powers for protecting its gold holdings which are possessed by the central or government banks of other nations. Fortunately, Congress was in session and at once levied increased taxes to prevent the trouble that always comes when the Treasury is poor in funds.

Clearing-house certificates were issued in twelve of the larger cities, but only for use in settling debit balances at the clearing-houses and not to circulate as currency, as had been done in many cities on previous occasions.

CLEARING-HOUSE CERTIFICATES ISSUED DURING EUROPEAN WAR CRISIS OF 1914[1]

Compiled by William J. Gilpin, Assistant Manager, New York Clearing-house

CLEARING-HOUSE	FIRST ISSUE	LAST ISSUE	FIRST CANCELLATION	FINAL CANCELLATION	AGGREGATE ISSUE	MAXIMUM AMOUNT OUTSTANDING	DATE OF MAXIMUM AMOUNT
New York	Aug. 3	Oct. 15	Aug. 26	Nov. 28	$124,695,000	$109,185,000	Sept. 25
Chicago	Aug. 4	Oct. 14	Oct. 2	Dec. 14	42,190,000	41,890,000	Oct. 14
Philadelphia	Aug. 3	Oct. 2	Oct. 16	Nov. 28	11,530,000	11,530,000	Oct. 2 to 16
Boston	Aug. 4	Oct. 5	Oct. 7	Nov. 24	11,385,000	11,385,000	Oct. 5–6
St. Louis	Aug. 5	Sept. 2	Sept. 8	Dec. 10	10,805,000	10,725,000	Sept. 2 to 7
Baltimore	Aug. 4	Sept. 15	Aug. 13	Dec. 9	2,350,000	2,225,000	Aug. 15 to 26
New Orleans	Aug. 4	Aug. 5	Aug. 23	Oct. 23	2,150,000	2,150,000	Aug. 5 to 23
St. Paul	Aug. 5	Aug. 18	Aug. 29	Nov. 7	2,040,000	2,040,000	Aug. 18 to 29
Minneapolis	Aug. 6	Aug. 29	Sept. 30	Nov. 5	1,915,000	1,915,000	Aug. 29 to Sept. 29
Detroit	Aug. 5	Aug. 13	Oct. 8	Nov. 9	1,350,000	1,350,000	Aug. 13 to Oct. 7
Louisville	Aug. 5	Aug. 5	Dec. 1	Dec. 1	1,200,000	1,200,000	Aug. 5 to Dec. 1
Des Moines	Aug. 6	Aug. 15	Aug. 15	Nov. 7	168,000	159,000	Aug. 15
					$211,778,000	$195,754,000	

NOTE. — Inquiries were sent to 100 clearing-houses. It is found that certificates were issued by only the twelve above. The same clearing-houses in 1907–1908 issued $200,551,000. The total issued in 1907–1908 (51 clearing-houses) was $255,536,300 and the maximum amount outstanding $227,114,100.

The emergency currency law, commonly called the Aldrich-Vreeland law, made it possible for the banks to get all the currency needed; a currency stringency, one of the usual embarrassments in a crisis, was entirely eliminated; the very energetic and efficient coöperation of William G. McAdoo, Secretary of the Treasury, enabled the banks to obtain this currency promptly and thus prevent any panicky feeling which otherwise surely would have developed. Under the Federal Reserve Law it will be possible to receive currency in times of emergency with even greater facility than was possible under the Aldrich-Vreeland act. The total amount of this emergency currency issued was $382,502,645; the first issues were made early in August; the retirement was very rapid as the money market eased; the large cities were the first to retire, the country finding a profitable use

[1] See page 353 for complete statement of clearing-house certificates issued by the New York Clearing-house from 1860 to 1914.

for the same for a longer period; the amount outstanding April 1, 1915, was $15,490,595.

All bankers and business men were compelled to take up all exchange drawn upon Europe, which bore their indorsement; drafts drawn upon both commercial and travellers' letters of credit were refused, and Americans abroad were subjected to such great inconvenience that our government furnished a warship, a fast cruiser, upon which the bankers sent gold abroad to redeem such drafts and relieve distress. The city of New York had negotiated $83,000,000 of short term revenue bonds or notes abroad, maturing in London and Paris from September to January; the city doubtless borrowed this money abroad at a slightly lower rate than was obtainable in New York, but the ultimate cost was much more, not to mention the embarrassment to every one occasioned by these large maturities accruing in such anomalous times. The banks of the city of New York formed a syndicate and furnished the gold and exchange to pay this city indebtedness.

So much was said and written about the payment of America's obligations abroad, in gold, that the impression became quite general that there was a large indebtedness abroad that was in default; not so, American obligations were paid as they came due, in gold or exchange equivalent.

One of the first results of the war was the almost complete demoralization of our international trade and banking arrangements. It became necessary to ascertain as nearly as possible the total amount of American obligations abroad, which would mature in the near future, in order that means might be devised to pay the same, however complicated the conditions might be. Albert H. Wiggin, Chairman of the New York Clearing-house Committee, at the request of the Federal Reserve Board, undertook to gather data upon which to approximate the above balance, and associated with him in this work were the Hon. Seth Low, President of the Chamber of Commerce of New York, and

Henry R. Towne, Director of the Federal Reserve Bank of New York. Letters were sent by Chairman Wiggin to all the institutions believed to be doing any foreign exchange business whatever, requesting confidential data as to the amount of their maturing indebtedness to Europe, and *vice versa,* as well as the character of such indebtedness. The response to this appeal to the institutions and individuals addressed was prompt and complete, and the assembled figures were of great use in determining the steps which were later taken with such good results.

Chairman Wiggin of the Clearing-house Committee later on acted as Chairman of the Gold Fund Committee which was the direct outcome of the information secured as above, and which showed the splendid coöperative spirit of the American bankers.

The Gold Fund was organized in September, 1914, to relieve the acute situation existing in the foreign exchange market and in our international trade relations. The plan was formulated by a committee acting with the approval of and in conjunction with the Secretary of the Treasury and the Federal Reserve Board. The Fund was administered by the Gold Fund Committee, consisting of the following: Albert H. Wiggin, Chairman; William Woodward, James S. Alexander, Francis L. Hine, Benjamin Strong, Jr., Frank A. Vanderlip, James N. Wallace, W. P. Holly, Secretary.

The first meeting of the Gold Fund Committee was held at the New York Clearing-house on September 21, 1914, and arrangements made for assembling a fund of approximately $100,000,000 in gold. Acting through the various clearing-house associations of the Central Reserve and Reserve cities of the country, the Gold Fund Committee succeeded in obtaining subscriptions in a remarkably short space of time, aggregating approximately $109,000,000. Of this amount New York City furnished $45,-000,000, Chicago $16,000,000, Philadelphia $8,000,000, Boston $7,000,000, St. Louis $5,000,000, San Francisco $3,250,000, Pittsburg $3,000,000, Cleveland $1,800,000, Portland, Ore.,

$1,500,000, Cincinnati $1,500,000, Minneapolis $1,250,000, and St. Paul, Milwaukee, Los Angeles, Kansas City, Denver and Baltimore $1,000,000 each, and the balance was contributed by thirty-six other cities.

A 25 per cent. call was made upon the subscribers in the latter part of October, and approximately $10,000,000 thereof was immediately shipped to Ottawa under an arrangement with the Bank of England by which a corresponding credit was established in London in favor of the Gold Fund Committee. Against this credit, exchange was sold by the Committee to all applicants who could show that they desired the exchange for a legitimate purpose.

When the Gold Fund was organized the foreign exchange market was demoralized. Sterling exchange was quoted at over $5 to the pound and was practically unobtainable. Europe was demanding that our maturing obligations be met by the shipment of gold. The effect of the establishment of the $100,000,000 Gold Fund and the actual shipment of a portion thereof was immediate. Sterling quotations began to drop and the congested condition of our export trade began to be relieved through normal channels. In other words, the very knowledge that this large fund was actually available was one of the chief stabilizing factors in the situation. The Gold Fund Committee never shipped any gold beyond the $10,000,000 above referred to, and even found it unnecessary to sell all of the exchange created by that $10,000,000. The Fund was finally terminated on March 12, 1915, exchange rates having been normal or below for many weeks.

The cotton crop amounted to 16,000,000 bales, but instead of a blessing it became a source of embarrassment, because of the lessened demand of the warring nations, the lessened ocean tonnage and the danger and expense of foreign shipments. It seemed certain that a very large portion of the crop would have to be carried over into the next year. To relieve the situation a

Cotton Loan Fund of $135,000,000 was created to be administered under the general direction of the members of the Federal Reserve Board acting as individuals. The actual operation of the Fund was in the hands of the Cotton Loan Committee, consisting of the following: Hon. W. P. G. Harding, Chairman, Hon. Paul M. Warburg, Albert H. Wiggin, New York, James S. Alexander, New York, James B. Forgan, Chicago, Festus J. Wade, St. Louis, Levi L. Rue, Philadelphia, William A. Gaston, Boston, W. P. Holly, Secretary. The first meeting of the Cotton Loan Committee was held on November 20, 1914, and the completed plan, as approved by the Federal Reserve Board, was declared operative on January 2, 1915. The total amount available to borrowers in the cotton-producing states was $135,000,000, which they could borrow on the security of cotton stored in warehouses and pledged at the rate of 6 cents per pound, the interest rate being 6 per cent. per annum. When the Fund was organized the cotton situation was most acute owing to the unusual volume of the crop and the almost complete stoppage of demand resulting from the war. Cotton was quoted at less than 5 cents per pound and was practically unsalable at any price. The establishment of the Cotton Loan Fund exerted an immediate stabilizing effect upon the market; the price was "pegged" at 6 cents per pound in the South and buyers who had been waiting for lower prices came into the market; the cotton exchanges, all of which had been closed, were presently opened; on February 1, when the time limit for making loans expired, only $28,000 of the $135,000,000 had been applied for and loaned; cotton was selling at 8 cents per pound with a good demand.

Of the $100,000,000 subscribed by the non-cotton-producing states, New York City contributed $53,000,000, Chicago $12,000,000, St. Louis $11,500,000, Philadelphia $5,000,000, Baltimore $2,500,000, Boston $2,000,000, Pittsburg $2,000,000, Detroit $1,200,000, Cleveland $2,000,000, Cincinnati $2,000,000,

Kansas City $1,200,000, Louisville $1,000,000, Washington $1,000,000, and the balance was contributed by 54 other cities. No call for payment under the subscription was ever made; the New York institutions with which the two members of the Cotton Loan Committee from that City were identified, viz., the Chase National Bank and the National Bank of Commerce, took over for their own accounts the $28,000 of loans actually made, — a splendid exhibition of the coöperative power of the banks.

CHAPTER XXVI

The War and Post-war Period

General Outline

The years that have followed August 1, 1914, have been more filled with significance for the historian of money, banking, and finance than any similar period in the world's history. The problem of selection from the great number of events becomes increasingly difficult. The writer must not only pick out the more significant developments in the field of money, credit, and finance, but he must also make frequent reference to military and political events and to changes in industry and commerce without which a strictly financial and monetary history would be unintelligible.

The past seven and a half years have been, on the whole, a vindication of the established principles of money and credit, though they have revealed the fact that our modern credit system can stand a much greater strain than would have been anticipated in the past, and that the possibilities of substituting credit for real capital, and of piling up liabilities without increasing assets, are much greater than bankers and economists in 1914 were ready to recognize. These years have not proved, however, that financial folly will not hang itself if given rope enough. They have merely proved that financial folly will take a great deal of rope. He would be a rash student, moreover, who would conclude from the experience of the past seven and a half years that the world can safely discard, or will discard in the future, the canons of sound finance. The probabilities are rather that the bitter experiences resulting from reckless disregard of sound finance will make creditors more cautious in the future and will mean more, rather than less, rigorous credit standards after the final reckoning is complete and a new financial equilibrium is restored.

In the United States, in Great Britain, and in most of the neutral countries of Europe, the battle for sound money and sound finance, though the issue has at times been doubtful, appears clearly to have been decided in favor of those who wished to adhere to established principles. There have been financial follies even in these countries, but, for the most part, the financial difficulties and the departures from strict compliance with sound canons have been forced by war necessity and by disturbances in the neighboring countries rather than by a deliberate relaxing of restraints at home. Only the United States have preserved the gold standard in its full integrity, but Great Britain and the Continental neutrals have held steadily in mind the necessity of a return to the gold standard, and have kept their financial houses in such order that there is little doubt that they will ultimately return to the gold standard at the old pars. The Continental belligerents, however, partly through the terrible pressure of war necessity, but even more through reckless financial policies, have involved themselves in the gravest difficulties—difficulties which only the most resolute, intelligent, and courageous statesmanship can hope successfully to deal with.

War between great industrial countries involves, on the one hand, a tremendous diminution in the productive output of a country as millions of its best workers are drawn into the army and navy, and, on the other hand, an immense increase in consumption and destruction as these millions of men not only require much more in the way of food, clothing, and other personal supplies than they would normally consume, but also because of the waste and destruction of munitions and other supplies which war involves. In the actual battle zone, moreover, property of all kinds is destroyed.

Since the great bulk of the world's wealth consists not of

goods available for immediate consumption, but rather of roads, bridges, houses, factories, and other fixed wealth, it is clear that modern war, involving many nations, must rapidly deplete the world's current stocks of goods and that acute shortages must speedily arise. Belligerent countries especially are quickly driven to desperate expedients to keep an adequate stock of goods going to the battlefront without actually starving their own people. A great increase in production is called for and a great curtailment of ordinary civilian consumption.

For the European belligerents the increase in supplies could be drawn from two sources. First, there were labor reserves—women, children, and old men. In France, moreover, it was possible to bring in from the African colonies laborers who could replace French soldiers who had gone to the front. A second great resource was goods produced abroad, and particularly goods produced in the United States. The Entente Allies, having command of the seas, were able to make use of this resource on a great scale. Germany, speedily shut off from the seas, could draw in goods only to a limited extent from foreign countries, and was quickly obliged to make the maximum possible use of internal labor reserves.

The outstanding fact in the first three years of the War, in so far as the War affected the monetary, financial, and economic life of the United States, was the ever-increasing volume of exports sent to Europe without a compensating backflow of goods. Down to the middle of 1916 we accomplished this rather readily. The outbreak of the War found the United States in a slack state of industry and the increased demands from Europe led first to an increase in our domestic production, rather than to shortages of supplies and rising prices. By the middle of 1916, however, we had used up our industrial slack and were producing at maximum capacity. From that time on every extra boatload of goods that went to Europe meant an additional tightening of the belt for consumers in the United States.

With our own entrance into the War the pressure was intensified greatly. Five million men were withdrawn from industry for the army and navy (partly replaced by women) and a very high proportion of the remaining civilian population was turned from ordinary peace-time production to the production of military and naval supplies, including merchant marine, aircraft, and so on.

Paralleling these changes in the physical direction of production, consumption, industry, and trade, financial events of the greatest magnitude and complexity took place. The first effect of the outbreak of the War was increased desire for liquid wealth. Long-run plans could not be made. Men, banks, and governments wished to get hold of gold and other cash resources so that they could readily meet emergencies and so that they could shift their plans as unforeseen developments might come. This tendency manifested itself well before the War. As early as 1912 German bankers began to increase their gold supplies. France and Russia made strong efforts to increase their gold reserves during the spring and summer of 1914. These three countries in the eighteen months preceding the outbreak of the War increased their gold holdings by about $360,000,000—a quiet process which, none the less, led to a tightening of the money markets of the world and led to an unusually large drain on the gold supply of the United States.

Following the assassination at Sarajevo on June 28, 1914, business men and banks generally in Europe began to convert securities into liquid cash in the form of bank balances. Heavy selling began on the Bourse of Vienna with the fall in the price of stocks of from 10% to 12% on July 13th and spread rapidly to the other great markets. There were panics on the bourses of Vienna, Berlin, and Paris which forced them to suspend operations. Then panic selling spread to London and New York and at the outbreak of the War all Europe was selling in New York, without limit of price, vast quantities of European holdings of American securities. On July 31st both the London and the New York stock exchanges were forced to close.

There was emphasized also a strong preference for hard money, including even silver, over bank notes in the countries of Europe.

We have seen in a preceding chapter the measures by which New York met this emergency, and the various devices by means of which credit was restored and finance enabled to function again. In later chapters we shall go somewhat into detail in dealing with some of these matters. The purpose of the present chapter is to give perspective and to place things in bold relief.

The problems of money, credit, banking, and public finance are a part of the larger problem of social control and social co-ordination. By means of money, credit, and finance, industry is guided and production and consumption are regulated. The problem facing a government when a great war breaks out is that of bringing to bear the maximum of force in a minimum of time upon the battlefront, at the same time preserving, as far as may be, the health and normal functioning of social and economic life behind the lines. There are in theory two main ways in which a government can control such a situation. It may, on the one hand, undertake a sort of military organization of the whole population, planning the whole life of the people, rationing out supplies, drafting men and plants for industrial purposes as well as for the army, and seeking to coördinate things in a comprehensive way. Practically a complete application of this system has never been successful and could not be expected to be successful since, even in war-time, a great population would resist any such degree of coercive control as this would require, and since, moreover, no government could be expected to have the intelligence requisite to carry it out. Chaos, rather than order, would result from the attempt. The other system is for the government to enter the markets as the dominating purchaser and employer, outbidding private individuals in the markets for labor and supplies and thus making use of ordinary commercial methods for diverting labor and supplies from non-essential to essential war industries. Practically, in varying degrees, in different countries both these methods were combined. The governments in all countries refused to compete in the labor markets for soldiers. They drafted the necessary soldiers at fixed rates of pay. Practically, also, they commandeered the necessary plants and equipment for making munitions in cases where such plants were not voluntarily placed at their disposal. They also introduced a great deal of rationing of supplies and a good deal of price-fixing, making an effort to pay high enough prices for the goods they took to give profits and wages of an adequate sort. It is probable that these measures in Great Britain and the United States reduced the cost of the War in considerable measure. They still left the governments, however, with the problem of raising funds on a gigantic scale.

Public treasuries may raise funds for war in five main ways:

(1) by taxation,
(2) by long-term bonds,
(3) by short-term treasury bills,
(4) by advances from a state bank of issue in the form of bank notes or deposit credits, and
(5) by direct issue of paper money by the government.

In preceding chapters we have seen the evil effects of the issue of legal tender notes (Greenbacks, especially) in American history. It is a last resort of financial weakness. We escaped the worst consequences of such weakness in this country by substituting, during the course of the Civil War, a strong loan and tax policy. We maintained this until we were able to resume specie payments.

When specie payment is suspended, however, and the state leans heavily on the state bank of issue, as is true of all the Continental belligerents, there is no practical difference between direct issue of government paper money and the issue of state bank notes.

There has been a great deal of discussion in comparing the methods of the loan policy and the tax policy during the War. Certain economists urged an all-tax policy. The argument is that, if the income of the people is taken up and turned over directly to the government, prices will not rise and that, as soon as the government spends more, the people spend less—precisely as much less—and, as the government consumes more, the people consume less. When bonds are issued, on the other hand, the people may use them as collateral at the banks and borrow money which they can use in competing with the government in the markets for labor and supplies. Prices are thus driven up.

Those who advocated the all-tax policy failed to realize adequately the dangers in a complicated business and credit situation, where every active business is both creditor and debtor, and failed especially to see the importance of not driving non-essential industries into bankruptcy at the same time that the government is curtailing their supplies and labor forces. It is far better that in the early stages of the war prices should rise sharply as a means of checking consumption and making it easy for the industrial transition to be accomplished. In the latter stages of the war, after the main transition is accomplished, taxes should be increasingly applied. A judicious combination of short-term treasury certificates, increasing taxes, and long-term funding loans seems clearly to be the right policy. While mistakes were made both by Great Britain and the United States in their financial policy, on the whole, war finance was a success in both of these countries, and modifications in detail of the expedients used by these two countries, rather than the effort to apply a drastic all-tax policy, would seem to be indicated as the proper programme for future national emergencies, if such unfortunately come.

The following chapters will deal, first, with the effects upon American industry, trade, and finance during the period from

1914 to our entrance into the War in 1917, centering about our export trade to Europe, the foreign exchange problem and the various financial expedients used in carrying our export balance; second, with the Federal Reserve System during the War; third, with the public finance of the United States during the War; fourth with the post-War boom and the great crisis of 1920; a final chapter will discuss the gold and rediscount policy of the Federal Reserve Banks with reference to the future.

CHAPTER XXVII

FOREIGN EXCHANGE DURING THE WAR

THE accumulation of gold by the central banks of Russia, Germany, and France which preceded the outbreak of the War led to drains on the gold stocks of the United States. We had an excess of exports over imports of gold in 1913 of over $28,000,000, while in 1914, to the end of June, we lost $84,000,000. The heavy selling of securities by Europe at the outbreak of the War, and the maturing of $80,000,000 of New York City short-term obligations, held by England and France, during the crisis of 1914 led to still further drains on our gold. The total loss of gold in 1914 was $165,000,000. After the outbreak of the War gold was not shipped to Europe directly but rather to the depository of the Bank of England at Ottawa.

In the fall of 1914 the very heavy volume of exports of commodities from the United States to the Entente Allies began which turned the tide of these gold payments. In October we lost $44,000,000 of gold, in November $7,000,000 and in December the tide definitely turned and we gained $4,000,000 in excess of imports over exports of gold. From December, 1914 to May, 1917, an unprecedented flow of gold came to the United States. We gained $421,000,000 in 1915, in 1916 over $530,000,000, and in 1917, over $181,000,000—a total of $1,132,000,000 in gold for the three years, 1915–1917, and a gain of more than a billion from the outbreak of the War, even when the net loss for the last half of 1914 is taken into account.

This tremendous influx of gold led to a prolonged period of excessively easy money. From January, 1915 to May, 1916, the range for call money at New York was from 1% to 2¼%, and the general average was from 1¾% to 2%. It was not until the vast financial operations of the United States Government during the War began in the summer of 1917 that call money got as high as 5% again.

Foreign demand, directed first toward grains and munitions in the fall of 1914, speedily included a very large number of American products. The following figures exhibit the changes in our export and import situation brought about by the War:

TOTAL EXPORTS, IMPORTS, AND BALANCE OF TRADE WITH WORLD
(In millions of dollars)

Calendar Year	Total Exports from U. S. A.	Imports into U. S. A.	Excess of Exports over Imports
1914	2,114	1,789	325
1915	3,555	1,779	1,776
1916	5,483	2,392	3,091
1917	6,234	2,952	3,282
1918	6,149	3,031	3,118

EXPORTS, IMPORTS, AND BALANCE OF TRADE WITH EUROPE
(In millions of dollars)

Calendar Year	Exports from U. S. A.	Imports into U. S. A.	Excess of Exports over Imports
1914	1,339	784	556
1915	2,573	546	2,027
1916	3,813	633	3,180
1917	4,062	551	3,511
1918	3,859	318	3,541

EXPORTS AND IMPORTS OF GOLD AND SILVER
(In millions of dollars)

Calendar Year	Gold			Silver		
	Exports	Imports	Excess −Exports +Imports	Exports	Imports	Excess −Exports +Imports
1914	223	57	− 165	52	26	− 26
1915	31	452	+ 421	54	34	− 19
1916	156	686	+ 530	71	32	− 38
1917	372	552	+ 181	84	53	− 31
1918	41	62	+ 21	253	71	− 181

Domestic Merchandise Exported from the United States
(In millions of dollars)

Calendar Year	Crude Materials for Use in Manufacturing	Foodstuffs in Crude Condition and Food Animals	Foodstuffs Partly or Wholly Manufactured
1914	490	275	309
1915	567	462	551
1916	721	421	648
1917	781	509	807
1918	953	547	1,406

Calendar Year	Manufactures for Further Use in Manufacturing	Manufactures Ready for Consumption	Miscellaneous	Total Value
1914 . . .	345	629	23	2,071
1915 . . .	476	1,315	123	3,493
1916 . . .	912	2,625	94	5,423
1917 . . .	1,315	2,706	52	6,170
1918 . . .	1,053	2,069	19	6,048

Merchandise Imported into the United States
(In millions of dollars)

Calendar Year	Crude Materials for Use in Manufacturing	Foodstuffs in Crude Condition and Food Animals	Foodstuffs Partly or Wholly Manufactured
1914	598	235	256
1915	696	243	273
1916	1,010	260	339
1917	1,268	386	352
1918	1,220	346	397

Calendar Year	Manufactures for further Use in Manufacturing	Manufactures Ready for Consumption	Miscellaneous	Total Value
1914 . . .	276	407	18	1,789
1915 . . .	261	292	14	1,779
1916 . . .	418	346	20	2,392
1917 . . .	537	392	18	2,952
1918 . . .	650	405	13	3,031

The figures for net gold imports compared with the figures for balance of trade make it clear that Europe was buying from us on credit on a colossal scale. From July 1, 1914 to November 30, 1918, the total excess of our merchandise exports over imports was $11,169,392,000. The balance with Europe alone was $12,272,-654,000. An early consequence of this very heavy excess of exports was a break in the exchange rates of leading European countries in New York. The very outbreak of the War had seen the exchanges of most of the European countries go high above par, since New York was indebted to Europe in consequence of the heavy selling of securities and could not get gold across the waters in view of the dangers from German and other cruisers. Before the end of the year, however, several of the European exchanges had gone below par and by March of 1915 every one of the European exchanges was at a discount in New York. Europe had departed from the gold basis and Europe had become a debtor on current items to the United States, though still heavily a creditor on investment account. Sterling broke to something like $4.50 a pound in the summer of 1915. Following this break in sterling and the more dramatic declines in other exchanges, a distinguished group of British and French financiers came over to the United States and arranged the Anglo-French Loan of half a billion dollars, the proceeds of which were to be used in protecting sterling and franc exchange and in paying for further exports which the French and British Governments might need. This was the largest foreign loan which had ever been placed in American markets, and virtually the whole financial community, under the leadership of J. P. Morgan & Co., took part in making a success of it. The response of American investors was good, and certain of the larger businesses which were receiving large orders from the British Government for munitions and other exports took a substantial part of the Anglo-French issue. In addition to that we repurchased from Europe something like $2,000,000,000 worth of American securities held abroad.

The following table exhibits the purchases by American investors of foreign government securities during the War:

FOREIGN GOVERNMENT SECURITIES PLACED IN THE UNITED STATES DURING THE WAR PERIOD—Aug. 1, 1914–Nov. 30, 1918

Country	Amount	
Europe:		
United Kingdom of Great Gritain	$700,000,000	
France	449,500,000	
City of Paris	50,000,000	
City of Bordeaux	12,000,000	
City of Lyons	12,000,000	
City of Marseilles	12,000,000	
Norway	5,000,000	
Russia	85,000,000	
Switzerland	5,000,000	
Total for Europe		$1,330,500,000
North and Central America:		
Dominion of Canada	175,000,000	
Canadian Municipal Loans	103,704,279	
Newfoundland	5,000,000	
Panama	3,450,000	
Total for North and Central America		287,154,279
South America:		
Argentina	30,000,000	
Bolivia	2,400,000	
Chile		
City of Valpariso	471,000	
Brazil		
City of Sao Paulo	5,500,000	
Total for South America		38,371,000
Asia:		
China	5,000,000	5,000,000
Grand Total		$1,661,025,279

EXCHANGE RATES AT NEW YORK

(Highest Rates for Months Indicated of Sight Drafts, 1914–1918 and of Cable Transfers, 1919–1922)

	London	Paris	Milan	Yokohoma	Berlin	Copenhagen	Madrid	Buenos Aires	India (Bombay)	Shanghai
Par of Exchange	$4.8665	$0.193	$0.193	$0.4985	$0.9528[1]	$0.268	$0.18[2]	$0.4245[3]	$0.3244[4]	$0.729[5]
1914, June	4.8910	.1942	.1937	.4990	.9544	.2690	.....	.....	.3300	.6400
Dec.	4.8925	.1957	.1912	.....	.9250	.2525	.....	.....	.....	.....
1915, June	4.7856	.1840	.1693	.4940	.8287	.2642	.1908	.4185	.3350	.5650
Dec.	4.7413	.1721	.1535	.5050	.7975	.2800	.1890	.4200	.3300	.6300
1916, June	4.7588	.1695	.1575	.5050	.7712	.3010	.2070	.4225	.3300	.7200
Dec.	4.7569	.1714	.1502	.5088	.7525	.2780	.2125	.4489	.3250	.8900
1917, June	4.7555	.1747	.1421	.5125	.....	.2925	.2365	.4426	.3250	.9238
Dec.	4.7525	.1745	.1252	.5180	.....	.3375	.2440	.4765	.3500	1.1000
1918, June	4.7550	.1750	.1129	.5290	.....	.3125	.2855	.4338	.3850	1.1350
Dec.	4.7585	.1834	.1575	.5325	.....	.2700	.2020	.4515	.3585	1.2500
1919, June	4.6450	.1600	.1277	.5213	.....	.2475	.2012[2]	1.0038[3]	.4300	1.2800[5]
Dec.	3.9950	.1010	.0812	.5075	.0245[1]	.2000	.1995	.9858	.4650	1.7075
1920, June	3.9950	.0840	.0622	.5175	.0276	.1725	.1675	.9693	.4375	1.1700
Dec.	3.5350	.0608	.0369	.5038	.0146	.1580	.1385	.8125	.2875[4]	.8575
1921, June	3.9100	.0847	.0530	.4825	.0158	.1785	.1337	.7326	.2525	.6765
Dec.	4.2295	.0822	.0472	.4799	.0061	.2093	.1519	.7614	.2796	.7638
1922, June	4.5095	.0915	.0523	.4798	.0037	.2218	.1587	.8332	.2918	.7995
Dec.	4.6799	.0761	.0513	.4899	.0002	.2099	.1579	.8637	.3111	.7207

[1] Par value of 4 marks in U. S. currency. The par used from 1919 on is 1 mark equals $0.2382.

[2] The average value of the silver peseta in 1913. In 1919, the par of exchange used in these statistics was changed to the gold peseta, its value being $0.193.

[3] In 1919, the par of exchange used in these statistics was changed to 1 gold peso, equals $0.9648.

[4] A new par of exchange was established in September, 1920, of 1 rupee equals $0.4866.

[5] The par of exchange used from 1914–1918, inclusive, is the average value of the Haikwan tael in 1913, $0.729. From 1919 on, the par of exchange used is the Shanghai tael, which equals $0.6685, and is based on the average value of silver in 1913.

CHAPTER XXVIII

The War and the Federal Reserve System

The Federal Reserve Board was not organized until August 12, 1914, after the outbreak of the War. The Federal Reserve Banks opened for business on November 16, 1914, after the main shock had been met by other agencies, described in a previous chapter. The Aldrich-Vreeland notes, clearing house certificates, which were good between the banks, and the close coöperation of banks, clearing houses, stock and produce exchanges, and the Federal Treasury prevented the crisis of 1914 from developing into a money panic. The flood of gold which came in beginning with December of 1914 created great monetary ease and there was little occasion for banks to rediscount at the Federal Reserve Banks until after the entrance of the United States into the War in April of 1917. Most of the Federal Reserve Banks found difficulty in meeting expenses, to say nothing of paying dividends. In certain of the rural Federal Reserve Districts, notably those centering around Dallas, Kansas City, and Atlanta, rediscounting began promptly. Of one of these districts it has been said that the "earning assets of the Federal-Reserve Bank were waiting at the front door on the day they began business." But the chief asset of most of the Federal Reserve Banks was the non-earning asset, gold, down to April of 1917. On December 22, 1916 the Federal Reserve Banks had only $32,000,000 of rediscounts, $125,000,000 of bills bought in the open market, $43,000,000 of United States Government long-term securities, $11,000,000 of United States Government short-term securities, making a total of earning assets of only $222,000,000. Foreseeing the probability of war from the beginning of 1917, the Federal Reserve Banks strengthened their position by reducing their earning assets and when the War broke out their earning assets were well under $200,000,000. They constituted a great reservoir of unused lending power, and were ready to expand loans and demand liabilities enormously as war finances required it. The table on page 462 makes clear how great was the expansion of Federal Reserve Bank credits in the period that followed April, 1917. The peak of this was reached in November of 1920, in the midst of the great crisis, since which time there has been a very great reduction.

At the outbreak of the War the total stock of gold in the United States was estimated at $3,089,000,000. The United States Treasury held $204,000,000 of this, the Federal Reserve System held $938,000,000 of it, and gold "in circulation," supposed to be largely held by banks, was placed at $1,947,000,000. In the eighteen months that followed about $1,100,000,000 of the gold "in circulation" was turned in to the Federal Reserve Banks being exchanged for Federal Reserve notes or deposit credits, chiefly the former. This was a matter of deliberate policy. The Federal Reserve authorities called on the banks of the country to accumulate and turn in gold and "yellow backs," or gold certificates. The banks responded loyally. Gold and gold certificates in their own vaults were largely turned over to the Federal Reserve Banks and the gold and gold certificates deposited with them were sorted out and turned over to the Federal Reserve Banks. It was demonstrated that gold in the hands of member banks and gold in the hands of the people constitute a true secondary reserve for the Federal Reserve System in emergencies. The same thing, it may be observed, was demonstrated by the War for Germany, France, and Great Britain. Gold in general circulation was turned in on a great scale to the central bank in all of these countries. The great joint stock banks in England, at the request of the Bank of England, turned over their gold to that institution. In France, between the out-

Condition of the Federal Reserve Banks[1] (In millions of dollars)

Date	Total Gold Reserves	Total Cash Reserves	Total Earning Assets	Total Resources	Total Deposits	Federal Reserve Notes in Circulation
1914						
Nov. 20	205	241	6	247	228	2.7
Dec. 31	229	256	11	278	256	10.6
1915						
Mar. 26	242	265	53	333	288	34
June 25	255	303	55	381	311	72
Sept. 24	290	313	79	418	345	116
Dec. 30	345	358	83	491	415	189
1916						
Mar. 31	335	345	135	523	458	163
June 30	377	404	172	625	559	152
Sept. 29	387	395	184	633	561	197
Dec. 29	454	471	222	768	698	275
1917						
Mar. 30	938	947	168	1,256	842	358
June 29	1,295	1,334	495	2,053	1,484	509
Sept. 28	1,408	1,458	505	2,204	1,434	700
Dec. 28	1,671	1,721	1,064	3,101	1,771	1,246
1918						
Mar. 28-29	1,816	1,874	1,202	3,446	1,901	1,453
June 28	1,949	2,006	1,345	3,872	2,050	1,722
Sept. 27	2,021	2,072	2,081	4,817	2,317	2,349
Dec. 27	2,090	2,146	2,318	5,252	2,313	2,685
1919						
Mar. 28	2,142	2,211	2,335	5,230	2,401	2,522
June 27	2,148	2,216	2,354	5,288	2,437	2,499
Sept. 26	2,118	2,188	2,503	5,632	2,542	2,655
Dec. 26	2,078	2,136	3,080	6,325	2,780	3,058
1920						
Mar. 26	1,935	2,057	3,191	6,048	2,542	3,048
June 25	1,969	2,109	3,183	6,075	2,473	3,117
Sept. 24	1,990	2,152	3,310	6,312	2,477	3,280
Dec. 30	2,059	2,249	3,263	6,270	2,321	3,345
1921						
Mar. 25	2,211	2,422	2,692	5,753	1,841	2,931
June 29	2,462	2,625	2,060	5,242	1,686	2,634
Sept. 28	2,726	2,879	1,666	5,107	1,717	2,457
Dec. 28	2,870	2,992	1,536	5,151	1,765	2,443
1922						
Mar. 29	2,975	3,103	1,180	4,816	1,805	2,182
June 28	3,021	3,148	1,180	4,905	1,939	2,124
Sept. 27	3,077	3,203	1,110	4,970	1,840	2,243
Dec. 27	3,040	3,149	1,334	5,305	1,900	2,464

[1] Annual Reports Federal Reserve Board 1914–1920. 1921–22 Weekly Statements.

break of the War and December 18, 1916, the Bank of France had been able to draw in 1,948,000,000 francs of gold from general circulation in exchange for its notes.

There grew up in the course of the War in certain very responsible banking quarters the theory that gold ought not to return to general circulation, but ought to be kept in great reserves where it would be instantly subject to the control of organized banking or public treasuries as a basis for credit. I regard this view as thoroughly unsound. Under normal conditions in a gold standard country, people will be seeing and handling a substantial amount of the actual yellow metal. They will respect their paper money more if they know that it actually represents gold and that gold can be got for it, instantly and without difficulty. The presence of a substantial amount of gold in general circulation has a splendid psychological effect and is a very important factor in combating money heresies. The ordinary man thinks in very simple terms, but is quite capable of understanding the true theory of paper money if that theory is emphasized in his daily practice. The true theory of paper money is that a piece of paper money is a demand promissory note, a promise to pay real money—gold—on demand. If the ordinary man has in his own practice an opportunity to test this principle, to present paper money for redemption, and to have it redeemed, to get gold when he wants it, and to turn in gold for paper when it is more convenient to use the paper, he is not easily misled by fiat money propagandists.

Moreover, it is surely not well that the full lending power of a banking system should be kept employed. There should be large reserves of lending power in ordinary times. If all the gold of the country is accumulated in central reservoirs, and if reserve percentages are allowed to run to extreme heights, the temptation to reduce money rates unduly in the effort to force out loans becomes very great, and political pressure upon central banks to make them reduce rates becomes very great. The theory so widely held, that rates and volume of loans should be dependent upon cash reserves instead of upon the general liquid assets of borrowers, has much too wide currency. It is a false theory. The true basis of credit is the volume of business being done, rather than the volume of cash reserves. When, however, the theory that credit should depend upon reserves is held, and when reserves are made artificially great, the tendency to make unsound loans and to tie up bank funds in illiquid advances is strong. It is better that a country should carry a large part of its cash reserves in the form of a secondary reserve, in the pockets of the people and in the vaults of its commercial banks, rather than all concentrated in the hands of its central bank, or Federal Reserve Banks, as direct reserve.

The Great War has demonstrated that gold in the hands of the people and the private banks is a true secondary reserve. Our Federal Reserve System in the future ought to adopt a flexible policy of paying out gold and gold certificates, and retiring Federal Reserve notes when the gold reserve gets too high and, on the other hand, of drawing back gold and gold certificates in return for Federal Reserve notes if the gold reserve gets uncomfortably low. The member banks would coöperate splendidly in a plan of this sort. It would work automatically. At a suggestion from the Federal Reserve Banks they might, on the one hand, sort out gold and gold certificates to pay into the Federal Reserve Bank in return for Federal Reserve notes, or, when the contrary suggestion is made, they could pay out gold and gold certificates into general circulation and turn into the Federal Reserve Bank the Federal Reserve notes. If it were necessary to give special inducement to the member banks to coöperate in this way, abundant precedent can be found in the policy of the Bank of England which, when it needs gold, makes advances of deposit credits without interest to gold importers who have gold in shipment for England, and which foregoes its right to charge a premium for gold coin over gold bullion when actual gold bullion is deposited with it. Member banks would find an adequate pecuniary inducement to turn in gold and gold certificates to the Federal Reserve Banks if they could thereby get an extra day or two of credit for deposits made in gold.

In the summer of 1917 the Federal Reserve Act was amended by reducing the reserve percentages required of member banks, and at the same time requiring them to carry all their legal reserves in deposits with the Federal Reserve Banks. Gold or "lawful money" held in their own vaults no longer counted as legal reserve. Member banks were thus enabled to use Federal Reserve notes as vault cash and had no longer any legal reason for holding gold or legal tender notes in their own vaults.

Certain of the more conservative banks have still continued to carry substantial amounts of gold and legal tenders in their vaults, particularly gold. This also I regard as good policy. It is good policy from the standpoint of the individual bank which does it as giving it a certain measure of independence of the Federal Reserve authorities in ordinary times, and it is excellent public policy when a good many large banks do it, since it means that when the Federal Reserve ratio goes dangerously low there remains in the hands of important member banks a substantial volume of gold and legal tenders which can be instantly thrown into the common pool, strengthening the Federal Reserve Bank reserve ratio and easing the situation.

It would be selfish and stupid also for a member bank to hold back gold and Federal Reserve notes if the time came when the last ounce of gold and the last dollar of legal tender were needed by the Federal Reserve System. But unadvertised reserves, mobile and instantly available, are a great asset both to banking generally and to a central bank in war and crisis. British financiers have long understood this. The best American bankers understand it. It is usually well to be stronger in fact than you appear to be. No honest banker will minimize his liabilities, but every prudent banker will be conservative in reckoning his assets.

No honest or prudent banking system dare minimize the extent of its demand liabilities, but it may very properly refrain from needlessly advertising the full extent of its liquid assets.

Another amendment in 1917 simplified the process of exchanging gold for Federal Reserve notes, and made it possible to count the gold in the system as reserve for either notes or deposits interchangeably. The original Federal Reserve Act provided that Federal Reserve notes might be issued against commercial paper, with a 40% gold reserve, by the Federal Reserve Agent. The Federal Reserve Banks had very little commercial paper and had an abundance of gold. It was further felt to be desirable that the new gold coming into the country should be concentrated in Federal Reserve Banks and that Federal Reserve notes should be put in circulation instead of the new gold. Had it been possible to take gold to the Federal Reserve Banks and turn it in in direct exchange for Federal Reserve notes it would have been desirable. In this case the Federal Reserve notes would have been almost equivalent to gold certificates.

But the law did not permit this simple exchange. An indirect method was therefore devised. The Federal Reserve Bank would turn over to the Federal Reserve Agent commercial paper to the amount of $100 and gold to the amount of $40, receiving in exchange $100 in Federal Reserve notes. The next step would be to turn in $60 in gold to the Federal Reserve Agent and receive back the commercial paper. The Federal Reserve note was then completely covered by gold and the Federal Reserve Bank was again in possession of its scant supply of commercial paper. The gold was safely impounded in the hands of the Federal Reserve Agent and the Federal Reserve notes were available for general circulation. The process could then be repeated. The same $100 of commercial paper with an additional $40 of gold could be given over by the Federal Reserve Bank to the Federal Reserve Agent in exchange for a second $100 worth of Federal Reserve notes and the commercial paper could again be redeemed by turning over to the Federal Reserve Agent an additional $60 of gold. By this clumsy, but thoroughly legal, process a good many hundred millions of dollars worth of Federal Reserve notes were issued, based on commercial paper and 40% of gold at the time they were issued, but ultimately based on dollar for dollar deposit of gold. Federal Reserve notes were thus outstanding far in excess of the total of commercial paper held by the Federal Reserve Banks.

In the summer of 1917, as stated above, an amendment to the Federal Reserve Act, permitting Federal Reserve notes to be issued directly in exchange for gold, made this cumbersome process unnecessary. This amendment was obviously merely a correction of an oversight in the original act. Central banks generally are only too glad to exchange their notes directly and simply for gold. It is obviously sound public policy that they should be permitted to do so.

The most important work of the Federal Reserve System during the War was in facilitating the financial operations of the United States Government. The finances of the United States Government preceding the war had involved the turnover of less than a billion a year, taken in as taxes and disbursed in payments. In connection with the First Liberty Loan, over $2,000,000,000 dollars were paid into the Federal Treasury in a very short time. In the summer of 1918 something like $4,000,000,000 in taxes was paid in in a few weeks. Every one of the great loans following the First Liberty Loan was of larger amount, the Fourth Liberty Loan producing something like $7,000,000,000. In anticipation of the Liberty Loans and tax payments there were billions of dollars of short-term Treasury Certificates issued. Our banking system, as it stood before the adoption of the Federal Reserve Act, could not possibly have handled transactions of this magnitude. Banks throughout the country having to make payments for their customers to the Federal Treasury would have drawn on their correspondents in reserve and central reserve cities, particularly in New York, and actual cash would have been transferred from the Reserve Banks to the Federal Treasury. Cash payments would have been instantly suspended, and our financial mechanism would have broken down with the First Liberty Loan.

With the Federal Reserve System, however, it was possible to accomplish these vast transactions largely by bookkeeping entries, with a minimum of disturbance in the money market. Call money touched 6% for a short time in June of 1917, falling speedily thereafter to 3% which was the maximum for the month of July, 2% being the minimum for that month. Even June saw a good deal of 2 % call money. Various expedients were employed in this connection. For one thing, the Sub-Treasury System was virtually abandoned. The Secretary of the Treasury had discretion as to whether he would deposit Government moneys with the Federal Reserve Banks, with other banks, or in actual cash in the vaults of the Sub-Treasuries. This discretion was admirably used. The Federal Treasury made deposits all over the country, picking out those sections and those institutions where strain was likely to develop because unusually large demands on loan account or tax account were likely to have to be made. Heavy withdrawals were balanced by heavy deposits so that the strain was very evenly distributed. In the second place, the Treasury policy of preceding the great loans and heavy tax payments by the marketing of short-term Treasury Certificates, which would mature on the dates when tax payments or payments of the Liberty Loans were due, greatly relieved the stress. The Government was making great disbursements in payment of maturing Treasury Certificates on the days when it was having large receipts from taxes or from the proceeds of Liberty Loans. The matter was made still simpler by arrangements under which the Treasury received maturing Treasury Certificates in payment for taxes or for Liberty Bonds, making it unnecessary in many cases to draw checks or to touch deposit balances.

Another device was the inauguration by the Federal Reserve Board of a gold settlement fund in Washington analogous to the gold fund on deposit in the New York Clearing House. This greatly reduced the necessity for the shipment of gold from one Federal Reserve Bank to another, since debits and credits at the gold settlement fund at Washington would serve instead. There still remained the necessity for gold shipments between the different Federal Reserve Banks and the gold settlement fund at Washington, but even this was much reduced by the use of "suspense accounts" and by the earmarking of gold held by a Federal Reserve Bank for the gold settlement fund, which might subsequently be released if a few days later the Federal Reserve Bank in question gained adequate credits at the gold settlement fund.

Most important of all, however, was the provision in the Federal Reserve Act under which the Federal Reserve Board could require one Federal Reserve Bank to rediscount for another. It was this provision which has made our Federal Reserve System really function as a true central banking system and has made possible the pooling of the gold reserves of the whole country to meet emergencies. Until this provision was inserted in the Federal Reserve Act the present writer and his associates in the American Bankers Association were opposed to the Federal Reserve System. When this provision was agreed to they withdrew their opposition.

The efficiency of the Federal Reserve System in handling the great problems of the War and the post-War crisis is a supreme vindication of this attitude on our part. So long as one Federal Reserve Bank had gold, all the Federal Reserve Banks had gold. If, on a given day, the bank at Boston found its gold reserves going below the safety point as heavy demands were made upon it in making remittances to the Federal Treasury, but at the same time the Federal Reserve Bank of Richmond found itself with more gold than it needed, the Federal Reserve

Board, informed by telegraph of the position of each bank, could direct the bank at Richmond to rediscount paper for the bank at Boston and credit the bank at Boston with part of its gold in the gold settlement fund. The bank at Boston would then ship commercial paper to the bank at Richmond and, even before the commercial paper was received, the reserve ratios of the two banks would be equalized by bookkeeping entries at Washington, and the situation left perfectly safe. After the inauguration of the daily settlement in connection with the gold settlement fund at Washington, which began on July 1, 1918, the Federal Reserve authorities at Washington were in daily telegraphic communication with the twelve Federal Reserve Banks, and were daily making such adjustments of rediscounts among the twelve Federal Reserve Banks as were necessary to keep their reserve ratios approximately equalized or, at all events, sufficiently equalized to prevent anyone from going below the point of safety. In the crisis of 1920 there were times when one or two of the weaker Federal Reserve Banks would have been almost completely denuded of gold had they been dependent entirely on their own gold reserves. With the system of inter-regional rediscounting, however, all were abundantly protected, all were safe at every stage, and all were put in a position to do their full duty in protecting their member banks.

The figures in the table on page 462 illustrate strikingly the expansion of rediscounts and of demand liabilities of the Federal Reserve Banks in connection with War finance and in connection with post-War boom and crisis. In a later chapter on the gold and rediscount policy of the Federal Reserve Banks a further analysis is given, showing the relation between member bank expansion and Federal Reserve Bank expansion, together with a discussion of the principles involved. The Federal Reserve Banks stood ready to rediscount paper, and particularly Government paper, to the full limit of the needs of War finances. They also, during the period of the War, inaugurated a system of discrimination in the matter of credit extension, seeking to reduce credits to non-essential industries and to increase credits for essential industries. They did this largely through advice and suggestions to member banks. An act of Congress, moreover, created the Capital Issues Committee of the Federal Reserve Board which sought to limit the issue of new securities by non-essential industries, subsequently turning over this work to the War Finance Corporation.

At two points the War policy of the Federal Reserve Board is subject to severe critisicm, though it is proper to state that at these two points the Federal Reserve Board was subject to control of the United States Treasury and really surrendered its policy to Treasury dictation. It is regrettable that political control of any kind should have entered the Federal Reserve System. The War emergency and the necessity for coöperation with all policies of the Government, whether expedient or inexpedient, may doubtless be urged in defense of the Board and urged with great force. It is with no desire to criticize individuals that the following comments are made. Rather, taking the War policy of the Federal Reserve Board, and of the Federal Treasury, as a whole, the writer would commend it highly, and he would wish to be understood as giving generous commendation to the able and patriotic men who handled vast problems so ably and honestly. But the historian must also be a critic if history is to be of use, and where mistakes were made they should be pointed out.

The first criticism is that the Federal Reserve authorities surrendered control of their discount policy during the War, and in the two years following the War, to the fiscal policy of the Treasury, and made rediscounts rates much lower than they should have been, in order to facilitate the Treasury's policy of borrowing as cheaply as possible from the people. There was an artificial ease in the money markets which increased the difficulty of denying credits to non-essential industries. This did serious harm during the War and did much worse harm after the restraints on non-essential borrowing were released in the boom period which followed the War.

The second criticism relates to the gold policy of the Federal Reserve System during the War. Control over shipments of gold to foreign countries was taken over by the Federal Reserve Board, and, with few and minor exceptions, gold shipments to foreign countries were stopped. Payments of gold in redemption of Federal Reserve notes were largely abandoned and manufacturing jewelers and others needing bullion in the country were greatly handicapped in getting it. In other words, even the United States for a time abandoned the gold standard during the War, and abandoned the gold standard at a time when the gold reserves in the hands of the redeeming agencies exceeded $2,000,000,000. It was an indefensible policy and a policy which would certainly have led to serious currency disorders had the War lasted much longer. Even as the matter stood, a premium on gold did appear in California and other Coast States, along the Mexican Border, and on the East Side in New York, In addition dollar drafts were allowed to go to a very great discount in Spain, in other European neutral markets, in the Argentine, in Valparaiso, and in Japan.

The two policies criticized were essentially connected. One of the reasons for preventing gold from leaving the country and for not paying out gold in redemption of Federal Reserve notes was to keep an enormously high reserve ratio in order that color of validity might be given to the policy of low rediscount rates. This was not the only reason for the suspension of gold payments or for control over gold shipments. Our American financial authorities were in part imbued with the unsound Continental doctrine regarding gold reserves. It is hardly a caricature of the Continental doctrine to say that it holds that gold reserves are to be accumulated, advertised, and admired. The British doctrine, on the other hand, has always been that gold reserves are accumulated in quiet times in order that they may be *used* in emergencies.

The present writer has never had any sympathy with failure to pay on demand. Reserves are to be used when needed. Bankers accumulate reserves in order that they may always be able to meet their demand liabilities on demand. Unless they intend to use them it is folly to accumulate them. The first duty of a banker or other debtor is to meet his obligations on demand and at maturity. It is strange reasoning which would lead a government or a central bank to feel that it can preserve its credit better by refusing to meet its legal obligations than by meeting them!

The Governmental policy of borrowing money at artificially low rates was pernicious from several points of view. In the first place it threw upon the money markets, as a patriotic duty, the burden of supporting the Liberty Bond market. Bankers and investors did this as long as they could, but in the great crisis which followed the War the pressure became so heavy that some of the Liberty Bonds went to a discount of 17% or 18%, at which price a great many holders, including both great banks and small holders, took their losses. Indeed, at the time of subscribing for most of the Liberty Loans, a great many well-informed investors bought the bonds knowing full well that they would have to take losses on them and in the expectation of taking their losses by selling at a discount as soon as they were sure that the Loan was oversubscribed.

Much more fundamental, however, is the point that artificially low money rates encouraged unnecessary borrowing and unnecessary spending, and discouraged capital accumulation. When capital is really scarce—and a great war necessarily makes a scarcity of real capital—it is vicious policy to create the false impression of abundance of capital through controlled money market operations.

Fortunately, as we shall later see, patriotic restraints led to a great deal of economy on the part of our people during the War, and while the War itself lasted the low rediscount rates did not do great harm. The chief evil came in the period that followed the War.

On October 13, 1917, the President of the United States issued an appeal to the State banks and trust companies to enter the Federal Reserve System as a war-time measure. Many of the leading State institutions, including the great trust companies of New York City, did so. Something like two-thirds in number of the thirty thousand banking institutions in the United States still remain outside the Federal Reserve System, but, measured in volume of resources and capital, by far the greater part of the banking power of the country is enrolled in the system.

Federal Reserve Banks have established various branches and agencies at home and abroad. The Bank of England and the Bank of France have become agencies of the Federal Reserve Bank of New York. The Federal Reserve Bank of San Francisco has made the Philippine National Bank its agent and has established branches at Seattle, Spokane, Portland, and Salt Lake City. The Federal Reserve Bank of Chicago has established a branch at Detroit. The Cleveland Federal Resérve Bank has placed branches at Cincinnati and Pittsburgh. Various other Federal Reserve branches have been established.

The Federal Reserve Act authorized national banks and member banks to establish foreign branches. A number of the leading institutions of the United States established branches in various foreign countries under this authorization, some of which have been closed as a result of unfortunate experiences in 1919 and 1920.

CHAPTER XXIX

CHANGES IN THE CURRENCY DURING THE WAR—MONETARY HERESIES

THE Great War and the coming of the Federal Reserve System have led to a number of interesting and significant changes in the circulating money of the United States. Two new types of paper money have been introduced: (1) the Federal Reserve note, and (2) the Federal Reserve Bank note. The former is a truly elastic bank note issued against deposits of gold or against discount of commercial paper, expanding and contracting with the needs of trade. This note is the largest single element in our circulation today. It has been adequately described in preceding chapters. The other note referred to is of minor and now diminishing importance and is issued by the Federal Reserve Banks on the principle of the old national bank notes. It is secured by approved Government securities, chiefly short-term certificates.

An Act, signed by the President on April 23, 1918, authorized the retirement of silver certificates, which had constituted the largest element in the paper money of the United States, and the melting down of the silver dollars, held dollar for dollar as reserve for these certificates. The purpose was to release silver for shipment to the Far East. Rupee exchange and exchange on Shanghai and Hong Kong had risen greatly as against both sterling and dollars, and in order to protect sterling and dollars in the Far Eastern markets it was regarded as desirable to ship silver to these countries. An opportunity was here presented largely to get rid forever of the anomalous silver certificates which were a heritage from the Bland-Allison Silver Act and the Sherman Silver Act. These silver certificates, although redeemable in silver coin, were really protected in value by the fact that gold lay behind them ultimately and that the Government has the responsibility of preserving all forms of money at a parity. The silver reserve was not the real reserve behind them. It was virtually a dead asset in the Treasury. The position of the Treasury would have been greatly improved had it been able, definitely and finally, to get rid of this old sore spot. The silver interests, however, were still strong enough to insist that the Government should continue to protect the silver markets, and representatives of the silver States were able to insert into the Pittman Act the provision that the Government should subsequently repurchase silver to an amount equal to the silver dollars melted down, at the fixed price of $1 an ounce and restore the silver, or silver certificates, to circulation.

No harm would be done in leaving actual silver dollars in circulation to the extent that the West and South desire them, but circulation of silver certificates might well have been dispensed with to the full extent that this situation made possible.

The turning in of silver certificates created a shortage of one dollar and two dollar bills. This was anticipated, and the Pittman Act provided for Federal Reserve Bank notes (not Federal Reserve notes) in denominations of one and two dollars to meet the shortage. This situation gave rise to the creation of most of the Federal Reserve Bank notes which were issued. The largest amount outstanding at any one time was $270,522,800 on January 7, 1920. After the Armistice the Treasury began the policy of buying domestic silver at a dollar an ounce. The volume of silver certificates was again increased and the volume of Federal Reserve Bank notes, *pari passu*, declined to a figure of $116,670,400 in January, 1922.

The shortage of one and two dollar bills was also made by a change in the denomination of the old United States notes (Greenbacks) as we have seen on page 376. By the Act of 1900 provision was made that Greenbacks under $10 were to be retired as smaller silver certificates were issued, but as a matter of convenience the small denominations of the Greenbacks were restored in 1917. During the fiscal year ending June 30, 1917, there were issued $10,304,000 in one dollar Greenbacks and $9,216,000 in two dollar Greenbacks.

The growth of the country and the growth of the country's gold holdings have made the old controversies over the Greenbacks and the silver currency matters of secondary importance. Both the Greenbacks and the silver constitute small fractions of our total circulation today. The fight for sound money, in so far as Greenbacks and silver are concerned, is won. Subtler forms of money heresies are now presenting themselves. One of these is the proposal of Professor Irving Fisher for a "stabilized dollar" regarding which the Currency Commission of the American Bankers Association (composed of A. Barton Hepburn, Chairman; James B. Forgan, Vice Chairman, M. T. Herrick, F. J. Wade, G. M. Reynolds, O. E. Dunlap, Luther Drake, Sol Wexler, Robert Wardrop, E. F. Swinney, A. J. Frame, J. F. Sartori, L. L. Rue, C. A. Hinsch, E. L. Howe) had the following to say in its report at the Washington meeting of the Association, October, 1920:

At the annual convention of the American Bankers Association in 1919, Dr. Irving Fisher, of Yale University, addressed the convention upon the subject of "Stabilizing the Dollar," and submitted a plan designed to accomplish such result. The Executive Council voted that the subject be referred to the Currency Commission for report.

The commission has been provided with literature for and against the proposition. The principal literature in favor of Dr. Fisher's plan for stabilizing the dollar is contained in his own book published by Macmillan Company, in which he discusses the subject with great force and clearness. He has approached the subject from all angles, raising and answering from his standpoint all possible questions or objections. We also put before the commission a briefer presentation and discussion by Dr. Fisher of his plan. The commission was also furnished with discussion of Professor Fisher's plan by leading economists and financiers who do not approve of the same. For instance, Dr. Carl C. Plehn, professor of economics, University of California; Dr. E. R. A. Seligman, professor of economics, Columbia University, and formerly president of the American Economic Association; Dr. David Kinley, president of the University of Illinois and formerly president of the American Economic Association; Dr. B. M. Anderson, Jr., economist of the Chase National Bank in New York; Dr. H. P. Willis, professor of banking at Columbia University and formerly secretary of the Federal Reserve Board; Dr. J. H. Hollander, professor of economics at John Hopkins University; Dr. F. W. Taussig, professor of economics, Harvard University, formerly president of the American Economic Association; Dr. J. L. Laughlin, emeritus professor of economics, Chicago University; Dr. David Friday, professor of economics, University of Michigan; Mr. Andrew J. Frame, economist, Waukesha, Wis.

The Currency Commission has given very careful study to Dr. Fisher's proposal. We have examined the literature bearing upon the subject, pro and con. It is our conclusion that Professor Fisher's plan, though interesting and ably worked out, is wholly impractical, and would involve grave dangers to the stability of our financial and monetary system. It would lead to foreign drains on our gold in any period of crisis, since the plan calls for lightening the gold behind the dollar when prices fall, and foreigners, foreseeing this, would draw down their balances in this country and sell "dollars" short, before the Government could make the change. The plan would also make difficult, if not impossible, the maintenance of gold redemption in periods of rapidly rising prices. If adopted at the present time it would perpetuate all the suffering which recipients of fixed incomes have experienced as a result of the rapidly rising prices of the war. It would be wholly out of the question for the United States alone to adopt it, as Professor Fisher proposes, and almost no other great country is in a position to meet gold obligations on demand. Had the plan been in operation at the outbreak of the great war in 1914, it would have broken down, as Professor Fisher now admits. It could not, therefore, have prevented the war-time rise in prices, and consequently most of the claims which Professor Fisher has made for it must be abandoned. The great economic evils of the war have grown out of wasteful consumption and destruction, demoralization and interruptions of transportation, and the withdrawal of many millions of men from production, the whole combining to create great scarcities of goods. No change in the monetary system could have prevented this evil. The plan could not, therefore, have been a remedy for social distress and discontent.

Professor Fisher's plan involves the modification of contracts calling for payment in "gold coin of the United States of the present weight and fineness," by substituting the "stabilized dollar" for the dollar of fixed weight and fineness. Your commission is not in sympathy with this feature of the plan.

Our judgment is, therefore, definitely adverse to Professor Fisher's plan.

Our judgment is further very definitely adverse to the proposal that the American Bankers Association should memorialize Congress to appoint a commission to investigate this matter and to determine whether a law embodying the plan should be adopted by Congress. We believe it is unwise to agitate changes in the gold standard at the present time. Proposals looking toward the creation of new currency systems divorced from the gold standard are being made in many places. Many of them are of an extremely wild and dangerous character. Professor Fisher's plan, to be sure, retains the element of redemption of gold, even though in a varying amount of gold. But there are many proposals whch involve the abandonment of gold altogether and the creation of *fiat* money pure and simple. It is our view that the banking profession should set itself firmly against agitation of any schemes of this sort. The next ten years will see a prolonged contest between the defenders of sound money and the advocates of unsound plans, especially in Europe, and it is our view that the banking profession of the United States should concern itself with the maintenance in the United States and restoration in Europe of the old-fashioned gold standard, rather than with any effort to introduce refinements and novelties.

In an appendix we submit various documents bearing upon Professor Fisher's plan. The plan itself is stated most fully by Professor Fisher in his book, "Stabililizing the Dollar," published by Macmillan in 1920. This book is ably and interestingly written, and members of the Association, who wish fullest information regarding Professor Fisher's proposal, are advised to consult this book.

We call your attention especially to the fact that the economists whom we have quoted and who have written in opposition to Professor Fisher's plan are among the very ablest men in the economic field. The weight of their combined judgment strengthens decidely our confidence in our own adverse conclusions regarding Professor Fisher's plan.

Should the convention print the data herewith submitted and made a part of this report, members of the Association will have at their command a very full and able presentation of both sides of the question.

Respectfully submitted,

CURRENCY COMMISSION,

A. Barton Hepburn, Chairman Advisory Board,
Chase National Bank, New York, *Chairman.*

Jas. B. Forgan, Chairman of Board,
First National Bank, Chicago, Ill., *Vice-Chairman.*

(In signing the report, Mr. Forgan added the following:

"I have read Dr. Fisher's book, 'Stabilizing the Dollar,' also the discussion of his plan by quite a number of authorities, the great majority of whom arrive at conclusions adverse to the plan.

"While it is possible that Dr. Fisher's plan might work out if established under normal conditions and if a guaranty could be had that normal conditions would permanently prevail, I am satisfied that it would break down whenever conditions came under any abnormal stress and would be a hindrance rather than a help when facing such sudden abnormality of conditions as were produced by the war and which still continue.

"Under our present system the government gold certificates of fluctuating redeemable value would, as do the present gold certificates of definite value, practically all find lodgement in the Federal reserve banks as the basic reserves for the credit structure which has been built up in the shape of Federal reserve notes, Federal reserve deposits and the deposits of the member banks. The actual circulation of these gold certificates themselves would be practically nil. I cannot, therefore, believe that a fluctuation, restricted to 1 per cent. a month, in the value of the gold forming the reserve basis for such a structure of credit as now exists would have much if any effect on the prices of goods and merchandise for which these various forms of circulating credits are exchangeable.

"When credits are expanded to the extent they now are and as long as merchandise can be bought and paid for, not by the gold certificates themselves, but by credit instruments for which the gold certificates are merely deposited as a small basic reserve, no slight change in the value of the metal represented by these certificates will, in my opinion, have the desired effect of lowering or raising the prices of merchandise.")

Another dangerous proposal was the so-called gold bonus plan dealt with by another committee of the American Bankers Association, composed of George M. Reynolds, Chairman; A. Barton Hepburn, and Lawrence E. Sands, in the following report:—

REPORT OF GOLD BONUS COMMITTEE

To the Administrative Committee, American Bankers Association,

We, the undersigned committee, appointed to consider and report our opinion of the McFadden Bill, submit the following as embodying our views:

The McFadden Bill, so-called, provides for a tax of fifty cents per pennyweight of fine gold for all gold manufactured, used or sold for other than coinage or monetary purposes, including jewelry and other purposes of ornamentation and dentistry (with some exceptions for children and charity cases). The bill provides further that out of the funds, thus collected and "any other funds in the Treasury of the United States not used for specified purposes" there shall be paid a bonus to the producers of new gold in the United States of $10 per fine ounce down to May 1, 1925, and that thereafter both the tax and the premium shall be readjusted annually by certain government officers in accordance with the commodity price index number, as determined by the Bureau of Labor Statistics. The tax and the premium are both to rise or fall after May 1, 1925, according as the index number rises or falls. In behalf of the bill it is argued that the general increase in prices and wages in the United States has raised the cost of gold production, while the price of gold is fixed at $1 for every 23.22 grains of fine gold; that as a consequence of the fixed price and rising costs the profits of gold production are cut and the mines where low grade ore is worked are in some cases being forced to close, with the result that gold production in the United States, which stood at about $89,000,000 in 1913, was cut to $58,488,000 in 1919—a reduction of around $30,000,000—whereas the industrial consumption of gold, which stood at about $45,000,000 in 1913, increased to over $80,000,000 in 1919. The result is that whereas we had a large surplus for monetary purposes in 1913, we were obliged to draw on our monetary stock of gold for industrial purposes in 1919 to the extent of about $22,000,000. It is urged that this consumption of gold money for industrial purposes, cutting into our gold reserve, constitutes a national emergency, and that a measure both to reduce the industrial consumption of gold (by taxation) and to increase the production of gold (by a bonus) is called for. It is further argued that if relief is not given to gold miners by some measure some gold mines will be abandoned permanently, particularly the deep mines which will fill with water and other mines where timbering will deteriorate to such an extent that the mines will become unsafe for operation.

CREDIT DEFLATION THE CURE

It can hardly be contended that the loss of $22,000,000 of gold per year from our monetary stock of around $3,000,000,000 constitutes a national emergency. When the gold embargo was removed the United States had the largest gold supply of any country in the world's history, a supply so abnormally great that every banker and economist knew that it could not be permanently held, and practically all students were agreed that it was desirable that a substantial part of it should leave the country. Its presence made possible an over-expansion of credit in the United States and the outflow which has since taken place of three or four hundred millions has actually made our situation far safer than it was, by imposing a check upon credit expansion. The best banking opinion of the country looks forward to a progressive and far-reaching contraction of our credit fabric and regards it as the only alternative to such a disastrous disruption of the credit system as Japan has recently seen. The proper course to take is not by artificial methods to seek to expand the gold basis of our credit system, but rather to contract the superstructure of credit to a point where it can be safely maintained under conditions of a normal distribution of the world's gold supply. The problem of gold production is an international and not a national problem. Our national stock of gold is dependent, not upon the difference between gold production and gold consumption in the United States, amounting to a few tens of millions, but rather upon the world-wide consumption and production of gold, and upon the course of international trade. If at any time the banking situation calls for more gold in the United States, we can purchase it in the international gold markets far more cheaply than we can obtain it by the doubtful method of an expensive bonus on new gold produced in the United States, which could at best make a difference of only two or three tens of millions per annum. Gold imports and exports of the United States in the first four months of 1920, running between two and three hundred million dollars, were far more significant than any difference that could be made by the gold bonus plan in our stock of gold would amount to in several years.

The increased industrial consumption of gold following the armistice, was partly temporary, a phenomenon growing out of the relaxation of war-time economies. Our people, who had repressed their desire for luxuries during the war, turned suddenly extravagant and bought jewelry of all kinds lavishly. This tendency may be undesirable and probably is. Extravagance of all kinds should be suppressed. The policy of a general tax on luxuries may be commended, and a tax on jewelry, as part of such a general tax, may well be advisable, but a *differential* tax on gold as a raw material of production is a different matter, and one which no national emergency calls for.

The essential elements of the gold standard are: (1) the instant convertibility of all forms of representative money in gold on demand; (2) the free coinage of gold bullion; (3) the unrestricted melting down of gold coin into bullion; (4) the uninterrupted flow of gold from money into the arts, and the uninterrupted flow of gold from the arts into money; (5) the free export and import of gold. A tax of this kind, interfering with the free flow of gold into the arts, thus violates one of the basic elements of the gold standard.

From the outbreak of the great war in Europe our industrial system has been under an increasing strain. Our markets have been drained increasingly of goods and supplies for Europe. The one-sided flow of commodities to Europe has been financed from the beginning, in considerable part, by expanding bank credit in the United States; the resultant shortage of goods, together with expanding bank credit, have raised prices high, and as a consequence costs of production of all kinds have risen. These conditions were intensified by our own entry into the war. Our government spent many billions of dollars, raised by taxes, bond issues and borrowings from the banks, resulting in increased shortages of goods and increased prices, which increased the strain on our industrial system. During the war four or five million able-bodied men were withdrawn from the ranks of industry and entered the military and naval service of the United States, while many more millions were diverted from the production of ordinary goods to the production of war-time materials and supplies. A labor shortage necessarily resulted, with a material increase in wages.

While some industries, owing to the rise in war-time prices, have made very large profits, many others have suffered. Among these were the gold mines producing low-grade ore. A number of these, because of the increased cost of production and labor shortage, were obliged to suspend. This was true, however, of copper and iron as well as gold. The well-known Treadwell mine, possessing a large volume of low-grade ore, was obliged to suspend. Others very likely suspended production from the same cause. Some continued, hoping for a change in conditions. But gold miners are not the only ones who have suffered. Traction companies, for example, having a stipulated fare, usually a nickel, have suffered severely. The different states having refused to make it possible for the traction companies to earn expenses by allowing them increased compensation for their service, somewhat in proportion to the general advance in costs. The steam railways have a just claim upon the public for increased compensation in order to enable them to maintain efficiency and to render the public good service. Universities and charitable institutions, with income derived largely from bonds, have found themselves in many cases in desperate plight as a consequence of the rise in prices, with no increase in income. Widows and orphans, trust funds, public officers, and in general all recipients of fixed incomes, have suffered.

A large body of other industries whose costs have risen faster than their prices have similarly suffered.

Recognizing that no national emergency exists calling for special treatment of the gold mining industry, it is difficult to make a case for singling out the gold mining industry for special relief from the government. That it has suffered is unfortunate, but it is one of the costs of the war. It is one among a large class of those which the war has injured.

Gold mining, however, though suffering under present conditions, enjoys a peculiar advantage which few other industries enjoy. As a consequence of the fact that gold is the standard of value, the price of gold in terms of gold money is necessarily fixed. The demand for gold, however, is always unlimited. The gold miner can always sell at a fixed price as much gold as he can possibly produce. He finds his costs rising in periods of boom and prosperity, and he suffers as a consequence. On the other hand, periods of adversity, depression and falling prices bring to the gold miner, as to no one else, increased profits. He has an unlimited market in the worst depression, and the more severe the depression the lower his costs of production tend to be. He is at present suffering in an intensified form from the upswing of prices and costs. He has in the past, however, enjoyed periods of prosperity when the rest of the community was suffering, and in the natural course of things he may look forward to the recurrence of similar situations.

In reality, the propaganda in favor of doing something for gold is exactly on a par with the propaganda in favor of doing something for silver, about which we heard so much a generation ago. It has no more stable foundation than did the silver propaganda. There is nothing to justify government interference in behalf of this industry, or to justify a government bounty upon the production of virgin gold. *Per contra*, there is very much to be said against such action on the part of the government.

ARGUMENTS AGAINST BONUS

We may pass briefly over the difficulties of the administration of such an act; the danger that frauds would be practiced upon the government; the difficulty of distinguishing virgin from old gold melted down. Gold which differs from other gold merely in having a special history, and which, by virtue of that special history rather than its intrinsic qualities, commands a high premium, presents an anomaly inconsistent with the normal functioning of a free gold market and the normal functioning of the gold standard. The temptation to *manufacture history* instead of mining gold would be very great.

Again the provisions in the McFadden bill, introducing the index number of commodity prices as a basis for fixing the rate of taxes on gold manufacture and of premium on gold mining, constitutes an opening wedge for the general introduction of the index number as a standard of value in the United States in accordance with Professor Irving Fisher's plan for "Stabilizing the Dollar." It is beyond the province of this paper to deal with that plan *in extenso*. Your committee believes in the gold standard and does not believe in tampering with it or interfering with it in the present critical condition of the world's monetary affairs. There is, moreover, another committee of the American Bankers Association, which is to make a detailed report upon the project. We shall content ourselves, for the present, with pointing out that, if this index number standard is to be adopted, it should be considered on its own merits and not introduced "by the back door" as a feature of the McFadden bill.

DANGER TO GOLD STANDARD

The greatest objection of all, however, lies in the danger which this measure would involve to the gold standard itself. Nearly all of the European states are on a paper basis. Only a few of the smaller countries of Europe are even approximately maintaining the gold standard. The United States, *par excellence*, and Japan as well, stand out conspicuously as nations maintaining the gold standard. All the world believes that our dollars are as good as gold. All the other nations of the world are struggling and hoping to get back to the gold standard. We enjoy a proud preëminence in this respect, and it should be zealously guarded and maintained. The belief which obtains in the world today that our dollars are as good as gold must be maintained. The whole world must be convinced that money can be deposited in this country at any time and withdrawn at any time in any form which the depositor may elect.

Offering to pay a premium for the production of gold in this country instead of strengthening our position would weaken it. Instead of assuring the world that the gold standard would be maintained by the United States, it would raise a doubt. Public sentiment throughout the world would at once assume that our position is weak, that we are in danger of going on a paper basis, and that it is in order to guard against this, we regard it as expedient to pay a premium on the production of gold. Great Britain, with far greater difficulties than we are facing, has resolutely refused to do anything of the sort in reply to the petition of her South African gold miners. Unable to maintain the gold standard in its integrity, she has frankly permitted an open gold market in which the depreciation of her paper money could be measured. The so-called "premium" on gold in London represents not a real premium on gold bullion in standard gold coin, but rather merely a "discount" on British paper money. Action of the kind proposed by the United States would be a red flag to the commercial world. The passage of the McFadden bill, instead of strengthening confidence in the position of the United States would weaken it. It would be considered as a confession of weakness. The McFadden bill should be opposed by every well-wisher of this country's credit and commercial and financial prosperity.

The present situation of high costs of production is abnormal and temporary. When our wholly abnormal balance of trade is reduced, leaving three or four hundred million dollars' worth of goods per month for our domestic markets to absorb, which they have not been absorbing; when labor gets over its illusion that prosperity can be maintained by the shortening of hours and by reduced efficiency, accompanied by higher wages; and when the strain in our money market is relaxed through reduced extravagance and increased savings on the part of our people, and their government, most of the present derangements in our industrial system will disappear.

Increase of gold mining will return with normal conditions. It must not be forgotten, however, that part of the automatic working of the gold standard depends upon an increase in gold production when prices are low and upon a decrease in gold production when prices are high. Increased gold production in a period of low prices and low costs makes it easier for prices to rise again, while diminished gold production in periods of high prices and high costs tends to reduce prices and costs again.

Moreover, the industrial consumption of gold tends to increase in a period of high prices, since the price of gold does not rise as other prices rise, while in a period of low prices the prices of gold manufactures are relatively high, and purchases of gold manufactures consequently tend to diminish. Variations in the consumption of gold thus also work toward diminishing the supply of free gold when prices are too high, and toward increasing the supply when prices are too low, thus tending to correct both the rise and the fall of prices. In this feature of gold production and consumption we have one of the stabilizing factors in the gold standard. The McFadden bill proposes to strike at this automatic regulator and corrective. It would aggravate the very conditions which it seeks to remedy.

GEO. M. REYNOLDS, *Chairman*
LAWRENCE E. SANDS
A. BARTON HEPBURN

Other dangerous proposals are dealt with in a later chapter on the gold and rediscount policy of the Federal Reserve Banks. Even the fiat money heresy, however, has recently reappeared in utterances by distinguished technologists and entrepreneurs, and it is probable that the time will never come when the sound banker and economist will not need to combat the idea that governmental fiat can create something out of nothing, that promises to pay on demand may be made without being kept, and that long time loans may properly be negotiated without interest payments.

CHAPTER XXX

THE POST–WAR BOOM AND THE CRISIS OF 1920

FEW of us realized, on Armistice Day, the extent of the financial, industrial, social, and political demoralization of Europe. Few indeed were pessimistic enough to anticipate the evils that were to follow. We expected that Europe would soon go to work again; that the tens of millions of soldiers would return to the ranks of industry; that the public treasuries would reverse their policies of extravagant expenditure, and would put through the necessary increases in taxation. We expected the enormous floating debts of the warring countries to be funded into long-time loans, and the greatly expanded issues of irredeemable bank notes to be reduced, as States paid their debts to the State banks of issue, so that the banks might work back to a policy of gold redemption. As a consequence of these policies in Europe, we expected Europe to cease to buy American goods on the war-time scale and we expected Europe to increase very greatly the export of her own products to this country, thus working back to a state of balanced trade. We recognized that for a time, it would be necessary for us to send unusual amounts of certain supplies to Europe, necessary for rehabilitation and even for current consumption, but in view of the creditor position which the United States had acquired during the war, we thought it probable that in a year or two the tide of exports would turn and the United States might be receiving an import surplus.

Anticipating these things, we expected a sharp drop in commodity prices following shortly after the Armistice and a rapid liquidation and readjustment in the United States, working toward pre-war levels. Business men and bankers, more or less generally, expected this and the country was braced for it. Had we had our post-war reaction and liquidation in its full rigor shortly following the Armistice, the country would have borne the shock easily.

Following the Armistice, there came a price reaction of from 8 to 10%, according to Dun's and Bradstreet's index numbers of wholesale prices. There came also a rapid liquidation of commercial loans to the banks and a very great contraction in the volume of Federal Reserve notes outstanding. The country was in a liquid position and a contraction of credits followed quickly on a contraction of business and falling prices. Early in February of 1919, I had occasion to remark that if it were not for the Government, which was marketing short-time Treasury certificates on a great scale, the banks would have no customers. Commercial loans were going down every day.

In March, however, the reaction was clearly slowing down. In April business sentiment began to change rapidly and in May the strong upward movement, of prices and volume of business and inquiry for bank loans, was unmistakable. In the year that followed, prices rose to levels well above those reached during the war itself. The volume of bank loans expanded something like 25% between May of 1919 and May of 1920, and we had the most feverish financial and industrial boom since 1837.

The explanation of this was largely given in certain private memoranda which the present writer and certain of his banking friends interchanged in May and early in June, 1919, although all the factors were not in evidence until the end of the year. The main explanation is to be found in the fact that Europe did not go back to work and that Europe continued to draw from the outside world gigantic supplies of goods for immediate consumption, including luxuries. Clear evidence of this was contained in the export and import figures for the early part of 1919. Our export balance had averaged $248,000,000 per month in the ten months preceding the Armistice. The export balance rose to $409,000,000 in January, 1919. It reached $442,000,000 in April, 1919. In June, 1919, our excess of exports reached the stupendous figure of $635,000,000; our exports, in that month, approaching one billion.

Down to the middle of May, 1919, this enormous excess of exports over imports was largely made possible by advances made by the United States Treasury to European Allies. Our Allies used these funds for a considerable part in supporting the exchange market, which made it possible for private importers in Europe to buy whatever they chose from private exporters in the United States. Thus, bills drawn in francs by New York exporters on Paris importers would be purchased by banking representatives of the French Government in New York with dollars drawn from the United States Treasury. In May and June, we expected that this process would come to an end as our Government ceased making these advances. We expected that the exchange rates would drop violently, and that the falling exchange rates would lead to a great contraction of European purchases. With the throwing back of $200,000,000 to $400,000,000 worth of goods a month on our domestic markets, we expected that domestic prices would break and a reaction would come. The exchange rates did break violently late in June, but the flood of exports went on for reasons that did not become clearly apparent until toward the end of the year.

Not only were expectations regarding Europe disappointed, but expectations regarding America were not realized. Our own Government continued its lavish expenditures. During the fiscal years 1918 and 1919 the disbursements of the Federal Treasury were about 24 billion dollars (not including net advances for these years to the Allies of eight and a half billion); and during the fiscal years 1920 and 1921, the disbursements amounted to about eleven and a half billion dollars. Government shipbuilding was maintained on a great scale and lavish expenditures of many kinds were continued.

The third disappointment was in the failure of American industry to expand its physical output when four million soldiers returned to the pursuits of peace. As a matter of fact, when output is measured in physical units, tons, yards, bushels, etc., we produced from five to seven per cent. less in 1919 than we did in 1918 when our soldiers and sailors were at war. The depression of early 1919 reduced output on the one hand and on the other hand, the very intensity of our efforts later in the year with strikes, labor troubles, high rate of labor turnover, and railroad congestion worked against larger output. Reduced managerial efficiency, reduced labor efficiency, and congestion at various other critical points all tended to hold down production. Finally, our own people, who had in many ways been economical during the war, relaxed at the close of the conflict, and an orgy of private consumption began in the United States. These various factors: increased export drain, continued Government expenditures, reduced domestic production and increased domestic consumption, all combined to cause greater scarcity of goods in 1919 than had been manifest in 1918. Add to this real scarcity the artificial scarcity, due to the activities of spectaculars who took goods off the market to hold for higher prices, and our post-War boom is fully explained.[1]

Adherents of the so-called *quantity theory* of money sought to explain the high prices of 1919 in a different way. They contended that prices could not fall, because there was so much money and bank credit to float in the country. The Harvard *Review oj Economic Statistics* in June, 1919, (following Professor Irving Fisher's theory) laid down the dictum that we were on a permanently high price level. They said prices might rise five or six per cent. above or fall five or six per cent. below this level, with future business cycles, but they maintained that the new level was permanent and safe. Prices thereupon rose 15 per cent. and then fell 49 per cent. Increased gold and greatly expanded bank

[1] Vide *Chase Economic Bulletin,* Vol. I, Nos. 1 and 3.

credit proved quite incapable of sustaining the price level once the underlying factors had spent their forces. The quantity theory of money has been very badly discredited as a result of these predictions by its adherents in 1919. New borrowing for non-productive purposes will raise prices and will cause bank credits to expand, but the mere existence of a large volume of bank credits will not sustain prices when new borrowing for non-productive purposes ceases or when abnormal demand falls off. In the relation between prices and bank credits and between prices and value of money, prices are much more apt to be causes than effect and the volume of bank credit is much more apt to be a resultant of price changes than it is to be an active cause of price changes.

Even after the United States Government ceased to advance funds to Europe for the financing of a one-sided export trade and even after the foreign exchange rates broke under the pressure of these exports, the exports continued and our boom based on the exports continued. Toward the end of 1919, the reason for this became apparent. London took over the burden of financing these exports when the United States Treasury gave it up. The London money market, always the great center of foreign exchange dealings, bought lire, francs, and other Continental exchange being created in the United States and other parts of the world. London sold dollars to the Continental buyers, pledging her credit in the United States to obtain the dollars. London bought great blocks of securities of one kind or another held on the Continent, giving in exchange sterling, or dollars in New York. In these and a variety of other ways, London took over the burden of keeping up the flow of goods to Europe. In the course of this, the banks of London expanded their loans even more rapidly than did the banks in the United States. As a result, sterling exchange broke very greatly, the pound falling to $3.18 in February, 1920.

British public finance was improving while the public finances of the Continental belligerents were growing steadily worse. Yet the depression of sterling was almost as startling as that of the Continental currencies. Sterling was depressed far below its real merits and the exchanges of the Continental belligerents were held far above their true values by this process.

United States exports to Europe continued, being no longer financed by long-time credits but merely going on short bills and open account credits. There thus grew up an unfunded debt of Europe to private creditors in the United States, which was estimated by the *Chase Economic Bulletin* at three and a half billion dollars, as of September 15th, 1920, and which was not less than four billion dollars at the end of 1921. This was partly an obligation of European debtors to American banks, but the bulk of it took the form of open account credits extended by American exporters and producers, and of purchases of European moneys by American exchange speculators, including especially purchases of German marks, whether in the form of actual German paper money or in the form of bank balances in Germany. Part of it, too, represented goods shipped to Europe but not taken by the importers or consignees and subsequently sold for much less than export prices. The losses by holders of this open account credit, whether through depression of European currencies, or through failure to collect for goods shipped, or through resale at prices much below export prices, have been enormous. In German marks alone, the losses have been gigantic, though it is practically impossible to determine the exact amounts.

In May of 1920, speaking before the Academy of Political Science in New York, the present writer remarked that "we have not only the underlying indicia of approaching crisis but also all the outward and visible signs." The crisis was inevitable and the problem was simply as to how we could soften its effects. Bank loans had expanded 25 per cent. due in very considerable part to the fact that American business men had tied up working capital in open account advances to Europe and had then been driven to replenish their working capital by borrowings from their banks. These were "frozen credits." In addition, railroad congestion had tied up a large volume of goods in transit, again creating "frozen credits." A "frozen credit" may be defined as a loan which the banker thought was a commercial loan at the time he made it but which later turns out to be an investment.

More significant than the great increase in bank loans was the great deterioration in the average quality of bank loans. This deterioration in quality was, to be sure, indicated by the very increase in quantity. Had the loans been truly liquid loans, the amount would not have piled up so rapidly. To the experienced banker, this is a familiar symptom of approaching crisis.

Financial troubles manifested themselves first in the countries which had the soundest monetary systems. It is easy to bolster up weak spots by expanding credits in countries with freely expanding irredeemable paper money; but in countries which have sound gold money the check comes earlier. It was thus no accident that Japan was the first great country to crack under the strain and that the financial strain manifested itself in the United States and in Great Britain long before it was felt on the Continent of Europe.

No mention has been made of the discount policy of the Federal Reserve Banks, as a factor in the boom and crisis. This topic is discussed in the chapter which follows on "The Gold and Rediscount Policy of the Federal Reserve Banks."

In the spring of 1920, bankers in the United States generally began to realize that conditions were very dangerous and that concerted policy was necessary to avoid disaster. The Federal Reserve Board had sounded a warning as early as August, 1919, and since it was free from the control of the Treasury, in the latter part of 1919 and early part of 1920, it had raised its rediscount rates as a means of imposing restraint on credit expansion.

Sound bank policy in meeting a crisis involves several elements. On the one hand, it is necessary that banks should restrict loans for the purpose of expansion and to limit advances to borrowers who do not pressingly need them. On the other hand, it is necessary that banks should expand loans readily to solvent borrowers who are caught in a tight position temporarily, which they can work out of if given time. The Bank of England has long since worked out a technique for dealing with such a situation. In a crisis period, it raises its discount rate as a means of checking unnecessary borrowing. On the other hand, it provides money freely to solvent borrowers who must have money. The third element in credit policy is the refusal of credit to definitely insolvent debtors. If there is reasonable prospect that they can work out if given time, the banks should protect them fully; but, if they are wholly insolvent, it is, of course, entirely unwise for the banks to throw good money after bad. The crisis is a period of liquidation during which unsound elements are eliminated and illusory hopes are cleared away.

Finally, sound credit policy in a crisis must recognize that even in the worst of crises and depressions, an enormous volume of ordinary business goes on and banks should continue to make loans that are necessary in order to enable the current flow of goods to continue. Banks should refuse to make loans to permit speculators to withhold goods from the market in the vain hope of realizing higher prices or of recouping losses incurred on a boom time market, but banks should continue regular lending to permit products not yet ripe for the market to be completed and brought up to a stage when they can be marketed.

With the Federal Reserve System, we were able adequately to carry out these policies. Despite the unprecedented break in commodity prices, amounting to 49%, according to Bradstreet's index number, we were able to prevent the crisis from degenerating into a money panic; we were able to prevent the insolvency of really solvent firms, and to accomplish so complete a liquidation that, by the end of 1921, a modest business revival had already begun to manifest itself.

We have been through no ordinary crisis and no ordinary business cycle. World disturbances continue; the public finances of Continental Europe grow worse rather than better. Europe has not resumed her place as the world's great manufacturing center. The regions producing articles for foreign trade and raw materials consequently lack, and will for a long time continue to lack, their normal markets. They are consequently unable and will for a long time be unable to buy manufactured goods in accustomed volume. The economic world is out of equilibrium. We, in the United States, will continue to be hampered and handicapped by this fact until real improvement comes to Europe. None the less, we are clearly through the worst of our economic and financial trouble. We can have living business in the United States, even though not good business.

But we must recognize that very great responsibility rests upon us. We shall not meet that responsibility by imposing a high tariff against European goods or by yielding to cheap money propagandists. We shall not meet the responsibility by washing our hands of Europe. Neither shall we meet it by making unsound loans to Europe in the absence of reforms on the other side of the water. We shall aid Europe best and serve ourselves best if we join with Great Britain and other solvent countries with surplus capital in urging financial and monetary reforms upon the Continent of Europe as conditions for making the loans which will help her to get on her feet.

EVENTS IN CRISIS OF 1920

1919

March 17. French Government removes support of exchange markets; rates decline sharply. Similar action taken by England on the 20th and by Italy on the 21st.

March 20. Sterling exchange drops to $4.71, lowest since 1915.

Nov. 6. Bank of England raises discount rate from 5 to 6%, first change since April 5, 1917.

Nov. 12. Call money loans at 30%, highest since panic of 1907. Violent collapse in security prices.

Dec. 12. Sterling exchange sells at $3.64½.

Dec. 29. Call money rates again advance to 25% due to low reserve ratio of Federal Reserve Banks. Time money 8½%, highest of the year.

1920

Wk. end'g Jan. 31. Sinshiu silk drops from high point $17.85 to $17.25.

Feb. 1. Bradstreet's index number reaches high point of 226.5.

Feb. 4. Collapse of foreign exchange market. Sterling 3.19, francs 15.15, Italian lire 18.82. Call money 25%.

Wk. end'g Feb. 9. Cotton falls $9 a bale. Fall in prices of corn, pork, and lard. Stocks slump 5 to 20 points.

March. During March Egyptian cotton falls from 92.50 pence a pound to 83.00 in the Liverpool market.

April 18. Dispatches from Japan report financial crisis in that country.

April 21. Practically all financial markets suffer a most severe slump.

Wk. end'g April 24. Iron and steel prices ease slightly.

May 1. Dun's index number reaches high point of 217.8.

Wk. end'g May 8. Big New York department store takes part in fight against high costs of living.

May 11. Furs drop 20 to 30% at St. Louis fur auction.

May 31. Further financial upset in Japan.

July 22. Spot cotton reaches high figure of 43¾ and then price moves downward.

Aug. 2. Sharp fall of grain and commodity quotations.

Aug. 25. Receiver appointed for Bethlehem Motor Corporation.

Latter part of Aug. Sinshiu No. 1 silk reaches low point of $6 a pound.

Aug. 31. Aug. bank clearings decrease 7¾% from previous month.

Sept. 9. American Woolen Company cuts prices 15 to 25%.

Sept. 21. Henry Ford announces reduction of 31% in automobile prices.

Sept. 22. Wholesale and retail price reductions nation-wide.

Sept. 24. Wheat breaks to below recent Government guarantee of $2.26.

Wk. end'g Sept. 27. Cotton reaches lowest price since Sept. 15, 1919. Dec. corn drops below $1. Recessions in hides and leathers are tremendous. Trend is downward in all commodies except oil and steel.

Sept. 29. Cut announced in some steel prices.

Oct. 4. Dec. wheat falls below $2 a bushel.

Oct. 10. Break in sugar prices caused Pres. of Cuba to declare 50-day moratorium. High level of 24 cents in July—since then a decline of 70%.

Oct. 18. Many industrial plants curtail operations, while others make drastic price reductions. Some mills reduce wages. Crisis in China.

Oct. 20. Sharp decline in pig iron prices.

Oct. 31. Failures increase $36^1/_3$% in number and $31^2/_3$% in amount of liabilities in October compared with September.

Nov. 4. Reduction in soft coal prices.

Nov. 22. Call money loans at 5%, lowest for 1920.

Dec. 8. Bradstreet's reports record decline in commodity prices in November.

Dec. 13. New England textile mills file notice of 22½% wage reduction.

Dec. 28. Anaconda Copper Co. passes quarterly dividend.

Dec. 31. Corn, flour, pork, coffee, sugar, iron, silver, lead, tin, copper, and cotton all sell at new records for year during the month of December.

1921

Jan. 4. Bethlehem Steel Corporation announces 10 to 20 % reduction in wages, effective Jan. 16.

Jan. 10. American Woolen Co. announces 22½% wage cut.

Jan. 13. Singer Company reduces wages 20%.

Jan. 25. U. S. Steel Corporation reports reduced earnings for fourth quarter of 1920.

Jan. 26. Ford Company announces cut in price of Fordson tractors.

Feb. 1. American Hide and Leather Co. passes preferred dividend.

Feb. 9. Independent steel mills cut prices below the U. S. Steel Corporation's.

Wk. end'g Mar. 7. Cotton touches $15^1/_3$, lowest point since 1914. Copper touches lowest point since the early days of the war. Woolen market shows some improvement. Sugar has recovered a bit.

April 12. United States Steel Corporation announces price reductions.

April 27. Pennsylvania Railroad cuts dividend rate on common stock from 6 to 4%.

May 3. U. S. Steel Corporation announces 20% reduction in wages. Credit situation is easier.

May 16. Iron and steel industry now operating at less than 40% activity.

June 1. Railroad Labor Board announces wage reduction of 12%, to become effective July 1. Bradstreet's index number reaches low point of 115.2.

June 7. Henry Ford announces reduction in price of automobiles ranging from $15 to $50.

Wk. end'g June 13. Iron and steel operations probably do not reach 30% of capacity.

July 1. Dun's index number reaches low point of 132.3.

July 11. Sharp reduction of iron and steel prices by U. S. Steel Corporation, bringing them down $4 to $10 a ton.

July. In July operations in iron and steel industry were 20 to 25% of capacity.

Aug. 25. U. S. Steel Corporation cuts sheet steel prices.

Aug. 27. U. S. Rubber Co. reports a deficit.

Sept. 1. Government estimates cotton condition at 49.3%.

Sept. 7. Price of cotton goes over 21 cents a pound in New York market, distant futures above 22 cents.

Sept. 19. Bureau of Labor's index shows rise in wholesale prices of 2.7% in August; first gain in fifteen months.

Oct. 10. U. S. Steel Corporation's unfilled orders show increase for first time since July 31, 1921.

Nov. 10. U. S. Steel Corporation's unfilled orders on books, smallest total since May, 1919.

CHAPTER XXXI

THE GOLD AND REDISCOUNT POLICY OF THE FEDERAL RESERVE BANKS[1]

FEDERAL RESERVE BANK policy is still in the making. Conditions since the inauguration of the system have been highly abnormal. A new system, working under wholly extraordinary conditions, could not apply simply and directly the traditional principles of European central banks to its operations, and was obliged to experiment with tentative policies. The present article is not primarily concerned with discussion or criticism of what the Federal Reserve Banks have already done. Our interest is rather in future policy. The effort will be made to draw from the experience of the great central banks of Europe and from the banking experience of the United States certain principles which should guide sound Federal Reserve Bank policy for the future. The center of interest is the question of what considerations should guide the Federal Reserve Banks in determining their rediscount rates. Closely related are the questions of the gold policy of the Federal Reserve Banks, and their policy governing the kind of paper they are prepared to rediscount. These three problems hang together and cannot be considered separately.

THE FIRST PRINCIPLE OF REDISCOUNT BANKING—"KEEPING ABOVE THE MARKET"

Since 1871 there has not been a single year when the official bank rate of the Bank of England was not above the market rate on yearly averages. It has occasionally happened for a very

[1] This chapter is reproduced from *The Chase Economic Bulletin* of July 20, 1921, issued by the Chase National Bank of New York. It was written by A. Barton Hepburn and Benjamin M. Anderson, Jr.

short period that the market rate might be fractionally above Bank Rate. This happened in November of 1919, but Bank Rate was promptly advanced to correct it. It happened in April of 1920. But again Bank Rate was promptly advanced to correct it. When Bank Rate was reduced at the end of April, 1921, from 7% to 6½%, the market rate stood at 6% to 6 1/8% on ninety-day bills, while sixty-day bills were as low as 5 5/8 % in the open market. When Bank Rate was subsequently reduced to 6%, the market for ninety-day bills was 5½ to 5 9/16%.

The reduction of the official rate of the Bank of Switzerland on May 2, 1921, was also in conformity with the principle of keeping the official rate above the market rate. The official rate was reduced from 5% to 4½%, but the market rate stood at 4% when this change was made. The following figures covering a series of years exhibit the relations on annual averages between official bank rates and market rates in France, England, and Germany.

DISCOUNT RATES

BANK RATE *vs.* MARKET RATE

	France		England		Germany	
	Bank Rate	Market Rate	Bank Rate	Market Rate	Bank Rate	Market Rate
1887	3.00	2.53	3.36	2.58	3.40	2.30
1889	3.16	2.60	3.56	3.25	3.68	2.63
1891	3.00	2.63	3.40	1.50	3.80	3.02
1893	2.50	2.25	3.05	1.67	4.08	3.17
1895	2.10	1.63	2.00	.81	3.15	2.01
1897	2.00	1.96	2.78	1.87	3.82	3.09
1899	3.06	2.96	3.75	3.29	4.98	4.45
1900	3.23	3.17	3.96	3.70	5.33	4.41
1901	3.00	2.48	3.72	3.20	4.10	3.06
1902	3.00	2.43	3.33	2.99	3.32	2.19
1903	3.00	2.78	3.75	3.40	3.84	3.00
1904	3.00	2.19	3.30	2.70	4.22	3.13

A similar policy has obtained for the Bank of Sweden, and in general the central banks of Europe have held almost without exception to the policy of keeping their official rediscount rates above the market rates.

A number of principles have been involved in the determination of the rediscount policy of the Bank of England:

1. A high reserve ratio has usually been regarded as occasion for a low Bank Rate, and a low reserve ratio for a high rediscount rate, but a good many exceptions to this can be found.

2. When sterling is at a premium, the bank is usually more ready to reduce Bank Rate than when sterling is at a discount. But exceptions to this again have been not infrequent.

3. When gold is leaving England in large quantities, the Bank of England will usually raise its rate substantially to check foreign borrowing in the British market and to turn the tide of gold back to London. The last two reductions in the Bank of England rate, however, have been in the face of an abnormally large outward flow of gold.

4. Bank Rate has usually tended to advance in periods of expansion and speculation, and has usually declined in periods of depression and slow business. It usually rises to a very high point in the crisis which intervenes between the period of prosperity and the period of depression.

5. The central principle, however, guiding the Bank of England in fixing its rediscount rate is clearly that, whatever else Bank Rate might do, it must not go below the market rate. To this principle, barring short intervals of a few days, there seems to have been no exception even during the wholly extraordinary disturbances of the war and the post-war period. It is the essential principle of rediscount banking, and it is the one sure principle which can prevent a reserve bank from demoralizing, instead of steadying, the money markets in the long run.

The basic idea involved in this policy of keeping above the market is that reserve bank money is for exceptional and unusual use—that it is not the province of a reserve bank to supply a substantial part of the ordinary funds employed in the market in ordinary times. Of course it is expected that a reserve bank shall make money for its stockholders and shall employ such of its funds as may be necessary to meet expenses and to pay dividends. One provision of the Federal Reserve Act, permitting open market operations on the part of the Federal Reserve Banks, was designed to give them discretion in this matter, whether the member banks should rediscount with them or not.

But the position of a reserve bank is a very peculiar one. If an ordinary bank makes a loan, checks come in against it, as a consequence of the loan, which it must meet out of its reserve unless it should happen that simultaneously new deposits are made with it of checks drawn on other banks. Loans made by a reserve bank, however, need not lead to drains on its reserve. When, in making a loan, it issues its notes or gives a deposit credit to a rediscounting bank, that note or a transfer of that deposit credit will be accepted as ultimate payment by some other institution. The deposit liabilities of the reserve bank count as ultimate reserve for the other banks of the country, and the volume of reserve money is consequently increased through a mere increase in the deposit liabilities of the reserve bank. With an increase in the volume of reserves of the member banks, there is an immediate tendency to a reduction in the general level of discount rates throughout the country, placing them below the level which open market conditions would otherwise call for and creating a temptation for the uneconomical use of bank funds. There is particularly a temptation to use bank funds in an excessive degree for capital purposes, and for the ordinary banks of the country, misled by the artificial excess of liquid cash, to tie up too great a part of their assets in non-liquid form. The reserve bank which makes rediscount rates too low, therefore, instead of performing its function of increasing the liquidity of the banking system, tends rather to destroy the liquidity of it.

It is the function of the reserve bank to hold the reserves of the country in central reservoirs, so that they may be available for emergencies. It is the function of the reserve bank to increase the supply of money in the country to meet seasonal variations in the demand for hand to hand cash. The reserve bank should at all times be prepared to supply additional funds for short-term operations. In crises, the reserve bank must, of course, supply further funds in sufficient volume to permit the member banks to keep a crisis from degenerating into a panic. In the wholly extraordinary emergencies which a great war begets, the reserve bank may well be justified in violating temporarily the ordinary canons of sound finance, because financial disorders are of less consequence than the losing of the war, and temporary expedients may be justified even though the long run cost be high. But under normal conditions, and under conditions when it is possible to take a long run view, the well established traditions covering a reserve bank's operations must be followed. The chief of these canons is that the rediscount rate of reserve banks should be kept above the market.

What is the "Market Rate" in the United States?

The problem at once arises as to what is meant by the market rate, above which the Federal Reserve Rate should be kept. If we take the situation of May, 1921, and look for quotations on commercial paper, we find the Federal Reserve Bank rate of 6½% in New York well above the market rate on acceptances, which stood at about 5⅞%, and at the same time we find the Federal Reserve Bank rate of 6½% well below the market rate on so-called commercial paper, which stood at 7% or above. We find, moreover, a special rediscount rate in the Federal Reserve Bank for acceptances. Acceptances could be rediscounted at 6%, where "commercial paper" was rediscountable at 6½%. It is necessary that we should know precisely what we mean by the market rate. If we look into the practices of the banks, we find, of course, a great diversity of rates. Banks in Western and Southern States may well be charging 8% or even 9%, when banks in the financial centers are charging 6% or less in discounting paper for their customers. Is there a "market" in the United States comparable to "the market" in London? Obviously, we cannot directly adapt London practice to American conditions without making modifications.

The market rate in London has a very definite meaning. It means the rate at which prime acceptances or bills of exchange, accepted by banks or acceptance houses (and occasionally by prime mercantile houses), will be bought in the open market. The market rate is a competitive rate, and it is a rate publicly known. There is an open, well established bill market.

The original theory of the Federal Reserve Banks was that they should chiefly rediscount acceptances, and the effort has been made by the Federal Reserve authorities to develop an open bill market in the United States, in the hope that a large volume of bills would be created which could be used for rediscount purposes. At the present time, however, these acceptances constitute a very small part of our total bank loans, and a very small part indeed of the total earning assets of the Federal Reserve Banks. On April 1, the total of bankers' acceptances outstanding was $664,000,000, as compared with the total volume of bank loans in the United States of approximately $30,000,000,000. The Federal Reserve Banks held only $122,491,000 of acceptances on this date, as against total earning assets of $2,613,183,000 and as against total rediscounts of $2,214,595,000. Obviously the published rate on acceptances in the United States is not to be taken as the basic market quotation.

The same may be said of the rates on "commercial paper," so-called. The amount of single name commercial paper sold through note brokers stood at only $730,000,000, as reported by the Federal Reserve Bank of New York on June 1. Moreover, the Federal Reserve Banks do not rediscount this paper at all, since it is four to six months' paper. They will rediscount it as it approaches maturity, but four to six months' commercial paper they do not rediscount. There is little gain, therefore, in connecting the Federal Reserve rediscount rates with the published rates on this paper.

In the United States the "market rate" is best represented by a body of loans, the rates on which are rarely published. "Line of credit" loans made to customers constitute the bulk of bank loans in the United States. Of these line of credit loans many are made at widely varying rates. But there is a large block of these loans which may be taken as the best representative of market conditions, namely, loans made by banks in the great cities to those of their customers who have deposit accounts and lines of credit with several banks.[1] The important businesses of the country usually have a number of bank accounts with borrowing privileges. They will frequently have accounts with New York, Boston, Chicago, Philadelphia, and other banks. They will borrow from several banks and in several cities. The rates on loans made to them thus involve competition among many banks and many cities. They are truly competitive rates. They respond quickly to changes in market conditions. They tend to be approximately the same in all the great cities of the country. Though the rates on these loans are not matters of published record, they are well known in the banking community, and they are, of course, well known to the authorities of the Federal Reserve System. They constitute the best index of changing market conditions.[2]

Our conclusion would be, then, that the principle that the Federal Reserve rediscount rate should be kept above the market

[1] Acknowledgment is made to Mr. M. Hadden Howell, Assistant Vice-President of the Chase National Bank, for valuable advice in this connection.

[2] The relation between these rates and the published rates on open market commercial paper sold through note brokers is fairly clear. In times of tight money the open market rates on paper sold through note brokers usually go well above the rates charged to customers. In times of exceedingly easy money, the open market commercial paper rates usually go somewhat below the rates charged to customers on line of credit loans. The open market commercial paper rates fluctuate more widely, in other words, than the market as a whole does.

means that the Federal Reserve rediscount rate should be kept above the rate which the great city banks charge to those of their customers who deal with several banks.

Further analysis, however, is called for. Not even in England does the bulk of bank loans consist of bills of exchange. Bills constituted not more than 25% of the total of "discounts and advances" of the chief British banks before the war. In 1920 they did not constitute more than about 20% of their discounts and advances. The "advances" of British banks, which are normally the largest item on the asset side of a British bank balance sheet, consist of customers' loans under line of credit, including overdrafts, loans on stock and bond collateral, a large body of loans on many kinds of commodity collateral, and other items. It is virtually impossible to get details as to just what elements enter into them and as to what the proportions among the elements are. Loans made by British banks under the head of "advances" are frequently made at a rate above the official rate of the Bank of England. In addition to discounts and advances, British banks lend large sums on call to discount houses and bill brokers on bill of exchange collateral, and they also make loans on "short notice" to stock exchange houses on stock exchange collateral—the so-called "contangoes," or loans until the next fortnightly settlement. These loans on call and the "contangoes" frequently are made at rates well below the market rate on bills.

It might be questioned on the basis of this whether the market rate on bills could be correctly taken as representing even the British market rate.

The significant point, however, is that the Bank of England rediscounts bills and does not rediscount advances. The official bank rate is the rate at which the Bank of England will rediscount bills. Indeed, it is a tradition that the largest banks in London do not rediscount at all except in the greatest emergiences. When one of the great banks wishes to replenish its cash, it can commonly do so by calling the loans to discount houses and bill brokers, which leads the discount houses and bill brokers to rediscount their bills with the Bank of England, so that the great banks replenish their funds from the Bank of England indirectly. They can also increase their cash very quickly by the simple expedient of ceasing to purchase new bills to replace the daily maturing bills which they hold. The Bank of England also makes loans on stock and bond collateral (Lombard loans), but when it does so, it commonly charges more than the official rate. In the United States, on the other hand, the great bulk of commercial rediscounts is made on line of credit loans. The member banks take over to the Federal Reserve Banks the single name paper of their customers, made under lines of credit, and rediscount it at the official commercial paper rate.

The essence of the principle that the rediscount rate should be above the market rate is that when a bank rediscounts paper with the Federal Reserve Bank, it should do so at a sacrifice. It should pay the Federal Reserve Bank more for the money it gets from it than the customer whose paper is being rediscounted pays the bank on his loan. This is always the case in England. The British house which to-day gets accommodation from the Bank of England at 6% does so by turning over to it a bill of exchange which it has discounted at 5½%. In New York, on the other hand, a member bank which has discounted a note for one of its corporate customers at 6¾% can rediscount that same note with the Federal Reserve Bank at 6%. The British house pays a premium for the extra cash which it gets through rediscounting. The New York bank makes a slight profit on the transaction.

Rates Correlated with Liquidity

We help clarify the matter if we recognize that instead of one rediscount rate and one market rate, we may have several rediscount rates and several market rates. Thus in England there is the official bank rate on bills, but there is a rate higher than this charged by the Bank of England when it makes loans on stock and bond collateral. In New York there is a rediscount rate on "commercial paper," which has frequently been different from the rediscount rate on acceptances. The rediscount rate and market rate on loans secured by government war paper may be different also. The principle of keeping above the market means merely that the rediscount rate on a given kind of loan should be higher than the market rate on that same kind of loan. If acceptances sell in the open market at 5¾% and the rediscount rate on acceptances is 6%, the principle is being maintained. If, at the same time, customers' loans, made under line of credit, are above 6% but can be rediscounted at 6% as "commercial paper," the principle is not being maintained.

Narrowing the discussion to that rate which is now of greatest importance at the Federal Reserve Bank, the Federal Reserve Bank rate on commercial paper, the principle would be that the commercial paper rate of the Federal Reserve Bank should be above the market rate which the great city banks charge on line of credit loans to those of their customers who deal with several banks.

The rediscount rate on commercial paper cannot be considered apart from the question of what kind of paper is eligible for rediscount. To the extent that rediscounts consists of truly liquid commercial paper, the rate may safely be much lower than when all manner of line of credit loans, which are in form short term loans, are eligible. The open market itself will give a preference to such paper. The market rate on such paper will tend to go relatively low, and the rediscount rate on such paper may safely be relatively low in full harmony with the principle of keeping the rediscount rate above the market.

To the extent that we can develop in the United States a broad acceptance market and to the extent that the acceptances are based on goods actually in transit or actually in process of being marketed, to the extent, moreover, that these bills grow out of international commerce and are capable of rediscount in foreign markets, the Federal Reserve Banks may safely, in full harmony with the principle of keeping above the market, make their rediscount rates on such bills low.

Prime sterling bills before the war did not look to London alone for their market. They were held in large volume by many foreign banks. The Austro-Hungarian Bank, for example, carried a very substantial part of its reserve in the form of bills payable in London. It preferred these bills to gold, because they bore interest. The National Bank of Belgium did likewise. Banking houses all over the world in greater or less degree purchased and held such bills, seeing in them a liquid resource almost as good as gold. If the volume of dollar bills payable in the United States grows great enough, if foreign bankers buy them, and if American banks throughout the country develop the practice of holding them in sufficient number as a secondary reserve eligible for rediscount at the Federal Reserve Bank, the time may come when the really important rate at the Federal Reserve Bank will be its rediscount rate on acceptances and when Federal Reserve Bank money will be available properly and safely at much lower rates than is now the case. Foreign bank holdings of dollar bills ought to increase greatly in the next few years, since such bills are almost the only bills payable in gold, and so can constitute a real reserve.

So long, however, as the chief item offered to the Federal Reserve Banks for rediscount is the one name line of credit paper of the customers of the member banks, our rediscount rates will have to be much higher than rediscount rates in Europe have usually been.

This is not to impugn the essential goodness of customers' loans under line of credit. They are good, but they are not as liquid as open market paper, which a bank may treat in a wholly impersonal way, which it may refuse to renew without giving offense, and for the maker of which it feels no responsibility. The quality of paper involves two elements: (1) essential goodness, and (2) liquidity. In general, to the extent that the Federal Reserve Banks supply "money" only, Federal Reserve Bank rates may safely be low. But to the extent that the Federal Reserve Banks are called upon to supply capital, it is necessary that their rates should be high.

In all cases it is necessary that their rates should be above the market rate for the particular kind of loan they are called upon to rediscount.

"Money" Versus Capital

The traditional theory of commercial banking has always been that banks should supply their customers with "money", but not with capital. A bank has not been supposed to supply the money needed for building or machinery or other fixed investment. It might, however, properly supply part of the funds for the purchase of raw materials and part of the wages of laborers working up these raw materials into finished products, since the prompt sale of the finished products would bring back cash with which the loan could be paid off. The strictest theory of commercial banking, however, would object to loans to manufacturers even for these purposes, and would hold that bank money should be employed only in financing goods actually ready for the market during the period of sixty or ninety days that would ordinarily be necessary for a merchant to turn them over. Bank loans of this character have been regarded as thoroughly liquid, since funds are automatically created for paying them off as the loans mature, and since a bank whose funds are invested in this form of loan can at any time, by declining to renew loans, almost automatically turn its resources into actual cash.

It is notorious that in the banking practice not only of America, but also of most parts of the world, we have gone far beyond this old view of banking. Banks, for example, have loaned large sums of money on stocks and bonds, and stocks and bonds represent the fixed capital of corporations. The stocks and bonds of a railroad ultimately represent roadbed, rails, terminals, bridges, rolling stock, and the like. The development of organized trading in securities, however, has made this form of loan also very liquid. The railroad as a whole cannot be sold, but the hundred dollar shares of the railroad can be sold at any moment. The crisis of 1920 demonstrated the fact that loans to the stock market were the most liquid resource which the New York banks possessed. At the end of 1919 the total of loans for stock market purposes in New York stood at about $1,750,000,000. By the end of 1920 it had been reduced to $700,000,000. During this same period there had been an actual increase in practically all the other forms of loans. Loans to the stock market proved to be an extremely valuable liquid resource, and the ability of the stock market to absorb securities, supplying the banks with new cash to lend for other purposes, eased the situation greatly.

These loans which have proved most difficult to liquidate have not been the loans on stock and bond collateral, but rather the so-called commercial loans to manufacturers, and even merchants, as well as the loans to agriculture. There are undoubtedly in the assets of American banks, in the form of three and six months' notes, a great many loans for capital purposes. These loans in general are good and safe, but they are slow. Banks cannot realize on them in emergencies. Banks know well enough that in emergencies they must protect the majority of their borrowers, even by making additional loans. They can do this safely only if among their assets they have a sufficient volume of truly liquid loans which they can refuse to renew, so that they may get the new cash they need to lend to their other borrowers. In the days before the Federal Reserve System was inaugurated, they had this resource (to the extent that they had it) in stock market loans and in paper bought through note brokers. They could call their loans in the stock market, and they could refuse to repurchase commercial paper bought through note brokers. By these means they could increase the funds which their local customers required. The mechanism broke down at times, but to the extent that there was liquidity in our system before the Federal Reserve System was inaugurated, it was to be found chiefly in these two elements.

With the coming of the Federal Reserve System the banks of the country found an additional immense source of liquidity in that paper in their portfolios which the Federal Reserve Banks were willing to rediscount. The original conception of the Federal Reserve System was that it would rediscount only truly liquid commercial paper. There was provision, of course, that it should rediscount loans based on Government securities and that it should purchase State and municipal warrants, but it was not expected that the volume of this would be great. The amount of paper in American banks that met the original requirements of the Federal Reserve Banks was probably not very great. As the pressure of war finance grew, however, and the volume of Government issues increased, the member banks came into possession of an immense amount of rediscountable paper based on Government securities. Moreover, as the Federal Reserve Banks sought increasingly to aid in handling the war and post-war problems, they relaxed in various directions their requirements as to what constituted commercial paper eligible for rediscount, and the member banks found that a very high proportion of their portfolios was eligible. In the last two years the Federal Reserve Banks have undoubtedly taken over from member banks a substantial amount of so-called commercial paper, which, in fact, represents capital loans. This has been particularly true in the expansion which prevented the crisis of 1920 from degenerating into a panic.

The emergency in 1920 required this. No criticism attaches to the Federal Reserve Banks for permitting it. Indeed, it would be subject to criticism if they had not done it. But the time has come for a gradual reversal of policy.

In emergencies, the Federal Reserve Banks should be prepared to supply both money and capital. But in order that they may be able to supply "capital" in emergencies, they should limit themselves to supplying "money" in ordinary times.

Various proposals for the employment of Federal Reserve Bank money for capital purposes as a permanent policy are at the present time being made. The suggestion has recently been made that the Federal Reserve Banks should be authorized and required to rediscount live stock paper running for two years and agricultural paper generally of nine months' maturity. Any such policy generally carried out by the Federal Reserve Banks in the agricultural districts would make them cease to be true reserve banks. Their assets might be sound, but they would be slow. They would lose their liquidity. From the standpoint of liquidity they would become parasites upon the general Federal Reserve System. We must protect our Federal Reserve Banks from proposals of this kind.

The Reserve Ratio as a Guide for Discount Rates

The view has often been expressed that the reserve ratio should serve as a regulator of the rediscount rate of the Federal Reserve Banks, and it seems to be a common impression that reserve banks and central banks in general make their rediscount rates low when their reserve ratio is high and make their rediscount rates high when their reserve ratio is low. This view rests on the assumption that there is a certain fixed reserve ratio at which central banks should aim, or do aim, and that, when the reserve ratio gets above this, it is desirable to bring it down by expanding credit, and that, when the reserve ratio gets below this, it is desirable to bring it up by contracting credit.

There is no clear justification for this view in the history of the great European banks. The Bank of France, for example, expanded its gold reserves by about 76% between 1899 and 1911, but increased its discounts and advances by only about 5% during the same period. The Bank of England has at times lowered its rediscount rate when reserves were very much lower than on other occasions when it was raising its rediscount rate. Other things equal, a large reserve would constitute an argument for lower rates, and a low reserve would constitute an argument for higher rates. But the reserve ratio as such is not, and should not be, the controlling factor. This is particularly true in the United States at the present time because the reserve ratio is abnormally high, as a consequence both of the extraordinary inflow of foreign gold, and of the war-time policy of the Federal Reserve Banks of drawing into their reserves the great bulk of the gold and gold certificates which had been in general circulation. There are very few gold coins or gold certificates in circulation in the United States at the present time as compared with conditions before the war. One rarely sees gold or gold certificates outside the banks.

THE GOLD POLICY AND THE RESERVE RATIO

The way in which the gold policy of the Federal Reserve Banks influences their reserve ratio will be made clearest by certain figures. The ratio of total reserves to combined Federal Reserve Note and deposit liabilities of the Federal Reserve Banks stood on June 8, 1921, at 58.3%. The total gold holdings of the Reserve Banks on that date stood at $2,431,000,000. Their holdings of legal tenders, silver, etc., stood at $162,000,000, making a total reserve of $2,593,000,000. Federal Reserve Notes outstanding were $2,711,000,000, and the deposit liabilities were $1,735,000,000, combined notes and deposits amounting to $4,446,000,000.

Let us assume that $1,162,000,000 of Federal Reserve Notes were cancelled, and in their place $1,162,000,000 of the reserve were returned to circulation; that is, a billion dollars of gold and all of the legal tenders, silver, etc. In this computation we will leave the deposits unchanged and the earning assets of the Federal Reserve System unchanged. The reserves (all gold) would then be reduced to $1,431,000,000, and the combined notes and deposit liabilities would be reduced to $3,284,000,000. The ratio of reserves to combined note and deposit liabilities would then stand at only 43.5%.

This ratio of 43.5% would much more accurately represent the real position of the Federal Reserve Banks than the figure of 58.3%, with the great bulk of the gold and gold certificates withdrawn from circulation. A country, soundly based on the gold standard like our own, will normally have a substantial amount of actual gold in circulation. A high reserve ratio may mean either of two things. It may mean that the Federal Reserve Banks have low demand liabilities, or it may mean that they have a very large reserve. At the present time the demand liabilities are abnormally large, but the reserves are also abnormally large, and the high reserve ratio is, therefore, misleading.

Since the entry of the United States into the war, there has been an enormous flow of gold into the vaults of the Federal Reserve Banks. As a matter of deliberate policy during the war and since, the Federal Reserve Banks have sought to draw into their vaults the gold (and gold certificates) in circulation in the country and the gold in the vaults of member banks, private banks, and other institutions. The response of the country to this policy of the Federal Reserve Banks has been exceedingly gratifying. It has been demonstrated that gold in the hands of the people or in the hands of the banking institutions of the country constitutes an admirable secondary reserve which can be drawn into the Federal Reserve Banks when needed. The war-time experience of Great Britain, France, and Germany demonstrated the same thing. Gold in the pockets of the people, and gold scattered among the numerous ordinary banking institutions, can be assembled and transferred into direct reserve when the central insitutions call for it.

The decline in the gold holdings of the Federal Reserve Banks in the period between May, 1919, and August, 1920, does not mean that gold ceased coming into the Federal Reserve Banks from the country at large. During this period the Federal Reserve Banks drew in an additional $150,000,000 of gold from circulation and from the ordinary banks of the country, which very substantially protected their gold holdings from the foreign drain upon our gold supply amounting to nearly $400,000,000 net. The new gold, which has come in from abroad since the tide turned in the latter part of 1920, has practically all gone to the Federal Reserve Banks. The power of the Federal Reserve Banks to draw in gold and gold certificates at will is, thus, not merely a war-time matter.

If the Federal Reserve Banks continue to draw in gold during the coming months, and if the liquidation of Federal Reserve notes, member bank deposits, and Federal Reserve earning assets continues, the reserve ratio could easily go to extreme heights. The liquidation of another billion dollars of member bank rediscounts, with the gold reserves of the Federal Reserve Banks held at the June 8, 1921, figure might easily give us a reserve ratio of over 75%. Liquidation of a billion and a half might place the ratio at 88%. With the idea generally entertained that a high reserve ratio should be a signal for low rediscount rates, it would be exceedingly difficult for the reserve banks to resist political pressure demanding very low rediscount rates, and demanding improper uses of Federal Reserve Bank money.

It is, therefore, under present conditions, imperative that we should combat the theory which makes a high reserve ratio a signal for low rediscount rates. Our present high reserve ratio and our prospective higher reserve ratio are wholly abnormal and misleading.

Trustees of the World's Gold

We hold an enormous proportion of the world's gold, and the world's gold is still flowing toward our shores. Much of this gold we cannot expect permanently to retain. We hold it as trustees. Europe will need it again from us in future years when she has sufficiently reorganized her public finances and her currencies to go back to the gold standard. We cannot treat it as a permanent possession, and we must hold it ready to give back to Europe when Europe is prepared to take it. We dare not make it the basis for non-liquid credits. We dare not use it in such a way that we cannot easily return it when Europe is able to take it back. The volume of it is so great that, if we could look forward to retaining it permanently, it would tend to depreciate upon our hands. The problem is not so much a problem of conserving the physical gold in one big pile as it is a problem of conserving its value and keeping it mobile.

The Ratio of Reserve Bank Expansion to Expansion by the Commercial Banks of the Country

To what extent may we expect the swollen volume of Federal Reserve Bank credits which the war and post-war boom brought about to be liquidated? Shall we soon return to a condition where the great bulk of the bank credit of the country is supplied by the ordinary banks of the country? Will the Federal Reserve Banks return to the position which they occupied prior to our entrance into the war in 1917, of true reserve banks with great unused lending power, ready to expand in emergencies? Or have we reached a situation in which the Federal Reserve Banks are permanently to contribute a large part of the ordinary bank credit in use in the country? A dogmatic answer to these questions should, of course, not be given. Much will depend upon the rediscount policy which the Federal Reserve Banks employ. If they make their rates low enough, they will doubtless find borrowers who will absorb regularly and all the time substantial amounts of their funds. In the present state of frozen credits, it is possible that a good many banks in important regions of the country may be obliged for a long time to rely upon them for accommodation. If, however, they adopt and persist in a policy of keeping their rates above the market, we may anticipate that any considerable increase in business activity, or other circumstance which permits the liquidation of frozen loans, will lead to a very sharp decline indeed in the total earning assets of the Federal Reserve Banks.

The theory has been heard in the course of the past year in certain circles that liquidation of Federal Reserve Bank earning assets will have to be slow, because an enormous liquidation of member bank loans must precede a moderate liquidation at the Federal Reserve Banks. The theory has been expressed that there is something like a 9:1 ratio between expansion of the banks of the country as a whole and expansion at the Federal Reserve Banks, and that there must consequently be a liquidation of $9 of general bank credits to secure a liquidation of $1 at the Federal Reserve Banks. This theory apparently rests on the assumption that on every dollar of reserve bank credit there can be, will be, and has been based an expansion of $9 of credit in the country at large, and that there is a fixed ratio between reserve bank credit and general bank credit of about 9:1. The doctrine apparently is that credit will be expanded by every bank in the system to the full limit of the potentialities of the system, and that the one factor governing bank credit is the possible volume of reserves.

An examination of the facts in this connection, as developed by our experience in the United States, is well worth while.

We may take as our starting point April of 1917, at which time the total earning assets of the Federal Reserve Banks were approximately $220,000,000. Since that time the expansion in the earning assets of the Federal Reserve Banks has been enormous, and it is interesting to see what parallel movements there have been on the part of the banks of the country as a whole, and whether or not any definite ratios can be ascertained between them.

Figures for the banks of the country as a whole are obtained annually in the reports made to the Comptroller toward the end of June.[1] These figures cover national banks, State banks, trust companies, savings banks, and private banks. We omit from them the figures for savings banks in our computations.

If we compare the increased earning assets of the Federal Reserve Banks with the increase in commercial bank deposits in the country, we find that fifteen months after the entrance of the United States into the war there had been a greater expansion of earning assets of the Federal Reserve Banks than there had been in deposits in the commercial banks of the country. Instead of a 9:1 expansion, the expansion had been 1:1.03. By the end of June 1919, Federal Reserve Bank earning assets had expanded $2,128,000,000, while deposits in the commercial banks of the country had expanded $5,908,000,000, as compared with the situation of April, 1917. At the end of two years and three months, in other words, the ratio of expansion stood, not 9:1, but 2.8:1. By the end of June, 1920, at a time when the expansion of the banks of the country was straining every possible limit, the ratio had gone to 3.2:1. Federal Reserve earning assets, by the end of June, 1920, had increased over April, 1917, $3,046,000,000, while deposits in the other banks of the country had increased $9,892,000,000. The comparison of bank deposits in the country with earning assets of the Federal Reserve Banks in the country gives no warrant to the view that there is any 9:1 ratio or that there is any fixed ratio. It does, however, demonstrate that the extreme limits of possible expansion of the banks of the country, based on Federal Reserve Bank expansion, are far below 9:1.

A similar result is obtained when the loans of the commercial banks of the country are compared with the earning assets of the Federal Reserve Banks. The loans of the banks of the country expanded from April, 1917, to the end of June, 1920,

[1] For 1917 we have converted these figures into May 5 figures by altering them to conform to the National Bank returns to the Comptroller on May 5—, the Comptroller's "call" nearest to the beginning of Federal Reserve Bank expansion.

by $10,362,000,000, giving a 3.4:1 ratio with the expansion of earning assets of the Federal Reserve Banks.

The ratio is greater when the increase in total loans and investments of the commercial banks of the country is compared with the increase in earning assets of the Federal Reserve Banks. In the three years and three months in question the total loans and investments of the commercial banks of the country increased $13,555,000,000, giving a ratio of 4.5:1.

When the growth of the total resources of the Federal Reserve Banks is compared with the growth of the total resources of all the banks of the country, a much lower ratio appears. The total resources of the Federal Reserve Banks increased $5,216,000,000 from April, 1917, to the end of June, 1920. The total resources of the commercial banks of the country increased $13,551,000,000 in the same period. The ratio of increase is 2.6:1.

The following comparison may be still more significant. We may add together the Federal Reserve notes outstanding and the deposits in the commercial banks of the country to obtain the total circulating bank credit of the country.[1] The items on the assets side of the Federal Reserve balance sheet corresponding would be the reserves of the Federal Reserve Banks and the earning assets of the Federal Reserve Banks. As these two items grow, Federal Reserve notes may increase and bank reserves lying behind commercial bank deposits may increase.

In the first fifteen months following April 6, 1917, the combined earning assets and reserves of the Federal Reserve Banks increased more rapidly than did the combined Federal Reserve

[1] This ignores the National Bank notes and the Federal Reserve Bank notes. These two items in combination, however, have not varied greatly in the period under consideration. The Federal Reserve Bank notes have been chiefly issued to replace silver certificates. Our results would be very slightly changed if these factors were taken into account. We do not bring into our figures member bank deposits with the Federal Reserve Banks, since drafts on these are used primarily for interbank settlements and do not circulate among the people or among business houses. They are merely a link between the Federal Reserve Banks' earning assets and reserves, on the one hand, and commercial bank deposits on the other hand.

notes and commercial bank deposits. The ratio was 1.05:1. Combined reserves and earning assets of the Federal Reserve Banks had increased $2,541,000,000; combined Federal Reserve notes and commercial bank deposits had increased $2,427,000,000. By the end of June of the following year, 1919, the ratio had risen to 1:2.1. Combined earning assets and reserves of the Federal Reserve Banks had increased in the two years and three months $3,760,000,000, while Federal Reserve notes and commercial bank deposits combined had increased $8,030,000,000. By the end of June, 1920, the increase over April 6, 1917, of combined earning assets and reserves of the Federal Reserve Banks was $4,572,000,000; and the increase in combined Federal Reserve notes and commercial bank deposits was $12,684,000,000, giving a ratio of 1:2.8.

The peak of expansion, both of the banks of the country as a whole and of the Federal Reserve Banks, was apparently reached in October of 1920. Detailed figures for all of the banks of the country since that time are, of course, not available. It is possible, however, to get some index from the figures of the reporting member banks of the Federal Reserve System, which would show the relation between liquidation by member banks and liquidation by the Federal Reserve Banks. From October 15, 1920, to May 25, 1921, the total earning assets of the Federal Reserve Banks declined $1,075,000,000. Deposits of member banks decreased less than earning assets of the Federal Reserve Banks decreased. The ratio, instead of being $9 of member bank deposits to $1 of Federal Reserve Bank earning assets, was actually less than 1:1. If total deposits be broken up into demand and time deposits, it appears that the demand deposits of the reporting member banks decreased $1,320,000,000 during this period, while their time deposits increased $245,000,000. The decrease in demand deposits of the reporting member banks thus moved somewhat faster than the decrease in earning assets of the Federal Reserve Banks, the ratio being something more than 1:1. The total loans and investments of member banks during this same period declined $1,938,000,000 as against a decline of $1,159,000,000 of the earning assets of the Federal Reserve Banks—a ratio of 1.7:1.

It is time to explode once for all the theory so widely prevalent in the text books, and so often used as the basis of wild computations, that a banker can expand his loans and deposits fourfold, sixfold, or ninefold for every increase in his reserves. It has often been gravely stated that for a given increase in the cash resources of a bank a several-fold increase in its loans may be made; and, since these loans will take the form of writing down deposit credits to the customers' accounts in the books, a several-fold increase in the bank's deposits may be made.

The banker knows that this theory is absurd. He knows that he can only lend what he has. If new cash is deposited with him, or if through rediscounting he obtains new cash in the form of deposit credits with the Federal Reserve Bank, he can lend that. If he lends more than that he will find checks coming in against him at the clearing house which it will embarass him to meet, or checks presented at the counter, calling for actual cash. For a given bank at a given time loans can expand, not in any multiple ratio with increasing reserves, but merely dollar for dollar with increasing reserves.

It is, of course, true that if all the banks of the country are simultaneously expanding so that they do not drain away one another's reserves, an expansion in a greater ratio than 1:1 may take place. If a bank could be sure that incoming checks at the clearing house would always be offset by checks on other banks deposited with it, it could forthwith increase its loans (and consequently deposits) in some multiple ratio with the increase in its reserves obtained by rediscounting. But no bank can ever be sure of this. The figures given above would seem to indicate the maximum possibilities in this matter in the period of greatest stretching of credit that the country has ever seen. In quiet times we may expect that a ratio of 3.2:1 (the ratio of expansion of the deposits of the commercial banks to the expansion of the earning assets of the Federal Reserve Banks) will probably never be attained. For any individual bank to attempt to build $3.20 of credit upon $1 of rediscounts would be suicidal. For any particular section of the country to attempt it would be suicidal. For the country as a whole to attempt it when the rest of the world was quiescent in the matter of credit expansion would ordinarily be speedily checked by foreign drains on our gold. It was possible in 1919 and 1920 because not only the whole country, but also the whole world, was straining every resource in credit expansion.

Fundamentally, the basis of credit is not reserves, but general assets. Credits may safely and properly grow as wealth grows, and particularly as the liquid part of wealth grows. The bulk of the wealth of the country is not gold, but real estate, factories, railroads, crops, live stock, work in process, goods on shelves, and the like. The mobile or liquid part of the wealth of the country, with the growth of which bank credits may properly grow, is such of these items as are easily salable. This includes not merely the goods in current movement and the work in process, but also that part of the wealth of the country represented by bonds and shares with a wide and ready market.

Our conclusion would be that with the restoration of normal conditions in the United States, and of a normal relation between the rediscount rates of the Federal Reserve Banks and the market rate, we should see an enormous reduction in the volume of rediscounts, in the earning assets of the Federal Reserve Banks, and in the demand liabilities of the Federal Reserve Banks. Even with the rediscount rates below the market rates, the member banks of the country are generally working hard to "get out of the Federal Reserve Banks," that is, to return to a position where their own capital and surplus and deposits supply the basis of their earning and investing operations.

The member banks were thoroughly justified in rediscounting liberally with the Federal Reserve Banks in order to assist the Treasury in financing the war. They would have been slackers had they not done so. They were under the most imperative obligation, also, to rediscount heavily with the Federal Reserve Banks during the crisis in order that they might take care of their customers and avert a panic. It was only a doctrinaire policy which could criticise lending by the banks or rediscounting by the banks in these two great emergencies. The banks which did not do it failed to do their duty to the community.

But the banks themselves are disposed to reduce their rediscounts as rapidly as they can without embarrassing their good customers. And with the restoration of the proper relation between the rediscount rate of the Federal Reserve Banks and the market rates, this process may be expected to go very far. The present volume of Reserve Bank credit is very much in excess of the amount outstanding in April, 1917, at a time when the general average of commodity prices in the United States was higher than it is today. If our position to-day were as liquid as it was then, we should have little occasion for much more credit from the Federal Reserve Banks than we had then. With the progressive thawing out of frozen credits and the gradual restoration of liquidity throughout the credit system of the country, we may expect the capital, surplus, and deposits of the commercial banks of the country to suffice for the great mass of bank accommodation required in the country, and may expect the Federal Reserve Banks to resume their normal position of reserve banks and emergency banks with greatly reduced assets and liabilities. Confident prediction cannot be made here. There will be banks, particularly smaller banks in country districts, where local rates of interest are much above the great city market rates, which will find it profitable to borrow substantially from the Federal Reserve Banks all the time. If rediscount rates are kept too low, even the great city banks may be tempted to do too much of this.

But with a sound policy at the Federal Reserve Banks, the liquidation process should go far.

The Rediscount Rate as a Stabilizer of Prices

One of the most dangerous proposals which has been made in connection with the rediscount policy of the Federal Reserve Banks is that they should seek by varying the rediscount rate to hold the general average of commodity prices in the United States at a fixed level. The plan proposed has been that rediscount rates should be raised as a means of checking a price advance and that they should be lowered as a means of checking a decline in prices, and that by this process prices should be stabilized.

An obvious danger in such a policy would be that if the Federal Reserve Banks were generally believed to have such a power, and if they should undertake to exercise such a power, they would at once become subject to irresistible political pressure in the interest, not of stable prices, but rather of "prosperity." The special interests, clamoring for higher prices for this, that, and the other commodity, are almost always much stronger and more effective politically than is the unorganized general consuming public, which desires lower prices. If it were generally supposed that the Federal Reserve authorities really had any such control over prices, the Federal Reserve System would at once become a football of politics. Even if the policy were concurred in, and the effort were made to stabilize prices by this device, there would be a tremendous political controversy over the composition of the average of prices of the index number which was to be kept stable, as various special interests sought to have a greater weight given to the prices of their particular products.

A much more fundamental objection, however, is to be found in the fact that this proposal involves a grotesque and absurd exaggeration of the influence of rediscount rates over commodity prices. The writer who has been most responsible for the theory that rediscount rates of central banks can control price levels is Professor Knut Wicksell of Sweden.[1] Wicksell argues that if the bank rate is lowered from 4% to 3%, a business man can pay one quarter of one per cent. more for goods which he expects to hold three months, and one per cent. more for goods which he expects to hold a year, even if he anticipates no increase in the prices of the goods which he sells. He can also afford to pay one quarter of one per cent. more wages on work in process to be marketed three months later and correspondingly more rent for land. Higher wages and other incomes, however, would lead to greater demand and to higher prices generally, which would mean that the business man could get more for his goods than before, which would make it possible for him to pay still more for the raw materials, labor, and other things which he has to buy. He argues that these higher prices will sustain themselves even if the bank rate goes back to 4%, because the business man's goods also have risen, and he both can and must pay more for his materials, labor, etc. If the rate should stay down at 3%, the prices would continue to rise still more. Wicksell has the idea of a natural rate of interest, adapted to a given situation, which will neither raise nor lower prices, and his contention is that the artificial manipulation of the bank rate above or below this natural rate tends to depress or to raise prices, a rising bank rate tending to depress them, a falling bank rate tending to raise them.

Wicksell admits, however, a host of limitations upon his doctrine. He admits that banks which make their discount rates too low will lose their gold to general circulation, to other banks, and to the arts, and that countries which make their discount rates too low will lose their gold to other countries. It would take a world-wide policy, worked out through all the central banks of the world, to regulate prices according to his scheme. He admits, too, that the industrial uses of gold, drawing away part of world bank reserves, would limit this policy. Finally, his reasoning implies,

[1] "Der Bankzins als Regulator der Warenpreise," Conrad's *Jahrbücher*, 1897.

and he indeed admits, that if the tendency of prices is strongly downward and business men expect prices to fall, say 8% in the course of a year, a reduction of the bank rate from 4% to zero would not check the fall. The banks in such a case would actually have to forego interest and in addition pay a premium to their borrowing customers of 4% in order to get them to borrow and spend enough money to prevent an anticipated fall of 8% in prices. Wicksell comes to the practical conclusion that in the real world, constituted as it is, the bank rate merely has a greater or less influence on prices, and that the central bank of no country could really control prices by its discount policy.

It is easy to trace the influence of the rediscount policy of the Federal Reserve Banks on prices, particularly in the period of the post-war boom and in the reaction which has followed. The Federal Reserve rediscount rates were too low in 1919. They were far below the market rates through most of that year. Prices would have risen and would have risen greatly even had Federal Reserve Bank rates been higher. The main factors making for rising prices during 1919 and early 1920 were: (a) the insatiable demand of Europe for goods in this country without limit of price or quantity; (b) the continued gigantic expenditures on the part of the American Government; (c) the wave of extravagance which spread over the American people; and (d) declining industrial efficiency, with the further shortening of supplies in the United States. With conditions of this sort in existence the demand for borrowed money was very great; and with the Federal Reserve Banks willing to supply this money on unduly easy terms, a good deal more money was borrowed than would otherwise have been the case. Credit was able to expand further than would have been the case otherwise in financing our dangerous boom. But the Reserve Bank's rediscount policy was not the main factor. It was a contributing factor in what would have been a dangerous boom even with a much better policy on the part of the Federal Reserve Banks.

Similarly, the raising of the rediscount rate by the Federal Reserve Banks helped to check the boom. It made the interest element in cost of business go higher, and consequently helped make profits disappear. It was not, however, the chief element in the rising costs which swamped profits in so many businesses and compelled reaction. Labor costs rose also on an appalling scale, partly through rising wages and partly through growing labor inefficiency. Rentals rose startlingly on new leases. Raw materials rose. Costs multiplied through declining managerial efficiency. Demoralization of railroad traffic made for a great rise in costs. Coal rose to great heights, etc. Moreover, long before the Federal Reserve Banks raised their rediscount rates, interest rates in the open market were very high. The shortage of real capital and the shortage of bank money reflected themselves in rapidly rising rates on all kinds of loans, well in advance of an increase in the rediscount rates of the Federal Reserve Banks. To attribute the rise in prices in 1919 to the low rediscount rates of the Federal Reserve Banks and to attribute the fall in prices in 1920 to the moderately higher rediscount rates of the Federal Reserve Banks, is to exaggerate in an absurd degree a minor factor in the general situation.

There is evidence enough in the utterances of Federal Reserve authorities that they neither claim to have the power to regulate prices, nor desire to have it, nor believe that they possibly could have it.

Much more reasonable than the proposal that the Federal Reserve Banks should seek to stabilize prices by their rediscount policy is the suggestion that they should properly consider the general business situation in governing their rediscount policy, and that they may consider the course of commodity prices as one factor in the general business situation. Very rapidly rising commodity prices may well constitute a danger signal which would justify them in raising sharply the question of whether new credits are soundly based and which would justify them in scrutinizing very closely loans offered for rediscount. If they are convinced that speculation is going dangerously far, they may properly place their rediscount rates higher as a means of checking it.

Usually, however, in a situation of this sort what is called for is not so much a *general* restriction of all kinds of credit, as a check on some particular kind of credit expansion, which is basic to the rest, and which is the root and origin of the general movement. This, for example, was to be found in 1919 and 1920 in the rapidly growing unfunded debt of Europe to the United States; and, had the Federal Reserve Banks been able to discriminate in their rediscounting against loans which contributed most directly to making this possible, they could have gone far in mitigating trouble, even apart from the general change in rediscount rates. It is perfectly legitimate, indeed it is exceedingly desirable, that the Federal Reserve authorities should be studying the business conditions of the country constantly, and that they should discourage unsound borrowing by higher discount rates and by discriminations of one or another kind.

It is, however, no part of the business of the banks or of the Federal Reserve Banks to make artificially easy money rates with the purpose of raising prices and creating "prosperity." Artificial money rates, like all other artificial prices, are pernicious. The normal tendency in a period of depression is for liquidation to proceed, borrowing to fall off, and funds to accumulate in the banks, which brings about sooner or later low natural discount rates, which, in conjunction with a general lowering of costs of production, lay the foundation for business revival. The revival is in order when costs of production of all kinds, including rentals, overhead, wages, raw materials, coal, and so on, have been shaken down until they are in line with the prices of finished products. It is necessary that this general shaking down should be thoroughgoing before a soundly based revival can be expected. The effort to offset the failure of certain costs to come down by making other costs artificially low is pernicious. Any revival based upon it would be unsound and short-lived.

When money rates are made artificially low, there is a reaction on long time rates of interest on investment money. They also tend to go lower. There is a temptation to use bank money as a substitute for investment money. The demand for capital is increased by the low rates, while the supply of capital is checked by the low rates. Men do not save as much for 3% as they will save for 6%. Businesses make less economical use of 3% capital than they make of 6% capital. A corporation which can float a 3% bond issue in an artifically easy money market will be tempted to pay out all its earnings in dividends and to increase its fixed charges. The same corporation, facing the necessity of paying 6% on a bond issue, will turn back its earnings to surplus, pay out lower dividends, and refrain from issuing bonds.

Natural prices are those prices which develop in open competition and which over reasonble periods of time are adequate to induce a normal supply of the thing demanded. Artificially high prices increase supply and check demand. Artificially low prices increase demand and check supply. Artificial prices, in either case, tend to destroy equilibrium, and to bring about congestion or stagnation. This is as true of money rates and of railroad freight rates as it is of the price of wheat or the price of cotton or other commodities.

Summary

The basic principle of rediscount banking, well established in the traditions of the central banks of Europe, is that the official rate of rediscount shall be above the market rate. This is essential if bank funds are not to be made superabundant and if general market rates are not to be forced so low as to be far below the natural rates of interest, leading to wasteful employment of bank funds on the one hand, while interfering with savings by investors and businesses on the other hand.

As applied to England, this means that the official bank rate shall be kept above the market rate on prime bills of exchange. The Bank of England has not varied from this policy on annual averages since 1871. If, for a few days, the market rate should rise above Bank Rate, Bank Rate is promptly advanced to correct it.

In the United States the bill market is relatively unimportant. The "market" is best represented *by rates on customers' loans made under lines of credit by the banks of the great cities to those of their customers who have borrowing accounts with several banks in several cities.* The rates on such loans are highly competitive. They are rarely published, but they are known in the banking community and to the Federal Reserve authorities. They tend to be uniform throughout the great cities of the country.

It is true that in England many of the "advances" of the banks are made to their customers at rates above the official bank rate. The significant point is, however, that the Bank of England does not rediscount advances to customers. It rediscounts only bills. In the United States, on the other hand, customers' loans are actually rediscounted with the Federal Reserve Banks. The essential principle involved in "keeping above the market" is that it shall cost a bank something to rediscount. It ought not to be possible for banks at the financial centers to borrow money from the Federal Reserve Banks and re-lend it at a profit.

There are really several rediscount rates at the Federal Reserve Banks: a rate on loans on Government war paper; another rate, which may be different, on commercial paper; a third rate, which may be still different, on acceptances. The important thing is that each of these rates should be above the market rates for each type of loan.

If we develop a wide discount market for acceptances; if bills drawn in dollars, growing out of actual self-liquidating commercial operations, increase in number; if foreign banks develop the practice of holding such bills as an interest-bearing substitute for gold reserves; and if banks generally throughout the United States make a practice of carrying substantial amounts of such bills in their portfolios as an especially liquid resource, then the rediscount rate on acceptances may become the most important rate at the Federal Reserve Banks. The rediscount rate on acceptances in such a case may safely go much below the rediscount rate for customers' line of credit paper, in full harmony with the principle of keeping above the market, since the market itself will discriminate in favor of such bills.

The reserve ratio under present conditions is no safe guide for rediscount policy. Five main factors have been considered by the Bank of England in fixing its rediscount rate:

1. Is the reserve ratio high or low?
2. Are trade and speculation expanding or are trade and speculation depressed?
3. Is gold coming into or going out of the country?
4. Are the exchanges favorable or adverse to England?
5. What is the market rate? Bank Rate must not fall below it, and is almost always above it.

Of these five considerations the dominant one has always been that of keeping above the market. When necessary to conform with this principle, rediscount rates have been raised in the face of high reserve ratios and, in harmony with this principle, have been lowered in the face of low reserve ratios.

The high reserve ratio in the United States to-day does not justify lowering rediscount rates: (1) because rediscount rates are already below the market rates (barring acceptances); and (2) because the present reserve ratio is abnormal and misleading. The reserve ratio is not high in the United States because the liabilities of the Federal Reserve Banks are low, but rather is high, despite abnormally high liabilities of the Federal Reserve Banks, *because the reserves are abnormally high.*

This is due partly to the unprecedented influx of foreign gold, and partly to the policy which the Federal Reserve Banks have pursued since our entrance into the war of drawing into their vaults the great bulk of the gold and gold certificates held by banks and individuals throughout the country. There is relatively little gold left in circulation. Under normal conditions, a gold standard country will have a substantial amount of gold in hand to hand circulation. If, for example, we returned the legal tenders now in the Federal Reserve Banks, together with a billion dollars of their gold (or gold certificates) to general circulation, with a corresponding cancellation of Federal Reserve Bank notes, the reserve ratio would stand, not at 58.3%, at which it stood on June 8, 1921, but rather at 43.5%.

The great excess of gold in our Federal Reserve Banks constitutes a real problem. The artificially high reserve ratio, which may easily go to extreme heights with further liquidation, constitutes a shining target for cheap money advocates, and constitutes a temptation to unsound employment of Federal Reserve funds. We must recognize that we hold much of our gold in trust against the time when Europe will need it to restore sound currency in Europe. We must not let it depreciate upon our hands or tie it up in illiquid credits.

The proposal that the Federal Reserve Banks should stabilize commodity prices by varying their rediscount rates, lowering the rates when prices fall to pull them up again, and raising the rates when prices rise to pull them down again, is thoroughly vicious and unsound. It is, in the first place, economically impossible. Rediscount rates are only a minor factor affecting prices. In the second place, any effort to apply this policy would at once make the Federal Reserve Banks a football of politics.

Our two most significant conclusions are: (a) that the rediscount rate should be kept above the market rate; and (b) that the high Federal Reserve ratio, due to an artificial and abnormal excess of gold, constitutes no justification at all for reducing rediscount rates.

Condition of the Federal Reserve Banks (In Millions of Dollars) [1]

Date	Total Gold Reserves	Total Cash Reserves	Total Earning Assets	Total Resources	Total Deposits	Federal Reserve Notes in Circulation
1914						
Nov. 20	205	241	6	247	228	2.7
Dec. 31	229	256	11	278	256	10.6
1915						
Mar. 26	242	265	53	333	288	34
June 25	255	303	55	381	311	72
Sept. 24	290	313	79	418	345	116
Dec. 30	345	358	83	491	415	189
1916						
Mar. 31	335	345	135	523	458	163
June 30	377	404	172	625	559	152
Sept. 29	387	395	184	633	561	197
Dec. 29	454	471	222	768	698	275
1917						
Mar. 30	938	947	168	1,256	842	358
June 29	1,295	1,334	495	2,053	1,484	509
Sept. 28	1,408	1,458	505	2,204	1,434	700
Dec. 28	1,671	1,721	1,064	3,101	1,771	1,246
1918						
Mar. 28-29	1,816	1,874	1,202	3,446	1,901	1,453
June 28	1,949	2,006	1,345	3,872	2,050	1,722
Sept. 27	2,021	2,072	2,081	4,817	2,317	2,349
Dec. 27	2,090	2,146	2,318	5,252	2,313	2,685
1919						
Mar. 28	2,142	2,211	2,335	5,230	2,401	2,522
June 27	2,148	2,216	2,354	5,288	2,437	2,499
Sept. 26	2,118	2,188	2,503	5,632	2,542	2,655
Dec. 26	2,078	2,136	3,080	6,325	2,780	3,058
1920						
Mar. 26	1,935	2,057	3,191	6,048	2,542	3,048
June 25	1,969	2,109	3,183	6,075	2,473	3,117
Sept. 24	1,990	2,152	3,310	6,312	2,477	3,280
Dec. 30	2,059	2,249	3,263	6,270	2,321	3,345
1921						
Mar. 25	2,211	2,422	2,692	5,753	1,841	2,931
June 29	2,462	2,625	2,060	5,242	1,686	2,634
Sept. 28	2,726	2,879	1,666	5,107	1,717	2,457
Dec. 28	2,870	2,992	1,536	5,151	1,765	2,443
1922						
Mar. 29	2,975	3,103	1,180	4,816	1,805	2,182
June 28	3,021	3,148	1,180	4,905	1,939	2,124
Sept. 27	3,077	3,203	1,110	4,970	1,840	2,243
Dec. 27	3,040	3,149	1,334	5,305	1,900	2,464

[1] Annual Reports Federal Reserve Board 1914–1920. 1921–22 Weekly Statements.

MISCELLANEOUS FINANCIAL STATISTICS

Year	Bank Clearings (millions) [1]		Savings Banks [2]		Failures [3]	
	New York	United States	Depositors (Thousands)	Deposits (Millions)	Number (Thousands)	Liabilities (Millions)
1915	90,843	163,009	11,286	4,998	22	302
1916	147,181	242,236	11,148	5,089	17	196
1917	181,534	305,044	11,367	5,418	14	182
1918	174,524	320,989	11,380	5,472	10	163
1919	214,703	387,912	11,435	5,903	6	113
1920	252,338	464,052	11,428	6,537	9	295
1921	204,082	374,825	10,738	6,018	20	627
1922	213,326	380,493	12,539	7,181	24	624

[1] Years ended Sept. 30.
[2] For reports nearest June 30 of each year.
[3] Calendar years.

FAILURES OF NATIONAL BANKS[1]

YEAR	NUMBER	CAPITAL	CLAIMS PROVED	PAID TO DATE	% PAID
1864-1873	34	$ 8,211,100	$14,820,455	$10,582,012	71.4
1874-1883	55	11,762,800	18,956,573	13,484,510	71.1
1884-1893	161	24,577,000	54,457,531	37,811,696	69.4
1894-1902	158	23,661,520	53,206,406	44,242,593	83.2
1903-1915	165	25,903,500	63,024,136	52,786,670	83.8
1916-1921[2]	55	4,005,000	15,465,061	6,202,278	40.1
Total	628	$98,120,920	$219,930,162	$165,109,759	75.1

[1] For later years, assets have not been entirely distributed.
[2] Oct. 31, 1921.

BANKING POWER BY SECTIONS

National, State, Savings, and Private Banks and Trust Companies.

STATES	CAPITAL, SURPLUS, PROFITS AND DEPOSITS[2] (MILLIONS OF DOLLARS)	PER CAPITA
	1921[1]	1921
New England	$ 4,775	$631.89
Eastern	16,853	670.37
Middle	10,603	350.63
Southern	4,389	148.94
Western	2,342	273.13
Pacific.	3,090	429.31
United States	42,052	388.74

[1] The total banking power of the United States on June 30, 1921 (31,270 banking institutions) is computed by the Comptroller of the Currency to be $48,-219,900,000, this including estimates for 446 non-reporting banks and amounts for 12 Federal Reserve Banks.
[2] Under deposits are postal savings deposits, including outstanding articles.

PRODUCTION OF GOLD AND SILVER

(In Millions of Dollars)

Year	World			United States		London Price of Silver[1]	Ratio	Bullion Value of Silver Dollar
	Gold	Silver		Gold	Silver			
		Commercial Value	Coining Value		Commercial Value			
1914	439	92	216	95	40	$0.55312	37.37	.427
1915	469	87	217	101	37	.51892	39.84	.401
1916	454	121	227	93	49	.68647	30.11	.531
1917	419	162	234	84	59	.89525	23.09	.692
1918	384	195	256	69	66	1.04171	21.00	.761
1919	366	198	228	60	64	1.25047	18.44	.867
1920	337	177	224	51	61	1.34649	20.27	.788
1921	330	111	227	50	53	.80522	32.75	.488

[1] Per fine ounce.

EXHIBIT OF GROWTH OF NATIONAL BANKS

(Expressed in Millions)

Date	Number	Capital	Surplus and Profits	Loans	Deposits	Circulation	Total Resources
1915. Nov. 10	7,617	1,069	1,040	7,234	7,446	713	13,236
1916. Sept. 12	7,589	1,068	1,048	7,860	8,446	674	14,412
1917. Sept. 11	7,638	1,090	1,123	9,055	10,185	666	16,543
1918. Nov. 1	7,754	1,108	1,208	10,097	12,151	676	19,821
1919. Sept. 12	7,821	1,138	1,301	11,085	13,192	682	21,615
1920. Sept. 8	8,093	1,248	1,456	12,416	13,649	693	21,885
1921. Sept. 6	8,155	1,276	1,566	10,978	12,144	705	19,014

CONDITIONS OF THE REPORTING MEMBER BANKS (In Millions of Dollars)

Date	Number of Reporting Banks	Total U. S. Securities Owned	Other Bonds, Stocks, and Securities [1]	Total Loans, Discounts and Investments [2]	Loans Secured by U. S. War Obligations	Net Demand Deposits	Accommodation at Federal Reserve Banks [4]
1917							
Dec. 7	607	1,763		9,916	374	8,391	
Dec. 28	630	892		10,134	388	8,570	
1918							
Mar. 29	682	1,805		12,094	312	9,201	
June 28	705	1,446		12,516	499	9,118	
Sept. 27	747	2,186		13,277	475	9,532	
Dec. 27	759	2,056		13,659	1,269	9,963	
1919							
Mar. 28	772	2,829		14,204	1,122	10,054	1,423
June 27	772	2,189		14,350	1,381	10,286	1,351
Sept. 26	776	2,243		15,297	1,333	10,839	1,476
Dec. 26	797	1,930		15,621	1,020	11,174	1,834
1920							
Mar. 26	811	1,548		15,775	1,170	11,493	2,114
June 25	814	1,561		15,728	1,026	11,344	1,946
Sept. 24	818	1,448		15,674	950	11,161	2,151
Dec. 31	821	1,391		15,287	909	10,942	2,098
1921							
Mar. 25	823	1,342	2,042	14,796	760	10,186	1,760
June 29	817	1,374	2,074	14,442	672	10,046	1,215
Sept. 28	809	1,362	2,022	14,307	577	9,866	875
Dec. 28	806	1,470	2,090	14,343	513	10,174	698
1922							
Mar. 29	804	1,610	2,092	14,372	394	10,309	268
June 28	799	2,101	2,395	15,120	285	11,124	165
Sept. 27	790	2,219	2,247	15,359	261	11,085	160
Dec. 27	782	2,549		16,152 [3]	290	11,255	369

[1] Not reported separately until 1921.
[2] Not including rediscounts with Federal Reserve Bank, except for Dec. 27, 1922.
[3] Includes rediscounts with Federal Reserve Bank.
[4] Not reported separately until 1919.

Circulation of Money in the United States
(Millions of Dollars)

July 1	Gold [1]	Silver [2]	Subsidiary Silver	U. S. Notes	Treasury Notes [3]	National Bank Notes	Federal Reserve Notes	Federal Reserve Bank Notes	Total	In Treasury and F. R. Banks [4]	In Circulation	Population Millions	Per Capita Circulation Dollars
1915..	1,986	568	185	347	2.2	819	84		3,989	728	3,261	101	32.38
1916..	2,450	568	189	347	2.1	744	176	9	4,483	892	3,591	102	35.06
1917..	3,019	568	198	347	2.0	715	547	13	5,408	1,559	3,849	104	36.96
1918..	3,076	500	232	347	1.9	724	1,848	15	6,741	2,405	4,336	106	40.96
1919..	3,113	308	243	347	1.7	719	2,688	188	7,605	2,810	4,795	106.1	45.18
1920..	2,709	269	259	347	1.7	719	3,406	201	7,910	2,578	5,332	106.4	50.11
1921..	3,298	289	271	347	1.6	743	3,000	151	8,099	3,256	4,843	108.1	44.80
1922..	3,785	381	271	347	1.5	758	2,555	80	8,177	3,803	4,374	109.7	39.86

[1] Includes cover for gold certificates.
[2] Includes cover for silver certificates and for Treasury Notes of 1890.
[3] Not included in "Total"; see footnote 2.
[4] Exclusive of metallic cover for gold and silver certificates and Notes of 1890.

EXPORTS AND IMPORTS OF MERCHANDISE, GOLD AND SILVER
(Millions of Dollars)

Fiscal Year	Merchandise			Silver				Gold		
	Exports	Imports	Excess Exports	Exports	Imports	Excess Exports	Excess Imports	Exports	Imports	Excess −Exports +Imports
1915	2,768	1,674	1,094	51	29	22		146	171	+ 25
1916	4,333	2,197	2,136	60	34	26		90	494	+404
1917	6,290	2,659	3,631	78	35	43		292	977	+685
1918	5,920	2,946	2,974	139	70	69		191	125	− 66
1919	7,232	3,095	4,137	301	79	222		117	63	− 54
1920	8,109	5,238	2,871	179	103	76		466	150	−316
1921	6,517	3,654	2,862	53	59		6	134	645	+511
1922	3,771	2,608	1,163	63	71		8	27	468	+441

CHAPTER XXXII

BIBLIOGRAPHY

It is proposed in this chapter to present a list of books and other publications to guide the reader who may desire to consult original records and study the discussions of the several questions at greater length.

The arrangement of the list will enable the reader to determine, without research and additional examination, which of the volumes are requisite for the pursuit of the specific subject upon which further information is desired.

The history of the Colonial and Continental periods is not voluminous, and the official records are not only scant but in many particulars fragmentary; nevertheless, much may be gleaned from the publications named below.

On the subject of Coinage, the extracts from the Journals and manuscript reports of the Continental Congress appear in: —

International Monetary Conference, 1878, Senate Ex. Doc., No. 58, 45th Cong., 3d Sess. (Washington, 1879).

This also contains Robert Morris's plan for a coinage system, Thomas Jefferson's Notes on the same, the Reports of the Board of Treasury and the Ordinance on Coinage of the Continental Congress, which established the dollar unit.

Unofficial publications are: —

History of American Coinage, David K. Watson, 1899.

Money and Banking, Horace White, 1902.

The Early Coins of America, Crosby.

United States Mint and Coinage, A. M. Smith.

Financial History of the United States, Albert S. Bolles, 1896, 3 vols.

Consult also the numbers of *Sound Currency*, semimonthly (later quarterly), published by the Reform Club, New York, 1895–1903.

Paper Currency legislation prior to 1789, from the Journals of Congress, is covered by the books mentioned below, and the data are compiled in the official Treasury publications: —

History of the Currency of the Country, etc., William F. DeKnight, 1897.

The Funding System of the United States, Jonathan Elliot, House Doc., No. 15, 28th Cong., 1st Sess.

Unofficial publications are: —

Historical Account of Massachusetts Currency, J. B. Felt, 1839.

History of Bills of Credit of New York, John H. Hickox, 1866.

Short History of Paper Money, etc., William M. Gouge, 1833.

Historical Sketches of the Paper Currency, etc., Henry Phillips, Jr., 2 vols., 1865–1866.

Currency and Banking in Massachusetts, A. McF. Davis, 2 vols., 1900.

History of American Currency, William G. Sumner, 1874; revised 1884.

The Financier and the Finances of the American Revolution, William G. Sumner, 2 vols., 1892.

Brief Account of Paper Money of the Revolution, J. W. Schuckers, 1874.

Short accounts will be found in: —

United States Notes, John Jay Knox, 1888 (3d edition, 1894).

Money and Banking, Horace White, 1902.

Money, Francis A. Walker, 1891.

Continental Currency, Byron W. Holt, *Sound Currency*, Vol. V., No. 7, 1898.

Statistics of the issue of Continental and State currency, during the Revolution, and of its fluctuation, are compiled from various sources in the DeKnight publication, in Phillips's and in Schuckers's mentioned above.

BANKING during the earliest period is discussed in: —

History of Banking in the United States, William G. Sumner (being Vol. I. of the New York *Journal of Commerce* publication, *History of Banking in all Nations*, in 4 vols.), 1896.

History of Banking in the United States, John Jay Knox, 1900.

Also the volumes of W. M. Gouge and Horace White noted above, and the *Sound Currency* publications.

The charter of the Bank of North America, the first incorporated bank, may be found in Clarke and Hall, *Legislative and Documentary History of Bank of the United States*, 1832.

The period from the adoption of the Constitution (1789) to the opening of the Civil War (1861) is in many respects the most important, covering as it does the formative era of the nation; and respecting the monetary system, the experiments which the people tried and repeated, notwithstanding the many sad experiences, serve as instructive guides to the proper understanding of the subject.

The constitutional provisions will be better understood by consulting: —

Elliot's *Debates of the Constitutional Convention.*

A Plea for the Constitution, etc., George Bancroft, 1884.

The laws will be found in the *Statutes at Large*, but the principal ones have been reprinted, laws of U. S. concerning money and banking 1778–1909, Doc. 580, National Monetary Comm. Report.

The general subject of MONEY is covered in: —

Finance Reports, being the reports of the Secretaries of the Treasury, including some special reports (many of the latter are, however, to be found elsewhere). These reports are, for the period 1789 to 1849, published in 6 volumes; thereafter in separate annual volumes, which also contain the reports of subordinate officers of the Treasury.

Messages and Papers of the Presidents, Vols. I. to V., covering this period. In the earlier messages little material is found; Madison, Jackson, and later presidents devote considerable space to the subject.

Congressional action is recorded officially in *Annals of Congress* (1789–1824), *Register of Debates* (1824–1837), and *Congressional Globe* (1838–1860); but for the period from 1789 to 1856 the material is digested in *Abridgment of Debates*, 6 vols., Thomas H. Benton.

Furthermore, Public Documents of Congress, embracing Executive and Miscellaneous Papers, Committee Reports, etc.

Executive action is also recorded in *American State Papers*, 5 vols.

Unofficial publications on the general subject are: —

American Statesmen, Andrew W. Young, 1857.

Statesman's Manual, Edw. Williams, 3 vols., 1858.

Money in Politics, J. K. Upton, 1884.

Money and Banking, Horace White, 1902.

Niles's Register, a weekly publication, 1811–1848.

Hunt's Merchant's Magazine, a monthly, 1840–1860.

Consideration on the Currency and Banking System of the United States, Albert Gallatin, 1831.

Suggestions on Banks and Currency, Albert Gallatin, 1841.

COINAGE is especially considered in Hamilton's *Report on the Establishment of a Mint*, found in *Finance Reports;* Crawford's in 1820,

Ingham's in 1830, and Gallatin's paper included in the latter. These and other important documents are reprinted in *International Monetary Conference*, 1878, already referred to. Secretary Corwin's Treasury Reports also contain valuable material. A concise review of the coinage history also appears in the *Report of the Director of the Mint* for 1895.

Congressional action is recorded in the *Annals* and *Debates* and in reports by: —

Sanford, Nathan, Senate Report No. 3, 21st Cong., 2d Sess., 1830.

White, Campbell P., House Reports, 1831, March 1832, June 1832, 1834; all of these are reprinted in the last-mentioned Report, No. 278, 23d Cong., 1st Sess., and are very valuable.

Hunter, R. M. T., Senate Report No. 104, 32d Cong., 1st Sess.

Benton's Abridgment of Debates.

Statistics of the composition of the coins and the volume of coinage from 1792 to date are annually printed in the *Reports of Directors of the Mint.*

Unofficial publications are: —

History of Bimetallism in the United States, J. Laurence Laughlin, 4th edition, 1897.

Thirty Years' View, Thomas H. Benton, 2 vols., 1854-1856.

Watson's *History of Coinage*, and White's *Money and Banking*, already referred to.

On Currency and Banking generally the official data for the early portion of the period are exceedingly meagre.

Gallatin's and Crawford's Treasury Reports and the latter's correspondence with State Banks, printed in *American State Papers;* Crawford's special report of 1820, and Elliot's *Funding System*, contain almost all the information prior to 1833, when Congress directed the Treasury to collect data on State Banks and their Currency.

Knox in *Report Comptroller of Currency*, 1876, compiled the data from the earliest days to 1863, in fairly satisfactory form. This was in large part reprinted in Senate Ex. Doc., No. 38, 52d Cong., 2d Sess.

Hepburn in the same Bureau's Report for 1892 materially enlarged the scope of the information, adding much valuable statistical material in the appendix.

After 1833 the *Finance Reports* contain much important material and the separate annual Treasury *Report on Condition of Banks* gives all the data obtainable at this time. Special mention should be made of the historical compendium on banking embraced in the appendix to Guthrie's Treasury Reports, 1855–1856, and of the reports of the condition of depositary banks, in appendices to the *Finance Reports*, 1835 and thereafter.

Discussions of the operations of State Banks of later date will be found in the *Messages of Presidents*, Jackson, Van Buren, Tyler, and Buchanan, and in the *Finance Reports* of their Secretaries of the Treasury.

The volume of money is discussed by Elliot, Gallatin, and Guthrie.

Unofficial publications of the early period include Gallatin's *Consideration of Currency and Banking System*, wherein a very detailed account of banks is given; Gouge's *Short History*, which is equally interesting.

The works above referred to of Sumner, Knox, Bolles, and White are valuable, the two former being quite comprehensive. See also *Treatise on Currency and Banking*, Condy Raguet, 1839.

In *Sound Currency*, monographs treating of the banks and note-issues of the several states are most instructive. See particularly the papers by Horace White and L. Carroll Root.

Special features are discussed in: —

The Suffolk Bank, D. R. Whitney, 1878.
The Banks of New York and Panic of 1857, J. S. Gibbons, 1859.
History of the Surplus Revenue of 1837, E. G. Bourne, 1885.
History of the Bank of New York, H. W. Domett, 1886.

Treasury Notes, aside from the several *Finance Reports* prior to 1861, are officially and comprehensively treated in DeKnight's volume already mentioned, and in *History of National Loans of the United States*, R. A. Bayley, 1881. (Also embraced in Vol. VII. of the 10th Census.)

It is also of interest to examine what Madison, Van Buren, and Tyler in their messages, and Crawford in his special report of 1820, say of the use of these notes as currency.

Unofficial publications include Knox's *United States Notes;* Sumner's several works, and Bolles's *History*.

Bank of the United States. The most comprehensive publication of official data from 1790 to 1832 is: —

Clarke and Hall, *Legislative and Documentary History*, embracing Hamilton's original plan; the debates in Congress, opinions of Hamilton and Jefferson on the question of constitutionality, the proposed and adopted charters; the Bank War; Gallatin, Dallas, Madison, Crawford, Webster, Clay, Calhoun, and others on the question generally; Congressional investigations; McDuffie's Reports; and the Supreme Court Decision by Marshall, on the Constitutionality (McCulloch *vs.* Maryland).

Finance Reports contain papers by Hamilton, Gallatin, Dallas, Rush, McLane, Taney, Woodbury, and others on the Bank.

Messages of Presidents, Madison, Jackson, Van Buren, Tyler, and Polk.

Benton's *Abridgment of Debates* and his *Thirty Years' View* also cover a great many points.

A concise review may also be found in *Report Comptroller of Currency,* 1876 (Knox), with statistics in the appendix.

Unofficial publications embracing valuable material are the already named Sumner's *History of Banking,* Knox's work of the same name, White's *Money and Banking,* Bolles's *Financial History,* Schouler's *History,* and Gallatin's *Consideration for a Currency System,* Williams's *Statesman's Manual, Niles's Register. Sound Currency,* Vol. IV., Nos. 7, 17, 18. *History of the United States of America,* Henry Adams, 1889–1891, 9 vols. *Constitutional and Political History of the United States,* H. E. Von Holst, 1877–1892, 7 vols. G. T. Curtis's *Constitutional History of the United States,* 2 vols.

Special features are treated in the works and writings of Hamilton, Jefferson, Madison, Gallatin, Dallas, Clay, Calhoun, Webster, and Woodbury, and in the Essays of Matthew Carey.

In Biographical Works, see Adams and Stevens on Gallatin; Schurz on Clay; Parton and Sumner on Jackson; Lodge, Morse, and Sumner on Hamilton; Shepard on Van Buren.

See also *Removal of Deposits from Bank of United States,* W. J. Duane, 1838; and on the same topic, Secretary Taney's separate Report in *Finance Report,* 1833.

General History of Banks, etc., T. H. Goddard, 1831, contains Cheves's report on the reorganization of the Bank.

THE SUBTREASURY SYSTEM is officially discussed by Van Buren, Tyler, and Polk in their messages, and by Secretaries Woodbury, Ewing, Walker, Guthrie, and Cobb, in the *Finance Reports.* Embraced in some of the later volumes will be found Wm. M. Gouge's reports of examinations of the Subtreasuries; see especially that of 1854.

The *Abridgment of Debates* covers the Congressional discussion.

Unofficial books on the subject include *Life and Times of Silas Wright,* R. H. Gillette, 1874.

Also Benton's *Thirty Years' View;* important references are also found in Webster's, Clay's, Woodbury's, and Calhoun's writings, and in the biographical monographs on Clay and Van Buren already referred to.

The Independent Treasury, etc., David Kinley, 1893, is quite a complete treatise.

The period after the Civil War is covered by a multitude of books, pamphlets, reports, etc.; mention is made here only of the principal ones, giving the reader an opportunity to consult those most effectively presenting the facts and discussions.

The official publications covering the entire field are: —

The *Congressional Globe* to 1873, and *Congressional Record*, 1874 to date, containing the debates in full; Congressional Documents, of which each house publishes a separate collection, including Executive and Miscellaneous Documents and Committee Reports, presenting the subjects prior to legislative action. A number of these documents are also published separately by the Executive Departments.

Messages and Papers of Presidents, Vols. VI. to X.; every incumbent of the presidency during the period has had occasion to discuss the money question.

Finance Reports, annually for fiscal years ending June 30, embracing the reports of Secretaries of the Treasury and subordinate officers, of which latter the most important are the *Reports of the Comptrollers of the Currency*, *Directors of the Mint* and *Treasurers of the United States*, which since about 1870 have also been published separately with exhaustive statistical appendices. The Mint Bureau also publishes, since 1880, annual *Reports on Production of Gold and Silver*, by calendar years. The Bureau of Statistics publishes monthly (formerly also quarterly) and annually *Reports on Commerce and Navigation;* the monthlies in the later years include besides the statistics of imports and exports, valuable statistical data on monetary subjects, and those statistics are, in digested form, reproduced in the *Statistical Abstracts of the United States*, annually, beginning in 1871.

A *Treasury Circular, No. 113*, in pamphlet form, containing a digest of the laws and statistics of coinage and currency, Washington, 1900. (Previously issued in 1896.)

Unofficial books covering all the subjects generally are: —

Money and Banking, Horace White, 1902.

Political History of the Rebellion, E. McPherson, 1864.

Political History of the Reconstruction, same author, 1871.

Handbook of Politics, biennially, 1870–1892, same author.

McPherson's works give the various measures and amendments, the votes on the several propositions, etc., constituting a valuable digest of the actions of Congress.

Speeches and Reports in Congress, John Sherman, 1881.

Recollections of Twenty Years, same author, 1895.

Twenty Years in Congress, James G. Blaine, 1884.

Financial History of the United States, Albert S. Bolles.

Thirty Years of American Finance, A. D. Noyes, 1898.

Money in Politics, J. K. Upton, 1884.

Money and Legal Tender, H. R. Linderman (sometime Director of the Mint), 1877.

Reports of Monetary Commission of Indianapolis Convention, J. Laurence Laughlin, Chicago, 1898. (Covers the entire field of our monetary history and recommends concrete reforms.)

The Natural Law of Money, William Brough, 1894.

Open Mints and Free Banking, same author, 1898.

Sound Currency, published semimonthly (afterwards quarterly) by the Reform Club, 1895–1903.

Men and Measures of Half a Century, Hugh McCulloch, 1889.

Monetary Systems of the World, M. L. Muhleman, 1896; a digest of laws and statistics.

Money and its Laws, Henry V. Poor, 1877.

Our National Currency and the Money Problem, Amasa Walker, 1876.

Principles of Money, J. Laurence Laughlin, 1903.

Financial History of United States, Davis R. Dewey, 1903.

COINAGE received but little attention during the decade, 1861–1870. The mint reports are almost the sole repositories of information.

International Monetary Conference, 1867, Report of Proceedings, by Samuel B. Ruggles, Senate Ex. Doc., No. 14, 40th Cong., 2d Sess., 1868, also reprinted in *International Monetary Conference*, 1878 (see below).

This conference was called for the purpose of considering the adoption of an international gold coin. The subject was further considered in Senate Reports of the Congress named, and discussed by Sherman in his *Speeches and Reports*.

Early in the decade, 1871–1880, the silver question developed. From the mass of publications which it called forth, the following are especially recommended: —

History of the Coinage Act of 1873, Senate Misc. Doc., No. 132, 41st Cong., 2d Sess. In this publication the progressive steps which omitted the silver dollar from the coinage system, improperly denounced as the "Crime of 1873," are fully set forth, refuting the charge. Reprinted in 1900.

United States Monetary Commission of 1876, Report and Testimony, 2 vols., Senate Report No. 703, 44th Cong., 2d Sess.

International Monetary Conference, 1878, Report of Proceedings, with appendix containing a mass of valuable material not found elsewhere, compiled by S. Dana Horton, Senate Ex. Doc., No. 58, 45th Cong., 3d Sess., 1879.

International Monetary Conference, 1881, House Misc. Doc., No. 396, 49th Cong., 1st Sess.

Bimetallism in Europe, E. Atkinson, Ex. Doc., No. 34, 50th Cong., 1st Sess., 1887, also printed in Consular Report No. 87. Contains translation of A. Soetbeer's remarkable statistical compilation of materials for the study of the coinage question.

British Gold and Silver Commission, Report of, reprinted as Senate Misc. Doc., No. 34, 50th Cong., 2d Sess., 1889.

International Monetary Conference, 1892, Senate Ex. Doc., No. 82, 52d Cong., 2d Sess.

Many reports from the Coinage Committee of the House and the Finance Committee of the Senate appear in the Congressional Documents; among the notable ones are Wickham and Bartine, House Report No. 3967, 51st Cong., 2d Sess.; Bland's House Report No. 249, 52d Cong., 1st Sess.

Most of the Presidents, beginning with Hayes (whose veto message, in February in 1878, is of special importance), referred to the silver question in their messages. Cleveland's special message in August, 1893, preceding the suspension of silver purchases, is of extraordinary interest. The Secretaries of the Treasury also touch on the subject almost continuously from 1878; the fullest consideration will be found in Manning's report for 1885 and Windom's for 1889. Technical and statistical information, as complete as could be desired, will be found in the reports of the Mint Bureau, that of 1895 containing a review of the coinage question from 1776.

Unofficial publications include: —

History of Bimetallism in the United States, J. Laurence Laughlin, 1892. (Unqualifiedly opposed to bimetallism.)

History of American Coinage, David K. Watson, 1899.

Nomisma or Legal Tender, Henri Cernuschi, 1877. (A leading exponent of international bimetallism, who published many pamphlets here and abroad.)

The India Commission Report (British), reprinted as Senate Misc. Doc., No. 23, 53d Cong., 1st Sess.

The Berlin Silver Conference (Germany), reprinted as Senate Misc. Doc., No. 274, 53d Cong., 2d Sess.

International Bimetallism, F. A. Walker, 1896.

The Silver Situation, Frank W. Taussig, 1876.

Silver in Europe, S. Dana Horton, 1890.

Silver and Gold, S. Dana Horton, 1877.

Consult also the numerous pamphlets on Silver in *Sound Currency*.

Economic Tracts, Soc. for Pol. Education, New York, 1884, includes numbers by McCulloch and others.

International Monetary Conference, H. B. Russell, 1898. (A review of all the conferences and connected history.)

If not Silver, What? J. W. Bookwalter, 1896.

An Honest Dollar, E. B. Andrews, 1889.

TREASURY NOTES AND LEGAL TENDER NOTES form the subject of discussion in the *Messages* of *Presidents* and *Finance Reports* throughout the period, and much space is devoted thereto in the congressional debates. Specially important are the reports of Chase, McCulloch, Sherman, Manning, and Carlisle.

Specie Resumption and Refunding of the Debt, Report by Secretary Sherman, Ex. Doc., No. 9, 46th Cong., 2d Sess., 1880; *National Loans of the United States*, R. A. Bayley, 1880; *History of the Currency of the Country*, W. F. DeKnight, 1897. The two last mentioned give the forms of notes, complete statistics, and brief statements of the legislative provisions.

On the specific questions of LEGAL TENDER, see *Supreme Court Reports*, 8th and 12th Wallace, and 110th U. S.

The unofficial publications besides those already mentioned are: —

United States Notes, John Jay Knox, 1884.

Life of Chase, J. W. Schuckers, 1874.

History of Legal Tender Paper Money, etc., E. G. Spaulding, 1869. (The author of the Greenback Law; gives abstracts of debates and a succinct historical account.)

A History of the Greenbacks, W. C. Mitchell, 1903.

Legal Tender, S. P. Breckinridge, 1903.

The legal tender decisions in full also appear in McPherson's *Handbooks*, and a historical discussion in Bancroft's *Plea for the Constitution*, 1884.

Special papers on the legal tenders and their cost, the premium on gold and prices as affected thereby, appear in *Sound Currency*.

The daily premium on gold during suspension of specie payments may be found in Homans's *Merchants' and Bankers' Almanac* (annual); also in a small volume published by the New York Gold Exchange (Mersereau). For the GOLD PANIC, 1869, see House Report No. 31, 41st Cong., 2d Sess.

BANKING AND BANK-NOTES. Chase's *Finance Reports*, in which the system is outlined, and the series of *Reports of Comptrollers of the Currency*, 1864–1902, give an adequate survey of the birth and history of the national banking system, with statistics more complete than ever attempted by any country. The original act of 1863 was published as "*The National Currency Act, 1863*"; the revised act with amendments from time to time appears separately (*National Bank Act*) and most complete in the one of 1900.

Certain of the Reports of Comptrollers contain special features; Knox in 1875 and 1876 reviews other banking systems, particularly state banks in the latter; Hepburn in 1892 devotes much space to state banks; Knox prepared a special report of the use of credit instruments, 1881; and Lacey in 1891, as well as Eckels, 1896, repeated this work. The latter also presented in 1896 a special report on deposits and depositors in banks. A useful digest of legal decisions affecting the banks will be found in each of the reports since 1876.

Congressional documents contain much valuable information, particularly the reports of hearings in the period from 1893 to 1901, when bank-note reform became a burning question, and the many plans suggested are printed in full in these volumes. See on this subject House Reports, No. 1508, 53d Cong., 3d Sess., and No. 1575, 55th Cong., 2d Sess.

Statistics of state banks appear in the *Reports of the Comptrollers of the Currency* since 1874, and in reports in the 90's appear digests of the laws of the states relating to banks.

The most valuable unofficial works are: —

History of Banking in the United States, W. G. Sumner, 1896.
History of Banking in the United States, John Jay Knox, 1900.
History of Modern Banks of Issue, Charles A. Conant, 1896.
Theory and History of Banking, Chas. F. Dunbar, 1894.

ASSET BANKING, branch banking, the Baltimore plan, and other features are specially discussed in a number of the pamphlets in *Sound Currency*, in the two last-named works and in *Report Indianapolis Monetary Commission*.

The reports of the proceedings of the annual meetings of the *American Bankers' Association*, 1875–1902, also contain much valuable material on the subject of banking and currency.

THE CLEARING-HOUSE SYSTEM is discussed in: —

The New York Clearing House, N. Squire, 1888.
Clearing Houses, James G. Cannon, 1900.
Federal Clearing Houses, Theodore Gilman.

AUXILIARY CURRENCY is well treated in *Sound Currency* by J. D. Warner, Vol. II., No. 6.

Consult also as to the SUBTREASURY —

The Independent Treasury of the United States, David Kinley, 1893, and White, *Money and Banking;* Sumner, *History of Banking in the United States.*

And on other pertinent topics: —

The Canadian Banking System, R. M. Breckinridge, 1894, reprinted in American Economic Association publications.
The Currency and Banking Law of Canada, W. C. Cornwell, 1895.

PRICE, WAGES, etc., in *U. S. Senate* (Aldrich) *Reports*, No. 986, 52d Cong., 1st Sess.; No. 1394, 52d Cong., 2d Sess.

The VOLUME OF MONEY is given in the *Statistical Abstracts* in the *Treasury Circular, No. 113* (1900), and in the *Finance Reports* in recent years. In *Reports of the Treasurer of the United States* will be found monthly statistics since 1878 in detail. Details are discussed also in Muhleman's *Monetary Systems.*

The PANIC OF 1893 and the subsequent years of monetary troubles, and the bond issues, are discussed in the *Messages of the Presidents* and in *Finance Reports* for the years, also by White, Noyes, Muhleman, and in numbers of *Sound Currency.*

INDEXES AND BIBLIOGRAPHIES. — The Congressional Library at Washington has compiled and printed a bibliography on *Currency and Banking*, and a bibliography on *The Monetary Question.* Since their publication, the Congressional Library has prepared supplementary typewritten lists of references of books and pamphlets on the monetary question and on the organization of the Federal Reserve Banks.

The List of References, 1913–1914, on the Federal Reserve Board, its organization, operation, etc., prepared by H. H. B. Meyer, Chief Bibliographer of the Congressional Library, and dated Feb. 3, 1915, contains references to 143 pamphlets, addresses, articles, etc.

In 1908 the New York Public Library published a *List of Works in the Library Relating to Money and Banking* (170 pages); and while this is comprehensive up to and including that year, it must be supplemented by reference to the card indexes for later years.

Students of this period, who desire to follow closely the course of events and the discussion thereon will be materially aided by using the indexes of the *Commercial and Financial Chronicle*, the *Bankers' Magazine*, and the *New York Times*.

STATISTICAL. — For statistics covering this period, consult *The Statistical Abstract of the United States*, the annual reports of the Comptroller of the Currency, the annual reports of the Director of the Mint, the annual reports of the New York Chamber of Commerce and the files of the *Commercial and Financial Chronicle*.

The Panic of 1907, the National Monetary Commission and the Federal Reserve Bank are treated in the following authorities: —

PANIC OF 1907. — The most comprehensive statement of the causes and effects of the panic of 1907 is given in the *History of Crises under the National Banking System* by O. M. W. Sprague of Harvard University (484 pages), issued by the National Monetary Commission. The panics of 1873, 1884, 1890 and 1893 are also treated in this book.

The proceedings of the American Academy of Political Science in 1908 contains a symposium on the lessons of the crisis of 1907, by George B. Cortelyou, Frank A. Vanderlip, William B. Ridgely, George E. Roberts, William A. Nash and others.

The fifth edition (1915) of *Modern Banks of Issue*, by Charles A. Conant, contains chapters relating to the panic of 1907 and the Federal Reserve Act.

The 1908 edition of *Monetary and Banking Systems*, by Maurice L. Muhleman, describes the effects of the 1907 panic.

Other authorities: E. R. A. Seligman on *The Crisis of 1907*, Columbia University Press; and Yves Guyot on *La Crise Americaine*, Paris, 1908.

NATIONAL MONETARY COMMISSION. — As the work of the National Monetary Commission created by act of Congress May 30, 1908, effectively prepared the way for the establishment of the Federal Reserve Act, so the publications of this Commission constitute the most comprehensive and valuable summaries ever printed of the banking and currency systems of the United States and other countries.

The publications of the Commission, issued as Senate Documents during the 61st Congress (1909–1910), are as follows: —

The Work of the National Monetary Commission, an address by Senator Aldrich before the Economic Club, New York, Nov. 29, 1909; an admirable outline of the banking systems of Great Britain, Germany and France (Doc. 406; pages 29).

Interviews on the Banking and Currency Systems of England, France, Germany, Switzerland and Italy (Doc. 405; pages 541).

Statistics for Great Britain, Germany and France, 1867–1908, by Sir R. H. Inglis Palgrave, F.R.S., and others (Doc. 578; pages 354).

The Credit of Nations, by Francis W. Hirst, editor of the London *Economist*, and *The Trade Balance of the United States*, by Sir George Paish, editor of the London *Statist* (Doc. 579; pages 213); authoritative statements on these subjects by two great experts.

Fiscal Systems of England, France, Germany and the United States, by J. O. Manson, Chief of Division of Accounts, Redemption and Issues (Doc. 403; pages 86); a report upon the methods of receiving and disbursing public moneys in various countries.

Notes on the Postal Savings Bank Systems of England, Canada, France, Italy, Belgium, Russia, Netherlands, Austria-Hungary, Sweden and Egypt (Doc. 658; pages 123).

The Discount System in Europe, by Paul M. Warburg (now member of Federal Reserve Board); the relation of the Central banks to the discount market is described (Doc. 402; pages 43).

Bank Acceptances, by Lawrence Merton Jacobs; a description of the European methods of borrowing by means of bank acceptances (Doc. 569; pages 20).

Statistics for the United States, 1867–1909, compiled by A. Piatt Andrew, formerly Assistant Secretary of the Treasury (Doc. 570; pages 280).

Special Reports from the Banks of the United States, 1909, compiled by Charles A. Stewart (Doc. 225; pages 90).

Laws of the United States Concerning Money, Banking and Loans, 1778–1909, compiled by A. T. Huntington and Robert J. Mawhinney (Doc. 580; pages 812).

Digest of State Banking Laws, by Samuel A. Welldon (Doc. 353; pages 746).

The First and Second Banks of the United States, by J. J. Holdsworth and Dr. Davis R. Dewey (Doc. 571; pages 311).

State Banking before the Civil War, by Davis R. Dewey and Dr. Robert E. Chaddock (Doc. 581; pages 338).

State Banks and Trust Companies since the Passage of the National Bank Act, by George E. Barnett (Doc. 659; pages 260).

Bank Loans and Stock Exchange Speculation, by Jacob H. Hollander (Doc. 589; pages 27).

The Origin of the National Bank System, by Andrew MacFarland Davis (Doc. 582, pages 213).

History of Crises under National Bank System, by O. M. W. Sprague, with articles by A. D. Noyes and A. Piatt Andrew (Doc. 538; pages 484).

Use of Credit Instruments in Payments in the United States, by David Kinley (Doc. 399; pages 229); a statistical study showing that 80 to 85 per cent of the total business of the country is done by checks and other credit instruments.

The Independent Treasury System of the United States and its Relations to the Banks of the Country, by David Kinley (Doc. 587; pages 399).

Seasonable Variations in the Demands for Currency and Capital, by Edwin W. Kemmerer (Doc. 588; pages 600); a statistical study (1890–1908) to determine the regularity and extent of seasonal demands for money and disclosing the lack of elasticity in the currency.

Clearing House Methods and Practices, by James G. Cannon (Doc. 491; pages 335).

Suggested Changes in Administrative Features of the National Banking Laws (Doc. 404; pages 374).

History of National Bank Currency, by A. D. Noyes (Doc. 572; pages 20).

History of Banking in Canada, by R. M. Breckenridge (Doc. 332; pages 310).

The Canadian Banking System, by Joseph French Johnson (Doc. 583; pages 191).

Interviews of the Banking and Currency Systems of Canada (Doc. 584; pages 209).

The English Banking System, by Hartley Withers, R. H. Inglis Palgrave and others (Doc. 492; pages 294).

History of the Bank of England, with introduction by H. S. Foxwell of the London School of Economics (Doc. 591; pages 297).

The Bank of France in its Relation to National and International Credit, by Maurice Patron, with an article on "French Savings" by Alfred Neymarck (Doc. 494; pages 181).

Evolution of Credit and Banks in France, by André Liesse (Doc. 522; pages 267).

History and Methods of the Paris Bourse, by E. Vidal (Doc. 573; pages 275); a valuable account of the Paris Stock Exchange.

The Reichsbank, a translation of a work published in Germany in 1900 (Doc. 408; pages 362).

German Imperial Banking Laws, edited by R. Koch (Doc. 574; pages 330).

The Great German Banks and their Concentration in Connection with the Economic Development of Germany, by J. Riesser (Doc. 593; pages 620); an excellent statement by a distinguished German banker.

Miscellaneous Articles on German Banking; twelve articles by prominent German experts (Doc. 508; pages 478).

The German Bank Inquiry of 1908; a translation of stenographic reports. Two volumes, pages 1162 and 1000 (Doc. 407).

Renewal of Reichsbank Charter, including discussions by R. Koch, Moriz Stroell and others (Doc. 507; pages 268).

The Swiss Banking Law, by Julius Landmann of the Swiss National Bank (Doc. 401; pages 269).

Italian Banks of Issue, by Tito Canovai, of the Bank of Italy, and Carlo F. Ferraris (Doc. 575; pages 350).

The Swedish Banking System, by A. A. Flux (Doc. 576; pages 248).

The National Bank of Belgium, by Charles A. Conant (Doc. 400; pages 238).

The Banking System of Mexico, by Charles A. Conant (Doc. 493; pages 284).

Banking in Russia, Austro-Hungary, Holland and Japan, by Profs. Idelson and Lexis, Robert Zuckerkandl, R. van der Borght, Marquis Katsura, Baron Sakatani, S. Naruse and O. M. W. Sprague (Doc. 586, pages 200).

Financial Diagrams, prepared by A. Piatt Andrew (Doc. 509); presents the operations of banks, movements of money and merchandise, etc.

Letter transmitting Report of the Commission (Doc. 243; pages 72).

Suggested Plan for Monetary Legislation (Doc. 784; pages 20).

THE FEDERAL RESERVE SYSTEM. — Following the preparatory work performed by the National Monetary Commission, the discussion, in and out of Congress, leading directly to the establishment of the Federal Reserve System, was begun in 1912 and carried on through all of 1913, the House of Representatives Committee on Banking and Currency beginning hearings on January 6, 1913, the Glass-Owen (Administration) bill being introduced in June, and the bill becoming a law December 23, 1913.

The Congressional Record; the printed record (31 pamphlets) of the Pujo Investigation from May 16, 1912 to Feb. 26, 1913; the reports of the Comptroller of the Currency, the American Bankers' Association, and the New York Chamber of Commerce, should be consulted for records of this great debate. Another aid to the investigator is the files of the *Commercial and Financial Chronicle.* The *Banking Law Journal* and the *Bankers' Magazine* may also be consulted to advantage.

For debates in Congress on the bill see *Congressional Record,* September to December, 1913, inclusive.

Since the enactment of the law, Thomas Conway, Jr., and Ernest M.

Patterson, of the Wharton School of Finance, have published (1914) a book on *The Operations of the New Bank Act.* While issued too soon after the event to be of the highest historical value, this work has a wide range and is helpful.

OTHER PUBLICATIONS. — Eighteen pamphlets issued by the National Citizens' League, 1911–1913: —

Banking Reform, by J. Laurence Laughlin, an argument for elastic and scientific banking, 1912.

Discussion of the Banking Problem, in the *Proceedings* of the American Academy of Political Science, 1910–1911.

The Federal Reserve Act, an address by Charles S. Hamlin, the first Governor of the Federal Reserve Board, before the New York Credit Men's Association, Jan. 15, 1914.

The Federal Reserve Act of 1913, its History and Digest, by Virginius G. Iden.

Clearing House and Domestic Exchange Functions of Federal Reserve Banks, an address by Joseph T. Talbert before the Academy of Political Science in New York, October, 1913.

The Functions of Centralized Banking, by Charles A. Conant, in *Bankers' Magazine,* October, 1914.

Origin, Plan and Purpose of the Currency Bill, by Senator R. L. Owen, in *North American Review,* October, 1913.

Commercial Paper and the Federal Reserve Banks, by O. M. W. Sprague, *Journal of Political Economy,* May, 1914.

The Currency Bill in the Senate, by Horace White, in *North American Review,* January, 1914.

The Federal Reserve Act, its Legislative History, Origin and Significance, American Economic Review, March, 1914.

The Currency Problem and the Present Financial Situation; a series of addresses by E. R. A. Seligman, Thomas F. Woodlock, A. Barton Hepburn, Albert Strauss, William A. Nash, James G. Cannon and Paul M. Warburg, delivered at Columbia University.

Banking Reform in the United States, an address by Senator Nelson W. Aldrich before the Academy of Political Science, New York.

NOTE. — For reports, reviews, trade and financial statistics disclosing in part the effect upon business of the country of the outbreak of the European War, a convenient record is the annual report for 1914–1915 of the New York Chamber of Commerce. Consult also the weekly issues of the *Commercial and Financial Chronicle.*

SUPPLEMENTARY BIBLIOGRAPHY

BANKING

Agger, E. E. *Organized Banking.* (New York: Holt. 1918)

Dewey, Davis R. and Shugrue, Martin J. *Banking and Credit.* (New York: Ronald Press Company. 1922)

Kane, T. P. *The Romance and Tragedy of Banking.* (New York: Bankers Publishing Company. 1922)

Laughlin, J. Lawrence. *Banking Progress.* (New York: Charles Scribner's Sons. 1920)

Scott, W. A. *Money and Banking.* (New York: Holt. 1916)

Westerfield, Ray B. *Banking Principles and Practice.* (New York: Ronald Press Company. 1921)

Willis, H. P. *Principles of Banking.* (New York: Harper. 1921)

MONEY

Anderson, B. M., Jr. *The Value of Money.* (New York: The Macmillan Co. 1917)

Foster, W. T. and Catchings, W. *Money.* (Newton, Mass.: Pollack Foundation. 1923)

Hawtry, R. G. *Currency and Credit.* (London: Longmans. 1919)

Marshall, Alfred. *Money, Credit and Commerce.* (London: Macmillan & Co., Ltd. 1923)

McCullough, Ernest. *Everybody's Money.* (New York and London: Putnam's Sons. 1923)

The Money Problem. Proceedings of the Academy of Political Science. Vol. X, No. 2. January, 1923. (New York: Academy, Columbia University. 1923)

FEDERAL RESERVE SYSTEM

Hepburn, A. Barton and Anderson, B. M., Jr. *The Gold and Rediscount Policy of the Federal Reserve Banks.* Chase Economic Bulletin. Vol. I, No. 5. 1921. (Reprinted as final chapter of the present volume.)

Kemmerer, E. W. *The A B C of the Federal Reserve System.* (Princeton: Princeton University Press. 1918)

Willis, H. P. *Federal Reserve System.* (New York: Ronald Press Company. 1923)

Reed, Harold L. *The Development of Federal Reserve Policy.* (Boston: Houghton Mifflin Co. 1922)

The Federal Reserve System—Its Purpose and Work. The Annals,

Vol. XCIX, No. 188. (Philadelphia: Am. Academy of Political and Social Science. 1922)

CURRENCY, BANKING, ETC., IN OTHER COUNTRIES

Baldy, E. *Les Banques d'Affaires en France depuis 1900.* (Paris: Lib. Général de Droit et de Jurisprudence. 1922)

Marion, M. *Histoire Financière de la France depuis 1715.* (Paris: Rousseau. 1921)

McCaleb, Walter Flavius. *Present and Past Banking in Mexico.* (New York: Harper & Brothers. 1920)

Spalding, W. F. *Eastern Exchange, Currency and Finance.* (New York: Pitman. 1917)

Subercaseaux, Guillermo. *Monetary and Banking Policy of Chile.* Carnegie Endowment for International Peace. Division of Economics and History. (Oxford: Clarendon Press. 1922)

Monetary Systems of Principal Countries of the World. 1916. Treasury Department document 2799. (Washington: Superintendent of Documents. 1917)

MISCELLANEOUS

Bergengren, R. F. *Coöperative Banking.* (New York: Macmillan. 1923)

Phillips, Chester Arthur. *Bank Credit.* (New York: The Macmillan Co. 1920)

Tucker, Donald S. *The Evolution of People's Banks.* Columbia University Studies in History, Economics and Public Law. Vol. CII, No. 1. (New York: Longmans, Green & Co. 1922)

EFFECTS OF THE WAR

Bibliographies.

European War. Financial Influence. Library of Congress: Division of Bibliography. Washington. September 1915.

List of references on the cost of the European war. Library of Congress: Division of Bibliography. Washington, 1918)

Anderson, B. M., Jr. *Effects of the War on Money, Credit and Banking in France and the United States.* Carnegie Endowment for International Peace Preliminary Economic Studies of the War, No. 15. (New York: Oxford University Press. 1919)

Ayres, L. P. *The War with Germany.* (Statistics Branch of the General Staff. Washington. 1919)

Bass, J. F. and Moulton, H. G. *America and the Balance Sheet of Europe.* (New York: Ronald Press Company. 1921)

Bendix, Ludwig. *Krieg und Geldmarkt.* (Berlin: L. Simion. 1915)
Bogart, E. L. *War Costs and their Financing.* (New York: Appleton. 1920)
Bogart, E. L. *Direct and Indirect Costs of the Great World War.* Carnegie Endowment for International Peace. Preliminary Economic Studies of the War, No. 24. (New York: Oxford University Press. 1919)
Cassel, Gustav. *The World's Monetary Problems.* (London: Constable & Co. 1921)
Cassel, Gustav. *Money and Foreign Exchanges after 1914.* (London: Constable & Co. 1922)
Decamps, J. *La Guerre et les Finances de la France.* (Paris: Tenin. 1918)
Diehl, Karl. *Über Fragen des Geldwesens und der Valuta Während des Krieges und nach dem Kriege.* (Jena: G. Fischer. 1921)
Fisk, H. E. *French Public Finance in the Great War and Today.* (New York: Bankers Trust Co. 1922)
Fisk, H. E. *English Public Finance.* (New York: Bankers Trust Company. 1920)
Foxwell, H. S. *Papers on Current Finance.* (London: Macmillan & Co. 1919)
Gibson, A. H. and Kirkaldy, A. W. *British War Finance During and After the War. 1914–1921.* Being the Results of Investigations and Materials Collected by a Committee of Section F. (Economics and Statistics) of the British Association. (London: Sir Isaac Pitman & Sons. 1921)
Guyot, Yves and Raffalovich, A. *Inflation et Déflation.* (Paris: F. Alcan. 1921)
Hantos, E. *Die Zunkunft des Geldes.* (Stuttgart: Enke. 1921)
Hawtry, R. G. *Monetary Reconstruction.* (New York: Longmans, Greene & Co. 1923)
Hepburn, A. B. *Financing the War.* (Princeton: Princeton University Press. 1918)
Hollander, Jacob H. *War Borrowing; A Study of Treasury Certificates of Indebtedness of the United States.* (New York: The Macmillan Co. 1919)
Kiernan, T. J. *British War Finance and the Consequences.* London: P. S. King & Son. 1921)
Laughlin, J. Lawrence. *Credit of the Nations.* (New York: Charles Scribner's Sons. 1918)

McVey, F. L. *The Financial History of Great Britain. 1914–1918.* Carnegie Endowment for International Peace. Preliminary Economic Studies of the War, No. 7. (New York: Oxford University Press. 1918)
Nicholson, J. S. *War Finance.* (London: King. 1917)
Rist, Charles. *Les Finances de Guerre de l'Allemagne.* (Paris: Payot & Cie. 1921)
Růžička, Ernst. *Das Ende der Kronenwährung; durch Devalvierung zur Konsolidierung.* (Wien: C. Konegen. 1921)
Vissering, G. *De Problemen van Geldwezen en Wisselkoersen op de Finantieele Conferentie te Brussel.* (The Haag: Van Stockum. 1920)
White, B. *The Currency of the Great War.* (London: Waterlow. 1921)
Report of the Committee on War Finance of the American Economic Association. The American Economic Review. Supplement No. 2. (March, 1919)
The Effects of the War on Credit, Currency, Finance and Foreign Exchanges. (London: British Association for the Advancement of Science. 1922)
Currencies After the War. A survey of conditions in various countries compiled under the auspices of the International Secretariat of the League of Nations. (London: Harrison. 1920)
Proceedings of the Brussels International Conference. (London: Harrison & Sons)

The following books are being prepared for publication by the Carnegie Endowment for International Peace.

Apostol, Paul N. *Russian State Credit During the War.*
Bernazky, Michæl B. *Currency in Russia During the War.*
Epstein, E. M. *Private Banks in Russia During the War.*
Hirst, F. W. *British War Budgets and Financial Policy.*
Jannaccone, Pasquale. *Currency Inflation in Italy and its Effects on Prices, Incomes and Foreign Exchanges.*
Michelson, Alexander M. *State Finances in Russia During the War.*
Popovics, Alexander. *Austro-Hungarian Banking and Financial History.*
Rasin, A. *Financial Problems and Policy of Czecho-Slovakia During the First Year After the War.*
Teleszky, John. *The History of Hungarian Finance During the War.*

Truchy, M. Henri. *War Finances.*
Van der Flier, M. J. *The Financial Effects of the War upon the Netherlands.*

A bibliography which listed all the important articles dealing with the war and the post-war period would be a book in itself, so no attempt has been made to include them here. The student is referred to the American Economic Review where he will find most of the important articles listed under the digest of periodicals.

The following magazines will be found especially helpful in giving accounts of the events in this period.

American Economic Review
Annalist
Annals—American Academy of Political and Social Science
Bradstreet's
Commercial and Financial Chronicle
Commerce and Finance
Dun's Review
Jahrbücher für Nationalökonomie und Statistik
Economic World
Economist (London)
Economic Journal (London)
Ekonomisk Tidskrift
Journal Des Économistes
Journal of Political Economy
Manchester Guardian
Political Science Quarterly
Proceedings—Academy of Political Science in the City of New York
Quarterly Journal of Economics
Statist (London)

Bank Publications

Chase Economic Bulletin. Chase National Bank of New York.
Commerce Monthly. National Bank of Commerce, New York.
Federal Reserve Bulletin
Monthly Letter of the National City Bank of New York.
Monthly Reviews of the Federal Reserve Banks of New York, Boston and Philadelphia.

INDEX